JEWELRY

2ND EDITION

A FULLY ILLUSTRATED PRICE GUIDE TO 19th- AND 20th-CENTURY JEWELRY, INCLUDING VICTORIAN, ART NOUVEAU AND COSTUME

CHRISTIE ROMERO

Volumes in the Encyclopedia of Antiques and Collectibles

Harry L. Rinker, Series Editor

Warman's Americana & Collectible, 6th Edition,
edited by Harry L. Rinker

Warman's American Pottery & Porcelain,
by Susan and Al Bagdade

Warman's Country Antiques & Collectibles, 2nd Edition,
by Dana Gehman Morykan and Harry L. Rinker

Warman's English & Continental Pottery & Porcelain, 2nd Edition,
by Susan and Al Bagdade

Warman's Furniture,
edited by Harry L. Rinker

Warman's Glass,
by Ellen Tischbein Schroy

Warman's Jewelry,
by Christie Romero

Warman's Oriental Antiques,
by Gloria and Robert Mascarelli

Warman's Paper,
by Norman E. Martinus and Harry L. Rinker

Cover photo by Christie Romero
Author photo by Chic Images

Back-cover photos: **Brooch/Pin**, silver, pearls, amethysts, garnet, c. 1910, circ disk with chased and hammered design, central garnet cab quartered by four amethyst cabs further quartered by four pearls on the rim, probably Eng, C-catch, tube hinge, 2-3/4" dia, **$300** (Terrance O' Halloran collection); **Brooch/Pin**, sterling vermeil, rhinestones, ptd enamel, depicting a bird on a branch with *pavé* colorless r.s. breast, branch and leaf tips, red r.s. eye, ptd details in green, yellow, orange, brown, black and red, mkd "Corocraft STERLING" on appl plaque, double-pronged hinged clip on rev, 2-3/8" w x 2-3/8", **$175** (Charles Pinkham collection).

Published by

700 E. State Street • Iola, WI 54990-0001
Telephone: 715/445-2214

Please call or write for our free catalog.
Our toll-free number to place an order or obtain a free catalog is 800-258-0929
or please use our regular business telephone 715-445-2214 for editorial comment and further information.

ISBN: 0-87069-768-4
Library of Congress: 94-25278
Printed in the United States of America

CONTENTS

Part I—Late Eighteenth and Nineteenth Century Jewelry

Part II—Turn-of-the-Century Jewelry

Part III—Twentieth-Century Jewelry

Part IV—Special Collectible Jewelry

ACKNOWLEDGMENTS

Once again, the list of credits is long. And once again, this book would not have been possible without the help, support, and encouragement of a great many people, including all of my dealer and collector friends and colleagues who lent jewelry and gave information, and my dedicated and loyal students, some of whom are or have become dealers, advanced collectors, friends and colleagues.

Some special people should be mentioned: I am once again indebted to Sam Gassman for providing me with an extraordinary array of jewelry and the information to go with it; and this time, many thanks also go to his sister, Jorese Dunham, for her much-appreciated assistance. To Lenore Dailey, Gail Gerretsen, Ellen Hoffs, Sue James, Carmelita Johnson, Neil Lane, Leigh Leshner, Richard Levey, Terrance O'Halloran, Kirsten Olson, Chuck Pinkham, Elaine Sarnoff, Pam Tonge and Dawn Usher, Diane White, and Sandra Willard, who willingly entrusted me with large quantities of jewelry from their inventories and collections, I am especially grateful. Patrick Kapty not only put his extensive collection at my disposal, but devoted hours upon hours to entering data into my database and to endless discussions about jewelry and the marketplace. I thank him for his efforts and for his enthusiasm for the subject. Thanks, too, to Jane Clarke, Jill Crawford, Bruce Healy, Terri and John Krantz, Karen Lorene, Julie Robinson, Amanda Triossi and Sharen and Nicholas Wood for their sharing of information and photographs. Co-instructor and friend Karen Lorene, N.A.J.A. associate director Joe Tenhagen and executive director Jim Holliff have been wonderfully supportive and helpful. To my e-mail "pen pal" and database compiler extraordinaire, Shari Miller, much appreciation for her in-depth research and original source material, and husband Jeff for help with photographs and both for their jewelry. I thank Ellen Hoffs for her jewelry, her reference material and first-hand information, and collector Munir Meghji for sharing many photocopied pages of original source material as well as his own wonderful collection. Gallery owner Steven Cabella also generously shared his extensive knowledge and contributed photographs. Peter Shemonsky, auction consultant, appraiser and jewelry historian, friend and associate, who knows jewelry backside and front, was and continues to be a never-ending source of information. Confrere (*consoeur*?), writer and researcher Elise Misiorowski likewise was always willing to lend a hand and a brain. To my esteemed colleague and friend Janet Zapata, heartfelt appreciation for her knowledge, answers to my questions, and continued support and encouragement, as well as photographs and jewelry. I continue to be grateful to Sherry Shatz for her unflagging friendship and support, and I thank her for her research and bibliographic contribution. Gilly Phipps remains my dear long-distance friend, as well as a contributor this time around. My pal Liz Hada contributed words of encouragement, as well as jewelry and gemological assistance. I am also deeply indebted to Mary Palmer for connecting me with jewelry people and places in London during my short stay there, and for sharing her experiences and jewelry.

To Joyce Jonas goes appreciation for giving me an opportunity to teach what I've learned in researching and writing my books to participants in the annual Antique Jewelry & Gemstones course. The Internet e-mail listserv Jewelcollect also deserves mention for being a forum for discussion and networking in the true sense of the word. Kudos to Isabelle Bryman for administering to such a large and varied group.

I must also thank several others anonymously who contributed jewelry or photographs but do not wish to have their names published. They know who they are, and that I value their contributions.

To the staff at Olson Photo and Imaging, who got used to seeing me on a near daily basis, thanks for being fast and accommodating. Brad Pettigrew and Dena George deserve praise for their marks illustrations. Dena and the rest of the staff at Rinker Enterprises: Dana, Kathy, Virginia, and Nancy, were always helpful and supportive, and I thank their boss, Harry L. Rinker, for his guidance and friendship, and for inviting me to teach at his Institute.

The staff at Krause Publications is to be commended for its efficiency and ability to work technological miracles with photographs. Thanks to Don Gulbrandsen, managing editor in the books division, for reassuring me that reformatting, retouching, and rearranging were "no problem," and kudos to Patsy Morrison in production for making everything look "right." Special thanks to my editor Kris Manty for coming on board as a "new recruit" and tackling this monumental project with aplomb. Warman's editor Ellen Schroy gave sage advice and counsel as well.

Several auction house personnel should be thanked for their assistance: Mary Borchert at Beverly Hills Auctioneers, Dana Ehrman at Sloan's, Gloria Lieberman at Skinner's, Brett O'Connor at Christie's Los Angeles, and Carol Elkins and Leslie Simone at Sotheby's Beverly Hills. In the research department, the staff at the G.I.A. Library aided me as well.

To my mother and stepfather, Peggy and Norm Levine, my father Sam Schultz, my brother Ron Schultz, sister-in-law Laura Sanderford–writers all–gratitude for their love and empathy.

And finally, to the Computer Wiz, my ever-supportive, ever-patient husband, Jimmie, who endured the seemingly endless process a second time around, this book is dedicated once again, to you, with love.

Christie S. Romero

INTRODUCTION

Warman's Jewelry 2nd edition is an expanded update of the first edition. It contains new information, new photographs and listings, but its basic purpose remains the same: It is a "field guide" to styles and types of antique, period, and vintage collectible jewelry currently on the market in the United States. It is for anyone who owns old jewelry, whether it is a collector's collection, a dealer's inventory, an heir's inheritance, a packrat's accumulation, or a garage-saler's finds.

No matter how they've acquired it, most people want to know the same basic things about a piece: how old it is, where and how it was made, who made it, what it is made of, and the ubiquitous bottom line, what it is worth. Jewelry has always been kept and worn, for many different reasons, but only within the last fifteen years or so has conscientious collecting (by style or period, material, country of origin, etc.) become a major reason to buy. As greater numbers of collectors have entered the field, there has been a growing need for more information about the many varieties of collectible jewelry being bought and sold today. *Warman's Jewelry* was written in response to that need. The second edition continues in that tradition.

The focus of this book is American: what was made here, and what is now available here. Americans tend to have an "inferiority complex" when it comes to competing with what was produced in Europe. This attitude is beginning to change with the burgeoning recognition and appreciation of American talents and ingenuity. Several categories are included which have not received a great deal of attention in other price guides: American Arts & Crafts, mid-century modernist American studio artists, '50s and '60s fine jewelry, and a Special Collectibles section which covers Native American jewelry, and the product of two regions which are closely tied to the U.S.: Mexican and Scandinavian jewelry.

Jewelry is the only art form where the "intrinsic" value of the materials from which it is made can have greater value than the work itself. Many beautiful and historically significant pieces have been destroyed for their stones and metal, particularly after a certain style becomes "outdated" or "old-fashioned." This usually happens before there is retrospective appreciation for the style, before it becomes "collectible."

Stones and metal are paint and canvas. Rare and beautiful stones can be used to great effect to enhance a jewel. However, supply and demand, and the public's perceptions, can alter value. For example, aluminum was once a rare and valuable metal, and platinum was looked down upon as "unripe gold." While our culture has consistently placed a higher value on gold and precious gemstones (diamonds, rubies, sapphires, and emeralds), other factors, such as craftsmanship, design and designer, and provenance, as well as rarity and desirability, can outweigh intrinsic value. The following table of seven criteria (3 **C**s, 2 **D**s, 2 **S**s), with questions to ask when evaluating a piece of jewelry, can be a useful aid:

Craftsmanship—Is it well-made, with attention to details and finish?

Condition—Are there any cracks, chips, dents, missing parts, metal corrosion, or other damage? Are all parts original? Has it been repaired? Is there evidence of lead solder on precious metal?

Color—Especially important in costume jewelry, is/are the color(s) currently fashionable, popular? In gemstones, is the color desirable for its kind?

Design—Can the style be attributed to the period in which it was made? Can it be attributed to a particular maker? Is the piece balanced and proportioned? Does it have "eye appeal?" (this is a subjective evaluation) Is it *wearable*?

Demand—Is the piece highly sought-after, currently in vogue?

Scarcity—Is this a rare item, or is it commonly available?

Size—Is it a large or small piece? Is the size appropriate for the style? (Large size is usually more desirable, but style and the wearer's proportions should also be taken into consideration).

Note that age alone does not make a piece valuable. A badly made and designed 150-year-old piece is worth no more today than it was when it was first produced. If it is in poor condition, it is probably worth less! A loupe or magnifier is an essential tool for examining a piece of jewelry. Ten power (10x) is the standard magnification. In addition to detecting alterations and repairs, a loupe is necessary to read hallmarks and maker's marks, to evaluate condition, and to analyze materials (stones, metal, enamel, etc.) and construction. It is important to scrutinize a piece thoroughly, both front *and* back, in order to detect the clues that will tell you what you need to know before you buy.

A word of caution is in order when buying gemstone-set jewelry. The public has been conditioned to believe that the intrinsic value of all gemstones is high and that jewelry set with them is expensive. To some extent this is true, but the range of gemstone values is wide and variables are many. Unless you have some gemological knowledge and have studied the complexities of the market carefully, you can easily get burned. Your best defense against rip-off is your *own* knowledge, but when in doubt, consult a gemologist (G.G., F.G.A., or C.G.A.) for gemstone identification, a qualified gemstone appraiser (who should also be, or be associated with, a gemologist) for values. Another caveat: Appraisers are not licensed or regulated by law, but some of them are credentialed by recognized national appraisal organizations. Make sure the appraiser you choose has had the proper training and experience.

In order to truly understand old jewelry, you must see and handle a *lot* of it. Readers are encouraged to avail themselves of every opportunity to do so, including attending shows, flea markets, museum exhibitions, and seminars, conferences, and classes on antique jewelry. A unique opportunity to enhance one's knowledge with lectures and hands-on experience takes place annually in July, formerly at the University of Maine, now held at Rhode Island College in Warwick, RI, near Providence: The Antique & Period Jewelry and Gemstones Course, directed by Joyce Jonas. Inquiries about the course may be sent to Joyce Jonas & Associates, Inc., 215 East 80th St., Suite 5K, New York, NY 10021-0539, (212) 535-2479, Fax: (212) 988-0721.

The Gemological Institute of America and three national appraisal organizations (American Society of Appraisers, International Society of Appraisers, National Association of Jewelry Appraisers) respectively provide specialized instruction in gemology and gems and jewelry valuation theory and techniques. A correspondence course in jewelry appraisal, The Master Valuer Program, is also available.

My own classes in antique, period and vintage jewelry are held in Southern California at Santiago Canyon College in Orange, CA and at other locations throughout the year, and annually at the Institute for the Study of Antiques and Collectibles in Emmaus, Pennsylvania.

Another opportunity to see, handle and closely examine antique and period jewelry is the auction preview. Christie's and Sotheby's in New York City hold "important" and "magnificent" jewelry sales at which historically and gemologically significant pieces are offered. If in-person inspection is not possible, the color catalogs for these sales, which include biographical and other pertinent information, are excellent reference resources. These and the other auction houses whose names and addresses appear on a following page, also offer a wide range of antique, period, and contemporary jewelry, and were the sources for much of the fine jewelry pictured and listed in this book. All of them hold previews of upcoming sales which are well worth attending. Their catalogs, with prices realized, provide up-to-date market information.

ORGANIZATION OF THE BOOK

Warman's Jewelry 2nd edition is divided into four main sections: Late Eighteenth and Nineteenth Century, Turn of the Century, Twentieth Century, and Special Collectibles. Within each section, the listings are arranged by category in the manner most appropriate and conducive to locating a particular type of piece. Within each category, the listings are alphabetical by type of piece (Bracelet, Brooch/Pin, etc.). A timeline precedes, and a glossary follows the main body of the book. The index cross-references by type of piece (e.g., all earrings listings), name of maker/designer (e.g., all pieces made by Eisenberg), material (e.g., all pieces made of jet), and motif (e.g., animals).

Timeline: One of the unique features of *Warman's Jewelry* is the Timeline. Its purpose is to aid in circa-dating and to put jewelry in context with other relevant historical events, discoveries and inventions. It also summarizes some of the information included in the text of each section. The dates can be used to set the earliest and/or latest possible circa date for a piece. For example, the lowering of karatages of gold to 15, 12, and 9 karat was made legal in Great Britain in 1854. Therefore, gold jewelry with the British designation "9 ct" would date to after 1854. In 1932, the British law was changed, eliminating 15 and 12 karat in favor of 14 karat gold, which gives us the latest date for a piece marked "15 ct" or "12 ct."

Construction methods, materials and findings, if unaltered, can also be helpful circa-dating clues. For example, commercially-made safety catches for brooches were introduced around the turn of the century (one version was patented in 1901, another in 1911). An original safety catch on a brooch, then, is a telltale sign of twentieth century manufacture. Care must be taken, however, to ascertain that the finding is in fact original. Alterations on old pieces are common.

Patents are another useful circa-dating tool, when used as a clue to a piece's age in addition to other factors, such as style and manufacturer's dates of operation. In the captions and listings, if a patent number is found on the back of a piece, it is given along with the corresponding year in which the patent was issued. (Prior to the 1930s, the patent's actual date of issue is more often stamped on a piece, rather than the number.) This is not necessarily the year in which the piece was made, as patents are valid for seventeen years (design patents for fourteen). The piece could have been made later, but it certainly could not have been made *earlier* than the year the patent was issued.

Clothing styles have often dictated or at least influenced types and styles of jewelry, so it is helpful to have some knowledge of fashion history when researching and dating a piece. Significant specific events related to fashion are listed in the Timeline, but space did not permit the inclusion of every stylistic change in clothing and jewelry fashion. Some of this information can be found in the text of each section, and, for further information, books on fashion history are included in the references.

The dates given in the Timeline are as accurate as could be ascertained. I attempted to confirm each date in two or more sources, using original sources or notations whenever possible. Research is never complete, however. New information continues to be discovered which sometimes contradicts previously published "facts." Indeed, the Timeline in this edition of *Warman's Jewelry* includes some newly researched dates for discoveries and inventions which were not known when the first edition was published.

Different dates are often given in various sources for the same event. Sometimes there is a span of a number of years between date of first invention and dates of patenting, perfecting, publishing results, commercialization, and common use. One source may cite, for example, the date a new manufacturing process was *patented,* but another may give the date it was *invented,* perhaps five years earlier. Or it may have taken its inventor five years to perfect, and may not have been available to the public for another five. The difficult task for historians is to decide which date is the most accurate, significant and helpful. We don't always agree. Analysis of history is often a matter of subjective interpretation.

History: Jewelry does not exist in a vacuum. Fashion and history have a cause-and-effect relationship to jewelry designs. Events, discoveries, inventions, social trends and fads play important roles in jewelry history. Each category of this book is prefaced by an encapsulated history, so that readers will understand why a particular piece of jewelry was made and worn during a given period. Design elements that identify a particular style or period, and well-known designers and manufacturers are also included.

It is not always possible to pinpoint the age of a piece exactly. A dated publication can help to circa-date a piece, but relying on only one piece of evidence can also be misleading. Some "models" (manufacturers' name for designs) continued to be made for many years, even decades, as long as they were popular and sold well. There is a "bell curve" to every style or trend–an ascension, peak, and tapering off in popularity. Styles evolve, coexist, and overlap. This is better understood when history is viewed as a continuum of *simultaneous* events, rather than as a linear succession of events.

Improved methods of communication have hastened the rate of influence and change over the past two centuries; today, trends come and go at breakneck speed. Historians used to record changes in fashion by the decade; now changes occur annually.

References: For further information, a number of books and other references that relate to specific jewelry topics are listed within each section and category. Those that cover several topics are listed under each relevant category. Because of growing interest and the constant need for updated information, new titles and new editions appear every year. At press time, the following books of a general nature were in print. Some of these and some out-of-print and specialized publications may only be available through book dealers who specialize in books on antiques and/or gems and jewelry. Many of them publish catalogs of their inventory, run ads in antiques trade papers, or sell at shows. Ask to be put on their mailing lists. Listed are author, title, most recent edition, publisher (if self-published, listed as "published by author"), and date of publication.

Lillian Baker, *100 Years of Collectible Jewelry, 1850-1950*, Collector Books, 1978, values updated 1993; Vivienne Becker, *Antique & Twentieth Century Jewellery*, 2nd ed., N.A.G. Press, 1987; Howard L. Bell, Jr., *Cuff Jewelry,* published by author, 1994; Jeanenne Bell, *Answers to Questions About Old Jewelry, 1840-1950*, 4th edition, Krause Publications, 1996; David Bennett & Daniela Mascetti, *Understanding Jewellery*, 2nd ed., Antique Collectors' Club, 1994; Roseann Ettinger, *Popular Jewelry, 1840-1940*, Schiffer Publishing, 1990; Stephen Giles, consultant, *Miller's Antiques Checklist: Jewellery*, Reed International Books Ltd, 1997; Duncan James, *Old Jewellery*, Shire Publications Ltd, Buckinghamshire, UK, 1989; Arthur Guy Kaplan, *The Official Price Guide to Antique Jewelry*, 6th ed., House of Collectibles, 1990, 1994 reprint; Karen Lorene, *Buying Antique Jewelry: Skipping the Mistakes*, Lorene Publications, 1987; Daniela Mascetti and Amanda Triossi, *Earrings From Antiquity to the* Present, Rizzoli International, 1990; Mascetti and Triossi, *The Necklace From Antiquity to the Present,* Harry N. Abrams, 1997; Donald S. McNeil, *Jewelers' Dictionary,* 3rd ed., Chilton Book Co., 1979; Anna M. Miller, *Buyer's Guide to Affordable Antique Jewelry*, Carol Publishing Group, 1993; Harold Newman, *An Illustrated Dictionary of Jewelry*, Thames & Husdson, 1987; Claire Philips, *Jewelry From Antiquity to the Present*, Thames and Hudson, 1996; Dorothy T. Rainwater, *American Jewelry Manufacturers,* Schiffer Publishing, 1988; Sheryl Gross Shatz, *What's It Made Of? A Jewelry Materials Identification Guide*, 3rd ed., published by author, 1996; Oppi Untracht, *Jewelry Concepts and Technology,* Doubleday, 1985.

Numerous books on diamonds and colored gemstones have been published, some of them consumer-oriented and non-technical. The catalog of the G.I.A. (Gemological Institute of America) Bookstore, 5355 Armada Drive, Suite 300, Carlsbad CA 92008-4698, (800) 421-8161, lists the ones in print, which can be ordered by mail.

The video cassette is a new medium for disseminating information in the antiques field. My video, *Hidden Treasures, A Collector's Guide to Antique and Vintage Jewelry of the 19th and 20th Centuries,* produced by Venture Entertainment Group, is the first of its kind on the subject.

Periodicals: Specialized periodicals are listed in the appropriate categories. Two that cover a broad range of jewelry topics are:

Gems & Gemology, the quarterly journal of the Gemological Institute of America (see address above). Occasionally includes articles on period jewelry.

Jewelers' Circular-Keystone/Heritage One Chilton Way, Radnor, PA 19089. Monthly trade publication of the retail jewelry industry and periodical report on antique and period jewelry and watches.

Two new publications:

The Estate Jeweler, the official magazine of the Estate Jewelers Association of America, 209 Post Street, Suite 718, San Francisco, CA 94108. Published quarterly.

Professional Jeweler, Bond Communications, 1500 Walnut St., Suite 1200, Philadelphia, PA 19102; (215) 567-0727. Internet web site: http://www.professionaljeweler.com. Published monthly, articles on period jewelry in every issue.

Another periodical is *Maine Antique Digest*, P.O. Box 1429, Waldoboro, ME 04572, (207) 832-4888. Internet web site: http://www.maineantiquedigest.com. Peter Theriault, FGA, GG, writes a monthly column on antique and collectible jewelry for Maine Antique Digest. He welcomes questions and press releases on related topics, addressed to him at 58 Bayview St., Camden, ME 04843; phone/fax: (207) 236-3933, e-mail: gemlab@midcoast.com.

Collectors' Clubs: Perhaps as an indication of the newness, and/or the diversity, of the field, there is no national organization with local chapters of jewelry collectors in general. However, a number of specialized jewelry-related clubs and societies exist in the United States. Most of these can be found listed under the appropriate category. A few for which there is no category, or which span several categories, are listed here:

American Hatpin Society, Beverly Churchfield, president, 2101 Via Aguila, San Clemente, CA 92672, (714) 498-1792.

The American Society of Jewelry Historians (semiannual newsletter, annual journal), Box 103, 1B Quaker Ridge Road, New Rochelle, NY 10804.

Bead Societies are located in a number of U.S. cities. A comprehensive listing can be found in Peter Francis, Jr.'s *Beads of the World,* Schiffer Publishing, 1994.

National Antique Comb Collectors Club (and newsletter), Belva Green, editor, 3748 Sunray Dr., Holiday, FL 34691.

National Cuff Link Society (newsletter "The Link"), Eugene Klompus, president, P.O. Box 346, Prospect Heights, IL 60070, (708) 632-0561.

Museums: As of yet, the U.S. does not have a museum with an extensive *permanent* collection of jewelry on display, comparable to museums in Great Britain and Europe. Specialized collections can be found listed under the appropriate category. A few other museums with unique collections are:

The Bead Museum, Prescott, Arizona; Miller Comb Museum, Homer, Alaska; Providence Jewelry Museum, Providence, Rhode Island (old jewelry-making equipment and other items related to the area's costume jewelry manufacturing industry).

Reproductions: Fakes, reproductions, and stylistic copycats are rampant in jewelry. Whenever a particular style or type of jewelry becomes popular, knockoffs proliferate. This has long been a common practice. Repros become especially problematic when they enter the secondary market after a number of years, with signs of wear making them difficult to distinguish from an original of the period. Notations on reproductions are included in the listings categories when applicable.

Marks: Categories with numerous maker's marks appear separately in an appendix, as do marks that span more than one category. Others are illustrated within their related categories. Marks that are names or initials which are easily read are described but not illustrated. Marks that would be otherwise difficult to identify are shown in drawings.

Attribution of unsigned pieces must rely on provenance, or documentation such as company catalogs or archives, and fashion magazines or trade publications which picture the item in question along with its maker's name. Most old jewelry is unmarked and unattributable, and must be evaluated solely on its own merits. Ideally, the same should be true of "signed" pieces, but the fact is that an "important" name on a piece scores points with collectors and adds value. Nevertheless, the name itself should not be the only or even the first thing taken into consideration when evaluating a signed piece. Marks and attributions are "the frosting on the cake," and are therefore listed at the end of the listings descriptions.

Listings: The variety of jewelry is so great that it would be impossible to include examples of every kind. Unlike some other collectibles, with jewelry, there is less likelihood of finding pieces identical to those shown or listed. In certain categories, such as mass-produced costume jewelry of the mid-20th century, multiples of the same design can still be found. What you will find more often are comparable pieces–from the same period, of the same style, made from the same materials. The prices listed are for specific pieces of specific quality and condition. It is important to make sure you are comparing "apples to apples." Although they may be beyond most budgets, "high-end" pieces are listed as a basis for comparison, and as sought-after examples. They set standards by which other pieces of their genre can be measured. However, it must be noted that the pieces in this book are not all necessarily the very best examples of their kind; rather they are representative of what is on the market today.

Watches are not included in the listings. Although a watch can often be a jewel, as well as a timepiece, the factors that determine value and collectiblity are too complex and specialized to fit within the scope of this book. Watch collectors already have a number of fine references at their disposal. However, watch accessories, such as chains, fobs, and pins, are included. Of necessity, some other categories were also omitted: most "generic" (undatable or otherwise unidentifiable) jewelry, ethnic jewelry (indigenous Middle Eastern, Oriental, African, etc.), and late twentieth-century jewelry. Several other jewelry books include pieces from the '80s and the '90s. While it is important to stay abreast of recent developments, it is often difficult to determine what tomorrow's collectibles will be from today's vantage point. Thirty years is considered a sufficient span of time for a clear perspective on what has "staying power" for jewelry collectors.

Now that the sixties are a firmly established era, collectors and historians are beginning to look at the seventies. The first edition of *Warman's Jewelry* covered the twentieth century up to circa 1965. The second edition extends its coverage to circa 1975.

Every effort was made to be consistent in the listings descriptions. However, it was not always possible to examine the jewelry firsthand, and information provided in catalogs was not always complete (e.g., weights, numbers and cuts of stones). The most detailed information on pieces sold at auction came from a semiannual report, *Auction Market Resource for Gems and Jewelry,* a comprehensive compilation of recent auction results from a dozen different houses, published by Gail Levine, G.G., listed on the Board of Advisors

Measurements are in inches, rounded to the nearest eighth. Width or diameter is at the widest point; total length includes any findings. Rings are measured shoulder to shoulder and top to bottom. Necklace and flexible bracelet lengths are clasp to clasp. Width of brooches, clips, earrings, and pendants is side to side, length is top to bottom as the piece is worn. Stone measurements are usually given in millimeters, weights in carats. Total weight for the entire piece, metal and gemstones if any, is in pennyweights.

Photographs: Unless otherwise credited, photographs were taken by the author. The captions for the photographed pieces in *Warman's Jewelry* are as detailed as the listings for pieces not pictured. The reasoning behind this is threefold. First, the reader will more clearly understand the terms used to describe a piece when they can be correlated to the photo, and thus understand the descriptions of pieces *not* pictured. Second, because we often look but don't see, the captions will call the reader's attention to details that might otherwise be missed, as well as to details not visible in the photos, such as findings, marks, and cuts of stones. Finally, these descriptions are given in hopes that they will help to further a common usage of terms whenever we attempt to describe an unseen piece. Terms that may be unfamiliar to the reader are further explained in the glossary.

Glossary: Jewelry has its own lexicon. Many jewelry terms are derived from the French, which became the language of choice when jewelry-making terminology was adopted internationally in the eighteenth century. This glossary lists terms used in *Warman's Jewelry,* and is necessarily incomplete. The general references list several jewelry dictionaries that the reader can use as supplements. Often there is more than one word that can be used to describe a piece of jewelry. For example, the word used to describe a piece of jewelry fastened to clothing by means of a pinning device is either *brooch* or *pin.* Some say that size determines which word is used, but no one has determined at exactly what size a brooch becomes a pin. Others say that *brooch* is the only correct term and *pin* is the word for the mechanism itself, the hinge or joint, pinstem, and catch. In this book, whenever more than one word can be used for a jewelry form, both are included in the listings, e.g., "Brooch/Pin."

PRICE NOTES: BUYER'S GUIDE, NOT SELLER'S GUIDE

Most of the pieces pictured and listed in this book were for sale, or sold at auction, in 1996 and 1997. Those that are from private collections were usually acquired at antiques shows, shops and malls, auctions, flea markets, and yard sales over the past several years, but are valued at current levels. Prices listed are *average retail,* the median of prices noted in various parts of the U.S., except for auction results, designated by (A), which are actual, rounded to the nearest dollar, including the 10% to 15% buyer's premium charged by the auction house. Regional retail prices may be higher or lower than average retail, and often depend upon the individual dealer. Auction prices are subject to a number of variables, and are not considered retail or wholesale. They represent the price that one person–a dealer *or* private party–paid at the time and place the piece was offered for sale.

In most cases, the prices in this book are those a buyer should expect to pay for a piece in excellent to very good condition. Pieces with flaws that affect value are so noted in the descriptions. Because prices are *average* retail (except for auction results), some collectors will consider the price on a particular piece a bargain and others will say it is exorbitant.. Everyone likes to think they are getting "a deal" when they buy. The tendency for most jewelry price guides is to overstate values, which has conditioned the collecting public to expect to see higher prices listed than what was actually paid for a piece. This is not the case with *Warman's Jewelry.* "Average retail" means just that: there will be times and places when *higher* prices will be asked and paid as well as lower than what is listed here.

The marketplace where a piece is sold affects price as much as other criteria, i.e., design, craftsmanship, condition, demand and scarcity, and intrinsic value of metals and stones in fine jewelry. Pricing data was gathered from all over the country, but differences were often a result of the *type* of marketplace (e.g., an urban retail shop versus a rural flea market) rather than its region or locale. Prices were compiled from a number of sources, including auction houses, appraisers, dealers, jewelry store owners, collectors, and that newest and most pervasive of marketplaces, the Internet.

If you see one of your possessions in this book (or a similar one) and wish to sell it–as a private party to a dealer, or as a dealer to a dealer–you should expect to receive approximately 35% to 40% of the value listed. If it cannot be resold quickly, expect even less; and it is possible that a dealer may not wish to purchase it at all. Collectors are very specialized; dealers work for years to assemble a list of collectors who will pay top dollar for an item. Try to be as objective about your item as possible. If it is an heirloom, its sentimental value may be greater than any dollar amount you could get for it.

BOARD OF ADVISORS

One person cannot be an expert in every type of jewelry. Many "specialists"–dealers, collectors, gemologists, appraisers, auction house directors, museum curators, researchers and historians–were consulted for the sections relating to their specialty. Some provided expertise in more than one field, or general gemological and/or historical information, as well as photos or items for photos and listings. Their names appear in the captions and at the end of their respective categories. Mailing and/or e-mail addresses and/or phone numbers are listed in the front of this book. If you wish to buy or sell an item in their field or fields of expertise, send a note, with a photograph or photocopy, description, and self-addressed stamped envelope (call or e-mail if no address given). If time and interest permit, they will respond.

OTHER CONTRIBUTORS

Other dealers and collectors who provided jewelry for the photos and listings are listed below. Note that the word "collection" in the photo captions can refer to a dealer who sells under his or her own name, or a collector (some people are both). Correspondence to any of them may be addressed in care of the author (see below).

Dealers: Julia Alberts, Claudette Beaulieu, Ron Belkin, Brett Benson, Maranda Blackwelder (Blackwelder's Antiques & Fine Art), Lenore Dailey (The Raven's Nest), DLW Antiques, Bill Faust, Gail Freeman, Gail Gerretsen, Elayne Glotzer, Diane Hanselman (Past and Present Jewelry), Kerry Holden, Neil Lane, Penny Lesch, Dawn Lowe (Xcentricities), Lis Normoyle, the Old Territorial Shop, Kirsten Olson, Mary Palmer, Connie Parente, Gilly Phipps (Phipps Antiques), Charles Pinkham, Benjamin A. Randolph (The Eden Sterling Co.), David Skelley (Boomerang), Pamela Tonge and Dawn Usher (Kindred Company), and Mary Williamson.

Several of my dealer-contributors (including some advisors) are members of the Internet e-mail listserv Jewelcollect and some of them also have websites: Jane Clarke (Morning Glory Antiques), Martha Exline (Metique), Terri and John Krantz (Lovejoy's), Leigh Leshner (Venture Entertainment Group), Beegee McBride (South Texas Trading Co.), Susan Morton (Noisy Boy and Disorderly Girl), Elizabeth Nyland. Links to their sites and many others can be found at list administrator Isabelle Bryman's website: http://www.lizjewel.com/jewelcollect/jc.html.

Collectors: Ellen Borlenghi, Gianna Cagliano, Cheryl Chang, Jill Crawford, Marisela Doria, Elizabeth Hada, Alice and Charlotte Healy, Sue James, Richard Levey, Elaine Sarnoff, Susan Shargal, Anne Tidwell, Yolanda Tisdale, Sandra Willard.

COMMENTS INVITED

Our readers are encouraged to send their comments and suggestions to Christie Romero, Center for Jewelry Studies, P.O. Box 424, Anaheim, CA 92815-0424. E-mail: CR4jewelry@aol.com.

STATE OF THE MARKET

In spite of economic recovery, the antique and period jewelry market continues to have its ups and down. While the middle market has remained weak, the high and low ends have held their own. Advanced collectors and foreign buyers who want the rarest and best still fuel the upper end, while the very inexpensive pieces sell to bargain-hunters, seekers of future trends, and beginners fearful of paying too much.

Never has it been more crucial to arm oneself with knowledge and experience. Reproductions abound, some only detectable if one knows their source. Once these pieces have circulated through the secondary market, it will be even more difficult to identify them. Skepticism is the watchword of the day.

Heading toward the next millennium, an air of uncertainty prevails. Trend-spotters are finding it difficult to pinpoint any one particular area of growth, perhaps because there are many. Workmanship, history, and beauty of fine antique jewelry in general has come to be appreciated by a growing segment of the market. No longer is it a given that a fine old gemstone-set gold jewel will be broken up for the intrinsic value of its components. Recutting of old European and old mine diamonds is no longer standard operating procedure amongst knowledgeable dealers.

Victorian jewelry remains popular, but prices have not increased significantly in most markets. Sentimental Victoriana (love tokens, memorial jewelry, hairwork, etc.) appears to be holding up well, gathering a growing collector base. There is even an Internet website for hairwork collectors!

The style known as Art Deco does consistently well at auction, signed or unsigned, but circa 1920s and 30s Cartier jewelry in particular usually sells well, due in part to a major exhibition and a European auction devoted exclusively to the firm's history and product. In fine jewelry, however, the Retro Modern style of the forties is, as one auction house representative put it, "dead in the water" - unless, of course, it is something unusual, spectacular, and signed.

Traveling exhibitions and catalogs have also fueled increased interest in handmade, one-of-a-kind or limited production pieces with unique, identifiable designs, from Arts & Crafts to Mid-Century Modern. Names carry weight in this segment of the market, too.

The jewelry of India, past inspiration for many a Western jewelry designer (but itself outside the scope of this book), is once again garnering attention, being worn by movie stars and others in the media spotlight.

One market maxim still holds true: a large segment of the collectible jewelry market is trend-oriented, and pricing is often dependent on the basic economic law of supply and demand - the currently "hot" and scarce pieces command the highest prices. Costume jewelry (see price notes in Designer/Manufacturer Signed Costume section) is particularly subject to the ins and outs of fads and trends. Some fads are short-lived, while others make a comeback. Sustained and growing collector interest in Bakelite and other plastics followed on the heels of the publication of several books and high-end auction catalogs. Prices have kept pace for the most sought-after and scarce items. Interest in signed costume jewelry still varies by region, but a great deal of trading takes place on the Internet, with a consequent nation-wide leveling of prices. Nationally distributed price guides, well-publicized auction results, and itinerant dealers have also contributed to this circumstance, which has affected the fine jewelry market as well. With few exceptions, a comparable piece *in a comparable marketplace* will generally carry a comparable price. Regional differences still exist in the *kinds* of jewelry that most readily *sell*, but even those differences appear to be narrowing. There will always be individualists who buck the trends, but increasingly, we have become a nation of trend-watchers. As word gets out at a faster and faster pace, the trends will come and go accordingly.

BOARD OF ADVISORS

Rosalie & Aram Berberian
ARK Antiques
P.O. Box 3133
New Haven, CT 06515
(203) 498-8572
American Arts & Crafts

Mary Borchert, G.G.
Beverly Hills Auctioneers
9454 Wilshire Blvd Suite 202
Beverly Hills, CA 90212
(310) 278-8115

Steven Cabella
The Modern i Gallery
500 Red Hill Ave.
San Anselmo, CA 94904
(415) 456-3960
e-mail: moderni@slip.net
Mid-Century American Modernist

Jill Crawford, Collector
(310) 457-8076
Mexican Silver

Ulysses G. Dietz
The Newark Museum
P.O. Box 540
Newark, NJ 07101
(973) 596-6661

Ruth Eller, Historian
(206) 365-6305
Late 18th and 19th Century

Samuel C. Gassman, G.G.
Foxe Harrell Jewelers
P.O. Box 444
Clinton, IA 52732
(319) 242-3580 (by appointment)
Late 18th and 19th Century

Bruce Healy, Collector
(303) 494-9222
Scandinavian

Ellen Hoffs
Before
P.O. Box 3637
Santa Monica, CA 90408
Mid-Century American Modernist

Mary Lee Hu
University of Washington
Art-Box 353440
Seattle WA 98195
Metalworking techniques

Carmelita Garceau Johnson, Collector
(818) 594-0695
Hair and Hairwork

Patrick Kapty, Dealer-Collector
(714) 530-1015
email: CK4ARTsAKE@aol.com
20th Century Costume & Silver

Keith Lauer
National Plastics Center and Museum
210 Lancaster Street
Leominster MA 01453
(508) 537-9529
Plastics

Gail Brett Levine, G.G., I.S.A.
Publisher, *Auction Market Resource*
P.O. Box 7683
Rego Park, NY 11374-7683
(718) 897-7305
e-mail: 76766.614@compuserve.com

Karen Lorene, G.G., I.S.A., N.J.A.
Facèré Jewelry Art
City Center, 1420 Fifth Ave.
Seattle, WA 98101
(206) 624-6768
e-mail: karenl@halcyon.com

Lynne Loube, G.G., Historian
7805 Old Georgetown Road, Suite 200-D
Bethesda, MD 20814
(301) 656-5787
e-mail: lintat@erols.com
18th Century American

Yvonne Markowitz
Museum of Fine Arts
Egyptian Department
465 Huntington Avenue
Boston, MA 02115
(617) 369-3348

Al Munir Meghji, Collector
(604) 251-5183
Vancouver BC, Canada
Mid-20th Century Modern

Anna Miller, G.G.
Director, Master Valuer Program
P.O. Box 1844
Pearland, TX 77588
(713) 485-1606
Cameos

Shari & Jeff Miller
Antiques & Eccentricities
(602) 952-1467
e-mail: DsrtTrader@aol.com
Mid-Century American and Native American

Elise Misiorowski, G.G., Historian
(310) 473-0529 (also fax)

Ginger Moro
P.O. Box 64376
West Los Angeles CA 90064
e-mail: modmoro@earthlink.net
European Costume, Scandinavian

Steve Nelson
Mountain Lion Trading Post
229 Avenue I #150
Redondo Beach, CA 90277
(310) 540-4428
Native American (Indian)

Gary Niederkorn
Niederkorn Gallery
2005 Locust Street
Philadelphia, PA
(215) 567-2606
American Silver

Terrance O'Halloran, G.G., J.M.A.
P.O. Box 230-0337
Encinitas, CA 92023-0337
(818) 782-9398
Arts & Crafts, Art Nouveau

Sigi Pineda
Reforma #52
Taxco, Gro. CP40230, Mexico
52 (762) 2-15-91
Mexican Silver

Charles Pinkham, Dealer
(909) 620-5805 (by appointment)
20th Century Costume and Silver

Julie P. Robinson, Historian
P.O. Box 744
Davidsville, PA 15928
(814) 479-2212
Plastics

Patsy Sanders Seal, Collector-Dealer
10 Rosewood Place
Joshua, TX 76058
(817) 295-4569
e-mail: Patstfy@aol.com
20th Century Costume

Gertrud Seidmann, FSA
Institute of Archaeology
36 Beaumont St
Oxford OX1 2PG England
18th, 19th Century engraved gems

Gail Roeshman Selig, G.G., Collector
(610) 776-0951
e-mail: roesh@itw.com
Scandinavian

Peter Shemonsky, G.G., I.S.A.
P.O. Box 594
East Boston, MA 02128
(617) 569-1502
e-mail: Pshemonsky@aol.com

Paula Straub, G.G., I.S.A.
Gemological Institute of America
5355 Armada Drive
Carlsbad, CA 92008
(760) 603-4000 ext. 7739
e-mail: pstraub@aol.com

Lucille Tempesta, Publisher/Editor
Vintage Fashion & Costume Jewelry Newsletter
P.O. Box 265
Glen Oaks, NY 11004
Fax: (718) 939-7988
e-mail: VFCJ@aol.com

Joseph W. Tenhagen, NGJA, FGA, GG
J.W. Tenhagen Gemstones, Inc.
36 NE First St, Suite #419
Miami, FL 33132
(305) 374-2411
Fax: (305) 374-2413
Diamonds

Amanda Triossi, F.G.A.
Sotheby's Institute
30 Oxford Street
London W1N 9FL England
44 (171) 462-3232

Caryl & Hal Unger
Imagination Unlimited
4302 Alton Rd. Suite 820
Miami Beach, FL 33140-2893
(305) 534-5870
e-mail: PopPop0818@aol.com
Georg Jensen

Ruth Levin Watters, Collector
157J Helm Road
Barrington Hills, IL 60010
(847) 428-1570
e-mail: jwatters@email6.starnetinc. com
Butterfly Wing jewelry

Alfred Weisberg, Executive Director
Providence Jewelry Museum
P.O. Box 9650
Providence, RI 02940
(401) 781-3100

Colin Williamson
Plastics Historical Society
1 Carlton House Terrace
London SW1Y 5DB England
e-mail: Smile Plas@aol.com
Plastics, Victorian compositions

Sharen and Nicholas Wood
The Silver Fox Gallery, Stand L
121 Portobello Road
London W11 England
44 (1892) 542167
Late Georgian, Early Victorian

Janet Zapata
Decorative Arts Consultant
(973) 376-7608 (by appointment)
American Fine and Silver, Tiffany

AUCTION HOUSES

Beverly Hills Auctioneers
Mary Borchert, GG
9454 Wilshire Blvd Suite 202
Beverly Hills, CA 90212
(310) 278-8115
(310) 278-5567 FAX

Butterfield & Butterfield
Jill Burgum, Jewelry
7601 Sunset Blvd
Los Angeles, CA 90046
(213) 850-7500 ext. 200
(213) 850-5843 FAX

Butterfield & Butterfield
Taryn Miller, Jewelry
220 San Bruno
San Francisco, CA 94103
(415) 861-7500 ext. 247
(415) 861-8951 FAX

Christie's
Simon Teakle, Jewelry
502 Park Ave. (at 59th St.)
New York, NY 10022
(212) 546-1133
(212) 980-8163 FAX

Christie's East
Susan Abeles, Jewelry
219 East 67th St.
New York, NY 10021
(212) 606-0400
(212) 737-6076 FAX

Christie's Los Angeles
Glenn Spiro, Brett O'Connor, Jewelry
360 North Camden Dr.
Beverly Hills, CA 90210
(310) 385-2666
(310) 385-9292 FAX

William Doyle Galleries
Susan Dalrymple, Jewelry
175 East 87th St.
New York, NY 10128
(212) 427-2730
(212) 369-0892 FAX

Joseph DuMouchelle
199 North Main St., Suite 204
Plymouth, MI 48170
(734) 455-4555
(734) 455-2403 FAX

Dunning's Auction Service
William Milne, Jewelry
755 Church Road
Elgin, IL 60123
(708) 741-3483
(708) 741-3589 FAX

Grogan & Co.
Peter Shemonsky, Jewelry
22 Harris Street
Dedham, MA 02026
(781) 461-9500
(781) 461-9625 FAX

R. G. Munn
Native American Art Auctions
P.O. Box 705, Cloudcroft, NM 88317
(505) 687-3676
(505) 687-3592 FAX

Phillips
Claudia Florian, Jewelry
406 East 79th St.
New York, NY 10021
(212) 570-4830
(212) 570-2207 FAX

Skinner, Inc.
Gloria Lieberman, Jewelry
The Heritage on the Garden
63 Park Plaza
Boston, MA 02116
(617) 350-5400
(617) 350-5429 FAX

Sloan's
Dana L. Ehrman, Jewelry
4920 Wyaconda Rd.
Bethesda, MD 20852
(301) 468-4911 (800) 649-5066
(301) 468-9182 FAX

Sotheby's
John D. Block, Jewelry
1334 York Ave (at 72nd St.)
New York, NY 10021
(212) 606-7000
(212) 606-7107 FAX

Sotheby's Beverly Hills
Carol Elkins, Tracy Sherman, Jewelry
9665 Wilshire Blvd
Beverly Hills, CA 90210
(310) 786-1864
(310) 274-0899 FAX

Sotheby's Chicago
215 West Ohio St.
Chicago, IL 60610
(312) 670-0010
(312) 670-4248 FAX

Treadway/Toomey Galleries
818 North Blvd
Oak Park, IL 60301
(708) 383-5234
(708) 383-4828 FAX

Weschler's
909 E St. NW
Washington, DC 20004
(202) 628-1281
(202) 628-2366 FAX

ABBREVIATIONS

Am	American
appl	applied
approx	approximately
bc	brilliant cut
bg	background
cab	cabochon
ct, cts	carat, carats (gemstones)
ct or c	karat gold (Eng)
C	century
c.	circa
circ	circular
constr	construction
curv	curvilinear
dam	damaged
dk	dark
diag	diagonal
dia	diameter
dwt	pennyweight
emb	embossed
Eng	English
engr	engraved
Fr	French
f.w.	freshwater (pearls)
geo	geometric
Ger	German
gf	gold-filled
gp	gold plated
grad	graduated
hmk	hallmark
hp	hand painted
h	height
imp	impressed
irid	iridescent
Ital	Italian
k	karat (gold)
lg	large
l	length
lt	light
mfr	manufacturer
mk	mark
mkd	marked
mm	millimeter(s)
mono	monogram
MOP	mother of pearl
No	number
#	numbered
oe	old European cut
om	old mine cut
orig	original
pr	pair
pat	patent
pc, pcs	piece, pieces
pl	plated
plat	platinum
ptd	painted
rect	rectangular
rev	reverse
r.s.	rhinestone(s)
rh pl	rhodium-plated
rc	rose cut
sgd	signed
sp	silver plated
st yg	silver-topped yellow gold
sm	small
sc	single cut
sq	square
ster	sterling silver
syn	synthetic
tl	total length
tw	total weight
turq	turquoise
wg	white gold
wm	white metal
w	width
yg	yellow gold
ym	yellow metal

PHOTO POSITION ABBREVIATIONS

L - Left
C - Center
R - Right
T - Top
B - Bottom
TL - Top Left
TC - Top Center
TR - Top Right
CL - Center Left
CR - Center Right
BL - Bottom Left
BC - Bottom Center
BR - Bottom Right

More than one piece in a position is assigned a number, reading left to right (or top to bottom), e.g., BL-1 is the first piece on the left at the bottom, BL-2 is the second piece on the left at the bottom (to the right of the first piece).

TIMELINE

Late Georgian Period

Date	General History, Discoveries & Inventions	Date	Jewelry & Gemstone History, Discoveries & Inventions
1760	George III becomes king of Great Britain	1760	American goldsmith Paul Revere begins making jewelry (c.)
		1764	Josiah Wedgwood introduces fine ceramic known as jasperware in plaques with relief decoration resembling cameos, mounted in cut steel manufactured by Matthew Boulton beginning in 1773.
1774	Louis XVI becomes king of France		
1775	American Revolution begins, Congress adopts the Declaration of Independence, 1776, cessation of hostilities declared, 1783		
1782	French scientist Antoine Laurent Lavoisier succeeds in melting platinum from its ore using pure oxygen		
		1786	Marc Étienne Janety, goldsmith to Louis XVI of France, crafts a sugar bowl out of platinum "Lover's eye" miniatures popularized by Prince George of England
1789	French Revolution begins, ends 1799 George Washington elected first President of the United States, dies 1799		
		1793	Seril Dodge of Providence, RI advertises offering of jewelry items made to order, sells business to half-brother Nehemiah, 1796
1799-1815	Napoleonic Wars		
1800	Thomas Jefferson and Aaron Burr tie in Presidential election Alessandro Volta invents the first battery, the Volta Pile Metallurgist Wm. H. Wollaston, chemist Smithson Tennant begin collaboration, create commercial-grade platinum, discover platinum family of metals (palladium, rhodium, 1802; iridium, osmium, 1803)		
1801	Robert Hare of Philadelphia invents oxyhydrogen ("gas") blowpipe Thomas Jefferson chosen President by House of Representatives	1801	E. Hinsdale establishes first American factory for the manufacture of fine jewelry in Newark, NJ
1804	Napoleon crowns himself Emperor of France	1804	Royal Ironworks of Berlin opens, jewelry production begins 1806
1811	George III declared insane; Regency period begins in Britain		
1812-1815	War between U.S. and Great Britain		
1813-1815	Prussian War of Liberation against Napoleon	1813-1815	Berlin iron jewelry made in Germany as patriotic gesture during War of Liberation: "*gold gab ich fur eisen*" [I gave gold for iron]
1817	A street in Baltimore, MD becomes the first to be lighted with gas from the first U.S. gas company	1815	Fortunato Pio Castellani established in Rome, begins study of granulation in ancient goldwork, 1827
		1819	*The Gas Blowpipe* by E.D. Clarke is published

Date	General History, Discoveries & Inventions	Date	Jewelry & Gemstone History, Discoveries & Inventions
1820	George III of Great Britain dies, George IV becomes king Platinum discovered in Russian Ural Mountains	1820s	Ancient goldwork discovered in Etruscan excavations
		1824	Pinmaking machine for straight pins patented in England by Lemuel Wellman Wright, by John Howe in U.S. 1832
1829-1837	Andrew Jackson is President of U.S.	1829	Sir Walter Scott's *Anne of Geierstein* is published, describing the opal as "misfortune's stone" French square hallmark for *doublé d'or* (rolled gold) introduced by Paris Mint
1830	"India rubber" elastic first appears in women's clothing *Godey's Lady's Book* first published French occupation of Algeria begins George IV of Great Britain dies, William IV becomes king		
1836	Edmund Davey discovers and identifies acetylene U.S. Patent Act passed. U.S. Patent Office issues Patent Number 1		

Early Victorian (Romantic) Period

Date	General History, Discoveries & Inventions	Date	Jewelry & Gemstone History, Discoveries & Inventions
1837	Victoria becomes Queen of Great Britain Louis J. M. Daguerre perfects daguerreotype photographic process The telegraph is patented by Cooke and Wheatstone, improved by Samuel Morse, first message sent 1844	1837	Enameled garter armlet made for Queen Victoria; Order of the Garter strap and buckle motifs become popular Charles Lewis Tiffany founds company in New York City; becomes Tiffany & Co. 1853
1839	Charles Goodyear invents and patents (1844) vulcanized rubber; displays products at Crystal Palace (1851)		
1840	Victoria weds Prince Albert	1840	Electroplating commercialized, patented by Elkingtons of Birmingham. Large-scale jewelry manufacturing begins in U.S. Process for permanently foiled pastes (faceted glass) discovered
		c. 1840	Scottish motifs in "pebble" (agate) jewelry popularized, continuing through the rest of the century Repoussé and machine stamping replace *cannetille* (gold filigree) Algerian knot motif introduced in Paris
		1841	Duty on imported jewelry and mounted gemstones levied by U.S.
1842	Gutta percha introduced in Paris Excavations of ancient Assyrian capital of Nineveh begin British kite-shaped registry mark introduced		
		1846	Riker, Tay & Searing founded in Newark, NJ, become Riker Bros. 1892
		1847	Cartier founded in Paris
1848	Balmoral Castle in Scotland purchased by Queen Victoria Formation of the Pre-Raphaelite Brotherhood in England Gold discovered in California	1848	Caldwell & Bennett becomes J.E. Caldwell & Co., Philadelphia Thomas H. Lowe of Birmingham introduces rolled gold plating process (a.k.a. gold filled) to Providence, RI manufacturers
1849	California Gold Rush The safety pin invented and patented by Walter Hunt of New York (patent # 6,281)	1849	Gold electroplating patented Opals first discovered in Australia
1850	High tariff placed on foreign goods imported into U.S.	1850	Tube-shaped ("trombone") safety catch patented by Charles Rowley of Birmingham England
1851	First international exhibition, the Great Exhibition of the Works of Industry of All Nations, held at The Crystal Palace in London. Gold first discovered in Australia Hard rubber (vulcanite) patented by Nelson Goodyear	1851	Artificial aventurine ("goldstone") exhibited at Crystal Palace

Date	General History, Discoveries & Inventions	Date	Jewelry & Gemstone History, Discoveries & Inventions
1852	Louis Napoleon becomes Napoleon III, beginning of French Second Empire	1852	Tiffany & Co. introduces the English sterling standard to the United States
			Machine for heat-pressing bog oak patented
1853	Commodore Matthew Perry sails American fleet into Japan, opens East-West trade relations	1853	Demantoid garnets discovered in Ural Mountains, identified as green andradite, 1864, named demantoid, 1878
	Crystal Palace Exhibition held in New York, modeled after London exhibition		
1854	Results of first commercially successful aluminum reduction process published by Henri Ste. Claire Deville	1854	Use of 15, 12, and 9-karat gold made legal in England
1855	Paris Exposition Universelle	1855	Theodor Fahrner founds jewelry factory in Pforzheim, Germany
	Aluminum articles first exhibited		First aluminum jewelry made in France (c.)
	R.W. Bunsen develops gas-air burner		
1856	Wm. Perkin accidentally discovers the first synthetic aniline (coal-tar) dye, mauve		
1857	Financial "Panic of 1857" affects all U.S. industries	1857	Snake-chain making machine patented in U.S.
	Furnace to melt platinum and its alloys developed by Henri Ste. Claire Deville		
		1858	Boucheron founded in Paris
1859	Construction of the Suez Canal begins	1859	Jewels of Queen Ah-Hotep of Egypt discovered
	Comstock Lode (silver) discovered in Nevada		First attempt at organized jewelers' union in U.S., not successful until 1900 (International Jewelry Workers Union of America)
		1860	Henry D. Morse opens first American diamond-cutting factory in Boston, develops standards for American round brilliant cut, 1872-75

Mid Victorian (Grand) Period

Date	General History, Discoveries & Inventions	Date	Jewelry & Gemstone History, Discoveries & Inventions
1861	U.S. Civil War begins [1861-1865]; Lincoln inaugurated	1861	Fortunato Pio Castellani turns business over to son Augusto
	Prince Consort Albert dies; Victoria enters prolonged period of mourning	1861-c.1880	The wearing of mourning (black) jewelry required at British court
1862	International Exhibition held in London	1862	Archeological Revival gold jewelry exhibited by Castellani of Rome at International Exhibition
			Reverse crystal intaglios by Charles Cook shown at Exhibition
			Japanese decorative arts exhibited for the first time in the West
1863	Edward, Prince of Wales, marries Alexandra of Denmark		
1865	Lincoln assassinated	1865	Sapphires found in Missouri River in Montana
1866	First transatlantic cable laid		
1867	Paris Exposition Universelle	1867	Egyptian Revival jewelry exhibited at Paris Exposition
			First authenticated diamond, the Eureka, discovered in South Africa
1868	Celluloid, the first successful semi-synthetic thermoplastic, invented in U.S. by John Wesley Hyatt; patented, trade name registered, 1870; commercial production begins, 1872	1868	Gorham Mfg. Co., Providence, RI, adopts sterling standard of 925 parts per thousand
1869	First transcontinental railroad from Omaha to San Francisco	1869	Henry D. Morse cuts the Dewey diamond, largest found in America to date (23.75 cts, cut to 11.70 cts)
	Suez Canal opened		"Diamond rush" begins in South Africa with discovery of the "Star of Africa"
			American Horological Jounal first published, merges with *The Jewelers' Circular* to become *The Jewelers' Circular and Horological Review,* 1873

Date	General History, Discoveries & Inventions	Date	Jewelry & Gemstone History, Discoveries & Inventions
1870	Fall of the French Empire British metallurgist George Matthey perfects lime furnace for platinum refining	1870	*The Jewelers' Circular* founded, first issue published February 15 Peter Carl Fabergé takes over father's business
1870s	Recession in Europe	1870s	Influx of European craftsmen and designers into U.S. Japanese craftsmen introduce metal-working techniques and designs to the West
1872	International Exhibition held in London	1872	Black opals first discovered in Queensland, Australia Ferdinand J. Herpers of Newark NJ patents six-prong setting for diamonds, introduced as the "Tiffany setting" by Tiffany & Co., 1886
1873	Universal Exhibition held in Vienna		
1874	Gold discovered in Black Hills of Dakota Territory		
1875	Arthur Lazenby Liberty founds Liberty & Co. of London	1875	The Celluloid Mfg. Co. begins jewelry production in Newark, NJ
1876	Centennial Exposition held in Philadelphia Wearing of swords banned in Japan Queen Victoria becomes Empress of India Alexander Graham Bell patents the telephone	1876	Alessandro Castellani presents and lectures on Etruscan Revival jewelry at Centennial Exposition Henry D. Morse and Charles M. Field obtain U.S. and European patents for steam-driven bruting (diamond-cutting) machines
1877	Advent of bottled oxygen (liquified and compressed)	1877	Successful experiments with chemical manufacture of very small rubies and sapphires in Paris, published by Frémy
1878	Paris Exposition Universelle	1878	Tiffany & Co. awarded gold medal for encrusted metals technique in the "Japanesque" style at Paris Exposition Tiffany Diamond discovered in South Africa Unger Bros. of Newark, NJ, begins the manufacture of silver jewelry
1879	T. A. Edison patents incandescent light bulb	1879	Gem expert George F. Kunz joins Tiffany & Co.

Late Victorian (Aesthetic) Period

Date	General History, Discoveries & Inventions	Date	Jewelry & Gemstone History, Discoveries & Inventions
1880	Rational Dress Society founded in Britain	1880	Cecil Rhodes establishes the De Beers Mining Company in South Africa (renamed De Beers Consolidated Mines in 1888) Mass production of wrist watches begins in Switzerland, introduced in U.S. 1895, U.S. manufacture 1907 (c.)
1881	The first electrically-lit theatre, The Savoy, opens in London		
1883	Metropolitan Opera House opens in New York City		
		1885	First appearance of the "Geneva" synthetic ruby
1886	Gold discovered in South Africa (Transvaal) Statue of Liberty dedicated	1886	Tiffany setting for diamond solitaires introduced Richard W. Sears starts a mail-order company to sell watches (second company to sell jewelry and watches founded in 1889)
1887	Queen Victoria's Golden Jubilee Hall-Héroult process for refining aluminum developed; first commercial production in Switzerland, value drops Celluloid photographic film invented by Hannibal W. Goodwin	1887	Gold extraction by cyanide process invented by John Stewart Macarthur and the Forrest brothers Birmingham (England) Jewellers' and Silversmiths' Association formed by manufacturers Tiffany & Co. purchases French crown jewels The Belais brothers of New York begin experimenting with alloys for white gold (c.); David Belais introduces his formula to the trade in 1917 (referred to as "18k Belais")
1888	George Eastman introduces the first commercial box camera, the Kodak	1888	C.R. Ashbee's Guild of Handicraft founded in London, the first crafts guild to specialize in jewelry-making and metalwork
1889	Paris Exposition Universelle - Eiffel Tower constructed, first structure to serve as landmark for an exposition	1889	Tiffany & Co. exhibits enameled orchid jewels by Paulding Farnham at the Exposition Universelle Black opals discovered in New South Wales, Australia

Date	General History, Discoveries & Inventions	Date	Jewelry & Gemstone History, Discoveries & Inventions
1890	Sarah Bernhardt plays Cleopatra on stage Charles Dana Gibson's "Gibson Girl" first appears in the humor magazine *Life*		
1891	The marking of foreign imports with the name of the country of origin in English required by the enactment of the McKinley Tariff Act, October, 1890	1891	Power-driven bruting (girdling) machine for cutting diamonds patented in Europe
1892	*Vogue* Magazine founded in U.S.	1892	Marcus & Co., formerly Jaques & Marcus, established in New York
1893	World's Columbian Exposition in Chicago	1893	Cultured pearls first developed by K. Mikimoto in Japan; first spherical pearls grown 1905
1894	Thomas Edison's Kinetoscope Parlor ("peepshow") opens in New York City	1894	Screwback earring finding for unpierced ears patented (U.S.)
1895	Samuel Bing opens his new Paris gallery of decorative art called *"L'Art Nouveau"* American Consuelo Vanderbilt marries the British Duke of Marlborough The wireless telegraph invented by Guglielmo Marconi (first transatlantic wireless signal in 1901)	1895	René Lalique exhibits jewelry at the Bing gallery and the Salon of the Societé des Artistes Français; begins work on a series of 145 pieces for Calouste Gulbenkian Daniel Swarovski opens glass stone-cutting factory in Tyrol, Austria Blue sapphires discovered in Yogo Gulch, Montana
1897	Queen Victoria's Diamond Jubilee Casein plastics marketed in Germany Boston and Chicago Arts and Crafts Societies founded	1897	Lacloche Frères established in Paris
1898	Alaska Gold Rush Spanish-American War		
1899-1902	Boer War (South Africa)	1899-1902	Diamond supplies curtailed by Boer War; prices for De Beers' reserve stock rise

Edwardian Period (*Belle Époque*)

Date	General History, Discoveries & Inventions	Date	Jewelry & Gemstone History, Discoveries & Inventions
1900	Paris *Exposition Universelle* U.S. officially adopts the gold standard with McKinley's signing of the Gold Standard Act (monometallism) Oxyacetylene torch invented by Edmund Fouché	1900	Synthetic rubies exhibited at Paris Exposition; Tiffany & Co. exhbits a life-size iris corsage ornament set with Montana blue sapphires Boucheron, Fouquet, Lalique, Vever and other French jewelers display their Art Nouveau jewels at Paris Exposition The Kalo Shop founded by Clara Barck Welles in Chicago, begins jewelry-making 1905, closed 1970 The diamond saw is invented in France (c.)
1901	Queen Victoria dies. Edward VII becomes king McKinley assassinated. Theodore Roosevelt becomes President. Pan-American Exposition held in Buffalo, NY Gustav Stickley begins publishing his periodical, *The Craftsman* (until 1916)	1901	Lever safety catch for brooches patented by Herpers Brothers of Newark Tiffany & Co. exhibits at Pan-American Exposition, special mark (beaver) used on exhibition pieces
1902	Vienna Secession Exhibition Edward VII coronation	1902	Flame-fusion process for synthesizing rubies presented in Paris by Verneuil, published and patented 1904 Cartier opens a London branch Process for setting rhinestones or metal in celluloid patented
1903	Wiener Werkstätte founded in Vienna, Austria by Koloman Moser and Josef Hoffmann	1903	Fabergé opens London branch, selling mostly "gentlemen's things"
1904	Louisiana Purchase Exposition held in St. Louis New York City subway opens Construction begins on the Panama Canal	1904	Louis Comfort Tiffany exhibits his jewelry for the first time at the St. Louis Exposition Marshall Field & Co., Chicago, establishes a craft shop for jewelry and metalware (closed c. 1950) Georg Jensen opens his silversmithy in Copenhagen, Denmark

Date	General History, Discoveries & Inventions	Date	Jewelry & Gemstone History, Discoveries & Inventions
1905	Albert Einstein proposes his theory of relativity Henri Matisse and other fauvist artists exhibit at *Salon d'Automne* in Paris	1905	Forest Craft Guild founded by Forest Mann in Grand Rapids, MI The Kalo Shop begins jewelry-making in Chicago Cullinan diamond (3,106 carats) discovered in Transvaal So. Africa, presented to Edward VII 1907
1906	San Francisco earthquake and fire Finland is first European country to grant women's suffrage	1906	National Stamping Act passed in U.S., requiring marking of gold and silver content, sterling standard established Van Cleef & Arpels founded in Paris
1907	First exhibition of cubist paintings held in Paris, including works by Pablo Picasso and Georges Braque Suffragettes demonstrate for the right to vote in London	1907	Tiffany & Co. establishes Art Jewelry Dept. with Louis Comfort Tiffany as director Benitoite discovered in California, declared official state stone, 1985
1908	Henry Ford introduces the first mass-produced automobile, the Model T Couturier Paul Poiret opens "Boutique Chichi," introduces corsetless dresses and the vertical line in fashion (c.)	1908	First spherical cultured pearls patented in Japan by Mikimoto (first grown in 1905, American patent granted in 1916)
1909	Leo H. Baekeland patents first entirely synthesized plastic, Bakelite The Wright brothers begin large-scale manufacture of the airplane (first flight 1903, patented 1906)	1909	Cartier New York opens
1910	The Ballets Russes production of *Schéhérazade* presented in Paris Edward VII dies, George V becomes king of Great Britain First major American women's suffrage parade held in New York City, demonstration in Washington, DC, 1913	1910	Eugene Morehouse invents the "bullet" safety catch for brooches, patented for B.A. Ballou & Co 1911 France classifies platinum as a precious metal, new hallmark (dog's head) issued 1912
		c. 1910-1920	Suffragette jewelry in green, white, and violet (first initials for "give women votes") is popular in Britain and U.S.
1911	George V coronation	1911	George V has Cullinan I and II set in Imperial State crown and scepter The Hope Diamond is purchased by Ned and Evalyn Walsh McLean from Cartier Synthetic blue sapphires patented in U.S by Verneuil
1912	The *Titanic* sinks	1912	Oscar Heyman & Bros. founded in New York
1914	World War I begins First ship through Panama Canal (completed 1913) The first U.S. fashion show is staged by Edna Woolman Chase, editor of *Vogue*	1914	Platinum declared a "strategic metal" during wartime, use in jewelry diminished
1915	Panama-Pacific International Exposition held in San Francisco	1915	U.S. patent #1165448 granted to Karl Gustav Paul Richter of Pforzheim Germany, for a white gold alloy of gold, nickel and palladium
1917	Theda Bara plays Cleopatra in first (silent) film version The U.S. enters the war Russian Revolution begins	1917	David Belais of New York introduces his formula for 18k white gold to the trade, known as "18k Belais" Cartier designs the Tank wristwatch, first public sale 1919
1918	First regular airmail service, between Washington, DC and New York City, begins, New York to San Francisco 1921 World War I ends Bohemia, Moravia and Slovakia become the Republic of Czechoslovakia		

The "Modern" Era

Date	General History, Discoveries & Inventions	Date	Jewelry & Gemstone History, Discoveries & Inventions
1919	Bauhaus founded in Germany by Walter Gropius The Eighteenth Amendment to the U.S. Constitution is ratified (Prohibition)	1919	Marcel Tolkowsky publishes *Diamond Design*, detailing the cut and proportions of the modern brilliant ("American" or "ideal" cut), following scientific standards first discovered and developed by Henry D. Morse, 1872-1875

Date	General History, Discoveries & Inventions	Date	Jewelry & Gemstone History, Discoveries & Inventions
1920	The Nineteenth Amendment, giving women the right to vote, is ratified		
	First regular radio programs begin broadcasting in Pittsburgh		
1922	Howard Carter discovers King Tutankhamun's tomb in Egypt	1922	Raymond C. Yard, Inc. founded in New York City
1923	Cartoonist John Held Jr.'s "Betsy Co-ed" and "Joe College" first appear on the cover of humor magazine *Life* (c.)	1923	Frederik Lunning comes to New York City, opens a shop for Georg Jensen, 1924
			Synthetic pearl essence for simulated pearls invented, called "H-scale"
		1924	Egyptologist Caroline R. Williams discovers the granulation technique used by ancient goldsmiths
1925	*Exposition Internationale des Arts Decoratifs et Industriels Modernes* held in Paris	1925	Synthetic spinel, inadvertently produced by flame fusion process 1908, in wide commerical use (c.)
	Josephine Baker appears in the *Revue Nègre* in Paris		Firm of Trifari, Krussman & Fishel established
1926	The first commercial injection molding machine patented by Eckert and Ziegler in Germany		
1927	Charles Lindbergh flies solo nonstop New York to Paris	1927	Cartier patents model with spring system for double clip brooch
	Motion pictures with sound first publicly shown (Al Jolson in *The Jazz Singer*)		
	Cellulose acetate, trade name Lumarith, introduced by Celluloid Corp.		
		1928	Schiaparelli establishes "Maison Schiaparelli" in Paris
			Paul Flato opens salon in New York
1929	The Great Depression begins with stock market crash	1929	Trabert & Hoeffer, Inc.-Mauboussin merger agreement
			Black, Starr & Frost merger with Gorham Corp., until 1966
1930	Formation of the *Union des Artistes Modernes* in Paris		
	Construction completed on Chrysler Building in New York		
1931	Empire State Building becomes New York's tallest	1931	The "Duette" pinback mechanism for double clip brooches patented by U.S. costume jewelry manufacturer Coro
	Exposition Coloniale held in Paris		William Spratling opens the first silver workshop in Taxco, Mexico
1932	Franklin D. Roosevelt elected President	1932	14k gold replaces 12k and 15k in Britain, by decision of the Worshipful Company of Goldsmiths, London
	Radio City Music Hall opens		Harry Winston opens a retail jewelry business in New York City
1933	Construction begins on Golden Gate Bridge in San Francisco (completed 1937)	1933	The "invisible setting" (*serti invisible)* patented by Cartier and Van Cleef & Arpels (introduced in U.S. 1936)
	Prohibition repealed		Lost wax process, used in dentistry since c.1910, reintroduced for mass production of jewelry castings with vulcanized rubber molds (c.)
	Gold taken out of circulation		
	"Century of Progress" World's Fair opens in Chicago		
1934	Cecil B. De Mille's "Cleopatra" starring Claudette Colbert in title role	1934	Ernest Oppenheimer creates the De Beers Consolidated Mines Ltd. diamond cartel
	Salvador Dalí exhibits surrealist paintings in New York City		Synthetic emeralds ("Igmerald") devloped by IG-Farben, Germany, first seen by gemologists
			Van Cleef & Arpels introduces the "Ludo" flexible strap bracelet
			Patent for clipback earring finding for unpierced ears granted to Eugene Morehouse for B.A. Ballou
1935	French luxury cruise ship *Normandie* arrives in New York	1935	D. Lisner & Co. introduces "Bois Glacé" jewelry, their trade name for colorless phenolic plastic (Bakelite) laminated to wood
	U.S. Works Progress Administration inaugurated		*The Jewelers' Circular* merges with *The Keystone* to become *Jewelers' Circular-Keystone*

Date	General History, Discoveries & Inventions	Date	Jewelry & Gemstone History, Discoveries & Inventions
1936	George V dies. Edward VIII of Britain abdicates the throne to marry American-born divorcée Wallis Simpson, becomes Duke of Windsor, succeeded by George VI Margaret Mitchell's novel, *Gone With The Wind*, is published BBC inaugurates television service; general broadcasting begins in U.S. 1941 *Life* magazine founded by Henry Robinson Luce		
1937	Du Pont de Nemours & Co. introduces acrylic plastic, trade name "Lucite"; also patents nylon fiber The International Exhibition of Arts and Techniques in Modern Life held in Paris First feature-length animated film, Walt Disney's "Snow White and the Seven Dwarfs"	1937	Van Cleef & Arpels makes "marriage contract" bracelet for Wallis Simpson, the Duchess of Windsor Boucheron, Cartier, Mauboussin, Van Cleef & Arpels and others display figural jewels of colored gold and gemstones at Paris exhibition Paul Flato opens his Los Angeles establishment
1939	"Gone With The Wind" premiers World War II begins in Europe First nylon stockings marketed The New York World's Fair, titled "The World of Tomorrow," opens	1939	First commercially successful synthetic emerald process marketed by Carroll Chatham of San Francisco CA ("Chatham Created Emerald" term first used 1963) The House of Jewels at the New York World's Fair is sponsored by Tiffany & Co., Black, Starr & Frost-Gorham, Udall & Ballou, Marcus & Co., and Cartier New York Van Cleef & Arpels opens an office in New York City Verdura opens his own shop in New York Sam Kramer opens shop in Greenwich Village
1940	France falls under German occupation	1940	The Bank of France bans all gold trading
1941	The U.S. enters the war with the Japanese bombing of Pearl Harbor *Craft Horizons,* the first national magazine for crafts, is published by the Handcraft Cooperative League	1941	10% luxury tax on jewelry in U.S., raised to 20% 1944 Jean Schlumberger opens shop in New York, joins Tiffany & Co. 1956
1942	Rationing of consumer products (sugar, coffee, gasoline) begins in U.S.	1942	Use of platinum for jewelry prohibited in U.S. White metal restricted by U.S. government, sterling silver used as substitute in costume jewelry
1943	Postal zones added to addresses of large cities in U.S.		
1945	Roosevelt dies. Harry Truman becomes President World War II ends United Nations is formed, holds first session 1946	1945	Suzanne Belperron forms partnership Herz-Belperron with Jean Herz in Paris Mexican government requires marking of sterling silver with "spread eagle" assay mark (c.)
		1946	First national exhibit of American studio artists' jewelry held at Museum of Modern Art in New York City Jerry Fels founds "Renoir of Hollywood" in Los Angeles, CA David Webb opens office in New York, salon in 1963
1947	Couturier Christian Dior introduces "The New Look" Copyright symbol © is part of law passed by U.S. Congress	1947	Synthetic star rubies and sapphires ("Linde") first marketed Metalsmithing workshop series for war veterans begins, ends 1951
1948	Jewish State of Israel declared, admitted to U.N. 1949 Truman elected to full term as President	1948	De Beers Diamond Corp. launches the slogan "a diamond is forever"
1949	German Federal Republic (West Germany) proclaimed	1949	Harry Winston purchases Hope diamond. His "Court of Jewels" exhibit opens in New York, tours U.S. for the next four years
1951	Color television is introduced in U.S.	1951	The Metal Arts Guild organized in San Francisco
1952	George VI of Britain dies; succeeded by Elizabeth II Dwight D. Eisenhower elected President	1952	Italian jewelers Buccellati establish a salon in New York City
1953	Marilyn Monroe sings "Diamonds Are a Girl's Best Friend" in "Gentlemen Prefer Blondes"	1953	Mamie Eisenhower wears Trifari faux pearls to inaugural ball

Date	General History, Discoveries & Inventions	Date	Jewelry & Gemstone History, Discoveries & Inventions
		1954	De Beers institutes the annual Diamonds International Awards for original designs in diamond-set jewelry First successful production of synthetic diamonds at General Electric, process patented 1960, large gem-quality crystals produced 1970
1955	Atomically generated power first used in the U.S. Disneyland amusement park opens	1955	Swarovski Corp introduces the "aurora borealis" color effect for rhinestones and crystal in collaboration with Christian Dior
1957	The U.S.S.R. launches the first "Sputnik" satellite on Oct 4 Jack Kerouac's *On the Road* published, coins the term "Beat Generation"		
1958	Universal Exhibition opens in Brussels, Belgium	1958	Harry Winston donates the Hope Diamond to the Smithsonian Institution
1960	John F. Kennedy elected President of U.S.		
1961	Audrey Hepburn stars in "Breakfast at Tiffany's" Soviets, U.S., put first men in space	1961	International Exhibition of Modern Jewelry (1890-1961) held in London U.S. National Stamping Act amended, requiring a maker's trademark
1963	Kennedy assassinated. Lyndon Johnson becomes President U.S. Post Office introduces the ZIP code Elizabeth Taylor stars in *Cleopatra*		
1964	The Beatles perform live for the first time in the U.S.		
		1974	Tsavorite garnet (green) discovered in Kenya, Africa

References: David Bennett & Daniela Mascetti, *Understanding Jewellery,* 2nd edition, Antique Collectors' Club, 1994; Shirley Bury, *Jewellery 1789-1910, The International Era*, Vols. I & II, Antique Collectors' Club, 1991; Ulysses G. Dietz, ed., *The Glitter & The Gold, Fashioning America's Jewelry,* The Newark Museum, 1997; Martha G. Fales, *Jewelry in America 1600-1900*, Antique Collectors' Club, 1995; Gemological Institute of America, *Gems & Gemology*, vol. 32 #2,Summer, 1996, Vol. 33 #3, Fall, 1997; Bernard Grun, *The Timetables of History*, revised 3rd ed., Simon & Schuster/Touchstone, 1991; David Federman, "American Diamond Cutting: The Untold Heritage," *Modern Jeweler,* vol. 84 #1 (January, 1985); Hans Nadelhoffer, *Cartier, Jewelers Extraordinary*, Harry N. Abrams, 1984; Kurt Nassau, *Gems Made By Man*, Chilton Book Co., 1980; Penny Proddow, Debra Healy, Marion Fasel, *Hollywood Jewels, Movies, Jewelry, Stars*, Harry N. Abrams, 1992; Dorothy Rainwater, *American Jewelry Manufacturers,* Schiffer Publishing, 1988; Joseph W. Tenhagen, "What is the "Ideal Cut" Diamond Today?," prepared for the National Association of Jewelry Appraisers Conference, 1998; Laurence Urdang, ed., *The Timetables of American History*, updated edition, Simon & Schuster/Touchstone, 1996; Alfred M. Weisberg, *Why Providence?* Providence Jewelry Museum, 1992; *Information Please Almanac,* Houghton Mifflin Co, 1991; *Microsoft Encarta Multimedia Encyclopedia*, 1997 (CD-ROM)

Advisors: Karen Lorene, Yvonne Markowitz, Elise Misiorowski, Peter Shemonsky, Joseph W. Tenhagen, Janet Zapata.

PART I

LATE EIGHTEENTH AND NINETEENTH CENTURY JEWELRY

INTRODUCTION

The first edition of *Warman's Jewelry* began with the reign of Queen Victoria of Great Britain. The second begins with the reign of George III, some 75 years earlier. The reason for this is simply that, in the past few years, more of what is termed Late Georgian jewelry has come onto the market in this country and in the U.K., and likewise more information has been recently published about jewelry of this period (see References). New books tend to both reflect and create greater interest in a topic.

Jewelry has always been worn for other purposes, in addition to social status. It can serve as a memento of loved ones living or dead. It also has a role as decorative and/or functional parts of clothing. A jewel can be worn as an expression of religious faith, and as a talisman or amulet to ward off evil and disease. Souvenir jewelry, and traditional jewelry symbolic of national or cultural origin or group membership, are also common. In fact, more non-status antique jewelry, often made from non-precious materials, survives today in its original form than does gemstone and gold jewelry. Anything with components of value was more likely to be broken up for its gemstones and precious metal and reworked into pieces in keeping with current fashion.

Fine and expensive high-karat gold and gemstone pieces from the late eighteenth and early nineteenth centuries certainly do turn up at auctions and high-end antique shows. However, most of the earliest accessible and affordable jewelry that exists today is memorial and sentimental jewelry. The first section is divided accordingly, covering what is known as the Late Georgian and Regency periods in Great Britain (the reigns of Georges III and IV), circa 1760-1837 (William IV reigned 1830-1837, but there is no "William period"). In the U.S., these periods correspond roughly to the late Colonial and Federal periods.

Although it may seem arbitrary, the year 1837 is generally recognized by jewelry historians as the beginning of a new era, although some types and styles of jewelry carried over from the previous decade. The time span of the period is lengthy, so it is usually divided into three sub-periods. While there is a difference of opinion as to the exact years when one sub-period ends and the next begins, there is general recognition of their names: They are called the Early or Romantic, the Middle or Grand, and the Late Victorian or Aesthetic Period.

In order to more easily understand the great diversity and quantity of Victorian jewelry, the listings in this section have been grouped by types and/or materials. Each category is listed under the sub-period most closely associated with it, but individual listings may have earlier or later circa dates. Jewelry doesn't always fit neatly into one or another time-slot or category. Styles tend to overlap, and newer versions of old designs continued to be made in later periods. Many materials were worn throughout the late eighteenth and nineteenth centuries, e.g., coral, cut steel, and diamonds; many motifs recurred, such as snakes, flowers, and hands, and many types or forms of jewelry continued to be worn, like watch chains, bracelets and cameos. Precise dating can be difficult, unless there are clues like maker's marks, hallmarks with date letters, or engraved dated inscriptions. More often than not, late eighteenth and nineteenth century jewelry is unmarked. Identifying construction techniques and original findings can help to narrow the date range. Some findings, however, like the "C"-catch (a simple hook) and the "tube" hinge of brooch pin assemblies, were in use for the entire period, and often continued to be used in the twentieth century. Furthermore, pieces with intrinsic value (precious metals and stones) do not always survive intact. Alterations are common.

Several thematic threads were woven into the fabric of society. Nature, history, symbolism, and above all, sentiment, were sometimes inextricably intertwined. In Victorian times, naturalism was expressed in jewelry with exact depictions of flora and fauna in gold and gemstones or other materials. Distasteful as it may seem today, real insects and birds' heads were sometimes made into jewelry. Flowers were symbols of sentiment and nature. Every flower had a specific meaning, and their definitions were catalogued in several flower dictionaries. One book, published in 1866, was appropriately called *The Language and Sentiment of Flowers.*

The second half of the nineteenth century was the age of the international exhibition–what later came to be known as World's Fairs and Expos. Their historical importance should not be underestimated. In a period lacking mass communications media like television, exhibitions were the mass marketing tool of the era. They made it possible for manufacturers and merchants to display their wares over a period of six months or more to hundreds of thousands of potential customers. The latest discoveries and developments, styles, and tastes were introduced to the general public at exhibitions. Instead of "as seen on TV," an item would be touted, for example, "as seen at the Paris Exposition." To have a booth at an exhibition conferred the highest status upon the goods and their maker. Jewelry was exhibited by such prestigious firms as Froment-Meurice of Paris and Phillips of London at London's Crystal Palace Exhibition in 1851, Castellani of Rome exhibited at the International Exhibition in London in 1862 and at the Philadelphia Centennial Exposition in 1876, Tiffany & Co. of New York was also at the Philadelphia Centennial and in the Paris Exposition in 1867, 1878, 1889, and 1900. The designs of these and other exhibitors became fashionable by word of mouth and through reports in periodicals. They inspired many imitators.

The period 1837-1901 is called Victorian in the United States as well as Great Britain. In spite of our country's independence from hers, Victoria's tastes influenced Americans as well as her own subjects. While the Western world looked to Paris for the latest styles and trends, English interpretations of French styles were acceptable to the more conservative American temperament. At times these styles were modified even further by American artisans and manufacturers.

When the young Queen ascended the throne of Great Britain in 1837, the United States was still a young country. Machine-made jewelry production had begun in New England and New Jersey, but a distinct American style had yet to emerge. Most of it was imitative of the English or French. Some jewelers in fact, tried to "pass" their items as European. Other types of jewelry that were worn were usually imported from Britain and the Continent.

In the early years of this country's history, patriotism and lifestyles in general discouraged ostentatious displays of wealth. Aristocracy and all that symbolized it like jewelry, was out. The Puritan work ethic was in. Many Americans wore little except sentimental jewelry until after the Civil War. Wives of statesmen and presidents, the elite of Boston, New York and Philadelphia, and other well-to-do Americans were the exception to this rule. Dolley Madison was known for her jeweled turbans, sent from Paris (the War of 1812 notwithstanding). In the 1840s, President John Tyler's new wife, Julia, was the closest thing to royalty this country ever saw. She wore crowns and diamond tiaras.

References: Vivienne Becker, *Antique and Twentieth Century Jewellery,* 2nd ed., N.A.G. Press, 1987; Jeanenne Bell, *Answers to Questions About Old Jewelry*, 4th ed., Krause Publications, 1996; David Bennett and Daniela Mascetti, *Understanding Jewellery*, 2nd ed., Antique Collectors' Club,1994; Shirley Bury, *Jewellery, 1789-1910, The International Era,* 2 vols., Antique Collectors' Club, 1991; Margaret Flower, *Victorian Jewellery,* A.S. Barnes & Co., 1951 (out of print); Duncan James, *Old Jewellery*, Shire Publications, 1989; Arthur Guy Kaplan, *The Official Identification and Price Guide to Antique Jewelry,* 6th ed., House of Collectibles, 1990.

The early history of a number of American manufacturers can be found in Ulysses G. Dietz, ed., *The Glitter & The Gold, Fashioning America's Jewelry,* The Newark Museum, 1997; Martha G. Fales, *Jewelry in America 1600-1900*, Antique Collectors' Club, 1995, and Dorothy Rainwater, *American Jewelry Manufacturers*, Schiffer, 1988. The problem for historians and collectors is that most early American pieces were unmarked and undocumented, so the surviving product of these early manufacturers cannot be readily identified.

For some excellent (and sometimes amusing) examples of nineteenth century fashions and jewelry worn by a cross-section of Americans, see Priscilla Harris Dalrymple, *American Victorian Costume in Early Photographs*, Dover, 1991; a comparable British work is Alison Gernsheim's *Victorian and Edwardian Fashion, A Photographic Survey*, Dover, 1981.

Museums: The Victoria and Albert and the British Museums, London, have a wonderful array of eighteenth and nineteenth century, as well as earlier, jewels on display. In the United States, the Peabody Essex Museum in Salem, MA, Museum of Fine Arts, Boston, MA, Walters Art Gallery, Baltimore, MD, Cooper-Hewitt Museum, New York, NY and National Museum of American History, Smithsonian Institution, Washington, DC. all have some jewelry of the period in their collections. Mount Vernon in Virginia has a collection of Martha Washington's jewelry.

Reproduction Alert: Manufacturers in Portugal, South America, Germany, Thailand, and the U.S. can and do reproduce late eighteenth and nineteenth century style pieces to any specification, using stones and findings identical to the originals. Unless you have one of their catalogs or are aware of the provenance of a piece, it is often extremely difficult to differentiate new from old.

LATE GEORGIAN JEWELRY, c. 1760-1837

A quick look at the beginning of the Timeline in the front of this book will hint at the social and political upheaval that took place in Europe and America during this time period: The American and French Revolutions, England at war with France, France with the United States. George III was declared insane. Louis XVI was beheaded. Napoleon overran Europe and crowned himself Emperor. Little wonder that changes in social customs, fashion and attitudes about personal adornment occurred at the same time.

At the beginning of the period, royalty and nobility were the primary wearers of jewels of high intrinsic value. In 1762, Queen Charlotte, wife of George III, posed for her portrait wearing, among other jewels, a diamond stomacher which covered her entire V-shaped bodice. (Evidence that diamond-set jewels were made and worn in America in pre-Revolutionary times has been presented, but little of it survives or is documented.) Low necklines and upswept hair suggested long earrings and short necklaces. The *girandole* (French for chandelier) and *pendeloque* were popular shapes for earrings. The former usually consist of three pear-shaped diamond (or colored gemstone) drops suspended from a central element and small surmount. Pendeloques are single pear-shaped drops, sometimes suspended from a central bow and single-stone or cluster surmount. Short necklaces of graduated collet-set diamonds or other gemstones, known as *rivières*, were worn through the first two or three decades of the nineteenth century. Diamonds began to be set *à jour* (open-backed) at this time, but colored gemstones such as garnets and topaz continued to be mounted in closed back settings lined with colored foil to enhance their natural color.

Large diamond-set bow brooches, known as *sévigné*, were fashionable when tight bodices were in style in the late eighteenth century, but when fashions changed, they were no longer wearable. The bow motif itself remained, however. Floral spray and feather brooches were also set with diamonds. These tended to be stylized and flat until Early Victorian naturalism gave them dimension and a realistic look.

The eighteenth century is commonly called the Age of Diamonds, but it could also be called the "Age of Paste" (a high lead content glass, invented by Georg Frédéric Strass in 1730). Those who could not afford to emulate the aristocracy still strove to imitate their style. Paste jewels were set in silver or gold closed-back mounts and foiled for added sparkle. A black spot was often painted on the culets of colorless brilliant-cut stones to further emphasize the look of diamonds of the period (now called "old mine cut," cushion-shaped with a small table and large culet, or bottom facet). The jewelry forms were identical to those set with diamonds and colored gemstones. Paste jewels were prized in their own right, not merely as a substitute or imitation, and were sold by many of the "best" jewelers of England, France, and in the Colonies before the American Revolution.

The American and French Revolutions, like most wars, were an impetus for change. Jewelry, a non-essential luxury, was one of the first things to go, sold or melted down for the war effort, or survival. In France, anything that smacked of aristocracy was frowned upon. Jewels were not part of the new republic's ideology. But by the end of the eighteenth century, a desire for personal adornment had returned, albeit in new forms.

Fashion changed drastically at the turn of the nineteenth century, when Napoleon's First Empire held sway. The late eighteenth century's full skirts, tight bodices and three-quarter sleeves with deep lace ruffles, gathered draped collars (berthas) or ruffled lace necklines were discarded in favor of the Neo-classical look of filmy, high-waisted and draped Grecian-style dresses with short puffed sleeves and deep *décolletage*. The style's simplicity and the fabrics' delicacy required changes in jewelry forms: out went stomachers and large, heavy brooches. In came necklaces of plaques and draped chains, small buckles for sashes worn just under the bosom, smaller gem- or paste-set brooches, and narrow link bracelets worn in multiples. Interest in Greek and Roman antiquities had been heightened by new archeological discoveries at Herculaneum and Pompeii in the mid-eighteenth century, and was kept alive by Empress Josephine's preoccupation with classical motifs. Cameos and mosaics were worn as necklaces *en esclavage*, the plaques joined with two or three lengths of swagged chain encircling the base of the neck.

In the 1820s, fashions underwent another change. Sleeves were longer and grew larger toward the end of the decade. Waists remained high but skirts were fuller and heavier, embellished with ruffles and trimmings. By 1830, the waist had returned to its natural position, tightly sashed and buckled. Tight bodices returned. Sleeves were voluminous, necklines cut straight across. Shoulders were often bared. Jewelry forms included long draped chains, wide buckles and bracelets, long earrings (the "torpedo" shape was popular), and fancy combs in elaborately-dressed hair. Cross pendants were also popular, especially Maltese crosses, which could be set with diamonds, carved from chalcedony or made entirely of gold. Gold was in short supply in the early nineteenth century, but the decorative technique known as *cannetille,* a type of scrolled filigree with tightly coiled spirals or rosettes, was used to make a small amount of gold go a long way. Substantial-looking chains were made of stamped thin gauge gold, and were very lightweight.

As the Industrial Revolution gave rise to more mechanized methods of production in the first three decades of the nineteenth century, more jewelry was made for the middle classes, making way for the profusion and variety of the Victorian era.

References: David Bennett and Daniela Mascetti, *Understanding Jewellery*, 2nd ed., Antique Collectors' Club,1994; Shirley Bury, *Jewellery, 1789-1910, The International Era, Vol. I.*, Antique Collectors' Club, 1991; Martha G. Fales, *Jewelry in America 1600-1900*, Antique Collectors' Club, 1995; M.D.S. Lewis, *Antique Paste Jewellery*, Boston Books and Art, 1970 (out of print); Diana Scarisbrick, *Jewellery in Britain 1066-1837*, Michael Russell Publishing Ltd., 1994; exhibition catalog: *Jewels of the Romanovs, Treasures of the Russian Imperial Court*, Corcoran Gallery of Art, 1997.

Advisors: Ruth Eller, Sam Gassman, Lynne Loube, Sharen Wood.

Bracelet

Bangle

Diamonds, silver, yg, c. 1820-30, central heart-shaped plaque flanked by scrolled foliate motif centering a lg oval rc diamond surrounded by one hundred twenty-three sm rc diamonds, set in silver and appl to yg bangle, possible marriage to late Victorian bangle, 1-1/4" w (at center), 2-1/4" (at top) .... 2,588 (A)

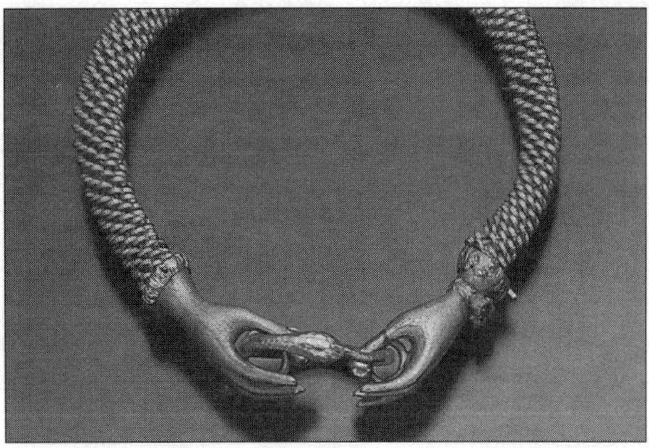

Bracelet, yg, gemstones, c. 1820, cylindrical woven mesh band terminating in a serpent ring clasped by two chased hands with cuffs, each with gem-set finger rings, one with a gem-set bracelet, 1/2" w (at center), 2-1/8" inside dia, **$4,025** [A]. (Photo courtesy of Christie's Images, New York, NY, 12/11/96).

Link

Malachite, vermeil, c. 1810, six oval malachite cabs in plain silver gilt bezel links, larger center stone, v-spring and box clasp, 3/4" w x 7" 550

Yg, rose gold, green gold, amethysts, emeralds, rubies, c. 1825, lg cushion-shaped clasp of floral and foliate motif in yg, rose gold, and green gold, with appl bead and wirework edges, centering a circ emerald surrounded by four lg oval amethysts alternating with four sm oval foiled rubies set in cut-down collets, on a band of three rows of circ links set alternately with sm circ emeralds and rubies, clasp 1-3/4" w x 1-3/4", 6-1/2" tl.............. 6,900 (A)

Brooch/Pendant

Rc diamonds, st yg, c. 1810-20, floral spray, flowerhead with lg rc diamond center set in cut-down collet, surmounted by a foliate branch, petals and leaves set throughout with sm rc diamonds, closed back st yg mount, later-added findings, lead solder, may have been element of larger piece, C-catch, tube hinge, hinged bail, 1-7/8" w x 1" 1,800

Brooch/Pin

18 yg, gemstones, hair, rock crystal, c. 1820, rect, with six cusped lobes framing six gemstones: ruby, emerald, garnet, amethyst, ruby, diamond (first initials spell "REGARD"), encircling oval compartment containing braided lt brown hair, beveled rock crystal cover, convex back, C-catch, tube hinge, extended pin stem, in fitted box, 1-1/8" w x 7/8" 2,650

Amethyst, 15k yg, c. 1810, twelve circ-cut amethysts surrounding lg faceted oval amethyst in cut-down yg collets, unmkd, C-catch, safety pin on chain, tube hinge, 1-1/4" w x 1-1/8" 400

Paste, glass, silver, c. 1790, navette-shaped, blue foiled glass framed by colorless pastes, colorless paste flowerhead cluster in center, C-catch, tube hinge, added loop, stickpin and safety chain, circ gf head with green paste and seed pearls, 1-1/8" w x 3/4", stickpin 3/8" dia, 2-1/8" tl 200

Paste, st yg, c. 1790-1810, lg cushion cut colorless foiled-back paste encircled by sm colorless pastes, cut-down collets, closed back, C-catch, tube hinge, extended pinstem, 3/4" w x 5/8"................................. 250

Rc diamonds, silver, c. 1800, open oval frame bead-set with rc diamonds centering a lg open quatrefoil with lg and sm rc diamonds in cut-down collets and flat-backed closed settings, foliate motif at four compass points, later-added pinback assembly, 2-3/8" w x 2" 2,000

Yg, emeralds, rubies, c. 1830, *cannetille* butterfly with "spots" of four bezel-set cushion-cut rubies and two emeralds, ruby head, body a vertical row of four emeralds, 1-5/8" w x 7/8" .... 1,725 (A)

Brooch/Pendant, yg, c. 1820-30, Maltese cross, allover granulation, *cannetille*, and spiked decoration, C-catch, tube hinge, extended pinstem, 1-3/4" w x 2" tl, **$750**. (Courtesy of E. Foxe Harrell Jewelers, Clinton, IA).

Brooch/Pendant, diamonds, st yg, c. 1820, Maltese cross, lg central om-cut diamond of approx 1.30 cts and four om-cut diamond openwork arms, with om-cut diamond bail, mounted in st yg (two sm diamonds missing), 1-3/4" w x 2-1/8" tl, **$10,350** [A]. (Photo courtesy of Christie's Los Angeles, CA, 10/3/96).

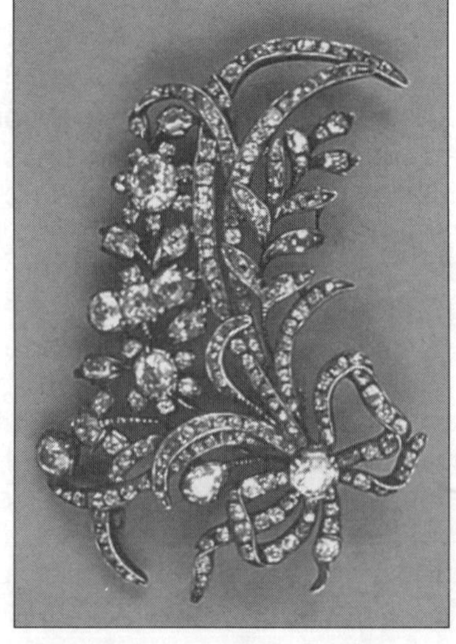

Brooch/Pin, diamonds, silver, c. 1790-1810, floral spray tied with a bow, set throughout with 184 om diamonds, approx 12 cts tw, in a closed back silver mount, later added pin back, lever catch, tube hinge, 2-3/4" w x 1-7/8", **$8,000**. (Private collection).

Brooch/Pin, emeralds, rc diamonds, st yg, c. 1790-1830, scrolled bow motif, three sq cut emeralds set in flowerhead centers, and set throughout with rc diamonds, cut-down collet settings, possible center pc of necklace, later-added trombone catch, flanged hinge, 1-1/2" w x 1", **$1,100**. (Courtesy of E. Foxe Harrell Jewelers, Clinton, IA).

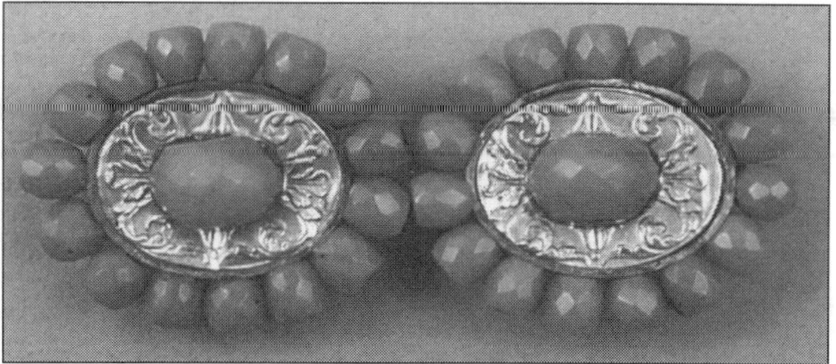

Buckle, coral, gp brass, c. 1810, pair of oval belt clasps with stamped foliate and scroll design encircled by faceted coral beads on outer edge and centered with one lg faceted coral bead, probably Fr, converted into two pins, each 1-1/8" w x 1", **$250**. (Private collection).

Brooches/Pins, late 18th century English and French paste:

TL, c. 1790, open scalloped frame of foil-backed colorless pastes, black spot on culets, enclosing star-shaped cluster of colorless pastes in closed-back silver mount, 1-1/2" dia, **$400**.

TC, c.1790, brooch/pendant, cruciform, four large cushion-shaped rc foiled yellow pastes interspersed with sm circ rc foiled yellow pastes set in domed closed-back gilt metal mount, 1-3/4" x 1-3/4", **$450**.

TR, c. 1790-1800, ring of foiled aqua-colored circ-cut pastes enclosing flowerhead cluster of foiled colorless pastes, engr yg star center, 1-1/4" dia, **$360**.

C, yg, c. 1780-90, *girandole*, central cluster of foil-backed colorless pastes with engr yg decoration, suspending three pear-shaped drops set with foil-backed colorless pastes in closed-back silver mount, Fr, 1-3/4" w x 2-1/2", tl, **$825**.

BL, c. 1780-90, rounded oblong faceted foil-backed citrine in an engr yg frame, encircled by circ-cut foil-backed rock crystal, black spot on culets, in engr yg collets and frame, in closed-back silver mount, 1-1/2"w x 7/8", **$495**.

BC, c. 1790, flower spray set throughout with foiled colorless pastes, black spot on culets, closed-back silver mount, 1-1/2" w x 7/8", **$280**.

BR, c. 1760-80, bracelet clasp, pierced oval with cluster center, set throughout with colorless foiled pastes, black spot on culets, in closed-back silver mount, 2" w x 1-1/2", **$740**.
(Photo courtesy of Sharen and Nicholas Wood).

Buckle, Cravat

Yg, blue enamel, c. 1820, open oval, blue enamel band within engr yg frame, double hasp on central swiveling rod, 1-1/4" w x 2-1/8" 125

Buckle, Shoe

Sterling, steel, c. 1800, cushion-shaped hollow silver frames, steel backings, Eng hmks, 2-1/2" w x 1-7/8", pr 250

Chatelaine

Silver, glass, c. 1830-40, guitar shape surmounted by wide band guitar strap, open filigreed wire decoration, faceted amber glass stone in sawtooth bezel setting at base of guitar, suspended wire loop with applied foliate plaque, inscribed "V.L.D. 3 Mai 1831," hinged flattened hook on rev, 1-3/4" w x 4" 500

Earrings, pendent

18k yg, c. 1820, "torpedo"-shaped drop, emb with allover star motif, appl cutout stars within filigree rosettes encircling the base, suspended from a round surmount with similar star and rosette appl decoration, fishhook earwires, probably Eng, 1/2" w x 2-1/4" tl, pr 660

Pendent Earrings, c.1790:

L, red-orange foiled topaz, oval-cut topaz surmount suspending pierced foliate motif with topaz center and three pear-shaped topaz drops in closed-back silver mount, back-hinged earwires, Fr or Spanish, 7/8" w x 2" tl, pr, **$660**.

C, *girandole,* an open trefoil set with lg oval and sm sc pink pastes, suspending three pear-shaped drops, each a lg pear-shaped paste surrounded by sm sc pastes, suspended from a single oval-cut pink paste surmount, silver earwires, probably Fr, 7/8" w x 2" tl, pr, **$535**.

R, flowerhead surmount suspending a larger floral/foliate motif, set throughout with lg, medium and sm colorless pastes with black spot on culets, silver fishhook earwires, probably Eng, 7/8" w x 1-3/4" tl, pr, **$660**.
(Sharen and Nicholas Wood collection).

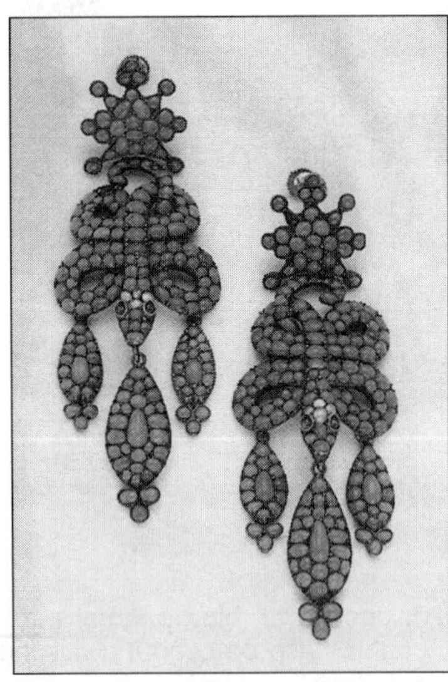

Pendent Earrings, turquoise, st yg, seed pearls, red stones, c. 1820-30, star-shaped detachable surmount suspending a snake motif forming a quatrefoil knot terminating in three pear-shaped drops tipped with sm trefoil clusters, pave-set throughout with sm turq cabs, seed pearl cluster on snake head, red stone eyes, later-added screwbacks, orig fitted box, 1" w x 2-7/8" tl, pr, **$1,725** [A]. (Photo courtesy of Butterfield & Butterfield, San Francisco and Los Angeles, CA, 6/25/97).

Pendant, chalcedony, tricolor gold, green beryl, split pearls, c. 1830, Maltese cross, equilateral arms of translucent white chalcedony, center set with a sq-cut foiled green beryl bordered by split pearls within a *cannetille* tricolor frame, engr foliate motif yg bail, glazed compartment on rev containing woven hair, 1-5/8" w x 2-1/4" tl, **$2,990** [A]. (Photo courtesy of Christie's Images, New York, NY, 4/8/97).

Diamonds, st yg, c. 1825, modified *girandole* style, a chain of paired foliate motifs alternating with single om diamonds in cut-down collets terminating in a pear-shaped foliate frame suspending an oe diamond drop in the open center, and three articulated drops of similar design to top chain, eighty-eight om-cut and rc diamonds, European backs, 5/8" w x 3-1/8" tl .... 3,450 (A)

Emeralds, rc diamonds, yg, c. 1750-60, floral motif set throughout with rc diamonds in yg surmounts, suspending pear-shaped emerald beads with rc diamond-set caps, replaced earwires, probably Spanish or Portuguese, 5/8" w x 1-3/4" tl, pr 2,800

Foiled pink topaz, silver, yg, c. 1770, inverted pear-shaped surmount topped by a single stone, suspending a foliated starburst center and elongated pear-shaped drop, set throughout with lg and sm collet-set circ-cut foiled pink topaz, black spot on culets, in a closed-back silver mount, yg bead decoration around collets, back-hinged earwire with attached loop for ribbon (for support when worn), Portuguese, 3/4" w x 3-1/4" tl, pr................ 2,640

Paste, silver, yg, c. 1750-70, three-dimensional floral/foliate motif silver drop set with colorless rc pastes, yg decorated back, suspended from paste-set trefoil surmount, yg earwire, probably Fr, 3/4" w x 1-3/4" tl, pr 740

Rc diamonds, silver, yg, c. 1790, open bow motif surmount suspending articulated center and scallop-edged oval drop, set throughout with rc diamonds in closed-back silver mount, yg accents and earwires, probably Fr, 1/2" w x 1-1/2" tl, pr 1,070

Vauxhall glass, yg, c. 1820, faceted dk red glass (appears black), lg and sm circ stones forming flowerhead surmount suspending three splayed rows of lg and sm circ stones and a cluster of marquise-shaped stones forming starburst motif drop, mounted on a black lacquered metal backing, yg earwires, probably Eng, 7/8" w x 2-1/4" tl, pr 495

Necklace

18k yg, topaz, pearls, turquoise, c. 1830, twelve grad flowerhead links with yg bead decoration, each link centering an oval foiled pink topaz surrounded by alternating split pearls and circ turq cabs in sawtooth bezels, beaded borders, interlinks of split pearls with appl bead decoration, in a fitted box (two pearls missing), 7/8" w (at center), 15" tl .... 2,875 (A)

Pendant

Diamonds, silver-topped rose gold, c. 1780, openwork Maltese cross with lg central om-cut diamond surrounded by four open arms each centering a lg om-cut diamond surrounded by oval and om-cut diamonds bead-set in a frame of silver-topped rose gold, provenance: formerly the property of The Trustees of the late 7th Duke of Newcastle, 2-3/8" w x 2-3/4" (with bail) .... 51,750 (A)

Ring

18k yg, c. 1800, pierced high relief engr foliate scroll band encircled by a raised center of similar motif, 1/2" w, size 7 .... 1,495 (A)

Diamonds, emeralds, green stones, st yg, 18k yg, c. 1830, central om diamond of approx 1.50 cts flanked by four sm om diamonds set in st yg, two sm circ-cut emeralds

Pendent Earrings, chalcedony, 18k yg, c. 1820-30, white chalcedony torpedo-shaped drops with concave centers, cusped scallop edge at base, appl yg floral motif, surmount of white chalcedony disks, appl floral motif, fishhook ear wires, 3/8" dia surmount, 5/8" w x 3" tl , pr, **$1,500**. (Private collection).

Ring, diamonds, enamel, st yg, c. 1810, blue enameled ellipse, rc diamond center encircled by sm rc diamonds set in st yg mounted on narrow engr yg shank, approx size 8, 7/8" w x 1-3/8", **$900**. (Courtesy of E. Foxe Harrell Jewelers, Clinton, IA).

and five sm circ-cut green stones set in 18k yg, mounted in cut-down collets on a split tapered shank, 3/8" w (at center), approx size 4 .... 2,166(A)

Foil-backed paste, yg, c. 1810, faceted oval paste, yellow foil, set in cut down collet, closed back, engr frame and split shank, approx size 8-1/2, head 1/2" w x 5/8".... 300

Suite: Brooch/Pin and Earrings

Pastes, silver, c. 1790, bow-shaped brooch with central floral motif of cushion, circ, and pear-shaped pastes set in closed-back silver mountings, pendeloque earrings with floral motif surmount, bow motif center, suspending pear-shaped drop, earring backs later-added, brooch probably missing a pendant drop, provenance: formerly the property of Anne Morgan, daughter of J.P. Morgan, orig fitted velvet box, brooch 2-3/4" w x 2-3/4", earrings 1-1/2" w x 2-1/4", suite .... 18,400 (A)

Suite: Necklace, Brooch/Pin, Earrings, and Ring

Yg, amethysts, aquamarines, rock crystal quartz, 1830, necklace of twelve oval *cannetille* links joined by repoussé floral interlinks, each link centering lg prong-set oval amethysts surrounded by sm circ rock crystal quartz and aquamarine alternating with appl textured yg beads, oval brooch centering an oval prong-set aquamarine surrounded by four lg oval amethysts alternating with four sm circ rock crystal quartz, pendent earrings with oval surmounts centering a prong-set oval amethyst suspending a pear-shaped drop with central pear-shaped amethyst surrounded by sm circ rock crystal quartz alternating with appl textured yg beads, ring similar to a single link of necklace, earring stud closures later-added, necklace 1" w (at center), 14-1/2" tl, brooch 2-1/2" w x 1-3/4", earrings 3/4" w x 1-3/4", ring 7/8" w x 1" (at top), suite .... 10,925 (A)

Suite: **Necklace, Pendant, Brooch**, yg, topaz, pearls, c. 1830, necklace of eleven grad floral and scroll motif *cannetille* links set with a total of sixteen lg oval bezel-set foiled pink topaz with pearl accents, suspended from a triple strand cable link chain to v-spring and box clasp decorated with one lg oval pink topaz and appl *cannetille* decoration, cruciform pendant and lozenge-shaped brooch of similar design, fitted box (missing earrings), necklace 1-1/4" w (at center), 15" tl, pendant 2-1/4" dia, brooch 1-1/2" dia, suite, **$2,588** [A]. (Photo courtesy of Dunning's Auction Service, Elgin, IL, 12/1/96).

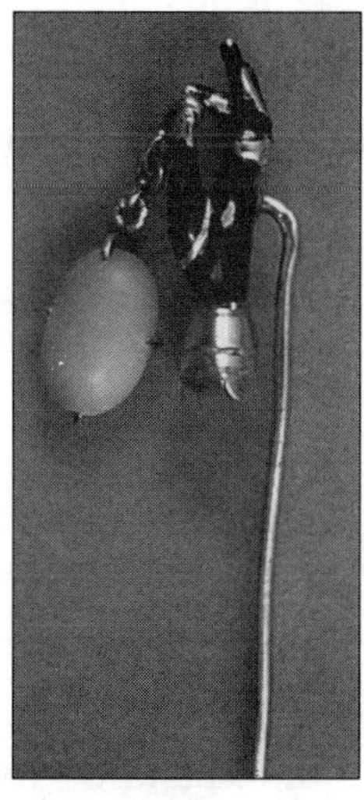

Scarf Pin/Stickpin, yg, enamel, coral, c. 1800, dk blue enameled yg cuffed hand holding pendent oval coral bead suspended from yg chain, yg pinstem, some enamel loss, hmk on pinstem (illegible), hand 3/8" w x 7/8", 3-1/2" tl, **$350**. (Courtesy of E. Foxe Harrell Jewelers, Clinton, IA).

Suite: Necklace, Pendant, Brooch

YG, topaz, pearls, c. 1830, necklace of eleven grad floral and scroll motif cannetille links set with a total of sixteen lg oval bezel-set foiled pink topaz with pearl accents, suspended from a triple strand cable link chain to v-spring and box clasp, box decorated with one lg oval pink topaz and appl cannetille decoration, cruciform brooch and pendant of similar design, fitted box (missing earrings), necklace 1-1/4" w (at center), 15" tl, pendant 2-1/4" dia, brooch 1-1/2" dia, suite .... 2,588 (A)

CUT STEEL, BERLIN IRON, SILESIAN WIRE WORK

History: Jewelry made from riveted faceted beads or studs of polished steel dates at least as far back as the sixteenth century. Cut steel jewelry had its heyday in the late eighteenth century, when some of the most delicate and intricate ornaments were made to imitate the sparkle of diamonds. But it persisted as a craft and a fashion into the twentieth century. Much of what survives today was made in France, especially in the form of buckles for shoes and waists.

Some sources say that circa dating can be determined by construction methods and the number of facets on the studs. Earlier pieces have numerous (up to fifteen) facets, while later ones have as few as five. Machine-stamped strips instead of individually riveted studs are an indication of later, lower-quality, manufacture. But, according to other sources, multi-faceted, individually-studded examples of higher quality can also date as late as the 1900s. England was a primary source for cut steel in the eighteenth century, the most well-known manufacturer being Matthew Boulton of Soho, near Birmingham. But factories in France were still turning out cut steel trinkets as recently as the 1940s.

Although buckles are the form most often seen today (for which there is less demand), bracelets, brooches, earrings, chains and necklaces can also be found. Considering the intricacies of their design and craftsmanship, and their relative scarcity, prices on these pieces remain quite reasonable.

Most of the black lacy cast iron jewelry known as Berlin iron was made in the early nineteenth century. Its manufacture began around 1804, but a quantity of it was made in Germany during the Prussian War of Liberation against Napoleon (1813-15). Some pieces continued to be made in the 1850s and were exhibited by German manufacturers at the Crystal Palace in 1851. Earlier pieces tended toward the Neo-classical, with cast cameo-like profiles mounted on polished steel plaques, sometimes framed in gold. By the 1820s and 30s, Gothic Revival was the stylistic influence. Gothic arches and tracery were cast into lace-like necklaces, bracelets, earrings, cross pendants and chains,. Today Berlin iron in any style is extremely scarce and expensive, but the Neo-Gothic forms are in the greatest demand. Berlin iron was sand-cast, then lacquered black.

Another unique type of iron and steel jewelry, associated with a part of Eastern Europe then known as Silesia (now mostly part of Poland, and parts of the Czech Republic and eastern Germany), is referred to as Silesian wire work. Wrapped and woven iron wire mesh was fashioned into bracelets, necklaces, brooches and earrings, sometimes decorated with cutout polished steel shapes known as "sequins" or *paillettes.* Little documentation or information is available about this work, including where it was made and by whom. Although a number of examples are shown in Anne Clifford's *Cut Steel and Berlin Iron Jewellery*, cited below, the author can only conjecture about its origin. As yet, twenty-seven years after that book's publication, no one has come up with any further information. Some theorize the work was done in England or France, but to date no documentation supports this theory.

Regardless of its origin, the intricacy of the workmanship is something to marvel at. Coupled with its rarity, Silesian wirework is certainly deserving of greater appreciation and respect than to be called "Brillo pad" jewelry, as once source would have it.

References: Vivienne Becker, *Antique and Twentieth Century Jewellery*, 2nd ed., N.A.G. Press, 1987; Shirley Bury, *Jewellery, 1789-1910, The International Era,* Vol. II, Antique Collectors' Club, 1991; Anne Clifford, *Cut Steel and Berlin Iron Jewellery,* Adams and Dart, 1971 (out of print); Ginny Redington Dawes & Corinne Davidov, *Victorian Jewelry, Unexplored Treasures*, Abbeville Press, 1991; Derek Ostergard, *Cast Iron From Central Europe, 1800-1850,* The Bard Graduate Center for Studies in the Decorative Arts, 1994.

Bracelet, flexible

Silesian wire, cast iron, yg, c. 1810, fine black wire mesh band terminating in oval cast iron clasp depicting a winged cherub (putto) riding a dog, set in millegrained bezel, 6-1/4" tl x 1/2" 450

Silesian wire, c. 1820, wire mesh strap, ornamental mesh slide, cut steel beads and bow-shaped twisted wire clasp, polished steel rosette with center fringe of five rod and coiled wire drops, 7" tl, clasp 2-1/4" w x 1-1/8" 750

Bracelet, link

Cut steel, sp brass, c. 1820-40, seven links of circ domed disks riveted throughout with sm multifaceted cut steel studs, encircled by frame of lg and sm cut steel studs, sp brass backing, v-spring and box clasp, probably Eng, 7/8" w x 7" tl 420

Link Bracelet, Berlin iron, gilt metal, c. 1820, pierced quatrefoil patterned segments alternation with cast floral/foliate motif segments, openwork ornamental front clasp surmounted by a cast draped seated female figure on a polished oval plaque mounted in a gilt frame within a cast floral border, attributed to Johann Conrad Geiss, Berlin (Ger), v-spring and box clasp, 2" w x 8" tl, clasp 1-1/8" w x 2-3/4", **$1,500**. (Courtesy of E. Foxe Harrell Jewelers, Clinton, IA).

Bracelet, Silesian wire, glass, ptd enamel, c. 1840, interwoven coiled wire strap, hook closure under oval central plaque of a rev ptd polychrome scene framed by coiled wire loops, interspersed with sm cutout steel starbursts (sequins), center 2-1/8" w x 1-3/4", **$550**. (Courtesy of E. Foxe Harrell Jewelers, Clinton, IA).

Brooch/Pin, Berlin iron, polished steel, yg, c. 1830, scrolling floral and foliate design flanking rosettes set in steel and yg disks, open scrolled fan and lacy star drop, C-catch, tube hinge, extended pinstem, 2" w x 1-3/8" tl, **$600**. (Courtesy of E. Foxe Harrell Jewelers, Clinton, IA).

Cut steel, late 18th and early 19th century:

T, Tiara, c. 1810, five evenly spaced domed disks separated by flowerhead-tipped C-scrolls, encrusted with multifaceted cut steel studs riveted to sp brass, attached to a velvet ribbon-wrapped wire headband with a double row of steel studs across the front, terminating in yg loops for ribbon attachment, probably Fr, 10" l x 1-1/2" at center, **$495**.

TC, Brooch/Pin, c. 1820, in the shape of a swallow, encrusted with multifaceted circ and marquise cut steel studs riveted to a brass backing, 2" w x 7/8", **$100**.

C, Suite, Brooch and Pendent Earrings, c. 1800-20, circ openwork brooch, clusters of multifaceted cut steel studs riveted to sp brass, surmounted by seven circ red glass cabs in millegrained collets with star-shaped cut steel centers, matching earrings with circ cut steel disk surmount suspending cut-steel-topped red glass cab linked to larger cut steel disk drop, probably Eng, brooch 1-3/4" dia, earrings 3/4" w x 1-3/4" tl, suite, **$395**.

BC, Brooch/Pin, 1790, in three layers, inverted teardrop-shaped clusters of lg and sm multifaceted cut steel studs forming fan shape, surmounting larger framework with sm flowerhead clusters and scrolls suspending fringe of seven teardrops, each tipped with single stud, riveted throughout with lg and sm cut steel studs, Fr or Eng, approx 2" w x 3" tl, **$600**.

BCLR, Pendent Earrings, c. 1800-10, fleur-de-lis surmount suspending lg open pear-shaped drop enclosing sm teardrop, lg and sm multifaceted cut steel studs riveted to sp brass throughout, later-added screwback findings, probably Fr, 5/8" w x 2" tl, pr, **$485**.

BLR, Pendent Earrings, c. 1790, star-shaped surmount of sm multifaceted cut steel studs suspending sm then lg inverted open heart shapes outlined in cut steel with star-shaped cluster centers, terminating in a fringe of five sm cut steel clusters, brass backing and earwires, probably Fr, 3/4" w x 2-1/4", pr, **$485**.
(Photo courtesy of Sharen and Nicholas Wood).

Bracelets, link

Berlin iron, polished steel, c. 1810-20, cast and lacquered black scrolled foliate links, box and v-spring clasp with ornamental top of central flowerhead and four fleurs-de-lis surmounting oval polished steel disk framed by sm shell motifs and scalloped wire, flanked by foliate motifs forming lozenge shape, 1-1/2" w, clasp 2-3/4" w x 1-3/4", 8" tl, pr 6,000

Brooch/Pin

Silesian wire, c. 1810, lobed oval shape, faceted cut steel center within wire rosette and fine wire mesh bow, mounted on polished steel backplate, C-catch, tube hinge, 2-1/4" w x 1-3/4" 800

Silesian wire, c. 1830-40, wire mesh rosette encircled by steel band and coiled wire spirals, polished steel rosette center, C-catch, 1-3/8" dia 175

Silesian wire, c. 1860, oval wire mesh wreath suspending coiled wire drop in open center, nine coiled wire drops, C-catch, 1-1/2" w x 1-7/8" 175

Silesian wire, steel, c. 1840, open coiled wire interlace, two central polished steel rosettes ("sequins"), C-catch, extended pinstem, 1-7/8" w x 1" 200

Bar

Cut steel, silver, c. 1810, in the shape of an arrow surmounted by a swallow, riveted throughout with multifaceted cut steel studs to silver back, probably Eng, 2-1/4" w x 1" 150

Earrings

Silesian wire, cut steel, c. 1830, finely coiled wire quatrefoil, faceted cut steel center, hinged wire (Fr back) finding, 7/8" w x 7/8" 600

Earrings, pendent

Cut steel, sp brass, silver, c. 1790-1810, one lg cut steel stud suspending five grad tiers, four rect plaques terminating in one pentagonal plaque suspending a fringe of three inverted teardrops, riveted throughout with sm multifaceted cut steel studs to sp brass backing, silver earwire, probably Eng, 1" w x 2-3/4", pr 480

Cut steel, sp brass, silver, c. 1790-1800, circ surmount, cluster outlined in marquise-shaped studs, suspending cusped and lobed open drop surmounted by foliate motif center of marquise-shaped and sm circ studs, riveted throughout with sm multifaceted cut steel studs to sp brass backing, silver earwire, probably Fr, 3/4" w x 2-1/4" tl, pr 450

Pendent Earrings, Berlin iron, c. 1820, cast ironwork, scrolled foliate and floral motifs in elongated cusped trefoil drops, unmatched surmounts (one replaced), Fr wires (hinged, from back), 1" w x 2-7/8" tl, **$600**. (Courtesy of E. Foxe Harrell Jewelers, Clinton, IA).

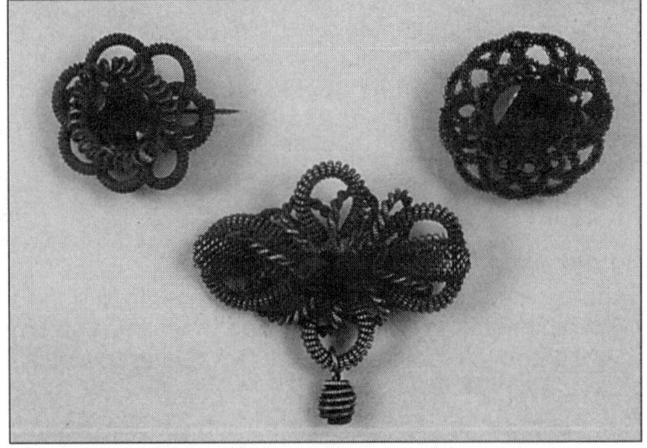

Silesian wirework brooches, c. 1850:

TL, rosette of coiled wire loops, black glass center cut with six-pointed star, encircled by sm coiled wire loops, C-catch, 1-1/4" dia, **$125**.

TR, open circle formed by wire mesh loops, faceted black glass center framed by twisted coiled wire, C-catch, 1-3/8" dia, **$175**.

BC, wire mesh loops forming open quatrefoil with faceted black glass center, suspending coiled wire drop, C-catch, 2-1/8" w x 2" tl, **$300**.
(Courtesy of E. Foxe Harrell Jewelers, Clinton, IA).

Silesian wirework brooches:

L, c. 1840, woven in an undulating design with polished steel sequins (several missing) forming navette shape, C-catch, 2" w x 1-1/2", **$250**.
(Private collection);

R, c. 1830, ptd polychrome Swiss enamel landscape with castle, water, mountains, trees, on oval porcelain plaque, ink-stamped "Chillon" (a castle in Switzerland) on rev, set in cross-looped Silesian wire frame studded with sequins (rusted), C-catch, extended pinstem, 1-5/8" w x 1-1/2", **$350**.
(Gilly Phipps collection).

Necklace, Berlin iron, c. 1820, a collar of linked pierced plaques, nine cast floral motifs within pierced oval frames alternating with nine lanceolate trefoils, v-spring and box clasp, 15" tl x 1-3/4", **$2,500**. (Courtesy of E. Foxe Harrell Jewelers, Clinton, IA).

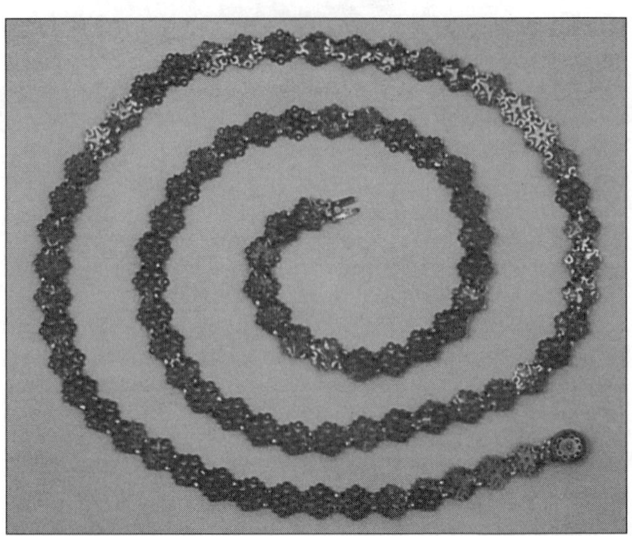

Neckchain, polished steel, cut steel, c. 1800-10, links of flat cutout six-pointed stars within circ frames terminating in circ clasp, probably Eng, 36" tl x 3/8", **$475**. (Courtesy of E. Foxe Harrell Jewelers, Clinton, IA).

Suite: Knee and shoe buckles, pr, Cut steel, leather, c. 1820, convex rounded rect, lg and sm faceted steel studs, shoe buckles with fittings mkd "L" and "R," black leather centers, knee buckles open with double hasps, fitted box, shoe: 2-3/8" w x 1-5/8", knee: 1" w x 1-1/2", **$450**. (Courtesy of E. Foxe Harrell Jewelers, Clinton, IA).

Watch Fob, polished steel, c. 1820, pairs of open rect links alternating with navette-shaped links with ropetwist decoration, terminating in lg split ring suspending watch keys, smaller split ring on opposite end, 10" tl x 1/2", **$200**. (Courtesy of E. Foxe Harrell Jewelers, Clinton, IA).

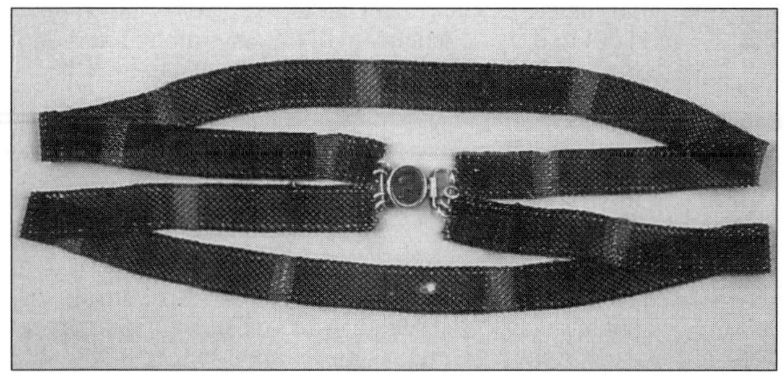

Necklace, Silesian wire, cast iron, yg, c. 1810, two fine wire mesh bands, black with gp sections, linked to oval cast iron clasp depicting a classical profile, set in yg bezel, 13" tl x 7/8" (both bands), **$750**. (Courtesy of E. Foxe Harrell Jewelers, Clinton, IA).

Cut steel, pink coral, sp brass, yg, c. 1790, circ flowerhead cut steel surmount suspending oval drop of pink coral plaque surmounted by flower design in cut steel, framed in circ and crescent-shaped cut steel, sp brass back, yg earwires, Fr or Eng, 7/8" w x 1-3/4" tl, pr 400

Cut steel, polished steel, c. 1820-30, open triangular surmount suspending a lg open pear-shaped drop enclosing a free-swinging smaller pear-shaped drop, riveted throughout with sm circ and larger navette-shaped faceted cut steel studs, polished steel backing, shepherd's hook earwire, 3-1/8" tl x 1" w, pr 350

Necklace

Silesian wire, c. 1820-30, fine wire mesh narrow band caught by crowned heart slide, terminating in scrolled openwork bow suspending bird motif drop, black lacquered tube clasp, evidence of repair, 16"l, 1-1/8" w x 1-3/4" tl at center.. 700

Pendant

Cut steel, sp brass, c. 1790-1800, openwork oval suspended from tapered bail, geo design suspending three long articulated drops, each terminating in a fringe of three sm drops, riveted throughout with lg and sm multifaceted cut steel studs to sp brass backing, probably Fr, 1-3/4" w x 5" tl 660

Pendant, Cross

Berlin iron, c. 1810, cast openwork cross with central appl rosette and fleur-de-lis terminals, repaired and relacquered, 2-5/8" w x 3-1/4"..................................... 1,200

Ring

Berlin iron, c. 1830, cut corner rect plaque, impressed crowned shield, cast floral design on tapered shank 275

Suite: Bracelet and Brooch

Silesian wire, c. 1840, bracelet an openwork coiled wire strap, hook closure under gathered and coiled wire mesh surmount in grape cluster motif, matching brooch, C-catch, tube hinge, bracelet 8" tl, top 1-5/8" w x 2", brooch 1-7/8" w x 2-1/4", suite 750

MEMORIAL, MOURNING AND HAIR JEWELRY

History: One of the most popular expressions of sentimentality, on both sides of the Atlantic, was the making and wearing of jewelry containing human hair, a practice which originated in the seventeenth century. These pieces were worn as memento mori (mourning) and also as love-tokens.

The earliest type of hair jewelry was made with glass or rock crystal-covered compartments to hold the hair of a loved one, living or deceased. These continued to be made and worn through the greater part of the nineteenth century, with some alterations in style. Eighteenth and early to mid-nineteenth century mourning brooches might depict an entire funereal scene painted on ivory, complete with weeping willow, urn, and a despondent maiden standing forlornly by. The sepia tones of the paint were often derived from using macerated hair as a pigment. This was strictly for reasons of sentiment, not because the hair provided a superior form of paint. Sometimes the scene was made three-dimensional with snippets of hair forming, for example, the branches of the willow.

In some pieces, the hair is formed into curls, called "Prince of Wales plumes," or made into wheat sheaves, mounted on a white background. Another technique was to lay strands of hair flat on "goldbeater's skin," a type of adhesive backing, and cut out individual floral motifs which were then assembled as a three-dimensional "picture" under glass.

More commonly, locks of hair were simply braided or coiled, sometimes using more than one color (from different family members), and placed in compartments set into a frame and covered with glass.

On mourning pieces, the outer or inner frame could include a snake motif, symbolizing eternity. Seed pearls, symbolic of tears, were sometimes added, along with gold thread or wire tied around the lock of hair. In late Georgian and early Victorian pieces, the backs are gold or gold-filled, and slightly convex. They were often engraved with names or initials, and dates of birth and/or death. This personalization of a piece is desirable to collectors, and of course it takes the guesswork out of placing the piece in its time-frame.

Late Georgian mourning brooches or pins were often navette-shaped, oval or oblong; circa 1820-40, they were small rounded rectangles, ovals, or crescents, often worn pinned to black ribbon as a necklace or bracelet. They were bordered with pearls, garnets, coral, French jet (black glass), or black enamel around the glass- or rock crystal-covered compartment. Later brooches were larger, worn at the throat or in the center of the bodice. Black onyx plaques or black enameled borders inscribed "In Memory Of" around a central hair compartment became standardized forms for mourning pieces.

Late Georgian mourning rings, like brooches, could also be navette-shaped or oblong, or wide bands with inscriptions encircling the outer surface. Others bore inscriptions around the outside of a narrow black-enameled shank surmounted by a hair compartment framed in garnets or pearls, or a gemstone. Victorian mourning rings might be simple bands with woven hair channel-set around the outside, or an enameled inscription. Fancier rings had cutout or enameled names on compartments containing hair.

References: Vivienne Becker, *Antique and Twentieth Century Jewellery*, 2nd ed., N.A.G. Press, 1987; Jeanenne Bell, *Collector's Encyclopedia of Hairwork Jewelry,* Collector Books, 1998; Shirley Bury, *An Introduction to Sentimental Jewellery*, Victoria & Albert Museum, 1985, and *Jewellery, 1789-1910, The International Era,* Vol. II, Antique Collectors' Club, 1991; Martha G. Fales, *Jewelry in America 1600-1900*, Antique Collectors' Club, 1995; Ruel Pardee Tolman, "Human Hair as Pigment," *Antiques*, December, 1925.

Advisor: Carmelita Johnson.

Brooch/Pin

10k yg, hair, glass, c. 1840-50, central oval glazed compartment containing braided lt brown hair, in a stamped scrolled relief navette-shaped frame, convex back, C-catch, tube hinge, extended pinstem, 1-3/4" w x 1-3/8".. 195

Gf, hair, glass, c. 1820-1840, rounded rect glazed compartment containing braided brown hair with quilted pattern

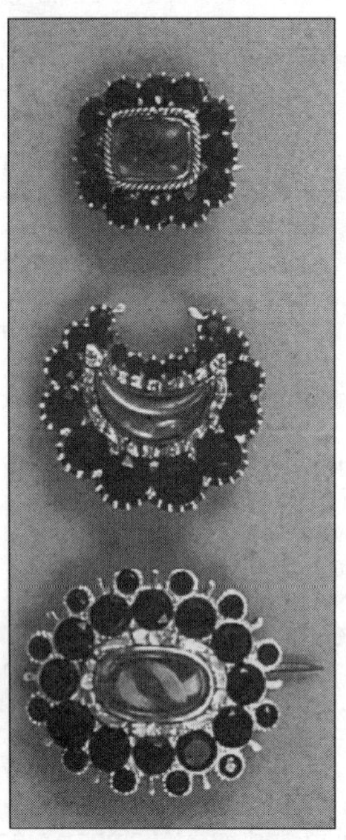

Memorial brooches, c. 1820-30, French jet, hair, yg:

T, cushion-shaped compartment containing brown hair with rock crystal cover surrounded by faceted black glass (Fr jet) in cut-down collets, rope-twist frame, convex back, C-catch, tube hinge, 1/2" sq, **$75**.

C, crescent-shaped compartment with braided brown hair and rock crystal cover framed by faceted black glass (Fr jet) stones set in cut-down collets, engr on rev "C.E. Ogden Obt 16th Aug't 1826 Ae 45," C-catch, tube hinge, 3/4" w x 5/8", **$95**.

B, oval compartment containing braided brown and blond hair with beveled glass cover surrounded by two rows of faceted black glass (Fr jet) set in cut-down collets, engr on rev "M.E.R.," C-catch, tube hinge, extended pinstem, 3/4" w x 5/8", **$110**. (Carmelita Johnson collection).

border set in scrolled and scallop-edged gf frame, C-catch, tube hinge, loop for safety chain, 1-1/4" w x 1" 200

Gf, hair, glass, c. 1840-50, deep glazed oval compartment containing flat-woven lt brown hair in basketweave pattern, set in open quatrefoil frame formed by engr hollow tubes with inner scrollwork accents, C-catch, tube hinge, extended pinstem, 1-3/4" w x 1-3/8" 175

Gf, hair, glass, c. 1860, oval glazed compartment containing braided blond hair set in gf frame, stamped and engr floral and foliate motifs at compass points, C-catch, tube hinge, 1-3/8" w x 1-1/8" 125

Hair, gf, glass, c. 1820, rounded rect glazed compartment containing braided blond hair, stamped and engr gf frame, C-catch, tube hinge, extended pinstem, 1" w x 1/2" 155

Hair, gf, glass, c. 1860-70, oval glazed compartment containing three grad braided knots of lt to dk brown hair mounted on ground of tightly woven brown hair, plain gf convex-backed frame, C-catch, tube hinge, 1-3/8" w x 1-5/8" 225

Hair, gf, rock crystal, c. 1800, convex elliptical gf frame with raised rim, central compartment containing braided blond hair, rock crystal cover, rev engr with initials "AA," C-catch, tube hinge, extended pinstem, 1" w x 1/2". 150

Hair, paste, st yg, glass, c. 1780-1820, navette-shaped glazed compartment containing flat woven strips of light brown hair, sq cut pastes bead-set in st yg frame, yg back engr "William Young," C-catch, tube hinge, ring for safety chain, 1" w x 1-1/2" 225

Hair, yg, glass, c. 1800, oval glazed compartment containing two knots of hair, blond surmounting brown, set in convex-backed yg frame, C-catch, tube hinge, extended pinstem, 3/4" w x 1/2" 175

Hair, yg, glass, c. 1800, rect glazed compartment containing braided hair, stamped and engr frame, scalloped edge, C-catch, tube hinge, extended pinstem, 5/8" w x 1/2" 175

Hair, yg, rock crystal, seed pearls, c. 1800, rounded rect central compartment containing brown hair, crystal cover, seed pearl and yg frame, initials "MAB" engr on rev, C-catch, tube hinge (on plate mounts), extended pinstem, 3/4" w x 5/8" 200

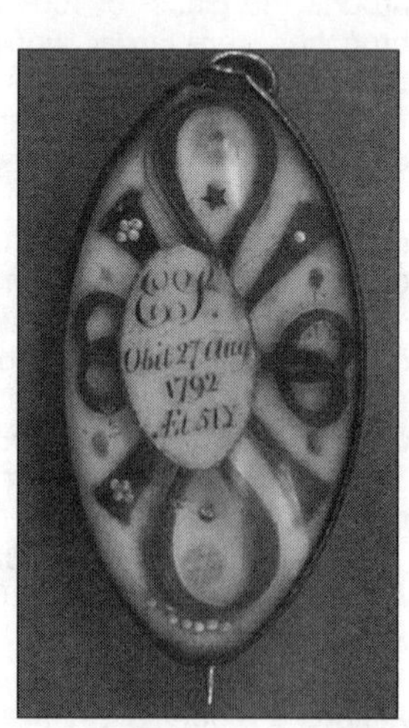

Mourning brooches, c. 1790-1800:

L, glass, hair, st yg, yg, c. 1800, oval foiled blue glass plaque, raised rn in white material and yg with flowers made from cutout shapes of adhesive-backed hair and white beads in three-dimensional design, C-catch, tube hinge, extended pinstem, loop for safety chain, 7/8" w x 1/4", **$400**.

LC, ivory, rock crystal, rolled gold, c. 1792, navette-shaped central ivory plaque inscribed "E T Obit 27 Aug 1792 AEt 51Y," domed rock crystal cover, appl loops of brown hair and sm white beads, rolled gold frame, C-catch, tube hinge, extended pinstem, loop for safety chain, 1-1/2" w x 7/8", **$400**.

(Carmelita Johnson collection).

RC, ivory, paint, gilt ym, glass, c. 1800, painting of woman holding a wreath, leaning and gazing upon an urn on a pedestal, set in navette-shaped gilt ym frame under glass cover, C-catch, tube hinge, extended pinstem, 1-1/16" w x 1-9/16", **$895** (Lenore Dailey collection)

R, ivory, yg, seed pearls, blue foil-backed glass, c. 1790, navette-shaped sepia-toned painting depicting a mourning angel, urn with initials "MB," framed by blue glass, seed pearl border, C-catch, tube hinge (converted bracelet clasp), 3/4" w x 1-3/8", **$550**.

(Courtesy of E. Foxe Harrell Jewelers, Clinton, IA).

Mourning brooches, hair paintings:
T, c. 1865, oval three-dimensional graveyard scene, tomb and willow of cut strands of brown hair, mounted on opalescent glass, glass cover, ropetwist and engr scallop yg frame, paper label on rev: "W.J. 1865" with rampant lion, C-catch, tube hinge, extended pinstem, lead solder at compass points, later-added attaching frame mkd "333," 1-5/8" w x 1", **$350**.
B, c. 1850, oval three-dimensional sepia-toned hair painting of grave scene, willow, flowers, cutout shapes and strands of hair forming tree, flowers and ground, glass cover, S-scrolled gf frame, C-catch, tube hinge, loop for safety chain, 2-1/8" w x 1-3/4", **$325**.
(Courtesy of E. Foxe Harrell Jewelers, Clinton, IA).

Brooches, three-dimensional floral bouquets on mother-of-pearl, c. 1840-50:
L, constructed from cutout shapes of adhesive-backed hair, set in lacquered ym frame and backing, ropetwist border, C-catch, tube hinge, 1-1/4" w x 1-1/2", **$300**.
(Lenore Dailey collection).
R, cut shapes of adhesive-backed blond and brown hair with added hp details, seed pearls in flower centers, set in an oval engr and *taille d'épargne* enameled yg frame, beveled glass cover, convex yg rev engr with mono, C-catch (repaired), tube hinge, 1-3/4" w x 1-5/8", **$475**.
(Author's collection).

Brooch/Pin, yg, enamel, hair, glass, c. 1841, weeping willow and white enameled urn motifs on black enamel ground, glazed compartment in urn center containing braided lt brown hair, set in engr scrollwork, yg frame, "In Memory Of John Dexter Page Obt 24th Sept 1841, at 26" engr on rev, C-catch, tube hinge, extended pinstem, 7/8" w x 1-1/16", **$350**. (Lenore Dailey collection).

Brooch/Pin, hair, yg, enamel, c. 1847, yg winged cherub head surmounted by swiveling rect compartment flanked by yg wings, one side black enamel ground with raised yg letters "IN MEMORY OF," verso glazed compartment containing interwoven flat bands of dk blond hair, engr inscription on yg frame "July 4, 1847 Willm Beaumaris Knifre," suspending interwoven swagged braided cords of lt brown hair capped with engr and black-enameled yg drops, C-catch, tube hinge, 1-3/4" w x 1-5/8" tl, **$750**. (Private collection).

Brooches, c. 1850, hair in oval glazed compartments, yg:
TL, sm octagonal frame, "IN MEMORY OF" encircling oval, initials "RHC" engr on rev, C-catch, tube hinge, extended pinstem, 5/8" w x 1/2", **$200**.
TR, braided brown hair, engr and enameled cusped and scrolled edge yg frame, C-catch, tube hinge, 3/4" w x 5/8", **$200**.
BC, ropetwist yg frame, C-catch, tube hinge, extended pinstem, 1" w x 1/2", **$150**.
(Courtesy of E. Foxe Harrell Jewelers, Clinton, IA).

Brooch/Pin, hair, yg, MOP, glass, Fr jet, c. 1850-60, hair on MOP painting of mourning scene, tomb under tree, beveled glass cover set in oval yg bezel and back, encircled by sm Fr jet lozenges in millegrained and beaded frame, replacement lever catch and tube hinge, ring for safety chain on rev, 1-1/2" w x 1-1/4", **$550**. (Lenore Dailey collection).

Brooch/Pendant, yg, hair, c. 1840, seven joined circ glazed compartments with beveled glass covers each containing braided hair in shades of gray, white, lt brown, and gray and brown, rev engr with family names: "Katherine Starkie," "Robert Herring," "Nicholas Starkie," "Christiana Starkie," "Nicholas Starkie Junr," "Katherine Edgar Obt 29 Ap'l 1811 Aet 71," and "Harriet Bence Obt 5 June 1815 Aet 56," C-catch, tube hinge, loop for chain, 1" dia, **$400**. (Carmelita Johnson collection).

Brooch/Pin, ivory, 18k yg, hair, glass, c. 1836, hp graveyard scene, with headstone inscribed "Eliza 1r D'c 1836," cross and tree painted with hair, cherub in corner, rev glazed compartment containing Prince of Wales plumes of dk brown hair, bezel-set with beveled glass covers in rounded yg frame, appl scrollwork at compass points, upturned hook on rev, C-catch, tube hinge, extended pinstem, 1-1/2" w x 1-1/4", **$895**. (Lenore Dailey collection).

Brooch/Pin, yg, hair, glass, c. 1840-60, central oval glazed compartment containing braided and looped lock of brown hair in segmented yg frame with engr floral and scrolled foliate motifs, suspending three heart-shaped lockets, each with an inner glazed compartment containing hair, scrolled engr both sides, initials and number on each: "CHM3," "RM2" and "CHM4," C-catch, tube hinge, 1-1/2" w x 1-3/4" tl, **$600**. (Courtesy of E. Foxe Harrell Jewelers, Clinton, IA).

Brooches/Pins, Prince of Wales plumes:

L, yg, black glass (Fr jet), enamel, MOP, glass, c. 1840, oval outer border of circ-cut black faceted glass stones in sawtoothed bezels, yg and black enamel striped tubular frame around MOP plaque surmounted by lt brown hair Prince of Wales plume caught with a band of three pearls, beveled glass cover, convex back, C-catch, tube hinge, extended pinstem, 1-1/4" w x 1", **$350**. (Private collection).

R, 14k yg, porcelain, seed pearls, glass, c. 1860, blond hair Prince of Wales plumes decorated with seed pearls and gold thread, mounted on white porcelain, beveled glass cover, set in swiveling yg bezel, inscribed "S.A. Whittimore" on side, open ropetwist outer frame, textured and scrolled engr, cross bar on rev to hold swivel in place, C-catch, tube hinge, 1-3/4" w x 1-1/4", **$325**. (Lenore Dailey collection).

Ivory, glass, foil, yg, seed pearls, c. 1790, carved relief of draped woman beside an urn on a pedestal inscribed "WIR WERDEN UNS WIEDERSEHN" (Ger: we will meet again), mounted on blue foiled glass ground, set in elongated yg frame, seed pearl border, beveled glass cover, added pin back assembly (converted from ring), C-catch and tube hinge, extended pinstem, 3/4" w x 1-1/4" 1,395

Yg, foiled enamel, pearls, c. 1850-60, circ cobalt blue-enameled yg plaque, split pearls at compass points within yg scroll decoration, cobalt blue-enameled knot motif in domed center set with a split pearl and four seed pearls, engr yg details, central glazed compartment on rev containing a lock of hair on a cloth ground, C-catch, tube hinge, extended pinstem, 1-1/2" dia............ 2,528

Chatelaine, yg, enamel, hair, wm, c. 1837, open, scrolled elongated rect frame with black and white enameled floral and foliate design, hinged wm belt clip on rev, suspending lozenge shaped drop, black enameled "IN MEMORY OF" around central lozenge-shaped glazed compartment containing woven strands of brown hair, rev engr "Hester Sandbach Ob: 27th Octr 1837," three soldered loops for appendages, 2-1/2" w x 2-1/4" tl, **$1,595**. (Lenore Dailey collection).

Yg, hair, cloth, glass, c. 1859, oval undulating yg ribbon frame engr with buckle and floral motifs, central oval swiveling glazed compartment containing braided brown and gray hair, woven dk brown cloth on rev, inscribed: "N.J.W. OBT AUGT 31ST 1856 AGED 54 YEARS," and "PD JV 18.59" (1859 patent date), C-catch, tube hinge, extended pinstem, 2" w x 1-5/8" 450

Yg, hair, seed pearls, glass, c. 1860, Prince of Wales plumes of brown and blond hair caught by a row of seed pearls and decorated with undulating gold thread, mounted on oval opalescent glass plaque, domed glass cover, plain yg bezel with appl open scrolled and engr yg frame, 2-1/2" w x 2" .... 316 (A)

Locket

Hair, glass, gf, c. 1850, oval beveled edge glass front and back, one side hinged, containing braided knot of gray hair, plain gf frame, C-catch, tube hinge, extended pinstem, 7/8" w x 1-1/8" 200

Locket and Chain

18k yg, turquoise, hair, glass, c. 1830-40, wide rounded circ chevron-patterned links suspending a heart-shaped locket with appl beads, multicolor gold floral motifs encircling a central turq-set forget-me-not motif of two intertwined flowers flanking an oval-cut red stone, opens to reveal a hair design in a glazed compartment, gem-set beaded barrel clasp, locket 1-1/8" w x 1-3/4" tl, chain 38-1/2" tl .... 2,300 (A)

Ring

15k yg, enamel, pearls, diamonds, c. 1801, flat black-enameled oval top with white enamel border, set with split pearls in an oval surrounding and flanked by three sm diamonds, tapering to a plain narrow shank, rev inscribed "[cross symbol] Mary Lejeuntson, Obt Dec 9th 1801," 1-1/2" w x 1/2" 640

18k yg, enamel, c. 1820, two bands of black enamel encircling a high relief floral/foliate repoussé design, 1/2" w, size 7-1/2 .... 1,380 (A)

18k yg, enamel, hair, c. 1830, black enameled rounded rect with central glazed compartment containing woven dk brown hair, continuing to tapered shank, black enameled block letters "In Memory Of" around outside, mkd "18ct" on inside shank, approx size 9-1/2, 1/2" w x 7/16"... 295

Black glass (Fr jet), turq, glass, gf, rock crystal, hair, c. 1830-40, eight circ-cut black glass stones set in cut-down collets around central glazed compartment containing braided brown hair, shank of grad turq and turq-colored glass cabs set in cut-down collets, 5/8" x 1/2", approx size 5 395

Ring, yg, hair, enamel, seed pearls, glass, c. 1817, swiveling rect center, glazed compartment containing braided blond hair, seed pearl frame on one side, black and white enameled urn and willow on rev inscription inside split shank "THOS. KINGSLEY, ESQ: OB 5 MAY 1817 AET. 30," approx size 11-1/2, swivel 1/2" w x 5/8", **$1,200**. (Courtesy of E. Foxe Harrell Jewelers, Clinton, IA).

Carnelian, yg, hair, glass, c. 1810, swiveling top, one side set with rect-cut carnelian, rev glazed compartment containing hair, mounted on U-shaped shoulders continuing to chain link design yg shank, 1/4" w x 1/2", approx size 6 500

"Mother" Memorial Rings, yg, hair:
TC, c. 1850-70, woven patterned blond hair channel-recessed in yg band surmounted by engr yg plaque with black enameled "Mother," inner engr inscription "Augusta," approx size 8, 3/16" w, **$275**.
BL, c. 1886, engr yg band, cutout and black enameled letters spelling "MOTHER," enclosing woven dk brown hair, inner inscription "L.W. Feb 18 _86 Apr 15_86," approx size 8, 5/16" w, **$250**.
BR, c. 1850-70, domed, engr yg cutout letters spelling "MOTHER," enclosing woven lt brown hair, tapered shank, engr inscription on inside (illegible), approx size 6, 5/16" w, **$275**.
(Carmelita Johnson collection).

Mourning rings, late 18th and early 19th century, yg:
TL, c. 1766, a plait of woven dk blond hair set under a rock crystal cover in an oval convex closed-back mount encircled by sm circ-cut garnets, on a narrow black enameled shank, raised yg letters around outside: "THOS OGILWY, OBT 19 NOV 1766 AE 28" (damage to enamel), 1/2" w x 3/8", approx size 8, **$700**.
(Author's collection).
BL, c. 1818, band of engr and chiseled floral/foliate motif, engr on inside: "VISC'T VALLETORT, OB'T 29 OCT'R 1818," 1/4" w, approx size 11, **$950**.
TR, c. 1772, cushion-cut amethyst in a rubbed-over closed back convex setting, mounted on a black enameled yg narrow shank with raised letters around the outside: "SAM'L PEARSON, OB: 7 OCT : 1772, AE'T 48," head 3/8" x 1/4", approx size 7-1/2, **$700**.
BR, date letter for 1832, black enameled 18k yg band, rect hair compartment and "IN MEMORY OF" in Old English letters around outside within raised engr floral border, inside inscribed "David Matthew, died 18 July 1832, aged 65," maker's mk "WK," London hmks, 5/8" w, approx size 5-1/2, **$350**.
(Courtesy of E. Foxe Harrell Jewelers, Clinton, IA).

Ring, ivory, yg, glass, c. 1790, navette-shaped sepia-toned painting depicting a mourning scene of a woman beside an urn, inscription above: "NOT LOST BUT GONE BEFORE," glass cover, black enameled shank with raised inscription : "PAULA SILMORE OB 6 MEE 1790 AE 58," size 6-1/2, 5/8" w x 1", **$1,100**. (Courtesy of E. Foxe Harrell Jewelers, Clinton, IA).

Ivory, 18k yg, glass, enamel, c. 1785, painting on navette-shaped ivory plaque depicting a woman in classical drapery resting on a shield, glass cover, mounted in yg, black enameled shank with raised letters inscribed "CHARLES HAWKINS, OBIT 15 MAY 1785, AT 36," Eng, 1/2" w 3/4", approx size 9 595

Ivory, 18k yg, glass, paint, c. 1790, painting on navette shaped ivory plaque depicting seated young girl in mourning under trees, King Charles spaniel at her side, in glazed compartment mounted in yg, plain narrow shank, rev inscription illegible, 1-1/4" w x 1-1/2 600

Sapphires, 18k yg, enamel, c. 1764, central oval flat-cut blue sapphire with faceted edge encircled by 13 sm circ-cut foil-backed blue sapphires in closed-back mount, domed on rev, mounted on white-enameled narrow shank, inscribed "ROBERT ERSKINE, OBT AT BOMBAY, FEB 20 1764 AT 31," eng, 3/4" dia 740

Yg, enamel, c. 1741, band of white enameled scrolls with raised lettering inscribed "WM. TAYLOR ESQ: OB 17 APR 1741 AE 44," maker's mk "W.W.," 1/8" w, size 8 .... 575 (A)

Yg, enamel, c. 1773, band with white enameled center, raised lettering inscribed "RICHARD JENNENS ESQ: OB: 3 MAR: 1773 AET 63," flanked by incised edges, maker's mk "M.G.," 1/8" w, size 7-1/2 .... 575 (A)

Yg, enamel, c. 1799, narrow band, black enamel with white enamel border, inscribed "MR. JOHN COLLISON, OBT FEB 1799 AT 69," 1/4" w 330

Yg, enamel, c. 1826, central recessed band of green enamel flanked by bands of engr floral yg, further flanked by thin bands of green enamel, inscribed on inside "Sir Edmund Antrobus Bart, died 6 Feb 1826, aged 74," 1/2" w, size 8-1/4 .... 322 (A)

Yg, enamel, hair, c.1830, bowed, cusped rect frame with black enameled "In Memory Of" around central rect glazed compartment containing woven strands of brown hair, rev engr "Sarah Roper Parnell, Oct 29th, 1830" continuing to a pierced and engr tapered shank, approx size 6, 9/16" w x 1/2" 395

Ring, yg, hair, seed pearl, c. 1870-80, engr yg circ compartment containing woven brown hair, cutout letters spelling "JENNIE" encircling seed pearl center, flanked by engr sawtooth shoulders, each surmounted by two yg beads, mounted over woven blond hair channel-recessed in yg shank, approx size 6-1/2, top 3/8" dia, shank 1/4" w, **$350**. (Carmelita Johnson collection).

Yg, garnets, glass, silk, straw, c. 1776, profile of a young woman in straw embroidery on silk, glass cover encircled by sm faceted garnets, mounted on a garnet-set yg shank, rev inscribed "Harriet Sprogg, died 7 May 1778, aged 43," Eng, 3/4" dia, approx size 6 660

Yg, hair, enamel, rock crystal, c. 1820, rounded rect yg compartment containing braided blond/gray hair, rock crystal cover, mounts on black enameled yg band, inscribed on outside: "JOHN BAYLIES OB 12 NOV:1777 AE:50" (top line) and "ELIZ. BAYLIES OB 22 JAN 1816 AE:85" (bottom line), approx size 8-1/2, 1/2" w x 3/8", shank 1/4" w 325

Yg, hair, rock crystal, c. 1700, oval compartment containing a flat sheet of blond hair surmounted by spiraling gold thread encircling gold thread cipher, covered by faceted rock crystal in yg bezel, later added shank mkd "10k" (converted slide for ribbon), approx size 7, head 7/8" w x 1" 500

Yg, ivory, sepia-tone paint, glass, c. 1783, elongated octagonal plaque with mourning scene of a weeping man standing beside an urn surmounting a pedestal inscribed "SARAH STARR OB 5 MAY 1783 AE 12 YRS" mounted in engr yg frame, glass cover, engr shoulders tapering to narrow shank, approx size 4-1/2, head 3/4" w x 1-1/4" 1,895

Yg, ivory, sepia-tone paint, glass, c. 1784, navette-shaped engr frame bezel set with ivory plaque painted with funereal symbols: urn, two doves, weeping willow, initials "RT" flanking urn, rev engr "FRANCES CUMBERS OB 5 NOVR 1784" mounted on engr shoulders tapering to narrow shank, approx size 7-1/2, head 3/4" w x 1-1/4" 1,585

Yg, rubies, parchment, glass, c. 1760-70, design of double hearts, one enclosing initial "G" the other the initial "W," suspended from a ribbon bow, painted on parchment within glazed compartment encircled by sm sq-cut rubies, closed domed back, mounted in yg, on split shank with scrollwork decoration, 3/4" dia, approx size 6 540

Scarf Pin/Stickpin

Paste, ster, rolled gold plate, hair, c. 1780-1820, sm rect glazed compartment containing tightly woven hair, ropetwist brass frame encircled by eight colorless pastes in cut-down silver collets forming star outline, rolled gold plate back (worn), head 1/2" w x 5/8", 2-3/4" tl 200

Slide

14k yg, hair, seed pearls, enamel, glass, c. 1790-1820, flattened hollow sphere, cutout section on opposing sides for ribbon, surmounted by circ glazed compartment containing braided blond hair, encircled by stripes of blue and white enamel, seed pearls, seed pearls, mono "MAC" engr on rev, 7/8" dia, 3/4" top to bottom 550

MINIATURES

Before the advent of photography, the miniature portrait was the only way to capture a wearable likeness of a loved one. These were another popular form of sentiment in the eighteenth and early to mid-nineteenth centuries. Some miniatures were worn as memorials to a deceased spouse or parent, but others were simply a way of keeping a likeness as a reminder of the object of one's affections. Queen Victoria wore a portrait of Albert as a bracelet clasp from the beginning of their marriage, which she of course continued to wear after his death. Bracelets and pendants were the most common way of wearing a miniature, but brooches were also worn. Portrait miniatures in painted enamel often have a lock of the portrayed loved one's hair enclosed in a compartment on the reverse.

Portraits are relatively easy to circa-date, if one is familiar with fashion history, and notes the clothing, hair and other details of the person depicted. These are usually rendered in the styles of the times.

Other types of miniatures have religious themes, some simply depict a pretty scene. The Swiss were known for painted enamels (sometimes called Geneva or Swiss enamel), most often depicting people, usually women, in regional dress against a scenic background. These were at the height of fashion in the 1830s. Sylvan scenic Swiss landscapes were also rendered in enamels during this period.

One of the rarest and most desirable forms of miniature is the so-called "lover's eye," said to have originated with George IV in 1785, while he was Prince of Wales. The eye portrayed was difficult to identify, giving rise to the idea of a "secret lover," always watching. Eye miniatures were worn through the first half of the nineteenth century, although by the 1820s the fashion had waned considerably. They are seldom seen on the market today (see Reproduction Alert).

By the second half of the nineteenth century, photographs began to supersede portrait miniatures, and were often inserted into one side of the swiveling compartment of a large gold or gilt metal brooch (see Manufactured Gold and Gold-filled section). The other side might contain a lock of the loved one's hair or a swatch of his or her clothing. An unusual example of a photograph incorporated into hairwork is shown on page 25. Photographs were also contained in lockets, a tradition that continues to this day.

References: François Boucher, *20,000 Years of Fashion*, Harry N. Abrams, 1987; Shirley Bury, *Jewellery, 1789-1910, The International Era*, Vols. I and II, Antique Collectors' Club, 1991; Martha G. Fales, *Jewelry in America 1600-1900*, Antique Collectors' Club, 1995

Reproduction Alert: Because they are scarce and sought-after, eye portraits have been faked, usually by taking the hair out of a brooch with a glazed compartment and replacing it with an eye. Some of the eyes aren't even actual paintings, rather they are printed. The small screened dots making up the picture are the giveaway.

Bracelets

Link, yg, rose gold, enamel, colored gemstones, pearls, turquoise, c. 1830, each bracelet of eleven links, each link centering an oval multi-colored Swiss enamel panel of a woman in regional dress with the name of the relevant Swiss Canton on the back, each panel in a plain yg frame with three gemstones in cut-down collets at top and bottom, each panel with a different arrangement of colored gemstones including turq and pearls, appl foliate, fruit, and bead decoration of yg and rose gold, an appl shell at top and bottom of each link, v-spring and box clasp, in signed fitted leather cases mkd "I.J. Mazure & Co., London," 1-5/8" w x 7-3/8" tl, pr.......... 14,950 (A)

Brooch/Pendant

Porcelain, yg, diamonds, enamel, colored stones, c. 1880, oval ptd porcelain portrait of a woman in engr yg frame encircled by radiating rect bars of blue enamel alternating with sm rc and om diamond clusters terminating in various collet-set multi-colored gemstones, pendant hoop, chips to enamel, 1-3/4" w x 2-1/4"........... 978 (A)

Brooch/Pin

15k yg, enamel, Early Victorian, rect plaque, multicolored Swiss enamel portrait of a young girl in native dress in a harvest scene with dog, trees in bg, bezel-set within a tubular rect frame, sm foliate scroll motifs at compass points, 1-3/8" w x 1-7/8" .... 1,150 (A)

Bracelet, ptd ivory, yg, c. 1780-1790, oval ptd miniature of an eighteenth century bewigged gentleman set and glazed in yg bezel, bracelet of eight yg chains terminating in v-spring clasps (top and bottom), natural skintones, blue jacket, ruffled white shirt, blue bg with clouds, 7-1/4" tl, 1-5/8" w x 2-1/4", **$700**. (Courtesy of E. Foxe Harrell Jewelers, Clinton, IA).

Bracelets, yg, ptd porcelain, c. 1860, engr yg band with central oval ptd miniature, each inscribed "Mary L. Emrich," sized for doll or baby, locking mechanism on rev, gold band cracked on one, 1-3/8" inside dia, 3/8" w at center, pr, **$200**. (Courtesy of E. Foxe Harrell Jewelers, Clinton, IA).

Earrings, yg, porcelain, c. 1850-60, oval porcelain plaques, each with a hp blonde female bust on black ground , yg ropetwist frame around bezels, larger ropetwist outer frames suspended from shepherd's hook earwires (lead solder), 1/2" w x 1" tl, **$225**. (Courtesy of E. Foxe Harrell Jewelers, Clinton, IA).

Enamel, yg, rc diamonds, c. 1880-90, circ multicolored Limoges enamel portrait of Elizabethan woman, blue ground, gold scrolled border set with four rc diamonds at compass points, C-catch, tube hinge, extended pinstem (damage to enamel), 1-1/8" dia 450

Porcelain, enamel, yg, c. 1860, oval Swiss enameled porcelain scene of a chateau on a lake in shades of blue, green, brown, white, beige, gray, orange, and black, in an oval yg frame with wiretwist decoration, extended pinstem, sgd on rev "Chateau de Thun, A. Golay-Leresche, Geneve," 1-5/8" w x 1-3/8" .... 805 (A)

Ptd MOP, yg, c. 1840-50, rect, Madonna and child, pierced scrollwork, yg frame, engr bezel, dark bg in yellow and red, C-catch, tube hinge, extended pinstem, 2-1/4" w x 1-3/4" 650

Ptd porcelain, silver, seed pearls, glass, c. 1850, oval ptd portrait of seated girl reading, shades of pink, white and blue, floral and foliate silver frame set with seed pearls, turq glass, swivel bail, C-catch, tube hinge, hinged safety, 1-1/8" w x 1-1/2" 450

Reverse-painted glass, gf, glass, c. 1830-40, rect plaque, rev-ptd rose and rosebuds, beveled glass cover, convex back, stamped and notched frame, C-catch, tube hinge, 1-1/4" w x 1-1/8 200

Pendant

Ptd ivory, yg, glass, fabric, c. 1850-60, oval portrait miniature of bespectacled young man in neutral tones of gray, black, white and sepia, glass cover, glazed compartment on rev containing fabric, engr yg frame, 1" w x 1-3/4" 400

Pendant, ptd ivory, yg, c. 1864, oval miniature portrait of young gentleman wearing a cravat, beveled glass cover, engr frame and back, natural skin colors, gray bg, black and white jacket and shirt, inscribed and dated on inside "June 6 1864 Binghamton To Mary Stew," box, 1-3/8" w x 2-1/4" tl, **$600**. (Courtesy of E. Foxe Harrell Jewelers, Clinton, IA).

Pendants, miniatures, ptd ivory and rolled gold plate, early 19th century:

L, c. 1810-20, circ portrait of couple in medieval dress, river, trees, castle on hill in bg, ptd in blues, greens, orange and brown, glass cover over hinged compartment, glazed compartment on rev, yg frame and bail, 1-7/8" dia, 2-1/4" tl with bail, **$350**.

R, c. 1810, oval portrait, full figure of woman in pink drapery in a landscape bg encircled by bands of black and white enamel, beveled glass cover front and back, rev hinged compartment containing pieces of brown silk, yg frame and bail, 1-3/4" w x 2-1/2" with bail, **$375**.

(Courtesy of E. Foxe Harrell Jewelers, Clinton, IA).

EARLY VICTORIAN (ROMANTIC PERIOD) c. 1837-1861

Queen Victoria set the tone for the era as the first female to rule Great Britain since Queen Anne (d. 1714). Like most women of her time, she was an incurable romantic–and she *loved* jewelry! The early years of her reign are aptly called The Romantic Period (also known as the Victoria and Albert period). Victoria married Albert in 1840, who became Prince Consort in 1857, and died suddenly in 1861. The twenty-one years of their marriage were filled with love, devotion, and the births of nine children. Symbols of romance were predominant in the jewelry that Albert designed and had made for Victoria. Her betrothal ring was in the form of a snake with its tail in its mouth, symbol of everlasting love, a motif that recurs throughout the nineteenth century. The snake also symbolized eternity, guardian spirit, and wisdom. Snake (or serpent) jewelry was especially popular in the 1840s. Gold snake necklaces, bracelets and rings were set throughout with small turquoise cabochons or partly enameled and gem-set.

Flowers in jewelry were both symbolic of Victorian sentiment and a reflection of interest in nature. Flower motif brooches in diamonds and paste carried over from Georgian times, but became more three-dimensional and realistic. Flower heads were often set *en tremblant*. Gold and colored gemstone flowers were also realistically rendered.

The hand is another recurring romantic symbol in Victorian jewelry. It had a variety of meanings depending on how it was depicted. Hands holding flowers conveyed the flower's message. Yew wreaths symbolized mourning. Clasped hands symbolized friendship. Good luck and "evil eye" hand gesture amulets were carved in coral, ivory, jet, and mother-of-pearl. Hands were also used as clasps for bracelets and neckchains, especially in earlier period pieces.

Sentiment prevailed in the gifts of jewelry Victoria exchanged with others. She fostered the widespread practice of giving and wearing jewelry made with the hair of the giver as a memento or love token. And no one thought it at all strange that she had a bracelet made from her children's baby teeth.

The Great Exhibition of the Industry of All Nations, held in London in 1851, was perhaps the single most important event of the early Victorian period. It was dubbed "The Crystal Palace" after the gigantic all-glass structure that housed it. Never before had there been a multinational exhibit of any kind, held anywhere. This monumental spectacle has been called "the focal point for the Victorian culture of the Western world." Its success spawned "Crystal Palace" offspring in Cork in 1852, New York and Dublin in 1853, Munich in 1854, and Paris in 1855. In 1854, the Crystal Palace itself was recreated at Sydenham, outside London. The jewelers who took part in these exhibitions were the most highly esteemed trendsetters of jewelry fashion. If it had been seen at the Crystal Palace, it was "in," In 1851, naturalistic diamond flower brooches and hair ornaments, Celtic annular (ring) brooches and Scottish "granite" bracelets, Berlin iron jewelry, and gemstone and enameled bracelets were among the jewels shown.

Early Victorian fashions determined the ways in which jewelry was or was not worn. The dresses of the period were full-skirted, worn with petticoats, and often had long-sleeves. Lace collars with brooches pinned at the throat were common. Necklines on dresses worn by younger women were cut low and wide across the shoulders. Velvet or silk ribbons were sometimes worn around the neck, crossed in front and pinned with a small brooch. Large jeweled brooches with pendent drops, called bodice brooches, were worn on low-cut gowns in the evening. Unless otherwise altered, early Victorian brooches have an extended pinstem (meant to be pushed back through the clothing to keep the brooch in place), C-catch and tube hinge. In the late 1840s and early 1850s, bonnets were worn during the day, and for evening wear, center-parted hair covered the ears in loops or ringlets, trimmed in ribbons or flowers. Consequently, earrings were seldom worn. Bracelets, worn in multiples on both wrists, were the most popular form of jewelry, especially snake-shaped coils or bangles. "Stretchy" expandable bracelets were introduced in the early 1840s, thanks to the invention of elastic, c. 1830. In spite of their prevalence, relatively few early Victorian bracelets survive today, having been subjected to considerably more wear and damage than brooches or necklaces might have been.

Romanticism inspired the beginnings of a revival of medieval and Renaissance motifs and decorative elements that was to continue throughout the century. Gothic architecture was translated into jewels. Gold was still in relatively short supply at the onset of the Early Victorian period. In the 1830s, gold was mostly hand-wrought filigree (*cannetille*), but by the 1840s filigree was out and hollow stamped or repoussé thin gauge metal was in, used as settings for gemstones, or as frames for portrait miniatures and enamels.

Seed pearl jewelry was often made with little if any gold at all. Tiny pearls strung on horsehair and mounted on cut-to-shape mother-of-pearl backings were made into entire suites of delicate and fragile jewels, typically of floral and foliate design. It is unusual to find individual pieces intact, and even rarer to come across intact suites, many of which were made in England in the first half of the nineteenth century. The fashion for seed pearls persisted longer in the United States. It was traditionally worn as bridal jewelry.

References: *The Crystal Palace Exhibition Illustrated Catalogue,* reprint of the original Art-Journal publication, Dover, 1970; David Bennett and Daniela Mascetti, *Understanding Jewellery,* 2nd ed., Antique Collectors' Club, 1994; Carolyn Goldthorpe, *From Queen to Empress, Victorian Dress 1837-1877,* Metropolitan Museum of Art, New York (exhibition catalog), 1988.

Advisors: Sam Gassman, Ruth Eller and Sharen Wood.

Bracelet, link

Yg, garnets, c. 1840, chased and repoussé yg Algerian knot motif front clasp set with five rect-cut garnets in scalloped bezels, on a flexible 3/8" w strap of overlapping segments flanked by ropetwist borders, clasp 2" w x 1-1/2", 7" tl .... 633 (A)

Brooch/Pin

14k yg, turquoise, c. 1840, stamped raised horizontal foliate scroll, center set with eleven med and sm circ turq cabs, suspending a similar pear-shaped drop set with five turq cabs (damage, evidence of repair), C-catch, tube hinge, extended pinstem, 1-1/4" w x 1-1/2" tl .... 248 (A)

Yg, green beryls, c. 1840-50, repoussé yg knot, engr floral/foliate motifs on stippled ground, two center segments each set with five, side segments each set with two, cushion-cut green beryls in deep pronged bezels, suspending a similarly decorated oval locket from one of three swagged snake chains, locket with glazed compartment on rev containing cloth, front set with two green beryls, C-catch, tube hinge, 2" w x 2-1/4" tl 2,237

Brooch/Pin, yg, pink topaz, c. 1840, die-struck and engr yg double-lobed foliate and scroll motif frame set with three foil-backed faceted oval pink topaz in pronged bezels (closed backs), suspending a foliate and scroll motif drop with one prong-set foil-backed faceted pear-shaped pink topaz, C-catch, tube hinge, 2" w x 4" tl, **$1,500**. (Courtesy of E. Foxe Harrell Jewelers, Clinton, IA).

Brooch/Pin, paste, silver, c. 1840, floral spray, two flowerheads mounted on springs (*en tremblant*), prong-set a jour pastes in center, bead-set throughout with pastes with fused foil backing (fused backing first developed c. 1840), Fr hmk, maker's mk in lozenge on stem, later-added safety catch, 2-1/4" w x 4-1/2", **$650**. (Julia Alberts collection).

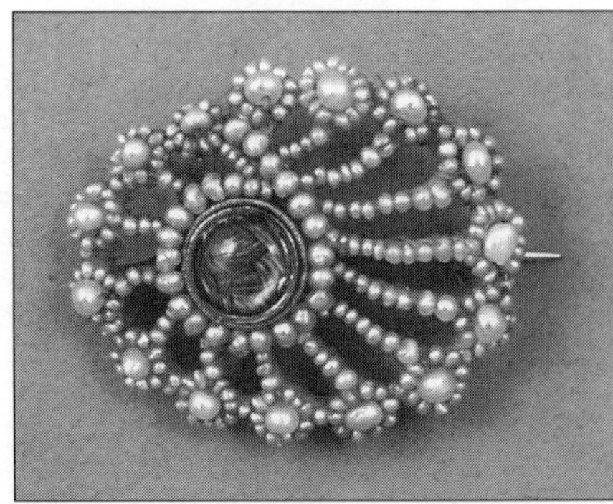

Brooch/Pin, seed pearls, MOP, hair, rock crystal, yg, c. 1840, seed pearls sewn onto oval pierced MOP plaque, circ glazed compartment containing gray-brown hair, rock crystal cover, C-catch, tube hinge (mounted on yg plaque on rev), extended pinstem, 1-3/8" w x 1-1/8", **$300**. (Carmelita Johnson collection).

Buckle, yg, citrine, amethyst, c. 1840, stamped scrollwork elements with central faceted oval citrine flanked by two faceted oval amethysts, converted to a brooch, C-catch, tube hinge, 2-1/4" w x 1-1/8", **$250**. (Private collection).

Yg, amethysts, c. 1840, navette-shaped die-stamped yg scrolled openwork with central faceted oval amethyst in open-backed pronged collet, suspending a scrolled openwork drop similarly set with elongated faceted pear-shaped amethyst, flat backing, C-catch, tube hinge, extended pinstem, safety chain with safety pin, 1-7/8" w x 2-1/2 tl 525

Rev ptd glass, gp brass, c. 1850, rect glass center depicting urn and willow, green bg, stamped curv gp frame, C-catch, tube hinge, 1-1/8" w x 1-1/4" 175

Neckchain

Yg, enamel, c. 1840, alternating links of sm chased and repoussé floral/foliate lozenges and open-ended lg lozenges with floral/foliate enamel in pink, green, white, blue, and black, Eng, 1/2" w x 50" tl .... 5,750 (A)

Necklace

14k yg, enamel, seed pearls, c. 1840-50, snake motif of grad scale-like links terminating in a turq-colored enameled snake's head front clasp, head set with seed pearls, suspending an inverted pear-shaped drop surmounted by an enameled fleur-de-lis motif set with seed pearls (some enamel loss), 15" tl .... 1,035 (A)

Yg, garnets, olivines, c. 1850, snake with engr head suspending a heart from its mouth, bezel-set garnet cab eyes, one lg oval prong-set garnet cab at top of head and in center of heart, a circ-cut and pear-shaped prong-set olivine on head, grad scale-like link chain, head 1/2" w x 1-3/4", chain 15-1/2" tl .... 1,380 (A)

18k yg, turquoise, c. 1840, in the form of a snake grasping its tail in its mouth, body of three rows of grad sm circ bezel-set turq cabs, yg head with sm circ turq cab eyes, v-spring and box clasp at mouth, 1/2" w (at head), 15" tl .... 2,185 (A)

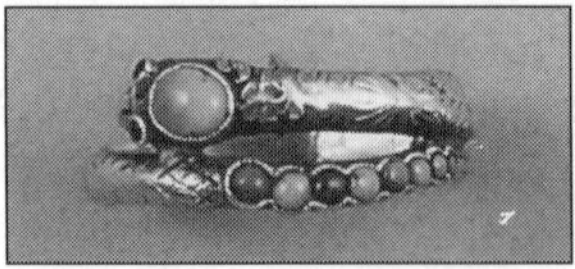

Rings, serpent motif, yg, st yg, and gemstones, c. 1840-50:

L, engr yg with bezel-set turquoise cabs and red glass eyes (one missing), mouth hinged, mkd "VIII" inside tongue, several dents, approx size 9-1/2, **$550**. (Private collection).

R, snake motif, seven rc diamonds set in st yg and lg pear-shaped turq cab in head, seventeen grad turq cabs on shank (five rc diamonds missing on tail), size 7-1/2, 3/16" head, **$900**. (Courtesy of E. Foxe Harrell Jewelers, Clinton, IA).

Ring

Bloodstone, yg, c. 1840-60, shield-shaped flat bloodstone plaque in engr yg mount, tapered shank, approx size 14, top 5/8" w x 3/4" 400

Yg, turquoise, c. 1840, band of appl scroll motif *cannetille* and beads centering a row of sm circ turq cabs, 1/4" w, size 6-3/4 .... 978 (A)

Yg, turquoise, rc diamond, c. 1840, a central cluster of five sm turq cabs forming flowerhead (forget-me-not) with rc diamond center, flanked by scroll and floral engr shoulders, tapering to a narrow shank, 3/8" center, approx size 6 150

Suite: Brooch/Pin and Pendent Earrings, seed pearls, MOP, horsehair, yg, c. 1850, brooch a three-dimensional plaque suspending a pear-shaped drop flanked by swags of strung pearls, design composed of five layers of seed pearls of varying size forming rosette clusters, strung on horsehair and attached to MOP backing, matching earrings of similar design, four layers of pearls, yg earwires, in orig box mkd "JOSEPH PERLINGTON, LIVERPOOL," Eng, earrings 1" w x 3" tl, brooch 2-1/2" x 4", suite, **$1,400**. (Photo courtesy of Sharen and Nicholas Wood).

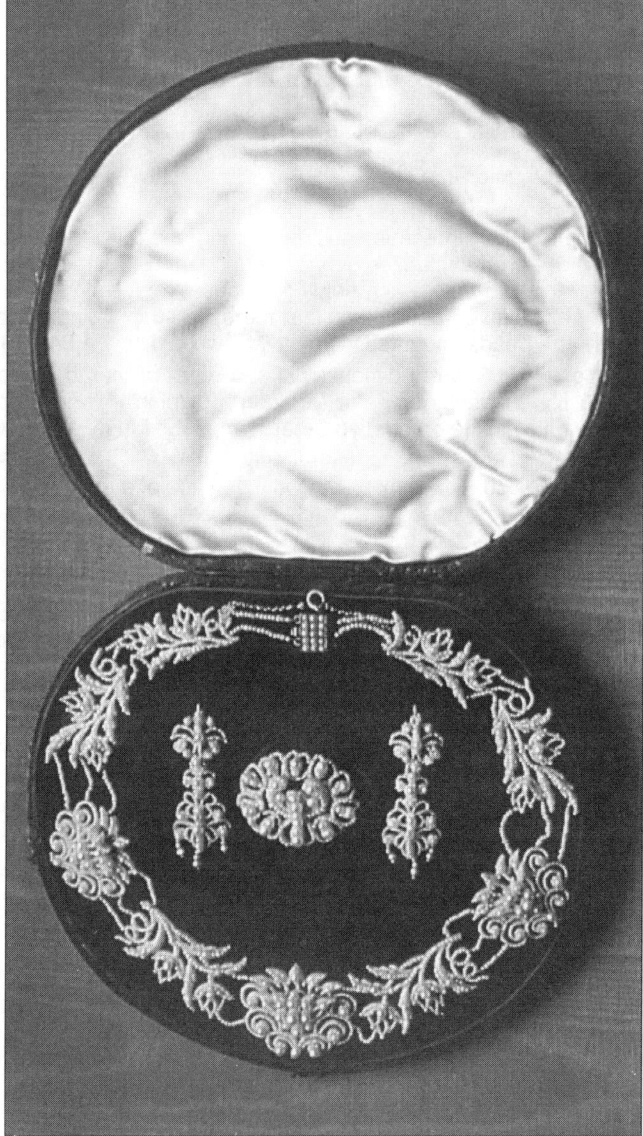

Suite: Necklace, Brooch/Pin and Pendent Earrings, seed pearls, MOP, horsehair, yg, c. 1840-50, necklace of openwork floral/foliate motifs alternating with scrolled pierced plaques, seed pearls of varying size strung on horsehair mounted on MOP, plaques joined with strung seed pearl strands, terminating in 18k yg v-spring and box clasp set with split pearls; earrings of openwork design interspersed with seed pearl rosette clusters, yg earwires; oval brooch of open seed pearl rings with larger seed pearl centers enclosing clustered seed pearl center, in orig box, Eng, necklace 1" at center x 18" tl, earrings 7/8" w x 2" tl, brooch 1-1/2" w x 1-1/8", suite, **$1,650**. (Photo courtesy of Sharen and Nicholas Wood).

Suite: Pendant and Earrings, Paste, yg, c. 1850, pendant prong-set with colorless cushion-cut pastes, mounted a jour in open circ yg frame, scallops forming prongs around outer circle of pastes, hinged bail, matching drop earrings, "honeycomb" frame around rosette cluster of lg oval and sm cushion-cut pastes, kidney earwires, pendant 1" dia, earrings 5/8" w x 1" tl, **$550**. (Courtesy of E. Foxe Harrell Jewelers, Clinton, IA).

Suite: Necklace, Brooch/Pin and Pendent Earrings

Seed pearls, garnet, MOP, horsehair, yg, c. 1800-20, necklace composed of three strands of seed pearls, top and bottom strand strung in clusters, center strand in open links, interspersed at equal intervals with grad foliate motifs in seed pearls of varying size strung on horsehair mounted on MOP, 18k yg v-spring and box clasp set with split pearls; matching earrings with cluster surmounts suspending foliate motif drops, yg earwires; oval brooch, double layers of seed pearls forming open scallops with pearl centers, surmounted by a central oval-cut garnet in closed-back mount, yg frame, in orig box, Eng, necklace 1-1/4" at center x 18" tl, earrings 7/8" w x 1-1/2", brooch 1-3/4" w x 1-1/4" 1,400

Tiara

Seed pearls, MOP, horsehair, 9k yg, c. 1850, grad floral sprays of seed pearls of varying size strung on horsehair and mounted on MOP plaques, yg wire mounts attaching sprays to yg circlet, looped terminals for ribbon attachment, in orig box, Eng, 12" circumference, 3-3/4" at center tapering to 1-1/4" 1,560

Brooch/Pin, ym, Mid-Victorian, pale pink V-shaped carving depicting the heads and wings of a pr of cherubs (putti) in high detailed relief, ym C-catch and tube hinge set into rev, 2-1/4" w x 1", **$1,275**. (Photo courtesy of Karen Lorene, Facèré Jewelry Art, Seattle, WA).

CORAL

History: Coral was popular throughout the nineteenth century. Children wore coral necklaces to fend off disease and evil spirits, because the Victorians held on to the ancient belief that coral had curative and protective powers. It also appealed to their interest in nature. Beads, carved cameos, floral motifs, good luck charms, and natural branches were made into jewelry of all types. Italy, particularly Naples, was the primary source for coral, and most carvers were Italian. Desirable, but rarer, colors were deep red and pale pink.

The most prevalent surviving forms are those in which the coral is protected by a metal mounting or frame, and beads. Intact examples of delicately carved all-coral pieces are more difficult to find.

References: Vivienne Becker, *Antique and Twentieth Century Jewellery*, 2nd ed., N.A.G. Press, 1987; Shirley Bury, *Jewellery, 1789-1910, The International Era*, Vol. I, Antique Collectors' Club, 1991; Martha G. Fales, *Jewelry in America 1600-1900*, Antique Collectors' Club, 1995.

Bracelet

Flexible

14k yg, c. 1850-60, central element with scalloped oval outline, engr yg frame forming undulating ribbon, enclosing carved coral floral and berries motif, mounted on heavy woven yg mesh strap, v-spring and box clasp with wiretwist and appl bead decoration, fitted box, center 2-1/4" w x 1-3/4", band 1" w x 7" .... 805 (A)

Brooch/Pendant, Cameo

14k yg, seed pearls, c. 1880, depicting the profile of a Bacchante in high relief, grad seed pearl frame, yg mount, 1" w x 1-1/4" .... 403 (A)

Yg, c. 1880, oval carving of a woman in profile bezel-set in a yg frame with engr floral scrollwork, pendant loop, 1-1/4" w x 1-5/8 tl .... 288 (A)

Brooch/Pin

14k yg, c. 1850-60, scalloped oval outline, engr yg frame forming undulating ribbon, enclosing carved coral floral and berries motif, wiretwist and foliate yg accents, 2-1/4" w x 1-7/8" .... 518 (A)

Yg, c. 1860, three-dimensional carving depicting the head of a woman flanked by grapes and leaves, ears of corn, and two putti, each holding a goose, three appl beads and carved double scroll at the base suspending three sm beads, mounted in yg , 1-7/8" w x 2-1/8"... 1,840 (A)

Yg, c. 1860, three-dimensional carving of a cherub and a fish in waves of water ("boy on a dolphin"), variegated pale pink to orange, yg C-catch and tube hinge, 1-1/4" w x 5/8" 688

Yg, c. 1850, pale pink carving in the shape of a feather with scrolled barbs, yg C-catch and tube hinge, 2-1/2" w x 3/4" 628

Corsage Ornament

Yg, diamonds, c. 1860-70, open shield-shaped swagged design, surmounted by a central scrolled yg knot motif with engr and *taille d'épargne* enamel decoration, bordered by a row of coral beads, surmounting a lg coral bead, suspending two swags of sm rc diamonds centering a third swag, all suspending yg braided wire fringe with black enamel yg cylindrical beads and oval coral bead terminals, fitted box, 4" w x 5-1/4" tl .... 8,050 (A)

Earrings, pendent

Seed pearls, yg, c. 1870, *girandole* style, circ coral cab surmount, suspending lg center circ coral cab bordered with three sm circ coral cabs alternating with seed pearls,

Pendent Earrings, yg, c. 1850, coral briolette, cutout engr yg cap suspended from faceted oval coral and yg surmount, kidney ear wires, 1/2" w x 2-1/2" tl, pr, **$700**. (Courtesy of E. Foxe Harrell Jewelers, Clinton, IA).

Necklace, yg, c. 1850-60, carved coral grapes and leaves in segments alternating with scarabs, suspending carved bacchantes' heads alternating with amphorae and grape vines from sm flowerheads, mounted on articulated yg armature, scarab surmounting box clasp, fitted case, 17" tl, 1-1/2" at center, **$4,000**. (Courtesy of E. Foxe Harrell Jewelers, Clinton, IA).

suspending three pear-shaped coral drops topped with seed pearls, with gold ropework swags, kidney earwires, 1" w x 2-3/8" .... 747 (A)

Pendant, Cameo

14k yg, diamonds, c. 1880-90, circ carving of a bacchante in profile, set in an open foliate motif frame with four sm circ diamonds prong-set at compass points, appl pendant loop at top, 1-3/8" dia .... 605 (A)

Suite: Brooch and Pendent Earrings

Yg, c. 1850-60, brooch a carved chrysanthemum flanked by and suspending carved foliage and blossoms, yg armature, matching earrings, fitted box, brooch 2-3/4" w x 3" tl, earrings 7/8" w x 2" tl including earwires..... 1,035 (A)

Pendant, yg, turquoise, c. 1840, carved coral hand holding a yg wire with attached carved coral cat drop, surmounted by a row of three bezel-set turquoise cabs, undulating yg wire work design with one bezel-set turquoise cab, plain yg wire bail, 1" w x 1-1/2" tl, **$300**. (Private collection).

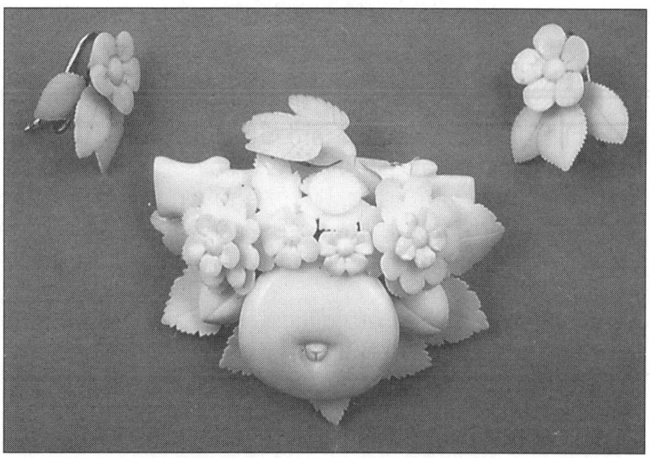

Suite: Brooch and Earrings, yg, c. 1850, brooch a carved pale pink and white relief floral and foliate cluster on a branch surmounted by carved bird, mounted on yg armature, C-catch, earrings each a flowerhead and three leaves, yg earwires, brooch 2-1/8" w x 2", earrings 3/4" w x 7/8", **$1,000**. (Courtesy of E. Foxe Harrell Jewelers, Clinton, IA).

HAIRWORK

History: Hairwork is another type of hair jewelry in which the entire piece is made of woven hair with the addition of gold or gold-filled fittings and decorative elements. These pieces were not necessarily meant for mourning. They were made by and for women and men out of their own or a loved one's hair and given as mementos or love tokens.

The technique involved the use of a type of worktable where individual strands of hair were weighted and woven together to form hollow tubes around a solid core of cording and/or wire. This core was sometimes removed, and the tubes were then tied or enclosed with gold rings at intervals to form spherical or elliptical hollow "beads." After processing and weaving, the hairwork could then be made into necklaces, bracelets, earrings, or brooches. A commonly found form is a watch chain in which the tube or rope of hair is woven in a spiral pattern, with an added gold or gold-filled swivel hook, bar and fob charms (sometimes also made of hair).

Recently published information indicates that hairwork jewelry dates back further than was previously thought. Documented examples survive going back to the late eighteenth century. But the height of hairwork's popularity was during the mid-nineteenth century, when it was made commercially as well as by "loving hands at home" from instructions found in women's magazines of the day, such as *Godey's Lady's Book* or *Peterson's Magazine*. Fittings for hair watch chains were advertised in Sears catalogs as late as 1911, but the practice of making and wearing hair jewelry had waned considerably by the 1880s.

While the thought of human hair jewelry may be distasteful to some, collectors find both the idea and its execution fascinating. In recent years, there has been a growing appreciation for this lost art, as well as interest in reviving it.

The value of hair jewelry is in the workmanship; solid gold fittings enhance value only slightly over gold-filled. Watch chains are the form most usually found, necklaces and earrings are scarce. Brown is the most common hair color, blond and white are scarce, and red is rare, not only because redheads are in the minority, but also because red hair was attributed to women of ill repute.

Damaged pieces are difficult to repair, so be sure to check condition carefully.

References: Jeanenne Bell, *Collector's Encyclopedia of Hairwork Jewelry,* Collector Books, 1998; Lilian Baker Carlisle, "Hair Jewelry," article in *The Antique Trader Weekly,* May 2, 1990; Anita and Phil Gordon, "Hair Jewelry: Much More Than Mourning," article in *Jewelers' Circular-Keystone /Heritage,* February 1990 (Chilton); Carmelita Johnson, *Ornamental Hair-Work,* published by the author (out of print), 1981; Jules and Kaethe Kliot, eds., *The Art of Hairwork, Hair Braiding and Jewelry of Sentiment* (reprint of book by Mark Campbell, 1875), Lacis Publications, Berkeley, CA, 1989.

Collectors' Club: Hairwork Society, P.O. Box 1617, Orem, Utah 84059 (send SASE for newsletter).

Internet: http://www.hairwork.com, web site of Marlys Fladeland (e-mail: marlys@hairwork.com), who also maintains a network of online collectors and dealers, as well as the above newsletter.

Museums: Bennington Museum, Bennington VT; Fleming Museum, Burlington, VT; Pine Forest Historical Museum, Edmore, MI; Henry Ford Museum and Greenfield Village, Dearborn, MI; Leila's Hair Museum, Independence, MO.

Advisor: Carmelita Johnson.

Bracelet

Gf, c. 1870, gray-brown hair woven in an expandable pattern, floral engr gf terminals hinged to loop-in-loop gf center with soldered ring for charm (bracelet stretches to go over hand), center 2" x 5/8" 200

Yg, c. 1840-60, hollow lt brown woven hair tube with dk brown core, engr yg snake head clasp, v-spring hinged to engr tail, 7-1/2" tl, 3/8" w 250

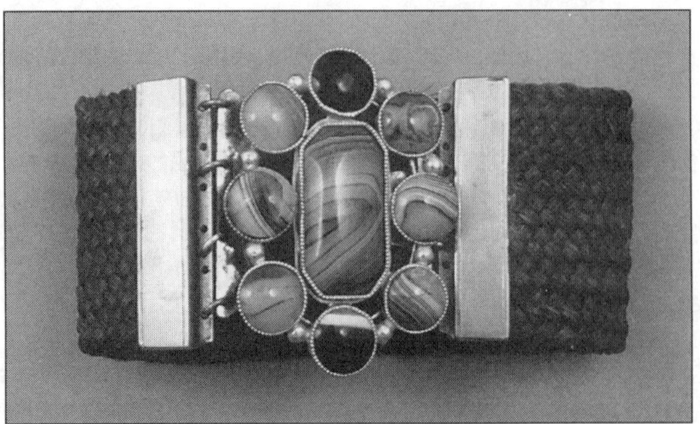

Bracelet, agate, gp metal, c. 1860, flat woven brown hair strap, v-spring front clasp set with banded agate cabs encircling central elongated octagonal agate cab, millegrained gp bezels, 8-1/2" tl, clasp 1-5/8" w x 2-1/8", **$650**. (Carmelita Johnson collection).

Bracelets, pr

Yg, c. 1880-90, bypass (crossover) bangles, tightly woven dk brown hair, engr yg terminals and sliding tubes, soldered loops for suspending charms, 2-1/4" inside dia, 3/4" at center, pr 550

Brooch/Pin

Yg, c. 1870, in the shape of a harp, engr yg "strings," yg frame, dk brown woven hair inserts, C-catch, tube hinge, 7/8" w x 1-1/2" 400

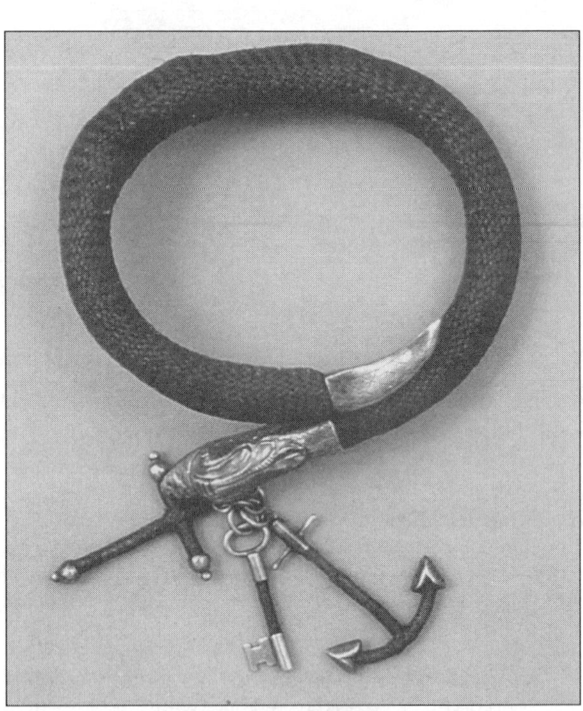

Bracelet, gf, c. 1840-60, tightly woven dk brown hair over wraparound spiral metal core, engr gf snake head and tail terminals, head suspending woven hair and gf anchor, cross, and key charms, 2-1/4" inside dia, 3/8" w, **$300**. (Carmelita Johnson collection).

Bracelet, yg, photograph, c. 1860-70, braided hollow tubes of woven brown hair terminating in a hinged rect yg front clasp with engr scroll design, locket compartment in clasp opens to reveal a photograph, 7-1/2" tl, 1-3/4" w, **$395**. (Photo courtesy of Lovejoy's Estate Jewelry, Bellingham, WA).

Braided Bracelets:

T, c. 1872, hollow and tight-woven brown hair tubes braided together and joined to a floral and scrollwork engr and *taille d'épargne* enameled hinged front clasp surmounted by scrolled and trefoiled wirework, three seed pearls in center, rev engr "Dolorita, Juin Le 22, 1872," 7" tl, clasp 1-5/8" w x 1-1/8", **$450**.

B, c. 1847, four linked segments, braided cords of woven brown hair, engr yg terminals, enameled black and white floral and foliate motifs, engr and enameled front clasp suspending engr and enameled heart charm, glazed compartment containing pink cloth on rev, clasp engr on rev: "W.B. Knipe July 4, 1847," 7-1/8" tl, 3/4" w, **$400**. (Carmelita Johnson collection).

Brooch/Pin, yg, c. 1870, blond and brown hair woven in plaid pattern, forming looped double bow with drops, yg caps and tips on drops, engr yg center, mono "S.A.," C-catch, tube hinge, 2-1/4" w x 1-3/8", **$350**. (Carmelita Johnson collection).

Brooch/Pin, yg, photograph, c. 1860-70, open yg crescent with woven lt brown hair center, framing circ sepia-toned photograph of woman in glazed compartment and engr frame surrounded by seven yg beads, surmounted by engr beveled yg sq, engr with mono "ST," suspending five cylindrical woven hair drops at bottom with yg tops and caps, C-catch, tube hinge, extended pinstem, 1-1/2" w x 2-3/4" tl with drops, **$375**. (Carmelita Johnson collection).

Brooches, c. 1850-70:

TC, acorn brooch, gf leaves, stems, and caps, woven brown hair acorns (frayed), C-catch, tube hinge, loop for safety chain on rev, 1-7/8" w x 1", **$275**.

BL, yg crescent with dk brown hair "berries" and yg caps, five loops for suspending charms on bottom edge, C-catch, tube hinge, extended pinstem, 1-1/4" w x 1", **$225**.

BR, gf crescent shape with woven blond hair acorns, engr gf tips, C-catch, tube hinge, extended pinstem, 1-1/4" w x 1", **$300**. (Carmelita Johnson collection).

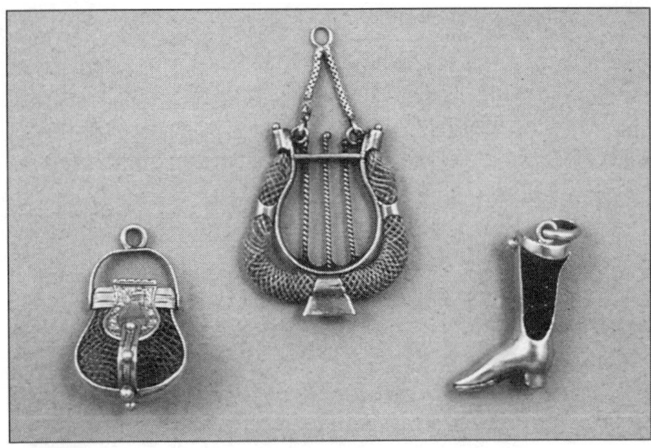

Charms, c. 1870-80:

TC, lyre, gf "strings" and frame holding woven hollow tube of blond hair, 7/8" w x 1-1/2", **$175**.

BL, purse, yg with woven blond hair insert, engr handle swivels, 1/2" w x 7/8", **$100**.

BR, boot, yg with woven dk brown hair inserts, 1/2" w x 1" tl, **$100**.

(Carmelita Johnson collection).

Pendent Earrings, c. 1870:

L, double hollow circ flowerheads in woven dk brown hair with engr yg star and seed pearl centers, fish hook earwires, 3/4" w x 1-3/4" tl, **$300.**

R, engr yg annular center with woven blond hair inserts suspending yg beads, oval hollow hair drops, fish hook earwires, 3/4" w x 1-3/4" tl, **$250**.

(Carmelita Johnson collection).

Earrings, yg, c. 1870, "day and night," detachable pear-shaped drops of woven brown hair in yg "cage," circ surmount, lg kidney wires, orig box, 1/2" w x 1-7/8" tl, **$400**. (Carmelita Johnson collection).

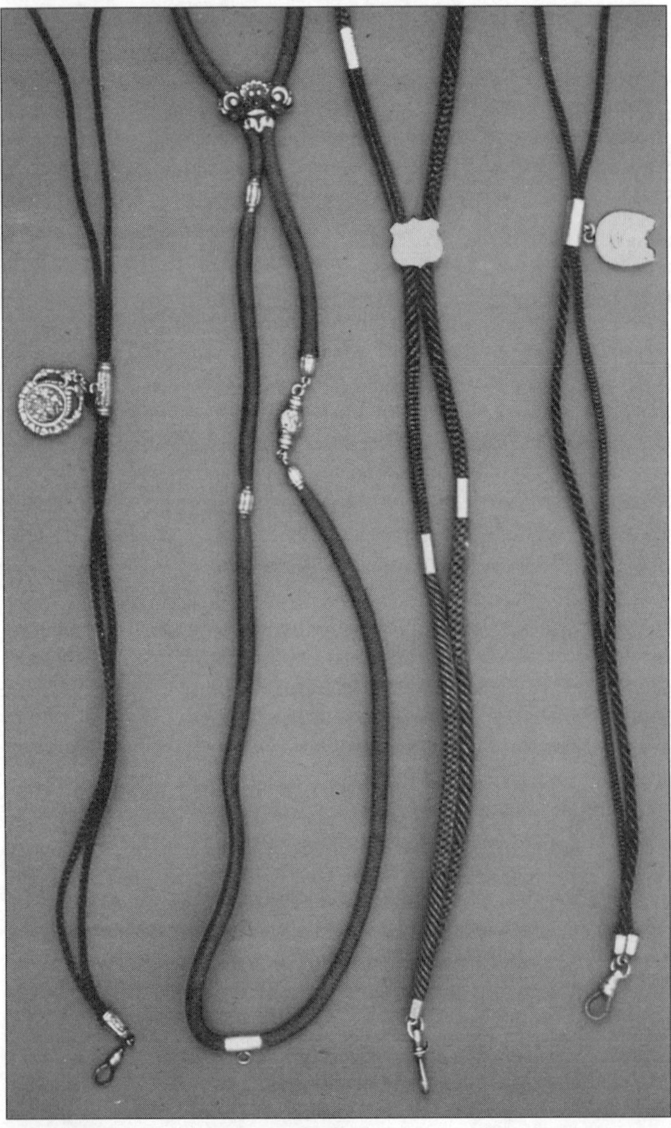

Longchains, c. 1870-90:

L, narrow chain of woven dk brown hair terminating in an engr gf cap and swivel, engr gf slide suspending gf fob charm set with black onyx disk, rev set with cluster of pyrite crystals ("fool's gold"), 67" tl, charm 3/4" x 1", **$250**.

LC, hollow tubes of woven brown hair joined with fluted gf terminals, tube clasp in one terminal, loop for swivel on another, joined at center with gf slide set with seven grad rc garnets, 44" tl, **$200**.

RC, c.1870, chain of lt brown hair, woven in segmented patterns separated by yg collars, shield-shaped engr yg slide with mono "A.H.," terminating in swivel hook, 49" tl, slide 5/8" w x 1/2", **$275**.

R, narrow chain of woven dk brown hair, gf slide suspending MOP and gf horseshoe fob charm terminating in gf cap and swivel, 55" tl, charm 3/4" x 3/4", **$265**.

(Lenore Dailey collection).

Necklace, yg, c. 1870, three strand blond hair necklace with one strand hollow woven, other two tightly braided, joined yg tube connectors, central element of opposed yg circ frames with woven blond hair inserts joined by rect hairwork and yg center, yg bead terminals, capped hollow hairwork beads top and bottom, swagged yg chain (loop for second chain) suspending segmented hollow hairwork drop, 1-3/4" w x 2-1/4" at center, 20" tl, **$400**. (Carmelita Johnson collection).

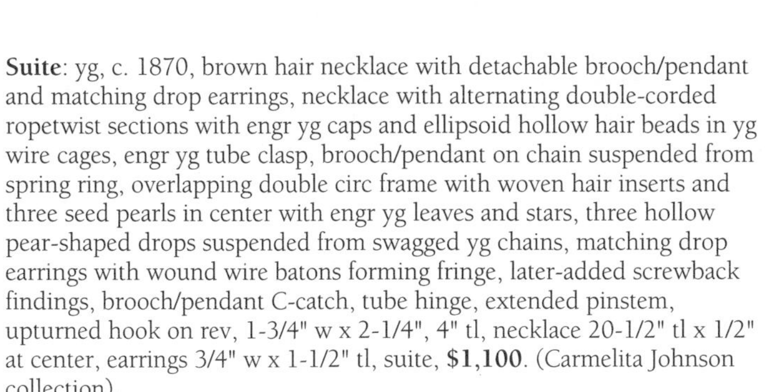

Suite: yg, c. 1870, brown hair necklace with detachable brooch/pendant and matching drop earrings, necklace with alternating double-corded ropetwist sections with engr yg caps and ellipsoid hollow hair beads in yg wire cages, engr yg tube clasp, brooch/pendant on chain suspended from spring ring, overlapping double circ frame with woven hair inserts and three seed pearls in center with engr yg leaves and stars, three hollow pear-shaped drops suspended from swagged yg chains, matching drop earrings with wound wire batons forming fringe, later-added screwback findings, brooch/pendant C-catch, tube hinge, extended pinstem, upturned hook on rev, 1-3/4" w x 2-1/4", 4" tl, necklace 20-1/2" tl x 1/2" at center, earrings 3/4" w x 1-1/2" tl, suite, **$1,100**. (Carmelita Johnson collection).

Earrings, pendent

Rose gold, c. 1860-70, open bell shape suspending rod and bead, woven brown hair inserts, later-added kidney wires, 1/2" w x 1-3/4" tl 250

Yg, c. 1870 , hollow bell-shaped woven dk brown hair, each with four hollow round hair beads, yg strips and caps, yg kidney wires, 1/2" w x 2" tl 225

Necklace

Yg, c. 1870, tightly woven rope of dk brown hair suspending anchor pendant of tightly woven hair around metal core with yg terminals and wrapped curb link chain, yg connectors and tube clasp, 17" tl, pendant 7/8" w x 1-1/2" 200

Pendant

Yg, glass, c. 1850-60, spiral-shaped snake of hair woven around solid core, blue glass cab eyes, engr yg head and tail, jump ring suspended from mouth, soldered ring at end of tail, 5/8" w x 2-3/4" tl 250

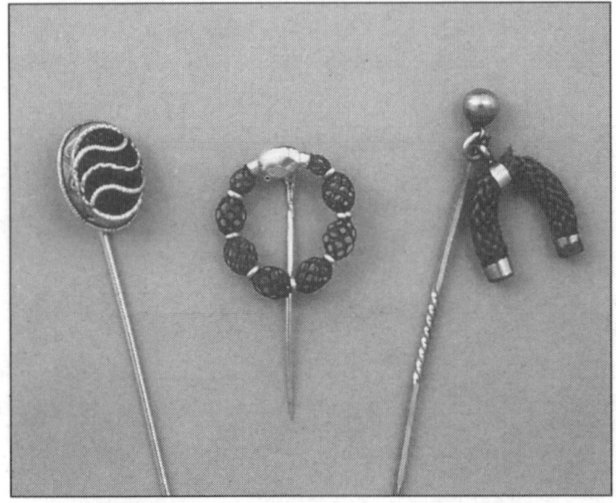

Stickpins, c. 1880:
L, engr oval yg frame and back, wiretwist border, three curv twisted wires forming "cage" over woven dk brown hair insert, yg pinstem, 1/2" w x 5/8", 2-7/8" tl, **$100**.

C, wreath of hollow open work brown hair tube, beads formed by yg rings, yg connectors, convex plaque at top, pinstem soldered to rev, 7/8" dia, 1-1/2" tl, **$95**.

R, horseshoe motif of tightly woven brown hair (slight damage), gf terminals, suspended from bead-tipped pinstem, 5/8" w x 5/8", 2-3/8" tl, **$120**.
(Carmelita Johnson collection).

Tiara, yg, red stone, turq, seed pearls, ribbon, c.1860 , woven dk brown hair in open mesh over wire framework, surmounted by cutout engr yg floral and foliate scrollwork, faceted cushion-shaped red stone in center collet flanked by two sm turq cabs in flower, two seed pearls at centers, engr yg terminals, loops for ribbon ties, wearable as necklace, in original fitted box, 1" w at center, approx 16" tl, **$1,375**. (Carmelita Johnson collection).

SCOTTISH JEWELRY

History: Gothic and Celtic Revivals were already well under way when Victoria ascended the throne. Her own romantic attachment to ancient and medieval history was certainly influential in furthering the public's preoccupation with the past. Britain's, particularly Scotland's, past was romanticized by historical novels, like those of Sir Walter Scott. And after Victoria purchased Balmoral, a castle in Scotland, in 1848, everyone became enamored of Scottish motifs. Circular Scottish plaid pins, heraldic crests, dirks and claymores (knives and swords), thistles and St Andrew's crosses (Scottish national emblems), the Order of the Garter strap and buckle (symbol of the chivalric order headed by Victoria)–all were made into jewelry with varieties of agates, cairngorms (dark yellow-amber faceted quartz) and amethysts set in engraved silver or gold.

Unless a piece is hallmarked with a British date letter (and many pieces are not; in fact, "purist" collectors say that "real" Scottish agate jewelry is never hallmarked), precise dating of Scottish jewelry is difficult. Earlier pieces tend to be more faithful to traditional Scottish motifs. Mid-Victorian pieces incorporated anchors, hearts, serpents, arrows, and other non-Scottish forms. Subtle differences can be seen in later 19th century pieces, such as the cut of the stones and the absence of ornate engraving. Some traditional forms continued to be made, and C-catches and tube hinges continued to be used as brooch findings well into the 20th century. But rhodium plating and cast mountings are sure signs of more recent vintage and lesser quality. Brooches are the most common form; bracelets are scarcer, but they do turn up; necklaces, earrings and buckles are rare. Scottish jewelry is very wearable with today's fashions, consequently demand is high, especially for larger pieces.

References: Vivienne Becker, *Antique and Twentieth Century Jewellery*, 2nd ed., N.A.G. Press, 1987;Shirley Bury, *Jewellery, 1789-1910, The International Era,* Antique Collectors' Club, 1991; Ginny Redington Dawes & Corinne Davidov, *Victorian Jewelry, Unexplored Treasures*, Abbeville Press, 1991, shows excellent (albeit mostly rare) examples, beautifully photographed.

Bracelet, link

Agate, silver gilt, Mid-Victorian, alternating links of paired octagonal cylinders and sq plaques of variegated agate with engr silver gilt caps and frames, 3/4" w x 7" .... 920 (A)

Agate, silver, c. 1860, central buckle motif flanked by hinged rect plaque links inlaid with striated gray agate in segmented sections outlined with engr silver (one sm pc missing), v-spring and box clasp, 1-1/8" w, 6-3/4" tl .... 316 (A)

Agates, silver, c. 1860, five linked elements of various colored and banded agates, a scalloped circ flowerhead with silver bead at center top and five silver wires radiating to hold the stone, alternating with a rounded and grooved rectangle with engr silver cap terminals surmounting a rounded cylinder, shield-shaped floral engr padlock clasp, 1" w x 7-1/2" tl .... 431 (A)

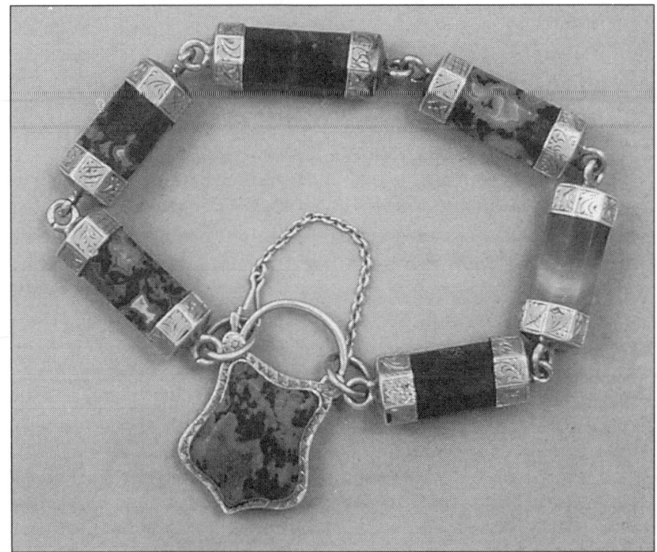

Link Bracelet, agate, silver, c. 1865, six cylindrical faceted (octagonal) agate links with engr silver caps, shield-shaped padlock clasp with cut-to-shape pink-orange-black agate in engr frame, oval glazed compartment containing dk brown cloth on rev, safety chain, 3/8" dia x 7-1/2" tl, padlock 7/8" w x 1", **$982**. (Mary Palmer collection).

Agates, silver, c. 1870, faceted cylindrical links of various agates each with engr silver caps, sm circ links, heart-shaped locket clasp with bezel-set heart-shaped agate plaque, 3/8" w x 7-1/4" tl .... 431 (A)

Malachite, silver, c. 1860-70, strap and buckle design, hinged sq silver links inlaid with malachite, engr borders, terminating in three links with "grommets" (center holes) and a triangular tip on one end, malachite inlaid buckle and silver hasp on the other, 8" tl x 5/8", buckle 1-1/4" w 575

Brooch/Pendant

Silver, agates, c. 1850, circ dome shape, circ cab of banded agate in center surrounded by four jasper, bloodstone and agate segments alternating with engr silver segments, engr "EB Matterson-Limerick" on rev, C-catch, tube hinge, 1-7/8" dia 375

Link Bracelet, agate, silver, c. 1850, carved banded agate, chalcedony and jasper oval links with figure-8 open centers alternating with similarly shaped silver links, triangular silver padlock clasp, one side engr with lyre design, other side set with agate, 8" tl, lock 1" w x 1-3/4", **$585**. (Courtesy of E. Foxe Harrell Jewelers, Clinton, IA).

Brooch/Pin, agates, citrines, 15k yg, c. 1850-60, Scottish dirk (dagger) shape, engr yg inlaid with jasper, carnelian, bloodstone, and citrines, surmounted by a prong-set faceted round citrine, 1/2" w x 1-1/2", **$850**. (Photo courtesy of Lovejoy's Estate Jewelry, Bellingham, WA).

Brooch/Pin

Agates, citrines, silver, c. 1850, outer ring of green agate with four oval faceted cairngorms (citrines) in pronged bezels interspaced between arms of appl silver cross inlaid with striated gray agate, engr silver mount, C-catch, tube hinge, 1-3/4" dia 350

Agates, gp brass, c. 1850, oval plaque inlaid with geo pattern of rect and sq banded agate, jasper, and bloodstone, slate backing, gp brass frame with appl stamped foliate scroll motifs at compass points, 1-1/2" w x 2" 295

Agate, wm, c. 1870, brown and white banded agate open-centered disk, two movable inner rings attached to disk by rect agate bar through open centers, C-catch, tube hinge, extended pinstem 1-3/8" dia.................. 165

Agates, 15k yg, c. 1860-80, open circle centering an equilateral cross with rect arms, set with various agates and engr entrelac design, 1-1/4" dia .... 633 (A)

Agates, 9k yg, tourmaline, quartz, c. 1860-80, scabbard design with three tapered agates in a chased yg mount, faceted tourmaline terminals, two sm circ-cut collet-set foil-backed quartz within a chased yg mount, 2-1/2" w x 3/4" .... 690 (A)

Brooches/Pins, agate, c.1860-70:
L, "target" brooch, segmented banded agate, bloodstone, and jasper, open center, scallop-edged, C-catch, tube hinge, extended pinstem, 2" dia, **$525**.
(Mary Palmer collection).
R, carnelian-colored banded agate annulus (ring shape) surmounted by a stamped and chased brass anchor, C-catch, 1-5/8" dia, **$195**. (Courtesy of DLW Antiques, Memphis, TN).

Brooches/Pins, malachite, silver, c. 1860-70:
L, scalloped edge open bow motif, bezel-set with cut-to-shape malachite plaques, suspending a shield-shaped malachite drop, C-catch, tube hinge, extended pinstem, 1-7/8" w x 1-1/2" tl, **$225**. (Author's collection).
R, oval strap and buckle motif (garter), malachite segments inlaid into silver frame, engr silver buckle, unusual double-sided screw locking catch mechanism for pin on rev, mkd "I. BRADFORD TORQUAY PATENT (crown symbol) VICTORIA PARADE," 1-3/4" w x 1-1/2", **$225**. (Courtesy of E. Foxe Harrell Jewelers, Clinton, IA).

Banded agate, silver, c. 1860-70, in the shape of an anchor, upper portion a faceted cylindrical cross of brown, white and black banded agate, engr silver cap surmounted by a ring and ropetwist wire spiraling around to the engr silver base, C-catch, tube hinge, 1-3/4" w x 3-1/4"...... 450

Sterling, bloodstone, red jasper, date letter for 1900, in the shape of a claymore (Scottish broadsword), circ hilt of red jasper overlaid with engr ster, tapered blade of bloodstone inlaid in engr ster, Birmingham (Eng) hmks, maker's mk "A & L Ld," C-catch, tube hinge, 1/2" w x 2-1/2".. 200

Wm, glass, c. 1885, Scottish plaid brooch, engr thistle motifs on open center disk, amber-colored prong-set faceted glass in center, C-catch, tube hinge, 2-3/4" dia 195

Necklace

Agate, silver, Mid-Victorian, a linked series of paired octagonal variegated agate cylinders with floral engr silver caps, shield-shaped padlock clasp set with a cut-to-shape agate plaque surmounted by a pyramidal lozenge-shaped agate, 7/8" w x 18" tl, clasp 7/8" w x 1" .... 1,150 (A)

Scarf Pin/Stickpin, silver, jasper, bloodstone, c. 1850-80, love knot motif, engr silver set with alternating red jasper and bloodstone segments, gp pinstem, 2-5/8" tl, 1/2" w x 3/8", **$150**. (Courtesy of E. Foxe Harrell Jewelers, Clinton, IA).

MID VICTORIAN (GRAND PERIOD) c. 1861-1880

The Romantic Period ended abruptly with the death of Prince Albert in 1861, and the beginning of the Civil War in the U.S.–causes for deep mourning on both sides of the Atlantic. The wearing of black was more than correct form for mourning; it became fashionable. Fashion, as always, played an important role in the changing look of jewelry. The voluminous skirt, supported by crinolines, or hoops, was introduced in the mid-1850s, and became the look of the 1860s. This wider silhouette required larger jewelry. Brooches were massive, bracelets widened, and were often worn in pairs, one on each wrist. Lower necklines prompted the wearing of necklaces and large lockets. Lockets and brooches often contained photographs, which gradually overtook portrait miniatures as a form of memorial jewelry. Hairstyles changed to once again reveal the ear; and earrings returned, growing to greater lengths towards the end of the period. Trains, bustles, ruffles, pleats, flounces, and fringe adorned the skirts of the 1870s. Tassels and fringe appeared in jewelry to complement the look.

For those who weren't in mourning, it was a colorful period. William Perkin discovered coal tar in 1856, which led to his accidental discovery of the first synthetic aniline dye. The first color he produced was purple, or mauve, which created such a sensation that it ushered in the era that followed, called the "Mauve Age." The fashion for bright colors continued through the 1870s. Colored gemstones and enamels complimented the look.

By the 1860s, Revivalism was in full swing. Women were piling on Etruscan-style amulets and other "classical" ornaments to the point of being satirized by the press. Revivalist Castellani's goldwork was displayed at the International Exhibition in London in 1862. Egyptian-style jewels were seen at the Exposition Universelle in Paris in 1867. Enameled Renaissance Revival jewels were seen in fashionably colorful social circles as well.

International exhibitions whetted appetites for exotic jewels from exotic places, like India. Mogul jewelry, Jaipur enamel, and gold-mounted tiger's claws from Calcutta became the rage in the 1870s, especially after Queen Victoria was proclaimed Empress of India in 1876. These pieces also inspired the work of English, European, and American jewelers.

After the Civil War, it became acceptable for American women to wear jewelry in greater quantities. Prosperity was growing, and with it the desire to display signs of wealth. What better way for a man to proclaim his status than to bedeck his wife in jewels? For the upper classes, at least, The Grand Period was indeed grand.

Working class women were also decking themselves in baubles, bangles and beads, although they were of the mass-produced "imitation" variety. Frankly fake costume jewelry was still an unheard of idea. Even if it wasn't "real," women wanted it to look like it was. Manufacturers were now capable of turning out machine-made goods in quantity to satisfy their demand. Electroplated trinkets set with glass "stones" were made to look like gold and diamond jewels.

Men continued to drape their vests with the requisite watch chains and fobs. Cuff links, also known as sleeve buttons, tie pins (also called scarfpins, stickpins, stockpins, cravat pins), signet rings, collar buttons and shirt studs were additional forms of male adornment. Most of these were gold or gold-filled. Gemstones were added on occasion, particularly to stickpins.

By the 1860s, Tiffany & Co. had established itself as America's most prestigious and reputable firm, first by importing the best of European goods, then by manufacturing their own wares of the highest quality. From 1867 until the end of the century, they exhibited and won medals at international expositions in Paris and the U.S. Tiffany promoted an appreciation of American craftsmanship and resources by exhibiting pieces with American themes, and newly discovered American gemstones, like Montana blue sapphires and Maine tourmalines. They also displayed newly discovered diamonds from South Africa and opals from Australia.

The Centennial Exposition in Philadelphia was a landmark event in American jewelry history. It gave Tiffany and other American jewelers the opportunity to "strut their stuff" in a grand manner and capture the world's attention. It furthered the recognition of the United States as an industrial nation with a talent for invention and production.

References: Joan Younger Dickinson, *The Book of Diamonds*, Avenel (Crown), 1965 (out of print); Penny Proddow & Debra Healy, *American Jewelry, Glamour and Tradition,* Rizzoli, 1987; Anne Schofield and Kevin Fahy, *Australian Jewellery, 19th and Early 20th Century*, Antique Collectors' Club, 1990; Kenneth Snowman, ed., *The Master Jewelers,* Abrams, 1990, chapter on Tiffany & Co. by Janet Zapata.

Brooch/Pin

Eagle talons, silver, c. 1870-80, opposed pr of talons, joined with engr silver band, flanked by ropetwist wire, swagged silver chain across front, C-catch, tube hinge, 2-1/2" w x 1-1/4" 200

Link Bracelet with locket, c. 1860, eight circ beads carved from quondong nuts (native to Australia), capped and linked with engr yg leaf motifs, suspending a quondong nut locket with two inner glazed compartments, 8" tl, 1-1/2" at center with locket, **$700**. (Courtesy of E. Foxe Harrell Jewelers, Clinton, IA).

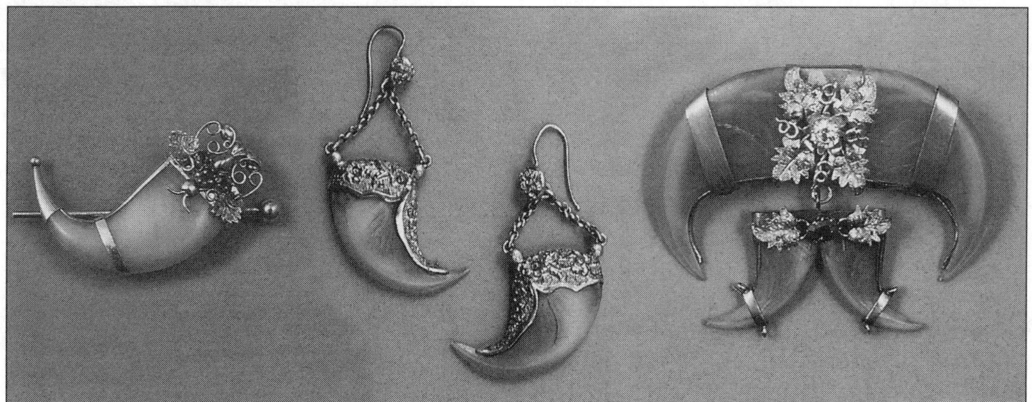

Tiger's claw jewelry, c. 1860-80:

L, Brooch/Pin, yg, sapphires, c. 1860, claw in yg frame capped with foliate and scrolled wire decoration prong-set with three sm circ-cut blue sapphires, mounted on a yg rod with single sphere terminal, C-catch, tube hinge, 1-1/2" w x 3/4", **$325**.

C, Earrings, c. 1880, claw mounted on floral motif gf frame suspended by two chains from floral motif surmount, shepherd's hook earwires, 3/4" w x 2" tl, pr, **$350**.

R, Pendant, c. 1875-80, pr of lg opposed tiger's claws joined in the center with yg band surmounted by cutout and engr yg grape leaves, prong-set diamond center, suspending opposed pr of sm tiger's claws, yg cap surmounted by two yg grape leaves, oval cut blue sapphire, two circ loops on rev, 2-1/8" w x 1-1/2", **$550**. (Courtesy of E. Foxe Harrell Jewelers, Clinton, IA).

BLACK JEWELRY

History: Sentiment was the glue that held Victorian lives together. It was also the preservative that has saved many pieces of jewelry from being discarded or sold for scrap. Surely one prevailing sentiment was that of bereavement. Victoria had an unswerving sense of propriety, and issued rules and regulations governing strict codes of behavior for herself, her family, her court and her subjects. These rules of etiquette included dress codes for all occasions, particularly for mourning, including the proper jewelry to be worn.

After Prince Albert died, Victoria went into a period of mourning that lasted for the rest of her life, a full forty years. For much of this time, all members of the royal court were required to wear black. This funereal atmosphere spread throughout the populace, creating a demand for black jewelry, the only color permitted during periods of full mourning. Jet was the material of choice. An entire industry grew up around the mining and carving of jet, a fossilized coal found near the town of Whitby in England. The area became famous for its artisans, and tourists went to Whitby to watch them work. They brought home jet souvenirs, sometimes personalized with the names of loved ones, not necessarily departed.

Brooches, bead necklaces, and bracelets were the most commonly worn types of jet jewelry. Bracelets were often of the "stretchy" type, strung on elastic, and usually worn in pairs (as were many types of bracelets). Pendent earrings were worn, but are not found as often today as are brooches and bracelets.

Jet jewelry became so popular that it spawned a number of imitations. Two of the most common were black glass, misleadingly called "French jet," and vulcanite, a hardened (vulcanized) rubber that is sometimes mistakenly called gutta percha. Gutta percha is a natural substance from the Malayan palaquium tree. It was occasionally used for jewelry, but it is not stable in air, so little survives. Other materials are also erroneously labeled gutta percha, including shellac-based compositions. Bog oak, from the peat bogs of Ireland, is sometimes included in this group of jet imitations, but although it is black to dark brown, and carved (usually with Irish motifs) or heat press-molded, it was never meant as a substitute for jet.

True jet tends to command higher prices than do comparable pieces made from its imitations. Many dealers do not know how to tell the difference. The word "jet" has become synonymous with "black," so any black shiny jewelry material may be misidentified as jet.

Black onyx is another material used in mourning jewelry, and about which there is some confusion. Gemologically, the correct name is dyed black chalcedony. Onyx by definition is a banded, or layered stone, most often seen carved into cameos. The black color is almost always a result of soaking in sugar solution and heating in sulfuric acid, a process that was known to the Romans.

At times it can be difficult to determine where mourning left off and fashion began in black jewelry. Massive necklaces, diamond-enhanced brooches, and elaborately carved bracelets might lead one to question the depth of the wearer's mourning. But considering that some women wore black for most of their adult lives, it is not surprising that they would want to enliven their "toilet" with a bit of fashionable elegance. Because it *was* fashionable, black jewelry was also worn by women who were not in mourning.

References: Sylvia Katz, *Early Plastics*, Shire Publications, Ltd., 1986. Includes information on vulcanite and other Victorian compositions; Helen Muller, *Jet Jewellery and Ornaments*, Shire Publications, Ltd., 1986, and *Jet,* Butterworths & Co Ltd, 1987. Both books contain extensive information on jet and its imitations, including history, sources, and identification. See also chapters on mourning and Celtic jewelry in Shirley Bury, *Jewellery, 1789-1910, The International Era,* Vol. II, and Vivienne Becker, *Antique and Twentieth Century Jewellery*, 2nd ed.; Ginny Redington Dawes & Corinne Davidov, *Victorian Jewelry, Unexplored Treasures*, Abbeville Press, 1991. For gemological information on jet and onyx, see Walter Schumann, *Gemstones of the World*, N.A.G. Press, revised and expanded edition, 1997.

Advisor: Colin Williamson (Victorian compositions).

Bracelet

Cuff

Vulcanite, celluloid, c. 1880, central molded vulcanite foliate branch with three berries, screw-mounted on a slightly flexible black celluloid tapered cuff with overlapping ends, 2-1/4" inside dia, center 1-1/2" x 1-3/4" 175

Link Bracelet, Vauxhall glass, lacquered metal, c. 1830, delicate floral and foliate links composed of faceted circ and foliate shapes of dark red glass (appears black) mounted on black lacquered metal backing, v-spring and box clasp, 5/8" w x 8" tl, **$495**. (Photo courtesy of Sharen and Nicholas Wood).

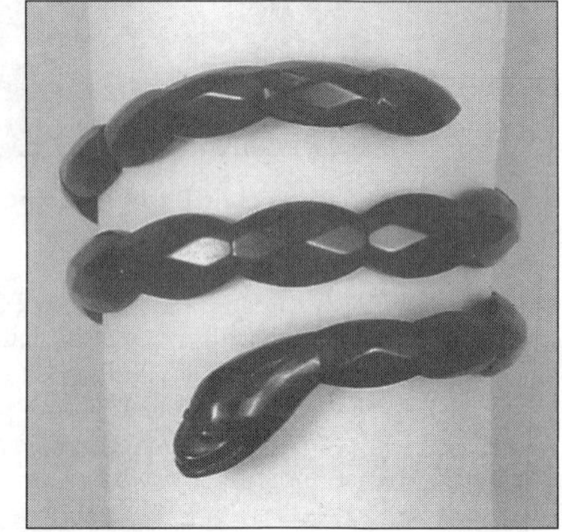

Bracelet, elastic (wraparound), vulcanite, c. 1860, grad faceted segments strung with black elastic terminating in snake's head and tail, 18" tl (stretched out) x 1/2" (head), **$395**. (Lenore Dailey collection).

Brooches/Pins, c. 1860-80:
T, Horn, press-molded in the shape of a cuffed hand with extended index finger, C-catch, tube hinge, 2-1/8" w x 3/4", **$155**.
C, Bar pin, bog oak, carved shamrock motifs, scallop edge, C-catch, tube hinge, extended pinstem, 2-1/8" w x 1/2", **$85**.
B, Bar pin, jet, vulcanite, yg, rect jet plaque laminated to vulcanite backing, surmounted by smaller jet rect, cross bars covered with engr yg strips suspending tablet-shaped drop with yg quatrefoil, C-catch, tube hinge, 1-3/4" w x 3/4", 1-1/2" tl, **$255**.
(Lenore Dailey collection).

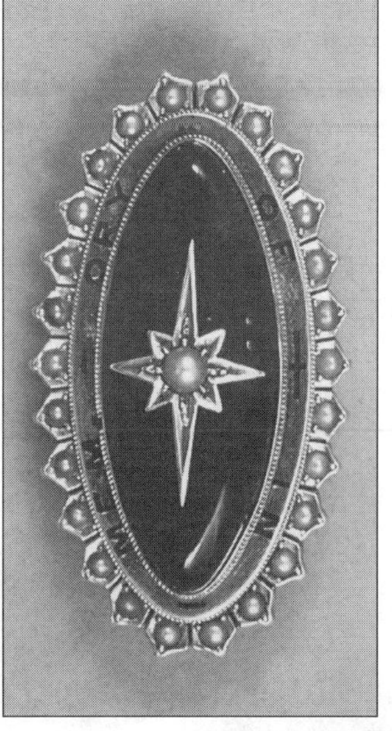

Brooch/Pin, black onyx, yg, seed pearls, enamel, glass, cloth, c. 1886, navette-shaped black onyx cab surmounted by a yg star center set with seed pearls, "IN MEMORY OF" in black enamel on frame set with seed pearls in serrated edge, rev edge engr "T.P. died 20th November 1886," glazed compartment containing cloth on rev, C-catch, tube hinge, 1-5/8" w x 1", **$240**. (Courtesy of E. Foxe Harrell Jewelers, Clinton, IA).

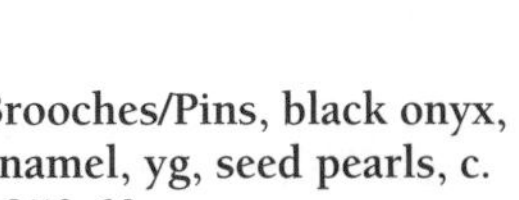

Brooches/Pins, black onyx, enamel, yg, seed pearls, c. 1850-60:
T, central concave navette-shaped onyx plaque, a seed pearl set in center, bezel-set in beaded frame with serrated border, encircled by "IN MEMORY OF" letters in black enameled lozenge shapes with white enameled stars around outer edge on 10k yg, glazed compartment for hair on rev, C-catch, tube hinge, extended pinstem, loop for safety chain, 1-1/2" w x 1-1/4", **$175**.
B, concave oval onyx disk surmounted by 14k yg star set with seed pearls, bezel-set in yg frame enameled with alternating black and white emblems, glazed fabric-lined compartment on rev, replacement safety catch, tube hinge, extended pinstem, loop for safety chain, 1-3/4" w x1-1/2", **$375**.
(Lenore Dailey collection).

Brooches/Pins, c. 1850-60:
T, bog oak, seed pearls, chalcedony, fabric, ym, glass, concentric ovals, serrated edge, crosshatch pattern carved bog oak frame, two rows of seed pearls, central concave chalcedony disk surmounted by oval glazed compartment containing tightly woven brown and black fabric bezel-set in engr ym frame, C-catch, tube hinge, 1-7/8" w x 1-5/8", **$245**.
B, black glass (Fr jet), garnet, seed pearls, 12k yg, open scallop edge set with grad faceted black glass stones encircling concentric rows of seed pearls and sm faceted black glass stones, oval cab garnet (carbuncle) in center, mounted in yg, C-catch, tube hinge, 1-3/4" w x 1-1/2", **$495**.
(Lenore Dailey collection).

Brooch/Pin, black glass (Fr jet), hair, ym, glass, c. 1820-40, modified Maltese cross, central sq glazed compartment containing braided dk brown hair, beveled glass cover set in scrolled gilt frame, mounted on cut-to-shape ym backing, soldered pin assembly, C-catch, tube hinge, 1-1/2" sq, **$175**. (Lenore Dailey collection).

Brooch/Pin, vulcanite, c. 1860, oval plaque with appl molded Cupid and lion (symbolizing "love triumphs"), C-catch, tube hinge, pinstem shortened, 2" w x 1-5/8", **$95**. (Private collection).

Brooch/Pin, shellac composition, wm, c. 1860-80, molded Buddhist knot of eternity, "MANTON'S PATENT" (for a shellac composition), and two swans imp on rev, wm pinstem imp "J.J. BLACKHAM'S PATENT," C-catch, flanged hinge, crazing and discoloration, 2-1/8" w x 1-3/8", $75. (Private collection).

Mourning brooches, c. 1860:

T, Vauxhall glass, gf, enamel, c. 1860, raised oval center, black and white enamel depicting grave and willow, encircled by ten flat circ cut black glass stones in millegrained bezels, C-catch, tube hinge, extended pinstem, 1-3/8" w x 1", **$225**. (Courtesy of E. Foxe Harrell Jewelers, Clinton, IA).

B, rev-painted glass, gilt metal, c. 1860, black ground with white painted tomb inscribed "MY DEAR CHILD" encircled by "IN MEMORY OF" set in oval gilt engr frame, C-catch, tube hinge, 1-3/4" w x 1-3/8", **$495**. (Lenore Dailey collection).

Buckle, horn, brass, c. 1880, pair of convex horn plaques, each surmounted by appl acorn and leaf motif on smaller rect plaque, brass findings, abraded upper left corner, 3" w x 2-1/2", **$75**. (Private collection).

Elastic

Bog oak, c. 1860-80, central domed disk, a lg press-molded shamrock in open center with ropetwist patterned frame, encircled by smaller shamrocks within cross-hatched border, continuing to a bracelet of thirteen carved I-beam shaped segments, each with two opposed press-molded shamrocks, drilled and strung on black elastic, center 1-3/8" dia, segments 3/4" w 250

Bracelets

Hinged Bangles

Onyx, seed pearls, yg, c. 1870-80, band of bezel-set rect onyx plaques, strap and buckle motif, buckle set with seed pearls, v-spring and box clasp, safety chain, 3/8" w, 2-1/4" inside dia, pr .... 684 (A)

Yg, enamel, c. 1890, plain black enameled yg band with yg edges, hinges and clasps engr with geo design, v-spring and box clasp, safety chain, 7/8" w, 2-3/4" inside dia, fitted case mkd "Shreve, Crump and Low, Boston." pr .... 2,760 (A)

Brooch/Pin

Bog oak, c. 1860, carved and pierced castle and landscape motif within oval foliate border, C-catch, tube hinge, extended pinstem, 2-3/8" w x 2" 195

Bog oak, c. 1860, cutout and carved castle motif within circ crosshatched border, C-catch, tube hinge, 1-1/2" dia 85

Horn, c. 1850, circ plaque with raised center, scalloped design around edges with arrow motif at compass points centered with appl arrow and target, replaced safety catch, 1-5/8" dia 75

Yg, enamel, seed pearls, glass, c. 1860-70, rounded-edge black-enameled yg disk with appl yg starburst set with seed pearls, glazed photo compartment on rev, 1-1/4" dia 275

Earrings

Jet, bog oak, Late Victorian, pendent acorns suspended from laurel wreath and log, later added ear wires mkd "14k" (possible marriage), 1-1/2" tl x 3/4" 45

Pendent Earrings, black onyx, yg, seed pearls, c. 1870, concave circ onyx disk surmount in millegrained yg bezel flanked by two sm beads, center set with a seed pearl, suspending an oval concave onyx disk surmounted by a yg bow with seed pearl center, framed by sm navette-shaped cut onyx in millegrained bezels (one repaired) alternating with half-round yg beads, trefoil drop of lg navette-shaped cut onyx flanked by two smaller navettes, yg bead tips, lg kidney earwires, 2" tl x 7/8" w, **$750**. (Author's collection).

Pendent Earrings, bog oak, 14k yg, c. 1870, carved spindle shape terminating in upturned six-lobed foliate motif and cusped knob, 14k earwires later added, 1/2" w, 2-1/2" tl, **$225**. (Lenore Dailey collection).

Locket and Chain, vulcanite, celluloid, c. 1880, oval hinged vulcanite locket with applied floral motif, imp designs on interior surfaces, celluloid chain, 1-1/2" w x 2", 42" tl, **$150**. (Elaine Sarnoff collection).

Pendant, Vauxhall glass, black lacquered metal, c. 1830-40, Maltese cross motif, four cut-to-shape black-appearing dark red glass plaques and one central disk encircled by sm faceted circ-cut glass stones, mounted on flat metal backing, pendant bail attached to top loop, 1-3/4"sq, **$95**. (Lenore Dailey collection).

Pendant, jet, glass, wm, c. 1860-70, oval scallop-edged plaque surmounted by an oval domed center framed by a multi-rayed carved sunburst, glazed compartment for photo on rev, suspended from inverted triangular jet bail, 1-1/2" w x 2-1/2" tl, **$250**. (Author's collection).

Locket and Chain

Vulcanite, lacquered metal, c. 1860, smooth domed oval locket surmounted by an appl molded floral motif enclosed by scrolled ribbon reading "IN MEMORY OF," locket interior imp with fleur-de-lis and scroll pattern on ridged ground, suspended from a lg hexagonal link vulcanite chain with oversize black lacquered metal spring ring side clasp, locket 1-7/8" w x 2-3/8", chain 1/2" w x 23" t .... 259 (A)

Necklace

Choker, jet, glass, c. 1880-90, central oval plaque flanked by five rect plaques alternating with five rounded trapezoidal plaques carved with bas-relief scrolling foliate motifs, strung with a double row of black glass bead spacers, possible elastic bracelet conversion, 13" tl x 1-3/8" 100

Pendant

Composition, c. 1870-80, molded oval with beaded edge and scrolled shell shapes at compass points, molded flower on plaque at center, rev emb, 2" w x 3" 75

Cross

Bog oak, c. 1860, relief carving of rose, rosebud and leaves, 1-5/8" w x 3-1/4" 150

Pendant and Chain

Onyx, seed pearls, 14k yg, cloth, enamel, c. 1870-80, rect onyx plaque pendant, diagonal geo design across upper corner, cattail motif in opposite lower corner, set with seed pearls in yg, oval glazed locket compartment on rev with black cloth inside plain yg frame, rect yg bail set with a row of seed pearls outlined in black enamel, scalloped onyx links with appl geo yg set with seed pearls, alternating with circ yg links, spring ring closure, locket 1-1/4" w x 2-3/8" tl (with bail), chain 19-1/2" tl .... 1,026 (A)

Ring

Black onyx, diamonds, yg, c. 1880-90, front half of three grad adjacent flowerheads, om diamond centers, approx .50 ct tw, encircled by circ-cut onyx in sawtooth bezels, tapered shank, 3/4" x 1/2" .... 517 (A)

Yg, enamel, c. 1870, plain yg band with black enameled words "FORGET ME NOT" encircling the outside, 3/8" w, size 7-3/4 .... 345 (A)

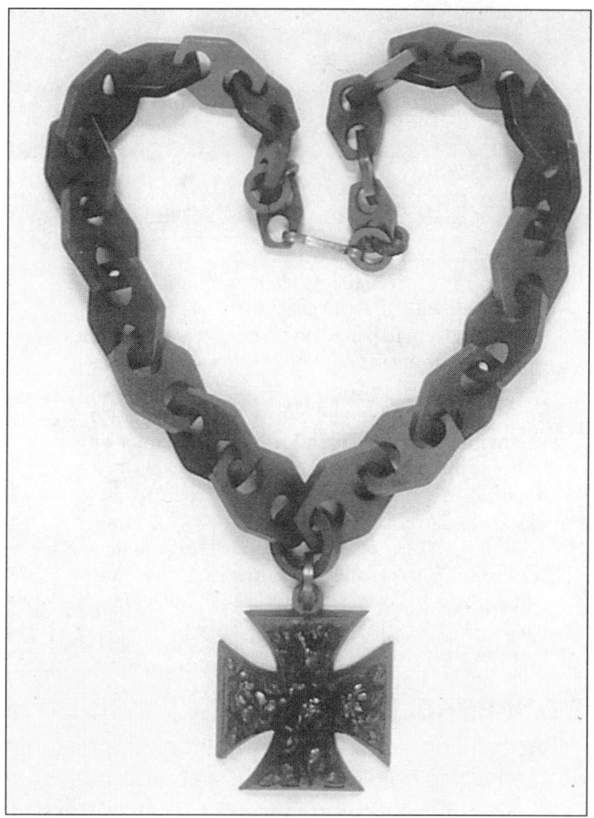

Pendant and Chain, vulcanite, c. 1860, chain of grad elongated hexagonal links, each with two circ holes, lg central circ link suspending molded Maltese cross with high relief floral and foliate motifs covering front surface, lacquered metal hook clasp, chain 20" tl, 7/8" w at center, cross 1-3/4"sq, **$395**. (Lenore Dailey collection).

Ring, yg, enamel, seed pearls, diamond, c. 1840-50, black enamel with thirteen seed pearls and one rc diamond in a floral design on a tapered dome top, receptacle for hair under bezel (no cover), tapered shank, some repair to enamel, approx size 6-1/2, 1/4" w at center, **$350**. (Private collection).

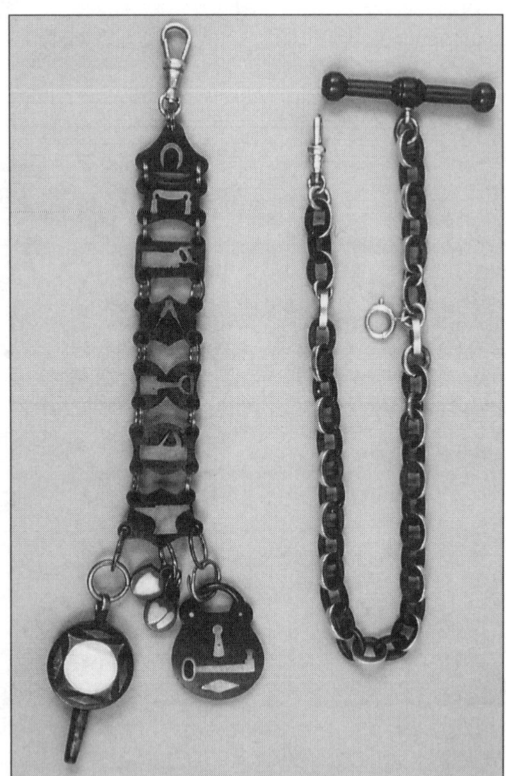

Watch Fob and Chain, vulcanite:

L, c. 1860, seven linked plaques of various shapes, each inlaid with silver in shapes of tools (compass, saw, shovel, anvil, plane, horseshoe) verso inlaid with geo shapes of silver, MOP, engr yg, suspending watch key, padlock, and two sm charms, 5/16" dia, each inlaid front and back, padlock with cross, keyhole and key motifs, watchkey with MOP disks, charms with hearts and star and shield motives, swivel hook at opposite end, 7" tl x 3/4", padlock 1" x 1-1/8", key 1-1/2" tl x 7/8"dia, **$695**.

R, c. 1870-90, oval link chain, alternate links banded in yg, suspending yg spring ring, vulcanite bar and yg swivel at opposite ends, 11" tl, links 1/4" w, bar 1-3/4" l, **$175**.

(Lenore Dailey collection).

TORTOISESHELL AND PIQUÉ

History: Tortoiseshell was another popular nineteenth-century jewelry material. It was also considered suitable for half-mourning. Lockets, hair combs, and bracelets were made from this natural plastic taken from the shell of the hawksbill turtle (now an endangered species).

A technique known as piqué, originally used in ornamental objects in the seventeenth century, was applied to jewelry and popularized in the mid to late nineteenth century. After softening it with heat, the tortoiseshell was inlaid with gold and/or silver in floral or geometric patterns. The technique using inlaid strips of metal cut into ornate designs is called *piqué posé*. *Piqué point* refers to dots or other small geometric shapes inlaid in an overall pattern.

Animal rights were not a big issue in Victorian times. Animals or parts of animals were used with impunity. It is now illegal to buy or sell tortoiseshell in this country. Antique pieces are exempt, but there are restrictions regarding import and export to and from other countries. Not all mottled brown lightweight material is tortoiseshell, however. Toward the end of the century, many hair combs and other jewelry and objects were made of celluloid in imitation of tortoiseshell.

References: Vivienne Becker, *Antique and Twentieth Century Jewellery*, 2nd ed.; N.A.G. Press, 1987; Ginny Redington Dawes & Corinne Davidov, *Victorian Jewelry, Unexplored Treasures*, Abbeville Press, 1991.

Bracelet, link

Gf, c. 1840-50, cable link bracelet with gf heart-shaped lock clasp die-stamped with garter motif decorated with engr scroll design, 8" tl, lock 3/4" w x 1-1/2"..................... 425

Silver, agate, c. 1840-50, lg cable links, silver heart-shaped lock clasp set with agate, verso engr, 6-3/4" tl, lock 3/4" w x 1-1/8" 425

Brooch/Pin

Cameo, silver, c. 1880, depicting the frontal bust of a woman with inlaid silver hair ornament and necklace in an engr oval silver frame, 1-3/8" w x 1-3/4" .... 403 (A)

Piqué, yg, silver, c. 1870-80, hexagonal tortoiseshell plaque, raised center inlaid with floral and geo motifs, outer frame inlaid with concentric straight and scalloped borders, C-catch, tube hinge, 1-1/2" x 1-1/2"........... 598

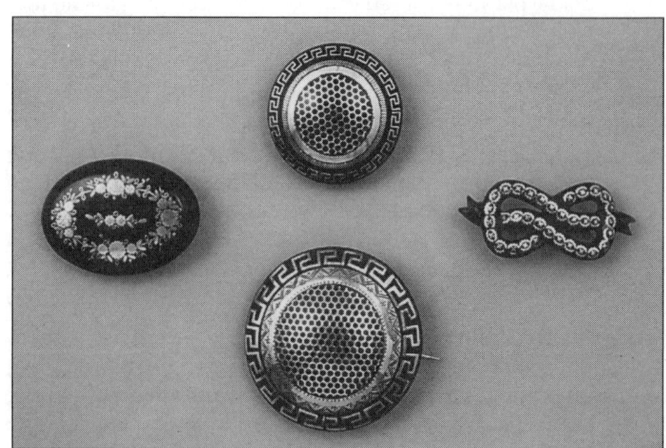

Brooches/Pins, tortoiseshell piqué, yg, c. 1850-60:

T, domed circle with central yg honeycomb pattern encircled by concentric yg bands, outer band in Greek key design, C-catch, tube hinge, 1-1/8" dia, **$275**.

B, domed circle with central yg honeycomb pattern encircled by concentric yg bands, engr inner band, outer band in Greek key design, C-catch, tube hinge, extended pinstem, 1-1/2" dia, **$375**.

L, convex flat-backed oval with floral and garland rose and yg inlay (*piqué posé*), later added safety catch, tube hinge, 1-3/8" w x 1", **$175**.

R, figure-eight ribbon inlaid with scalloped ovals and X's, C-catch, tube hinge, 1-1/2" w x 5/8", **$295**.

(Courtesy of E. Foxe Harrell Jewelers, Clinton, IA).

Earrings, piqué, silver, yg, c. 1865, domed oval surmount suspending three concentric oval hoops inlaid with silver and yg circles and disks, fishhook earwires, 7/8" w x 1-3/8" tl **$920** [A]. (Photo courtesy of Skinner, Inc., Boston, MA, 6/10/97).

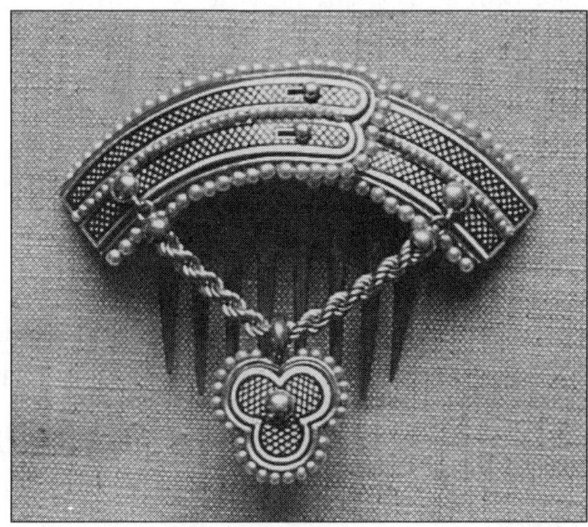

Hair Comb, gp metal, enamel, seed pearls, c. 1860-70, arched gp top decorated with *taille d'épargne* -enameled trellis pattern, overlapping at the center, depicting a cuff with two buttons, outlined in seed pearls strung on wire, suspending a rope-twist chain with an enameled trefoil drop outlined in seed pearls, mounted on a hinge attached to a blond tortoiseshell comb, 6" w x 5" tl, **$570**. (Photo courtesy of Sharen and Nicholas Wood).

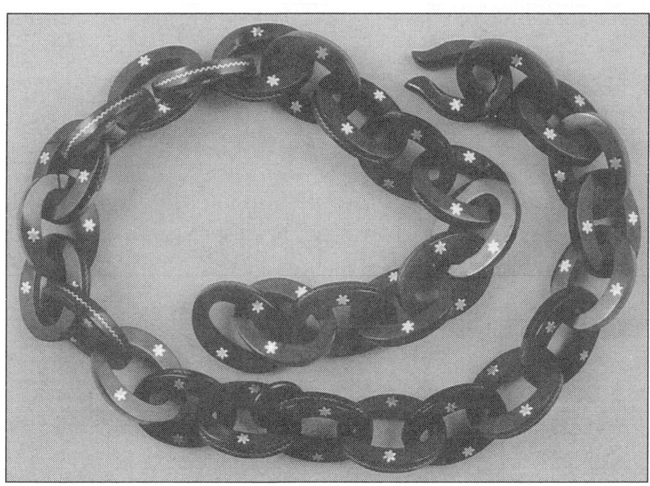

Neckchain, piqué, yg, c. 1860-70, lg tortoiseshell chain links with yg star *piqué point* on fronts and backs and meander piqué on edges, thirty-two links including horseshoe-shaped closure, 21" tl x 3/4" w, **$750**. (Private collection).

REVIVALIST JEWELRY

History: Victorians were fascinated with ancient history. For them, history meant revivals. Archeological discoveries and published accounts of ancient historical events and epics prompted revivals of jewelry styles from ancient and medieval cultures: Assyrian, Celtic, Egyptian, Etruscan, Gothic, Hellenistic and Roman, Mogul (India), Moorish, and Renaissance. Exact copies were favored over interpretations. With some exceptions, originality and creativity were not notable characteristics of Revivalist style, although exquisite workmanship and attention to details often were.

A number of noted jewelers of the mid to late nineteenth century worked in the Revivalist mode, copying ancient forms. Among these, the most famous were the Castellani family of Rome, and Carlo Giuliano and sons Carlo and Arthur of London.

Etruscan

Castellani

Revivalism reached its height during the 1860s and 70s. A mania for all things Italian promoted the popularity in particular of Etruscan Revival jewels, most closely associated with what is generically called the "archaeological style," which also includes copies of Roman cameos and intaglios, mosaics and "Hellenistic" (of Greek history, language and culture, 4th to 1st century BC) gold jewelry. The discovery of gold treasures from antiquity in Tuscany, in west-central Italy, near Rome, instigated the attempt to copy the ancient technique of granulation. Minute beads of gold were applied side-by-side to a gold surface to create a design. The difficulty lay in soldering the beads to the surface without melting them. Fortunato Pio Castellani, while unable to duplicate the technique exactly, came closest to perfecting it. Twisted, or "corded," wirework was also applied to gold jewels in the Etruscan style. Others made the attempt at granulation and wirework, but were usually less successful.

The ancient jewels themselves were copied by the Castellani as well as the techniques. The bulla, a two-sided round pendant worn by the Etruscans as an amulet, and the fibula, a safety-pin type of brooch used to fasten garments, were among the favorite forms.

The popularity of the Castellani's work was of course a motive for their imitators, copyists of copyists, as it were. Skill in craftsmanship, or the lack of it, is what separates the "wheat from the chaff." Some craftsmen were very skilled indeed, but the range of quality in Etruscan-style jewels is wide. Although quality workmanship is of primary consideration, a signature can add a great deal of value. The Castellani marks, back-to-back overlapping C's, are important ones to know. It is also important to note that their marks as well as their techniques were copied.

Large numbers of pieces in the archaeological style were produced by anonymous manufacturers throughout the last half of the nineteenth century. Many unsigned examples of varying quality can be found today of Etruscan decoration on gold and gold-filled pieces.

Renaissance

The Giulianos were Revivalists of another sort. They specialized in jewels in the Renaissance style, and were famous for their enameling. One trademark was an enameled white background with black dots, or black with white dots. Carlo Giuliano's work reached its peak in the 1870s. Although he too, employed granulation as well as other ancient techniques, unlike most Revivalists, he was an interpreter of the style. He improved upon techniques and forms with original ideas rather than exact copies. He signed his pieces C.G. in an applied or impressed oval plaque.

John Brogden

Sons Carlo and Arthur (mark: C.& A.G.) carried on after their father's death in 1896, but changing styles affected their business. Early twentieth century pieces were not as successful. The business closed in 1914. Both Giuliano marks have been counterfeited.

Other noted archaeological and Renaissance Revivalist jewelers were John Brogden of London, Ernesto Pierret of Rome, and Jules Wièse and son Louis of Paris.

Austrian and Hungarian Renaissance Revival jewelry was produced in quantity in the late nineteenth and early twentieth centuries. It is cruder in execution and materials–usually silver gilt, enamel, low-quality gemstones (sometimes glass) and freshwater pearls. Nevertheless, these pieces have a certain appeal, and are of growing interest, particularly among collectors of costume jewelry. Accordingly, prices have risen. Most pieces are unmarked, but sometimes a piece will have an Austro-Hungarian silver quality hallmark, usually a dog's head in a coffin-shaped lozenge (see Marks on Metals appendix; for other less commonly seen Austrian hallmarks, see Tardy, *International Hallmarks on Silver*, English translation, Paris, 1985.)

Egyptian

The discovery of the tomb and treasures of Queen Ah-Hotep and the start of construction of the Suez Canal in 1859 (completed ten years later) inspired the return of the Egyptian style, which had been revived once before in the late 18th and early 19th centuries. Familiar Egyptian symbols—scarabs, pharaohs, lotus blossoms, falcons and vultures—found their way into jewels by Castellani, Giuliano, Brogden, Robert Phillips, and several famous French jewel houses, including Froment-Meurice and Boucheron. These pieces were worked in gold, enamel, gemstones, and mosaics in much the same manner as other Revivalist jewelry.

Revivalism caught on in the United States too, although somewhat later. When Alessandro Castellani exhibited his family's work at the 1862 International Exposition in London, America was in the throes of the Civil War. But in 1876, at the Centennial Exposition in Philadelphia, Castellani presented his ideas and his jewelry to the receptive American public. Soon after, classical motifs and "Etruscan" worked gold began making their appearance in American-made jewelry, most of it mass-produced.

Today it is not unusual to find American pieces, both signed and unsigned, that reflect the widespread appeal of the past during the mid to late Victorian era.

References: Bennett and Mascetti, *Understanding Jewellery*; Shirley Bury, *Jewellery, The International Era*, Vol. II; Geoffrey Munn, *Castellani and Giuliano, Revivalist Jewellers of the Nineteenth Century*, Trefoil, 1984 (out of print); Kenneth Snowman, ed., *The Master Jewelers*, Abrams, 1990 (chapter by Geoffrey Munn). See also Tom R. Paradise, "Jewelry's Archaeological Style," Jeweler's Circular-Keystone/Heritage, November 1990 (Chilton); Elise B. Misiorowski, G.G., "The Magnificent 1800s, Inspiration for Gothic and Renaissance Revival Style Jewels," Jewelers' Circular-Keystone/Heritage, February, 1998.

Museums: The Villa Giulia in Rome houses a collection of 600 pieces of Castellani jewelry (limited public access). Some of the ancient jewels that inspired the Castellani can be seen at the British Museum in London. A selection of Giuliano's work is at the Victoria and Albert Museum, London, which has an extensive collection of Revivalist jewels.

Reproduction Alert: Faked signatures and repros are common. Signed pieces should be authenticated by an expert.

Bracelet

Bangle, hinged

Yg, garnets, diamonds, c. 1860-70, tapering front half, central lg bezel-set circ garnet cab (carbuncle) surmounted by an incised yg and rc diamond star motif, flanked by four grad oval bezel-set garnet cabs, wirework and appl bead and bar decoration, twisted wirework border, 1" w, 2-1/4" inside dia... 1,955 (A)

Bracelet, 15k yg, c. 1850, Etruscan Revival, fine mesh strap surmounted by a central circ openwork element with convex sq and trefoil center, granulation and wirework decoration, flanked by three joined rings on each side, v-spring and box clasp, orig fitted box, 6-1/2" l, **$975**. (Courtesy of E. Foxe Harrell Jewelers, Clinton, IA).

Yg, pearl, c. 1870, appl domed oval central star motif bead-set with one lg half pearl encircled by black enamel and engr geo design, opens to reveal glazed compartment, further encircled by appl beads and open scrolls, appl beads at sides of bangle to half-way, v-spring and box clasp, 16.4 dwt, 2-1/2" w x 1-1/2", 2-1/4" inside dia .... 748 (A)

Link

18k yg, c. 1860, six circ links with floral centers and ropetwist borders joined by figure-eight links, maker's mk for Castellani (interlocking adorsed C's), 1/2" w x 6-1/2" .... 6,325 (A)

Bracelet, yg, red stone cab, c. 1880, Etruscan Revival, hollow tube hinged bangle with twisted wirework and granulation-decorated terminals, three-dimensional head of a panther, suspending a granulation- and wirework-decorated sphere from a wiretwist loop opposite a similarly decorated sphere terminal, mkd with two patent dates: "Pat. Oct 25 . 76" and "Pat. June 29 . 80," head 1/2", inside dia 2-1/4", 2-1/2" w x 2-1/8", **$900**. (Yolanda Tisdale collection).

Bracelets, hinged bangles, 15k yg, c. 1870, Etruscan Revival, band with trefoil pattern appl wire border, beaded edges, centering tapered sections with appl vertical wire ridges flanked by lg and sm appl beads on smooth bloomed surfaces, v-spring and box clasp, 1-3/4" w, 2-3/8" inside dia, pr, **$4,025** [A]. (Photo courtesy of Sotheby's Beverly Hills, CA, 5/21/96).

Brooch/Pendant, silver, yg, c. 1875, bust of bearded man on pedestal in silver within an elaborate pierced and engr silver and yg frame, safety catch later added, 1-1/4" w x 2-5/8", **$1,500**. (Courtesy of E. Foxe Harrell Jewelers, Clinton, IA).

Bracelets

Bangle, hinged

Enamel, 14k yg, c. 1870, Gothic Revival, band of repeating arched motifs of wiretwist and appl beads, decorated with lt blue and white enamel, 1/2" w, 2-1/4" inside dia, pr .... 1,495 (A)

Brooch/Pendant

Citrine, 18k yg, enamel, pearls, diamonds, c. 1900, Egyptian Revival, a lg oval high relief carved citrine cameo of a full-face woman's head with Egyptian headdress, flanked by rows of sm rc diamonds in orange, blue, and white enameled rect plaques, surmounted by five grad pearls each with a sm rc diamond at the base, white enameled scrolled rect frame at bottom, rc diamond and pearl center, suspending five cone-shaped red enamel drops terminating in round pearls, 2" w x 3-1/4" .... 4,600 (A)

Brooch/Pin

Amethyst, seed pearls, yg, diamonds, c. 1900, Egyptian Revival, three-dimensional carved amethyst frontal bust of Cleopatra, yg bird headdress, sm rc diamond headband, necklace, and earrings, flanked by scrolling yg lotus motif, bezel-set within a yg breastplate, suspending a fringe of yg chains terminating in seed pearls, C-catch, extended pinstem, 1-3/4" w x 2" tall x 1" deep 8,625 (A)

Enamel, moonstones, 14k yg, c. 1870, Renaissance Revival, a circ Limoges enameled disk depicting a woman in Elizabethan dress, framed by prong-set moonstone beads in a yg mount, 1-3/8" dia .... 1,093 (A)

Enamel, pearls, 14k yg, c. 1870, a blue *en grisaille* Limoges enameled domed circ plaque depicting a *putto* playing the flute, set in a plain yg bezel, framed in split pearls, 1-1/4" dia .... 1,380 (A)

Brooch/Pin, yg, enamel, c. 1850, winged haloed St. Mark's lion with paw on book in polychrome enamel, inscription in black enamel "RICORDO DI VENEZIA" (Ital, "Souvenir of Venice") above and below, blue enameled Greek key border around scallop edge quatrefoil plaque, textured yg ground, C-catch, tube hinge, 1-1/2" w x 1-1/2", **$550**. (Courtesy of E. Foxe Harrell Jewelers, Clinton, IA).

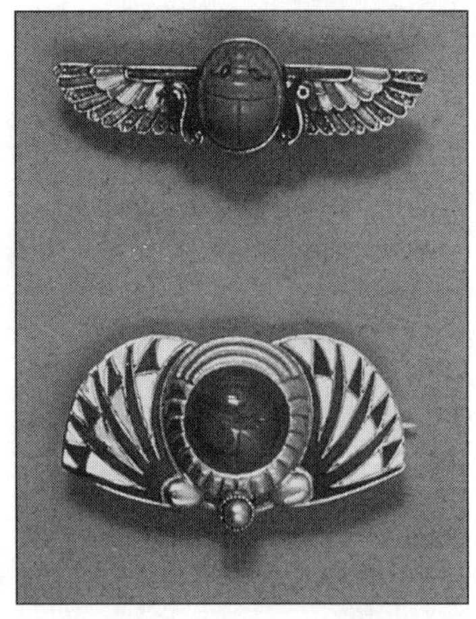

Brooches/Pins, yg, Egyptian Revival, winged scarab motif, c. 1890-1900:
T, bar pin, carved turquoise center flanked by yg S-scrolled dolphin motifs with rc diamond eyes surmounting wings, partially enameled in green, white, and red above alternating textured and smooth "feathers" with wiretwist borders, C-catch, tube hinge, mkd "O.R.G.M., N.N.v.S." on appl plate on rev, illegible mark stamped above plate, 1-1/2" w x 1/2", **$800**.
B, watch pin, engr circ blue star sapphire center within a wide stepped and ridged yg frame surmounting a millegrained bezel-set pearl, flanked by yg "antennae" and green, red, and white enameled wings, upturned hook for watch on rev, C-catch, flanged hinge, extended pinstem, 1-1/2" w x 7/8", **$1,250**. (Courtesy of E. Foxe Harrell Jewelers, Clinton, IA).

Earrings, pendent

18k yg, c. 1860, Etruscan Revival, rounded rect surmount suspending sm and lg circ plaques with C-scroll borders, bead and wiretwist decoration throughout, bead and wire rosette in center of lg plaque, shepherd's hook earwires, 5/78" w x 1-1/2" tl, pr .... 2,128 (A)

Garnets, yg, diamonds, c. 1860-70, a circ garnet cab surmount and drop, each with an incised star motif set with rc diamonds, surmount suspending central yg crossed keys motif with appl wirework and bead decoration with sm circ central garnet cab, later-added screwbacks, 5/8" w x 1-5/8" .... 1,610 (A)

Hair Comb

18k yg, seed pearls, enamel, c. 1880, curved pedestal-shaped top, seed pearl cluster border, six sm circ black enameled disks surmounted by appl yg flowers at the apexes of seed pearl swags framed by yg bands over a yg mesh bg, surmounting a yg comb, Fr hmks, 4" w x 4-1/4" tl .... 1,725 (A)

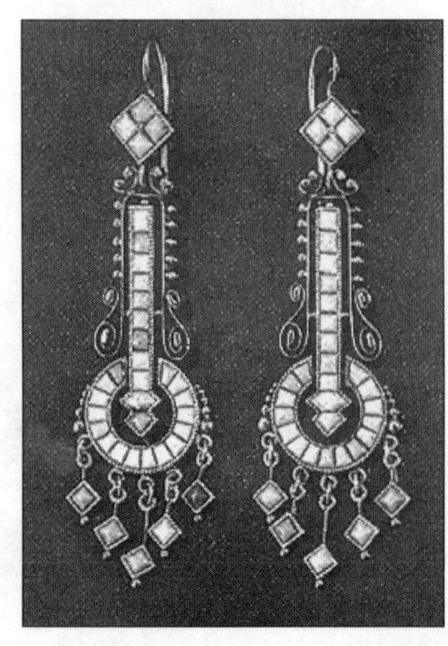

Earrings, turquoise, yg, c. 1870, Archeological Revival, sq surmount turned 45 degrees suspending an arrow shape piercing an open circle, beads and S-scrolls bordering shaft, a tapering fringe of five sq drops suspended by corners from circle, set throughout with a total of seventy bezel-set sq and calibré-cut turq cabs, shepherd's hook earwires, 3/4" w x 2-1/2", pr, **$1,265** [A]. (Photo courtesy of Dunning's Auction Service, Elgin, IL, 12/1/96).

Locket, 15k yg, c. 1870, Etruscan Revival, shield-shaped scroll-edged hinged locket, glazed compartment on rev, appl geo and shell shapes, granulation and scrolled wirework decoration, cusped pentagonal bail, 7/8" w x 1-3/4" tl, **$600**. (Elaine Sarnoff collection).

Necklace

18k yg, hardstone, c. 1875, Egyptian Revival, seven grad bezel-set carved hardstone scarabs in wiretwist frames, mounted on two trace link chains accented with appl disks, mkd "C.G." for Carlo Giuliano, 3/4" w (at center), 14-1/2" l .... 4,600 (A)

Necklace, yg, onyx, nicolo, c. 1880, Etruscan Revival, nine yg rams' heads suspending oval carved intaglios of alternating onyx and nicolo engr with images of Greco-Roman deities, each intaglio with appl wiretwist, bead, and floral decoration on yg frame, on a woven yg chain. serpentine clasp, appl shield-shaped plaque with mono for Ernesto Pierret, 2-3/4" w (at center), 17-1/2" tl, **$23,000** [A]. (Photo courtesy of Sotheby's Beverly Hills, CA, 5/21/96).

Pendant, enamel, diamonds, pearls, st yg, red stones, c. 1870, Renaissance Revival, navette-shaped foliate motif, centering an oval polychrome Limoges enameled plaque depicting a putto, set in a yg frame, surrounded by twelve pearls and numerous sm rc diamonds, red stone accents, suspending a pear-shaped drop with sm rc diamonds, rc diamond-set bail, 1-1/4" w x 3" tl, **$920** [A]. (Photo courtesy of Skinner, Inc., Boston, MA, 9/23/97).

18k yg, turquoise, c. 1870-80, Etruscan Revival, fringe of leaves suspended from rosettes, alternating with turq beads suspended from circ beads on jointed stems, appl wiretwist decoration, 7/8" w x 14" tl .... 1,495 (A)

Pendant

14k yg, chalcedony, rubies, diamonds, c. 1870-80, Egyptian Revival, depicting the head of a pharaoh with a ruby and diamond-set headdress, mounted in the center of a circ chalcedony cab within a beaded frame bordered with scrolled wirework and foliate motifs, diamond accents, cusped bail, 1-3/4" w x 2-3/8" .... 2,530 (A)

Lapis lazuli, yg, pearls, c. 1860-70, Etruscan Revival, lg bezel-set circ lapis cab within a circ yg ornate frame with appl bead and wirework decoration, six bezel-set pearls in balustered box frames evenly spaced around the edges, surmounted by adorsed three-dimensional ram's heads, open V-shaped bail with appl bead and wirework, 1-3/4" w x 3-1/4" tl .... 1,840 (A)

Locket

Yg, seed pearls, c. 1860-70, Etruscan style cartouche shape, a central horizontal row of four seed pearls within appl bead and scrolled wirework design, ropetwist border around oval locket compartment, 10.9 dwt, 1-1/4" w x 2-1/4" tl .... 632 (A)

Pendant, locket, yg, enamel, c. 1870, Greco-Roman Revival, oval enameled miniature depiction of a classical female, a dove on her hand, a putto at her side, in shades of white, beige, red and blue with white and blue enameled border, within an elaborate wiretwist and beaded yg frame surmounted by a cusped and scrolled pediment and tapered beaded bail, cusped at the base, locket compartment, attributed to Eugène Fontenay, 1-1/2" w x 3" tl, in a fitted case, **$4,025** [A]. (Photo courtesy of Christie's Images, New York, NY, 4/8/97).

Pendant and Chain

Black opal, enamel, 18k yg, diamonds, rubies, c. 1890, Egyptian Revival, central carved black opal scarab with inset rows of sm rc diamonds and rc diamond eyes, in a bead and wirework decorated yg frame, flanked by white enameled snakes with sm bezel-set ruby eyes, suspending an oval collet-set ruby, suspended from a stylized inverted lotus motif enameled in red, green, and white with sm ruby and diamond accents, plain yg loop bail, on an 18k yg oval link chain, 1" w x 2" tl .... 3,680 (A)

18k yg, c. 1860-70, Etruscan Revival, domed circ pendant with appl bead and wiretwist decoration, lg foliate motif hinged bail, suspended from a similarly decorated oval mesh chain, European hmks, 16" tl, pendant 1-3/8" dia, 2-1/2" tl with bail .... 1,725 (A)

Pendant/Brooch

15k yg, diamonds, spinel, c. 1870, cartouche shape centering a flowerhead of one lg om diamond, approx 1.00 ct, encircled by eight sm rc diamonds, framed by eight sm oval-cut red spinels, enclosed by a notched arcing frame at top and scrolled shell motif at base, appl bead and wirework decoration, suspending a grad flexible fringe, hinged bail at the top, fitted box, 1-1/2" w x 4-1/2" tl .... 3,737 (A)

Suite, Pendant/Brooch and Earrings

18k yg, MOP, paint, seed pearls, c. 1860-70, Renaissance Revival, oval MOP plaque with ptd scene of two cherubs within multicolored floral branches, bezel-set in engr yg frame encircled by six carre-set seed pearls surmounting twisted coiled wire, appl scroll motifs at compass points, engr bail, matching pendent earrings, each with circ surmount centering a seed pearl, scrolled wirework suspending smaller ptd oval plaque with a cherub, Fr hmks, shepherd's hooks, fitted case, pendant 1-1/2" w x 2-1/4 tl, earrings 1" w x 2-1/2" tl, suite .... 3,450 (A)

CAMEOS AND INTAGLIOS

History: The cameo has come to be known as a classic form of jewelry, the epitome of the "old-fashioned" look. But its widespread popularity began in the nineteenth century as a tourist souvenir. Hardstone cameos date to ancient Rome; shell cameos to the Renaissance. Late eighteenth century Neo-classicists revived the art, inspired by Napoleon's preoccupation with Roman Imperialism. But it was the Victorians who popularized (some say vulgarized) the cameo made from a variety of materials–shell, lava, coral, ivory, jet, as well as gemstones–as a part of a Greco-Roman Revival that remained in vogue from mid-century onward.

Travelers touring Europe (on guided excursions organized and conducted by the West's first travel agent, Thomas Cook) helped promote cameo-carving to the point of mass production. Italy was a favorite destination, especially, due to the Victorian preoccupation with ancient history, the ruins of Pompeii at Mount Vesuvius. "Lava" cameos were purchased as souvenirs. The material, actually a form of limestone mixed with volcanic particles called "pyroclastics" (real lava is molten rock), was found in the region, and associated with the volcano that was Pompeii's downfall. Nearby, in the seaside town of Torre del Greco, Italian cameo carvers made shell and coral cameos for the tourists, as they continue to do today.

A true cameo is a miniature sculpture in relief, carved from a single piece of material. When the material is layered, as are agate (onyx) and shell, the carver uses the light and dark layers as contrasting background and foreground. When a design is carved into only the thin white layer of onyx with a thick black layer underneath, the background of the design appears translucent bluish-white. This is called "nicolo." The subject matter of cameos can range from classic mythological and Biblical scenes, floral bouquets and landscapes, to the more commonly seen heads or busts of women or men. Male cameos predominate the Neo-classical period.

A woman's profile is the motif most closely associated with cameos by their wearers today. These can date anywhere from 1840 to the present. Their look is usually in keeping with the style of the times. One favorite technique for circa-dating is to look at the nose of the woman in profile. Aquiline, or Romanesque noses are found on the classic beauties of the mid-nineteenth century. Pert, turned-up noses are found on twentieth-century interpretations of female attractiveness. It's important to remember that carvers could only carve what they knew; "dead giveaway" motifs, such as the biplane in the cameo on p. 44, are the surest clues to a cameo's age, but hairstyles and attire can also help in circa-dating.

The most common material for cameos is shell, which is soft and easy to carve. Portrait cameos were sometimes made with the depicted woman wearing a necklace or other jewelry set with a small diamond. These are called cameos *habillés* (French for "dressed up"), and are still being made.

Nineteenth century lava and coral cameos are also found today, although not as abundantly. While most shell cameos are carved in bas-relief, due to the relative shallowness of the material's layers, lava and coral, being monochromatic, can be and often are carved in high relief. The protruding noses on these cameos are most susceptible to damage.

Some of the best and most highly prized cameos are made from hardstone. These cameos are more difficult and time-consuming to fashion, and require a great deal of skill with lathe-held tools. Cameo experts point out that the word "carved" is technically incorrect when applied to stone cameos and intaglios. The correct word is "engraved." The art of engraving gemstones is called "glyptics" or "the glyptic arts." Hardstone cameos are occasionally engraved within a concave depression in the stone, where the edge of the stone is level with the highest part of the cameo itself. *Chevet* or *chevée*, *cuvette* or *curvette* are the terms, used interchangeably, for this type of cameo. The British term is dished.

The quality of a cameo's carving can range from breathtaking to abysmal. Values also range widely, depending on the skill of the carver, depicted subject, size, and the materials used for the cameo and the mounting or frame. Quickly-made mass-produced shell cameos (most of which come from Idar-Oberstein, Germany, not Italy) are of little value. Ultrasonic machine-made stone cameos have been produced for the past twenty-five years. These have a faintly textured surface referred to as the "fresh-fallen snow" syndrome by author Anna Miller (see References below). Their quality and value are low. Pseudo or assembled cameos are molded from natural or synthetic materials and laminated to a backing or set in a metal frame.

Brooches are the usual form, but cameos can also be found set into necklaces, bracelets, earrings, rings, and stickpins.

Intaglios, which actually preceded cameos in ancient times, are the opposite of cameos, in that the design is recessed, engraved into the stone, below the surface. The most common association is with fob seals, or signet rings, in which the intaglio is used to create an impression in relief when pressed into sealing wax. These fobs and rings are also worn for ornamental purposes, but the design is less perceptible than that of a cameo. Intaglios are engraved in hardstone, never shell or other soft material. Molded glass imitation intaglios are found in inexpensive jewelry.

Reverse-painted rock crystal intaglios were popular in the mid to late nineteenth century, especially in sporting jewelry featuring animal motifs. Dogs, horses, or other animals were engraved into the backs of rock crystal quartz cabochons. The intaglios were then painted in realistic colors and backed with mother-of-pearl before setting. From the front, the animals appear three-dimensional. These were later imitated with molded and painted glass.

References: Vivienne Becker, *Antique and Twentieth Century Jewellery*; Anna M. Miller, *Cameos Old & New,* Van Nostrand Reinhold, 1991; Monica Lynn Clements and Patricia Rosser Clements, *Cameos: Classical to Costume*, Schiffer Publishing, 1998..

Museums: Boston Museum of Fine Arts, Boston, MA; J. Paul Getty Museum, Malibu, CA; Indiana University Museum, Bloomington, IN; Lizzadro Museum of Lapidary Arts, Elmhurst, IL; Metropolitan Museum of Art, New York, NY; University Museum, University of Pennsylvania, Philadelphia, PA; Walters Art Gallery, Baltimore, MD; see Anna Miller's book, above, for further information on these and other cameo collections.

Advisors: Anna Miller, Gertrud Seidmann.

Bracelet

Bangle, hinged

18k yg, nicolo onyx, c. 1880, open engr scrolled band centering a rect onyx plaque with a recessed oval blue and white nicolo cameo (*chevet*) depicting *putti* at play, set in a plain yg bezel, flanked by appl yg stylized shell motifs, mounted on an engr and pierced cagelike yg band, sgd "Tiffany & Co.," v-spring and box clasp, safety chain, 5/8" w, 2-1/4" inside dia .... 11,500 (A)

Charm

9k yg, rolled gold, hardstone, oval link 9k yg chain suspending nine mixed gold and rolled gold-framed hardstone intaglio seal fobs in various motifs, c. late Georgian and early Victorian, spring ring closure, safety chain, 1-1/2" w (at center), 7" tl .... 3,680 (A)

Link Bracelet, lava, 18k yg, c. 1830, six rounded rect carved and pierced lava plaques, each a different color (white, gray, tan, blue, lavender, black) and carved with a different classical theatrical mask in the center framed by S-scrolls and fleur-de-lis motifs, set in plain yg frames, v-spring and box clasp, mounted in England, in orig box, 1" w x 8" l, **$1,000**. (Photo courtesy of Sharen and Nicholas Wood).

Link

Lava, silver, c.1860-80, ten linked carved cameos, heads of men and women, shades of gray, tan, brown, and white, 6-3/4" tl x 5/8" 400

Brooch/Pendant

Coral, 14k yg, c. 1900, lt orange oval carving of a woman's profile bezel-set in wide engr yg frame, lever catch mkd "14k," hinged bail, 1-1/8" w x 1-1/4" 600

Hardstone, yg, enamel, c. 1876, oval white hardstone profile of a woman in Elizabethan dress mounted in blue enameled bezel, scroll and bead motif filigree frame, etched on rev "Centennial Exposition, Philadelphia, 1876, Starr & Marcus, New York," #777, C8, formerly the property of socially prominent Jesse Wright Barr, in a fitted leather case mkd "Starr & Marcus" on the inside and "J.R.B. Jan 1st 1877" on the outside, 1-7/8" w x 2-3/8" .... 4,830 (A)

Onyx, seed pearl, 18k yg, c. 1870, gentleman's profile within wiretwist frame with seed pearl border, compartment on rev, 1-3/4" w x 2" .... 748 (A)

Sardonyx, diamonds, pearls, yg, c. 1870, oval white on brown profile bust of a woman with pearl-entwined headdress, off-the-shoulder drapery and wing-like projections on her shoulders, prong-set in yg, bordered by alternating om diamonds and pearls and suspending a pearl drop, glazed locket compartment on rev (repaired), 1-3/8" w x 2-1/4" tl .... 2,530 (A)

Brooch/Pendant, 15k yg, hardstone, seed pearls, c. 1870, sardonyx cameo depicting classical woman's profile, multiple pronged setting within an engr shield-shaped beaded edge frame, suspended by a hinge from a cutout rect yg plaque surmounted by a trefoil (fleur-de-lis) set with seed pearls, flanked by foliate scrolls, beaded edge hinged bail, C-catch, tube hinge, 1-3/4" w x 3-1/8" tl, **$2,200**. (Lenore Dailey collection).

Brooch/Pin

Chalcedony, diamonds, plat-topped yg, c. 1890, a convex-sided rect chalcedony tablet with an oval chevet (recessed) cameo depicting a Venetian gondola scene, framed by om diamonds in plat-topped 18k yg, 1-5/8" w x 3/4" .... 6,950 (A)

Hardstone, 14k yg, c. 1850, white on brown profile of a helmeted male, helmet decorated with a winged horse (Pegasus) in dark brown and white, bezel-set within an independent yg wire frame of a later date, wound wire at compass points, lever catch, mkd "14k," 1-1/4" w x 1-5/8" 750

Hardstone, 18k yg, c. 1880, high relief cameo of woman's profile within a plain 18k yg frame, fitted box, 1-1/2" w x 2" .... 2,415 (A)

Hardstone, yg, Mid-Victorian, oval three-layered carving, classical woman's profile, white on black, a lg stemmed floral spray in her hair, bezel-set, encircled by a row of yg beads within a yg frame, enclosed C-catch, tube hinge, 1-1/8" w x 1-1/2" 1,700

Hardstone, yg, Mid-Victorian, three-layered circ carving depicting Mercury's profile, white on black, rust-brown wing in his wavy hair, yg frame, 7/8" dia 1,674

Bangle Bracelet, hinged, shell, wm, c. 1915, queen conch shell cameo of a woman's profile in WWI Red Cross headdress set in a narrow japanned wm tubular bracelet, mkd with an iron cross and additional illegible mk, cameo 7/8" w x 1-1/16", bracelet 2-3/8" inside dia, **$300**. (Private collection).

Brooch/Pin, lava, yg, c. 1840-60, rounded rect, two hounds, long and short haired, carved in relief in gray-brown monochrome, set in plain yg bezel and frame, C-catch, tube hinge, extended pinstem, 2-5/8" w x 1-7/8", **$1,500**. (Courtesy of E. Foxe Harrell Jewelers, Clinton, IA).

Hardstone cameo brooches, early 19th century:
L, c. 1800, high relief three-quarter profile of a bearded man, irregular cusped shape, plain yg conforming frame, C-catch, tube hinge, extended pinstem, 3/4" w x 1-1/8", **$1,800**.
R, c. 1830, low relief bearded man's profile, set in oval beaded-edge yg frame, C-catch, 7/8" w x 1-1/8", **$950**.
(Courtesy of E. Foxe Harrell Jewelers, Clinton, IA).

Brooch/Pin, hardstone, 18k yg, c. 1860-70, oval white on dk green, woman's profile in classical dress with flowers in her hair, bezel-set in wiretwist yg frame, C-catch, 2" w x 3", **$2,450**. (Photo courtesy of Lovejoy's Estate Jewelry, Bellingham, WA).

Brooches/Pins, lava, yg, c. 1860-70:
T, ochre-colored oval, deeply-carved high-relief profile of a bacchante, lg grape leaves and three-dimensional vines in her hair, in plain yg frame, C-catch, tube hinge, 1-1/2" w x 1-3/4", **$700**.
(Martha Exline collection).
B, carved black full face of Diana, goddess of the hunt, flanked by two dogs' heads, left side dog's nose and Diana's moon headdress chipped, 2-1/2" w x 1-1/2", **$600**.
(Private collection).

Brooches/Pins, male cameos, c. 1860-70:
L, hardstone, yg, high relief bust of bearded man set in oval frame flanked by rod and scroll motifs, replacement lever catch, tube hinge, 1-1/8" w x 7/8", **$1,800**.
R, sardonyx, 14k gold, depicting a classical man's bust, head crowned in laurel leaves, later made oval frame and pin assembly, safety catch, 1-1/8" w x 1-3/8", **$1,500**.
(Courtesy of E. Foxe Harrell Jewelers, Clinton, IA).

Brooch/Pin, shell, sterling, c. 1915-20, oval cameo depicting a woman with "bob" hairstyle holding a rose and looking up at circa WWI airplane, filigree frame mkd "Sterling," slight crazing in center of cameo, safety catch, flanged hinge, 1-7/8" w x 1-1/2", **$450**. (Private collection).

Brooch/Pendant, labradorite, yg, c. 1880, circ carved frontal head of a lion, pronged setting, hinged bail, lever catch, later mount, 1-1/4" dia, **$800**. (Courtesy of E. Foxe Harrell Jewelers, Clinton, IA).

Ivory, brass, c. 1850, oval, frontal bust of a woman, carved ropetwist border, C-catch, tube hinge, brass safety chain and pin, 1-1/8" w x 1-3/8" 350

Lava, gf, c. 1840-60, khaki-colored oval high relief frontal bust of a classical woman, plain bezel, chain-link frame, C-catch, tube hinge (lead solder), 1-1/8" w x 1-1/4" 200

Lava, gp wm, c. 1880, buff-colored oval, profile bust of a woman in classical drapery, bezel-set in a plain gp frame, C-catch, 1-1/2" w x 1-7/8" 350

Lava, rolled gold plate, c. 1860-70, woman's profile in white, floral and foliate motif, ropetwist decoration on frame, later added safety catch, tube hinge, 7/8" w x 1" 175

Lava, 14k yg, Mid-Victorian, chocolate brown monochrome depicting a mythological embracing couple in high relief with well-detailed drapery and features, plain yg frame, Russian hmks, 1-1/2" w x 2" .... 2,070 (A)

Lava, yg, c. 1830-40, gray monochrome depiction of an angel holding two babies with a winged cherub in bg, set in oval beaded-edge frame, converted bracelet clasp, C-catch, tube hinge, 1-5/8" w x 1-3/8"...................... 500

Lava, yg, c. 1860, charcoal gray woman's profile, some wear, yg frame, C-catch, tube hinge (worn), 7/8" w x 1-1/8".. 185

Lava, yg, c. 1860, oval grayish-beige depiction of three women in classical dress with spinning implements, plain yg frame, illegible hmk on yg pinstem, C-catch, tube hinge, extended pinstem, 2-1/8" w x 1-1/2"...... 400

Pâte de verre, gp, c. 1860, tan molded glass woman's profile glued to oval tan glass plaque, plain frame and bezel, C-catch, tube hinge, 1-1/2" w x 1-7/8"...................... 200

Reverse intaglio, rock crystal quartz, yg, cloth, c. 1890, circ rev-painted crystal of a pheasant in black, red, green, blue and white on a cloth bg in a circ yg bead and wirework frame, C-catch, 1" dia.................................... 500

Sardonyx, 18k wg, c. 1880, oval white on red-brown, woman's profile with floral-decorated hair, bezel-set in later engr wg frame, 1-1/2" w x 2" 1,650

Shell, gp metal, c. 1870, high relief three-dimensional cameo of woman wearing foliate hair ornament and Grecian hair style, mounted in later gp base metal frame with ropetwist decoration, lever catch, 1-1/4" w x 1-1/2" 250

Shell, yg, c. 1860, oval high relief carving of a frontal portrait of Jupiter above his symbol, an eagle grasping a thunderbolt, bezel-set within an open three-dimensional engr foliate and scroll frame, (nose broken, discoloration evident), 2-3/4" w x 3-1/4".................................. 2,760 (A)

Shell, yg, c. 1870, oval cameo of a classical woman's profile with ribbon-tied hair, bezel-set in an oval yg frame with appl bead and wiretwist decoration, some damage evident, 1-7/8" w x 2-1/4"....................................... 403 (A)

Earrings, pendent

Hardstone, yg, seed pearls, c. 1860, navette-shaped drops, each centering a woman's profile, white on black, within a floral scrollwork frame with beaded border, seed pearl accents, fishhook earwires, 1/2" w x 1-1/2", pr .. 863 (A)

Lava, gp brass, c. 1860-70, oval surmount suspending pear-shaped drop, each set with a woman's 3/4 profile in gilded brass frames, 3/4" w x 1-1/2", pr 275

Hair Comb

Sardonyx, yg, tortoiseshell, c. 1870, cutout yg foliate scroll motif framing one lg flanked by four sm oval cameos of a woman in profile surmounting attached tortoiseshell comb, 4" w x 4-1/4" tl .... 5,520 (A)

Pendent Earrings, shell, yg, c. 1830, navette-shaped cameos, profiles of two gentlemen suspended from unique surmounts, wiretwist decoration, threaded center turns to open and close attachment for unpierced ear (c. 1860-70), 1-7/8" tl x 1/2" w, pr, **$450**. (Courtesy of E. Foxe Harrell Jewelers, Clinton, IA).

Brooch/Pin, reverse intaglio, rock crystal quartz, MOP, 14k yg, c. 1900-10, circ rev-painted crystal depicting a collie's head in brown, black and white, MOP backing, mounted at compass points inside ropetwist frame, maker's mk for Enos Richardson & Co., Newark NJ, mkd "14k," unusual lever catch mkd "Pat'd," later-added engr "Ray 1936" on rev, 1" dia, **$1,100**. (Courtesy of DLW Antiques, Memphis, TN).

Pendent Earrings, *pâte de verre*, gp brass, c. 1830, navette-shaped molded blue glass drops each a classical figure, one Minerva, the other Venus, bezel set in gp frames, later screwbacks, 3/4" w x 2-1/2", pr, **$350**. (Courtesy of E. Foxe Harrell Jewelers, Clinton, IA).

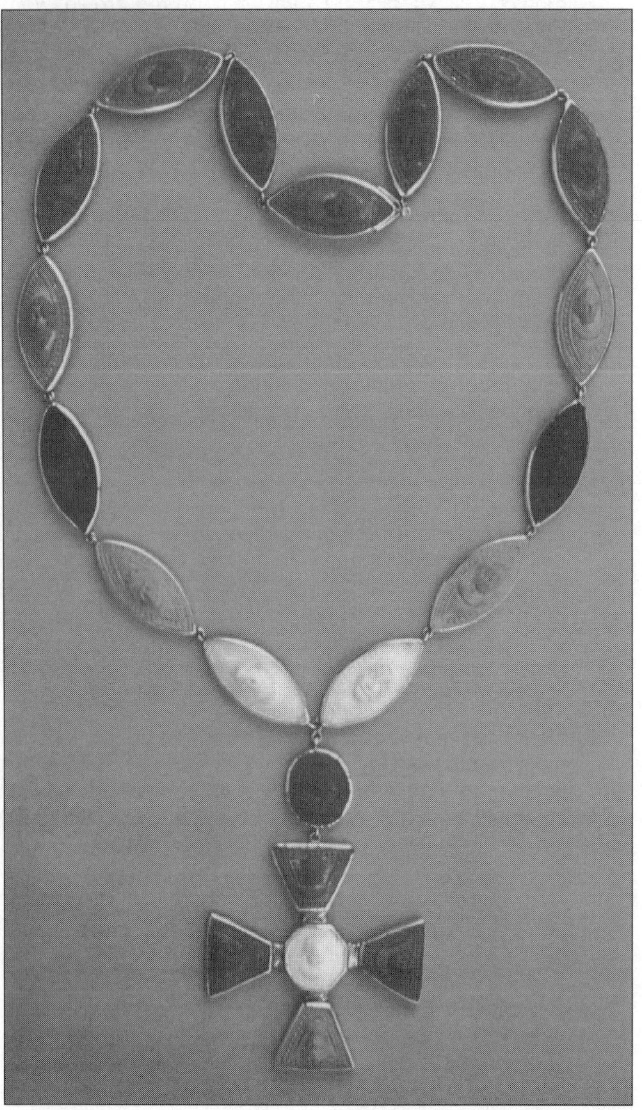

Necklace, lava, yg, c. 1820-30, chain composed of navette-shaped links of yg set with lava cameos, busts in four shades of brown, blue, white, and black, suspending a circ link with inset dk brown lava cameo and Maltese cross of four brown and central white cameo, v-spring and box clasp, 1/2" w x 16-1/2" tl, pendant 1-1/2" dia, **$1,450**. (Courtesy of E. Foxe Harrell Jewelers, Clinton, IA).

Necklace

Shell, yg, c. 1830, five grad oval shell cameos of classical figures in profile, including Athena and Mercury, each set in plain yg bezels, joined *en esclavage* by swagged double chains, central cameo 1-1/8" w x 1-3/8", 16" tl .... 2,645 (A)

Shell, 14k yg, c. 1860-70, seven graduated oval cameos depicting mythological scenes, in engr frames with scrolls surmounted by bead finials at top and bottom, alternating with swagged chains suspending inverted pear-shaped and spherical bead drops, joined by pierced scalloped-shaped bars (solder, repair and small breaks to chain), 3" w (at center), 14" tl .... 5,865 (A)

Ring

Garnet, yg, c. 1790, third century intaglio of a deer set in late eighteenth century mount, rubbed over irregular bezel, mounted on split shank, approx size 6-1/2, 1/2" w x 3/8" 850

Yg, hardstone, Early Victorian, a cartouche-shaped yg plaque with an oval cameo of a man's profile flanked by two smaller circ cameos of men's profiles, in a plain mount on a tapering shank, 5/8" w x 1" .... 518 (A)

Scarf Pin/Stickpin

Lava, c. 1860-70, carved three-dimensional reddish brown bust of Dante Alighieri on brass pinstem, 2-5/8" tl, 3/8" w x 5/8" head 200

Suite: Cuff Links and Stickpin

Reverse intaglio, rock crystal quartz, paint, 14k yg, c. 1900, double-sided cuff links, each a circ bezel-set rev-ptd crystal intaglio, a man on horseback on one side, a fox on the other, 1/2" dia, stickpin a rev-ptd intaglio of a horse's head, sgd "MARCUS & CO.," 1/2" dia, 2-1/2" tl, suite .... 3,795 (A)

Pendant, reverse intaglio, rock crystal quartz, MOP, paint, gilt metal, Late Victorian, rev-painted, depicting a coach and four with coachman and two footmen, two female and three male passengers, road and grass, MOP backing, plain gilt metal mount, pendant bail, 2-1/4" dia, **$2,500**. (Courtesy of E. Foxe Harrell Jewelers, Clinton, IA).

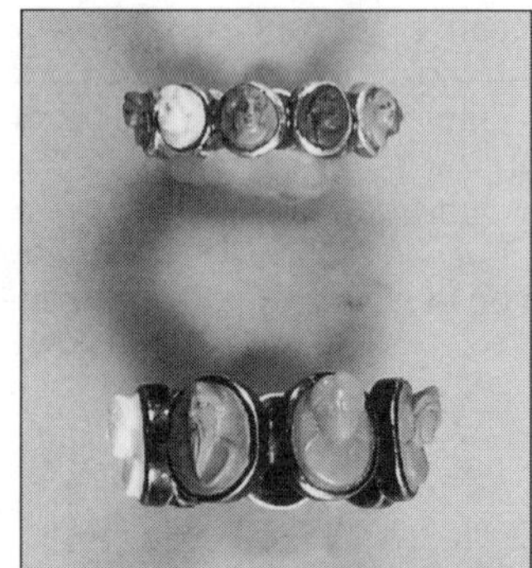

Rings, yg, c. 1860:
T, lava, ten sm individually carved bezel-set cameos in shades of tan, brown, beige and gray, approx size 7, 1/4" w, **$450**.
B, lava, coral, seven individually carved bezel-set cameos in shades of tan, brown, white, coral and gray, approx size 10, 3/8" w, **$700**. (Courtesy of E. Foxe Harrell Jewelers, Clinton, IA).

Ring, onyx, yg, colorless stones, c. 1880, oblong black and white onyx floral intaglio with yg wire stem, colorless faceted stones (one rc diamond replacement) at compass points, vase and grain decoration at the shoulders, mkd "18," tapered shank, approx size 6-1/2, 1/2" w x 3/4", **$275**. (Private collection).

Scarf Pin/Stickpin, banded agate, yg, c. 1880, man in the moon and star intaglio, black over white, beaded circ frame, 3-1/8" tl, 7/8" dia, **$250**. (Courtesy of E. Foxe Harrell Jewelers, Clinton, IA).

Suite: Pendant/Brooch and Pendent Earrings

Sardonyx, pearls, diamonds, 18k yg, st yg, c. 1870, pendant a brown sardonyx cameo depicting a seated woman with spinning implements in oval floral and foliate motif frame, black and white pearl and rc diamond accents, earrings each a brown sardonyx cameo depicting a different woman's opposed profile in an oval rc diamond-set frame with meander and scroll decoration, suspended from three link and pearl bead chains joined to larger pearl surmount, shepherd's hook earwire, five rc diamond and pearl drops at base, rc diamond accents, Fr import mks, orig fitted box, brooch 1" w x 2-1/4" tl, earrings 3/4" w x 2-1/4" tl, suite......................... 12,650 (A)

Watch Fob Seal

Carved glass, gilded brass, c. 1810-30, oval intaglio of kneeling nude male with an urn, 3/4" w x 7/8" x 1-1/8"h 200

Suite: Brooch/Pin and Pendent Earrings, hardstone, 14k rose gold, seed pearls, c. 1860-70, brooch an oval white on black, woman's profile bezel-set in fancy geo frame with a vertical row of three seed pearls at the base, C-catch, brooch 1" w x 1-3/4", matching pendent earrings 1/2" w x 3/4", suite, **$895**. (Photo courtesy of Lovejoy's Estate Jewelry, Bellingham, WA).

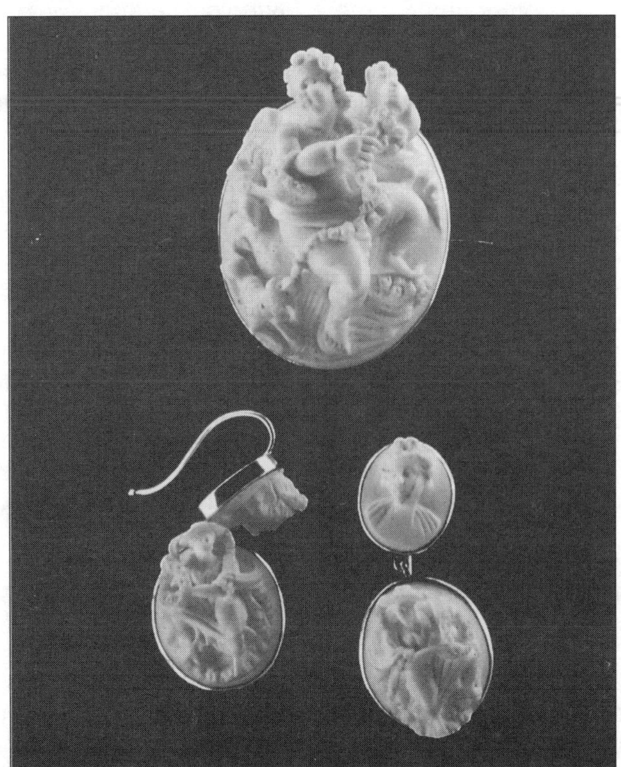

Suite: Brooch/Pin and Pendent Earrings, lava, yg, c. 1860, all white, oval brooch a high relief undercarved scene of a winged cherub, basket on his arm, holding a garland, a dog at his feet pulling at the garland's end, plain yg frame, C-catch, tube hinge, extended pinstem, 1-1/4" w x 1-1/2", each earring oval surmount a frontal bust of a woman, suspending an oval drop of a high relief undercarved woman wearing a hat and a draped shawl, holding a wreath, each a slightly different pose, plain yg frames, shepherd's hook earwires, 5/8" w x 1-1/2", suite, **$2,880**. (Photo courtesy of Karen Lorene, Facèré Jewelry Art, Seattle, WA).

MOSAICS IN JEWELRY

The rise and fall of mosaics developed along parallel lines to that of cameos. Also based on ancient Roman techniques and revived by Neo-classicists, mosaics of the late eighteenth and early nineteenth centuries were miniature works of art in glass or stone, resembling paintings. Like cameos, mosaics reached their height of popularity in the mid-nineteenth century, during the Revivalist rage for all things Italian. And like cameos, too, it was the tourist trade that brought them to that height, and was their downfall in terms of quality.

There are two types of Italian mosaics: Roman, in which tiny bits of colored glass called *tesserae* are pieced together to form a picture, held in place with cement in a glass or stone background; and Florentine, or *pietra dura* (literally, "hard stone," plural: *pietre dure*), in which thin slices of colored stones are cut in shapes and fitted together like a jigsaw puzzle to produce a picture, usually using a bed of black marble as the foundation.

The subject matter for mosaics is also of two distinct types. Roman mosaics, catering to the tourist trade, often depict Roman ruins and landscapes, or are copies of ancient mosaics, like the Capitoline doves, often called "Pliny's doves." King Charles spaniels were another favorite motif. Mythological and religious figures are also seen in Roman mosaics. Florentine mosaics most commonly have floral motifs, but other figurative motifs, such as butterflies and birds, are found as well.

Value depends on quality of workmanship and condition. Mosaics are easily cracked or otherwise damaged. In Roman mosaics, the size of the tesserae helps determine age and quality. Micromosaics that look less like pieces of glass and more like a painting to the naked eye are usually earlier, and better.

Entire parures, or suites, of jewelry were made from both types of mosaics. Demi-parures of pendant or brooch and earrings are also found. The brooch is the most common single form of mosaic jewelry. Mosaics continue to be made in Italy today, still for tourists, but with much larger tesserae and much lesser workmanship.

References: *The Art of Mosaics, Selections from the Gilbert Collection,* Los Angeles County Museum of Art, 1982; Vivienne Becker, *Antique and Twentieth Century Jewellery,* 2nd ed., N.A.G. Press, 1987; Lael Hagan, "Mosaic Jewelry: Heir to a Long Artistic Tradition," in *Jewelers' Circular-Keystone/Heritage*, November, 1991.

Brooch/Pin

Micromosaic, 18k yg, c. 1870, circ domed top, polychrome mosaic of two birds perched on a quiver of arrows, floral bg, yg beaded frame encircled with mosaic stars, bottom and sides with appl clusters of three sm mosaic stars, suspending three paired lengths of ropetwist chain interspersed with sm mosaic stars, forming three interlaced Vs terminating in three circ disk drops, center drop with floral mosaic, two sides with stars, 1-3/4" w x 3-1/4" tl .... 1,840 (A)

Micromosaic, 18k yg, c. 1870, oval mosaic still life bouquet of peonies and wildflowers, in a braided ropetwist yg frame, 2-1/4" w x 1-3/4" .... 5,463 (A)

Micromosaic, 18k yg, malachite, c. 1860-80, an oval polychrome mosaic depicting a King Charles spaniel in a landscape, inlaid in malachite (cracks), conforming yg frame with appl bead and wiretwist decoration, 1" w x 1-1/4" .... 345 (A)

Micromosaic, 18k yg, onyx, enamel, c. 1860-70, oval polychrome mosaic depicting Roman ruins in a black onyx ground, mounted in a bead and wirework bezel within a lobed and concave/convex rect yg frame, engr with blue enameled foliate scroll decoration, 1-3/4" w x 1-1/2" .... 920 (A)

Link Bracelet, micromosaic, 18k yg, c. 1860-70, six oval linked plaques each centering an oval mosaic with various scenes of Rome, set in an oval black onyx ground, bezel-set in appl wiretwist and bead yg frames, floral motif capped interlinks, Vatican hmks, v-spring and box clasp, 1" w x 6-1/4" tl, **$3,680** [A]. (Photo courtesy of Skinner, Inc., Boston, MA, 9/23/97).

Micromosaic, black glass, gf, c. 1850-60, rect black glass ground inlaid with oval mosaic of building, stamped scrollwork gf frame, C-catch, tube hinge, 1-7/8" w x 1-5/8" 950

Pietra dura, silver, gf, brass, c. 1880-90, circ disk of black marble, inlaid with central flower motif in shades of white, gray, brown and green, brass backing, silver frame encircled with gf beading, C-catch, tube hinge, 1" dia 125

Pietra dura, sp brass, c. 1870, beveled oval pietra dura plaque with the word "Karlsbad" in center, ropetwist bezel, engr boxes at compass points with beads connecting between (one missing), plating loss, C-catch, tube hinge, 1-3/8" w x 1-1/4" 125

Cuff Links

Micromosaic, 10k yg, c. 1870, each circ disk depicting a classical site in shades of brown, beige, green and white within a blue ground, in fitted leather box, 7/8" dia .... 805 (A)

Brooches/Pins, c. 1850-60:

T, mosaic, 14k yg, glass, figure of a peasant woman, polychrome on black ground inlaid into red glass, stamped oval filigree frame mkd "Birks 14k," lever catch mkd "14k," flanged hinge (later frame, replaced assembly), 1-1/4" w x 1-1/2", **$750**.

B, micromosaic, black onyx, yg, polychrome floral bouquet inlaid in oval black onyx plaque, beveled edge, wiretwist frame, C-catch, tube hinge, 1-1/2" w x 1-3/4", **$900**.

(Courtesy of E. Foxe Harrell Jewelers, Clinton, IA).

Brooch/Pin, micromosaic, yg, goldstone glass, c. 1850, polychromatic Roman mosaic depicting St. Peter's Square set in goldstone glass, plain oval yg frame, replacement pin assembly, 2" w x 1-5/8", **$950**. (Courtesy of E. Foxe Harrell Jewelers, Clinton, IA).

Bar Brooch/Pin, micromosaic, 15k yg, c. 1870-80, Egyptian Revival, central cut-corner rect bar flanked by smaller vertical cut-corner rect plaques, each depicting pharaoh's' heads flanked by scrolled floral/foliate motifs in white, red, and lt brown on lt green ground, C-catch, 2" w x 1/2", **$850.** (Photo courtesy of Lovejoy's Estate Jewelry, Bellingham, WA).

Brooch/Pin, mosaic, 800 silver gilt, c. 1900-20, Egyptian Revival, winged insect with shades of green mosaic wings and body, silver wire legs and antennae, C-catch, tube hinge, 1-7/8" w x 7/8", **$450**. (Courtesy of E. Foxe Harrell Jewelers, Clinton, IA).

Brooch/Pin, *pietra dura*, yg, c. 1850, rect plaque depicting two butterflies in mottled brown, green, orange, yellow and white, one with inlaid "spots," on a black marble ground, in a plain yg grooved-edge frame, later-added pin back assembly, 1-3/4" w x 1-1/4", **$1,400**. (Courtesy of E. Foxe Harrell Jewelers, Clinton, IA).

Micromosaic, 18k yg, c. 1860-70, circ disk, polychrome mosaic depiction of a swan in a floral bg, blue and white geo border, yg bead and wiretwist decoration, yg mount, 7/8" dia, pr .... 748 (A)

Earrings, pendent

Micromosaic, 18k yg, c. 1870, circ yg surmount with bead and wire decoration surmounting a horizontal bar with appl beads at each end, suspending a central inverted balustered conical drop, flanked by balustered tubular rods suspending a circ disk centering a polychrome mosaic of a man's profile in one, a woman's profile in the other, terminating in a round yg bead, shepherd's hook findings, 3/4" w x 2-1/4" tl, pr .... 2,760 (A)

Micromosaic, 18k yg, c. 1870, circ disk surmount with quatrefoil mosaic, suspending a rect plaque surmounted by a horizontal balustered rod, flanked by two balustered rods with circ disk terminals, plaque lobed at the base, inlaid with a polychrome mosaic depiction of a classical draped female figure, terminating in a circ disk drop, disks inlaid with floral motif mosaic, 3/4" w x 2-1/8" tl, pr .... 4,600 (A)

Necklace

Micromosaic, silver gilt, c. 1870, a fringe of alternating cusped shield-shaped and vasiform plaques, the former with blue mosaic ground and polychrome mosaics depicting a variety of flowers and birds, the latter with red mosaic ground and white floral motifs, suspended from a chain of reeded tubular silver gilt links, 1" top to bottom, 15-1/2" tl .... 2,875 (A)

Buckle, mosaic, brass, c. 1880-1900, multi-lobed oval shape, floral motif mosaic in blue, white, yellow and green, brass double hasp, mkd "800", 1-1/2" w x 2-1/4", **$75**. (Mary Palmer collection).

Cuff buttons, mosaic, glass, yg, c. 1860-80, black glass disks, mosaics of winged lions (St. Mark's) one paw resting on shield, shades of brown, green, blue and white, plain bezel setting, 3/4" dia, pr, **$400**. (Courtesy of E. Foxe Harrell Jewelers, Clinton, IA).

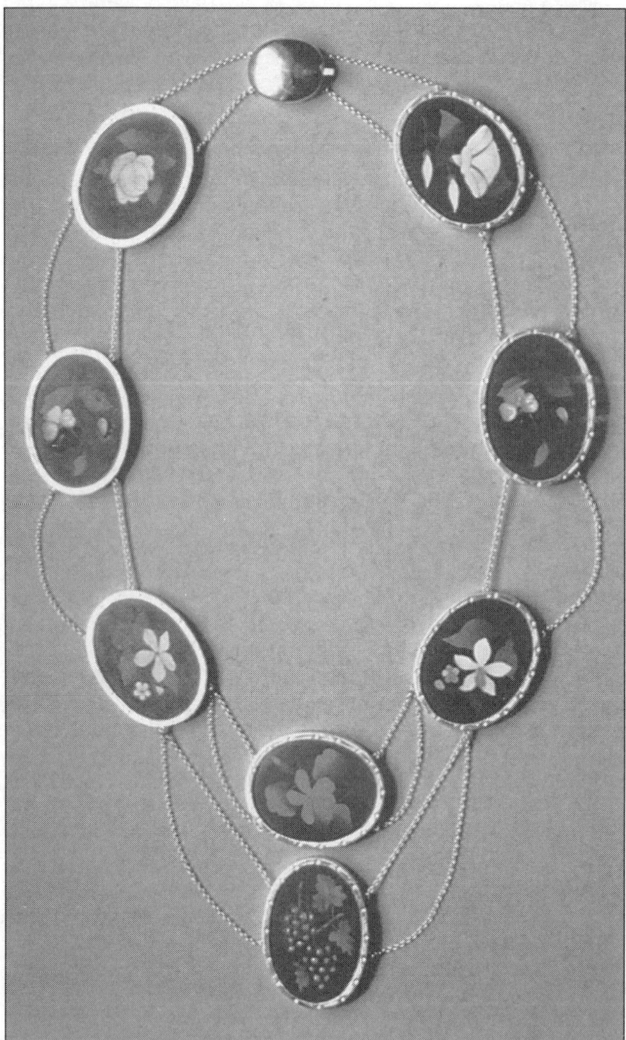

Necklace, *pietra dura*, 18k yg, c. 1810, oval plaques, each depicting a different floral motif (one at bottom center with grapes and leaves) in shades of white, green, red, blue and purple on black marble ground, set in notched yg frames and joined *en esclavage* with double lengths of fine yg swagged chain, terminating in an oval yg v-spring and box clasp, 16-1/2" tl, approx 2-1/2" top to bottom at center, **$2,000**. (Photo courtesy of Sharen and Nicholas Wood)

Ring, glass, mosaic, yg, c. 1840, elongated hexagonal purple glass inlaid with polychromatic mosaic of floral and foliate motif, bezel-set and mounted on narrow split shank, approx size 10-1/2, 5/8" w x 1-1/4", **$900**. (Courtesy of E. Foxe Harrell Jewelers, Clinton, IA).

Suite: Brooch and Earrings, micromosaic, yg, c. 1860, brooch an oval polychrome mosaic depicting scene of ruins, river, bridge, inlaid in black glass, yg frame, wiretwist border, later added pin assembly (safety catch), oval drop earrings, one depicting the Temple of Vesta, the other, the Forum, later added earwires (solder) brooch 1-3/4" w x 1-1/2", earrings 7/8" w x 1-1/8", **$2,250**. (Courtesy of E. Foxe Harrell Jewelers, Clinton, IA).

Suite: Bracelet, Brooch/Pin, and Earrings

Pietra dura, 14k yg, c. 1860, bracelet of five oval plaques alternating with foliate motif capped interlinks, each plaque a different polychrome floral motif inlaid in black marble, set in wiretwist decorated yg frames, v-spring and box clasp, brooch and each earring an oval of similar design, fitted box, bracelet 1-1/8" w x 5-1/4" tl, brooch 1-1/4" w x 1", earrings 5/8" w x 3/4", suite .... 2,530 (A)

Suite: Brooch/Pin and Earrings

Micromosaic, yg, glass, c. 1870, circ depiction of the Coliseum, polychrome tesserae on black glass ground, in a circ yg frame with wiretwist decoration, matching circ earrings, brooch 1-7/8" dia, earrings 1" dia .... 862 (A)

MANUFACTURED GOLD, GOLD-FILLED, GOLD-PLATED

History: The Revivalists inspired an interest in goldwork. All-gold jewelry was a novelty in the mid-nineteenth century. Before discoveries in California and Australia in 1849 and 1851 made larger quantities of gold more accessible, gemstones were the focal point of most jewelry. Gold was used sparingly in very thin filigree (*cannetille*) or repoussé work in the early part of the century. Later, heating, rolling and pressing, and electroplating, made a little gold go a long way, and gave machine-made articles the look of gold without the expense.

By the 1830s, the Industrial Revolution had come to jewelry manufacture. Birmingham became a major center for machine-made goods in England. The invention of electroplating in 1840 helped launch what was to become a huge costume jewelry industry in England and the United States (although the term "costume" jewelry wasn't coined until the early twentieth century).

The rolled gold plating process was brought to the U.S. from Great Britain in 1848 and was a big hit with New England jewelry manufacturers. Unlike electroplating, which was applied to a finished base metal article, rolled gold was a mechanical process for sheet and wire which was then used to manufacture a finished piece. The technique was derived from Sheffield plate, developed in 1743, which was copper clad with silver and rolled to the desired thickness. Rolled gold is copper or brass clad with gold, known as gold-filled in the U.S., and called *doublé d'or* by the French, who began using the technique as early as the 1820s. The metal "sandwich" was treated exactly the same as karat gold: stamped, engraved, and fashioned into pieces that were identical to their sold gold counterparts.

In the U.S., manufacturing centers grew along the Eastern seaboard: in Philadelphia, New York, Boston, and especially, in Providence, Rhode Island and the neighboring towns of Attleboro and North Attleboro, Massachusetts, and in Newark, New Jersey. Some of these manufacturers are still in business today.

It is worth noting that during the height of mid-Victorian Revivalism, several Newark firms produced quality pieces in Revivalist styles, comparable to those made in Europe. These jewels met with acceptance, however, only when they were sold as French or English-made. America's well-to-do believed their own country's product was inferior to that of Europe. Perhaps this was because Americans excelled in the mass production of inexpensive gold and gold-filled or plated items. Many of the factories that made these items were in Providence and the Attleboros, but Newark produced a sizable portion of them as well. Although the pieces were mass-produced, there was still some craftsmanship involved. The forms may have been die-stamped by machine (the preferred method at the time), but engraving, enameling, and finishing were done by hand.

Stamped jewelry backed with a flat plate is sometimes called "hollow work," and resembles hand-raised repoussé metalwork, in which the metal is worked from the back to create a design in relief. Engraving or chasing may be added to the front of the piece. This is the type of work that many people today consider typically Victorian, probably because it was produced in such quantities that a great deal of it has survived. Often, particularly in American pieces, the engraved depressions were partly filled with black enamel to enhance the design, called *taille d'épargne,* or "black enamel tracery."

The addition of gold fringe or bead-tipped foxtail chain tassels was common in pieces of the 1870s, a time when women's dresses were trimmed with abundant quantities of fringe. Long pendent earrings were in vogue, and were especially well-suited to tassels and fringing.

Garter bracelets, or *jarretières,* of gold or gold-plated brass mesh with fringed and tasseled ends, were worn in pairs. The bracelets were secured with an ornamental slide, often engraved and enameled, or set with a small cameo. They are sometimes referred to as slide bracelets, which can be confusing. Another type of bracelet is also called a slide bracelet, because it is made up of a collection of slides from longchains (see below)–a practice that began earlier in this century, after longchains went out of fashion. These slide bracelets became (and still are) popular enough to have been reproduced. The repros are fairly easy to detect. They don't have the "hodgepodge" look of a piece made up of old parts, as the originals are. Sometimes each slide is hallmarked in exactly the same way–a dead giveaway.

Bracelet, hinged bangle, 14k yg, enamel, c. 1860-70, oval, allover textured engr surface with central engr and *taille d'épargne* enameled floral/foliate, cusped and scrolled motif , 2" w, **$785**. (Photo courtesy of Lovejoy's Estate Jewelry, Bellingham, WA).

Hinged hollow bangles, both gold and gold-filled, are another kind of bracelet that remained popular throughout the Victorian period. They have become a classic form, and are still made today. Widths and decorative elements vary from wide and ornately engraved or decorated to narrow and plain. The "bypass" or "crossover" design, in which decorated ends of a narrow tubular bangle cross parallel to one another at the top, gained favor in the later part of the century.

One variety of necklace of typically Victorian manufacture is called a "bookchain" necklace. Stamped, flat, folded-over rectangles, resembling the shape of a book, form the links of a double-sided chain, usually engraved or decorated on both sides. The chain is held together in front by an ornate clasp or slide, often with a small cameo set in it, the ends extending like tassels. The design may have evolved from the practice of wearing a ribbon around the neck, pinned with the ends crossed in front.

Bracelets, hinged bangles, gf, c. 1870-80, hollow ovals, gf strips, beads, sm trefoils appl to front half, scalloped beaded borders, safety chain, 2-3/8" inside dia, 1/2" w, pr, **$195**. (Lenore Dailey collection).

Gold and gold-filled longchains and slides were practical as well as popular. A watch, lorgnette, or other useful (or decorative) item could be attached by means of a swivel hook and suspended from the chain. The ornamental slide was drawn up and the pendent piece pinned or tucked into a pocket or belt, causing the chain to drape attractively.

Lockets, another classic jewelry form, were popular throughout the nineteenth century, varying in size and shape. Large oval gold and gold-filled lockets on wide or thick chains were in keeping with style proportions of the Grand Period, 1860-80. Round and somewhat smaller lockets appeared toward the end of the century.

Gold-filled and electroplated jewelry was affordable to nearly everyone. Since it was manufactured in the same forms and styles as solid gold jewelry, unless there is enough wear on a piece to reveal base metal (usually brass), jewelry should be tested to determine if it is gold or gold-filled. Gold-filled pieces sell for a little more than half the price of their all-gold counterparts.

Occasionally, one hears the term "pinchbeck" used to refer to gold-filled or gold-plated brass jewelry (more commonly heard in Britain). This is a misnomer. In reality, pinchbeck is an alloy of copper and zinc formulated in the early eighteenth century by Christopher Pinchbeck as an inexpensive imitation gold. It fell out of favor as a substitute for gold when electroplating was invented (c. 1840), and truly met its demise when 9 karat gold was made legal in Britain in 1854. Most pinchbeck jewelry was made in England. It was imported by American jewelers, although some work was done here. Pre-Victorian pieces made from real pinchbeck are rarely seen today, despite some dealers' claims. If genuine, they are highly collectible, and expensive. The problem for collectors is that there is no readily available test for pinchbeck, as it closely resembles brass, only differing in proportions of copper to zinc.

The California Gold Rush of 1849 was followed by gold discoveries in Australia in 1851, the Black Hills of the Dakota territory in 1874, South Africa in 1886, and Alaska in 1898, thus ensuring a more plentiful supply of gold for the rest of the century. Two unique types of gold jewelry are directly connected to gold discoveries in the above-mentioned places, and to gold-mining in general. A sort of commemorative or souvenir jewelry came out of the mining industry. Pieces sometimes depicted picks and shovels and other accouterments of mining, and/or were set with small gold nuggets. These can be marked "Native Gold," "Alaska Gold," or other place name phrase.

Jewelry set with gold-in-quartz is a second type of mining-related jewelry, most closely associated with California. Quartz is the usual host mineral for gold, but it was more expensive to extract gold from the hard-rock mines than from placer mining, where natural forces had already separated the metal from its matrix. Gold-in-quartz was therefore called "rich man's gold." Jewelry set with polished pieces of it was considered status-symbol jewelry, now highly collectible, especially in California.

Nineteenth century gold jewelry is often unmarked. If hallmarks are present, however, they can help determine age and country of origin. The U.S. had no legal standards until 1906, but 14 and 10 karats were the most common alloys for mass-manufactured gold of the Victorian period. A few prestigious firms, such as Tiffany & Co., used 18k exclusively, others used it occasionally. The British used 9, 12, and 15 karat gold after 1854, when standards were lowered from 18 karat. According to some experts, unassayed (unmarked) gold before 1854 can be lower than 18k. Britons spell karat with a c; the abbreviation is "c" or "ct." If a British piece is hallmarked, the date of assay is indicated by a letter.

Assayed French gold is never lower than 18k; the hallmark is an eagle's head. Maker's marks are in a lozenge. Other European countries use three-digit numbers that are karat equivalents in thousandths, e.g., 750 equals 18k, 585 is 14k, etc. (see appendix, Marks on Metals).

References: Jeanenne Bell, *Answers to Questions About Old Jewelry,* 4th ed., Krause Publications, 1996; Ulysses G. Dietz, ed., *The Glitter & The Gold, Fashioning America's Jewelry,* The Newark Museum, 1997; Martha G. Fales, *Jewelry in America 1600-1900*, Antique Collectors' Club, 1995; Duncan James, *Old Jewellery*, Shire Publications, 1989; Yvonne Markowitz and Janice Staggs, "Goldmines, Goldrushes and Nugget Jewels," in *Metalsmith*, Vol. 16, No. 5, Fall 1996. **Marks:** Any book on English hallmarks can decipher them, but the venerable *Jackson's Hallmarks*, Ian Pickford, ed., Antique Collectors' Club, 1992, is now published in a portable pocket-sized edition. French and many other countries' hallmarks on gold and platinum are in Tardy's *Poinçons D'Or et de Platine*, Paris, 1988 (in French, no translation). Dorothy Rainwater, *American Jewelry Manufacturers*, Schiffer, 1988, is an indispensable source of information on American-made jewelry and marks. See also appendix, American Manufacturers.

Museum: Providence Jewelers' Museum, Providence, RI.

Bracelet

Bangle, hinged

14k yg, enamel, c. 1850-60, strap and buckle motif, allover floral/foliate engr, blue enameled ribbon striping on open oval buckle , 19.7 dwt, 1-1/4" w x 2-1/2" .... 1,495 (A)

14k yg, enamel, c. 1860-70, wide strap and buckle motif band with engr floral and foliate design, *taille d'épargne* enamel accents, v-spring and box clasp, safety chain, 32.0 dwt, 1-1/4" w (at top), 2-3/8" inside dia ... 1,035 (A)

14k yg, enamel, c. 1870, wide band, strap and buckle motif, allover engr floral design highlighted with black enamel tracery (*taille d'épargne)*, two panels added to enlarge bracelet, v-spring and box clasp, safety chain, 1-1/8" w, 2-1/4" inside dia... 575 (A)

14k yg, garnets, c. 1860-70, hinged triple coiled snake motif, faceted tubular yg terminating in snake head engr with floral/foliate scroll motif, sm circ garnet cab eyes and lg pear-shaped garnet cab at top, 1-1/2" w, 2-1/8" inside dia .... 805 (A)

14k yg, c. 1880, strap and buckle motif with appl beads and wiretwist decoration, two rows of appl wiretwist on the band, in a fitted box mkd "Crosby, Morse & Foss," v-spring and box clasp, safety chain, 1-1/8" w, 2-1/4" inside dia, pr.......... 1,840 (A)

Yg, c. 1880-90, top half with appl beads and wire along edges of central polished band flanked by ridged bands with ropetwist wire borders, v-spring and box clasp, 1" w, 2-3/8" inside dia .... 1,840 (A)

Gf, c. 1875, stamped and engr floral/foliate design on stippled ground, front half surmounted by appl stamped and engr buckle and strap motifs, inside imp "PATD AP'L (?) 1872," v-spring and box clasp, safety chain, 2-3/8" inside dia, 3/4" w 275

Flexible

Yg, enamel, diamonds, c. 1860-70, wide honeycomb mesh band, lg oval blue enameled front clasp, lg central incised star motif set with sm rc diamonds, surrounded by single star-set rc diamonds, tubular yg frame with scroll and wirework decoration, damage to enamel, clasp 2-1/4" w x 2-7/8", band 1-3/4" w x 6-1/2" tl...... 2,530 (A)

Garter

14k yg, enamel, c. 1870-80, a mesh link strap, circ disk slide surmounted by a lg engr and enameled loop with "doorknocker," engine-turned surface with outer band of black enamel, terminating in a bead-tipped foxtail chain fringe, 1/2" w .... 550 (A)

14k yg, enamel, seed pearls, c. 1880, chain mesh strap, cusped oval slide with four seed pearls, engr *taille d'épargne* enameled frame, foxtail chain tassels suspended from engr *taille d'épargne* enameled caps, damage to fringe, slide 1" w x 3/4", mesh 3/8" w .... $513 (A)

Gf, tiger's eye, c. 1870-80, chain mesh strap, 1/2" w, stamped shield-shaped cap terminating in bead-tipped foxtail chain fringe, stamped and engr rect slide with scalloped and cusped edge bezel-set with a rect tiger's eye cameo of a helmeted warrior, slide 1" x 7/8"..... 200

Link

14k yg, stone, Early Victorian, textured and pierced chain links alternating with polished fancy links, clasp a hand with gemstone ring and floral motif cuff, 1/2" w x 7" tl .... 1,150 (A)

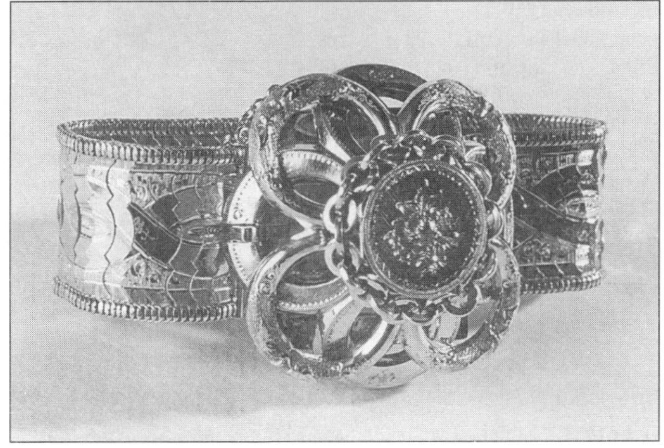

Bracelet, flexible, 14k yg, c. 1860, engr flexible mesh strap with front clasp a lg double open quatrefoil (one surmounting the other) stamped and engr, surmounted by a central circ hinged locket compartment with raised floral motif, within a chain link frame, 1-3/4" w, front clasp 2" x 2", **$975**. (Photo courtesy of Lovejoy's Estate Jewelry, Bellingham, WA).

Bracelet, slide, yg, gf, gemstones, made up of twelve assorted yg and gf late Victorian longchain slides set with a variety of gemstones (turq, seed pearls, sm rc diamonds, opals, sm rubies) alternating with yg bead spacers, strung on double chain, foldover clasp mkd "U.S.A. 10 k G.F. top" and maker's mk "JB" in a triangle, safety chain, 6-1/4" tl x 3/8", **$1,200**. (Courtesy of E. Foxe Harrell Jewelers, Clinton, IA).

Yg, enamel, turquoise, c. 1880-90, seven rect hinged plaques with floral and scroll motif enamel in shades of blue, red, and white, a larger rect plaque at each end, one end terminating in a semi-cylindrical link of similar motif, thirty-eight sm circ bead-set turq cabs throughout, bracelet folds up to become a book charm with each link a page, end links forming the binding and covers, safety chain, v-spring and box clasp, 1-1/4" w x 7" tl .... 1,093 (A)

Bracelets

Bangles, hinged

14k rose gold, enamel, c. 1870, engr and *taille d'épargne* enameled scroll and geo decoration on textured ground, 1" w, approx 2-1/8" inside dia, pr .... 1,150 (A)

14k yg, enamel, c. 1870, bands with engr floral, foliate, and scroll motifs, *taille d'épargne* enamel tracery (worn away), v-spring and box clasp, 1/2" w, 2-3/8" inside dia, pr .... 863 (A)

18k multicolored gold, c. 1880, band of appl floral and foliate motif, edges decorated with appl openwork, wiretwist, and beads, in a Tiffany & Co. box, 5/8" w, 2-1/4" inside dia, pr .... 3,450 (A)

Yg, rubies, c. 1880-90, of narrow tubular bypass form, each with one terminal an appl coiled snake with sm ruby cab eyes, the other a ball terminal with appl bead decoration, safety chains, approx 2-7/8" dia x 3/4", pr.......... 690 (A)

Brooch/Pin

10k yg, gold-in-quartz, seed pearls, enamel, Late Victorian, rounded-edge circ disk, center horizontal row of three

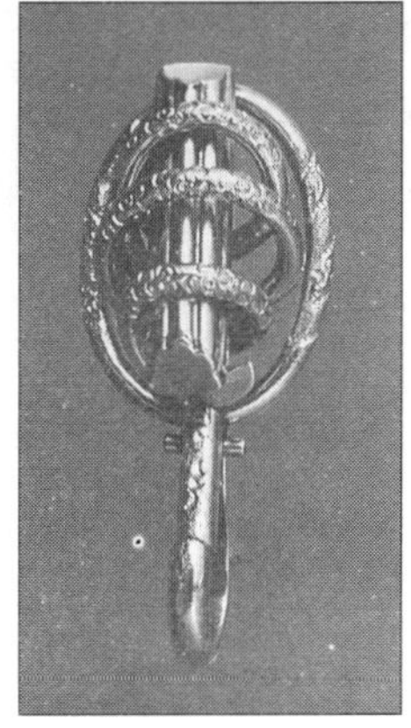

Brooch/Pin, Watch pin, yg, c. 1890-1900, open oval hollow tube frame, stamped and engr textured surface, continuing to a spiraling hollow tube around center fluted column , surmounting a hinged hook for a watch, 5/8" w x 1-1/2", **$125**. (Sue James collection).

split pearls flanked by two white mottled gold-in-quartz tablets within engr yg, vertical band of *taille d'épargne* enamel through center (slight damage), C-catch, tube hinge, 7/8" dia .... 633 (A)

Gilt metal, tinted photograph, glass, cloth, c. 1860-70, oval swivel with hp photograph of a mustachioed gentleman set under glass, glazed compartment containing cloth on rev within scalloped heavy wire outer frame, C-catch, tube hinge, 1-5/8" w x 1-7/8" 195

MOP, gf, c. 1880-90, "cake server" brooch with MOP handle, illegible mono on front, engr on rev "St. John 153," C-catch (bent), loop on end for chain, 1/2" w x 1-5/8" 90

Yg, enamel, ruby, c. 1875, undulating open oval snake motif, engr and dk blue enameled scales (some enamel loss), ruby eye, later-added pinback assembly (converted from a buckle), 2-1/8" w x 1-1/4" 500

Brooches/Pins

Gold-in-quartz, 14k rose gold, gold nugget, Late Victorian, one depicting a sq shovel, the other a pickax, handles inlaid with gray mottled gold-in-quartz, a gold nugget surmounting the shovel and pickax blades, C-catches, tube hinges, shovel 3/4" w x 2-3/8", pickax 1-1/4" w x 2", pr .... 3,450 (A)

Brooch/Pin, gf, photograph, c. 1880, swivel locket compartment, one side photo of young woman in c. 1880s dress, verso tintype of gentleman in c. 1840s dress, within undulating hollow tube and bead frame, C-catch, tube hinge, soldered loop for safety chain, 1-3/4" w x 2-1/4", **$200**. (Elaine Sarnoff collection).

Brooches/Pins, crescent and navette-shaped bars, yg nugget frames, fossil ivory centers, Alaska Gold Rush souvenirs, c. 1895-1900:

T, mkd "NATIVE GOLD," lever catch mkd "10k," 1" w x 7/8", **$225**.

TC, mkd "NATIVE GOLD NUGGETS," C-catch, 7/8" w x 3/8", **$125**.

BC, mkd "ALASKA GOLD," C-catch, 1-5/8" w x 1/2", **$200**.

B, mkd "NATIVE GOLD NUGGETS,", lever catch, 2-1/2" w x 3/8", **$300**. (Courtesy of E. Foxe Harrell Jewelers, Clinton, IA).

Watch pins, gf, c. 1880-90:

L, open oval wirework "wings," each with center bead-tipped wire, hook on rev for pendent watch, mkd "GGH Co," 1-3/8" w x 1/2", **$95**.

C, scrolled openwork trefoil shape with engr textured surface, hook on rev for pendent watch, 1" w x 1", **$65**.

R, open trefoil flanked by open cusped terminals, hook on rev for pendent watch, mkd "CT" on hook, 1" w x 1", **$65**. (Sue James collection).

Chatelaine, handkerchief holder, yg, enamel, c. 1880-1900, black enameled engr scallop shell and fleur-de-lis motif tongs with sliding ring closure, suspended from cable link chain and finger ring, 4-1/2" tl, tongs 1/2" w x 1-3/4" tl, **$300**. (Courtesy of E. Foxe Harrell Jewelers, Clinton, IA).

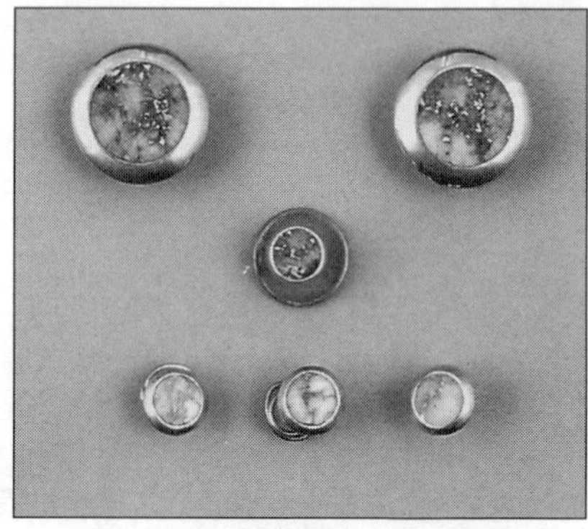

Dress Set, gold-in-quartz, rose gold, c. 1890-1900, pr of cuff links, collar button and three studs, flat circ disks of gold-in-quartz set flush in rose gold mounts, button-style (disk) backs on cuff links, 7/8" dia, and collar button 3/8" dia, spiral wires on studs, 1/4" dia, set, **$650**. (Charles Pinkham collection).

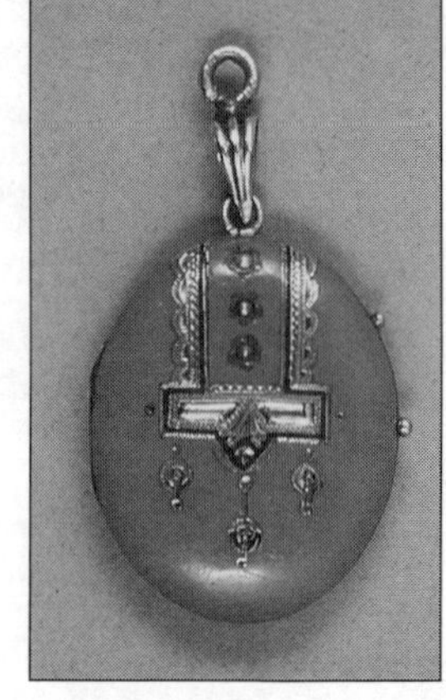

Locket, enamel, gf, c. 1900, sky blue enameled oval locket, engr and *taille d'épargne* enameled design, vertical row of three seed pearls set in flower head design, 7/8" w x 1-1/2", **$150**. (Elaine Sarnoff collection).

Cuff Links

14k yg, c. 1900, double-sided oval yg plaques with raised figures of putti playing golf, maker's mk for Eckfeldt & Ackley (an acorn), Newark, NJ , 1/2" w x 3/4" .... 1,265 (A)

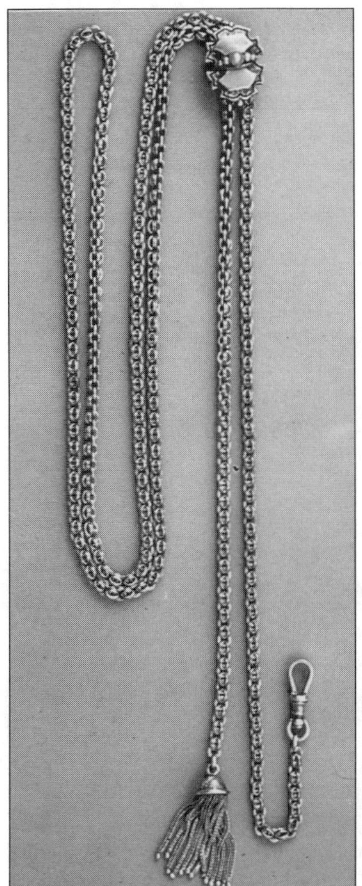

Longchain, yg, enamel, seed pearl, c. 1870-80, reeded double circ links terminating in a bead-tipped foxtail chain tassel with engr and enameled cap at one end and a swivel at the other, notched shield-shaped engr slide, *taille d'épargne* border, slide 5/8" w x 7/8", chain 44" tl, **$1,000**. (Yolanda Tisdale collection).

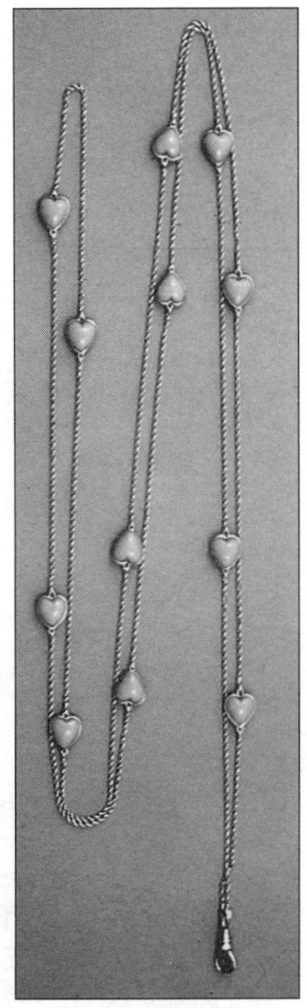

Longchain, 9k yg, glass, c. 1900, ropetwist yg chain interspersed with collet-set heart-shaped turq-colored glass double cabs, terminating in a swivel hook, 30" tl, **$350**. (Paula Straub collection).

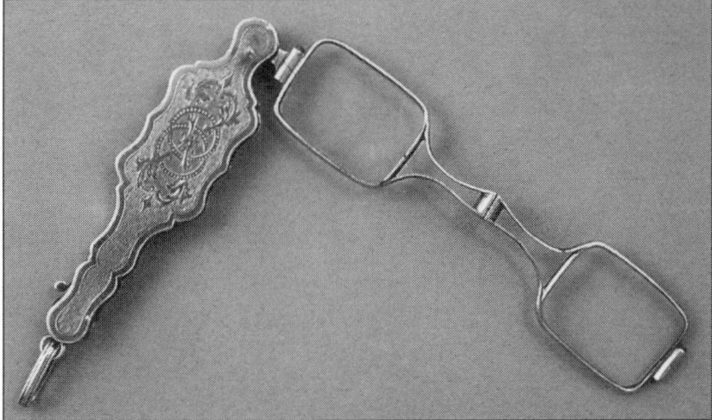

Lorgnette, yg, glass, c. 1880, scalloped and cusped outline, foliate engr yg case containing a pr of folding spectacles, oval link bail at one end, trigger (spring-loaded) mechanism, spectacles 4" w open, 3/4" w x 3-3/8" tl, **$450**. (Yolanda Tisdale collection).

Dress Set

Gold-in-quartz, 14k yg, Late Victorian, dumbbell-type cuff links, each set with a lg and sm oval gold-in-quartz cab, 5/8" x 1/2", three shirt studs, each with a circ disk of gold-in-quartz, 1/2" dia, set .... 1,265 (A)

Hatpin

Yg, c. 1900, hollow sphere with pierced scrollwork design (slightly dented), 5/8" dia, yg pinstem, 6" tl 125

Locket

14k rose and yg, seed pearls, c. 1870, cusped and scrolled shield shape, appl beads and wiretwist, vertical row of seed pearls above concave flowerhead with pearl center, compartment on rev containing a dried flower, 1-3/8" w x 2-1/4" tl... 805 (A)

Locket and Bookchain Necklace

Gf, enamel, c. 1880, die-stamped and engr tapered rect links, double spring rings at the ends of front two-link extension suspending an engr and *taille d'épargne* enameled oval locket (possible marriage), locket 7/8" w x 1-5/8", bookchain 19-1/2" tl x 1/2" w 350

Lorgnette

Yg, opal, rock crystal quartz, c. 1890, shell and S-scroll motif border, monogrammed in the center, suspended from a swivel hook on a yg chain interspersed with seven opal and rock crystal quartz rondelles, 1" w x 3-3/4" .... 1,380 (A)

Neckchain

Yg, c. 1860, interlocking engr circ links with four circ clasps, 1/2" w x 22" tl .... 1,840 (A)

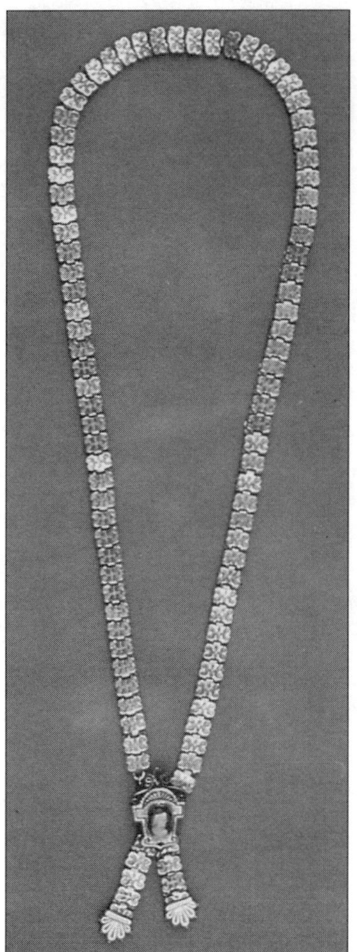

Necklace, Bookchain, gf, hardstone cameo, c. 1870-80, stamped rounded rect links, shield-shaped stamped, eng and *taille d'épargne* enameled front clasp surmounted by a sm cameo, scrolled wirework at top border, terminating in two ends stamped to look like tassels, 18" tl x 1/4", clasp 5/8" w x 3/4", **$250**. (Author's collection).

Yg, c. 1880-90, quatrefoil links, central bead with appl circ braided wire and circ interlinks, 1/4" w x 42" tl .... 1,840 (A)

Longchain

14k yg, enamel, seed pearls, c. 1870, splayed circ links suspending two foxtail chain tassels, engr and *taille d'épargne* enameled sq slide set with seed pearls, 62" tl, 48.0 dwt.. 1,955(A)

Gf, yg, opals, c. 1890, ropetwist gf chain terminating in a swivel hook, rect yg slide with heart-shaped center set with three sm circ opals, 49" tl, slide 3/8" w x 1/4" ... 150

Pendant, rose and yg, pearls, c. 1870-80, cushion-shaped filigree and beaded frame around alternating rose and yg stamped and engr leaves enclosing central berries and leaves motif in beading, pearls and similar larger rose and yg leaves, filigree bail, 1-7/8" w x 2-3/4" tl, **$800**. (Courtesy of E. Foxe Harrell Jewelers, Clinton, IA).

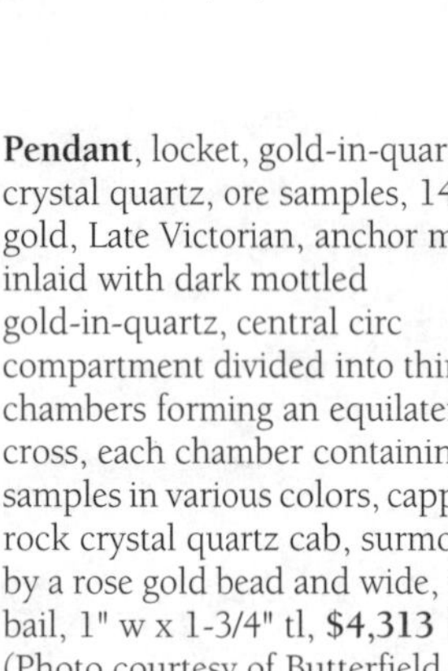

Pendant, locket, gold-in-quartz, rock crystal quartz, ore samples, 14k rose gold, Late Victorian, anchor motif inlaid with dark mottled gold-in-quartz, central circ compartment divided into thirteen chambers forming an equilateral cross, each chamber containing ore samples in various colors, capped by a rock crystal quartz cab, surmounted by a rose gold bead and wide, tapered bail, 1" w x 1-3/4" tl, **$4,313** [A]. (Photo courtesy of Butterfield & Butterfield, 6/25/97).

Pendant, cross, yg, rc garnets, c. 1850, die-stamped two-sided (hollow) reeded and scrolled yg front set with central rc garnet cluster, three rc garnets in millegrained bezels set in each scrolled terminal, 1-7/8" w x 2-3/4", **$900**. (Courtesy of E. Foxe Harrell Jewelers, Clinton, IA).

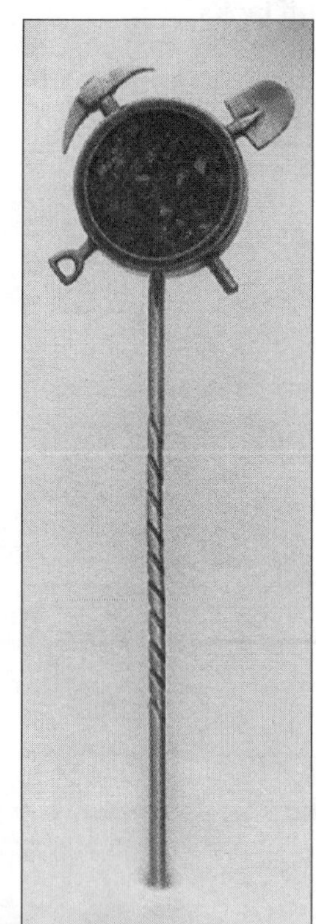

Scarf Pin/Stickpin, gold-in-quartz, ore samples, 14k rose gold, Late Victorian, segmented circ compartments (four on each side) containing eight ore samples, rose gold crossed pick and shovel motifs mounted on outer frame, in a fitted box mkd "Tiffany & Co.," 3/4" dia x 3-3/8" tl, **$3,738** [A]. (Photo courtesy of Butterfield & Butterfield, 6/25/97).

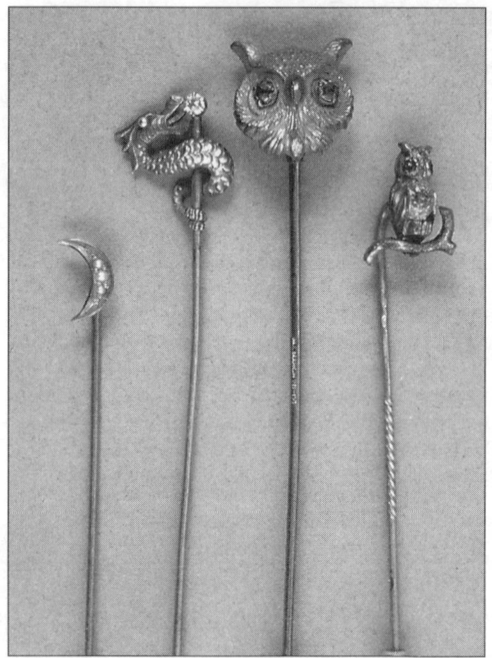

Scarf Pins/Stickpins, yg and gp, c. 1900:

L, 10k yg, crescent moon set with seed pearls, 1/4" w x 3/8", 2-1/8" tl, **$95**.

CL, 14k yg, dragon motif, prong-set with sm oe diamond, rev imp "14k," maker's mk for Carter, Gough & Co., Newark NJ, 1/2" w x 5/8", 2-3/4" tl, **$300**.

CR, Gp base metal, glass, owl's head mounted *en tremblant*, colorless r.s. eyes, pinstem mkd "PAT MARCH 20 –00," head 1/2" w x 1/2", 2-3/4" tl, **$100**.

R, Gp base metal, owl on branch, 3/8" w x 1/2", 2-1/4" tl, **$50**.

(Elaine Sarnoff collection).

Muff Chain

Yg, green stone, Early Victorian, overlapping and spiraling circ links with stamped star design, clasp a matte finish hand wearing a jeweled ring and engr floral design cuff, 1/2" w, 83" tl .... 10,120 (A)

Yg, red stone, Early Victorian, loop-in-loop circ links with beaded textured surface, clasp a matte finish hand wearing a red stone jeweled ring, engr floral cuff, 3/8" w x 57-1/2" tl .... 7,475 (A)

Yg, red stone, Early Victorian, overlapping circ links with stamped geo design, clasp a matte finish hand wearing red stone jeweled ring, engr floral cuff, 3/8" w, 45-1/2" tl .... 7,475 (A)

Yg, ruby, colorless stone, Early Victorian, alternating rope and chased links in interwoven spiraling design, clasp a matte finish hand with colorless stone jeweled ring and elaborate foliate cuff with triangular bezel-set ruby, 3/8" w x 22" tl .... 3,680 (A)

Necklace, sautoir

Yg, c. 1880-90, scalloped mesh band with pear-shaped ribbed terminals flanked by beads and scrolls suspending foxtail chain tassels, 1/2" w x 39" tl .... 1,840 (A)

Pendant and Chain

14k yg, enamel, amethyst, seed pearls, c. 1880, engr shield-shape with cusped sides and top, central oval prong-set amethyst flanked by six seed pearls, wirework and *taille d'épargne* enamel accents, on a fancy link chain, converted from longchain and slide, pendant 1-3/8" w x 1-1/8", chain 27" tl .... 855 (A)

Pendent Earrings

15k yg, c. 1870, round chased surmount, suspending a chased open yg knot, terminating in two bead-tipped foxtail chain tassels with engr caps, shepherd's hook findings, 3/4" w x 2", pr .... 1,380 (A)

Suite: Brooch and Pendent Earrings

14k yg, c. 1870, brooch with wiretwist-decorated double horizontal brackets, top surmounted by a shell motif flanked by scrolled wirework, four lozenge-shaped terminals flanking central disk surmounted by a quatrefoil motif, suspending a fringe of grad rods, center rod terminating in a lozenge, side rods with bead terminals, matching pendent earrings, each a domed rect surmount suspending a single bracket terminating in lozenges and beads, shepherd's hook earwires, brooch 1-1/4" w x 2-1/2" tl, earrings 5/8" w x 1-1/4", suite .... 1,093 (A)

Gf, c. 1870, brooch an arched rectangle with appl and engr foliate motifs and with drops at terminals, suspending lg central pendant with engr and appl foliate motifs and three drops, C-catch, tube hinge, 1-3/8" w x 2-1/2" tl, earrings same as central drop of brooch, replaced ear wires, 5/8" w x 2" tl, suite 400

Suite: Brooch/Pin and Earrings

18k tricolor gold, c. 1870, brooch an arched top with appl foliate decoration and scrolled wire and bead terminals, surmounted by inverted overlapping triangles, suspending an openwork concentric ovals drop held together with triangular and rect brackets at top and sides, further suspending a wide open oval drop with appl foliate motifs, looping around concentric ovals from front to back, appl bead and wiretwist decoration, matching earrings of similar design with annular surmounts, in a fitted box mkd "Tiffany & Co.", brooch 1-1/2" w x 2-1/4" tl, earrings 1" w x 1-7/8" tl, suite .... 2,645 (A)

Suites: Brooches and Pendent Earrings, yg, c. 1870:
T, rect yg bar, wiretwist, mesh and beaded decoration suspending a woven yg basket filled with sm coral beads, C-catch, tube hinge, pendent earrings, each a basket with coral beads suspended from coral bead cluster, yg frame and earwire, brooch 1-1/2" w x 1-5/8" tl, earrings 5/8" w x 1-3/4" tl, suite, **$1,000**.
B, brooch an arcing yg top set with an inner border of calibré-cut turq in an inverted U shape, surmounted by scrollwork flanking four lozenge-shaped turq mounted on wires, opposed C-scrolls suspending a lg yg bead and a pendant of a scrolled shield-shaped frame with 3 lozenge-shaped turq flanked by S-scrolls and beading around outside edge, enclosing an articulated beaded-edge lozenge-shaped drop set with calibré-cut turq, C-catch, tube hinge, upturned hook on rev for safety chain and pin, 1-1/2" w x 3-1/4" tl, earrings match pendant portion of brooch, suspended from lg yg bead surmounts, lg kidney earwires, 3/4" w x 2-1/2" tl, suite, **$2,200**. (Courtesy of E. Foxe Harrell Jewelers, Clinton, IA).

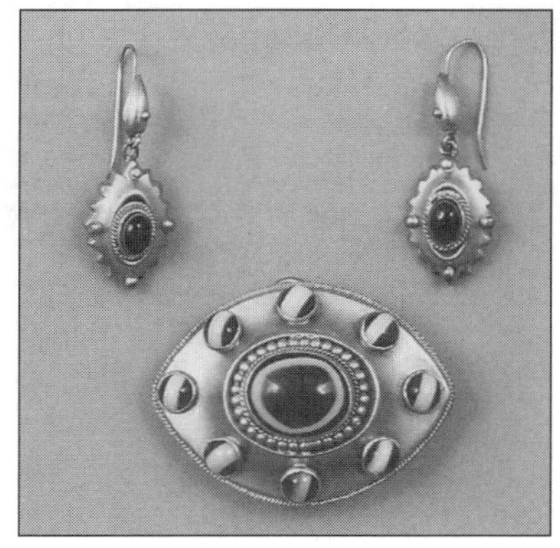

Suite: Brooch and Earrings, yg, banded agate, c. 1870, navette-shaped brooch, center bezel-set with oval black and white banded agate cab surrounded by bead trim and outer row of eight smaller bezel set circ banded agate cabs, compartment for hair on rev, matching earrings, each with one central agate cab, suspended from teardrop-shaped surmount, brooch, C-catch, tube hinge, jump ring for safety chain, 1-3/4" w x 1-1/4", earrings, hook earwires, 1/2" w x 1-1/4" tl, suite, **$495**. (Courtesy of E. Foxe Harrell Jewelers, Clinton, IA).

Watch Chain

14k yg, c. 1880, elliptical open links with foliate motif centers alternating with sm circ links, 16.7 dwt, 1/2" w x 8-1/2" tl .... 488 (A)

Watch Chain and Fob

14k yg, agate, gp brass, c. 1880, open rounded rect links, terminating at one end with a swivel hook, the other with a T-bar, and suspending a double-sided oval banded agate tablet in a gp brass frame, chain 16" tl......... 741 (A)

Watch Fob

9k yg, glass, brass, c. 1860-70, engr oval links terminating at one end in a swivel hook clasp, the other with a brass T-bar, suspending a brass fob with citrine-colored glass, 3/8" w x 15" tl .... 285 (A)

LATE VICTORIAN (AESTHETIC PERIOD) c. 1880-1901

By the 1880s, Victorian society was beginning to change. In celebration of 50 years on the throne in 1887, Queen Victoria was willing to relax her strict rules of mourning a little, much to the relief of her subjects. Fashions had changed, too. Victoria was no longer as influential as her beautiful daughter-in-law, Princess Alexandra, who was already a trend-setting fashion plate.

In keeping with a new "aestheticism," lines were simpler, fabrics lighter. Flounces and trains were abandoned in favor of smooth curves. Delicate lace replaced heavy fringe. After a short period of protruding emphasis, the bustle became a vestige of its former self as fullness transferred to "leg-o'-mutton" and "balloon" sleeves. Collars grew higher and tighter. The tailored look was in vogue. Women were becoming more active, in the work force and at leisure, and required proper attire. Their only remaining extravagance was their headgear. Hats were large and decorated profusely with bows, ribbons, lace, flowers, plumes and feathers–sometimes entire birds. Ornamental hatpins grew to great lengths to keep them in place.

Attitudes about jewelry were also affected. Elaborate ostentation gave way to refined simplicity. Heavy, dark, somber, massive and ornate jewelry was losing favor. Lighthearted, light-colored and delicate pieces took its place. Silver replaced gold for daytime wear. Many female aesthetes–early feminists rebelling against constricting fashions and protesting the notion of woman as decorative object–no longer wore any jewelry at all during the day. Diamonds continued to be the evening jewels of choice amongst most ladies of wealth and status, however.

Jewelry in general was reduced in dimension even when worn in quantity. Brooches were smaller, often worn in multiples. Crescents and stars were popular motifs. Some had utilitarian purposes as veil, lace, hat, bodice, skirt, or cuff pins. These were also called "handy pins" or "beauty pins." Earrings shrank to diminutive proportions. Sometimes they were nothing more than a single small stone, pearl, or stud. Until the 1890s, earrings were made for pierced ears. By the end of the century, however, women were beginning to look upon ear-piercing as a barbaric practice. The screwback finding was invented as a solution. The earliest "attachment for holding ear-jewels" for unpierced ears was patented in 1894. Its use gradually superseded the earwire and stud post; by the 1920s, screwbacks were predominant.

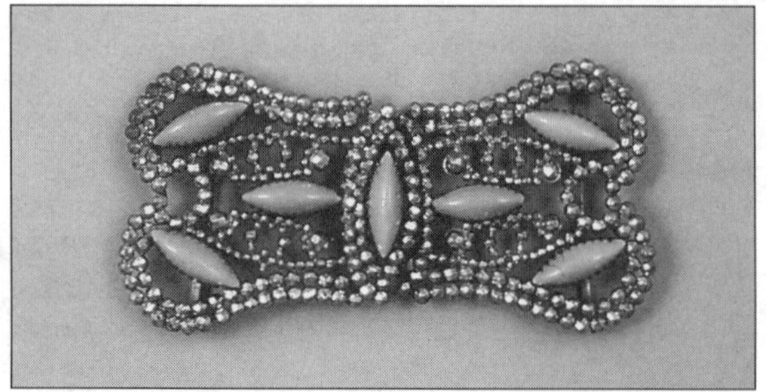

Buckle, cut steel, glass, brass, c. 1890, turq colored glass marquise cabs set in two pc bow-shaped frame, riveted throughout with cut steel studs, 3-7/8" w x 2", **$125**. (Courtesy of E. Foxe Harrell Jewelers, Clinton, IA).

Necklaces were fringes or festoons of linked gemstone drops and chains. Princess Alexandra was the instigator of the dog-collar necklace, a high, wide choker, usually of diamonds and/or pearls, which became an Edwardian trademark when she became Queen. In the U.S., the American "royal," Consuelo Vanderbilt (who became the Duchess of Marlborough in 1895), popularized the look with her dog collar of nineteen rows of pearls and diamond clasps. Both ladies had the requisite long slender necks for wearing such a jewel. Bracelets continued to be worn in multiples, growing narrower toward the end of the period. Bangles were tubular or open knife-edge wires joined by an ornamental device in front. Curb-link bracelets in gold or silver were also fashionable, often joined with a heart-shaped padlock clasp. Small waists were a fashion focal point; wide belts and ornamental buckles were commonly worn.

Chatelaines, derivatives of a chain worn by medieval keepers of keys, were once again in fashion, having returned in a slightly altered state from those of the early nineteenth century. Perhaps this was because of the focus on the waist, but it was also because Alexandra favored them. Late nineteenth century chatelaines performed a number of different specialized utilitarian and decorative functions. Various implements were suspended by chains from a decorative clasp that hooked over a belt or waist sash. They were a sort of housewife's tool kit. Scissors, needle cases and other sewing tools, notepads and pencils, match safes, coin purses, spectacles cases, and other assorted useful items could be hung from swivel hooks on a chatelaine. Most of these were decorated with repoussage, stamping or engraving. Those made of silver appealed to aesthetic tastes, especially after the trend-setting Princess Alexandra was seen wearing one.

Chatelaine, sp brass, fabric, c. 1890, spectacles case, Beaux-arts style, ornately stamped and pierced with foliated scrolls, appl female head on waist plaque, lions' heads and a shield on fabric-lined case suspended from stamped ornate quatrefoil link chain, adjustable hook on rev of waist clasp, 1-1/2" w x 9-3/4" tl, **$350**. (Martha Exline collection).

Sporting jewelry grew in popularity as women became more involved in outdoor activities. Horseshoes and animal motifs - fox and hounds, horses, game birds, etc.–were worn with tailored clothing. Both women and men wore reverse-painted crystal intaglios, an often-used decoration for stickpins, cuff links, and small brooches.

Animal and bird motifs showed up in gem-set novelty brooches and stickpins. The ubiquitous snake was joined by lizards and salamanders, bats, frogs, mice, butterflies and other insects, and swallows.

Japanese motifs and designs gained approval after new trade relations were opened with Japan in the 1850s, and Japanese decorative arts and crafts were introduced to the West at international exhibitions in the 1860s and 70s. Interest in things Japanese coincided with the growth of the Aesthetic Movement in Britain, France, and the U.S. The tenets of the movement embraced the Oriental approach to design: simplicity of form and inspiration from nature. Japanese fans, bamboo, scenes, and other ornamental devices, collectively referred to as *japonaiserie* (also called "Japanesque" and "japonisme"), began to crop up in jewelry, particularly in silver and mixed-metals, imitating metalworking techniques used in Japanese sword-making. Tiffany & Co. won the Grand Prix for their "Japanesque" mixed-metals designs in silverware at the Paris Exposition of 1878. They applied the same techniques to jewelry.

In 1876, Japan banned the wearing of swords and ended the feudal system, thus sounding the death knell for the samurai warrior. But the masterful metalwork of Japanese sword-makers lived on in jewelry. Sometimes the sword fittings themselves became jewelry, and were exported to the West. The Japanese also made jewelry to suit Western tastes. It is important to clarify the meanings of the Japanese words "shakudo" and "shibuichi": these are words for Japanese metal alloys (not the decorative metalwork technique itself), similar to the English word "sterling" for an alloy of silver and copper. Japanese metalworking techniques have a number of different names, but what Westerners erroneously refer to as "shakudo" is usually a raised design with gold and silver inlaid into a background metal (*shakudo* or *shibuichi*), a technique known as damascene work in Western culture. The general Japanese term for this type of work is "*zogan,*" but each variation of the technique has a different name. Japanese inlay is often imitated with die-stamped designs in shakudo or shibuichi overlaid with thin gold and silver foil accents.

International expositions continued to play an important role in the dissemination and marketing of new ideas and trends in fashion and jewelry. Two more Expositions Universelles were held in Paris in 1889 and 1900. The World's Columbian Exposition in Chicago in 1893 was another exhibition that brought international prestige and recognition to the U.S. Tiffany and Gorham each had their own pavilion, and numerous other American and European manufacturers were well-represented with displays of jewelry.

References: Genevieve E. Cummins and Nerylla D. Taunton, *Chatelaines, Utility to Glorious Extravagance*, Antique Collectors' Club, 1994; Oppi Untracht, *Jewelry Concepts and Technology,* Doubleday, 1985.

Brooch/Pin

Paste, sp brass, c. 1880-90, open oval of colorless circ cut pastes encircling one lg and 6 sm colorless pastes forming flowerhead, cut-down collet mounts, open back (a jour), C-catch, tube hinge, extended pinstem, 1-1/2" w x 1-1/4" 100

"Vauxhall" glass, c. 1880-90, marquise-cut foiled red glass (red under colorless glass) stones, overlapping layers forming flowerhead, japanned metal backing, C-catch, tube hinge, foiling off one stone (outside edge chipped), 1-3/8" dia 175

Scarf Pin/Stickpin

Brass, enamel, c. 1880, disk with black and white enameled swallow, surmounting an easel, 3-1/4" tl, 1/2" w x 7/8" 45

Gp brass, r.s., c. 1900, three-dimensional die-stamped head of man with cap, r.s. eyes, 2-7/8" tl, 5/8" w x 5/8" 75

Sp brass, c. 1890-1900, stamped three-dimensional woman with plumed hat, 2-3/8" tl, 1/2" w x 5/8" 60

Black glass, c. 1900, molded skull and cross bones, 2-1/8" tl, 3/8" w x 1/2" 75

EARLY CELLULOID

History: The first uses for the first commercially successful semi-synthetic plastic, invented in 1868 and dubbed Celluloid by its inventor, John Wesley Hyatt, were utilitarian. The initial motive for its invention was as a substitute for ivory billiard balls. Although that use proved impractical, celluloid was in fact an acceptable material for other uses, such as for detachable collars and cuffs, piano keys, and hair combs. Manufacturers of the latter took advantage of celluloid's ability to imitate tortoiseshell, a natural plastic. Makers of inexpensive jewelry found a use for celluloid too, as imitation coral and ivory. The earliest jewelry was made by the Celluloid Manufacturing Co. in 1875. It wasn't until the 1920s that "frankly fake" celluloid jewelry was made (see Plastics and Novelty section).

References: Shirley Bury, *Jewellery, 1789-1910, The International Era*, Vol. I; Sylvia Katz, *Early Plastics*,

Shire Publications, Ltd., 1986; Keith Lauer and Julie P. Robinson, *Celluloid, A Collectors' Reference and Value Guide*, Collector Books, 1998.

Advisors: Keith Lauer, Julie P. Robinson.

Bracelets, Bangles, hinged, celluloid, gf, wm, c. 1880, matched pr, ivory-colored celluloid inlaid with gf and wm, front half of each decorated with three sm floral motifs flanked by borders of notched and straight strips (a notched strip missing from one), imitating pique work, gf clasp, safety chain, pr, **$375**. (Author's collection).

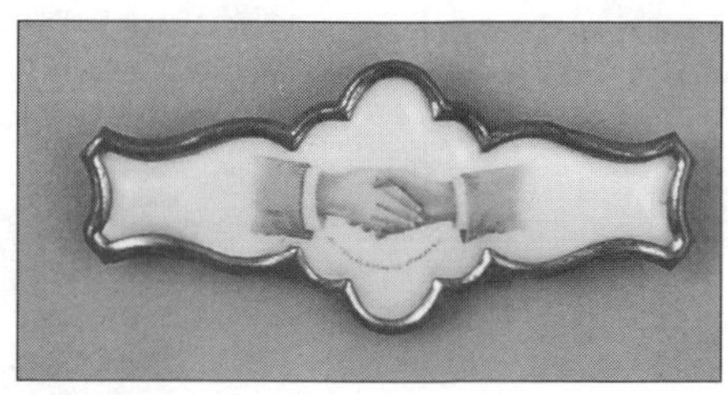

Brooch/Pin, Bar, celluloid, gp brass, c. 1895, lobed, convex/concave outline gp frame holding cut-to-shape ivory-colored celluloid plaque with central transfer print of clasped hands, sm print underneath reading "Whitehead & Hoag Co. Newark N.J.," bent wire pin back on rev surmounting a second blunt-ended wire assembly for holding a wide ribbon, rev imp "The Whitehead & Hoag Co." and "Pat. Oct. 18 '92, Mar. 7 '93," patents for badges with ribbons for societies or groups with insignias, this one being for the mfr itself, 2-7/8" w x 1-1/4", **$75**. (Author's collection).

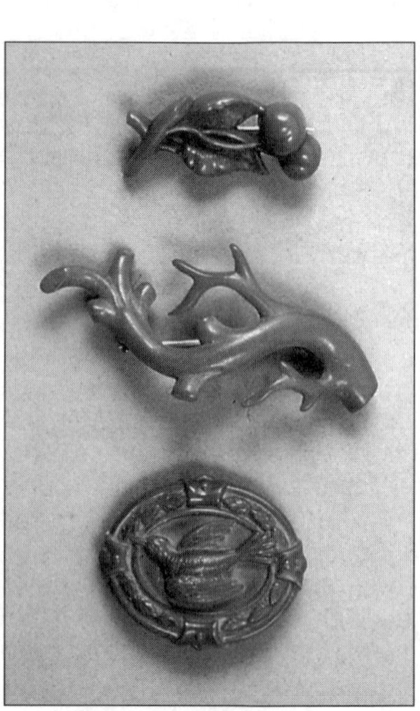

Brooches/Pins, imitation coral (early celluloid), metal, c. 1880:

T, pair of cherries, leaves and branch, metal pin assembly, C-catch, tube hinge, 1-5/8" w x 5/8", **$85**.

C, imitation coral "branch," metal pin assembly, C-catch, flanged hinge, 2-3/4" w x 1-1/4", **$150**.

B, oval medallion, molded pheasant motif in center, 1-5/8" w x 1-3/8", **$125**. (Courtesy of E. Foxe Harrell Jewelers, Clinton, IA).

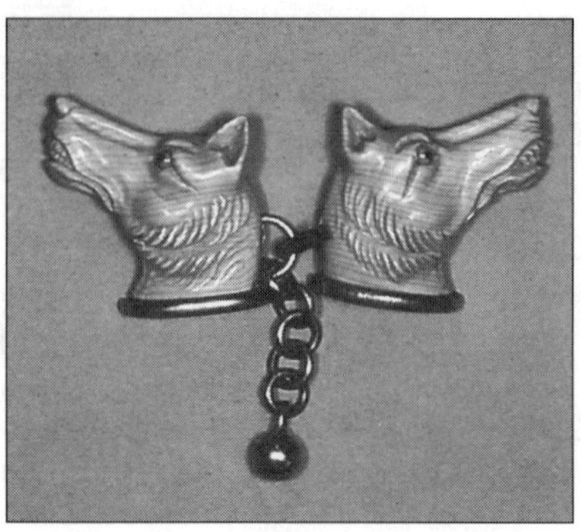

Cape Clasp, celluloid, glass, wm, paint, c. 1880, molded in the shape of three-dimensional ivory-colored and grained wolfs' heads with ptd black glass eyes, wm collars, chain and hook closure, unmkd, attributed to the Celluloid Co. of Newark, NJ, 3-1/2" w x 1-1/2", **$200**. (Photo courtesy of Julie P. Robinson).

Necklace, Bead, celluloid, brass, c. 1890, sm central celluloid and brass disk flanked by ovoid and round coral-colored celluloid beads with stamped brass filigree caps interspersed with sm cylindrical beads, continuing to a chain of cylindrical coral-colored celluloid beads strung on brass eyepins, suspending a drop of two linked grad round coral-colored celluloid beads with ornate stamped filigree brass caps, 2" w (at center, 38" tl, **$200**. (Photo courtesy of Julie P. Robinson).

SILVER AND MIXED METALS

History: Silver as a metal for jewelry has fluctuated in popularity and application. In the eighteenth and nineteenth centuries it was customarily used for setting diamonds and colorless paste, or, disguised with gilding, for making "imitation" jewels look "real." It wasn't until the latter part of the nineteenth century that silver came into its own as a material to be used for its aesthetic and sculptural qualities alone. Changing fashions, historical events and discoveries, and the Aesthetic Movement itself contributed to the metal's appreciation.

The discovery of the Comstock Lode in Nevada in 1859 made silver readily available to manufacturers in the U.S. and Britain. Its relatively low cost meant that silver jewelry was now affordable to almost everyone. The *japonaiserie* craze of the 1870s and early 80s led British and American manufacturers to produce stamped silver "trinkets" engraved with Japanese motifs. In the U.S., it was permissible to include copper in a fashion similar to the way in which Japanese alloys of copper and silver (*shibuichi*) and copper and gold (*shakudo*) were used, but assay laws prohibited British manufacturers from doing so. Touches of rose and yellow gold were added to silver for a "mixed-metals" effect.

The locket and the hinged bangle were favorite forms in silver. They were stamped, engraved, and embellished with beaded edges and applied motifs such as buckles, flowers and leaves, crosses and anchors. Pastes continued to be set in silver brooches and buckles.

After a decline in the wearing of daytime jewelry in the mid 1880s, silver jewelry regained favor in the waning years of the century. Message and "love brooches" were all the rage amongst the working class. These were stamped and engraved with the names of loved ones or other endearing terms. A Biblical reference, "Mizpah," sent the message: "The Lord watch between me and thee when we are absent one from another." The language of flowers was also used to send sentimental signals to loved ones: forget-me-nots (remembrance), ivy (friendship), and a different meaning for every variety of rose. Other popular symbols were the anchor of hope, the cross of faith, the heart of charity, the good-luck horseshoe, and lovebirds. Silver coins were also used for "love tokens," engraved with ciphers or names of family members or loved ones and made into bracelets or brooches. Jubilee jewelry was another sentimental working-class favorite, commemorating Queen Victoria's Diamond Jubilee, the sixtieth anniversary of her reign. Brooches would usually bear Victoria's cipher (VR or VRI) and the years 1837 and 1897 along with other engraved decoration. Touches of gold might be added. Those who could afford it wore gem-set versions.

Silver belts, buckles, clasps and chatelaines were frequently worn during the Aesthetic period, emphasizing the tiny corseted waist that women suffered so much to achieve.

Only a few American makers are associated with silver jewelry of this period. Those that are made jewelry as an adjunct to their other silver wares, notably Tiffany, Gorham, and George W. Shiebler. Tiffany's and Gorham's pieces were generally in keeping with the style of the times, mostly buckles and bracelets in the aesthetic taste. Shiebler's work followed a different bent, which proved successful enough to be imitated by others. Most well-known is Shiebler's "curio medallion" series, depicting profiles of Greek and Roman deities, which can be found on brooches, bracelets, cuff links, and also on the handles of flatware. Greek lettering was sometimes added. According to an article on Shiebler by Janet Zapata and D. Albert Soeffing (cited below), this series was produced from about 1880 to 1900. A quote from an 1892 article about the firm in Jeweler's Circular says that the pieces were designed to look like they had been "unearthed at Pompeii and Herculaneum." It seems Revivalism was still alive and well in the 1880s and 90s, but in a new form, with hand-crafted overtones. The company also produced quirky designs from nature, such as insects and spiders on leaves, sea shells and sea creatures, and other flora and fauna. Shiebler pieces are usually marked "sterling" with a winged S (see appendix, American Manufacturers), and numbered.

Brooches/Pins, sterling, "curio medallion," George W. Shiebler & Co., New York NY, imp with maker's mk (winged S), c. 1880-90:

TL, irregular cutout key shape, profile of Roman god Mercury at one end, incised Greek letters "XAPIE," suspending a circ medallion with profile of helmeted Roman god, rev mkd "STERLING # 729," C-catch with half-tubular "safety," tube hinge, 2-3/8" w x 1-1/4", **$350**.

TR, cutout shepherd's hook motif suspending lg circ medallion of Greco-Roman profile, incised Greek letters "TOEV" on front, rev mkd "STERLING #588," C-catch with half-tubular "safety," medallion 1" dia, pin 3" w x 1-3/4" tl, **$400**.

C, three lg circ overlapping medallions, profiles of Greco-Roman deities, mkd "STERLING #1093," C-catch with half tubular "safety," tube hinge, 3-1/4" w x 1-3/8", **$425**.

BL, ropetwist bar with Greco-Roman medallions at each end, suspending four medallions, each 1/2" dia, mkd "STERLING # 602," replacement safety catch, tube hinge, 3" w x 1-1/8" tl, **$325**. (Elizabeth Nyland collection).

BR, irregular cutout key shape with incised Greek letters "MNHMON," Greco-Roman profile at one end, mkd "STERLING #1020," C-catch, replacement hinge and pinstem, 2-3/8" w x 7/8", **$325**.

(Courtesy of The Eden Sterling Co.).

A technique known as "niello" was applied to silver ornaments in the late nineteenth century. Based on a medieval Russian technique, niello is a grayish-black mixture of silver, lead, copper, and sulfur that is applied to engraved designs on the silver's surface, then fired and polished smooth. Allover geometric or floral patterns yielded the best effect. An alloy of 800 silver (parts per thousand) was usually used because it withstands firing temperatures better than higher grades of silver.

Like gold, nineteenth century silver jewelry is not always hallmarked. When marks are found, however, they can be helpful clues. The American standard for silver was 900 parts per thousand until 1906. Pieces marked "standard" or "coin" are 900 silver of American origin. Some manufacturers, such as Tiffany, Gorham, and Shiebler, used the British sterling standard of 925 considerably earlier, and marked pieces "sterling." The British mark for sterling is a "lion passant," or walking lion. The place of assay and date letter hallmarks correspond to those used on gold. European countries used alloys ranging from 750 to 950 with various devices as indications of silver content for hallmarks (see appendix, Marks on Metals).

References: Vivienne Becker, *Antique and Twentieth Century Jewellery*, 2nd ed., N.A.G. Press, 1987; Ginny Redington Dawes & Corinne Davidov, *Victorian Jewelry, Unexplored Treasures*, Abbeville Press, 1991; Janet Zapata and D. Albert Soeffing, "Artistic Wares of George W. Shiebler, Silversmith," in *The Magazine Antiques*, July, 1995; **Marks**: *Bradbury's Book of Hallmarks* (on British and Irish silver, gold and platinum), J.W. Northend Ltd., 1987; Ian Pickford, ed., *Jackson's Hallmarks*, Antique Collectors' Club, 1992; Tardy, *International Hallmarks on Silver,* English translation, Paris, 1985. Includes the silver hallmarks of many European countries and Great Britain.

Advisors: Gary Niederkorn, Janet Zapata.

Bangle Bracelets, hinged, sterling, c. 1880-85:
T, date letter for 1882-83, strap and buckle motif with engr floral/foliate design, appl ster beads around strap terminal, rolled edge, v-spring and box clasp, Chester (Eng) hmks, maker's mk "GWD," 1" w, 2-1/4" inside dia, **$300**.
C, date letter for 1881-82, strap and buckle motif with engr foliate design, appl ster beads around strap terminal, v-spring and box clasp, dents, Birmingham (Eng) hmks, maker's mk "HW," 1-1/4" w, 2-1/4" inside dia, **$350**.
B, c. 1880-90, elaborate allover engr scroll motif flanked by crenelated and beaded border, v-spring and box clasp, 1-1/4" w, 2-1/4" inside dia, **$350**.
(Penny Lesch collection).

Bracelet

Sterling, c. 1890-1900, coiled snake, tightly woven mesh body, repoussé tail and head, red stone eyes, open mouth showing teeth and tongue, mkd "STERLING, 935," approx 14" tl (uncoiled), head 5/8" w x 1-3/8 .... l, 375

Bangle

Sterling, 14k yg, c. 1900, forged ster inlaid with yg medallion heads, mkd "STERLING" and "14k," maker's mark for George Shiebler, New York, NY, 5/8" w .... 1,380 (A)

Sterling, c. 1892, die-struck design on outside with Spanish words "*Recuerdo De La Reina Ysabel* 1492 [crowned] F [Maltese cross] [crowned] Y 1893 *La Esposición De Chicago*," ("Souvenir of Queen Isabel, 1492-1893 Chicago Esposition") mkd on inside of bangle "GORHAM MFG CO REGISTERED STERLING 1892," maker's mk for Gorham, 2-3/4" inside dia, 1/4" w.. 200

Sterling, date letter for 1882, open rolled-edge flexible bangle, heart-shaped terminals with raised beaded centers, die-rolled beading and ropetwist decoration on shoulders, Birmingham (Eng) hmks, 2-3/8" inside dia, terminals 3/4" w... 165

Bangle, hinged

Sp brass, c. 1880, a *manchette* (cuff), front half shaped and decorated to look like a shirt cuff, double-lobed on one edge, a central vertical row of three round bead "buttons" and twisted wire "buttonholes" surmounting allover engr foliate design, tapering to a plain back band, side hinge, inside imp "H H." v-spring and box clasp, 2-1/4" inside dia, 1-5/8" to 7/8" w 200

Charm

Sterling, c. 1880-90, curb link chain with alternating polished and textured links, single irregular circ charm medallion of woman's profile at end of chain, incised Greek letters "TOEV" on rev, mkd "STERLING #8," maker's mk for George Shiebler (winged S), charm 1-1/4" dia, chain 1/4" w x 8" 400

Link

Shakudo, 18k yg, silver, c. 1880, six alternating sq and circ linked *shakudo* plaques inlaid with silver and yg in designs of birds and insects in naturalistic setting, set in conforming yg mounts, European hmks and "K18 MS," v-spring and box clasp, ring for safety chain (missing), 5/8" w x 6-1/8" tl .... 1,955 (A)

Brooch/Pin

Arrowhead, sterling, c. 1880-90, ancient Native American arrowhead wrapped in ster "twine" and attached to ster bar at back, mkd "STERLING," maker's mk for George Shiebler (winged S), C-catch with half tubular "safety," tube hinge, 2-3/4" w x 7/8" 600

Shakudo, yg, c. 1890, *shakudo* plaque depicting three overlapping fans, folding and circ, uppermost in center decorated with marsh scene, waterbird and foliate motifs, flanked by floral and foliate motifs, raised design accented with yg overlay, 2-3/4" w x 1" 1,100

Bangle Bracelet, hinged, sterling, amethysts, citrines, rhodolite garnets, smoky quartz, c. 1850, an open shield-shaped plaque surmounted by an engr crown set with a central lg oval-cut citrine encircled by nine sm circ-cut stones, alternating amethyst, citrine, and rhodolite garnet, three sm smoky quartz cabs bezel-set in the spikes of the crown, flanked by engr Celtic knot motifs and beaded border shoulders, tapering to a v-spring and box clasp and hinge at sides, continuing to engr back section, illegible Eng Registry mk on rev, 2" w x 3" (at top), 2-1/4" inside dia, **$650**. (Penny Lesch collection).

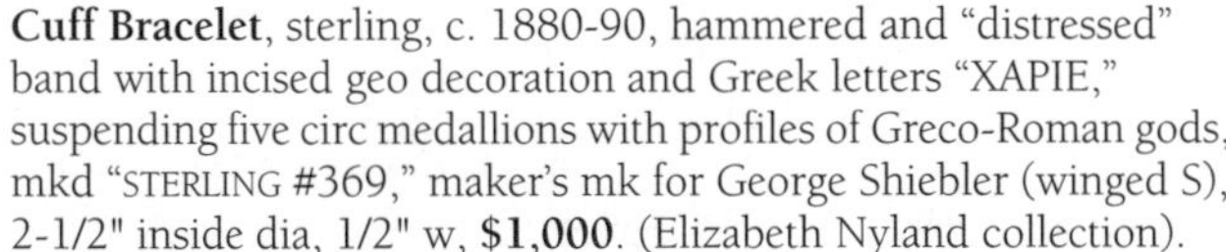

Cuff Bracelet, sterling, c. 1880-90, hammered and "distressed" band with incised geo decoration and Greek letters "XAPIE," suspending five circ medallions with profiles of Greco-Roman gods, mkd "STERLING #369," maker's mk for George Shiebler (winged S), 2-1/2" inside dia, 1/2" w, **$1,000**. (Elizabeth Nyland collection).

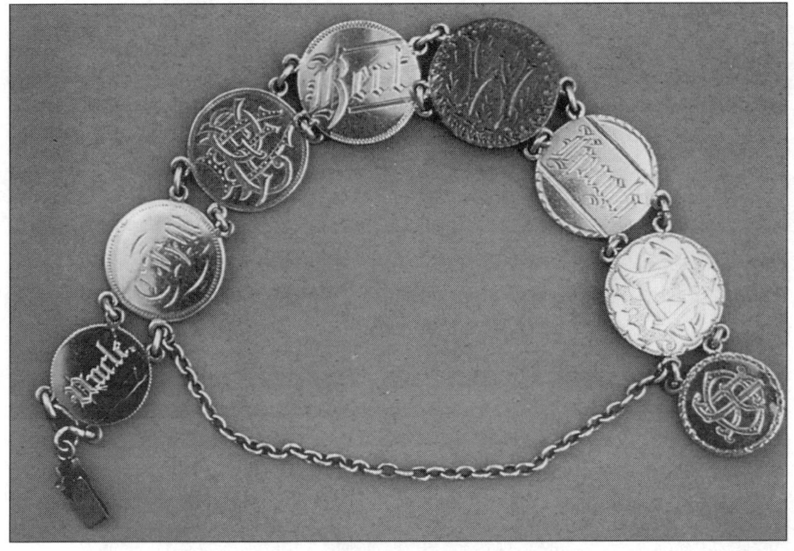

Bracelet, link, silver, gold, copper, enamel, c. 1890, "love tokens" made of eight U.S. coins dated from 1856 to 1887, engr with assorted names and ciphers, one engr "1888," one gold coin enameled "Amor," safety chain, v-spring and box clasp, 6-1/2" tl x 1/2", **$285**. (Courtesy of E. Foxe Harrell Jewelers, Clinton, IA).

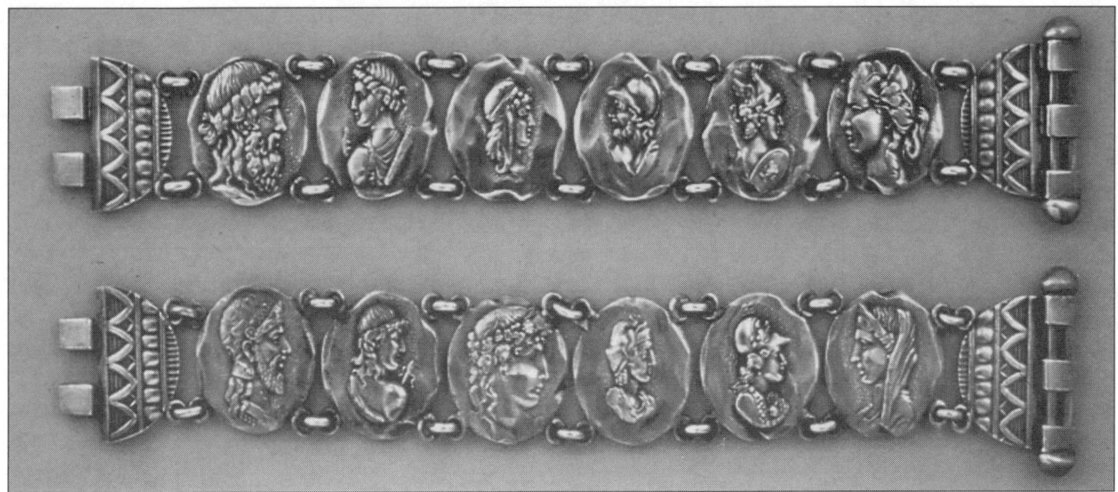

Bracelets, link, sterling, c. 1880-90, linked circ medallions, each depicting the profile of a different Greco-Roman deity, terminating in half disks stamped with geo design, hingepin clasps, rev imp with maker's mk for George Shiebler, New York, NY, #569, "STERLING," 6-3/4" tl, 7/8" w, pr, **$1,500**. (Gilly Phipps collection).

Bangle Bracelet, hinged, silver, niello, rose gold, c. 1880-90, narrow tubular bypass design with niello "candy striping," enclosed by a central appl horseshoe motif with niello and rose gold overlay on silver, v-spring and box clasp, safety chain, 5/8" w (at center), 2-1/4" inside dia, **$140**. (Penny Lesch collection).

Shakudo, yg, silver, c. 1880-90, circ *shakudo* disk, inlaid gold and silver decoration depicting a man pulling a rickshaw with a woman holding a parasol, floral sprays in bg, C-catch and tube hinge appl to cruciform yg pronged mount on rev, loop for safety chain, 1-1/8" dia......... 300

Brooch/Pin, silver, niello, rose gold, celluloid, c. 1880-90, two side-by-side circ photo frames with celluloid covers encircled by a figure-8 tubular silver frame with niello striping, rose gold center bead, four evenly-spaced rose gold rings around each frame, 2" w x 1", **$85**. (Penny Lesch collection).

Brooch/Pin, *shakudo*, colored gold, silver, c. 1880, oval *shakudo* plaque with appl raised and inlaid silver and colored gold depiction of two birds, floral and foliate motifs, sterling backing with later-added safety catch, 1" w x 1-3/4", **$375**. (Photo courtesy of Lovejoy's Estate Jewelry, Bellingham, WA).

Brooch/Pin, pastes, silver, c. 1880-90, in the shape of a winged insect set throughout with colorless pastes, red paste eyes, Fr hmks, C-catch, 1-3/4" w x 1-1/2", **$495**. (Photo courtesy of Lovejoy's Estate Jewelry, Bellingham, WA).

Brooches/Pins, sterling, c. 1880-90:

T, horseshoe shape, die-struck, replaced C-catch, tube hinge, extended pinstem, 1" w x 1-1/8", **$75**.

C, rect with engr bird, butterfly and foliate design, stamped to resemble a picture frame with serrated edge, flat backing, unmkd, later added safety catch, tube hinge, extended pinstem, 1-1/2" w x 1-1/4", **$95**.

RC, oval plaque with engr floral and foliate motifs, rose and yg overlay, beaded edge, openwork wire frame with circle motifs, C-catch, tube hinge, 1-3/4" w x 1-1/8", **$125**.

LC, oval frame with central plaque engr with Japanese crane in bullrushes, encircled by punched star decoration, C-catch, tube hinge, extended pinstem, 1-3/8" w x 1-1/8", **$95**.

B, date letter for 1898-99, bar with arcing serrated wire above and below, engr die-struck swallow flanked by two flowerheads and engr leaves, Birmingham hmks, C-catch, tube hinge, 1-3/4" w x 5/8", **$80**.

(Elaine Sarnoff collection).

Silver, c. 1880, oval plaque with appl cusped border, beaded outer edge, central engr scene of St. Paul's Cathedral London (backing missing), added C-catch, tube hinge, 1-1/2" w x 1-1/4" 67

Sterling, c. 1885-95, three-dimensional beetle on a branch with leaves, mkd "STERLING # 2," maker's mk for George Shiebler (winged S), C-catch, 1" w x 3" 650

Sterling, c. 1900, two overlapping irregular circ disks with facing classical profiles, hammered ground, maker's mk for Lewis Bros. (L inside a foliate wreath), Providence, RI (in business 1896-1915), mkd "STERLING," C-catch, 2-1/2" w x 1-1/2" 400

Sterling, date letter for 1878, name brooch, circ pierced center with cutout and engr floral/foliate motifs surrounding "Edith," within notched and beaded-edge frame, rev imp with maker's initials "S B & S," Birmingham (Eng) hmks, C-catch, tube hinged, extended pin stem, 1-1/2" dia 175

Brooch/Pin, sterling, yg, date letter for 1896-97, Jubilee pin, crossed branches with chain ring encircling cutout and engr yg crown, mono "VR," flowers and scroll engr "1837-1897" flanked by two yg ivy leaves near branch ends, Birmingham hmks, mkd "S. Bros," C-catch, tube hinge, 1-7/8" w x 3/4", **$200**. (Private collection).

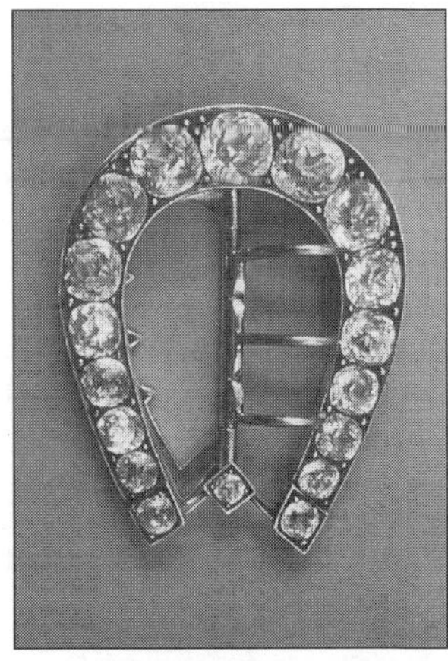

Buckle, silver, paste, c. 1880, horseshoe shape, row of grad circ-cut colorless pastes, bead-set in silver frame, gp three-pronged hasp bearing Fr hmks: boar's head, maker's mk in a lozenge (V et M), 1-3/4" w x 2-1/4", **$225**. (Courtesy of E. Foxe Harrell Jewelers, Clinton, IA).

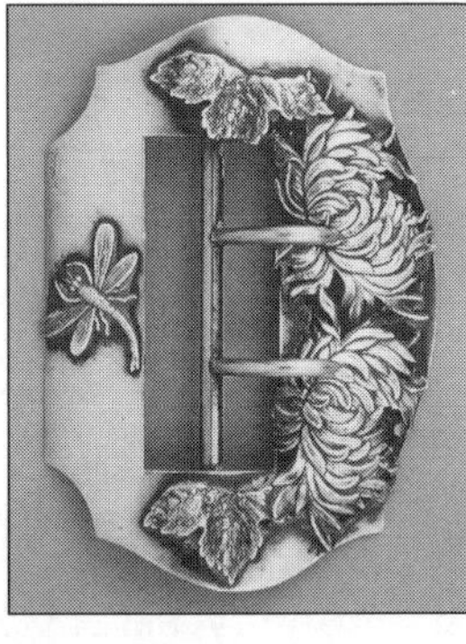

Buckle, sterling, c. 1880-1900, rounded cusped rect with open center, appl chrysanthemum and dragonfly motifs, imp with maker's mk for George Shiebler, New York, NY, "STERLING" #2431, double hasp, 2" w x 3", **$550**. (Janet Zapata collection).

Bar

Silver, c. 1880-90, narrow half-cylindrical bar, center appl strip of raised sq beading, suspending three "love tokens," U.S. coins dated 1873, 1875, 1877, one side of each engr with different ciphers, C-catch, tube hinge, 2-1/4" w x 1" tl 85

Sterling, c. 1880-1890, five irregular overlapping grad plaques, each with a different classical profile, hammered-textured ground, maker's mk "W&H" for Wood and Hughes (in business until 1899), New York, NY, mkd "STERLING #3731," C-catch, 2-1/2" w x 7/8" 450

Locket

Shakudo, 18k yg, hair, c. 1870-80, oval shakudo plaque, Japanese raised metal inlay depicting a peacock in a floral and foliate ground, set in an 18k yg Etruscan Revival frame with appl bead and wiretwist decoration, compartment with a lock of hair on rev, 1-1/4" w x 1-3/4" (including bail) .... 1,323 (A)

Lockets, c. 1880-90:

L, sterling, date letter for 1881-82, oval locket with engr floral and foliate motifs and sm bird, crenelated and beaded edge, Birmingham hmks on rev, 1-5/8" w x 2-1/2" tl, **$275**.

C, sterling, oval locket with stamped and engr foliate pattern, crenelated and beaded edge, convex back, suspended from a reeded cable-link and beaded chain, lg spring ring front clasp, locket 1-1/2" w x 2-3/8" tl, chain 3/8" w x 17-1/2" tl, **$400**.

R, sp base metal, oval locket in Japanese "Blue Willow" pattern scene, die-struck and emb, gp interior, 1-3/8" w x 2-1/4" tl, **$150**.

(Elaine Sarnoff collection).

Sterling, c. 1885, oval locket with engr geo foliate and scroll design, small dent on front, 1-1/4" w x 2-1/4" with bail 240

Locket and Chain

Sterling, c. 1880-90, oval locket engr with lattice and leaf pattern one side, floral-foliate and ribbon design on other, suspended from a wide flat pierced link chain, spring ring front clasp, locket 1-5/16" w x 1-1/2", chain 16" tl x 3/8" w 250

Sterling, c. 1880-90, scroll and foliate engr front, containing two photographs: the first a woman wearing a pierced, engr name brooch "Annie"; the second a child, suspended from fancy pierced, cutout and beaded ster chain with double spring rings and extension, locket rev imp with Birmingham hmks, date letter illegible, 1-3/4" w x 2", chain 18-1/2" tl x 3/4" w 525

Sterling, sp brass, c. 1880-90, oval locket, three dimensional stamped and engr, floral, foliate, beaded and engr scrollwork on rev, crenelated border, susp from sp wide fancy link beaded edge chain, locket 1-1/2" w x 1-7/8", chain 18" tl, 5/8" w 295

Necklace, Dog Collar, sterling vermeil, c. 1885-95, thirteen rect gp plaques and two half plaques at the closure, hammered textured surface, each closure plaque with Chinese characters, others with bamboo, serpents, bat, cattails, insect, mermaid with cattails, butterfly, arrowhead plant, bird, and seahorse, maker's mk for George Shiebler (winged "S"), New York, NY, and "STERLING # 625," sliding hinge pin closure, 1" w x 13", **$3,500**. (Private collection).

Necklace

Silver, c. 1890, fancy link chain with a heart-shaped slide with appl floral and foliate decoration, terminating in two cushion-shaped open drops with appl floral and foliate decoration, maker's mk for Gorham, slide 1" w x 7/8", drops 1-1/8" w x 1-1/4" .... 1,150 (A)

Scarf Pin/Stickpin

Silver, enamel, brass, c. 1900, sq silver head with blue enameled swallow on textured ground, mkd "P & B" for Paye and Baker, North Attleboro, MA., brass pinstem, 2-1/4" tl, 1/2" w x 1/2" 65

Watch Chain

Shakudo, silver, yg, c. 1880, double strand of sm circ links with floral motif tops, appl silver and yg details, swivel hook clasp, 1/4" w x 56" tl .... 2,185 (A)

Suite: Cuff Buttons and Bar Pin, sterling, Shiebler, c.1890-1900: T, seashell shapes, one with appl silver fish, other with appl copper seahorse, maker's mk for George Shiebler, New York, NY, mkd "STERLING CL," 7/8" w x 1", pr, **$650**. B, five overlapping three-dimensional sea shells, maker's mk for George Shiebler, mkd "STERLING #1243," C-catch, 1" w x 2-1/2", **$850**. (Janet Zapata collection).

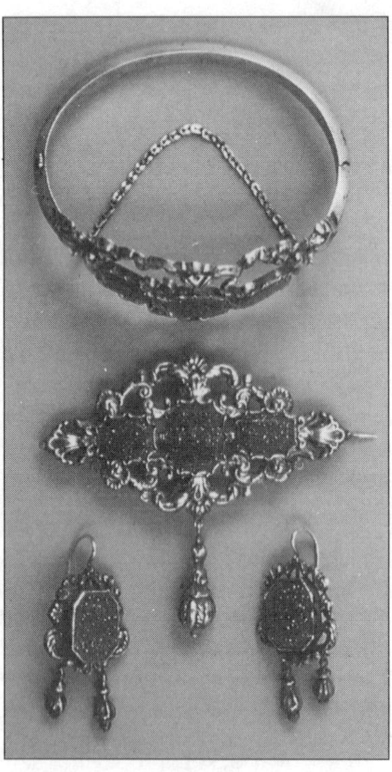

Suite: Hinged Bangle, Brooch/Pin, Earrings, silver, goldstone glass, c. 1850, die-struck openwork foliate and scroll motif, three beveled edge rect goldstones in bracelet and brooch set in crimped bezels, brooch and earrings suspending die-struck hollow drops (two missing from brooch), flat backings, Dutch hmks on bracelet and brooch "934-833" and maker's mark "VBG4," original fitted box, brooch: C-catch, tube hinge, extended pinstem, 2-3/4" w x 2-1/2" tl, bracelet: safety chain, 2-1/2" inside dia, 2-3/8" w x 1-3/8" at center, earrings: earwires, 1-1/2" tl, 7/8" w, **$750**. (Courtesy of E. Foxe Harrell Jewelers, Clinton, IA).

Suite: Bar Pin and Pendent Earrings, *shakudo*, gold, silver, c. 1880, rect plaque, cut-to-shape center depicting a circular handled fan overlapping an open folding fan, raised Japanese motifs overlaid with gold and silver leaf: a Japanese sailboat on water, Mt. Fuji, a pr of cranes under a cherry tree with blossoms, fans flanked by two quail amid floral/foliate decoration, appl C-catch and tube hinge, triangular drop earrings a pr of partially folded fans, one with a crane, the other a pr of quails, under cherry trees, fishhook earwires, bar pin 2-5/8" w x 3/4", earrings, 1-1/4" tl x 5/8" w, suite, **$450**.(Author's collection).

DIAMONDS AND COLORED GEMSTONES

History: The diamond has been the stone of choice among nobility and the wealthy for centuries. Although the eighteenth century has been called The Age of Diamonds, improved cutting and setting techniques to enhance the diamond's brilliance were developed in the nineteenth and twentieth centuries. Until the use of platinum found favor as a metal for setting diamonds at the end of the nineteenth century, silver was used to complement the stone's whiteness, almost always laminated to a yellow gold backing (sometimes called silver-topped yellow gold).

Closed-back and foiled settings were still in use at the beginning of the century. Open-backed (*à jour*) mounts gradually replaced them. It was discovered that brilliance was increased when light was reflected from the back as well as the front of the stone. The shape and cut of the diamond also evolved. Flat-backed rose cuts and cushion-shaped "old mine" cuts were eventually outnumbered (but not entirely replaced) by the circular "old European" brilliant cut toward the end of the century.

Credit for the development of the modern brilliant cut usually goes to Marcel Tolkowsky, who published his treatise "Diamond Design" in 1919. But the work of a little-known American diamond cutter, Henry D. Morse (1826-1888), preceded Tolkowsky's by more than forty years. It was Morse who first discovered the scientific principles and precise cutting angles of what has come to be known as the "American" or "ideal" cut. And it was Morse's foreman, Charles M. Field, who developed and patented with Morse the first steam-driven diamond cutting machines in 1874 and 1876, which preceded the European bruting (girdling) machine by sixteen years. Unfortunately, to date no known pieces of nineteenth century jewelry set with Morse's brilliants have been identified.

The discovery of diamonds in South Africa in 1867 increased the stone's availability. Subsequent discoveries led to greater supplies and lower prices in the early 1880s. In spite of a world-wide depressed economy, diamond-encrusted jewels were well-represented at the 1889 Paris Exposition, and found favor among the wealthy. By the 1890s, the De Beers Company had begun to control prices and dominate the South African diamond market, as it does today.

Diamonds have always been considered formal jewels for important occasions, usually reserved for nighttime wear. The Victorians had strict rules of etiquette concerning when diamonds should be worn and who should wear them. They were considered inappropriate for unmarried young women; most married matrons reserved them for balls and court appearances. However, toward the end of the century, when both diamonds and wealth were in greater supply in the United States, most rules were forgotten.

When electric lighting was introduced in the 1880's, sparkling diamond-set jewelry became even more desirable. Fashion would never be the same after electric lights began brightening up homes and public places, like the Savoy Theatre in London, opened in 1881, and the Metropolitan Opera House in New York, in 1883, where the privileged class went to see and be seen, decked in diamonds. The first tier of the Met was christened "The Diamond Circle" in reference to its bejeweled patrons. At the turn of the century, the fashion for pale fabrics and colorless platinum-set jewels further heightened the demand for diamonds.

Diamonds found their way into every conceivable form of jewelry, from tiaras to rings. The diamond brooch lent itself to a variety of motifs that reflected the Victorian preoccupation with nature. Flower bouquets and sprays were worn throughout the nineteenth century, sometimes with parts mounted *en tremblant*, on springs or wires that trembled when the wearer moved. Animal and insect motifs were popular in the 1880s and 90s, as were crescents and stars. These were often worn scattered about the neckline, or as veil or lace pins. Figural motifs remained in vogue through the turn of the century.

In 1886, Tiffany & Co. introduced the "Tiffany setting" for diamond solitaires. The high-pronged mount elevated the stone to show off its brilliance to the best advantage. It became the standard setting for engagement rings. This type of setting was originally patented by Ferdinand J. Herpers of Newark, NJ in 1872. It is perhaps not coincidental that the fourteen-year interval between Herpers' patent and Tiffany's setting is the length of time for which a design patent is granted. However, if it weren't for the prestigious firm's promotions, not only of solitaires, but of all diamond jewelry (including their purchase of a major portion of the French crown jewels in 1887), Americans might have worn far fewer diamond-set jewels.

Other gemstones were in and out of style according to the vagaries of fashion. In the 1830s, the romantic notion of the "language of stones," like that of flowers, gave rise to pieces with messages spelled out by the initial letter of the stone's name. "Regard," the most commonly expressed sentiment, was represented by ruby, emerald, garnet, amethyst, ruby, and diamond. This idea was revived at the end of the century.

Pavé-set small turquoise cabochons were used extensively in jewelry of the 1840s, particularly in snake motifs. Turquoise made a return appearance in the 1890s.

Besides their familiar use in Scottish jewelry, agates, variegated varieties of quartz, are found in other types of Victorian jewelry. Factories in Idar-Oberstein, Germany (the actual suppliers of many a "Scottish" pebble), have been the primary centers for the cutting and polishing of agates for three centuries. The soaking and heating processes for staining the stones has been done there as well. During the mid to late nineteenth century, color-enhanced banded agates were formed into beads and figural or geometric shapes. Although agate's value as a gemstone is low, Victorian agate jewelry is valued for its design, craftsmanship and collectibility.

Both faceted and cabochon garnets had their day at various times. There are several varieties and colors of garnets. Among them, the types most closely associated with the Victorian period are the reddish-brown pyrope, and the reddish-purple almandite. In the early nineteenth century, memorial brooches were often set with flat-cut pyrope or almandite garnets around a compartment containing hair. Large almandite cabochons, called carbuncles, are most often seen in mid-Victorian Revivalist pieces. In the later part of the century, small faceted rose-cut and single-cut pyropes (also called Bohemian garnets) were set in low-karat gold and gilt base metal or silver. This type of jewelry was mass-produced in Bohemia, and is being reproduced today. Green demantoid garnets were discovered in the Ural Mountains of Russia in 1853, but were not identified as a variety of andradite until 1864, and not named "demantoid" (diamond-like, referring to the stone's luster) until 1878. Demantoids are found in late nineteenth and early twentieth century pieces. The green color was especially favored for the salamander and lizard brooches that were in vogue at the time. The Russian Revolution of 1917 curtailed mining there, and by the 1920s, supply had dwindled. Demantoids are rarer, more desirable and more costly than most other varieties of garnet. Pyropes and almandites are the least expensive, but the quality and style of a piece set with these garnets may outweigh the stones' intrinsic value.

Opals were also popular in the late Victorian era, their wearers having overcome the superstition that the stone brought misfortune. In keeping with the pale look of the period's fashions, moonstones were worn, sometimes carved as cameos. The "man in the moon" was a favorite motif. Pearls, another pale gem, were worn as necklaces alone or in combination with diamonds, setting the tone for what would become the classic Edwardian style of the early twentieth century.

References: Vivienne Becker, *Antique and 20th Century Jewellery;* David Bennett and Daniela Mascetti, *Understanding Jewellery,* 2nd ed., Antique Collectors' Club, 1994; Eric Bruton, *Diamonds,* 2nd. ed., FGA, 1978; Joan Younger Dickinson, *The Book of Diamonds,* Avenel (Crown), 1965 (out of print); Ulysses G. Dietz, ed., *The Glitter & The Gold, Fashioning America's Jewelry,* The Newark Museum, 1997; Martha G. Fales, *Jewelry in America 1600-1900*, Antique Collectors' Club, 1995; David Federman, "American Diamond Cutting: The Untold Heritage," *Modern Jeweler,* vol. 84 #1 (January, 1985); Margaret Flower, *Victorian Jewellery*, A.S. Barnes & Co., 1951 (out of print); George E. Harlow, ed. *The Nature of Diamonds*, Cambridge University Press, catalog of an exhibition at the American Museum of Natural History, New York NY, 1998; Gilbert Levine and Laura L. Vookles, *The Jeweler's Eye, Nineteenth-Century Jewelry in the Collection of Nancy and Gilbert Levine*, catalog of an exhibition at The Hudson River Museum, Yonkers, NY, 1986; Wm. Revell Phillips and Anatoly S. Talantsev, "Russian Demantoid, Czar of the Garnet Family," *Gems & Gemology*, Summer, 1996; Herbert Tillander, *Diamond Cuts in Historic Jewellery 1381-1910*, Arts Books International, 1995; Basil Watermeyer, *Diamond Cutting*, 4th ed., Johannesburg, 1991 (self-published; includes history of cuts).

Museums: The most extensive collections are British, housed at the Victoria and Albert and the British Museums, London; in the U.S., the Cooper-Hewitt and Metropolitan Museum of Art, New York, and the Smithsonian Institution, Washington, have noteworthy collections.

Reproduction Alert: Late Victorian-style garnet jewelry is mass-reproduced. Wholesalers advertise in antique trade papers such as *The Antique Trader Weekly*; some participate in jewelry trade shows. Most of them have catalogs with photographs. Other gemstone-set repros are imported from Portugal, South America, Germany, and Thailand. Some pieces are good enough to fool the experts.

Advisors: Gertrud Seidmann, Joseph W. Tenhagen.

Bracelet

Bangle, hinged

14k yg, diamonds, seed pearls, c. 1890, narrow yg tube surmounted by a bead-tipped yg lozenge, center prong-set with a circ-cut diamond, six seed pearls interspersed throughout, flanked by two pierced ovals, each prong-set with an om diamond, ropetwist wire spiraling around front portion of bangle, 1/4" w, 2" inside dia...... 495 (A)

Jadeite, diamonds, emeralds, rose gold, Late Victorian, a lg oval mottled apple green jadeite cab encircled by thirty oe and sc diamonds, approx 1.25 cts tw, further encircled by thirty sm circ green beryl cabs, flanked by scrolled wirework set with two circ emerald cabs and two oe diamonds, mounted on a narrow sq-edged rose gold band, safety chain, 1" x 1-1/4" at center, 2-1/4" inside dia .... 1,725 (A)

Moonstones, diamonds, st yg, Late Victorian, front half surmounted by seven circ moonstone cabs separated by prs of om diamonds, surmounting a narrow sq-edged yg band, safety chain, 1/2" w x 2-1/4" inside dia .... 2,070 (A)

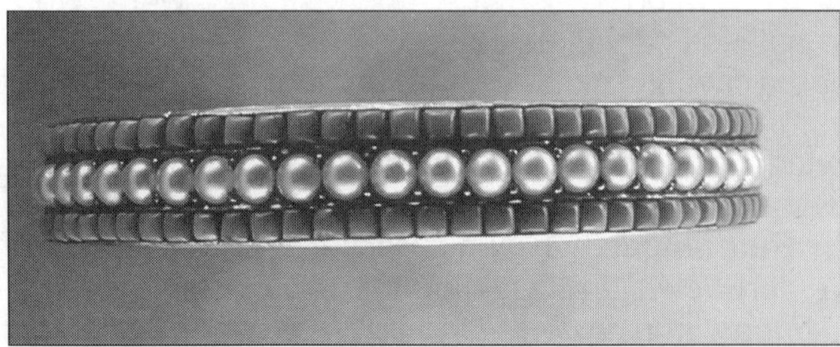

Bangle Bracelet, hinged, turquoise, pearls, 14k yg, c. 1890-1900, oval, double hinged at the sides, top half set with a center row of split pearls flanked by a row of sq-cut turq, back yg bands terminating in v-spring and box clasp, 2-1/4" inside dia, 3/8" w, **$2,424**. (Photo courtesy of Karen Lorene, Facèré Jewelry Art, Seattle, WA).

Link

18k yg, pearls, enamel, c. 1880, rect hinged yg panels with pierce scrollwork, each with one letter spelling the name

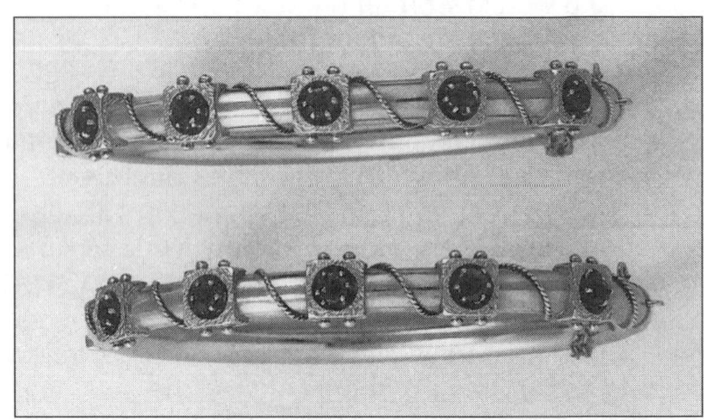

Bangle Bracelets, hinged, 14k yg, emeralds, c. 1880-90, narrow tubular form, each top half prong-set with five evenly spaced circ-cut emeralds set within textured sq box frames with appl beading, a spiral of ropetwist wire wrapped around top half in between frames, 3.8" w, 2-1/2" inside dia, pr, **$1,380** [A]. (Photo courtesy of Sotheby's Beverly Hills, CA, 11/18/96).

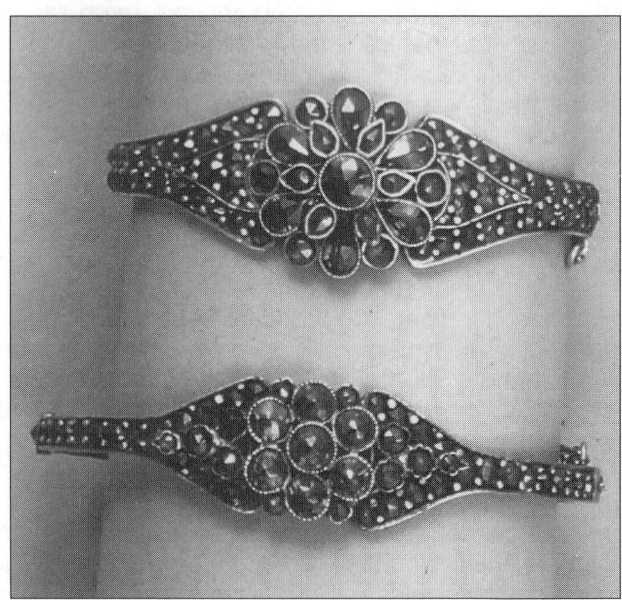

Bangle Bracelets, hinged, garnets, gp brass, c. 1890-1900:

T, cluster of rc circ and pear-shaped garnets forming central flowerhead, flanked by tapering band of bead-set garnets, v-spring and box clasp, safety chain, inside dia 2-1/8", 3/4" w at center, **$575**.

B, seven rc garnets in millegrained bezels forming central cluster, flanked by tapering sections of bead-set garnets, continuing to a single row of bead-set garnets around bracelet, v-spring and box clasp, safety chain, inside dia 2-1/2", 5/8" w at center, **$485**.

(Courtesy of E. Foxe Harrell Jewelers, Clinton. IA).

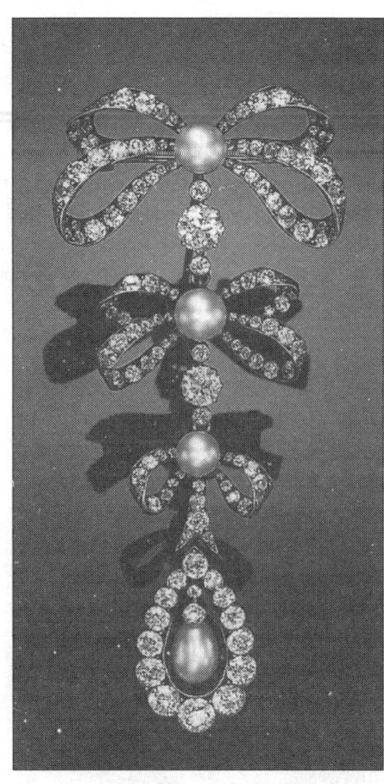
Brooch/Pendant, diamonds, pearls, st yg, c. 1870, a grad descending articulated vertical row of three bows and a pear-shaped drop, lg bow at top centering a pearl of approx 7.70 mm set with om and oe diamonds, suspending a smaller bow centering a pearl of approx 7.40 mm and set with om and oe diamonds, the last smallest bow centering a pearl of 6.30 mm and set with om and oe diamonds, each bow spaced by a chain of one lg flanked by two sm oe diamonds, terminating in a pear-shaped drop centering a pear-shaped pearl of approx 10.00 x 6.80 mm, within an open frame of grad oe diamonds, 1-3/4" w x 3-3/4" tl, **$34,500** [A]. (Photo courtesy of Christie's New York, NY, 10/23/96).

Brooch/Pendant, sapphire, diamond, st yg, c. 1890, shield-shaped, open beaded and scrolled wirework surmounted by an engr and beaded bow, circ-cut central sapphire in beaded bezel, bead-set rc diamonds interspersed throughout, hand made safety catch and bail, tube hinge, 1-1/4" w x 1-7/8", **$875**. (Courtesy of E. Foxe Harrell Jewelers, Clinton, IA).

"Beatrice," terminating in slightly larger engr panels and a blue *champlevé* enameled half cylinder set with three rows of split pearls, panels fold together to form a book, the enameled half-cylinder the spine, 1" x 7" tl .... 1,150 (A)

Yg, enamel, turquoise, c. 1880-90, seven rect hinged plaques with floral and scroll motif enamel in shades of blue, red, and white, a larger rect plaque at each end, one end terminating in a semi-cylindrical link of similar motif, thirty-eight sm circ bead-set turq cabs throughout, bracelet folds up to become a book charm with each link a page, end links forming the binding and covers, safety chain, v-spring and box clasp, 1-1/4" w x 7" tl .... 1,093 (A)

Brooch/Pendant

18k yg, enamel, diamonds, c. 1890, a bow motif top suspending a heart-shaped locket, allover turq-colored enamel, appl diamond-set butterfly motif surmounting bow, diamond-set flower surmounting heart, fitted box (minor enamel repair), 1-1/8" w x 1-1/2" tl.......... 805 (A)

Diamond, seed pearls, yg, c. 1890, multirayed sunburst motif centering one prong-set oe diamond of 4.34 cts, undulating yg rays bead-set with one hundred twenty half and full seed pearls, pendant loop, 2" dia .... 10,638 (A)

Diamonds, amethysts, st yg, Late Victorian, a central cushion-shaped amethyst cab bezel-set within rc diamond-set foliate scrolls, suspending a high-domed amethyst cab acorn motif with sm paired diamond-set leaves, 1-5/8" w x 2-1/2" .... 1,380 (A)

Diamonds, platinum, yg, c. 1890, openwork star shape centering lg collet-set and sm prong-set om diamonds surrounded by sm om diamonds bead-set in plat, pendant hoop, sgd "TIFFANY & CO.," 1-3/4" w x 1-3/4" .... 23,000 (A)

Opal, 10k yg, c. 1890-1900, starburst centering a circ opal cab of 6 mm, surrounded by yg rays, in box, pendant loop, 1" dia .... 80 (A)

Brooch/Pin

14k yg, seed pearls, diamond, c. 1890-1900, crescent with foliate motif, fifteen seed pearls and a sm circ diamond, C-catch, 1/8" w x 1-1/8"..................................... 110 (A)

Diamonds, silver, 18k yg, c. 1890, depicting a dog *en tremblant* in silver bead-set throughout with sm rc diamonds, jumping through an 18k yg hoop, Fr hmk (eagle's head) for 18k gold, maker's mk "GK" in a lozenge, fitted box, 1-1/2" w x 1-1/8" .... 2,990 (A)

Diamonds, rubies, demantoid garnets, st yg, enamel, c. 1897, Jubilee commemorative, a crown motif set with sm diamonds, rubies and demantoid garnets surmounting enameled floral symbols of England (a rose), Ireland (a shamrock) and Scotland (a thistle), flanked by cutout numbers "18" on the left and "97" on the right, surmounting diamond-set open navette shapes, 1-1/8" w x 1-1/2" .... 805 (A)

Diamonds, emeralds, st yg, c. 1890, four leaf clover motif centering one lg om diamond, each leaf centering a bezel-set oval emerald cab surrounded by om diamonds, a lg om diamond flanking one side of diamond-set stem, mounted in silver-topped 18k yg, Fr hmks, (one emerald cracked), 1-1/2" w x 1-3/8" .... 5,175 (A)

Diamonds, pearl, rubies, st yg, c. 1890, in the shape of a butterfly, the body a lg pear-shaped diamond and a button pearl, two ruby cab eyes, the wings set throughout with oe diamonds, 1-1/2" w x 1-1/4"................ 5,463 (A)

Brooches/Pins, garnets, gp brass, c. 1890:

TL, crescent moon encircling a floral motif of bead-set garnets and flanked by single garnets, C-catch, tube hinge, 1-1/2" w x 1-1/8", **$275**.

TR, star shape with lg central circ collet-set garnet surrounded by six pear-shaped garnets and outer row of sm circ bead-set garnets, C-catch, tube hinge, 1-1/4" dia, **$285**.

BC, horseshoe shape of bead-set garnets, later added stickpin (converted from brooch), 1-1/8" w x 1-1/4", **$200**. (Courtesy of E. Foxe Harrell Jewelers, Clinton, IA).

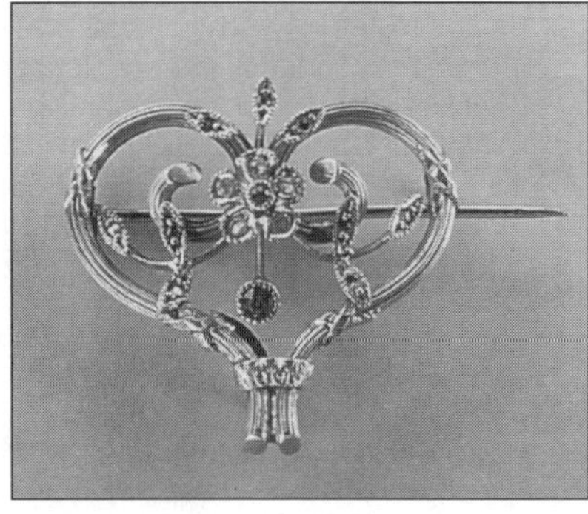

Brooch/Pin, 18k yg, rc diamonds, rubies, platinum, c. 1900, scrolled reeded yg frame forming an open heart shape, enclosing floral/foliate motif, set throughout with rc diamonds in plat, one lg and one sm circ-cut ruby in yg millegrained collets, Fr hmks, C-catch, tube hinge, extended pinstem, 1-1/4" w x 1-1/8", **$1,585**. (Photo courtesy of Karen Lorene, Facèré Jewelry Art, Seattle, WA).

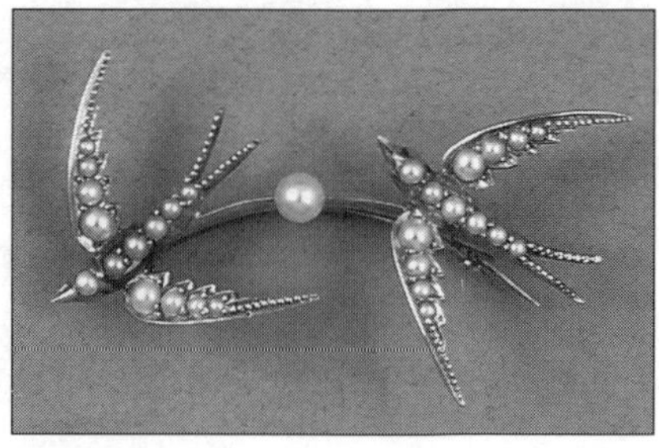

Brooch/Pin, 14k yg, seed pearls, c. 1890, pr of swallows flanking a central pearl, on a textured branch, swallow bodies and wings set with graduated pearls, beaded wingtips and tails, lever catch, flanged hinge, curved pinstem, 1-3/4" w x 1", **$450**. (Courtesy of E. Foxe Harrell Jewelers, Clinton, IA).

Brooch/Pin, diamonds, st yg, c. 1890, flowerhead with rc diamond-set petals surrounding prong-set oe diamond center, beaded and textured petals, removable pin back assembly, extended pinstem, C-catch, 1" dia, **$1,000**. (Courtesy of E. Foxe Harrell Jewelers, Clinton, IA).

Brooch/Pin, yg, st yg, red stones, tiger's eye quartz, enamel, c. 1900, three-dimensional yg bee with st yg wings set with sm rc diamonds, the body centering a prong-set oval tiger's eye quartz cab surmounting four rows of sm circ red stones alternating with bands of black enamel, red stone eyes, 2" w x 1-1/2", **$1,265** [A]. (Photo courtesy of Sotheby's Beverly Hills, CA, 5/20/97).

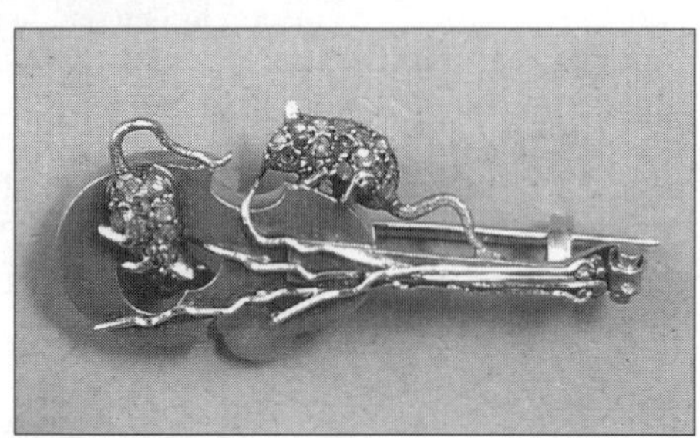

Brooch/Pin, 18k yg, rc diamonds, rubies, c. 1880-90, depicting a violin surmounted by two mice, one chewing a string, the other crawling into center hole in violin, mice pave-set with rc diamonds, ruby eyes, probably Eng, C-catch, tube hinge, 1-5/8" w x 3/4", **$2,000**. (Private collection).

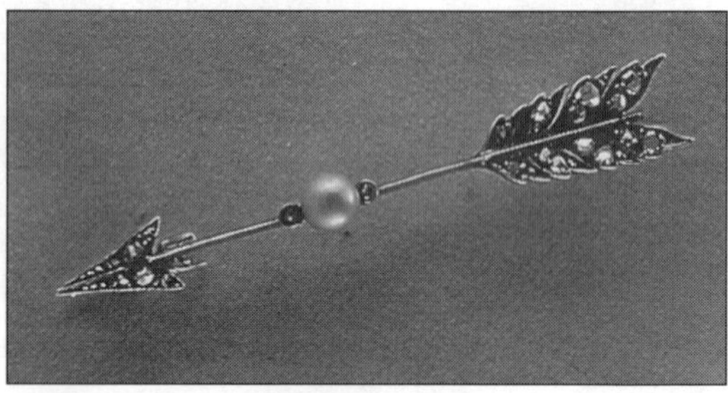

Bar Brooch/Pin, diamonds, pearl, yg, st yg, c.1900, in the shape of an arrow, yg shaft surmounted by a natural pearl flanked by two rc diamonds, arrowhead and feather set throughout with rc diamonds in st yg, Fr hmks, maker's mk in a lozenge, hinged safety mechanism on catch, 2-1/4" x 3/8", **$1,620**. (Photo courtesy of Karen Lorene, Facèré Jewelry Art, Seattle, WA).

Brooch/Pin, diamonds, black onyx, ruby, st yg, c. 1880, in the shape of a swallow on a branch, rc diamonds bead-set in leaves, branches and body of bird, ruby eye, carved black onyx folded wings (one chipped), Fr hmks on pinstem (eagle's head), replaced catch, 1-1/8" w x 1-1/8", **$850**. (Private collection).

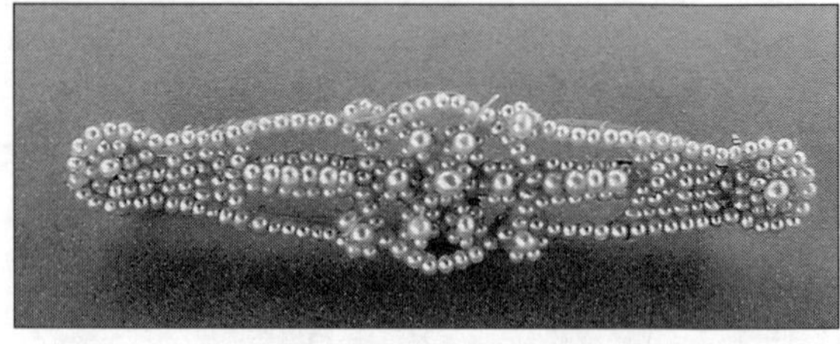

Bar Brooch/Pin, seed pearls, MOP, 14k yg, c. 1900, tapered and lobed bar, openwork flowerhead design in seed pearls strung with horsehair, mounted on cut-to-shape pierced MOP plaque, yg pinstem mkd "14k," lever catch, flanged hinge, 2-1/4" x 1/2", **$585**. (Photo courtesy of Karen Lorene, Facèré Jewelry Art, Seattle, WA).

Diamonds, pearl, st yg, c. 1890, a flowerhead with pearl center encircled by collet-set diamond stamens, diamond-set petals surmounting yg petals, Fr hmks on rev, 1-1/2" dia .... 1,150 (A)

Diamonds, peridot, st yg, c. 1860, a pear-shaped prong-set peridot measuring approx 20.50 x 18.00 x 12.80 mm, suspended within a conforming open om diamond-set frame, in the center of scroll and floral/foliate motif openwork surmounted by a ribbon bow, set throughout with lg and sm om and rc diamonds, terminating in three prong-set pear-shaped diamond drops, 2-5/8" w x 4-7/8" tl .... 51,750 (A)

Diamonds, plat-topped yg, c. 1900, narrow crescent set with a line of oe diamonds in plat-topped yg, yg pinstem, 3-1/4" x 1/8".. 2,070 (A)

Diamonds, rubies, st yg, c. 1880, openwork butterfly set throughout with om and rc diamonds and cushion-cut rubies in st yg mount, 2-5/8" w x 1-3/4"............ 18,400 (A)

Diamonds, st yg, c. 1880, multirayed starburst set throughout with om and rc diamonds mounted in st yg, 1-1/2" dia .... 3,450 (A)

Diamonds, st yg, c. 1880-90, open scrolled fleur-de-lis motif, center and three volute terminals prong-set with four om diamonds, .60 ct tw, and set throughout with rc diamonds, 1-3/8" w x 1-3/4" .... 1,725 (A)

Diamonds, st yg, c. 1890, floral spray of two six-petal flowerheads with lg rc diamond centers and five leaves set throughout with sm rc diamonds, 2" w x 3" .... 863 (A)

Diamonds, st yg, c. 1890, crescent-shaped, grad om and oe prong-set diamonds, approx 3.50 cts tw, pierced gallery, set in silver-topped 18k yg, 1/4" w x 2-1/4"..... 2,565 (A)

Emeralds, diamonds, rubies, rose gold, silver-topped rose gold, c. 1890, in the shape of a butterfly, two lg bezel-set circ emerald cabs for body, two sm emerald eyes, outer cusped edges of wings set with lg circ emeralds and lg oval rubies in rose gold, sq and rect diamonds bead-set in silver-topped rose gold, 1-3/4" w x 1-5/8".... 1,150 (A)

Opals, diamonds, st yg, c. 1890-1900, crescent-shaped, seventeen oval and circ grad opals with sm rc diamond accents, 3-3/8" w x 1/4".................................. 1,150 (A)

Bar

Diamonds, pearls, st 15k yg, c. 1880-90, arrow suspending a central foliate swag, forty-five sm rc diamonds throughout, a horizontal row of four sm pearls along shaft, sm pearl at center of swag suspending a pear-shaped pearl drop, 2-3/4" w x 1-1/8" tl.................................... 570 (A)

Yg, diamonds, c. 1880, centering an open horseshoe motif carré-set with eight om diamonds, flanked by chevron shapes to ball terminals with appl bead and wiretwist decoration, 2-1/4" w x 3/4" .... 690(A)

18k yg, f.w. pearl, enamel, c. 1890, a yg "safety pin" surmounted at one end by a duck motif, f.w. pearl body, enameled head and neck in green, blue and brown, Fr hmk (eagle's head) on pinstem, 1-7/8" l x 5/8" w..... 980

Corsage

Diamonds, silver-topped 18k rose gold, c. 1885, floral spray of rc and om diamonds, centering a similar flower center mounted *en tremblant*, tied with a rc diamond ribbon, with an assortment of hair and brooch fittings, Fr hmk (eagle's head) for 18k gold, in an initialed fitted leather case sgd by Alphonse Fouquet, Paris, 6" w x 3-1/2" .... 23,000 (A)

Earrings, pendent

Almandite garnets, pearls, 18k yg, Mid-Victorian, tapering foliate motif of circ, oval, and pear-shaped prong-set garnets around a central vertical row of sm split pearls, Fr hmk (eagle's head) for 18k gold, shepherd's hook findings, 1/2" w x 1-5/8" tl, pr .... 1,265 (A)

Amethysts, seed pearls, 14k yg, c. 1890, oval surmount centering an oval bezel-set amethyst in a beaded frame, suspending a scrollwork yg link leading to a round amethyst bead, leading to two scrollwork yg links, attached at either side of an octagonal yg frame centering a lg rect bezel-set amethyst surrounded by a row of seed pearls, stud and clutch findings, 5/8" w x 2" tl, pr........... 912 (A)

Sapphires, diamonds, yg, Late Victorian, a collet-set cushion-cut blue sapphire surmount suspending a flexible line of paired foliate motifs collet-set with rc diamonds alternating with single collet-set oe diamonds, terminating in a larger prong-set cushion-cut blue sapphire drop, each approx 2.50 cts, earwires, 3/8" w x 1-5/8" tl, pr .... 5,750 (A)

Hair Comb

Yg, pearls, iron, c. 1880, curved bar with appl three-dimensional filigree floral and foliate motif, sm pearl cluster and lg prong-set pearls (some pearls missing), surmounting a hinged iron five-toothed comb, 4-3/4" w x 4" tl .... 1,150 (A)

Hatpin

Amethyst, yg, c. 1900, pear-shaped amethyst bead set in a tapering scallop-edged yg collar, 1/2" w x 1-1/4", yg pinstem 7" tl 310

Yg, rock crystal, pearl, c. 1900, split crystal bead with faceted rondel spacer encased in cutout yg "cage," floral, scroll and fleur-de-lis design, surmounted by sm pearl, 1/2" w x 1", yg pinstem, 6-1/2" tl.............................. 225

Jabot Pin

Diamonds, st yg, yg, c. 1880-90, sword surmounted by crown, hilt and scabbard bead and prong-set throughout with sm om diamonds, yg rope chain swag, 1" w x 4-1/8".. 265 (A)

Locket

18k yg, pearls, coral, c. 1870, smooth yg oval surmounted by a curved row of sm circ coral cabs at top, from which descend five vertical rows of alternating bezel-set pearls and lozenge-shaped coral cabs, bail set with three seed pearls and a tapered oval coral cab, 1-1/4" w x 2-1/4" tl .... 747 (A)

Garnet cab, gf, c. 1860, two opposed garnet cabs (carbuncles) bezel-set in hinged ropetwist gf frame, 3/4" w x 1" 250

Yg, pearls, c. 1860, oval with central appl grape motif pearl cluster surrounded by conforming seed pearl border, opening to reveal two photo compartments, surmounted by a cutout scroll motif and pearl-set bail, one hundred five natural pearls total, 1-1/4" w x 2-1/2"........... 747 (A)

Necklace

Diamonds, emeralds, yg, st yg, Early Victorian, floral/foliate and scroll motif, segmented with detachable components, set throughout with rc diamonds in st yg, interspersed with thirty-two sq-cut emeralds pronged bezel-set in yg, central bow shape with pinback assembly, detaches for wear as a brooch, suspending a detachable hexagonal pendant with detachable pear-shaped emerald drop, 15" tl assembled, brooch 2" w x 3/4", pendant 2" w x 2-1/2" tl.................. 11,400 (A)

Diamonds, st yg, c. 1850, diamond-set crescent-shaped links suspending a knife-edge fringe, each set with three oe diamonds, cut-down collet terminals, twenty-one oe diamonds, approx 6.50 cts tw, fifty sm oe diamonds, approx 5.00 cts tw, rc diamond accents, Fr hmks, 1-1/2" w (at center), 16" tl.. 12,650 (A)

Diamonds, spinel, silver-topped 18k yg, c. 1875, *rivière* of fifty-three grad om and oe diamonds in prong settings, with a floral motif clasp centering a cushion-cut red spinel encircled by om diamonds, approx 52.00 cts diamonds tw, Fr hmks (eagle's head) for 18k gold, 1/2" w (at center), 16" tl, clasp 5/8" dia .... 112,500 (A)

Turquoise, yg, c. 1875, a fringe of lozenge shapes, sm ones bezel-set with a single lozenge-shaped turq cab alternating with larger ones set with a cluster of four lozenge-shaped turq cabs within one bezel, suspended by short and long yg rods from tubular reeded yg links alternating with sq turq cabs in hollow sq bezels, strung on chain, 1-3/8" x 16" tl .... 4,600 (A)

Pendant

14k yg, enamel, diamonds, c. 1890, tiger's head enameled in shades of white, orange, brown, black, and red, with sm oe diamond eyes, and one sm oe diamond in mouth, in a yg mount (enamel damage), 7/8" w x 1" tl... 345 (A)

Garnet, diamonds, pearls, st yg, Late Victorian, oval centering a bezel-set garnet cab measuring 19.5 mm by 28.54 mm, surrounded by scrolled filigree and a ring of sm sc diamonds bead-set in st yg quartered by four bead-set half pearls, each flanked by foliate motif set with sm sc diamonds, lozenge-shaped bail set with four sm sc bead-set diamonds, 1-3/8" w x 2-1/8" .... 863 (A)

Locket

Diamonds, enamel, 15k yg, c. 1890, heart-shaped, central inverted pear-shaped rc diamond encircled by a rayed oval of black enamel, eleven sm rc diamonds around scalloped edge, glazed locket compartment on rev, pendant loop at top, 1" w x 1-1/4" .... 1,088 (A)

Pendant and Chain

Diamonds, ruby, st yg, c. 1890, puffed heart shape of pavé-set om diamonds centering a lg cushion-cut ruby, later-added 14k wg chain, diamond set bail, 1-1/4" w x 1-1/2" tl, chain 18" tl .... 9,200 (A)

Necklace, diamonds, st yg, c. 1840, articulated floral and foliate motif links, love knot at center flanked by lg flowerhead and love knot, set throughout with rc diamonds, hinged bail at center for pendant, flowerhead surmounting v-spring clasp, 15-1/2" tl, **$7,500**. (Courtesy of E. Foxe Harrell Jewelers, Clinton, IA).

Necklaces, garnets:

L, seed pearls, silver gilt, c. 1840, *girandole* rc garnet cluster, starburst center flanked by foliate motifs set with seed pearls, suspending one lg and two sm garnet drops with seed pearl centers continuing to a chain of rc garnet links alternating with garnet and seed pearl clusters, terminating in v-spring and box clasp, safety chain, 1-1/2" w x 1-7/8" at center, 17-3/4" tl, **$1,600**.

R, gp brass, c. 1920, Bohemian (pyrope) garnet floral clusters with one lg central cluster flanked by grad clusters alternating with chain links to v-spring and box clasp mkd "Czech," safety chain, 1-1/8" w, 15" tl, **$595**. (Courtesy of E. Foxe Harrell Jewelers, Clinton, IA).

Ring, diamonds, st yg, c. 1840, flowerhead cluster, center rc diamond encircled by nine smaller rc diamonds, set *à jour* in silver, yg shank, approx size 6, possible earring conversion, head 1/2" dia, **$375**. (Courtesy of E. Foxe Harrell Jewelers, Clinton, IA).

Ring, opals, diamonds, rubies, yg, c. 1895, navette-shaped plaque, pavé-set diamond ground pierced with four petal-shaped openings radiating from om diamond-set center flanked by four sm oval opals and two sm marquise-cut rubies, two lg marquise-shaped opals top and bottom, mounted on a narrow shank, Fr hmks, 5/8" w x 1-1/2", size 7, **$2,300** [A]. (Photo courtesy of Christie's New York, 4/8/97).

Ring

9 kt yg, seed pearls, date letter for 1893, slightly tapered band, a horizontal row of seed pearls bead-set across top, Birmingham (Eng) hmks, 1/4" w, approx size 5 110

Amethyst, rose gold, c. 1870-80, faceted oval pale amethyst ("rose de France") mounted in a multipronged setting with C-scroll die-rolled gallery flanked by stamped vertical bars appl to engr shoulders on 1-1/4" wide shank, inscribed inside "Laura L. Klotz," head 3/8" w x 1/2", approx size 6-1/2 250

Amethyst, seed pearls, 14k yg, c. 1890, lg rect-cut amethyst in an octagonal bezel framed by a row of seed pearls, set in an octagonal scalloped yg frame with appl bead and foliate motif decoration, openwork shoulders, narrow shank mkd "14k", 3/4" w x 7/8", approx size 5.... 684 (A)

Diamonds, 14k yg, c. 1890, lozenge-shaped engr yg plaque set with nine om diamonds, approx 1.30 cts tw, plain shank, 1/2" w x 3/4", approx size 5 .... 912 (A)

Garnets, 14k yg, c. 1880-90, engr band centering three grad bezel-set garnets, 3/4" w x 3/8", size 10.... 316 (A)

Opals, demantoid garnets, diamonds, 14k yg, c. 1890, slightly convex horizontal oval mount centering a row of four oval opal cabs surrounded by sm circ-cut demantoid garnets, bordered with sm oe diamonds, illegible maker's mk, 5/8" w x 3/8", size 6-1/2 .... 1,495 (A)

Scarf Pin/Stickpin

Diamonds, moonstone, 14k yg, c. 1890, a crescent moon and star, central carved moonstone depicting the man in the moon, surrounded by a crescent of pave-set sm oe diamonds in a yg mount, a diamond-set star suspended from top terminal, 1/2" w x 5/8", 2-1/2" tl........ 1,495 (A)

Pearls, diamond, yg, c. 1900, a quatrefoil of four pearls with oe diamond center, mounted on yg pinstem, 1/2" x 1/2", 2-1/2" tl .... 138 (A)

Suite: Bracelet and Earrings

Ivory, 14k yg, c. 1880-90, bracelet of central lg oval and five sm oval carved ivory plaques in high relief floral bouquet motif, set in wiretwist-decorated yg bezels, matching oval earrings, v-spring and box clasp, bracelet 1-1/2" w (at center), 7-1/4" tl, earrings 3/4" w x 1", suite .... 690 (A)

Suite: Brooch/Pin and Bracelet

Yg, green gold, seed pearls, c. 1885, brooch a scalloped lozenge shape centering a lg cluster of seed pearls in grape motif flanked by engr green gold grape leaves, surmounted by a yg grape leaf flanked by two sm seed pearl grape clusters, within an open yg textured frame, C-catch, extended pinstem, matching bracelet of nine links, the central link with a lg seed pearl grape cluster surrounded by four lg green gold engr leaves and two sm yg engr leaves, flanked by sm circ links with a sm cluster of seed pearls and a green gold engr leaf, continuing to grad links surmounted by engr leaves, v-spring and box clasp, brooch 2-1/2" w 2", bracelet 1-1/2" w (at center), 7-1/2" tl, fitted case, suite .... 2,875 (A)

Suite: Necklace and Brooch/Pin

18k yg, chrysoprase, c. 1860-70, nine lg shield-shaped yg foliate scroll motif plaques, each framing a lg bezel-set chrysoprase tablet with faceted sides, alternating with eight sm yg grape cluster motif links, suspending a central bezel-set navette-shaped chrysoprase drop in a scrolling yg frame surmounted by a grape cluster, two flanking pendent sections missing, matching brooch/pin, in a fitted box, necklace 3-1/2" w (at center), 15-3/4" tl, suite .... 3,105 (A)

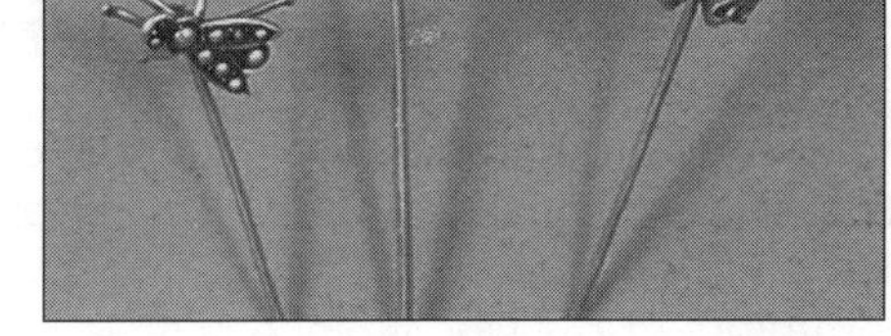

Scarf Pins/ Stickpins, yg, c. 1880-1910:
L, 10k yg, seed pearls, winged insect set with seed pearls, wire legs, 2" tl, 1/4" w x 5/8", **$145**.
C, three-dimensional tiger's head, diamond eyes and ruby in mouth, mkd "Pat Ap'ld For," 2-7/8" tl, 3/4" w x 5/8", **$400**.
R, 10k yg, repoussé lion's head in profile with seed pearl in mouth, 2-1/2" tl, 5/8" w x 5/8", **$200**.
(Courtesy of E. Foxe Harrell Jewelers, Clinton, IA).

Scarf Pins/Stickpins, garnets, silver gilt c. 1880-1900:
L, trefoil flower, larger garnets in millegrained bezels in flower petals, smaller garnets bead-set in leaf shapes, 2-5/8" tl, 3/8" w x 5/8", **$100**.
R, leaf and berry motif, lg garnet in millegrained bezel, several smaller garnets bead-set in leaf shapes, 3" tl, 5/8" w x 3/4", **$200**.
(Courtesy of E. Foxe Harrell Jewelers, Clinton,

Part II

TURN-OF-THE-CENTURY-JEWELRY

INTRODUCTION

The year 1900 did not signal the beginning of a new era so much as the continuation of the old and the continuing evolution of the new. The Victorian age did not end with the Queen's death in 1901; Victorianism held sway until World War I. But while a large proportion of the populace continued to cling to late Victorian fashions, three more stylistic trends emerged to establish themselves among various segments of society by the turn of the century.

This did not happen overnight. What is usually referred to as the Edwardian style had already begun to make its mark on fashionable society long before Edward became king. Aesthetic influences that led to the *Arts and Crafts* Movement and the beginning of modernism had made their presence felt as early as the mid nineteenth century. And the "New Art" had made its debut in Paris in the 1890s. So, in fact, at the turn of the century, there were four concurrent jewelry styles: Victorian, Arts and Crafts, Art Nouveau, and Edwardian.

This section is divided into the three latter styles. As with nineteenth century jewelry, it can be difficult to clearly identify turn-of-the-century pieces as one particular style or another. At times, two or more styles are commingled in a single piece of jewelry. Historians, collectors, and dealers seem to have a need to pigeonhole and label everything. It may be hard to accept that this is not always possible. A label for a style always crops up after the style has come and gone. It is artificial by nature. While an attempt has been made to categorize the pieces in the following sections, individual interpretations vary. Up until recently, historians usually grouped all turn-of-the-century "art" jewelry under Art Nouveau. Now, most make a distinction between Art Nouveau and Arts and Crafts. (Even more recently, a new label has come into use: Beaux-arts– see Art Nouveau section). But one person's Arts and Crafts is another's Art Nouveau. Edwardian pieces sometimes include Art Nouveau elements. Some stylistic details clearly belong in one or the other camp. These will be described in the sections that follow. What is important is to understand the part that each style played in jewelry history, to recognize its characteristic components, to see how the styles influenced one another, and how designs evolved over time.

As always, events and fashion trends played an important part in the evolution of *fin de siècle* jewelry design. The pace of change was quickened by new developments. The advent of the automobile and the airplane revolutionized transportation and increased mobility. "Motoring" became a fashionable pastime. The wireless telegraph and the telephone improved communication. The motion picture industry made its humble debut as the "peepshow" at Thomas Edison's Kinetoscope Parlor in New York City. By 1910, thousands of movie theaters were showing films whose stars were already influencing fashion. Jewelers advertised their wares in the new trend-setting fashion magazine, *Vogue.*

In the years between the turn of the century and World War I, several advances were made in the jewelry industry. The diamond saw was invented, making it possible for a cutter to get two diamonds out of an octahedron rough crystal instead of one. The National Stamping Act was passed in 1906, requiring the marking of gold and silver content on American-made jewelry.

Patents were granted for two kinds of safety catches for brooches, the first in 1901, issued to Herpers Bros. of Newark, NJ, for a catch with a lever to project and retract the closure. The second patent, granted in 1911 to Eugene Morehouse for B.A. Ballou of Providence, RI, was for the type of safety still in use today, which swivels around to enclose the pinstem. Synthetic rubies and sapphires were patented in 1904 and 1911 by Auguste Victor Louis Verneuil.

In 1915, a new alloy for white gold was patented by Karl Gustav Richter (see Edwardian section). A U.S. patent for spherical cultured pearls was granted to Kokichi Mikimoto in 1916.

The 1900 Paris Exposition Universelle heralded the pinnacle of Art Nouveau. Sarah Bernhardt's stage jewels by René Lalique and Georges Fouquet inspired many designers. The 1904 St. Louis Exposition showcased the remarkable jewels of Louis Comfort Tiffany for the first time.

In 1890, artist Charles Dana Gibson introduced the public to what was to become the epitome of turn-of-the-century American womanhood, the Gibson Girl. Her hair, figure and attire were considered the height of fashion in a trend that continued through the early 1900s.

The head and neck were emphasized with large hats, upswept bouffant hairdos, and high collars for day, décolleté for evening. Hatpins, hair combs, tiaras, "dog collar" chokers, and delicate lace pins and watchpins complemented the look. Festoon necklaces, pendants and their diminutive form, the lavalier, also focused attention on the neck. The lorgnette, usually worn suspended from a chain, became a symbol of period sophistication. Corsage, or bodice, ornaments decorated "pouter pigeon" bosoms. The waist was a focal point of the "hourglass" silhouette, and anything that adorned it was fashionable. One- and two-piece buckles, sewn onto fabric or leather belts, were often-worn accessories, as were belts of swagged chains linking small plaques. Large brooches known as sash ornaments or pins were also worn at the waist. Many have open centers; some include a simulated hasp. The pinstem is invisible when the brooch is pinned to a ribbon or belt, and the brooch imitates the look of a buckle. Cuff links and scarf pins continued to be worn by both sexes. Mainstream and avant-garde designs alike were rendered in these forms, made from both precious and non-precious materials.

References: Lillian Baker, *Hatpins and Hatpin Holders, An Illustrated Value Guide*, Collector Books, 1983, values updated 1992, and *The Collectors' Encyclopedia of Hatpins and Hatpin Holders*, published by the author,1988; Vivienne Becker, *Antique and Twentieth Century Jewellery*, 2nd ed., N.A.G. Press, 1987; Shirley Bury, *Jewellery 1789-1910, The International Era*, Vol. II, Antique Collectors' Club, 1991; Deanna Farneti Cera, ed., *Jewels of Fantasy, Costume Jewelry of the 20th Century*, Harry N. Abrams, 1992; Charlotte Gere, *American & European Jewelry, 1830-1914*, Crown Publishers, 1975 (out of print); Alison Gernsheim, *Victorian and Edwardian Fashion, A Photographic Survey*, Dover Publications, 1981; Malcolm Haslam, *Marks & Monograms, The Decorative Arts 1880-1960* (all media), Collins & Brown, London, 1995; Penny Proddow and Debra Healy, *American Jewelry, Glamour and Tradition*, Rizzoli International, 1987; Christie Romero, "Dates to Remember," Jewelers' Circular-Keystone/Heritage, February, 1997; A. Kenneth Snowman, ed., "The Master Jewelers," Harry N. Abrams, 1990; Janet Zapata, "Authenticating Tiffany Jewelry," article in Jewelers' Circular-Keystone/Heritage, August, 1988.

ARTS AND CRAFTS c. 1890-1920

History: Arts and Crafts was more than a style. It was called a Movement, which encompassed a philosophy, an attitude, and a way of living. The practitioners of the Movement were revivalists of a sort, but unlike the Etruscan and Greco-Roman Revivalists, they were not copyists; they were interpreters of the past. They revived the *ideas* of handicraft, of medieval guilds and individual craftsmanship. Their philosophical point of view influenced their creative impulses, which found expression in a number of different forms and incorporated a variety of stylistic elements. So Arts and Crafts is not one style, but many.

Historians usually classify the various interpretations of Arts and Crafts by country of origin. While it may be that an identifiable characteristic approach to design is shared by artisans of the same nationality, it is dangerous to generalize. Without documentation or identifying marks–and many Arts and Crafts pieces are unmarked–attribution to country or maker is a guessing game at best. In terms of history, however, it can be useful to trace the movement as it developed from it origins in Great Britain and spread to Europe and the United States.

Liberty & Co.

Liberty & Co., Cymric Ltd. (1903 only)

Murrie, Bennett & Co.

Great Britain

As early as the 1870s, when Victorian Classical Revivalists were in the majority, the seeds of dissent were germinating. The dissidents were counter-revolutionaries to the Industrial Revolution. They rebelled against increased mechanization and mass-production, and the consequent loss of the human touch in the making of decorative and utilitarian objects. They also rebelled against the excesses of Victorian ornament, setting the stage for the advent of modernism at the beginning of this century. The rebellion had its roots in Great Britain, then the greatest of industrial nations. The Crystal Palace Exhibition of 1851 had shown the world the achievements of the British in the use of the machine. For some, it was the beginning of the end of craftsmanship. John Ruskin and William Morris, generally recognized as the instigators of the insurrection, went on to formulate a rather utopian philosophy which would gather steam and become the Arts and Crafts Movement. The earliest application of the philosophy was in architecture, interior design and furnishings. Jewelry-making wasn't included until C.R. Ashbee founded his Guild of Handicraft in London in 1888.

The Aesthetic Movement of the 1870s may have given impetus to Arts and Crafts and Art Nouveau. The influence of Japanese art began with the aesthetes, and also found expression in the later styles. The adherents of the Aesthetic movement were a splinter group of intellectuals that included the Pre-Raphaelites of the art world and the advocates of dress reform, such as members of The Rational Dress Society in Britain and The Free Dress League in the U.S. While mainstream fashion kept women tightly corseted, boned and laced into "hourglass" figures, clothing reformists attempted to liberate fashion from the confines of the corset. Reform dress for Arts and Crafts proponents was loose and high-waisted in the medieval or Renaissance style. This was part of their preoccupation with the past–recalling simpler, idealistic times in hopes of liberating themselves from the dehumanizing mechanized world. Types of jewelry made to complement the clothing were primarily necklaces and pendants, buckles, sash ornaments and brooches. Hatpins, hair ornaments and tiaras, an important part of period fashion, were also interpreted by Arts and Crafts designers. Rings and bracelets were less commonly made, earrings rarely.

The prime directive of the Arts and Crafts Movement purists was for one artisan to make everything entirely by hand from start to finish. No matter how varied the style, the one thing they all had in common was the desire for their handcraftsmanship to be apparent. Hammer marks and irregularities were left intact as evidence of human handiwork. Simplification of line and form, and the use of stylized organic motifs were also common threads.

Staunch social idealists, the leaders of the movement hoped to bring art to the people "in an acceptable form at realistic prices." In jewelry, the intrinsic value of the materials was of secondary importance to design and workmanship. Most Arts and Crafts artisans preferred silver to gold, and inexpensive cabochon gemstones like turquoise and moonstone to faceted diamonds and rubies. Enameling was a favorite technique of many. Some worked in brass, copper, and glass.

Although the materials were inexpensive, the time and workmanship involved in producing entirely handmade pieces made them too labor intensive to be affordable for any but the well-to-do. The rejection of the use of all machinery made production in multiples difficult and expensive. The guild artisans were unable to produce sufficient quantities of jewelry to supply the "masses." The irony of the situation was that the very manufacturers whose techniques they rejected were successful where the purists failed. British firms such as Liberty & Co., W. H. Haseler, Murrle, Bennett & Co., and Charles Horner commercialized the style, but in so doing made it affordable.

Foremost among the success stories was Liberty & Co., founded by Arthur Lazenby Liberty in 1875 as an importer of Near and Far Eastern goods, just as the *japonaiserie* craze was in full swing. The company's own popular "Cymric" (pronounced "kim´-rik," from the word for the Celts of Wales) line of metalware and jewelry was first exhibited in 1899. Liberty employed a number of designers to create what were then called "modern" designs. The "Liberty Style," which really *was* the people's style, was mass-produced interpretations of one-of-a-kind handmade pieces, and much more accessible and affordable to the middle and working classes. The prototypes for these pieces were designed by talented artists whose names were kept from the public at the time, but who are well-known today. Liberty's principal designer, whose work is most sought-after, was Archibald Knox (1864-1933).

Knox's work is characterized by Celtic knot motifs (also called *entrelac)* and whiplash curves in silver and enamel. In his pieces, he popularized the use of intermingled "floating" blue and green enamels pooled in central depressions. He occasionally worked in gold.

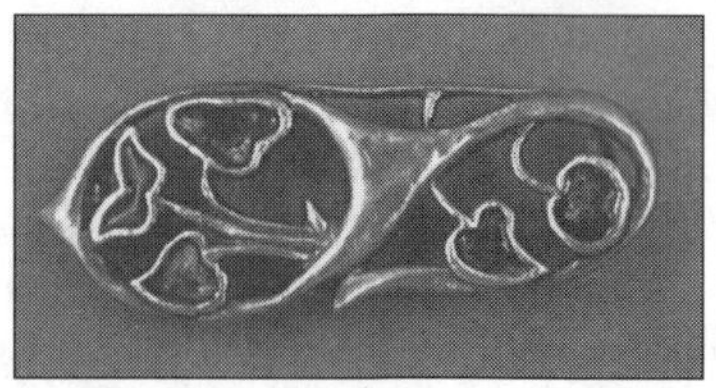

Brooch/Pin, silver, enamel, c. 1900, elongated openwork curv design with blue and green enameled leaves, mkd "CYMRIC" for Liberty & Co., C-catch, flanged hinge, 1-3/4" w x 1/2", **$450**. (Terrance O'Halloran collection).

Some other known designers who worked for Liberty were Jessie M. King, Oliver Baker, and Arthur and Georgie Gaskin. These same designers also worked independently, creating entirely handmade pieces. When Liberty appropriated their designs, the pieces were made by machine, but with hand-finished details. They retained the look of the handwrought designs, and, except by purists' standards, are still considered Arts and Crafts. Unfortunately, the pieces were only marked with one of several Liberty hallmarks ("L & Co.," "Ly & Co.," "LC&C Ld"). Attribution is based on characteristic motifs and techniques, and at times, archival documentation in the form of drawings and company records.

W. H. Haseler and Murrle, Bennett & Co. also produced designs for Liberty's retail establishment. In 1901, W. H. Haseler, a Birmingham manufacturer, formed a partnership with Liberty to produce their Cymric line. Pieces can be marked for Liberty or "W.H.H." for Haseler. Murrle, Bennett was founded in 1884 as wholesale distributors. They were based in England, but also had manufacturing connections in Pforzheim, Germany, where they imported pieces for Liberty and

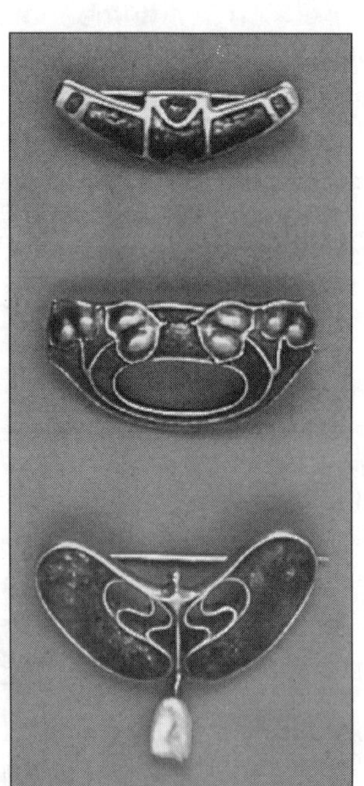

Brooches/Pins, silver, enamel, Eng, c. 1900-1910:

T, date letter for 1909, curved wing-shaped plaque, segmented sections filled with purple and green mingled enamel and blue enamel, mkd "CH" for Charles Horner, Chester hmks, C-catch, flanged hinge, 1-3/8" w x 3/8", **$225**.

C, irregular shape around cutout oval center, mingled blue and green enamel ground surmounted by two pairs of heart-shaped repoussé silver leaves, mkd "MBC" for Murrle, Bennett & Co. and "950," C-catch, 1-1/2" w x 3/4", **$450**. (Elaine Sarnoff collection).

B, wing-shaped plaque enameled in mingled green, orange and yellow, pierced heart-shaped center with four opposed S-scrolls flanking central vertical bar, suspending a f.w. pearl, rev mkd "W H H" for W.H. Haseler, Birmingham Eng, "SILVER," C-catch, tube hinge, extended pinstem, 1-1/2" w x 1-1/8" tl, **$350**. (Author's collection).

also worked with Theodor Fahrner. Their mark is a conjoined "MB" inside a large C, followed by a small o, which is often used together with British hallmarks or Fahrner's marks. Some pieces are marked "M.B. & Co." World War I brought association with Fahrner to a halt, and Murrle Bennett ceased to be known as such in 1916. The company was renamed White, Redgrove and Whyte.

Charles Horner was a mass-marketed manufacturer in Halifax, which produced silver and enamel jewelry that was entirely made by machine, but maintained the appearance of Liberty-style Arts and Crafts. They were known for small brooches, pendants and chains, and hatpins. The winged scarab, Celtic knot, and thistle were favorite motifs. Pieces are marked "C.H.," usually with Chester assay marks and date letters. For more on these four firms, see "Liberty and His Rivals" in Becker's *Antique and 20th Century Jewellery*.

Theodor Fahrner (Germany)

Wiener Werlstätte (Austria)

Germany and Austria

By the late 1890s, The Arts and Crafts Movement had found its way across the English Channel to Europe, where it was interpreted and renamed by German, Austrian, and Scandinavian artisans. In Germany and Austria, it was called *Jugendstil* ("young style"). Scandinavians called it *skønvirke*, which is described in the section on Scandinavian jewelry. The Italians mostly stuck with classic revivalism, but its few practitioners called the new style *Stile Liberty*.

German *Jugendstil* has been classified both as Arts and Crafts and as Art Nouveau, but it can also be viewed as the genesis of modernism. It seems best to analyze each piece individually rather than make a judgment call on the entire body of work. Certain pieces exhibit English Arts and Crafts influence while others take inspiration from French Art Nouveau. If it is possible to generalize at all, the *Jugendstil* "look," whether abstract or figural, is characterized by strong lines and bold designs. A number of individual artists worked independently or anonymously. Several manufacturers also produced *Jugendstil* jewelry. The most well-known of these was Theodor Fahrner of Pforzheim, who brought the work of many individual designers to the attention of the general public.

Theodor Fahrner could be called the Liberty of Germany, in terms of *modus operandi*, although Fahrner manufactured jewelry exclusively, while Liberty traded in a variety of goods. What the two had in common was employing skilled freelance designers to produce "modern" designs for a commercial market. The designs themselves were sometimes the same, thanks to the connection with Murrle, Bennett & Co. Unlike Liberty, however, many of Fahrner's pieces produced between 1900-1919 were also signed by the designers. Most of these designers came from the Darmstadt Colony, an artists' community founded on the same philosophical ideals as the British guilds. It is during this period that Fahrner's *Jugendstil* jewelry was produced. Today it is highly sought-after, especially if it is artist-signed. Some important designers were Patriz Huber, Max Gradl, Franz Boeres, and Georg Kleemann.

Founded in 1855 in Pforzheim, the company's distinctive mark, a conjoined "TF" in a circle, was not introduced until 1901. The death of Theodor Fahrner (Jr.), son of the company's founder, in 1919 brought changes to the factory. Keeping up with new styles under new ownership, the company went on to become known as a producer of Art Deco fashion jewelry in marcasite, enamel and gemstones set in silver. The firm closed in 1979. A great deal of information, painstakingly compiled by its authors, can be found in the book on Fahrner cited below.

Heinrich Levinger (Germany)

Heinrich Levinger was another Pforzheim manufacturer which is not as well-known as Fahrner, but the pieces the company made are equally desirable to collectors. They were noted for stylized organic forms in *plique à jour* enamel and silver. They made designs attributed to Viennese designer Otto Prutscher (1880-1949), but unlike Fahrner, no designer's mark was put on the pieces. In fact, sometimes the maker's mark is absent.

In Austria, Vienna was the center of Jugendstil activity. Among its practitioners, the best-known is a guild of multi-media craftspeople who were part of the Vienna Secession, the Wiener Werkstätte (Viennese Workshop). Founded in 1903 by Josef Hoffmann (1870-1956) and Koloman Moser (1868-1918), it was patterned after C.R. Ashbee's Guild of Handicraft. The style that evolved there is geometric and simplified, a harbinger of modernism. Jewelry by any of the Wiener Werkstätte designers, especially the work of Hoffman and Moser, is now highly collectible. The most of-

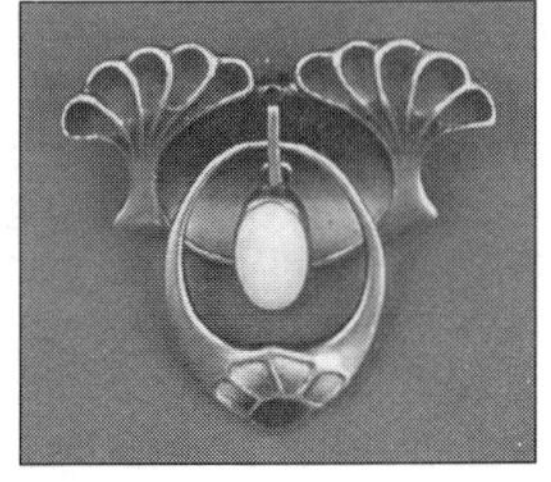

Brooch/Pin, 935 silver, enamel, opal, c. 1901, oval plaque, *champlevé* enameled in dk blue shading to lt green, flanked by stylized tree motifs, upper portions *plique à jour* enameled in similar colors, front-mounted top-center loop suspending a bezel-set oval opal within an articulated open oval frame extending below plaque, wider bottom portion of five irregular *champlevé* enameled segments in lt green to dk blue, design attributed to Rudolf Bosselt, rev imp with maker's mk for Theodor Fahrner, "935, DEPOSÉ," 1-1/4" x 1-1/4", **$2,000**. (Gail Gerretsen collection).

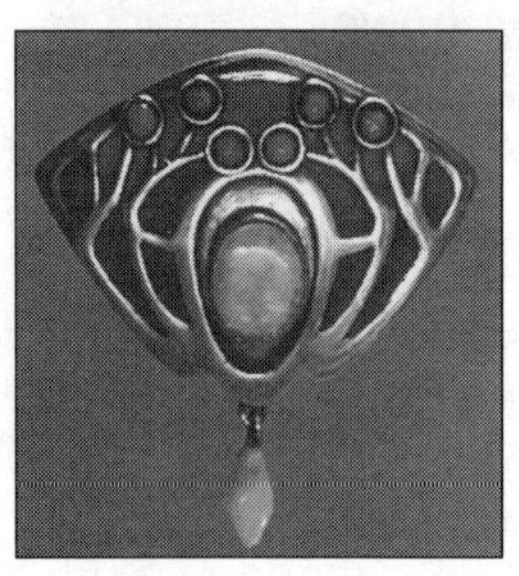

Brooch/Pin, silver, enamel, opal, f.w. pearl, c. 1900, shield-shaped plaque, stylized branchlike motif bezel-set with six sm circ blue-green opal cabs across top, enclosing lg oval bezel-set opal with predominantly red play-of-color, on a green *plique à jour* enameled ground, f.w. pearl drop, rev mkd "*DEPOSÉ,*" Fr import mk stamped on C-catch, attributed to Heinrich Levinger, Pforzheim (Ger), 1-1/4" w x 1-1/4" tl, **$1,200**. (Ann Tidwell collection).

ten-seen of the shop's marks is a superimposed "WW." An extensive history and examples of both German and Austrian Jugendstil can be found in Becker's *Art Nouveau Jewelry,* listed in the references below.

Some of Moser's designs were executed by the Viennese firm Georg Anton Scheid before the founding of the Wiener Werkstätte. The mark is "G.A.S." with Austrian hallmarks. The Scheid pieces tended to be non-representational Art Nouveau in style.

The United States

British and European Arts and Crafts jewelry has been well-documented in several books. American Arts and Crafts jewelry, however, has been given relatively little attention. Aside from brief chapters in two books, the only other sources of information are articles in periodicals, exhibition catalogs, and the semiannual sales catalogs published by Rosalie and Aram Berberian of ARK Antiques. There are a great many more extant, accessible examples of American Arts and Crafts jewelry than some historians would lead one to believe. Consequently, the listings in this book are weighted heavily toward them. Some examples are by makers about whom very little published information exists, but whose work is available on the market today.

The Art Silver Shop

The handicraft aesthetic caught on a bit later in the United States, and lasted longer. Some say it never ended, but that is a matter of personal interpretation. It began with guilds of craftspeople inspired by and patterned after British models. The most well-known are the Roycrofters and Gustav Stickley's Craftsman group. Perhaps because these guilds were not known for jewelry-making explains why some collectors are unaware that American Arts and Crafts jewelry was made by many others. The movement's jewelry makers were concentrated in the Northeast (Boston, New York), the Midwest (especially Chicago), and California. Arts and Crafts Societies were founded in several major cities, and promoted the work of their members.

In Boston, the Society of Arts and Crafts was the guiding light of the movement. Founded in 1897, the Society began conferring the award and title of Medalist to their most highly skilled members in 1913. Four of these Medalists were jewelers whose oeuvre is recognized today as the best of American Arts and Crafts. This Boston group seems to have been directly inspired by the British in terms of design and execution, if not use of materials. Their pieces incorporate organic motifs, wire and beadwork in open, delicate and refined designs. Unlike their British counterparts, however, they worked primarily in gold, and used faceted stones of high intrinsic value, as well as cabochon gemstones and pearls. They relied on stones and metal for color, rather than enamel. But like the British, their pieces are not always signed. Documentation in the form of drawings or photographs in the Society's archives have aided attribution.

Among the earliest recipients of the Medalist award was Josephine Hartwell Shaw (1865-1941), to whom it was given in 1914. Examples of her work are rare and sought-after today. Margaret Rogers (? - c. 1945) became a Medalist in 1915. She exhibited in Boston and at the annual exhibitions sponsored by the Art Institute of Chicago. Frank Gardner Hale (1876-1945) studied at C.R. Ashbee's Guild of Handicraft in England and in Europe. His work reflects the influence of his studies. He too, won the Medalist award in 1915. Edward Everett Oakes (1891-1960) studied under both Shaw and Hale.

The youngest and most prolific of the four, Oakes was awarded the Society's medal in 1923. Even though he was a latecomer, his pieces retained the motifs and the aesthetic of Arts and Crafts. He developed distinctive repoussé leaf and flower forms that were combined with wire tendrils and beadwork in layers around gemstones. He used his own alloys of colored gold, particularly green gold, and also worked in combinations of gold and silver. His mark is his last name within an oak leaf, but, like the others, he did not always sign his work.

An increasing amount of attention is being paid to a woman who, like Oakes, worked in a mode that wasn't in keeping with the period in which she lived. Mary Gage (1898-1993) was behind, not ahead of, her time. Her style is much more akin to Arts and Crafts, but the period in which she worked corresponds with that of modernist studio artist-jewelers. She began silversmithing in the mid-1920s in New York City, then later moved to New England, ending up in Portland Maine. She continued to make jewelry until her death at the age of 94 in 1993. Because her style varied little over the years, it's difficult to pinpoint circa-dates for her pieces exactly. Large flower and lily pad motifs were her specialty.

Another later-than-its-heyday example of Arts and Crafts is the work of a woman who is still living, but no longer working, Lillian Foster of Philadelphia. The cruciform brooch with strapwork details on page 83 has a central ceramic plaque depicting an angel painted in a naïve style. She also made silver or gold and gemstone pieces more reminiscent of the Boston school.

In New York, the eccentric artistic genius Louis Comfort Tiffany (1848-1933), son of the founder of Tiffany & Co., turned his attention from interior design to jewelry after his father's death in 1902. His pieces were first exhibited at the St. Louis Louisiana Purchase Exposition in 1904. Until 1907, his jewelry was made by his own firm, Tiffany Furnaces. After 1907 and until 1933, all L.C.T. pieces were made by and marked Tiffany & Co. There is ongoing controversy over the identification of L.C.Tiffany jewelry made after 1907, particularly when a Tiffany & Co. piece of the period comes up for sale at auction. An authentic, identifiable piece of Louis Tiffany jewelry sold at auction today may bring tens of thousands of dollars.

Perhaps because of his association with the most prestigious jewelry firm in the country, some may find it difficult to reconcile Tiffany's jewelry with the Arts and Crafts Movement's tenets. Many classify it as Art Nouveau, along with his glass, lamps, and other decorative art objects. Jewelry historian and L.C.Tiffany biographer Janet Zapata points out that his sources and influences were many, including Oriental, Islamic, Egyptian and Byzantine motifs, and, especially, the colors and forms found in nature. Tiffany was such an individual artist, that the diverse body of his work defies classification. However, Zapata considers his jewels to be very much in keeping with Arts and Crafts philosophy: "Louis's conception of jewelry was at odds with the pieces being made at Tiffany & Co. To him, color was paramount; gemstones were to be selected for their polychromatic effects, not for their monetary value." (p. 40, op. cit. below). She goes on to state that "each piece was hand-crafted...nothing was stamped out or cast. This craftsmanship ideal was followed at the time by Arts and Crafts designers in England and Boston." (ibid., p. 100).

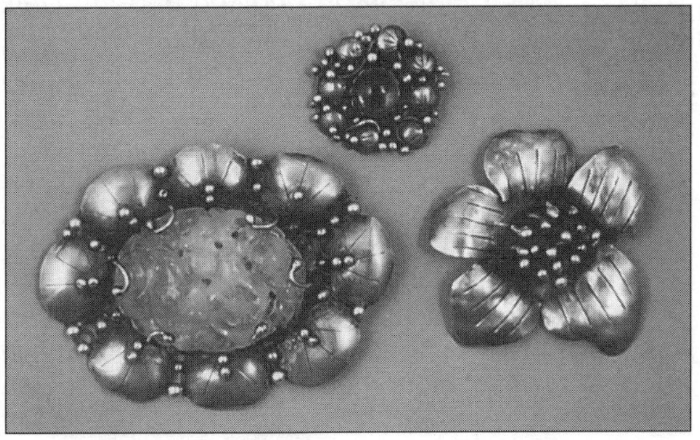

Brooches/Pins, sterling, Am, Mary Gage, c. 1930-40:

T, rock crystal, convex circ foliate motifs interspersed with undulating wire and beading, encircling central round rock crystal cab, rev imp "MARY GAGE STERLING," safety catch, flanged hinge, 1-3/8" dia, **$350**.

BL, sterling, rose quartz, eight engr stylized lily pad motifs encircling oval pierced and carved rose quartz (possibly Chinese) held in place with bead-tipped wire prongs, silver bead-tipped wires interspersed throughout, mounted on ster wire frame, appl plate imp "MARY GAGE STERLING," 3-5/8" w x 2-5/8", **$600**.

BR, sterling, five-petaled flowerhead with bead-tipped wire "stamen" in center, engr petals, rev imp "HANDWROUGHT NARY GAGE STERLING," 2-1/8" w x 2-1/2", **$250**.

(Gail Gerretsen collection).

Marcus & Co. was a New York firm whose output included both British-influenced Arts and Crafts and French-influenced Art Nouveau. They are noted for their enameled gold, gemstone and pearl jewels. They occasionally made sterling pieces.

Another latecomer who worked in the Arts & Crafts idiom was Peer Smed (1878-1943) of Brooklyn NY. Smed came to the United States from Denmark around 1904, having apprenticed with the well-known Danish firm A. Michelsen. Little information has been recorded about him or his work. He is known to have designed for Tiffany & Co. from his own studio in the 1930s. He made sterling flatware and holloware as well as jewelry. He followed the Arts & Crafts philosophy in producing individual pieces made by hand from start to finish by one person (he employed a few Scandinavian silversmiths in his shop). He marked his pieces with his name and the words "handwrought" or "hand chased."

In upstate New York, Heintz Art Metal Shop of Buffalo made jewelry and decorative objects of patinated bronze with sterling overlay in cutout patterns. They were in business from 1906 to 1929. Their style is so distinctive that although their mark was not used on jewelry, it is readily identifiable.

The Chicago Arts and Crafts Society was founded in 1897, the same year as Boston's. Chicago fostered a number of Arts and Crafts silversmiths and jewelers (many of them were both). Collectors were made aware of their work as a result of an exhibition and catalog entitled *The Chicago Metalsmiths,* sponsored by the Chicago Historical Society in 1977. The catalog is still the best source of information on this group of artisans and shops. The largest and best-known of them is The Kalo Shop, in operation from 1900 to 1970. Their early jewelry designs are the essence of simplicity in line and form. Most are sterling, often set with blister or baroque pearls, mother of pearl or abalone shell, coral, moonstones or other inexpensive gemstones. Pendants are suspended from handmade "paper clip" chains, so called because of the elongated oval shape of the links. This is a typical type of chain used by turn-of-the-century Arts and Crafts designers. In the twenties and thirties, the Kalo look changed to cutout and pierced repoussé floral and foliate motifs with engraved details. The word "KALO" in block letters is found as part of the mark on all of their pieces. Some are numbered with order or design numbers.

Some other noted Chicago shops and silversmiths who also made jewelry were the Art Silver Shop (later Art Metal Studios, still in business), the T.C. Shop, James H. Winn, Madeline Yale Wynne, Frances Glessner, and Matthias W. Hanck. Lebolt & Co., a retail jewelry establishment founded in 1899, installed a workshop around 1912 to produce their own line of handwrought silver and jewelry.

Marshall Field & Co., a Chicago department store, catered to the demand for handcrafted metalware and jewelry by opening its own Craft Shop around 1904. They made jewelry in silver and brass using acid-etching and patination, techniques that were apparently unique to American Arts and Crafts jewelry. These two processes were usually combined to create a design on a shaped plaque of hammered raised metal. The ef-

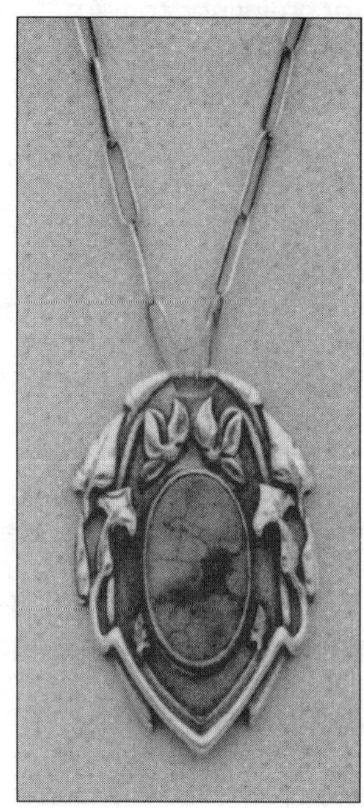

Pendant and Chain, sterling, turquoise, c. 1915, cusped oval open frame, an oval turq cab bezel-set in center surrounded by stylized floral/foliate motifs, suspended from a 16" paper clip chain, sgd "KALO," 1" w x 1-1/2", **$1,200**. (Photo courtesy of ARK Antiques, New Haven, CT).

fect was an "antique," aged look, more crude and rough in appearance than the polished, refined pieces of the Boston jewelers.

Other Midwestern shops made brass, copper, and nickel silver ("German silver") jewelry of the same genre: Carence Crafters of Chicago (who also made sterling and gemstone pieces), George W. Frost of Dayton, Ohio, and the Forest Craft Guild in Grand Rapids, Michigan, founded by Forest Mann around 1905. Most, but not all, pieces are marked.

Carence Crafters

George W. Frost

There were a number of other lesser-known American guilds or shops based outside of Boston and Chicago. Several of them were in other parts of the northern Midwest, particularly in Ohio: In Cleveland, Potter Studios, founded by Horace Potter, and the Rokesley Shop, founded around 1907. The latter produced pleasing designs in silver, enamel, pearls and gemstones. They were one of the few American shops to use enamel in the English manner.

Pasadena California silversmith Clemens Friedell (1872-1963) worked for Gorham Co. in Providence Rhode Island before coming to California in 1910. His style has the Art Nouveau overtones of that company's "Martelé" line. His earlier work was mostly commissioned silverware. He opened a retail shop in 1929 that carried jewelry as well as a large array of decorative silver objects and holloware.

The work of "unknowns" and unsigned pieces which exhibit an Arts and Crafts aesthetic are also illustrated in this section. As with any other type of jewelry, one should always evaluate an Arts and Crafts piece on its own merits, regardless of where, when or by whom it was made. Because so much Arts and Crafts jewelry is unmarked, and often unattributable, this may not be just the first, but the only method of evaluation. Many an amateur hobbyist made handcrafted jewelry in the Arts and Crafts mode. Some of it is well-done, some is not.

References: Edith Alpers, "Edward Everett Oakes (1891-1960), a master craftsman from Boston, Massachusetts," *Jewellery Studies* Vol. 3, The Society of Jewellery Historians, Great Britain, 1989, and "F.G. Hale: Master Craftsman/Jeweler," article in *Jewelers' Circular-Keystone/Heritage*, August, 1989; Vivienne Becker, *Art Nouveau Jewelry*, E.P. Dutton, 1985 (out of print); Malcolm Haslam, *Collector's Style Guide: Arts and Crafts*, Ballantine Books, 1988; Sharon S. Darling, *Chicago Metalsmiths,* Chicago Historical Society, 1977; Charlotte Gere and Geoffrey C. Munn, *Pre-Raphaelite to Arts and Crafts Jewellery*, Antique Collectors' Club, 1996; Wendy Kaplan, *"The Art that is Life": The Arts and Crafts Movement in America, 1875-1920*, Museum of Fine Arts, Boston, 1987; Janet Kardon, ed., *Craft in the Machine Age, 1920-1945*, exhibition catalog, American Craft Museum, Harry N. Abrams, 1996; Elyse Zorn Karlin, *Jewelry & Metalwork in the Arts and Crafts Tradition*, Schiffer Publishing, 1993; Catherine Kurland and Lori Zabar, *Reflections: Arts and Crafts Metalwork in England and the United States*, exhibition catalog, Kurland-Zabar, New York, 1990; Mervyn Levy, *Liberty Style, The Classic Years: 1898-1910*, Rizzoli International, 1986; Gloria Lieberman, "Artistic Adornment, Arts and Crafts Jewelry," article in *Antiques & Fine Art*, May/June 1990; Don Marek, "Light and Line: The Art of Forest Emerson Mann," *Arts and Crafts Quarterly,* Vol. VI, No. 3; Stephen A. Martin, ed., *Archibald Knox*, Academy Editions, 1995; Kevin McConnell, *Heintz Art Metal*, Schiffer Publishing, 1990; Joseph Sataloff, *Art Nouveau Jewelry*, Dorrance & Co., 1984; Nancy Schiffer, *Silver Jewelry Designs: Evaluating Quality*, Schiffer Publishing, 1996; Ulrike von Hase-Schmundt et al, *Theodor Fahrner Jewelry, between Avant-Garde and Tradition*, Schiffer Publishing, 1991; Janet Zapata, *The Jewelry and Enamels of Louis Comfort Tiffany*, Harry N. Abrams, 1993.

Periodicals: *Style 1900, The Quarterly Journal of the Arts and Crafts Movement,* 17 South Main St., Lambertville, N.J. 08530; *Fine Early 20th Century American Craftsman Silver, Jewelry & Metal* (semiannual catalog with prices), ARK Antiques, Box 3133, New Haven, CT 06515.

Museums: Birmingham Museums and Art Gallery, Birmingham, the Fitzwilliam Museum, Cambridge, and The Victoria and Albert Museum, London, England, British Arts and Crafts jewelry; The *Schmuckmuseum*

(Jewelry Museum) in Pforzheim, Germany has an extensive collection, including examples of both German and Austrian Jugendstil; Museum of Fine Arts, Boston, MA, American Arts and Crafts jewelry;

Advisors: Rosalie and Aram Berberian (American), Gail Gerretsen, Terrance O'Halloran (British), Janet Zapata (American) .

Bracelet

Link

14k yg, c. 1925, alternating lg and sm chamfered corner rect linked plaques, each depicting a different naturalistic scene of birds, fish, floral and foliate motifs in appl raised design, maker's mk for Edward Everett Oakes ("OAKES" in an oak leaf), Medalist of the Boston Society of Arts & Crafts, 3/4" w x 7-1/2" .... 4,830 (A)

18k yg, lapis lazuli, sapphires, c. 1925-30, alternating lapis disks and sq foliate plaques, each with scrolled wirework flanking a collet-set sapphire, by Edward Everett Oakes, clasp sgd "OAKES" in an oak leaf, 5/8" w x 7-1/2" tl .... 3,105 (A)

Silver, enamel, seed pearls, blue stones, c. 1910, four rect plaques, each with a rounded *plique à jour* enameled stylized design of weblike netting in shades of blue, green and red, radiating from a sq-cut lt blue stone at the base, corners set with seed pearls, plaques joined at equal intervals with seven lengths of cable link silver chain, sliding hingepin closure, illegible hmk and maker's mk, probably Ger or Austrian, approx 1-1/2" w x 7" .... 2,300 (A)

Sterling, c. 1930, alternating links of repoussé and engr five-petaled flowerheads and paired foliate motifs with raised beads, mkd "KALO," v-spring and oval box clasp, safety chain, 7" tl x 1" w 700

Sterling, enamel, c. 1915-20, five rect links, circ centers enameled with floral/foliate motifs in lavender and blue, maker's mk superimposed "T" over "N," 6-1/2" tl x 3/4" 225

Bracelet, Link, 950 silver, amethyst, yg, c. 1910, sq hammered links with raised beads ("rivets") encircling circ-cut amethysts in yg bezels, alternating with rect links of pierced interlocking strapwork (*entrelac*), maker's mk for Murrle, Bennet & Co., mkd "950," safety chain, spring ring clasp, 7-1/2" l x 1/2" w, **$850**. (Gail Gerretsen collection).

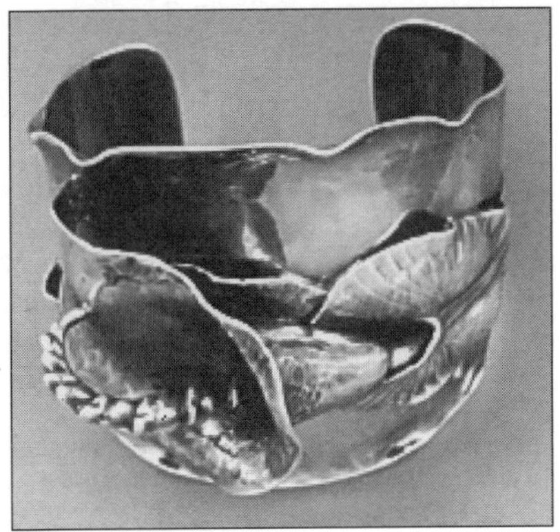

Bracelet, Cuff, sterling, c. 1935, hammered irregular surface with appl three-dimensional floral and foliate motif, mkd "PEER SMED STERLING HANDWROUGHT," 2-1/4" inside dia, 2" w (at center), 7/8" height, **$750**. (Janet Zapata collection).

Brooch/Pin

14k yg, lapis, c. 1910-15, lg oval lapis cab bezel-set in a navette-shaped frame, flanked by two seed pearls within geo cutouts at cusped ends, 1-3/4" w x 7/8" 475

18k yg, enamel, peridot, c. 1910, cushion-shaped yg plaque centering a sq step-cut peridot, surrounded by wiretwist filigree with green *plique à jour* enamel, designed by Louis Comfort Tiffany, Julia Munson, director in charge, sgd "TIFFANY & CO.," 1-1/4" w x 1-1/4" .... 2,300 (A)

800 silver, amber, c, 1910, open floral/foliate design, a small circ amber cab center flanked by two lg repoussé roses surmounted by beaded scrolls, beaded leaves below suspending a single repoussé rose drop, flat backing imp "*geschutzt*" (registered), "800," Ger crescent moon and crown hmk, maker's mk "A" within two concentric circles, 2" w x 3" tl 500

Silver, pearls, amethysts, garnet, c. 1910, circ disk with chased and hammered design, central garnet cab quartered by four amethyst cabs further quartered by four pearls on the rim, probably Eng, C-catch, tube hinge, 2-3/4" dia 300

Amber, silver, dyed green chalcedony, c. 1910, lg oval opaque amber cab surmounted by appl scrolled silver cutouts flanking a sm central bezel-set dyed green chalcedony cab, in a raised foliate motif silver frame, C-catch, flanged hinge, 2" w x 1-1/8" 450

Brooches/Pins, Am, Billiken motif (elfin character originally designed and patented by Florence Pretz, trademarked by the Craftsman's Guild of Chicago, 1908), patinated brass, c. 1910:

TL, circ disk, hammered and acid-etched with die-stamped figure of a Billiken, rev imp with sm billiken and "TRADE MARK BILLIKEN," wide C-catch, flanged hinge, 2" dia, **$185**.

TR, oval hammered and acid-etched disk, lg die-stamped Billiken in center, wide C-catch, flanged hinge, 2-1/2" w x 1-7/8", **$185**.

BL, hammered and acid-etched rect scallop edge plaque, die-stamped Billiken in center, wide C-catch, flanged hinge, 2-5/8" w x 2", **$185**.
(Gail Gerretsen collection).

BR, rounded lozenge-shaped plaque with raised and indented corners, appl pierced navette-shaped Celtic motif in open cutout center, flanked by a bezel-set lg circ green glass cab on one side, a raised Billiken motif on the other, on an acid-etched, abstract pattern ground, appl disk on rev mkd "TRADE MARK BILLIKEN" around imp Billiken mk, wide C-catch, flanged hinge, 3" w x 2-1/8", **$185**.
(Author's collection).

Brooch/Pin, Cross, moonstones, silver, c. 1910, openwork cross with braided and beaded decoration, foiled blue moonstone cabs prong-set in ropetwist frames in center and at terminals, closed backs, attributed to Mary Thew, Scotland, later-added safety catch, flanged hinge, extended pinstem, 1-1/2" w x 2-3/8", **$600**. (Terrance O'Halloran collection).

Brooch/Pin, silver, enamel, labradorite, c. 1910, openwork curv lilypad and blossom design in green, yellow, white and blue enamel suspending a labradorite briolette, unmkd, C-catch, flanged hinge, 1" w x 1-1/2", **$275**. (Terrance O'Halloran collection).

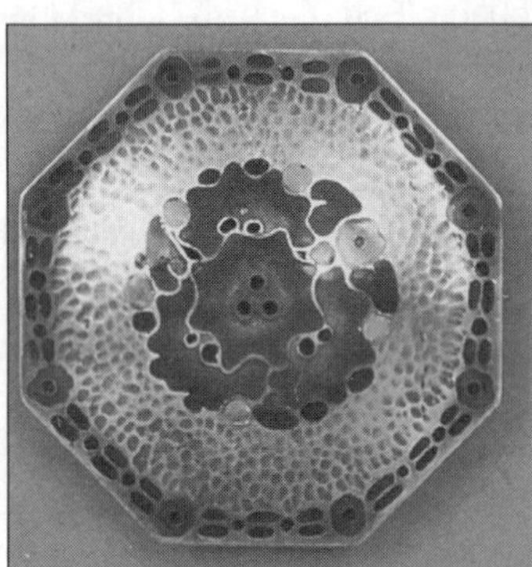

Brooch/Pin, sterling, enamel, c. 1910, octagonal raised and hammered plaque, central stylized floral design in blue, green, yellow and black *champlevé* and *basse-taille* enamel, border of dots, dashes and flowerheads in blue, green and black, design attributed to Hermann Häussler, maker's mk for Theodor Fahrner (Ger) "DEPOSÉ 935," C-catch, 1-7/8" w x 1-7/8", **$1,500**. (Gilly Phipps collection).

Bar Brooch/Pin, 18k yg, citrines, seed pearls, c. 1910, navette-shaped openwork bar with appl foliate and vine motif surrounding three collet-set circ-cut citrines, interspersed with seed pearls, C-catch, 3" w x 3/8" at center, **$450**. (BeeGee McBride collection).

Brooch/Pin, silver, enamel, citrines, c. 1910, convex rounded triangular shape with black matte enamel ground and beaded edge, surmounted by three silver heart-shaped leaves and vine motif with five collet-set citrines, unmkd, attributed to Theodor Fahrner (Ger), C-catch, flanged hinge, 1-3/4" w x 1-1/4", **$450**. (Terrance O'Halloran collection).

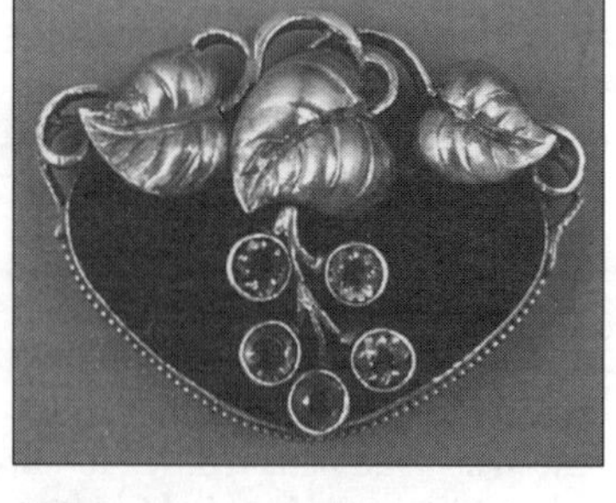

Brooch/Pin, bronze, sterling, c. 1910, heart-shaped sterling overlay with foliate motif at top appl to a domed bronze plaque, attributed to Heintz Art Metal Shop, Buffalo, NY, wide C-catch, flanged hinge, 1-1/8" w x 1", **$185**. (Courtesy of E. Foxe Harrell Jewelers, Clinton, IA).

Brooch/Pin, sp brass, glass, c. 1900-10, pierced circ plaque with projecting pierced "wings" and "tail," oval blue and green peacock eye glass cab in center, three sm blue glass cabs on sides and at base, unmkd, probably Ger, C-catch, tube hinge, 1-3/4" w x 1", **$250**. (Elaine Sarnoff collection).

Brooch/Pin, porcelain, sterling, c. 1910, circ jasperware cameo depicting scene of two women testing Cupid's arrow of love in white on blue bg, hand wrought ster foliate motif frame, cameo incised on rev: "Hartford Porcelain Cameo," C-catch, flanged hinge, extended pinstem, 2-1/4" dia, **$300**. (Private collection).

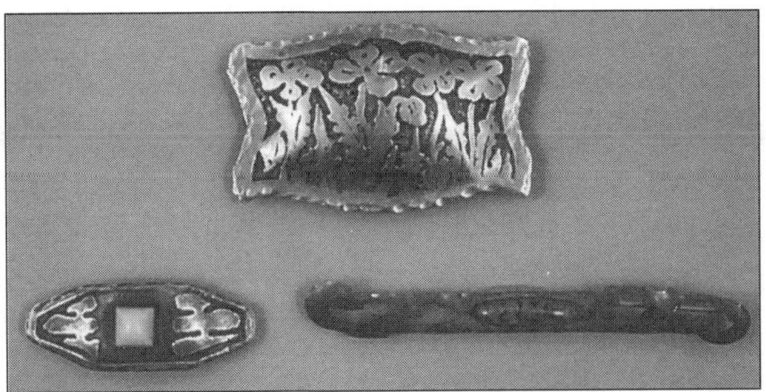

Brooches/Pins, Am, c. 1910:

T, patinated brass, hammered rounded rect plaque, acid-etched field of flowers motif, hammered edges, imp on rev "FROST" in triangle for George Winfield Frost, Dayton, OH, wide C-catch, flanged hinge, 2-1/2" w x 1-1/2", **$300**.

BL, patinated brass, glass, elongated octagon, central sq coral-colored glass cab, acid-etched oriental design, mkd on rev "FOREST CRAFT GUILD," Grand Rapids, MI, 1-7/8" w x 3/4", **$175**. (Elaine Sarnoff collection).

BR, Bar, copper, glass, hammered copper bar with rounded ends, four irregularly-shaped cutouts flanking elliptical mottled green glass cab bezel-set in center, rev imp "FOREST CRAFT GUILD," C-catch, flanged hinge, 3-5/8" w x 1/2", **$275**. (Author's collection).

Brass, enamel, c. 1915-20, stylized cartoonlike figure of a man with body and face in red, white and black enamel, cutout brass hands and feet, illegible mark, attributed to the Wiener Werkstatte, safety catch, 1" w x 2-1/8" 600

Brass, glass, c. 1910, acid-etched patinated brass rect plaque with indented edges, bezel-set green glass cab, appl circ disk in imitation of ancient coin with bust of man and the word "CICERO" at top, Am, wide C-catch, flanged hinge, 2" w x 1-3/4" 95

Brass, glass, c. 1910, green patinated hammered circ disk, abstract acid-etched design around an opaque cobalt blue glass cab center, wide C-catch, flanged hinge, Am, 2" dia 185

Sterling, c. 1920, oval chased and repoussé opposed stylized floral motifs, swirled with cutout center, mkd "STERLING HAND WROUGHT KALO" (Chicago), 2" w x 1-3/4"... 295

Sterling, c. 1930, cutout and pierced scallop edge oval with raised and engr floral and foliate motifs, rev imp "HAND WROUGHT STERLING KALO," safety catch, 2-3/8" w x 2" 450

Brooches/Pins, acid-etched brass, Am, Carence Crafters, Chicago, IL, c. 1910:

L, sp brass, irregular shield-shaped hammered and raised plaque, acid-etched winged insect motif on oxidized ground, rev imp with maker's mk for Carence Crafters, wide C-catch, flanged hinge, 2-5/8" w x 1-3/4", **$250**. (Author's collection).

R, waisted cut-corner rect plaque, acid-etched abstract design, rev imp with maker's mk for Carence Crafters, wide C-catch, flanged hinge, 1-5/8" w x 2-1/4", **$300**. (Elaine Sarnoff collection).

Brooch/Pin, sterling, c. 1935, rounded rect plaque, chased and repoussé cornucopia motif, mkd "PEER SMED STERLING HAND CHASED," safety clasp, 2-1/2" w x 2", **$750**. (Janet Zapata collection).

Sterling, c. 1930, cutout raised engr lobed feather motif, rev imp "KALO STERLING," 2-3/8" w x 7/8" 350

Sterling, c. 1940, five-lobed flowerhead with appl beads and engr decoration, sgd "MARY GAGE HANDWROUGHT STERLING," 2-1/2" dia 150

Sterling, carnelian, lapis lazuli, c. 1910, irregular oval ster plaque centering an oval bezel-set carnelian cab with beaded frame, encircled by foliate and scrolled vine motifs with sm bezel-set lapis cabs at compass points, maker's mk for Theodor Fahrner, Pforzheim, Germany, 1-5/8" w x 1-1/2" .... 690 (A)

Sterling, citrines, c. 1910, openwork oval, appl foliate motifs with scrolled wire, four collet-set citrines, maker's mk for Theodore Fahrner (Ger), 1-3/4" w x 1-1/4" .... 633 (A)

Sterling, zircon, c. 1920-25, oval frame with openwork design of appl foliate motif and scrolled wire accented with collet-set zircons, attributed to Edward Oakes, 2-1/2" w x 1-3/4" .... 1,380 (A)

Sterling, c. 1925-30, raised pierced oval plaque with a center cutout cluster of three chased and engr acorns framed by three chased and engr oak leaves, sgd "KALO," 2" w x 1-1/8" 325

Brooch/Pin, sterling, rock crystal, c. 1930-40, lg open oval frame surmounted by numerous sm engr grape leaves with appl beads mounted on undulating bead-tipped wire, sawtooth bezel-set circ rock crystal cab in center, rev imp "MARY GAGE, STERLING," 2" w x 2-3/4", **$350**. (Photo courtesy of The Noisy Boy & Disorderly Girl).

Brooch/Pin, silver, ceramic tile, c. 1940, cutout equilateral cross with strapwork motif decoration, center circ disk of stylized angel, orange ground, blue, white, yellow, rev imp "L.R. FOSTER" for Lillian Foster, Philadelphia, PA, safety catch, flanged hinge, 2-1/8" sq, **$350**. (Gail Gerretsen collection).

Bar

Sterling, rose quartz, c. 1915, irregular elongated slightly convex ster pierced plaque, bezel-set oval rose quartz cab off center, rev imp "STERLING," maker's mk for Carence Crafters (Chicago IL), wide C-catch, flanged hinge, 1-7/8" w x 1/2" 450

Sterling vermeil, carnelian, c. 1915, elongated plaque, abstract piercework, sq carnelian cab bezel-set on one end, rev imp "STERLING," maker's mk for Carence Crafters, wide C-catch, flanged hinge, (worn plating), 1-3/8" w x 5/8" 450

Buckle

Silver, enamel, c. 1900, two-pc, two rect silver plaques with floral design enameled in shades of blue, green and white, 2-1/2" w x 2" 350

Sterling, amethyst, c. 1910, two-pc, geo cutout openwork plaques, a volute with a sm circ bezel-set amethyst cab at each terminal, maker's mk for Theodor Fahrner, Pforzheim, Germany, 2-7/8" w x 1-1/2" .... 690 (A)

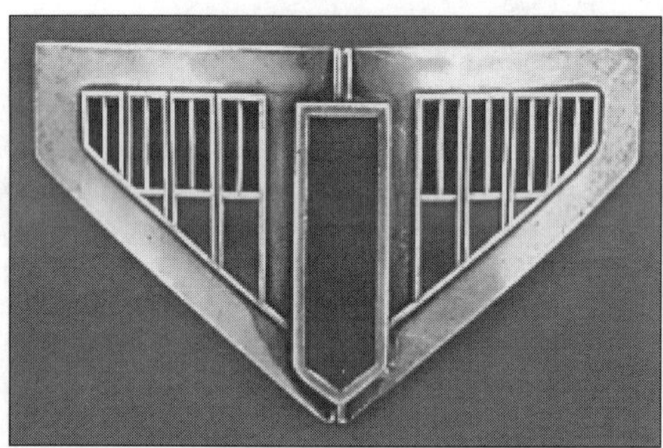

Buckle, 935 silver, enamel, c. 1905, two pcs forming cut-corner inverted triangle, surmounted by a blue *champlevé* enameled narrow pentagonal plaque, flanked by rect pierced sections surmounting blue *champlevé* enameled quadrangular panels tapering toward center, hook and eye closure, appl bars for belt attachment, design attributed to Franz Boeres, rev imp with maker' mk for Theodor Fahrner, "935 *DEPOSÉ*," 3" w x 1-7/8", **$1,400**. (Gail Gerretsen collection).

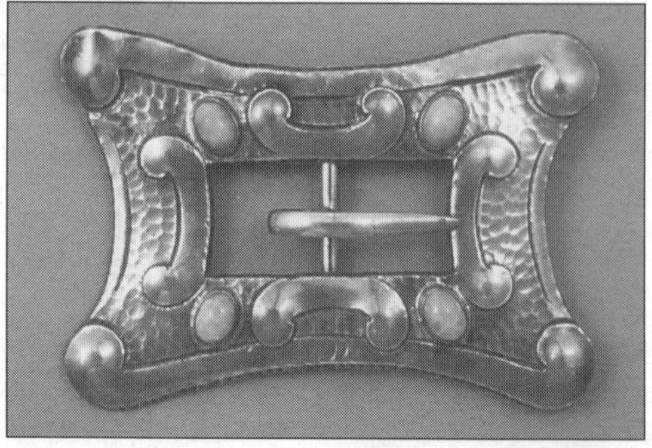

Buckle, sterling, glass, c. 1900, rounded rect with cutout center, indented sides, four coral-colored glass cabs at corners of central cutout, incised and hand-hammered decoration, rev mkd "STERLING," #3190, maker's mk for R. Blackinton & Co., No. Attleboro MA (superimposed B over a sword) on oval plaque, "HANDWROUGHT" on separate appl rect plaque, single hasp on swivel post, 2-5/8" w x 1-7/8", **$145**. (Leigh Leshner collection).

Sterling, enamel, date letter for 1905, two pieces forming slightly convex truncated lozenge shape, cusped corners, uneven textured surface with lg and sm central depressions filled with mingled blue and green *champlevé* enamel (slight damage), rev mkd "CYMRIC," maker's mk for Liberty & Co. ("L & Co" in adjacent lozenges) on one pc, engr "London 1905" on the other, Birmingham (Eng) hmks, #23 on both pcs, appl hook and eye, bars for belt attachment, 3-1/8" w x 2-1/8" 600

Cuff Links

Sterling, c. 1950, double-sided ovals, the fronts depicting an engr design of Kukla on one, and Ollie on the other (puppets from the popular 1950s children's television show, "Kukla, Fran, and Ollie"), sgd "KALO" for The Kalo Shop, Chicago, IL, 5/8" w x 3/4" .... 316 (A)

Sterling, enamel, green stones, c. 1900-10, each a pr of linked oval domed plaques with enameled geo design in blue, yellow, green and red on textured ground, sm circ-cut green stone in center of each oval, maker's mk for Gorham Mfg. Co., imp "STERLING," #225 enclosed in a rectangle, indicating a special order, 1/2" w x 5/8", pr 1,200

Earrings

Sterling, c. 1940, each a stylized concave lilypad motif with engr lines, surmounted by appl beads and wire, partially legible mks "STER..," "MAR ..E" for Mary Gage, screwbacks, 7/8" w x 3/4" 85

Hatpin

German silver, c. 1910, raised flowerhead motif, oxidized ground, in the center of an oval disk, 5/8" w x 7/8", 5-q/2" tl 65

Necklace

Yg, opals, diamonds, c. 1910, five grad linked yg plaques, the center an openwork shield shape, scrolled wire and cutout foliate motifs framing lg central bezel-set oval white opal encircled by ten sm collet-set om diamonds, four sm circ opals and three om diamonds above, one om diamond below, flanked by two cusped rect and two lozenge-shaped plaques of similar design set with sm opals and om diamonds, suspended from a twisted fetter and curb link chain, sgd "F.G. HALE" for Frank Gardner Hale, Medalist of the Boston Society of Arts & Crafts, 1-5/8" center top to bottom, 16-1/2" tl (modified chain) .... 12,650 (A)

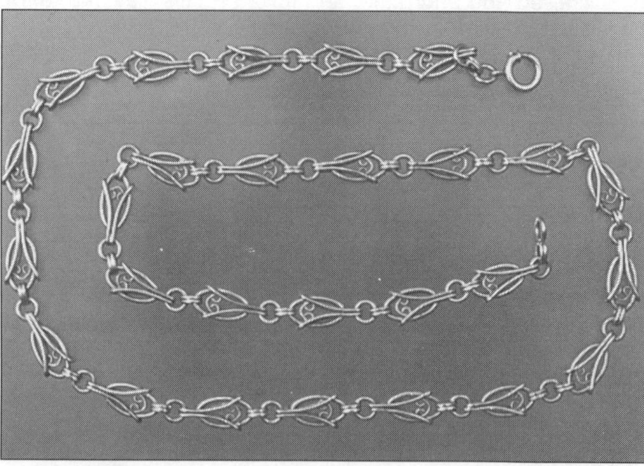

Neckchain, 18k yg, c. 1910, open oval links, each surmounted by two wires forming V-shape enclosing a C-scroll, alternating with circ links, reeded oval jump rings, spring ring clasp, mkd "18K," 1/4" w x 21" tl, **$1,200**. (Ann Tidwell collection).

Necklace, silver, green beryl, yg, c. 1910, five grad handwrought silver foliate and yg floral motifs, each terminating in bezel-set oval green beryl cab, suspended from paper clip and foliate motif chain, hook clasp with bezel-set green beryl, 14-1/2" l, 1-1/2" w at center, **$2,400**. (Gail Gerretsen collection).

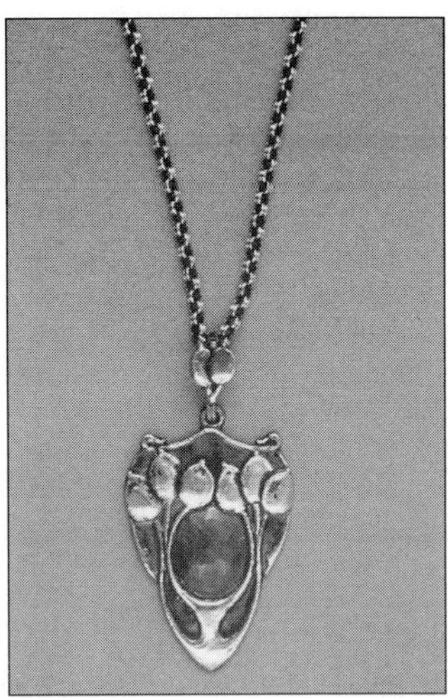

Pendant, silver, enamel, c. 1903, inverted lobed and cusped triangular plaque, raised floral design in silver, green enamel bg, central blue enamel dome, silver flower surmounting bail, mkd SILVER, maker's mk in quatrefoil for Liberty & Co. (used only in 1903), original box (added chain), 1-1/8" w x 2" tl including bail, **$800**. (Elaine Sarnoff collection).

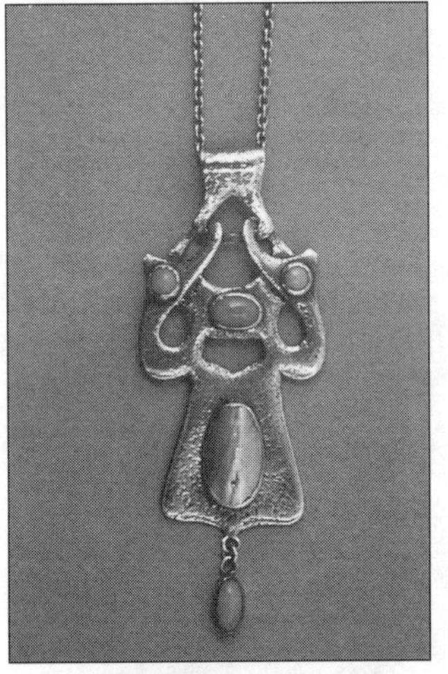

Pendant, silver, coral, blister pearl, c. 1910, pierced plaque set with three oval coral cabs, *entrelac* incorporating bail above lobed section bezel-set with blister pearl, suspended oval coral cab, rev imp "ALLEN" for Kate Allen (Eng), chain added, 1-1/8" w x 2-3/4" tl, **$350**. (Elaine Sarnoff collection).

Sterling, c. 1935, links of overlapping leaf shapes, central double leaf link with appl silver ball, mkd "PEER SMED HANDWROUGHT STERLING," hook closure with sliding safety, 1/4" w x 15-1/2" tl 600

Festoon

Sterling, "Swiss lapis" (dyed jasper), c. 1910-15, lg central dyed blue jasper circ cab suspending a sm circ cab terminating in a sm ster paired dolphin motif and a pear-shaped jasper drop, flanked by three swagged chains joined to two open ster trefoils, continuing to two swagged chains joined to two circ jasper cabs, paired dolphin motifs and single chain to spring ring clasp, rev mkd "STERLING," 17" tl, 4" top to bottom at center 200

Pendant

Amethyst, seed pearls, silver, c. 1900, shield-shaped beaded silver filigree with three central oval bezel-set amethyst cabs and one pendent amethyst cab drop, flanked by bezel-set seed pearls and seed pearl drops, illegible mks, 1-1/4" w x 2-1/4" 200

Silver, enamel, c. 1905, oval-shaped openwork plaque, center and four flowerheads at base enameled in violet and green, rev counterenameled in blue and white, suspending a sm enameled drop, 3/4" w x 1-5/8" 350

Silver, enamel, date letter for 1909, vasiform plaque with raised central silver curv Y-shape flanked by orange and green enameled leaves, suspending a sm navette-shaped enameled drop, mkd "S&5" Birmingham (Eng) hmks, 1-1/4" w x 2" 400

Sterling, enamel, blister pearl, date letter for 1905, blister pearl in center of hammered surface covered with translucent orange and green enamel, cobalt blue enameled arc below suspending lt blue enameled cusped drop, Birmingham hmks, illegible maker's mk, 1" w x 2" tl..... 150

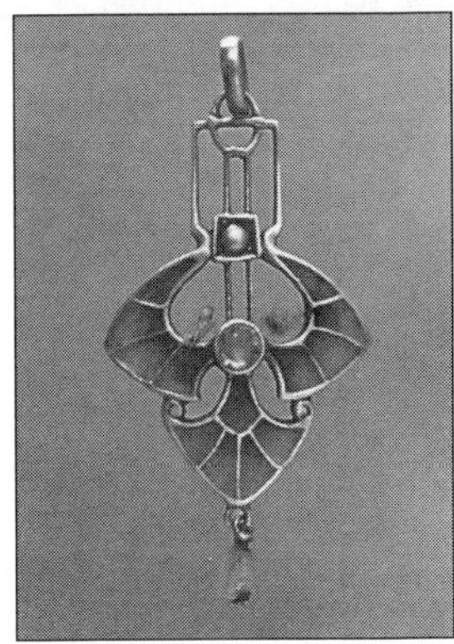

Pendant, silver, enamel, glass, pearl, c. 1910, open geo trefoil with three panels of green *plique à jour* enamel around a collet-set faceted blue glass stone, suspending a baroque pearl drop, mkd "EA" in an oval on rev, 7/8" w x 1-3/4" (with bail), **$450**. (Terrance O'Halloran collection).

Pendant and Chain

14k yg, opal, pearls, c. 1910, cutout open yg Tau cross, a rect bezel-set opal cab suspended lengthwise from its base, flanked by two pearl drops, a semi-circ bezel-set opal cab at cross junction, joined by two short chains to a triangular bezel-set opal cab, suspended from a trace and cable link chain and spring ring clasp, mkd "14K," 3/4" w x 2-1/4", 21" tl 750

950 silver, amethyst, f.w. pearl, yg, c. 1910, cutout and hammered cusped shield-shaped convex plaque, lg central faceted oval amethyst in yg bezel, flanked by two rivets, suspending f.w. pearl, Eng, maker's mk for Murrle Bennett & Co. (conjoined MB enclosed in C o), "950" imp

on rev, curb link chain mkd "IFB 925," chain 24", 1" w x 1-3/4" tl 950

950 silver, amethyst, yg, c. 1910, hammered and pierced pear-shaped ster plaque, a central oval faceted amethyst set in a yg bezel, encircled by MacGregor rose motifs, surmounted by a trefoil and suspended from three linked volutes and a trace and paper clip chain, T-bar clasp, pendant rev mkd "950," makers mk for Murrle, Bennett & Co., Eng, 7/8" w x 1-3/8", 2-3/4" tl, chain 16-1/2" tl 900

950 silver, amethysts, yg, c. 1910, cutout and hammered oval plaque, strapwork and rivet design, stones set in yg bezels: one lg central faceted oval amethyst flanked by two sm circ-cut amethysts on outer frame suspending med faceted oval amethyst, suspended from an elongated oval and curb link chain, T-bar clasp, maker's mk for Murrle Bennet & Co., "950" on rev, 1" w x 1-3/4" tl, chain 17" 900

Silver, enamel, c. 1910, oval convex plaque with Viking sailing ship motif enameled in shades of blue and white, beaded frame, pendant 3/4" w x 1", chain 16" tl 400

Sterling, agate, c. 1910, oval dyed blue agate bezel-set in the center of a lobed oval frame with pierced geo design, suspended from a paper clip chain, maker's mk for The Art Silver Shop, Chicago, IL, 18" tl, 1" w x 1-1/2 595

Sterling, enamel, date letter for 1908, geo shield shape with cutout sides and base, convex hammered surface, rect enameled center in mingled turq and cobalt blue, Bir-

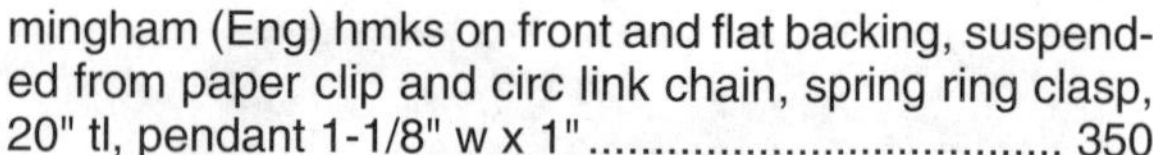

mingham (Eng) hmks on front and flat backing, suspended from paper clip and circ link chain, spring ring clasp, 20" tl, pendant 1-1/8" w x 1" 350

Sterling, enamel, date letter for 1909-10, central hammered-surface lt blue and green enameled rounded plaque flanked by angular silver branches, two enameled flowerheads on each side, pear-shaped enameled drop from center, suspended from two short chain lengths to a sm rounded triangular enameled plaque, continuing to spring ring closure, mkd "C.H." for Charles Horner, Chester (Eng) hmks, 1-1/4" w x 2-3/4" (from top plaque to end of drop), chain 14" tl 600

Sterling, enamel, date letter for 1909-10, oval openwork Celtic knot plaque enameled in violet and blue, suspended from sm circ enameled disk, fine cable link chain, spring ring closure, hmks for Chester (Eng), mkd "CH" for Charles Horner, 1" w x 7/8", chain 15" tl 500

Sterling, enamel, date letter for 1911, enameled thistle in green and purple on cutout and engr flat plaque suspending green enameled drop, trace chain caught in jump ring and bail above pendant, paper clip chain, Birmingham hmks, illegible maker's mk, 1-1/8" w x 2-1/2" tl to bail, chain 16" tl, ... 125

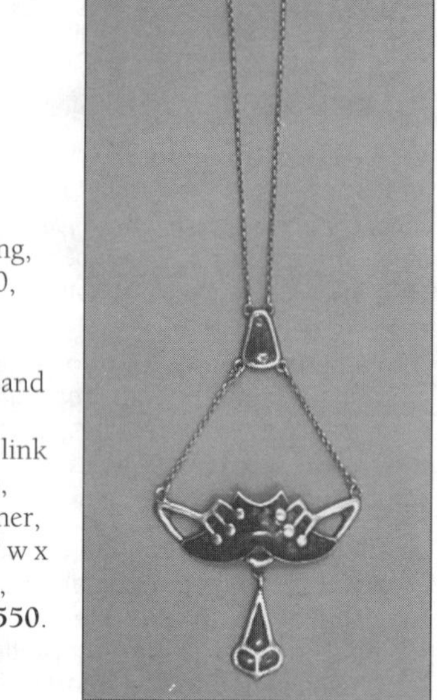

Pendant and Chain, sterling, enamel, date letter for 1910, branch-like silver motifs flanking "winged" enamel plaque suspending cusped and lobed triangular enameled plaque continuing to cable link chain and spring ring clasp, mkd "CH" for Charles Horner, Chester (Eng) hmks, 1-1/2" w x 2-1/2" l top plaque to drop, chain 17" tl from plaque, **$550**. (Elaine Sarnoff collection).

Pendant and Chain, silver, enamel, pearl, c. 1905-10, geo winged scarab motif in blue and white enameled sections alternating with orange spots, suspending a baroque pearl drop, rev mkd "W.H.H." for W. H. Haseler, sq plaque on hook bail suspended from a rod and circ link chain, pendant 1-1/4" w x 1-3/4", chain 19-1/2" tl, **$600**. (Terrance O'Halloran collection).

Pendant and Chain, silver, enamel, photograph, c. 1905, cusped disk enameled in shades of blue and green around a raised silver floral design surrounding a circ glazed compartment containing a photo, v-spring and tube clasp, mkd "W.H.H." for W.H. Haseler, Birmingham (Eng), chain mkd "STERLING," pendant 1-1/4" w x 2" (with bail), chain 15" tl, **$950**. (Terrance O'Halloran collection)

Pendant and Chain, silver, garnets, opals, pearl, c. 1900, teardrop-shaped drop depicting a crowned and robed Madonna and child set with five sm opals and four sm garnets, surmounting a winged head suspending a collet-set blister pearl further suspending a garnet cab drop; pendant suspended from a paper clip chain interspersed with beaded open quatrefoils, spring ring closure, unmkd, probably Eng, pendant 3/4" w x 4" tl, chain 22" tl, **$600**. (Terrance O'Halloran collection).

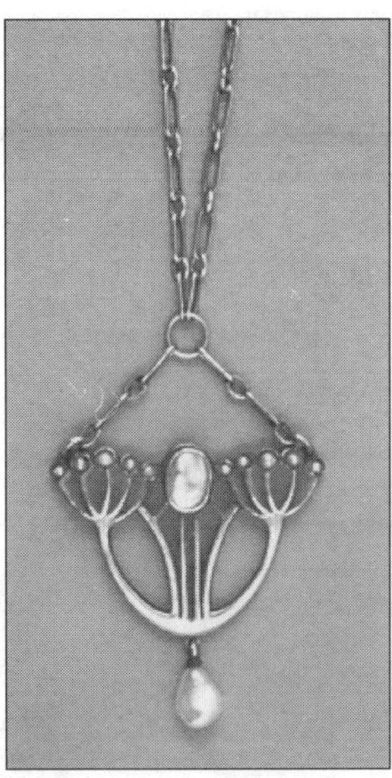

Pendant and Chain, 900 silver, enamel, c. 1910, yellow-green shading to violet *plique à jour* enamel, blister pearl flanked by ten seed pearls (five each side) in a Queen Anne's Lace floral motif, suspending f.w. pearl drop, paper clip chain caught in jump ring above pendant continuing to tube clasp, maker's mk for Heinrich Levinger, Pforzheim (Ger), mkd "DEPOSÉ 900," 1-1/2" w x 2" tl, 17" tl chain, **$1,150**. (Elaine Sarnoff collection).

Pendants and Chains, silver, *plique à jour*, c.1900-1915:

L, stylized butterfly motif, an open navette shape centering an oval dyed green chalcedony cab mounted on a vertical wire, surmounted by fan-shaped sections of *plique à jour* enamel shading from lt to dk green, bezel-set with four circ dyed green chalcedony cabs, two inverted triangular *plique à jour* enameled sections at the base, joined by two curved wires, one suspending a f.w. pearl drop, pendant suspended from four short lengths of fine chain attached to three rings at top, continuing to a paper clip chain with spring ring closure, rev mkd "DEPOSÉ 900," conjoined "HL" for Heinrich Levinger, Pforzheim (Ger), 1-1/4" w x 2-1/4", 21" tl, **$1,600**.

R, inverted pear-shaped open ster frame, bead-set with colorless pastes, bisected by a vertical wire set with a circ-cut prong-set amethyst above one sm circ collet-set colorless paste, flanked by scallop-edged stylized floral motifs *plique à jour* enameled in shades of violet, green, and white, terminating in a f.w. pearl drop, suspended from two lengths of cable link chain attached at top sides, joined to a sm circ colorless paste flanked by post-set pearls, continuing to v-spring and tube clasp, mkd "STERLING," 1-1/4" w x 1-3/4", chain 14" tl, **$650**. (Ann Tidwell collection).

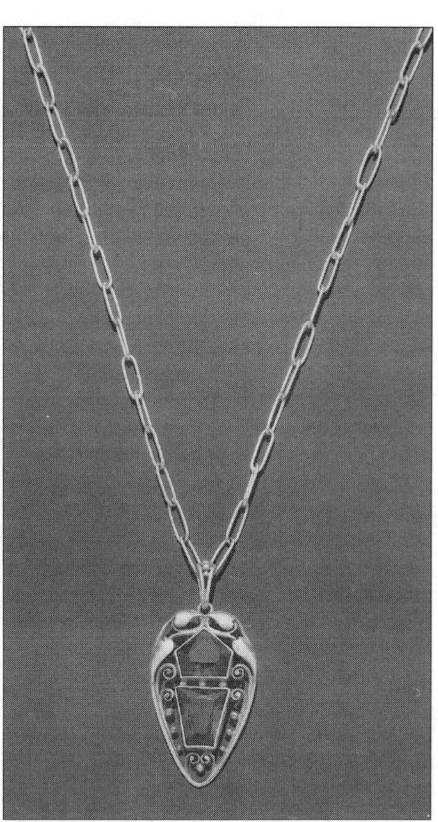

Pendant and Chain, 14k and 18k yg, tourmalines, c. 1910, tapered ovoid open 14k yg frame, a pentagonal-cut and a trapeze-cut green tourmaline bezel-set vertically in center, flanked by scroll and beadwork, surmounted by stylized foliate motifs, open bead-set bail, by Frank Gardner Hale, Boston, MA, suspended from a newly handmade 18k paper clip chain with T-bar closure, 17" tl, pendant 7/8" w x 1-3/8", **$3,300**. (Photo courtesy of ARK Antiques, New Haven, CT).

Pendant and Chain, moonstone, yg, peridot, seed pearls, sapphires, diamonds, c. 1925, a lg rounded oblong blue moonstone set in a yg frame with openwork foliate motifs tapering out and above the stone, surmounted by a lg circ-cut peridot and four clusters of three seed pearls, three sm Montana blue sapphires, and two sm circ-cut diamonds within scrolled yg wirework and sm leaves, suspended by jump rings at the top from two lengths of fine yg chain, by Edward Everett Oakes, 1-1/4" w x 1-7/8", 17" tl, **$6,400**. (Photo courtesy of ARK Antiques, New Haven, CT).

Sterling, enamel, date letter for 1912-13, central oval enameled plaque in blue to green enamel within a pierced geo shield shape, suspending an enameled pear-shaped drop, suspended from two short chain lengths to silver bail and chain, mkd "CH" for Charles Horner, hmks for Chester (Eng), pendant 7/8" w x 1-1/2", chain 17" tl 500

Ring

14k yg, sapphires, diamonds, platinum, c. 1925, pear-shaped notched yg frame with appl plat foliate motifs, asymmetrically set with a pear-shaped sapphire and three circ-cut diamonds, sapphire and diamond-set shoulders, sgd "OAKES" for Edward Everett Oakes, 5/8" w x 3/4" .... 2,070 (A)

Pendant and Chain, yg, star sapphire, sapphires, enamel, c. 1910, domed circ pendant with indented base, ropetwist border, circ bezel-set star sapphire center framed by blue and green enameled feather motifs and sm collet-set sapphire cabs, suspended from a ropetwist yg chain interspersed with prs of openwork filigreed and green and blue enameled cushion-shaped plaques flanking collet-set sapphire cabs, sgd "Tiffany & Co.," #835, designed by Louis Comfort Tiffany, produced under supervision of Julia Munson, director of Tiffany's Art Jewelry Dept., 1907-1914, chain 17" tl, pendant 1-3/8" dia, **$25,300** [A]. (Photo courtesy of Christie's New York, 4/ 8/97).

14k yg, tourmalines, garnets, pearl, c. 1925, 6.5 mm pearl center flanked by circ-cut green tourmalines, hessonite and rhodolite garnets bezel-set in the corners of a cushion-shaped openwork foliate mount on a narrow shank, attributed to Everett Everett Oakes, 3/4" x 3/4" .... 978 (A)

18k yg, opal, c. 1910, a lg navette-shaped opal cab bezel-set within a beaded yg frame, flanked by beaded yg trillium leaf motifs on shoulders, tapered shank, sgd "MR" (conjoined) for Margaret Rogers, Medalist of the Boston Society of Arts and Crafts, 7/8" w x 1-1/8", size 4-1/4 4,200

Chalcedony, baroque pearl, silver, c. 1900, open foliate design with central bezel-set dyed green chalcedony cab and baroque pearl flanked by appl silver leaves, 3/4" w, size 8-1/2 125

Sterling, c. 1940, foliate motif, sgd "MARY GAGE HANDWROUGHT," 3/8" w, approx size 8-1/2 100

Sterling, agate, c. 1910-15, a pear-shaped brown agate cab bezel-set in the center of a tapered band with arched and geo piercing, maker's mk for Carence Crafters, Chicago, IL, 1/2" w, size 5-3/4 695

Sterling, glass, c. 1940, central oval lt blue glass cab set in wirework frame and shank with appl beads, attributed to Mary Gage, approx size 8-1/2, top 3/4" w x 1" 125

Sterling, turquoise, c. 1930-40, lg slightly convex plaque in the shape of a lily pad, engr lines radiating from appl bead and wire cluster surmounting lobed side of plaque, an oval turq cab bezel-set off-center, mounted on a wire shank with beaded shoulders, unmkd, attributed to Mary Gage, 1-1/4" x 1", approx size 6-1/2 125

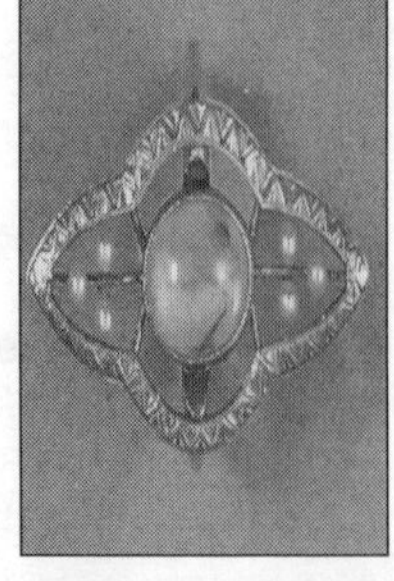

Ring, 14k yg, moonstone, seed pearls, c. 1910, lobed navette-shaped open engr yg frame, oval moonstone center, cluster of three seed pearls above and below, mounted on narrow tapering shank, approx size 5-1/2, imp superimposed "HV," mkd "14k," 5/8" w x 1-3/8", **$650**. (Gail Gerretsen collection).

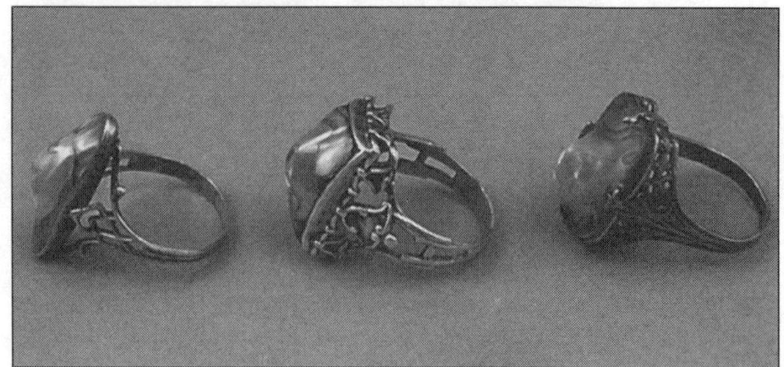

Rings, abalone shell, mkd "STERLING," c. 1910-20:
L, cut-corner rectangle, stamped filigree, engr scrolled design on shank, size 6, 3/8" w x 3/4", **$125**.
C, bezel-set rect plaque, wire and bead openwork gallery, size 5, top 3/8" w x 3/4", **$135**.
R, elongated oval abalone plaque, stamped filigree setting, scrolled openwork gallery, size 6-1/2, top 1/2" w x 3/4", **$125**. (Sue James collection).

Ring, sterling, glass, c. 1930, lg step-cut prong-set lt blue glass stone surrounded by appl foliate motif, mkd "STERLING DORIS CLIFF HANDWROUGHT," top 3/4" w x 1", **$250**. (Charles Pinkham collection).

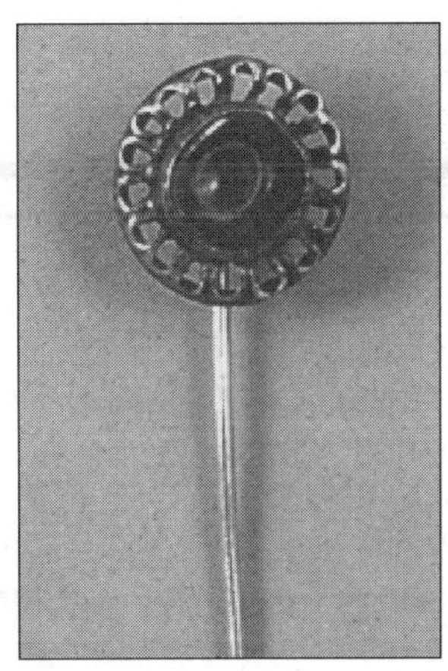

Scarf Pin/Stickpin, silver, azurmalachite, c. 1890-1900, pierced circ head with central azurmalachite cab, ym pinstem, probably Eng, 5/8" dia, 3" tl, **$175**. (Courtesy of E. Foxe Harrell Jewelers, Clinton, IA).

Scarf Pin/Stickpin

Brass, wm, c. 1910, slightly concave oval disk, acid-etched stylized serpent design in center, mounted on wm pinstem, Am, head 1/2" w x 3/4", 2-3/8" tl 65

Brass, c. 1910, inverted hammered triangular plaque, rounded apex, acid-etched and green patinated abstract design, rev imp "FROST" in a triangle for George W. Frost, Dayton, OH, head 5/8" w x 3/4", 2-5/8" tl 75

Suite: Bracelet and Brooch/Pin

Sterling, c. 1950, bracelet of five links of foliate and berry motif, engr details, hook clasp, sgd "LA PAGLIA" for Alphonse La Paglia, #145, brooch a double foliate motif with berries, mkd "INTERNATIONAL STERLING, LA PAGLIA DESIGNED" #145, bracelet 3/4" w x 6-1/2" tl, brooch 1-1/8" w x 1-5/8", suite .... 230 (A)

Suite: Brooch/Pin and Earrings, sterling, c. 1930, open oval raised floral/foliate motif with engr details, screwback earrings each a single flowerhead, mkd "KALO STERLING," brooch 2" w x 1-1/2", earrings 1/2" dia, **$375**. (Photo courtesy of Lovejoy's Estate Jewelry, Bellingham, WA).

Suite: Necklace, Bracelet, and Earrings

Silver, c. 1930, link necklace centering a lg shield-shaped pierced and engr plaque of cherry and foliate motif, flanked by sm oval plaques of similar design, bracelet of lg circ plaques of similar motif, earrings of three cherries with one leaf, sgd "KALO," necklace, 15" tl, bracelet 1-1/4" w x 7-1/2" l, earrings, 3/4" w x 1", suite .... 1,093 (A)

Suite: Link Bracelet and Earrings

Sterling, c. 1930, five circ pierced, raised and engr links, cherries motif, oval box and v-spring clasp, rev imp "HAND WROUGHT STERLING KALO," safety chain, 7-1/4" l x 1-1/8" w, bunch of three cherries and leaf matching earrings, screwbacks, mkd, 3/4" w x 1", suite 1,000

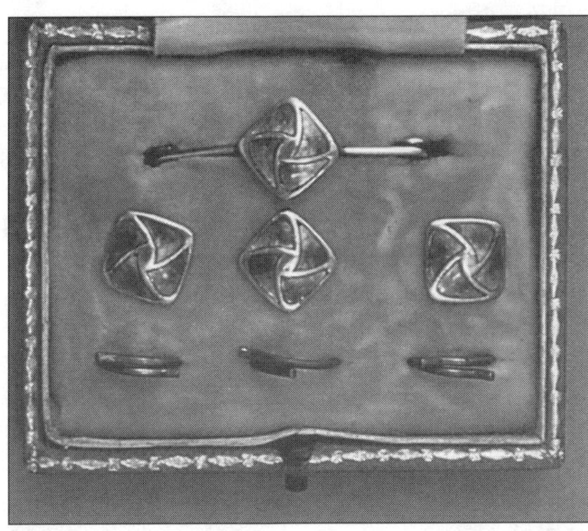

Suite: Shirt Studs and Tie Pin, silver, enamel, c. 1900, three rounded sq enameled shirt buttons with matching tie pin, pinwheel design enameled in shades of green and blue, mkd on back of pin "SOLID SILVER, REAL ENAMEL," findings for studs, orig fitted box, probably Eng, each 3/8" sq, suite, **$225**. (Terrance O'Halloran collection).

Watch Fob, Silver, enamel, leather, c. 1900, hammered and engr cusped geo silver plaques with stylized arrow motifs at each end of a leather strap, surmounted by intertwined engr silver stylized initials "JV" flanked by two engr silver bars, suspending a shield-shaped drop with blue, white, and black enameled diagonal stripes, short chain and swivel hook suspended from opposite end, eastern European hmks, 1-1/2" w x 4-1/2", **$345**. (Photo courtesy of Lovejoy's Estate Jewelry, Bellingham, WA).

ART NOUVEAU c. 1895-1910

History: In 1895, Samuel Bing (1838-1905) converted his Oriental art gallery in Paris into a gallery for a new style, which gave the style its name, *L'Art Nouveau.* The Art Nouveau style caught fire and burned with a passion for a short while at the turn of the century before it flamed out and died. Its rise and fall spanned less than twenty years, but Art Nouveau had quite an impact on jewelry history. The quintessence of Art Nouveau was distilled by the French, but the ingredients for its heady mix of line and form came from the British Arts and Crafts Movement. It was the British insistence upon artistic integrity and individual expression that inspired the French to break away from constricting, traditional, imitative realism. This may explain the difficulty in determining which elements constitute which style.

The two have much in common: the use of inexpensive gemstones and other materials, enameling, the "whiplash" curve, motifs taken from nature, Japanese influence. But something changes in the translation from English to French. French pieces are figural, more three-dimensional and asymmetrical. The female face and body (naked and clothed) are predominant subjects for Art Nouveau interpretation, nearly absent in Arts and Crafts. Other Art Nouveau favorites include dragonflies and butterflies–some with female bodies, writhing snakes and mythical creatures (chimera). The peacock and peacock feathers have been interpreted by both the British and the French in different ways. Irises, poppies, winged sycamore seeds, waterlilies and trailing vines are part of the botanical repertoire of Art Nouveau.

Arts and Crafts floral and foliate motifs are stylized, the designs more abstract and controlled. Art Nouveau motifs have an element of fantasy, with exaggerated lines and sensual overtones. It might be oversimplifying to say categorically that if it's British, it's Arts and Crafts, if it's French, it's Art Nouveau. It would be fair to say, however, that the British retained too much of their Victorian sensibility to embrace Art Nouveau wholeheartedly. The French, on the other hand, were more than willing to take off in Art Nouveau's exuberant and, some say, decadent direction. Other countries followed: Belgium, Spain, and to a lesser extent, Russia. In Germany, Austria, and the United States, both British and French influences were felt.

Although there were many practitioners of the style in France, the work of one man has come to represent everything that Art Nouveau jewelry is about: René Lalique (1860-1945). His life has been well-documented and his work well-preserved (see references below). A student of jewelry history should be familiar with his work because to understand Lalique is to understand Nouveau at its finest. An important sale of forty-three pieces of jewelry by Lalique was held at Sotheby's Geneva in November, 1996. Among the offerings were some of Lalique's most celebrated work.

Other important French Art Nouveau designers and houses include Maison Louis Aucoc, under whom Lalique apprenticed, Georges Fouquet, Lucien Gaillard, Lucien Gautrait, and Vever. Examples by some of these artists were offered for sale by Sotheby's New York in June, 1996.

A number of other recent auctions have included significant examples of French Art Nouveau. A few of them are included in this section. A brooch by Paris sculptor and jeweler Paul Liénard (b. 1849) is on page 93. Liénard exhibited regularly at the Paris Salons (a series of decorative arts exhibitions) after 1900, but his best work was made circa 1905-1910.

The pendant on page 98 was made by Frédéric Charles Victor de Vernon (1858-1912), a medallist and engraver whose work was sold in Paris by Cartier, and made by Maison Duval and Lacloche Frères. He exhibited every year at the Paris Salons and was awarded a first class medal in 1895. He specialized in Art Nouveau medal-jewels with religious themes, often enhanced with *plique à jour* enamel.

Enameling is one the most important decorative elements in Art Nouveau jewelry. One of the techniques that Lalique was noted for, and which became closely associated with Art Nouveau, is *plique à jour* enameling. The usual explanation is that it looks like a stained glass window; a piece has no metal backing and the enamel colors are translucent. *Plique à jour* is particularly effective when used to depict insect wings (butterflies, dragonflies) and landscapes with sky and water. It is a difficult technique, and the results are fragile. Intact pieces are scarce.

When an enameled piece does have a backing, or groundplate, there are several other possible techniques, all of which were used in Art Nouveau as well as other styles of jewelry: *basse-taille, champlevé, cloisonné,* and Limoges, or painted enamel are the ones most commonly seen. An explanation of these techniques can be found in the Glossary. *Basse-taille* and *champlevé* enameled flowers on sterling or brass plaques, resembling miniature paintings, are often found in American Art Nouveau brooches and sash ornaments.

The style itself was a departure from what had gone before, but jewelry forms followed fashion's dictates. Hatpins, hair combs, necklaces and pendants, ornamental *plaques de cou* for dog collars, brooches, sash ornaments and buckles, and to a lesser extent, bracelets, cuff links, rings, and stickpins, were all interpreted by Art Nouveau designers. Another commonly seen form is sometimes referred to as "medal" jewelry (see reference to Vernon, above). This was a French idea that was also popular in the U.S. It replaced the classic cameo with a medallion in gold or silver of the profile, full face, or torso of a woman or man in repoussé, stamped or cast relief. Borders and backgrounds were appropriately decorated with undulating vines, leaves, and flowers in the Art Nouveau style. The medallion could be a pendant, locket, brooch, or scarf pin. Less expensive versions were made in gilt base metals.

In the U.S., Americans were torn between English pragmatism and French *chic.* In New York City, Tiffany & Co. and Marcus & Co. produced beautiful enameled and gemstone-set Art Nouveau jewels that rivaled most French pieces. And, although Arts and Crafts jewelry was gaining popularity in Boston, Chicago, and other cities, Newark, New Jersey jewelry makers were turning out pieces influenced by Art Nouveau.

In the spirit of American entrepreneurship, the style was commercialized with great if short-lived success, particularly by two Newark silver manufacturers, Wm. B. Kerr and Unger Bros. Both firms were noted for their die-stamped relief designs that imitated repoussé handwork. They are easily recognized and circa-dated. The pieces are backed with flat soldered-on sterling plates that bear the companies' marks. Kerr used a fasces, a bundle of rods bound around a battle-ax; Unger Bros'. mark is their interlaced initials, UB. Typical motifs were women's faces with flowing hair, and flowers, particularly poppies, waterlilies and irises. Kerr was purchased by Gorham in 1906, retaining their name, but not their style, for some time afterward. Unger Bros. stopped making Art Nouveau designs in 1910. Pieces by either firm sell in the low to high three-figure range today. Other manufacturers, some based in Providence, Rhode Island and Attleboro, Massachusetts, produced similar die-stamped jewelry in sterling and silver-plated brass. The quality varies. Inexpensive pieces are usually made from a single thin sheet of unbacked metal.

Several notable Newark manufacturers specialized in gold jewelry in the Art Nouveau style, often enameled and/or set with gemstones: Alling & Co., Carter, Howe (later Gough) & Co., Krementz & Co., Larter & Sons, Riker Bros, Sloan & Co. and Whiteside & Blank, to name a few. See appendix, American Manufacturers, for marks on the companies' pieces which are shown or listed in this book. These and many other Newark makers' marks, can be found in Dorothy Rainwater's *American Jewelry Manufacturers.* Details on the companies' histories, compiled by Janet Zapata, are given in *The Glitter & the Gold,* cited below.

All turn-of-the-century jewelry made in Newark was not made in the Art Nouveau style, however. A new term has entered the jewelry historian's vocabulary, taken from architecture: Beaux-arts, as delineated by Ulysses Dietz and Janet Zapata in their article on Newark jewelers for *The Magazine Antiques,* also cited below. This is a term for a turn-of-the-century style that cannot be called Art Nouveau, Arts and Crafts or Edwardian, and is clearly derived from the Revivalist styles of the previous few decades, particularly those that came from a Viennese design source book called *Die Perle,* published in 1879. Finely detailed griffins, cherubs, scroll and foliate motifs often show up in circa 1890-1910 pieces by Kerr, Riker Bros., Krementz, Alling & Co. and others, which up until now have been called Art Nouveau, even though the name didn't fit. "Beaux-arts" seems to fill the need for a label for this style.

The commercialization of Art Nouveau also brought about its demise. Perhaps its stylistic excesses, like a rich dessert, became cloying and difficult to digest in large quantities. After 1910, relatively little Nouveau jewelry was produced. By 1915, it was completely out of fashion.

References: Lillian Baker, *Art Nouveau & Art Deco Jewelry,* Collector Books, 1981, values updated 1990; Vivienne Becker, *Art Nouveau Jewelry,* E.P. Dutton, 1985 (out of print); Vivienne Becker, *The Jewellery of René Lalique,* exhibition catalog, Goldsmiths' Company, London, 1987; Ulysses G. Dietz, ed., *The Glitter & the Gold, Fashioning America's Jewelry,* The Newark Museum, 1997; Ulysses G. Dietz and Janet Zapata, "Beaux-arts Jewelry Made in Newark, New Jersey," *The Magazine Antiques,* April, 1997; Alistair Duncan, *The Paris Salons, 1895-1914, Jewellery,* 2 vols., Antique Collectors' Club, 1994; Elyse Zorn Karlin, *Jewelry & Metalwork in the Arts and Crafts Tradition,* Schiffer Publishing, 1993; M. Koch et al, *The Belle Époque of French Jewellery 1850-1910,* Thomas Heneage & Co. Ltd., 1990; David Lancaster, *Art Nouveau Jewelry, A Connoisseur's Guide,* Bullfinch Press, Little, Brown & Co., 1996; Elise Misiorowski and Dona Dirlam, "Art Nouveau: Jewels and Jewelers," article in *Gems & Gemology,* Winter 1986; Gabriel Mourey et al, *Art Nouveau Jewellery & Fans,* Dover Publications, 1973 (reprint of 1902 *Modern Design in Jewellery and Fans*); Joseph Sataloff, *Art Nouveau Jewelry,* Dorrance & Co., 1984; Janet Zapata, "The Legacy of Value from Newark Jewelers," *Jewelers' Circular-Keystone/Heritage,* November 1993.

Museums: The Walters Art Gallery, Baltimore MD; Metropolitan Museum, New York NY; Musée des Arts Décoratifs, Paris, France; The Calouste Gulbenkian Museum in Lisbon, Portugal, houses the René Lalique collection created for its namesake between 1895-1912.

Reproduction Alert: Since the 1960s revival of Art Nouveau, many cast knockoffs of die-stamped period pieces have been made, especially in sterling. The repro pieces are solid instead of hollow, and the details are not as sharp. Reproductions of gold and gemstone Nouveau jewels can be cast or stamped, but also lack detail and signs of wear. Enameling is not as skillfully done.

Advisors: Ulysses G. Dietz, Elise Misiorowski, Janet Zapata.

Bracelet

Bangle

Yg, amethysts, c. 1910, openwork oval, scrolled yg foliate motifs enclosing a row of seven grad collet-set circ-cut amethysts, knife-edge frame tapering to an open grid at the back, maker's mk for Wordley, Allsopp & Bliss, Newark, NJ (conjoined WAB), 2-1/2" inside dia, 3/8" w 1,395

Bracelet, 14k rose and green gold, diamonds, c. 1900-10, undulating outline with die-struck iris motif in bi-colored gold, three sm diamonds in center of three cartouches, mkd "14k" and maker's mk for Riker Bros, Newark, NJ, safety chain, 2-1/8" inside dia. 1/2" w, **$1,300**. (Private collection).

Link

14k yg, citrines, seed pearls, c. 1910-15, open navette-shaped floral/foliate links, each centering a bezel-set circ-cut citrine, alternating with sm circ links set with seed pearls, maker's mk for Bippart, Griscom & Osborne (a torch), Newark NJ, 3/8" w x 7" .... 748 (A)

14k yg, diamonds, c. 1910, rect linked plaques with undulating borders, pierced openwork curv floral/foliate motif, four plaques surmounted by a three-dimensional lizard motif with a row of sixteen oe diamonds down the back, maker's mk for Riker Bros (R over a scimitar), Newark, NJ, 5/8" w x 6-1/4" .... 4,887 (A)

14k yg, sapphires, c. 1910, five circ lavender sapphire cabs bezel-set in open foliate frames, evenly spaced along double lengths of fine cable link chain, spring ring clasp, 1/2" w x 7" .... 1,035 (A)

Yg, sapphires, c. 1900, thirteen scrolling wirework links forming quatrefoils, each centering a bezel-set blue circ-cut sapphire, set in bloomed 14k yg, v-spring and box clasp, 3/8" w x 7" tl .... 1,840 (A)

Brooch/Pendant

14k yg, opal, diamonds, enamel, c. 1905, open circ floral and foliate motif with oval prong-set opal cab bud at top, sm oe diamond accents, polychrome opalescent enamel leaves, maker's mk for Krementz, Newark, NJ (a collar button), lever catch, 1" dia .... 748 (A)

Sterling, 14k yg, c. 1910, Egyptian Revival, central yg scarab flanked by ster wings, attributed to George Shiebler, mkd "STERLING & 14K," pendant loop on rev, 3" w x 5/8" .... 690 (A)

Yg, enamel, diamonds, sapphires, rubies, c. 1890-1900, three-dimensional butterfly with *plique à jour* enameled wings in shades of dk and lt blue, violet, and green, partially outlined by sm rc diamonds, each wing bezel-set with a blue sapphire cab, central sapphire cab in body, ruby eyes, rows of sm rc diamonds on lower body, engr yg legs and antennae, a total of one hundred thirty-eight rc diamonds, 3-1/8" w x 2-1/8......................... 8,050 (A)

Yg, sapphires, diamond, c. 1900, Beaux-arts style, depicting a three-dimensional griffin with a collet-set circ-cut blue sapphire in its mouth, pierced scrolled circ frame surmounted by a collet-set circ-cut sapphire and suspending a collet-set circ-cut and a pear-shaped sapphire drop surmounted by a sm om diamond, 1-1/2" w x 2-1/4".. 3,680 (A)

Brooch/Pendant and Chain

Yg, enamel, diamonds, c. 1900, open scrolled foliate yg frame enclosing and supporting three floral/foliate motifs enameled in shades of purple, green and yellow, center prong-set with an oval Dutch rc diamond, suspending a pear-shaped Dutch rc diamond drop, two lengths of detachable trace and curb link chain caught by a circ Dutch rc diamond in a pronged mount, 17" tl, brooch 1-1/2" w 1-5/8" tl .... 2,875 (A)

Brooch/Pin

14k yg, c. 1900, Beaux-arts style, a winged griffin impaled on a sword, sm diamond on wing, unmkd, 7.80 dwt, 1-3/4" x 1-3/4" .... 805 (A)

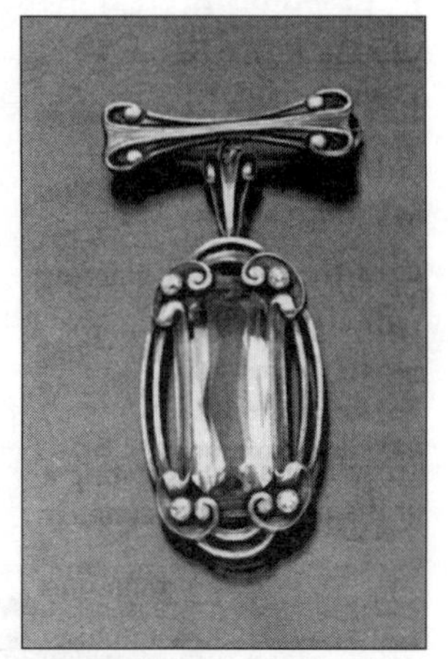

Brooch/Pendant, citrine, 14k yg, diamonds, c. 1910-15, open oval foliate design pendant centering a lg rect-cut citrine in a yg frame with four sm circ-cut diamonds within foliate C-scrolls at corners, suspended and detachable from a waisted rect foliate yg bar brooch, maker's mk for the Brassler Company, Newark, NJ, 1909-31 ("14 B" within a double oval), 1-1/8" w x 1-7/8", **$1,035** [A]. (Photo courtesy of William Doyle Galleries, New York, NY, 12/4/96).

Brooches/Pins, enamel, sterling, Am, c. 1910:
T, rounded navette-shaped ster plaque, iris motif in violet, yellow, and green translucent *basse-taille* enamel, mkd "STERLING, JEB Co." possibly for James E. Blake Co. Attleboro, MA, and C-catch, 1-1/8" w x 3/4", **$65**. (Leigh Leshner collection).
B, elliptical plaque, *basse-taille* enameled poinsettia motif in shades of red, green, and yellow, white ground, rev mkd "GENUINE CLOISONNÉ, STERLING," maker's mark for Watson, Newell & Co, Attleboro, MA (crown, Old English W and lion), 1-1/4" w x 5/8", **$75**. (Author's collection).

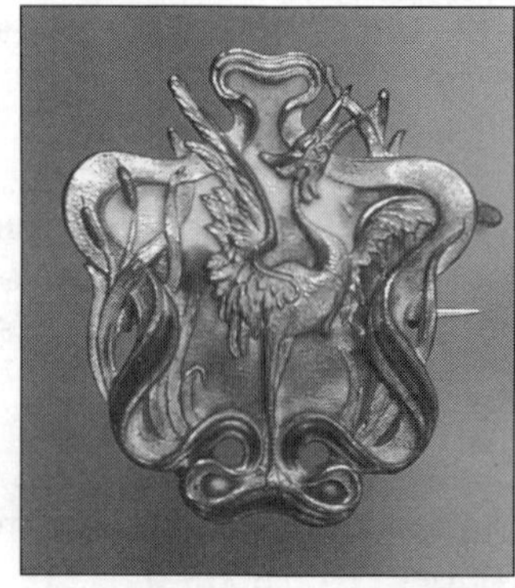

Brooch/Pin, gp brass, enamel, c. 1910, stamped shield-shaped gp brass plaque depicting a waterbird in a marsh with cattails, within an undulating frame, ptd enamel bg in shades of blue, pink, and green, wide C-catch, 1-1/2" w x 1-7/8", **$125**. (Ann Tidwell collection).

Brooch/Pin, moonstone, enamel, f.w. pearl, diamonds, 18k yg, c. 1905, central carved moonstone female face, surrounded by a flowerlike headdress of opalescent and pale green *plique à jour* enamel, om diamond and matte black enamel accents, suspending a lg f.w. pearl drop, sgd "P. Liénard" for Paul Liénard, Paris, Fr hmk (eagle's head) for 18k gold, 1-3/4" w x 3-1/8" tl, **$32,200** [A]. (Photo courtesy of Christie's New York, NY, 10/23/96).

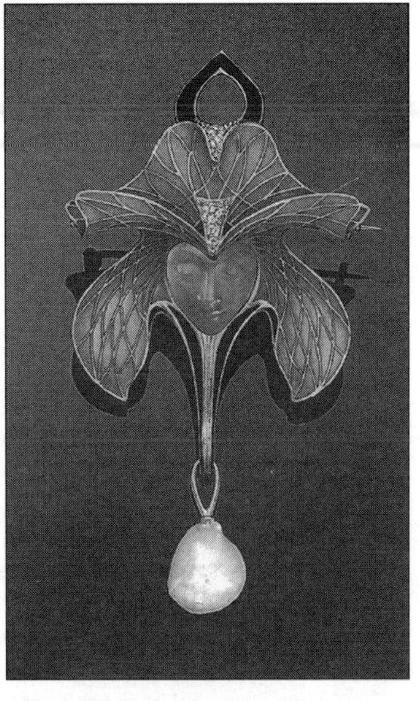

Watch pins, c. 1900-20:

L, gf, c. 1900-10, scroll and trellis design, engr mono "S" on central oval plaque, upturned hook on rev, mkd "P S Co" for Plainville Stock Company, Plainville, MA, lever catch, flanged hinge, 1-1/8" w x 3/4", $100.

C, gf, opal, seed pearls, cutout and die-struck and engr scroll motifs, surmounted by central fleur-de-lis with circ opal center flanked by eight seed pearls in two arcing horizontal rows, C-catch, upturned hook on rev, 7/8" w x 7/8", **$95**.

R, 14k yg, seed pearl, scrolling vine and floral motif with seed pearl center, upturned hook on rev, later added safety catch, 7/8" w x 7/8", **$150**.

(Elaine Sarnoff collection).

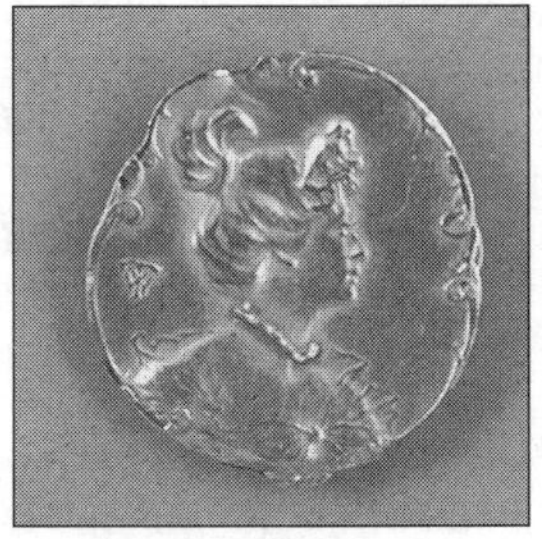

Brooch/Pin, yg, c. 1900, 14k, irregular circ medallion of woman's profile with scrolled border, maker's mark superimposed "TW" on front, C-catch, tube hinge, 1-1/8" dia, **$425**. (Courtesy of E. Foxe Harrell Jewelers, Clinton, IA).

Brooch/Pin, sterling, c. 1900-10, die-struck woman's profile with peacock entwined in flowing hair, maker's mark for Unger Bros imp on rev, wide C-catch, flanged hinge, 2-1/4" w x 2-1/2", **$650**. (Cheryl Chang collection).

Brooch/Pin, yg, c. 1900, Beaux-arts style, repoussé design depicting a griffin grasping a prong-set om diamond in its mouth, within a lozenge-shaped scrolled foliate motif open frame, C-catch, flanged hinge, Fr hmk (eagle's head) for 18k on rev, illegible maker's mk in lozenge on C-catch, 1-3/4" w x 1-1/4", **$1,500**. (Ann Tidwell collection).

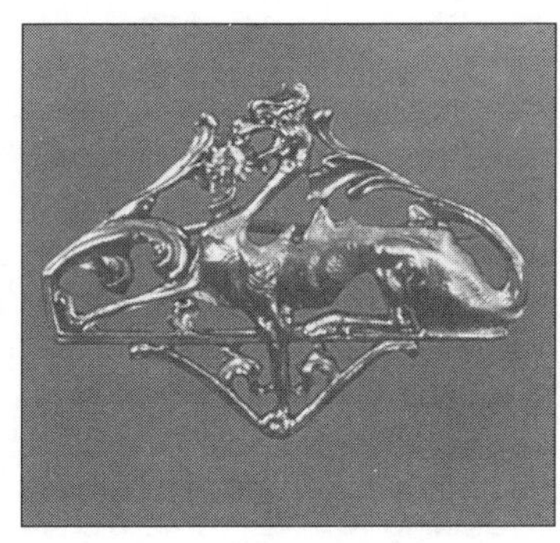

Brooches/Pins, die-struck sterling, c. 1900-10:

L, circ depiction of woman with flowers in flowing hair holding pan pipes, hair compartment on rev, mkd "STERLING," C-catch, 1" dia, **$125**.

C, unbacked woman's profile encircled by flowing hair intertwined with leaves, wide C-catch, 1-1/2" w x 1-3/8", **$75**.

R, circ woman's profile with flower in flowing hair, encircled by flowers and leaves, flat backing with imp maker's mk for Unger Bros., C-catch, flanged hinge, 1-1/8" dia, **$175**.

(Elaine Sarnoff collection).

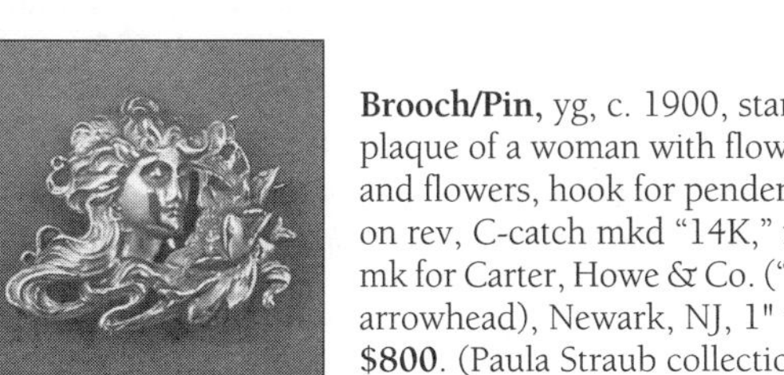

Brooch/Pin, yg, c. 1900, stamped plaque of a woman with flowing hair and flowers, hook for pendent watch on rev, C-catch mkd "14K," maker's mk for Carter, Howe & Co. ("C" in an arrowhead), Newark, NJ, 1" w x 1", **$800**. (Paula Straub collection).

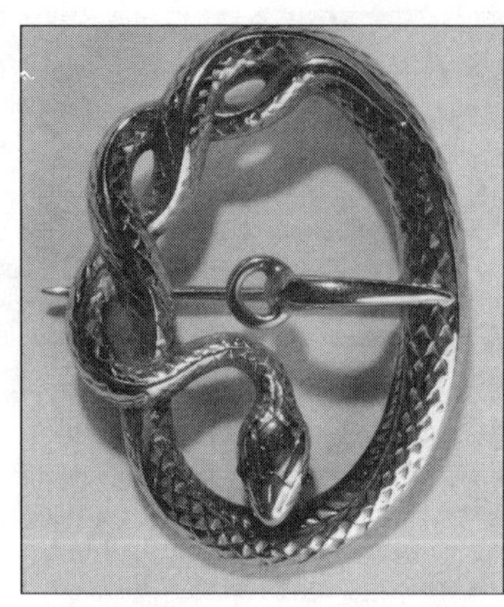

Brooch/Pin, Sash Ornament, 14k yg, rubies, c. 1900, open oval undulating snake motif, stamped and engr, simulated hasp, ruby eyes, Am, mkd "14K," C-catch, 1" w x 1-1/2", **$295**. (Photo courtesy of Lovejoy's Estate Jewelry, Bellingham, WA).

14k yg, diamonds, c. 1890-1900, Beaux-arts style, in the shape of a winged griffin impaled on a sword, sm diamond-set wing and sword, engr details, maker's mark for Riker Bros, Newark, NJ, 1-1/4" x 1-1/4" .... 1,093 (A)

14k yg, enamel, amethyst, seed pearls, c. 1910, "suffragette" colors of green, white, and violet ("give women votes"), opposed C-scrolls enclosing two pearl-tipped scrolled wires, flanking sm green enameled trefoil, surmounted by a faceted pear-shaped amethyst, suspending seed pearl and pear-shaped amethyst drop, maker's mk for Krementz & Co., Newark, NJ (collar button symbol), 14k imp on lever catch, 1-1/8" w x 1-1/4" tl ... 1,200

14k yg, enamel, diamond, c. 1900, circ pierced disk depicting a water bird among lily pads and bulrushes, setting sun, *plique à jour* enamel bg of blue, green, red, and yellow, sm diamond set in center lily pad, unmkd, attributed to Riker Bros., 1" dia .... 1,955 (A)

14k yg, enamel, diamond, c. 1910, floral lady slipper motif, transparent green enameled petals with one sm oe diamond "dewdrop," maker's mk for Bippart, Griscom & Osborne (torch), Newark, NJ, 1-1/2" w x 1" .... 431 (A)

14k yg, enamel, pearls, diamonds, c. 1900, central green *guilloché* enameled multilobed leaf set with five sm om diamonds and two natural pearls, enclosed by an undulating yg vine, 1" w x 1-3/8" .... 632 (A)

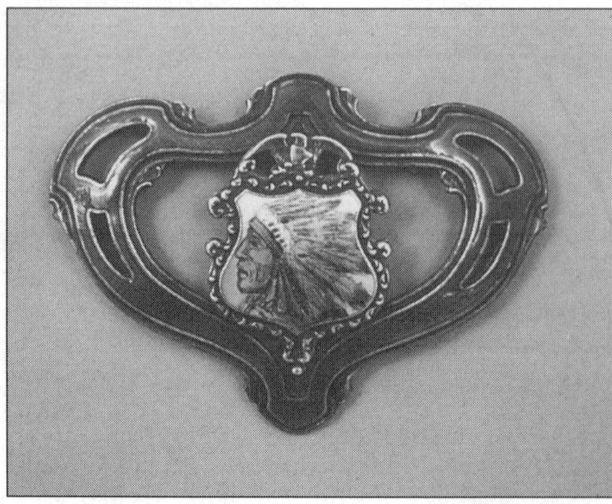

Brooch/Pin, Sash Ornament, sterling, enamel, c. 1910-15, red *basse-taille* enameled shield-shaped open frame, appl shield-shaped Limoges enameled plaque of Native American chief in blue, green, black, white, red, and beige, mkd "STERLING," maker's mks for Watson, Newell Co., Attleboro, MA (after 1910), wide C-catch, flanged hinge, 2-1/4" w x 1-1/2", **$200**. (Charles Pinkham collection).

14k yg, faience, enamel, diamonds, rubies, c. 1900, Egyptian Revival, open shield shape centering a blue-green faience scarab surmounted by one oe diamond and foliate and lotus motifs in blue and green enamel, undulating yg wire frame interspersed with alternating oe diamonds and sm circ-cut rubies, diamonds approx 0.65 cts tw, 1-1/2" w x 1-3/4" .... 2,850 (A)

18k yg, c. 1900, circ medallion of a young woman's profile in an elaborate floral and foliate scroll frame, Fr hmk (eagle's head) for 18k gold, 1-1/8" w x 1-3/8" .... 920 (A)

18k yg, diamond, plat, c. 1900, circ, bird in flight framed by a tree branch with an oe diamond accent, sgd "GG," approx 8.20 dwt, 1" dia .... 863 (A)

Opal, 14k yg, diamonds, enamel, c. 1910, lg oval white opal prong-set in a pave-set om and oe diamond oval plaque bordered with blue enamel, yellowish-green enameled yg outer frame with paired scrolls top and bottom, 1-5/8" w x 1-1/2 .... 5,520 (A)

Opal, yg, demantoid garnets, pearl, c. 1890, Beaux-arts style, an oval opal with matrix flanked by opposed yg griffins with entwined tails around the bottom, demantoid garnet eyes, a sm pearl between their open mouths, 1" w x 1-1/4" .... 575 (A)

Brass, glass, c. 1900, in the shape of a feather with peacock-eye glass cab at one end, C-catch, flanged hinge, 1" w x 3-3/4" 200

Sp brass, c. 1900, heart-shaped die-struck plaque, torso of a nude woman with flower in flowing hair floating in water, a flying bird near her mouth, undulating flower and vine border, C-catch, flanged hinge, 1-1/2" w x 1-5/8" 145

Sp brass, c. 1900, oval unbacked die-struck plaque of a woman holding up her hair with a flower, surrounded by water and lily pads, undulating vine border, C-catch, flanged hinge, 2-1/4" dia 125

Sterling, c. 1910, die-stamped woman's front-facing head with deeply waved loops of hair, rev mkd "STERLING," C-catch, extended pinstem, 1-1/8" w x 1-3/8" 225

Sterling, yg, c. 1905, depicting the profile of a woman with flowing hair and floral headdress in raised yg on a ster plaque with a C-scrolled border, maker's mk for George Shiebler (winged S), New York, NY, 1-3/4" w x 2" .... 575 (A)

Sterling, Am, c. 1900, die-stamped in the shape of a frontal bust of a woman wearing a lg hat, 2-1/2" w x 2" 400

Sterling, Am, c. 1900, die-stamped in the shape of a woman's profile, wearing a lg hat decorated with flowers, mkd "STERLING," maker's mk for Unger Bros., Newark, NJ, 2" w x 1-1/2" 650

Sterling, wm, c. 1900, die-stamped woman's head facing front wearing a mortarboard in a border of scrolls and flowerheads, mkd "STERLING SILVER FRONT," C-catch, 3/4" w x 1" 125

Sterling, wm, c. 1900, die-stamped woman's head with drapery headcovering, mkd "STERLING TOP," C-catch, 7/8" w x 1" 250

Bar

14k yg, enamel, amethyst, seed pearls, c.1910, two elongated foliate motifs *basse-taille* enameled in orange shading to yellow and green, stems scrolling around a central bezel-set circ-cut amethyst, surmounted by a seed pearl top and bottom, maker's mark for Krementz & Co., Newark, NJ (collar button) and "14k" imp on lever catch, 1-5/8" w x 1/2" 1,027

Sash Pin/Ornament

Enamel, sterling, c. 1910, open oval green and white *basse-taille* enameled frame with riveted plaques, central shield-shaped plaque with maple leaf center surmounted by crown, *basse-taille* enameled in shades of blue, white, green, yellow and orange, flanked by two butterflies in shades of blue and white on green leaves, rev mkd "925 R (lion motif)" and "STERLING," probably Canadian, C-catch, 2-1/4" w x 1-1/4" 85

Gp brass, c. 1910, lozenge-shaped stamped brass, openwork floral and foliate motif, oval plate on rev mkd "C & R" flanking a triangle, C-catch, flanged hinge, 3" w x 2-1/4" 65

Watch pin

Sterling, c. 1910, die-stamped circ plaque depicting an American Indian chief with feather headdress, flat backing with maker's mk for Unger Bros., later added safety catch, upturned hook for watch on rev, 1" dia 300

Sterling, c. 1910, circ medallion with Minerva in profile wearing a helmet surmounted by a griffin, maker's mk for Unger Bros, hook for watch on rev, C-catch, flanged hinge, 1" dia 300

Buckle

Sterling, c. 1900, lg open chain link oval, maker's mk, possibly for Howard Sterling Co., Providence RI, double hasp, 2-1/2" w x 3-1/4" 150

Sterling, c. 1900-10, two-pc, opposed open-mouthed snakes with curvilinear bodies, engr details, maker's mark for Wm B. Kerr (fasces), "STERLING" and design number on appl oval plate, hook and eye closure, bars for belt removed (converted to earrings), 5" w x 1-5/8" 400

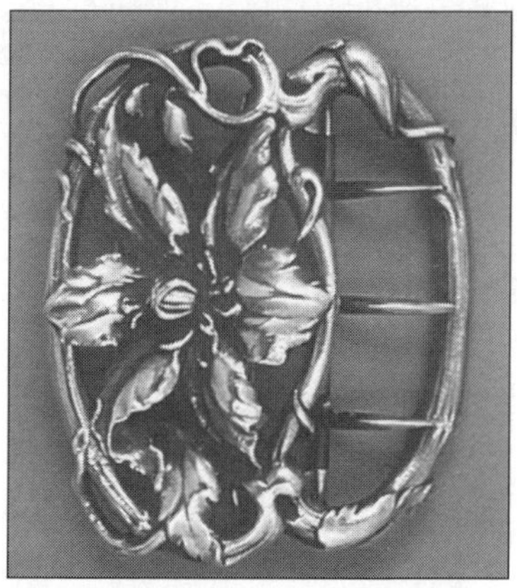

Buckle, silver, c. 1900, appl three-dimensional flower head and twining vine on open oval frame, Fr hmk (boar's head) and maker's mk "EL" flanking a bird motif in lozenge on swiveling triple hasp, bar for belt attachment on rev, 2-3/4" w x 2-1/4", **$450**. (Cheryl Chang collection).

Buckle, sterling, copper, c. 1901, woman's full face in copper surrounded by undulating waves of hair in sterling, separate clasp attachment for belt, maker's mk for Gorham Mfg. Co., mkd "STERLING, OTHER METALS," "B1402, copyrighted 1901" on rev hook, and "Pat. Apld. For" on both pcs, 2-3/8" w x 2-1/2", **$1,200**. (Private collection).

Buckles, sterling, Am, c. 1900:

TL, an irregular cusped and notched open-centered leaf shape, engr veins on convex/concave surface surmounted at compass points by four insect motifs: a beetle, a fly, a bee and a butterfly, swiveling double hasp in center, rev imp with maker's mk after 1896 for Frank M. Whiting & Co., North Attleboro, MA (W in a circle flanked by trefoils), "STERLING" #47, 2-1/2" w x 3-1/4", **$650**.

TR, open rounded-corner rectangle decorated with a series of foliated beaded scrolls on slightly undulating surface, swivel double hasp in center, rev imp "TIFFANY & CO" #5679M and 5433 "STERLING," 2-3/8" w x 3-1/4", **$750**.

B, central butterfly motif, wings set with two lg oval and eight sm circ opals, within an open double oval frame surmounted by undulating vines, leaves and flowers, hook on rev imp with maker's mk for Gorham Mfg. Co., Providence, RI, "STERLING" #B1422, bar mkd "PAT APLD FOR," 2-3/4" w x 1-3/8", **$1,500**.
(Janet Zapata collection, photo by Robert Weldon).

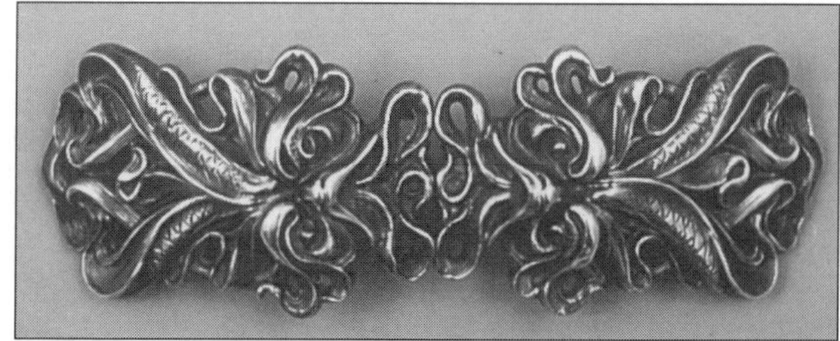

Buckle, sterling, c. 1900, 2-pc stamped relief design of opposed stylized dolphins with undulating whiskers and streamers, mkd "STERLING" #826, maker's mk for Wm. B. Kerr & Co. (fasces), Newark, N.J., hook and eye closure, bars for belt attachment, 3-1/2" w x 1-1/2", **$600**. (Lis Normoyle collection).

Sterling, c. 1901, open-centered circle formed by two engr feather motifs surmounting a scroll motif, maker's mk for Gorham Mfg. Co, mkd "STERLING, COPYRIGHTED 1901, B1432," and "PAT. APPLIED FOR," double hasp, hook on rev swivels, separate clasp for belt, 2-1/4" w x 2-3/8" 500

Sterling, c. 1905, two-pc, each pc a full-blown flowerhead and paired leaves in die-stamped high relief, hook and eye closure, appl double bars on rev for belt attachment mkd "PATENTED JUNE 25, 1901," flat backing with appl oval disk imp with maker's mk for Wm. B. Kerr & Co., Newark, NJ, "STERLING" #1564, 4-7/8" w x 1-1/2" 400

Buckles, sterling, c. 1900-10, Beaux-arts style, Wm. B. Kerr & Co., Newark,NJ:
T, two-pc, two die-struck cherubs each within a scroll and foliate cartouche, flat backing with appl oval plate mkd "STERLING" #5, maker's mk for Wm. B. Kerr & Co., hook and eye closure, bars for belt attachment, 2" w x 1", **$250**. (Elaine Sarnoff collection).
B, two-pc floral and foliate double wreath with a center bow, flat backing with appl oval plate mkd "STERLING" #20, maker's mk for Wm. B. Kerr & Co., hook and eye closure, bars for belt attachment on rev, 2" w x 1", **$200**.
(Sue James collection).

Sterling, c. 1908, open oval, engr on front "Lila" at top and "America 1908" at bottom, double hasp, hook on rev swivels, maker's mk for William B. Kerr, dents, 2-5/8" w x 2-1/8" 150

Chain

Sterling, c. 1900, oval links interspersed with four oval plaques of swirling water design, plaques 1" w x 1/4", chain 32" tl 275

Chatelaine Top

Gp brass, c. 1900, die-stamped circ flower motif plaque with central woman's profile, wide hook with attached safety pin on rev, 1-5/8" dia 75

Cuff Links

14k yg, c. 1900, oval disks with chased bulldog design, 5.3 dwt, hmk for Bippart, Griscom & Osborne (torch), Newark NJ, 1/2" w x 3/4", pr.......... 374 (A)

18k yg, c. 1900, double-sided, each a pr of tapered cusped cylinders with embossed floral motif, chain connectors, Fr hmk (eagle's head) for 18k gold, 5/8" w x 1/8", pr .... 258 (A)

Sterling, c. 1910, convex oval plaques with raised swirl design surrounding central domed bead, maker's mark for Unger Bros, imp "STERLING 925 FINE," 1/2" w x 3/4". 350

Cuff Links, silver, c. 1890, irregular circ disks with die-stamped design of dragonfly, cattails and water, mono "TR" on front, hinged cuff button mkd "PAT'D AUG 24, 1880," 1" dia, pr, **$175**. (Richard Levey collection).

Hatpin, 14k yg, rubies, gp wm, c. 1900-05, Beaux-arts style, engr yg depicting one head of Cerberus, the three-headed dog guarding the gates of Hades, "Roman" (matte or frosted) gold finish, ruby eyes, gp pin stem, base of head imp with maker's mk for Sloan & Co. (a lyre), Newark NJ, "14K," head 1" x 3/4", 4-5/8" tl (possibly cut down), **$1,200**. (Private collection).

Hatpin

Yg, enamel, f.w. pearls, ym, c. 1890, wreath of green enameled yg leaves enclosing four f.w. pearls, ym pinstem, 1/2" w x 8" tl .... 920 (A)

Yg, pearls, green stones, c. 1890, an open mushroom-shaped frame enclosing a horizontal row of seven pearls on yg stems surmounting a bezel-set green stone on front and back, 1-1/8" w x 7" tl .... 920 (A)

Brass, glass, c. 1900, pierced cusped shell-shaped plaque with central bezel-set circ peacock-eye glass cab, top 1" w x 1-1/4", 13-1/4" tl 165

Locket

Gf, c. 1900, circ, die-stamped bust of a flowing-haired woman, raised arm and hands holding flowers at her head and bosom, 1" dia 165

Gf, c. 1910-20, circ, die-struck floral wreath with undulating border, scrolled-edge polished convex center, engr mono on rev, 1-1/4" dia 85

Gf, c. 1910-20, cushion-shaped, die-struck scroll and foliate design, engr gallery, mkd "1/20 14k" on bail, 1" sq 65

Gf, glass, c. 1910-20, circ, die-struck with scrolling foliate motif, circ-cut and crescent-shaped purple glass set in center, side-sliding closure, 1" dia.......... 85

Gf, rhinestone, c. 1910-20, circ, die-struck scrolled vine and orchid motifs, r.s. center, mkd "3 B C O" inside locket frame, 1" dia 90

Gf, rhinestones, c. 1910-20, circ, profile of woman with flowing hair in draped border, replaced r.s. around lower edge, engr mono on rev, mkd "W & H Co." in heart shape for Wightman & Hough Co., Providence, RI, 1-1/4" dia 95

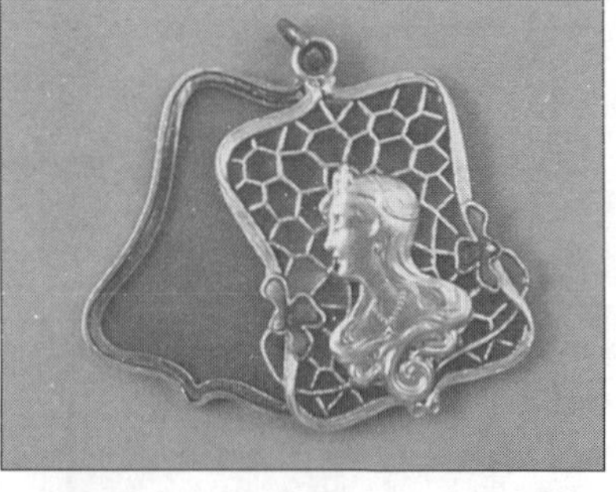

Locket, silver gilt, enamel, c. 1890-1900, waisted shield shape, appl woman's profile with flowing hair flanked by two flowers over irregular honeycomb bg of *plique à jour* enamel in shades of lilac, turq and blue, swivels open, glazed inner compartment, mkd "900" on rev front, later-added inscription on rev: "An Milly von Harry dein Natt VII 21 1934," probably Ger or Austrian, 1-1/4" w x 1-3/4", **$1,400**. (Courtesy of E. Foxe Harrell Jewelers, Clinton, IA).

Lockets, gf, Am, c. 1910-20:

L, bombé cusped corner rect, entrelac and floral motif set with r.s., engr mono "M" on rev, mkd "L.M. & Co." for Leach & Miller Co., of Attleboro MA inside back center, 1-1/4" w x 2-3/8" tl, **$115**.

CL, elongated cusped oval with fleur-de-lis, swag and foliate motifs, engr floral and foliate motif on rev, mkd "F & B" for Theodore W. Foster & Bro. Co., Providence, RI, 1-1/4" w x 2-1/2", **$125**.

CR, elongated oval locket set with sm colorless r.s. and lg lozenge-shaped faceted purple glass stone in center, meander and fleur-de-lis motifs top and bottom, engr mono "OC" on rev, mkd "S.H. Co.," 1-1/4" w x 2-1/2", **$100**.

R, cusped shield-shaped locket, stamped and engr *entrelac* and floral motifs, engr mono "MRW" on rev, mkd "FLS" on inside frame for F.L. Shepardson & Co, North Attleboro, MA, 1" w x 2-1/4", **$110**.

(Elaine Sarnoff collection).

Gp brass, glass, c. 1910, circ Greek Revival medallion/locket of Athena, r.s. around edge and on helmet, mkd "SOB & Co." for S.O. Bigney & Co., Attleboro, MA., inside frame, 1-1/4" dia 75

Lorgnette

14k yg, c. 1900, Beaux-arts style, foliate and scroll decorations on handle continuing to border of cover for lenses, spring mechanism for releasing folded spectacles, small dent, 1-1/4" w x 5-1/2" tl .... 748 (A)

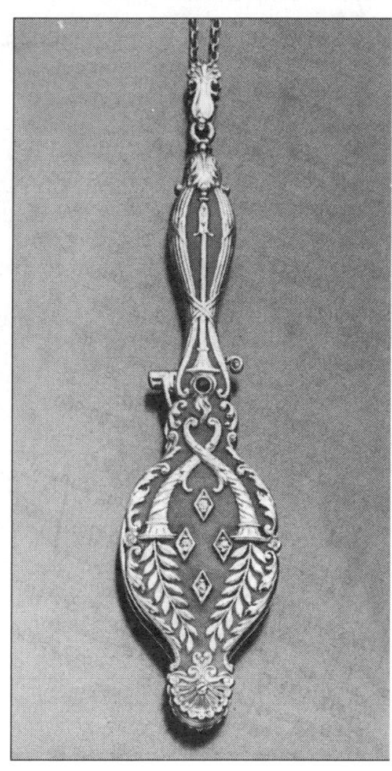

Lorgnette, 14k yg, enamel, diamonds, rubies, c. 1900, Beaux-arts style, double cornucopia design with foliate scroll surround on a translucent green enamel ground, enclosing four sm lozenge shapes set with sm circ diamonds, a circ-cut ruby in the flame of a torch motif on handle, suspended from a long chain with fancy enamel links set with sm circ diamonds and rubies, 1-1/8" w x 4-1/2" tl, **$3,450** [A]. (Photo courtesy of William Doyle Galleries, New York, NY, 12/ 4/96).

14k yg, c. 1900, raised design depicting a woman's face with flowing hair surmounting an iris motif enclosed by whiplash curv foliate motifs, maker's mk for Krementz, Newark, NJ, 1" w x 5" .... 1,038 (A)

Lorgnette & Chain

14k yg, glass, c. 1900, Beaux-arts style, repoussé handle with putto and scroll motifs, exposed hinged lenses with dolphin nose piece, suspended from a 14k yg trace link and baton chain, lorgnette 1-1/2" w (at lens) x 4-1/4" (closed), chain 25" tl .... 920 (A)

Necklace

Coral, 14k yg, f.w. pearls, c. 1900, horizontal foliate yg C-scroll set with three f.w. pearls, suspending five pear-shaped coral drops from elongated trumpet-shaped floral yg links and short trace chains, each end drop surmounted by a f.w. pearl, and linked to a trace and cable link chain, 18" tl, sgd "SHREVE & CO.," San Francisco, CA, 2" w (at center), 2-1/2" tl .... 1,725 (A)

Yg, tourmaline, peridot, c. 1900, twining foliate motif, central wreath with a lg circ-cut collet-set pink tourmaline center, flanked by two sm collet-set peridots, suspending pear-shaped bezel-set pink tourmaline drop flanked by leaves, twining foliate links each with a sm collet-set pink tourmaline to one side, 1-3/4" w (at center), 17" tl .... 2,530 (A)

Festoon

14k yg, pearls, c. 1900, centering an open heart shape with central sm post-set pearl and suspending a lg pink pearl drop, flanked by two smaller open circ motifs each suspending a pearl, attached by triple swagged chain, double chain to pearl bead, single chain to closure, 1" w (at center), 16" tl .... 1,840 (A)

Yg, rhodolite garnets, pearls, c. 1910, central collet-set rhodolite garnet suspending an open wirework drop surmounted by a round pearl, suspending a f.w. pearl,

Necklace, festoon, yg, f.w. pearls, enamel, glass, c. 1890-1900, central green enameled jack-in-the-pulpit floral motif flanked by seed pearl-set banches and green-enameled leaves suspending three collet-set red glass and baroque pearl drops, linked by double chains to foliate motif yg plaques with central bezel-set faceted oval red glass stones, single chain to closure, 2" w (at center), 15" tl, **$1,380** [A]. (Photo courtesy of Christie's Images, New York, NY, 12/11/96).

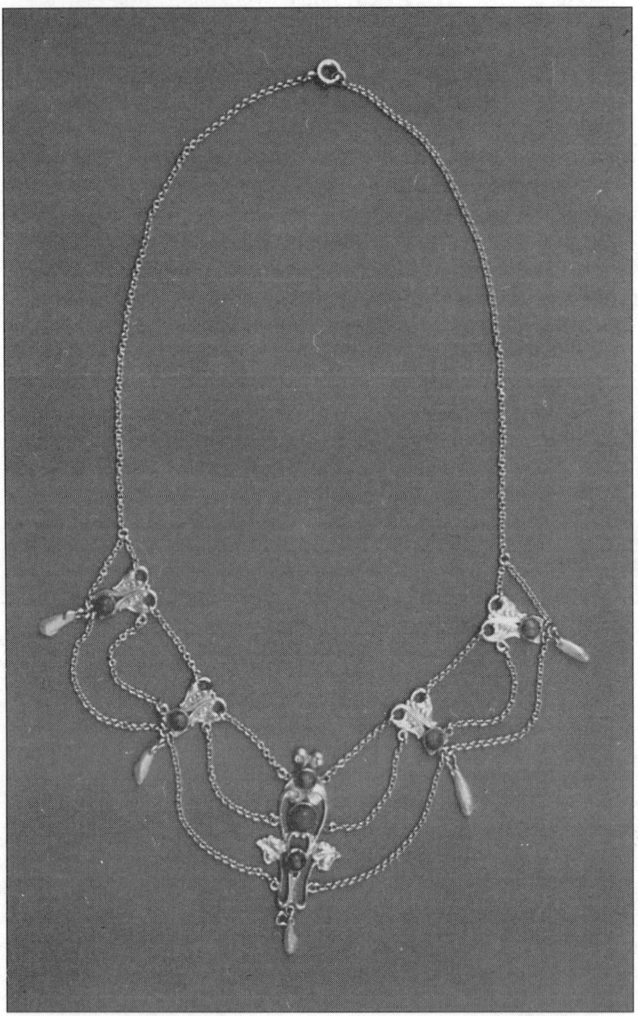

Necklace, festoon, gp brass, glass, c. 1900-10, central scroll and foliate motif stamped openwork gp plaque, sawtooth bezel-set with a vertical row of three green glass cabs, suspending f.w. pearl drop, flanked by four smaller stamped gp plaques, each set with one green glass cab and f.w. pearl drop, linked by three fine cable link swagged chains, continuing to a single chain, spring ring clasp, 2" at center, 17" tl, **$300**. (Terrance O'Halloran collection).

flanked by two fine cable link swagged chains leading to a collet-set garnet with f.w. pearl drop, single chain to spring ring closure, 1-1/2" w (at center), 18" tl 450

Sautoir

Seed pearls, glass, diamonds, enamel, 18k yg, c. 1899, braided seed pearl chain with blue enameled yg terminals, suspending two freeform curv rc and om diamond-set frames enclosing molded opalescent glass stylized poppy blossom motifs in shades of blue and gray suspended from cream-colored enamel stems, sgd "LALIQUE," Fr hmk (eagle's head) for 18k gold, in a fitted suede case, provenance: from the Barbra Streisand collection, pendants each approx 1-1/2" w 3", chain 25" tl .... 96,000 (A)

Pendant

18k yg, enamel, diamonds, platinum, c. 1900, central pear-shaped plaque with an enameled design of water, waterlilies, and a sunrise in pastel shades of yellow, blue, green, and orange, the sun a lg rc diamond with sm rc diamond rays, a lily pad set with sm rc diamonds, framed by chased yg pelicans, suspending a lg pear-shaped rc diamond drop set in plat, lg oe diamond at top center flanked by pelicans' outstretched wing, total of forty-six diamonds in bead and bezel settings, Fr hmk (eagle's head) for 18k gold, maker's mk for Antoine Bricteux, 1-7/8" w x 2-1/2" tl .... 28,750 (A)

Yg, enamel, diamonds, c. 1900, figure of a woman holding two sm circ-cut prong-set diamonds in her outstretched hands, surrounded by a diaphanous billowing robe with a scale-like pattern of *plique à jour* enamel in shades of lt pink and green, plain yg bail, 1-1/8" w x 1-3/8" tl .... 4,025 (A)

Locket

18k yg, diamonds, platinum, c. 1890, swiveling locket, front oval repoussé plaque depicting the upper torso of a woman in profile wearing rc diamond jewelry, surrounded by floral/foliate and scroll motifs, rc diamond-set plat-topped yg frame and bail, Fr hmks, 2" w x 3-1/2" (with bail).. 6,325 (A)

Pendant, platinum, ivory, enamel, seed pearls, diamonds, c. 1912, six-lobed circ platinum frame and backing, a central carved ivory madonna surrounded by seed pearls pave-set within a star-shaped border, encircled by a *plique à jour* enameled bg of grey-blue shading to amber (cracks and crazing), rc diamond-set bail, ivory sgd "VERNON" for Paris medalist Frédéric de Vernon (1858-1912), Fr hmk for platinum after 1912 (dog's head), illegible maker's mk in lozenge on rev, 1-1/8" dia, 1-1/2" tl with bail, **$5,000**. (Susan Shargal collection).

Pendant and Chain, 18k green gold, enamel, pearl, diamonds, emeralds, opal, c. 1900, open design of a woman's head in profile facing a crescent moon, blue and green *plique à jour* enameled undulating hair and floral motifs, headdress of a row of grad emeralds and one lg circ-cut bezel-set diamond, a row of grad sm circ-cut diamonds outlining the moon, four heart-shaped bezel-set emeralds and one opal interspersed, suspending a lg round pearl, suspended from two short lengths of trace link chain at the sides leading to scrolled fan shaped *plique à jour* enameled plaque, continuing oval link chain to closure, Fr, sgd on rev "L. Gautrait" for Lucien Gautrait, Paris, 2" w x 3-3/4", 16" tl, **$19,550** [A]. (Photo courtesy of William Doyle Galleries, New York, NY, 9/11/97).

Pendant and Chain

Black opal, 14k yg, diamonds, demantoid garnets, c. 1910, two triangular opals, one inverted at the top, 10.1 x 7.4 x 2.6 mm, flanked by C scrolls and two oc diamonds, surmounted by a curved row of five sm oe diamonds, enclosed in a conforming yg frame with whiplash decoration, the other opal, 16.1 x 12.3 x 4.8 mm, suspended from a tapered rod, flanked by two shorter knife-edged wires with collet-set diamond centers, sq-cut demantoid garnet terminals, fetter and cable link fine chain, pendant 1-1/4" w x 2-1/2" .... 4,250 (A)

Yg, enamel, diamonds, ruby, pearl, c. 1900, depicting a semi-nude dancing woman, lower torso clad in a diaphanous gown, arms overhead holding a tambourine, gown of pink *plique à jour* enamel bordered with rc diamonds, bg plaque in green *plique à jour* enamel, undulating yg border, heart-shaped terminal set with a ruby, suspending a pearl, suspended from two lengths of knot-like link chain attached at top sides, caught by a sm open cusped and lobed lozenge-shaped plaque with diamond-set paired wings through the center, Fr, 2" w x 2-3/4" .... 4,600 (A)

Pendant and Chain, silver gilt, enamel, pastes, f.w. pearls, c. 1910-15, two opposed cusped and scrolled triangular plaques, each depicting a flower with a paste set in center and on stem, *plique à jour* enameled in shades of violet shading to pale blue, on a blue-green ground, suspending a f.w. pearl, linked to a central sm circ collet-set colorless paste, three linked collet-set sm circ colorless pastes surmounting each plaque leading to chain, v-spring and tube clasp, Fr hmks on jump ring, 1-1/2" w x 2-1/4", 19" tl, **$650**. (Ann Tidwell collection).

Pendant and Chain, gp brass, glass, rhinestones, seed pearls, c. 1910, central stamped gp brass element in the shape of a stylized owl in flight, green glass cab eyes, wings set with amber-colored r.s. and seed pearls, on an open oval wire frame above a bezel-set faceted oval citrine-colored glass stone, suspending three bezel-set faceted oval yellow glass drops, one from the base, flanked by two from baton links on the sides, three short lengths of cable link chain at the top joined to a bezel-set circ-cut citrine-colored glass stone linked to two long lengths of chain and a T-bar clasp, unmkd, possibly Am, pendant 2-5/8" w x 2-1/2" tl, chain from top stone 16-1/2" tl, **$350**. (Private collection, photo by Robert Weldon).

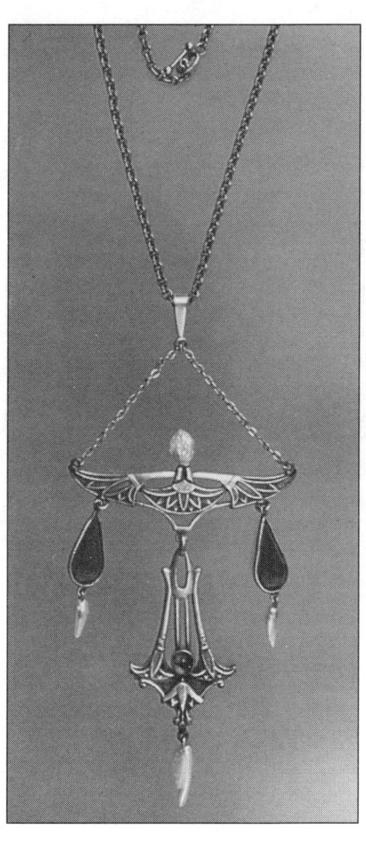

Pendant and Chain, brass, glass, f.w. pearls, c. 1910, Egyptian Revival, upper plaque three fanned lotus blossoms surmounted by a f.w. pearl, suspending a central drop of openwork lotus blossoms with a red glass cab and a f.w. pearl drop flanked by two marquise-shaped red collet-set glass stones with f.w. pearl drops, short lengths of chain attached at either side of top plaque leading to bail, mkd "F & B" for Theodore W. Foster and Bro., Providence, RI, T-bar clasp, pendant 2" w x 4-1/4", chain 17" tl, **$350**. (Sue James collection).

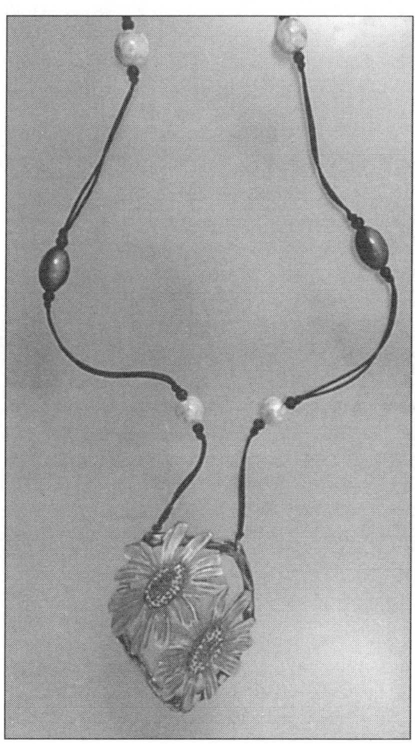

Pendant and Cord, clarified horn, silk cord, glass beads, c. 1900, two carved daises within open shield-shaped branch-like frame suspended from cord interspersed with two brown horn and four amber-colored glass beads, Fr, rev sgd "E. Bonté" for Elizabeth Bonté, bottom drop missing, 2-1/8" w x 2-3/4", cord 34" tl, **$500**. (Sue James collection).

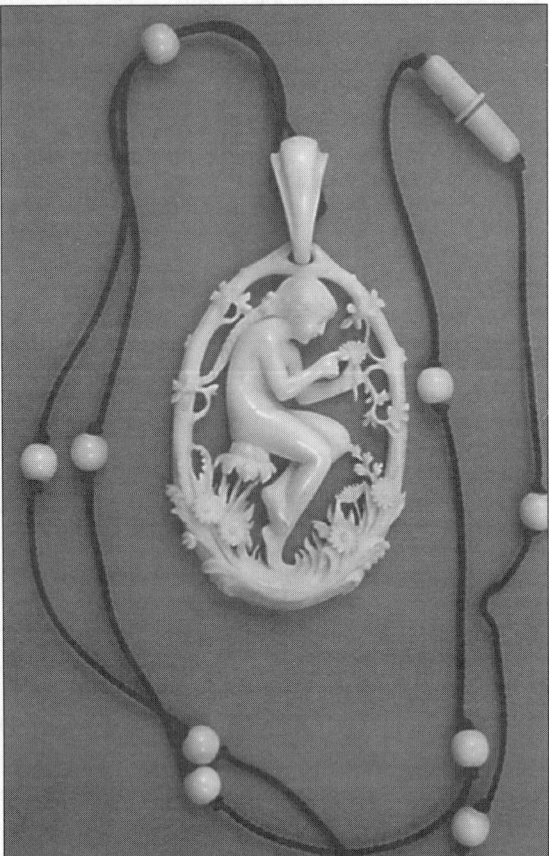

Pendant and Cord, Ivory, silk cord, c. 1910-20, pierced and carved oval plaque depicting a nude nymph-like female seated on a flower, holding a daisy, daisies and leaves intertwining around branch-like frame, suspended from a thin black silk cord interspersed with sm round ivory beads, ivory barrel clasp, pendant 1-1/2" w x 3" tl, cord 28" tl, **$400**. (Claudette Beaulieu collection).

Ring

18k yg, enamel, c. 1890-1900, pine bough motif sculptural band of mixed *plique à jour* and opaque enamel in shades of green, blue, and white, Fr hmks, maker's mk for Lalique, 1/2" w, size 8 .... 6,900 (A)

Aquamarine, diamonds, enamel, 18k yg, c. 1900, oval-cut aquamarine flanked by green-enameled foliate motifs continuing to shoulders, a spray of collet-set sm rc diamonds at top and bottom, mounted on a narrow yg shank, Fr hmks, maker's mk "LD," approx 3/4" w x 1" .... 2,645 (A)

Opal, diamonds, 18k yg, c. 1900, central marquise-shaped opal cab with four sm circ-cut diamonds at compass points, set in a pierced floral motif yg mount, Fr maker's mk, 7/8" w x 1-1/8", size 6-1/2......................... 1,840 (A)

Yg, amethyst, c. 1900, central circ bezel-set amethyst cab in a domed and tapered yg mount decorated with flowerheads and female faces with flowing hair, 3/4" w x 3/8", size 5-3/4.. 805 (A)

Ring, turquoise, diamonds, 14k yg, enamel, platinum, c. 1900-10, shield-shaped plaque, undulating scrolled foliate yg border and gallery, with a central rounded rect turq cab bezel-set on a blue shading to green *basse-taille* enameled ground, four circ-cut diamonds in plat collets at compass points, mounted on a narrow shank, probably Am, mkd "14k," size 6, 1/2" w x 3/4", **$700**. (Diane White collection).

Suite: Buckle, Hatpins, Buttons, gp brass, enamel, c. 1900, tapered and scalloped rect 2-pc buckle in gilt metal with pierced floral and foliate motif *basse-taille* enameled in dk green, lt green, blue, and peach, two hatpins and six buttons with circ enameled disks of similar motif, in orig fitted box with fittings for buttons, buckle mkd "METAL GILT," probably Bohemian, buckle 2-3/4" w x 1-1/2", hatpin 3/4" dia, 9-7/8" tl, buttons 1/2" dia, suite, **$350**. (Terrance O'Halloran collection).

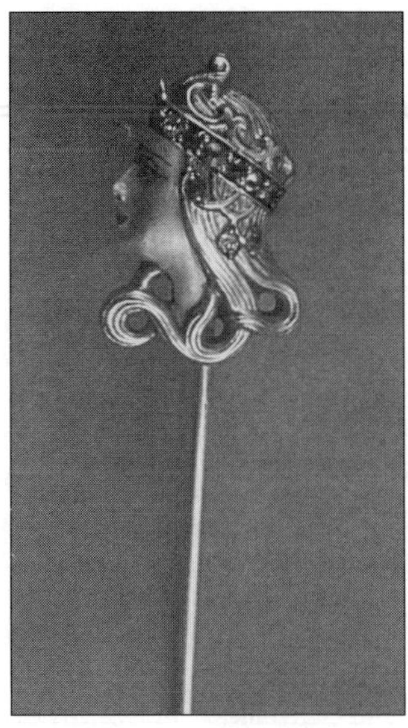

Scarf Pin/Stickpin, 14k yg, enamel, diamonds, rubies, c. 1900, depicting the profile of a woman with flowing hair and crown set with sm sc diamonds and rubies, enameled features, yg pinstem mkd "14k," Am, head 1/2" w x 3/4", 2-3/8" tl, **$850**. (Courtesy of E. Foxe Harrell Jewelers, Clinton, IA).

Scarf Pin/Stickpin

14k yg, enamel, c. 1900-10, depicting a male head in three-quarter profile, enameled features, yg draped turban, 1/2" w x 5/8", 2-1/2" tl .... 633 (A)

14k yg, enamel, c. 1900-10, depicting the head of a Viking, realistically enameled bearded face, yg winged helmet, 5/8" w x 3/4", 2-5/8" tl, ... 805 (A)

14k yg, enamel, diamond, c. 1900-10. full-face turbaned and bearded male head, yg face, red, white, blue and green patterned turban with diamond collet-set in center, 5/8" x 3/4", 2-5/8" tl .... 633 (A)

14k yg, enamel, diamonds, seed pearl, c. 1900-10, woman's head in profile, long flowing hair with diamond and seed pear-set headdress, enameled features, 5/8" w x 7/8", 3" tl.. 633 (A)

18k yg, enamel, diamond, c. 1900, depicting the head of a rooster in polychrome enamel, rc diamond eye, Fr hmks,1/2" w x 5/8", 3-1/4" tl .... 460 (A)

Black opal, 18k yg, c. 1900-10, an oval black opal, 12.50 mm x 16.00 mm in a plain yg frame (slight crazing), mkd "M & Co." for Marcus & Co., New York, NY, 5/8" w x 3/4", 3-1/8" tl... 2,645 (A)

Gf, c. 1910, oval plaque, die-stamped undulating snakes motif, mkd "gold top," 1/2" w x 3/4", 3" tl 90

Moonstone, enamel, diamonds, 18k yg, c. 1915, Egyptian Revival, oval bezel-set moonstone in a frame flanked by serpent and lotus motifs, two sm oe diamonds, enamel accents, sgd "T.B. STARR" for Theodore B. Starr, New York, NY, 1/2" w x 2-1/2" tl................................ 431 (A)

Sapphire, diamonds, yg, c. 1910, cushion-cut blue sapphire, approx 5.00 cts, in a textured scrolled yg frame, three sm oe diamonds at top and sides, Am, sgd "MARCUS & CO," #11743,1/2" w x 5/8", 2-3/4" tl....... 4,370 (A)

Tiara

18k yg, glass, enamel, diamonds, c. 1900, forest green enamel on a yg band surmounted by om and rc diamond-set yg thorned branch motifs, interspersed with lg and sm molded opalescent glass wildflowers, sgd "LALIQUE," Fr hmk (eagle's head) for 18k gold, provenance: from the Barbra Streisand collection, 1" w (at center), 13" tl .... 23,000 (A)

Watch Fob

Sterling, date letter for 1899, three linked medallions, each depicting a woman's profile, suspended from a T-bar, Birmingham (Eng) hmks, 1-1/4" w x 4-1/4" tl ..... 115 (A)

Yg, c. 1900, open shield-shaped intertwined floral and foliate motif suspending an unengr seal, short chain at opposite end terminating in a swivel hook, in a fitted leather, silk, and velvet box stamped "Spaulding & Co., Jewelers and Silversmiths, 36 Avenue de l'Opéra, Paris," 1" w x 5-1/4" tl .... 2,875 (A)

Watch Fob, 14k yg, lapis lazuli, ribbon, c. 1900-10, Egyptian Revival, black grosgrain ribbon suspending scrolled foliate motif loop and pendant of opposed pharaoh's heads surmounting oval frame with reversible center, carved lapis lazuli scarab one side and engr demotic (post-hieroglyphic) script the other, maker's mark for Carter, Howe & Co., Newark, NJ, 1" w x 2-1/4", **$3,000**. (Private collection).

Watch Fob, brass, c. 1910, Egyptian Revival, linked plaques, two triangles flanking two squares, stamped designs, different on each side, depicting Egyptian burial figures with hieroglyphic borders, suspending circ stamped disk depicting the Sphinx, verso an Egyptian god, 1" w x 5" tl, **$85**. (Sue James collection).

EDWARDIAN c. 1890-1920

History: Historically, the Edwardian period lasted for only the nine years that King Edward VII was on the throne, 1901-1910. The *style* most often referred to as Edwardian, however, began to evolve more than ten years earlier and continued to be seen for about ten years after Edward's death. By the time Edward and Alexandra became king and queen, they were past middle age, and the style they influenced was firmly entrenched.

The period was a time of social reform, but it also saw the rise of an incredibly wealthy upper class, even within the so-called "classless" democracy of the United States. Unlike Victoria, who was the people's queen, Edward and Alexandra set the tone for an international high society separated from the lower classes by a social whirl of balls, sporting events, yachting, and all the other accouterments of the well-to-do. Elegance and delicacy were the watchwords of the day. Jewels, of course, were an important part of the trappings.

Edwardian jewelry contrasts markedly with other concurrent styles. While Arts and Crafts and Art Nouveau were part of the aesthetic avant-garde, Edwardian jewelry clung to tradition. The former attracted the intellectual elite, the latter, the social elite. Arts and Crafts and Nouveau emphasized design and workmanship over intrinsically valuable materials. Edwardian emphasized diamonds, pearls, and platinum, in skillfully worked designs. Arts and Crafts and Art Nouveau jewelers used enamels and gemstones in a palette of colors. Edwardian jewels were monochromatic, mostly white or colorless.

Arts and Crafts was inspired by the medieval and Renaissance periods; Edwardian looked back to the Neo-classical and Rococo of the eighteenth century and the French courts of Louis XV and particularly, Louis XVI. Not so much the jewelry of that time, but rather the ornamental motifs found on furniture, architecture, and decorative objects: bows, tassels, lace, and the foliate wreaths and swags that gave the style a name: the garland style.

One of the most distinctive aspects of Edwardian jewels is their lacy, delicate appearance, made possible by the use of platinum, an extremely strong and ductile metal. Although platinum had been used earlier, demand for it–and consequently its value–was not as high, nor was it worked in the same way as it was at the turn of the century.

For a while, jewelers continued to treat platinum as they had silver, laminating it to gold. This was unnecessary, because platinum does not tarnish, and is strong enough to be used alone. The speculation is that jewelers were striving to maintain the tradition of nineteenth century diamond jewels set in silver-topped gold.

Platinum was not considered a precious metal until its advantageous qualities for setting diamonds were more widely recognized. Platinum wasn't *officially* recognized by the French government as a precious metal until 1910–years after platinum had become the metal of choice for setting diamonds. The French hallmark for platinum, a dog's head, wasn't introduced until 1912 (see appendix, Marks on Metals).

The Edwardian look is characterized by "knife-edge" platinum wires joining millegrained collet-set diamonds in openwork designs, and saw-pierced platinum plaques set throughout with diamonds. The colorless all-diamond and pearl-and-diamond jewels complemented the all-white and pale pastel feminine fashions of the period, which were made of lightweight fabrics and lace.

While we are accustomed to referring to this style as Edwardian, as noted by Penny Proddow and Marion Fasel in their book, *Diamonds, a Century of Spectacular Jewels* (see References), "Edwardian" is not an entirely accurate appellation. For one thing, the style has French derivations, and the French would *never* name a style after an English king! And while it's true that King Edward VII was a well-known patron of the delineator of the style, Cartier, whom he dubbed "the king of jewelers and the jeweler of kings," he himself would not have called the style Edwardian. As Proddow and Fasel note, other names, while French, are also found lacking: *belle époque* (beautiful era) covers a much longer period, and includes Art Nouveau. *Fin de siècle,* turn of the century, must also include other styles. "The garland style," *style guirlande* in French, is perhaps the most appropriate or evocative name, but there is certainly no consensus on its use.

We usually think of what to call a style after some distancing of elapsed time has occurred, so it should come as no surprise that, according to Judy Rudoe in the exhibition catalog, *Cartier 1900-1939,* it was Hans Nadelhoffer, author in 1984 of the comprehensive book, *Cartier, Jewelers Extraordinary,* who first christened diamond and platinum Louis XVI-inspired jewelry "the garland style." Cartier was at the forefront in developing the style, introducing it in 1899. But they were not alone.

The style's emphasis on diamonds coincided with improvements in diamond-cutting technology, which gave rise to new cuts, such as the marquise or navette, the emerald cut, and the baguette. The term "calibré cut" was used to refer to any stone cut to a special shape to fit a setting. The briolette cut, a three-dimensional teardrop shape, was often used for stones meant to be suspended, e.g., in earrings or lavaliers. All of these cuts were also used for other transparent gemstones. Colored stones were often combined with diamonds and pearls in Edwardian jewelry, particularly amethysts, peridot (Alexandra's and Edward's favorites, respectively), blue sapphires, demantoid (green) garnets, alexandrites, rubies, opals and turquoise.

The motifs of the garland style combined floral and foliate swags with bows, tassels and lace motifs to produce the jewelry forms of the day: dog collars, fringe and festoon necklaces, brooches, corsage ornaments and larger bodice ornaments (also called "stomachers," as they were in the eighteenth century), tiaras, lavaliers, pendants, and earrings.

The *négligée* pendant and the *sautoir* were uniquely Edwardian jewels of the period. A variation on the lavalier, the defining feature of the *négligée* is a pair of pendent drops suspended from unequal lengths of fine chain, usually joined to a small gem-set plaque. The drops are often pear-shaped pearls or gemstones. The *sautoir* is a long necklace terminating in a tassel or pendant. The necklace can be a rope or woven band of seed pearls, or a platinum chain interspersed with diamonds; the tassels are usually of pearls with diamond-set caps, the pendants pierced diamond-set plaques.

The probable originator of the garland style was Louis Cartier (1875-1942), who designed for an international clientele of the rich, royal, and famous. American bankers and industrialists, as well as French aristocrats and English nobility, commissioned jewels from Cartier's *atelier* in Paris. The firm was so successful with their new line of garland style diamond and platinum jewelry, that they soon expanded, opening branches in London in 1902 and New York in 1909.

Other famous French houses working in the same mode were Lacloche Frères, Boucheron, Chaumet and Mellerio. Georges Fouquet and Lucien Gautrait, also known for their Art Nouveau designs, made garland-style jewels as well.

Peter Carl Fabergé (1846-1920), the celebrated jeweler of the Russian Imperial court, was noted for his objects of vertu. Most of his jewels could be classified as Edwardian, but others have definite Art Nouveau lines and motifs. He was a master of enameling and a technical perfectionist, capable of great versatility. His clientele, however, tended toward the traditional in jewelry, and his jewels reflect a certain restraint. Because the Fabergé name on a piece brings high prices, there are many fakes and forgeries to beware of.

Although the style was predominantly white, pastel colors were also in fashion. Enameling played an important part in lending color to Edwardian jewels. Fabergé was the firm with which this type of enameling was most closely associated, called *guilloché* enamel, which was a transparent colored enamel over a machine-engraved repeating pattern. Cartier was also a proponent of enameling in the Russian taste - which was still very much in keeping with Louis XVI themes.

In the United States, by the first decade of this century, Tiffany & Co, Marcus & Co., Black, Starr & Frost, Udall & Ballou, and Dreicer & Co. all had retail establishments on Fifth Ave in New York, where their garland style jewels found favor with the wealthy denizens of that prestigious neighborhood.

For those unable to afford the opulence of Cartier et al, more modest adornments were available. Even if she owned no other piece of fine jewelry, a woman might have a diamond and platinum or white gold ring in the elongated oblong or navette shape and pierced scrollwork of the Edwardian style. Bar brooches were very much in vogue; stars and crescents, sporting and novelty jewelry continued to be popular, as were slim bangles, narrow flexible and link bracelets with pierced or filigree plaques; inexpensive gold lavaliers were prevalent. Most of these pieces were set with small diamonds and seed pearls. Moonstones, opals, peridots, demantoid garnets and amethysts were also used. Synthetic rubies were introduced in 1902, and synthetic sapphires made their appearance after 1911. White gold came into common usage during World War I when platinum was appropriated for the war effort and banned for use in jewelry, and necessity prompted a search for a workable substitute. Karl Gustav Richter was granted a patent for his ternary (three-part) formula for white gold in 1915. The Belais Brothers of New York came out with their formula for white gold in 1917, dubbed "18k Belais," which can sometimes be found marked on white gold jewelry of the late teens and twenties.

Less expensive still was "imitation" jewelry (the word "costume jewelry" had yet to be coined) in colorless rhinestones ("paste"), glass and silver made in exactly the same styles as "real" jewelry. It has been overlooked by many of today's costume jewelry collectors because of its small size and delicacy. Non-precious jewelry in the Edwardian or garland style has not survived in quantity. Whether little was made to begin with, or it was discarded, is unclear. Edwardian-era pieces made of non-precious materials are grouped separately in the listings, because they forecast the development of costume jewelry as an accepted form of ornament and a major collectible classification.

The latter part of the period, c. 1910-20, interrupted by war, saw both gradual and abrupt stylistic changes. It has been called a transitional period, from Edwardian to Art Deco, in both fine and costume jewelry. The transitional style continued through the twenties, becoming more geometric, but retaining the open, lacy filigree and white or pale palette of high Edwardian, moving toward Art Deco's stronger contrasts in black and white, and red and white. Aiding this change was what is considered a landmark event: the presentation in Paris of the Ballets Russes *Schéhérazade* in 1910. The ballet's Oriental-inspired costumes, stage design, and vibrant colors influenced trend-setters such as Paul Poiret, the progressive couturier, whose designs changed the fashion silhouette from curvilinear to vertical. Tassels and turbans were favorite Poiret accessories, and tasseled pendants and long pendent earrings were complementary jewelry forms. The sautoir evolved into long diamond-set geometric chain links and pendants, eventually reaching the masses as tasseled "flapper beads" in faceted glass.

At the same time that Paris was being swept away by the Ballets Russes, women in England and the United States were battling it out on the political front for women's suffrage. The suffragists had a secret color code which they translated into jewelry: green, white and violet, which stood for "give women the vote." Green peridots, white pearls and violet amethysts were all popular period gemstones. Many Edwardian and Art Nouveau style jewels were made with these stones. In the U.S., gold was sometimes used for the "g" instead of a green stone. Enamel was also used. Even today, it is difficult to say if a particular brooch or lavalier was meant for wear as a suffragist "badge," or is just a typical period piece.

References: David Bennett and Daniela Mascetti, *Understanding Jewellery*, Antique Collectors' Club, 1989; Franco Cologni and Eric Nussbaum, *Platinum by Cartier, Triumph of the Jewelers' Art*, Harry N. Abrams, 1996; Ulysses G. Dietz, ed., *The Glitter & the Gold, Fashioning America's Jewelry,* The Newark Museum, 1997; Joyce Jonas, "The Elegant Edwardians," *Jewelers' Circular-Keystone/Heritage*, August 1988; Michael Koch et al, *The Belle Époque of French Jewellery 1850-1910*, Thomas Heneage & Co. Ltd, 1990; Elise Misiorowski and Nancy Hays, "Jewels of the Edwardians," *Gems & Gemology*, Fall 1993; Hans Nadelhoffer, *Cartier, Jewelers Extraordinary*, Harry N. Abrams, 1984; Penny Proddow and Marion Fasel, *Diamonds, A Century of Spectacular Jewels,* Harry N. Abrams, 1996; Judy Rudoe, *Cartier, 1900-1939*, Harry N. Abrams, 1997; Diana Scarisbrick, *Ancestral Jewels*, Vendome Press, 1989; A. Kenneth Snowman, *Fabergé Lost and Found*, Harry N. Abrams, 1993; Géza von Habsburg, *Fabergé in America*, Thames and Hudson, 1996; Alexander von Solodkoff, *The Art of Carl Fabergé*, Crown Publishers, 1988.

Advisor: Elise Misiorowski.

Bracelet

Bangle, Hinged

18k yg, diamonds, sapphires, platinum, c. 1910, front half a serrated stair-step pattern of eleven cushion-shaped sapphires alternating with eleven om diamonds, approx 2.00 cts tw, twenty-four sm rc diamonds at sides, tapering to a narrow yg back, Fr hmks, v-spring and box clasp, safety chain, 3/8" w, 2-1/4" inside dia .... 4,600 (A)

Flexible

Diamonds, sapphires, platinum, c. 1915, tapered band pave-set throughout with circ-cut diamonds, central marquise diamond framed by calibré Fr-cut sapphires, flanked by two horizontally oriented marquise diamonds, the three outlined in a crossover ribbon of sm circ-cut diamonds terminating in two short horizontal rows of calibré Fr-cut sapphires, tapering to flexible diamond-set segments, 9.00 cts diamonds tw, v-spring and box clasp, safety chain, approx 5/8" w at center, 6-1/8" tl .... 7,762 (A)

Platinum, diamonds, rubies, emeralds, yg, c.1915, a line of very narrow rect box plat links, center surmounted by two intertwined opposed snake motifs, tails spiraling around links, om and rc diamond-set heads framing a millegrained collet-set om diamond, bodies alternately set with calibré-cut rubies and emeralds set in yg, 3/8" w x 7-1/4" tl .... 2,645 (A)

Link

Yg, platinum, enamel, seed pearls, diamonds, c. 1915, three strands of linked blue and white enameled yg tubes and seed pearls joined with plat eyepins to prs of blue enameled opposed C-scrolls, centers set with a row of sm rc diamonds, alternating with vertical blue enameled and rc diamond-set spacer bars, terminating in a rect blue and white enameled box clasp, 1/2" w x 8" tl .... 3,450 (A)

Bracelets

Ribbon, diamonds, platinum, c. 1910, each a band of -black satin ribbon outlined in sm rc diamonds set in plat, sgd "Cartier" # 3406, v-spring and box clasps, in a fitted leather case, each 5/8" w x 7" tl, 6-5/8" tl, pr .... 20,700 (A)

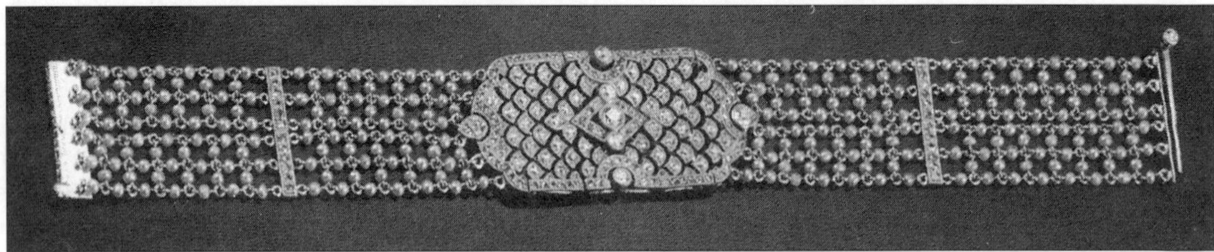

Bracelet, flexible, diamonds, seed pearls, platinum, c. 1915, central flexible cusped rounded rect plat plaque, pierced fish-scale pattern with three center collet-set diamonds in a lozenge-shaped frame, bead-set diamonds and millegrained accents throughout, pear-shaped collet-set diamonds at either end, flanked by openwork bands of seed pearls woven on plat wire, plat spacer bars set with sm rc diamonds, Fr hmk (dog's head) for plat, sliding hingepin closure, 7/8" w x 6-1/2" tl, **$7,475** [A]. (Photo courtesy of Skinner, Inc., Boston, MA, 12/9/97).

Link Bracelet, yg, diamonds, enamel, c. 1900, rect openwork plaques with bombe sides, each with blue *guilloché* enameled navette-shaped center with beaded and white-enameled border centering a collet-set diamond, alternating with navette-shaped openwork plaques, blue-enameled ground, white-enameled inner frames, and decorated throughout with Louis XVI-style ribbons, urns and floral and foliate motifs, plaques joined with om diamond-set collet links, Fr, sgd "L. Gautrait" for Lucien Gautrait, 1" x 7-1/2" tl, **$12,650** [A]. (Photo courtesy of Christie's Images, New York, NY, 4/8/97).

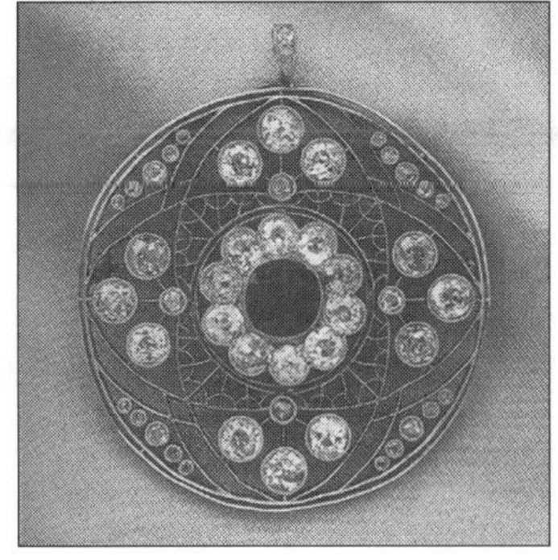

Brooch/Pendant, diamonds, platinum, sapphire, c. 1910, circ plaque with pierced quatrefoil design centering a circ-cut blue sapphire, 8.00 x 7.50 x 5.00 mm, encircled by oe diamonds, with trefoil clusters of three lg oe and one sm oe diamonds at compass points, approx 5.50 cts tw, short grad rows of rc diamonds mounted inside frame between clusters, hinged bail, lever catch, 1-3/4" dia, **$5,463** [A]. (Photo courtesy of Butterfield & Butterfield, Los Angeles & San Francisco, CA, 9/25/97).

Brooch/Pendant

14k wg, diamonds, blue stones, c. 1915-20, stepped and cusped rect plaque of stamped geo filigree, central horizontal row of three carré-set om diamonds alternating with two kite-shaped bezel-set blue stones, 1-3/4" w x 7/8" .... 542 (A)

Diamonds, pearls, plat-topped yg, c. 1900, open scrolled stylized fleur-de-lis motif, small pearl at top and bottom, set throughout with thirty-three circ-cut diamonds, approx 1.00 ct tw, sgd "T.B. STARR" for Theodore B. Starr, New York, NY, 1-1/4" w x 1-3/8" .... 1,495 (A)

Diamonds, platinum, c. 1900, open ribbon bow motif set throughout with seventy-three rc, om, and sm circ diamonds, pendant hook, 2" w x 1-1/4" .... 4,600 (A)

Diamonds, platinum, c. 1910-15, pierced plat circ disk, cusped quatrefoil quartered by four lotus motifs around outside edge, bead-set center and throughout with sixty-one oe diamonds, 2.60 cts tw, pendant loop, replaced pin back, 2-1/4" dia .... 1,380 (A)

Porcelain, enamel, diamonds, platinum-topped yg, c. 1905-10, oval ptd enamel porcelain portrait of a woman encircled by ninety-two bead-set sm oe diamonds, pendant bail and brooch fitting, 1-3/4" w x 2" .... 2,645 (A)

Brooch/Pin

14k yg, seed pearls, enamel, sapphire, c. 1900, open circ frame centering one circ-cut collet-set sapphire surrounded by eight seed pearls on knife edge yg wires, encircled by a ring of blue enamel, further encircled by a ring of engr yg, 1" dia .... 330 (A)

Brooch/Pin, diamonds, pearls, platinum, c. 1900, floral and foliate garland swags surmounted by a bow, one lg central pearl drop, approx 12.6 mm, one sm pearl drop, approx 6.7 mm suspended from lower swag, flanked by two button pearls, six lg collet-set om diamonds and sm rc diamond accents approx 4.70 cts tw, 2-1/4" w x 2-1/2", **$9,775** [A] (photo courtesy of Sotheby's Beverly Hills, CA, 5/20/97),

14k yg, seed pearls, sapphires, c. 1900, open-centered circle of yg filigree with four seed pearls on the outer edge at compass points, one sm circ-cut sapphire on the inner edge at compass points, mkd "14K" on catch , 1" dia .... 250 (A)

Aquamarine, diamonds, st yg, plat-topped yg, c. 1900, a lg pear-shaped aquamarine bezel-set in a conforming plat-topped yg diamond-set frame, lobed at the bottom, surmounted by an oe diamond, flanked by a pr of st yg wings set throughout with rc diamonds, 2-1/8" w x 1-3/4" .... 3,335 (A)

Aquamarine, seed pearls, platinum-topped 14k yg, c. 1915, a rect-cut aquamarine, approx 13.60 x 18.50 x 9.90 mm, mounted in a rect frame of seed pearls, geo filigree, and seed pearl border, 1" w x 7/8" .... 1,265 (A)

Brooch/Pin, alexandrite, diamonds, platinum, c. 1910, pierced openwork convex-sided rect plat plaque centering a natural-colored cushion-shaped alexandrite, 8.64 cts, flanked by scroll, fan and cusped quatrefoil motifs set throughout with oe and sc diamonds, approx 2.85 cts tw, 1-3/4" w x 1-1/8", **$26,450** [A]. (Photo courtesy of Sotheby's Beverly Hills, CA, 11/24/97).

Brooch/Pin, diamonds, platinum, sapphires, c. 1910, a cusped-cornered rounded oblong plaque with floral motif saw-piercing centering a collet-set oe diamond, approx 2.35 cts, flanked by six sm blue sapphire cabs, four curved rows of sm circ-cut diamonds forming inner truncated lozenge with four marquise diamonds at compass points, circ-cut diamonds at side terminals, a line of sm calibré-cut blue sapphires at four terminals, bordered by a pierced diamond-set frame, approx 3.00 cts tw diamonds, pierced gallery, lever catch, 2-1/4" w x 1", **$10,925** [A]. (Photo courtesy of Christie's Los Angeles, CA, 3/13/97).

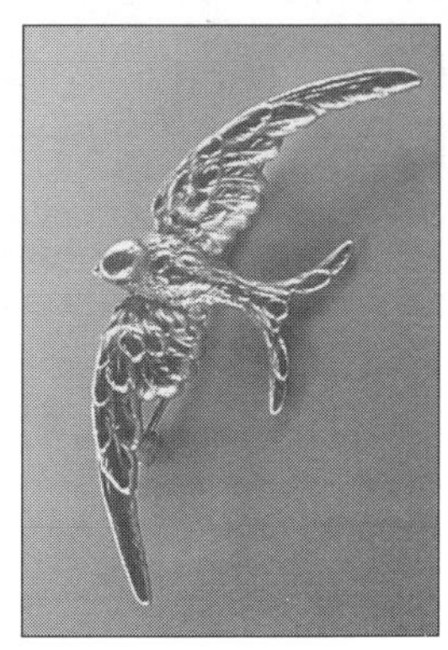

Brooch/Pin, 14k yg, c.1900-1905, in the shape of a swallow in flight, detailed engraving throughout, maker's mk for Carter, Howe & Co., Newark, NJ (C inside an arrowhead), 14k imp on lever catch, 2" w x 7/8", **$638**. (Photo courtesy of Karen Lorene, Facèré Jewelry Art, Seattle, WA).

Diamonds, pearls, platinum-topped yg, c. 1915, open fleur-de-lis motif, central sm pearl flanked by two lg oe diamonds, approx 1.85 cts each, suspending a pearl drop of approx 6.26 mm, accented by twenty-three sm oe bead-set diamonds, sgd "MARCUS & CO.," 1" w x 1" .... 10,350 (A)

Diamonds, platinum, c. 1910, circ pierced openwork plat plaque, "snowflake" pattern, six diamond-set scallops encircling six diamond-set trefoils, lg central diamond within inner circle of sm collet-set diamonds, approx 6.00 cts tw, 2" dia .... 12,650 (A)

Diamonds, platinum, c. 1915-20, cusped scallop-edged navette-shaped pierced plat plaque centering one lg collet-set oe diamond, approx 0.85 ct, surrounded by sm oe diamonds, approx 4.50 cts tw, 2-3/4" w x 1-1/8" .... 3,450 (A)

Diamonds, platinum, c. 1915-20, pierced stepped rect plat plaque, central prong-set oe diamond, 1.20 cts, flanked by two bead-set oe diamonds, approx 0.50 ct tw, and set throughout with sixty-four sm bead-set diamonds, approx 2.75 cts tw, 1-7/8" w x 3/4" .... 3,737 (A)

Diamonds, platinum, emeralds, c. 1915, cut-corner rect plaque pavé-set with sm oe and circ-cut diamonds, lg marquise diamond center framed by cusped brackets of calibré-cut emeralds, pierced curved lines radiating from center, oe diamond-set frame with calibré-cut emerald accents in corners, 1-1/4" w x 7/8" .... 5,980 (A)

Diamonds, platinum, syn sapphires, c. 1915, scrolled pierced U shape, set throughout with circ-cut diamonds, approx .50 ct tw, three larger circ-cut diamonds, .75 ct tw, at terminals and in center flanked by vertical rows of sm calibré-cut syn sapphires (one missing), filigree inside border, 1-1/4" w x 1-3/8" .... 1,495 (A)

Diamonds, platinum, c. 1910-15, lozenge-shaped plaque, central pierced rectangle with appl pedestaled flower basket motif, sm diamonds throughout, sgd Charlton, New York, NY, approx 1.75 cts tw, 2" w x 1-1/8" .... 8,625 (A)

Diamonds, platinum-topped 18k yg, c. 1905, open scalloped oval pavé-set with sm oe diamonds with six clusters of three sm collet-set oe diamonds interspersed at top and bottom, 2-3/8" w x 7/8" .... 1,840 (A)

Diamonds, platinum-topped 14k yg, opal, c. 1900, open tapered rounded rect frame, a circ white opal cab in the center of a sunflower motif flanked by splayed columnar motifs and floral/foliate stalks, set throughout with sm rc diamonds in a millegrained plat-topped yg mount, Austrian hmks, 1-7/8" w x 1" .... 1,725 (A)

Diamonds, platinum-topped 18k yg, c. 1900-10, open foliate motif with thirty-one om diamonds and six rc diamonds, approx 6.50 cts tw, safety catch, 1-1/2" w x 1-3/4" .... 3,300 (A)

Brooch/Pin, enamel, diamonds, platinum-topped 14k yg, c. 1900-10, polygonal plaque with cusped sides and chamfered corners, dk blue *basse-taille* enameled ground with central appl plat flower basket motif set throughout with ninety-eight sm rc diamonds, pierced geo design plat-topped 14k yg frame set with forty-five sm rc diamonds, lever catch, two diamonds missing, 1-3/4" w x 1-3/8", **$2,850** [A]. (Photo courtesy of Beverly Hills Auctioneers, Inc., CA, 9/21/97).

Brooch/Pin, diamonds, plat, c. 1910, open central foliate wreath flanked by two overlapping smaller open circles, a lg collet-set oe diamond at top and bottom of the wreath, approx 0.70 ct tw, sm circ-cut diamonds throughout in a plat mount, 1-5/8" w x 1-1/8", **$1,495** [A]. (Photo courtesy of Skinner, Inc., Boston, MA, 9/23/97).

Diamonds, platinum-topped yg, c. 1900-10, openwork crown motif set throughout with ninety-nine oe diamonds in bead and bezel settings, approx 5.00 cts tw, 2" w x 1-1/2" .... 4,255 (A)

Diamonds, rubies, pearls, platinum-topped 18k yg, c. 1905-10, open circle centering an open lozenge set with twenty sq-cut rubies, encircled by sixty sm rc diamonds and four collet-set om diamonds, four post-set sm white pearls at compass points, with box, mkd "14K" on lever catch, 1-1/8" dia .... 1,650 (A)

Diamonds, seed pearls, platinum, yg, c. 1910, open circle with alternating diamond-set paired leaf motifs and seed pearls, mkd "B S & F" for Black, Starr and Frost, New York, NY, 1" dia .... 575 (A)

Mabé pearl, 18k yg, demantoid garnets, diamonds, rubies, c. 1910, in the shape of a turtle, the shell of one lg oval mabé pearl, bordered by overlapping semi-circ yg plates, each set with demantoid garnets, the head and feet set with five oe diamonds, circ-cut ruby eyes, sgd "B.B.&B." for Bailey, Banks & Biddle, Philadelphia, PA, # 26403, 1-1/4" w x 2" .... 6,612 (A)

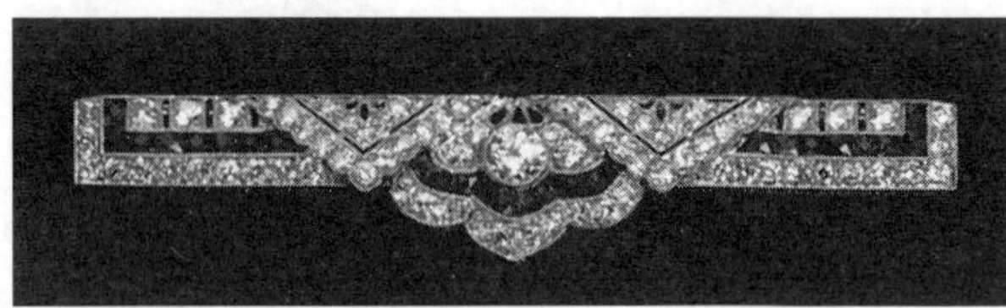

Bar Brooch/Pin, diamonds, sapphires, platinum, c. 1915-20, rect bar centering a draped lace handkerchief (*"lambrequin"*) motif in oe diamonds, approx 2.45 cts tw, calibré Fr-cut blue sapphires forming border, pierced plat mount, 2-7/8" w x 1/2", **$3,737** [A]. (Photo courtesy of Sotheby's Beverly Hills, CA, 5/20/97).

Bar Brooch/Pin, sapphires, seed pearls, 14k yg, c. 1900, crescent-shaped, with alternating circ prong-set blue sapphires and post-set seed pearls, mkd "14K" and maker's mk for Krementz & Co., Newark, NJ, 1-7/8" w x 1/4", **$400**. (Paula Straub collection).

Opal, diamonds, 14k yg, c. 1900, crescent-shaped yg mount set with alternating prong-set grad circ opal cabs and oe diamonds, 2.32 cts tw, 2-1/2" w x 1/4" 1,380 (A)

Seed pearls, 14k yg, diamonds, platinum, c. 1900, horseshoe shape, seven oe diamonds bead-set in appl plat sqs, alternating with seed pearls, maker's mk for Riker Bros., Newark, NJ, 1" w x 1-1/2" .... 288 (A)

Seed pearls, platinum-topped 14k yg, c. 1905-10, crescent set with seventeen sm seed pearls, C-catch, 1/8" w x 1-1/2" .... 110 (A)

Turquoise, diamonds, platinum-topped yg, c. 1900, seventeen bezel-set oval and pear-shaped turq cabs (some discolored) mounted on yg wires interspersed throughout a triangular openwork plat-topped yg floral/foliate motif bead-set with ninety-four rc and oe diamonds, 3" w x 2-1/2" .... 1,150 (A)

Bar

14k yg, platinum, seed pearl, c. 1905-10, cusped open bar, circ center, millegrained plat-topped yg foliate filigree, seed pearl in quatrefoil center, pierced yg gallery, lever catch mkd "14k," maker's mk for Taylor & Co., Newark, NJ, 2" w x 1/4" 150

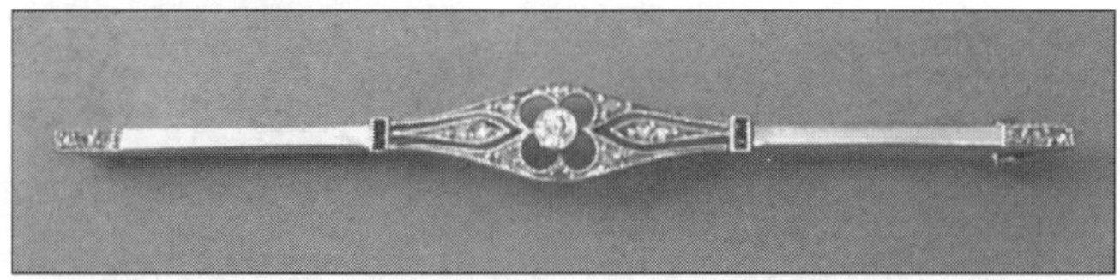

Bar Brooch/Pin, diamonds, sapphires, plat-topped 18k yg, c. 1905, central oe diamond of approx .15 ct within a cutout quatrefoil in a navette-shaped pierced and millegrained center bead-set throughout with sm rc diamonds, flanked by vertical rows of two sm sq-cut blue sapphires, tapering to a polished sq bar with three sm circ-cut diamonds at terminals, Eng, mkd "18 ct." on pinstem, shorter second pinstem, sheathed lever catch, 3-3/8" w x 3/8" (at center), **$900**. (Paula Straub collection).

Bar Brooch/Pin, 14k yg, sapphire, seed pearls, c. 1910, narrow open rectangle surmounted by paired yg foliate motifs flanking central circ-cut blue sapphire, four crossbars, each set with three seed pearls, lever catch imp with maker's mk for Taylor & Co (T flanked by 14 and K), Newark NJ, 2-3/4" w x 1/4", **$750**. (Photo courtesy of Karen Lorene, Facèré Jewelry Art, Seattle, WA).

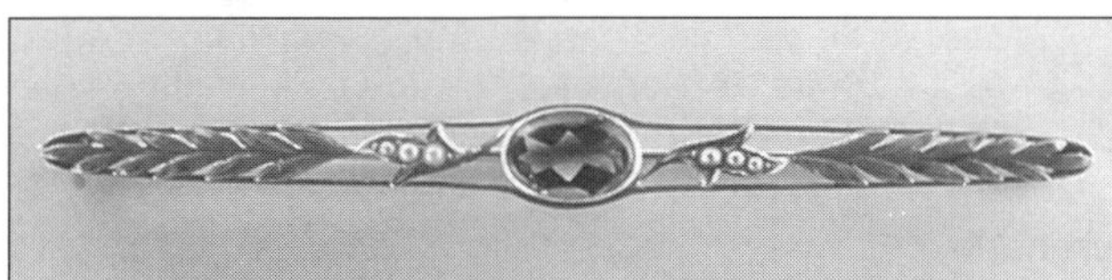

Bar Brooch/Pin, 14k yg, amethyst, seed pearls, c. 1910, open narrow tapered frame, oval buff-top amethyst bezel-set in center flanked by sm foliate motifs set with seed pearls, terminating in yg wheat ear motifs, rev imp with maker's mk for Hussey Co., Providence RI (lg H, T above crossbar, Co below; out of business by 1915), lever catch, 3-1/8" w x 3/8", **$800**. (Photo courtesy of Karen Lorene, Facèré Jewelry Art, Seattle, WA).

Diamonds, platinum-topped 18k yg, c. 1905-10, tapered ellipse, open foliate motif set with twenty-five oe diamonds in bead and bezel settings, approx 1.00 cts tw, 3" w x 1/2" .... 1,083 (A)

Pearl, diamonds, platinum, c. 1910, central pearl, 11.2 mm, flanked by open tapered crossover S-scroll plat bands bead-set with thirty sm oe diamonds, sgd "Cartier New York," 1-3/8" w x 3/8" .... 2,875 (A)

Pearls, diamonds, platinum, 14k yg, c. 1910, open elongated rect frame centering a millegrained collet-set oe diamond encircled by a ring of post-set pearls, alternating pearls and diamonds to terminals set with diamond trefoils, total of twenty pearls, twenty-five oe diamonds, approx 2.35 cts tw, 3-3/4" w x 1/2" .... 1,610 (A)

Platinum, diamonds, pearl, c. 1910-15, tapered elliptical plat bar, center set with a half-pearl flanked by a row of om diamonds, within pierced filigree network, cusped terminals pave-set with om diamonds, 18 diamonds, approx 1.00 ct tw, lever catch, 2-1/2" w x 3/8" .... 855 (A)

Buckle

14k yg, c. 1900, rounded lobed open rectangle with allover floral/foliate engraving, single hasp on central rod, 18.10 dwt, 3" w x 2" .... 489 (A)

Cuff Links

Platinum-topped 14k yg, sapphires, diamonds, c. 1915-20, double-sided octagonal plaques with engr geo border centering a bezel-set rect-cut blue sapphire on one side and a sc diamond on the other, mkd "PLAT. ON 14k," 1/2" dia, pr .... 200 (A)

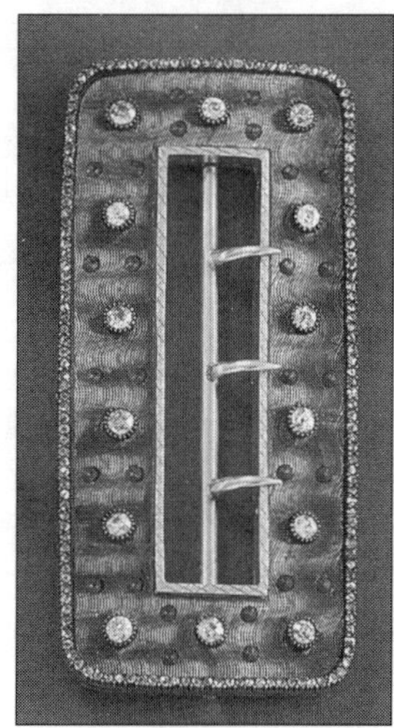

Buckle, diamonds, enamel, yg, st yg, c. 1890, open-centered rectangle, lt blue *guilloché* enameled ground set with 14 oe diamonds, approx 1.40 cts tw, border of rc diamonds set in st yg, yg inner frame and triple-pronged hasp, sgd "Fabergé" (Cyrillic letters), mks for workmaster Wilhelm Reimer, 1-3/8" w x 2-7/8", **$4,025** [A]. (Photo courtesy of Sotheby's Beverly Hills, CA, 5/21/96).

Cuff Links, platinum, yg, MOP, diamonds, c. 1915, circ disks inlaid with MOP with bc diamond centers within reeded and foliate engr plat frames, yg links to lenticular yg backs, Fr hmks, 1/2" dia, **$690** [A]. (Photo courtesy of Phillips New York, NY, 10/26/97).

Pendent Earrings, diamonds, platinum-topped 14k wg, c. 1915-20, each a single oe-cut diamond surmount suspending a paired foliate motif articulated shank and an open pear-shaped drop set with nineteen circ-cut diamonds, in plat-topped 14k wg, later-added 14k wg threaded posts, 1/4" w x 7/8", **$1,710** [A]. (Photo courtesy of Beverly Hills Auctioneers, Inc. CA, 9/21/97).

Earrings, pendent

Diamonds, platinum, yg, c. 1910, prong-set oe diamond drops, approx 3.79 cts and 4.10 cts, suspended from knife edge bar tops, each with two sm prong-set oe diamonds, approx 0.50 ct tw, plat mounts, yg fittings, Fr hmks, 1/2" w x 1-1/8" tl, pr .... 42,550 (A)

Lavalier

14k wg-topped 14k yg, diamond, c. 1915-20, cusped trefoil-shaped pierced plaque centering one oe-cut carre-set diamond, engr trefoil bail, maker's mk for Krementz & Co., Newark, NJ, mkd "14K" on bail, 5/8" w x 1-3/4" tl .... 171 (A)

Lavalier, opals, diamonds, platinum-topped yg, platinum, c. 1905-10, a pear-shaped pierced plat-topped yg plaque set throughout with rc diamonds, centering a pear-shaped black opal, suspended by a collet-set rc diamond chain from a cusped triangular pierced plaque set with rc diamond and millegrain accents centering an oval black opal, two sm collet-set rc diamonds at each top corner attached to a trace link plat chain 16" tl, boxed, 3/4" w x1-5/8", **$2,415** [A]. (Photo courtesy of Skinner, Inc., Boston, MA, 9/23/97).

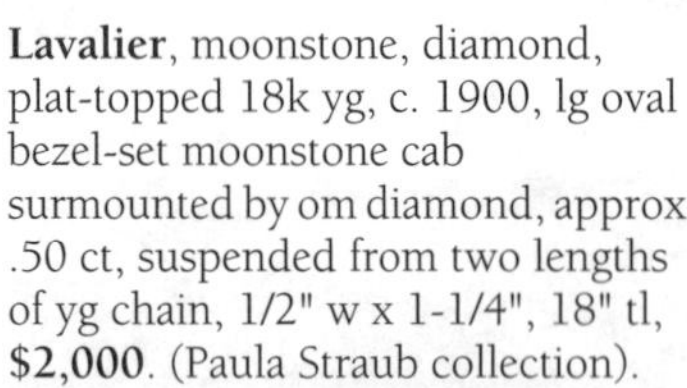

Lavalier, moonstone, diamond, plat-topped 18k yg, c. 1900, lg oval bezel-set moonstone cab surmounted by om diamond, approx .50 ct, suspended from two lengths of yg chain, 1/2" w x 1-1/4", 18" tl, **$2,000**. (Paula Straub collection).

Pearls, diamonds, platinum, c. 1900, central shield-shaped plat plaque set with sm oe diamonds around a lg button pearl, suspending *négligée* two chains of navette-shaped filigree alternating with collet-set oe diamonds, terminating in lg pear-shaped pearl drops, suspended from a similar diamond-set chain of navette-shaped filigree, each set with a sm central oe diamond, alternating with collet-set oe diamonds, GIA report stating pearls of natural origin and approx 15, 17, and 18 mm, orig fitted box mkd "J.F. Hayward, Boston," 3" top to bottom at center, 17" tl.................... 18,975 (A)

Diamonds, plat-topped yg, silver, c. 1900, pierced kite-shaped drop, folded handkerchief motif, a circ-cut diamond, approx 1.00 ct suspended from a short diamond-set chain in open center, three collet-set diamond chain from drop to pierced Y-shaped plaque and collet-set diamond chain, plaque and drop set throughout with om and rc diamonds in plat-topped yg, continuing to a fine cable link silver chain, 16" tl, 3/4" w x 1-3/4" tl .... 1,725 (A)

Locket and Cord

14k yg, enamel, plat, diamonds, silk cord, glass, c. 1915-20, rect double locket of yg entirely covered in black enamel with appl plat open lozenge bead-set with twelve full-cut diamonds in one corner, opening to reveal two locket frames, suspended by an engr plat bail from a black silk cord with plat caps, rings, and spring ring, inside inscribed "Mrs. R. Soribner, Toledo Ohio," slight damage to enamel on outside, one locket glass broken, 1-1/8" w x 1-1/2".. 627 (A)

Lorgnette

Platinum, diamonds, c. 1900-10, pierced openwork geo design, handle set with a central vertical row of sm circ-cut diamonds, suspended from an oval link chain, spring ring clasp to chain, 1-1/4" w x 3-1/2".............. 1,380 (A)

Platinum, diamonds, c. 1915-20, pierced openwork geo and foliate motif plat handle set throughout with oe and sc diamonds on both sides, the open lenses rimmed in feather pattern engr plat, 1-1/2" w x 4".................... 2,990 (A)

Neckchain

Diamonds, platinum, c. 1905, line of one hundred six collet-set oe diamonds, approx 26.00 cts tw, alternating with sm circ plat links, spring ring closure, 1/4" w, 32" tl .... 26,450 (A

Diamonds, platinum, c. 1910, sixty-one om diamonds linked in alternating sq and circ collets, provenance: from the estate of Greer Garson Fogelson, 1/4" w x 15-1/2" tl .... 12,650 (A)

Platinum, diamonds, c. 1910, fine curb link plat chain interspersed at equal intervals with prong-set diamonds in open circ frames, grad in size, approx 10.00 cts tw, 36" tl, 8,62 .... (A)

Platinum, diamonds, c. 1910-15, diamond-set openwork lozenge-shaped links alternating with pierced plat bar links, central diamond-set triangular link, approx 1.75 cts tw, 1/4" w x 20" tl .... 2,530 (A)

Necklace

Choker

Ribbon, pearls, 14k yg, c. 1915, three horseshoe-shaped yg slides set with split pearls on a 1-1/8" w black velvet ribbon, 11-1/2" tl .... 498 (A)

Dog Collar

Pearls, diamonds, st yg, c. 1900-10. *plaque de cou* an openwork foliate motif rectangle, center cluster of four pearls flanked by diamond-set leaves enclosed by pearl and diamond-set C-scrolls, a pearl in each corner and at sides, in the center of an eighteen strand seed pearl collar with rc diamond-set spacer bars, 2" w x 12-1/4" tl .... 3,450 (A)

Seed pearls, platinum, c. 1900, latticework of plat chains forming open rectangles, vertically set rows of seed pearls at the intersections, 1-3/8" w x 13-1/2" tl .... 5,462 (A)

Pendant and Chain

Jadeite, diamonds, pearls, platinum, c. 1915, foliate carved and pierced tapered rect jadeite pendant with diamond and pearl-set plat bail, suspended from a double chain of pearl and plat links, pendant 1" w x 2-3/4" tl, chain 28" tl .... 4,370 (A)

Topaz, diamonds, platinum-topped yg, c. 1905, ribbon motif of sm bead-set diamonds with central collet-set diamond, suspending a sm collet-set diamond and a lg faceted oval pink topaz in a millegrained collet, trace link chain, pendant 7/8" w x 1-1/2" .... 1,840 (A)

Pendant and Chain, diamonds, platinum-topped yg, c. 1890-1900, pendant an openwork scrolled trefoil with twelve oe diamonds, approx 6.00 cts tw, and one hundred forty-seven oe diamonds, approx 8.75 cts tw, on a chain (not pictured) set with fifty-two oe diamonds, approx 10.50 cts tw, 14" chain detachable, pendant 3-1/2" w x 3", **$14,950** [A]. (Photo courtesy of Sotheby's, Beverly Hills, CA, 5/21/96).

Pendant and Chain, diamonds, pearls, platinum, c. 1910, chain of collet-set diamonds suspending an octagonal openwork flowerhead plaque, pearl center surrounded by collet and bead-set diamonds, a large natural pearl drop with a floral surmount, pendant 1-1/4" w x 2-3/4" tl, chain 16-1/2", pendant 1-1/4" w x 2-3/4" tl, **$21,850** [A]. (Photo courtesy of Christie's Los Angeles, CA, 10/3/96).

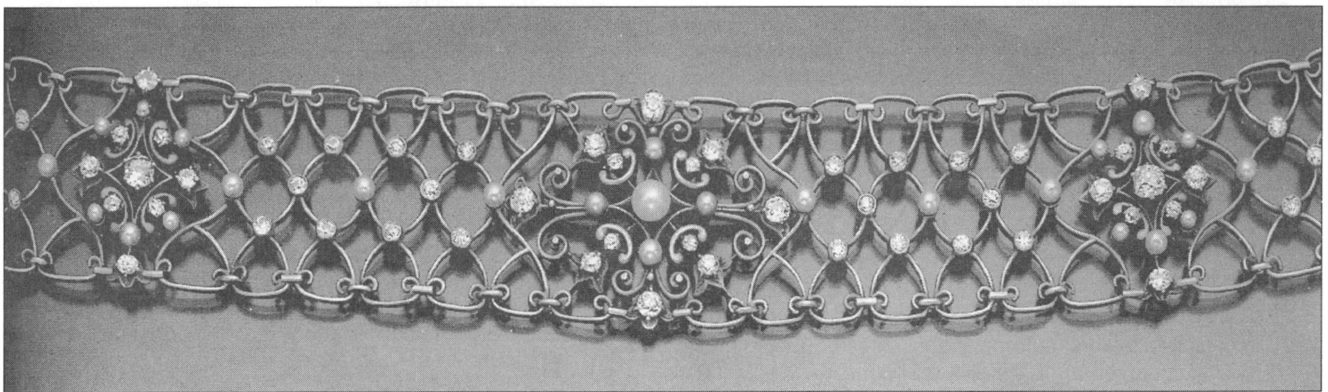

Necklace, Dog Collar, yg, pearls, diamonds, c. 1900, open latticework yg wire links, center section set with collet-set om diamonds alternating with sm post-set pearls, linking five evenly spaced floral scroll motifs, central motif set with lg central pearl and four sm pearls at compass points, surrounded by om diamonds in a lozenge shape, side motifs with central lg om diamond surrounded by lg and sm om diamonds and pearls, 1-3/8" w (at center), 14-3/4" tl, **$10,580** [A]. (Photo courtesy of Christie's Images, New York, NY, 12/11/96).

Pendant Necklace, diamonds, seed pearls, sapphire, platinum, c. 1915, an articulated open lozenge-shaped plat plaque set with sm oe diamonds in V-shaped rows, centering a circ bezel-set blue sapphire cab flanked by a horizontal row of sm circ-cut collet-set diamonds, suspended from and suspending articulated diamond-set fleur-de-lis and collet-set oe diamonds, flanked by two seed pearl and plat chains with oe diamond drops, joined at a diamond bail to a seed pearl and plat chain, 1-5/8" w x 4", 22" tl, **$18,400** [A]. (Photo courtesy of Christie's, New York, NY, 10/23/96).

Ring

14k yg, demantoid garnets, seed pearls, green stones, c. 1910, flowerhead cluster, prong-set circ-cut demantoid garnet center encircled by sm green stones, seed pearls set in scalloped border, mounted on a narrow tapering shank mkd "14k," illegible maker's mk, 1/2" dia, approx size 6 250

9 kt yg, ruby, sc diamonds, date letter for 1915, circ-cut ruby carré-set in center flanked by two sc diamonds, tapered shank, Birmingham (Eng) hmks, 5/16" w, approx size 7 110

9k yg, rc diamonds, ruby, date letter for 1919, six sm rc diamonds encircling sm ruby, forming flowerhead flanked by engr scrollwork, tapered shank, Chester (Eng) hmks, 1/4" w at center, approx size 5-1/2 110

Alexandrite, diamonds, platinum-topped yg, c. 1910, prong-set cushion-shaped mixed-cut yellow-green alexandrite of 2.00 cts, surrounded by twenty-one sm circ bead-set sc diamonds totaling approx .50 ct, 1/2" w x 3/4" (top), size 7-1/4 .... 2,850 (A)

Ring, demantoid garnets, diamonds, pearl, platinum, yg, c. 1900, navette-shaped plaque, center set with a button pearl flanked by two pear-shaped demantoid garnets set in yg bezels, framed by fourteen circ-cut diamonds set in plat, mounted on a narrow yg shank, 3/8" w x 3/4", approx size 6-1/2, **$880** [A]. (Photo courtesy of Beverly Hills Auctioneers, Inc., CA, 6/22/97).

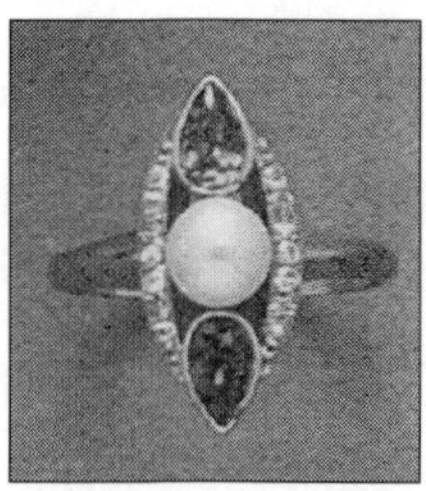

Diamonds, demantoid garnets, yg, c. 1910, a row of three om diamonds alternating with two demantoid garnets prong-set in a tapering yg band with scroll engr shoulders, Eng hmks, 1/4" w, size 6-1/2, ... 920 (A)

Diamonds, emeralds, platinum, c. 1910-15, a marquise diamond, approx .60 ct, framed by calibre-cut emerald baguettes in a pierced plat mount set throughout with sm circ-cut diamonds, narrow shank, 1/2" w, size 9 .... 4,370 (A)

Diamonds, platinum, emeralds, sapphires, c. 1915, a tapered cartouche-shape pierced plat plaque, a central carré-set om diamond flanked top and bottom by two horizontal rows of calibré-cut sapphires and stepped baguettes tipped with sq-cut emeralds and set throughout with sc diamonds, mounted on a narrow engr shank, 3/4" w x 1-1/8", size 8 .... 1,610 (A)

Diamonds, platinum, c. 1910, vertical row of three lg oe diamonds surrounded by sm diamonds set in an openwork plat mount, 3/4" w x 1-1/8" .... 23,000 (A)

Diamonds, platinum, emeralds, c. 1900, central prong-set om diamond, approx 1.50 cts, framed by fifty-two sm oe and sc diamonds in bead settings, engr mounting with pierced openwork set with eight sm calibré-cut emeralds in curved rows at shoulders, 3/4" w x 1/2", size 6-1/2 .... 2,875 (A)

Diamonds, platinum-topped 14k yg, c. 1905-10, central marquise-cut bezel-set diamond, approx 1.50 cts, framed by twenty sm oe diamonds, mounted on a narrow yg shank, 3/4" w x 3/8" .... 5,462 (A)

Diamonds, platinum-topped 18k yg, c. 1900, cusped navette shape of nine om prong-set diamonds, approx 5.75 cts tw, thirty sm rc diamonds on shoulders (one missing), mkd "TIFFANY & CO.," 3/4" w x 1" .... 8.625 (A)

Diamonds, platinum-topped yg, c. 1905, central marquise oe diamond, approx 3.10 cts, flanked by fourteen sm bead-set oe diamonds, scrolling mount, 7/8" w x 5/8", size 6-3/4 .... 16,100 (A)

Diamonds, platinum, emeralds, c. 1915, pierced navette shape set throughout with oe and sc diamonds, central open navette shape outlined in small calibré-cut emeralds with an oe flanked by two sm sc diamonds in center, mounted on a narrow shank, 5/8" w x 1-1/8", size 7 .... 1,035 (A)

Scarf Pin/Stickpin

14 k yg, platinum, sapphire, c. 1905-10, engr plat-topped yg spoked wheel motif with circ-cut blue sapphire center, yg pinstem mkd "14k," 3/8" dia, 2-5/8" tl 125

Pearl, 14k wg, yg, c. 1915, pear-shaped filigree mount centering a half pearl, yg pinstem, 3/8" w x 2-1/2" tl .... 124 (A)

Platinum, yg, diamonds, c. 1910, circ pierced plat disk with sm diamond-set center and border, yg pinstem, 1/2" dia, 2-1/2" tl .... 173 (A)

Seed pearls, diamonds, blue stone, platinum-topped 14k yg, c. 1905, open circle centering a collet-set circ blue stone surrounded by four rc diamonds and four seed pearls, yg pinstem, maker's mk for Carter, Howe & Co., Newark, NJ, 1/2" dia .... 124 (A)

Scarf Pins/Stickpins, yg, c. 1900-1910:
L, tapered yg bead with allover "vermicelli" decoration, 1/4" w x 1/2", 2-1/2" tl, **$200**.
R, open shield shape with central f.w. pearl, surmounted by a bow motif, mkd "14K," 1/2" w x 5/8", 2-1/2" tl, **$200**. (Paula Straub collection).

Tie Tack, reverse intaglio, rock crystal quartz, platinum, 18k yg, MOP, diamonds, c. 1915, reverse-painted intaglio of a biplane, MOP backing, set in plat and yg, four sm collet-set circ-cut diamonds at compass points within an open circ plat frame. 3/4" dia, **$2,300**. (Photo courtesy of Karen Lorene, Facèré Jewelry Art, Seattle, WA).

"IMITATION" COSTUME JEWELRY, c. 1900-1920

Brooch/Pin

Rh pl metal, enamel, rhinestones, c. 1915-20, cusped oval shape, openwork floral motif, central marquise-shaped open enamel design with colorless r.s. center, C-catch, 1-3/8" w x 1/2" 45

Rh pl metal, rhinestones, c. 1915-20, chamfered-corner rect openwork plaque of geo foliate design with lg prong-set colorless r.s. in center, safety catch, 1-1/4" w x 3/4" 55

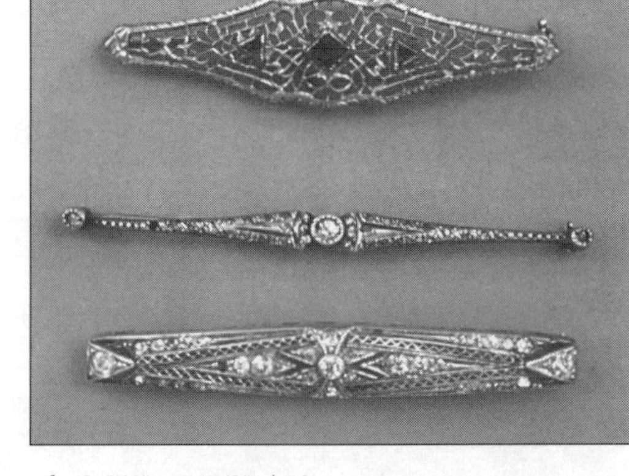

Bar pins, c. 1915-20:
T, rh pl wm, glass, stamped floral and foliate motif filigree cusped navette-shaped plaque centering one sq-cut and two triangular green glass stones, safety catch, 2-1/4" w x 5/8", **$50**.
C, sterling, rhinestones, bead and scroll-patterned sectioned bar, tapered from central millegrained bezel-set colorless r.s. to two colorless r.s. at terminals, mkd "Coro Sterling," 1/4" w x 2-1/2", **$45**.
B, sterling, rhinestones, slightly tapered stamped trellis-pattern filigree bar with oe colorless r.s. accents, mfr's mk for Fishel, Nessler & Co., New York, NY: "STERLING" inside a fish holding an "L" in its mouth, safety catch, 2-1/2" w x 3/8", **$75**.

Bangle Bracelet, hinged, sterling, rhinestones, c. 1915-20, stamped filigree foliate and geo design with central scalloped section, centering three sm oe-cut r.s. in cusped sq bezels, mkd "925" on v-spring, box clasp, 1-1/4" w (at center), 2-1/2" inside dia, **$125**. (Patrick Kapty collection).

Brooch/Pin, rhinestones, sterling, c. 1915, dragonfly with lg green r.s. center, set throughout with oe colorless r.s., C-catch, mkd "STERLING" in a fish-shaped reserve, 2-1/2" w x 1-7/8", **$125**. (Patrick Kapty collection).

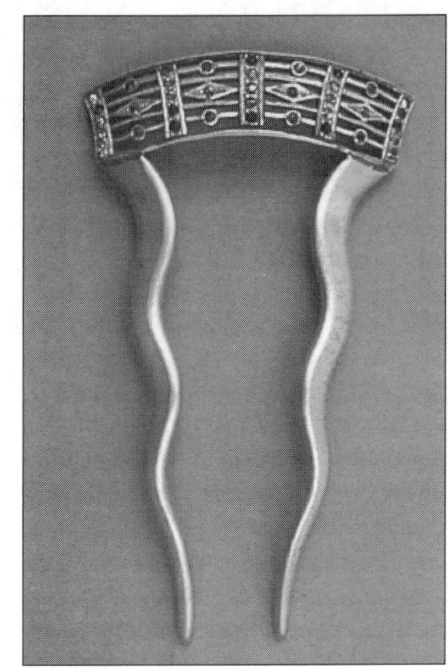

Hair Comb, aluminum, rhinestones, c. 1915, double-pronged hair comb with geo cutout section at top, collet-set oe-cut r.s. accents, 2-1/2" w x 4", $75. (Patrick Kapty collection).

Necklace, Dog collar, rose quartz, moonstones, silver, c. 1900-10, central bezel-set oval rose quartz cab flanked by two lg circ and two sm circ rose quartz cabs, alternating with bezel-set oval moonstones, joined with five, then four rows of cable link silver chain suspending a central circ moonstone and pear-shaped rose quartz drop flanked by two lg and two med pear-shaped rose quartz drops from swagged chain, continuing to a v-spring and box clasp surmounted by a circ rose quartz cab, 13" tl, 3-1/2" center top to bottom, **$1,200**. (Elizabeth Cook-Hada collection).

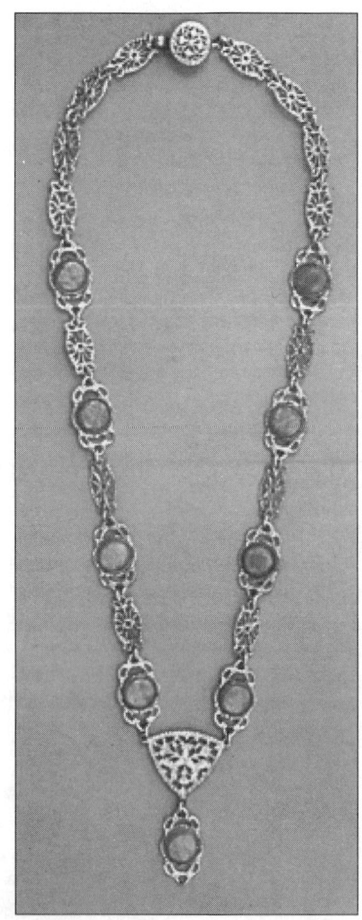

Necklace, rh pl wm, glass, c. 1915-20, triangular stamped wm filigree plaque suspending a navette-shaped pierced plaque drop bezel-set with molded Oriental motif green glass disk, continuing to a necklace of similar navette-shaped plaque links alternating with sm stamped pierced plaques of radiating pattern, v-spring and circ stamped filigree box clasp, 3/8" w, 17" tl, **$95**. (Patrick Kapty collection).

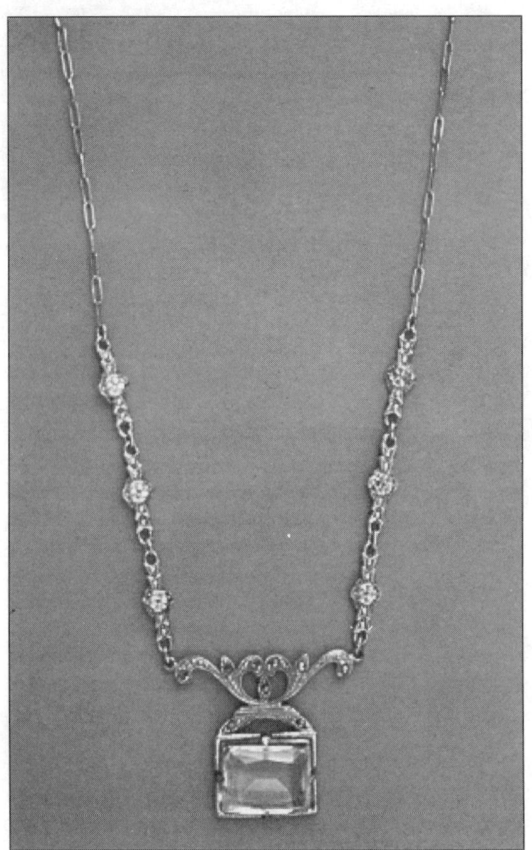

Necklace, rh pl metal, glass, rhinestones, c. 1915-20, lg central colorless sq-cut glass set a jour surmounted by scroll motif rh pl metal with sm white r.s. accents, flanked by rh pl metal links set with sm colorless r.s. leading to chain, spring ring closure, 1-1/4" w x 1-1/8" (central element), chain 16" tl, **$65**. (Terrance O'Halloran collection).

Pendant, rhinestones, ster, c. 1915-20, cutout handled vase shape set throughout with sm colorless r.s., mkd "STERLING," stamped design on bail, 1" w x 1-1/8", **$85**. (Leigh Leshner collection).

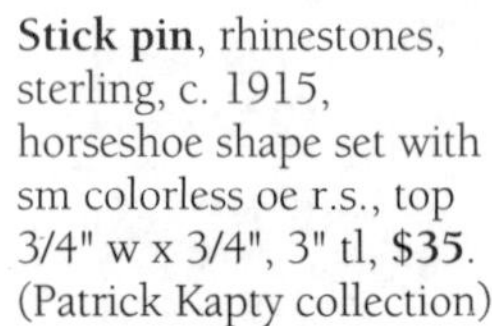

Stick pin, rhinestones, sterling, c. 1915, horseshoe shape set with sm colorless oe r.s., top 3/4" w x 3/4", 3" tl, **$35**. (Patrick Kapty collection).

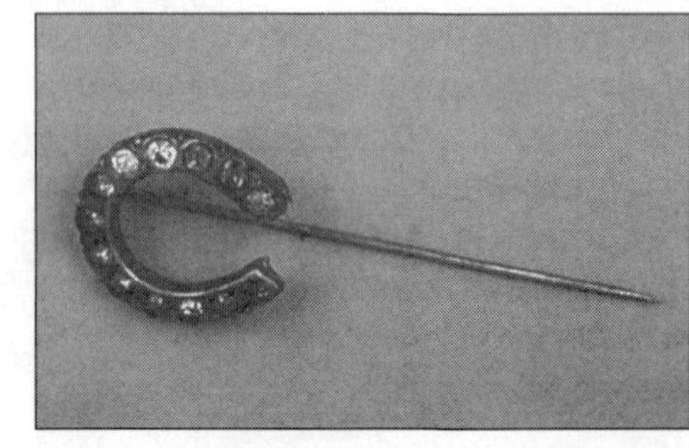

Part III

TWENTIETH-CENTURY JEWELRY

INTRODUCTION

The twentieth century truly began with World War I, a cataclysmic event that transformed society. Women would never be the same after "the war to end all wars." When the smoke cleared, the Gibson Girl had become Thoroughly Modern Millie. Her fashions, her attitude, her way of life, were marked departures from all that had gone before. The war, and–at last–the right to vote gave American women a stronger voice in the affairs of the country, and a greater awareness of the affairs of the world. This worldly sophistication was aided by the advent of radio, the growth of fashion magazines and popular culture periodicals, and perhaps most importantly, the motion picture industry. Changes in fashion occurred at an ever-accelerating pace.

Although Paris continued to be regarded as a fashion mecca through the mid-century, British and European royalty were no longer as influential as America's Hollywood elite. Movie stars were the new queens. What they wore was closely monitored, reported, and emulated. Purveyors to these new "royals" achieved instant fame and success by association. Names of designers attained new importance, and "name-dropping" became a pastime of a new social class.

Indeed, "new" and "novelty" were watchwords of the day. The latest was considered the best. In jewelry, new designs and materials were incorporated into manufacturers' repertoires. Except for a hiatus during World War I, diamonds and platinum still ruled, but the avant-garde opted for chrome, rock crystal, glass, and that most novel of materials, plastic. Costume jewelry was given its stamp of approval by Coco Chanel and other haute couturiers. It was no longer looked down upon as a mere imitation of the real thing, although there were surely many rhinestone and rhodium-plated knockoffs masquerading as diamonds and platinum. Frankly fake jewels, however, were now being worn to complement one's outfit, or costume.

A method for producing dental castings, introduced in 1907, led to a new application of the ancient art of lost-wax casting in the 1930s: the mass-production of both fine and costume jewelry. Multiple copies of one design were made possible with the aid of vulcanized rubber molds, using the vulcanization process invented by Charles Goodyear in 1839, along with the development of an improved casting investment plaster in 1932.

Stylistic trends evolved more rapidly in the twentieth century. Whereas a nineteenth century style could span several decades, after WW I, each decade was characterized by a different "look". And while the general term "modernism" can be applied to the entire era, we tend to group the changing styles within it by ten-year periods, i.e., the twenties, thirties, forties, fifties, etc. This is not necessarily an accurate classification, nor are the appellations Art Deco, Streamline Moderne, or Retro Modern, correctly applied to each decade. These are styles, not periods, which, as always, tend to overlap and coexist along with revivals and traditions. It can be said for example, that Art Deco was a popular style in the '20s, but certainly not the *only* style. Consequently, rather than label each of the following subdivisions of twentieth century jewelry with a style name, they are divided by period, with a prefacing explanation of the predominant styles in each.

In this section, it is also necessary to introduce a separate classification based on certain materials from which some jewelry was made. "Costume jewelry" is too all-encompassing and unwieldy a term for the several types of non-precious jewelry that proliferated from the twenties onward. Therefore there is a special category for plastic and novelty jewelry, the whimsical and "fun" costume jewelry that does not fall clearly into any other stylistic category. Costume jewelry that imitates fine jewelry is grouped separately in its respective period. The classification of "designer signed" costume jewelry, however, spans several decades.

References: Vivienne Becker, *Antique and Twentieth Century Jewellery*, 2nd ed., N.A.G. Press, 1987, and *Fabulous Costume Jewelry*, Schiffer Publishing, 1993; David Bennett and Daniela Mascetti, *Understanding Jewellery*, 2nd ed., Antique Collectors' Club, 1994; Barbara Cartlidge, *Twentieth-Century Jewelry,* Harry N. Abrams, 1985 (out of print); Deanna Farneti Cera, ed., *Jewels of Fantasy, Costume Jewelry of the 20th Century*, Harry N. Abrams, 1992; L. Eleuteri, ed., *Twentieth Century Jewelry, Art Nouveau to Modern Design,* Electa/Abbeville, 1994; Roseann Ettinger, *Popular Jewelry, 1840-1940,* Schiffer Publishing, 1990; Peter Hinks, *Twentieth Century Jewellery, 1900-1980*, Faber & Faber, London, 1983; Graham Hughes, *Modern Jewelry, an International Survey, 1890-1967*, Crown Publishers, 1968 (out of print); Daniela Mascetti and Amanda Triossi, *Earrings from Antiquity to the Present*, Rizzoli International, 1990, and *The Necklace from Antiquity to the Present*, Harry N. Abrams, 1997; Jane Mulvagh, *Costume Jewelry in Vogue*, Thames and Hudson, 1988 (out of print); Penny Proddow and Debra Healy, *American Jewelry, Glamour and Tradition*, Rizzoli International, 1987 (out of print); Penny Proddow, Debra Healy, and Marion Fasel, *Hollywood Jewels,* Harry N. Abrams, 1992; Penny Proddow and Marion Fasel, *Diamonds, A Century of Spectacular Jewels,* Harry N. Abrams, 1996; Jody Shields, *All That Glitters, The Glory of Costume Jewelry*, Rizzoli International, 1987 (out of print); Oppi Untracht, *Jewelry Concepts and Technology*, Doubleday, 1985.

FINE JEWELRY c. 1920-1935

History: After a period of wartime austerity, the twenties woman burst forth with a frenetic exuberance. She cut off her hair, her sleeves and her hems, bound her chest and dropped her waistline to become *la garçonne*, the female boy. She celebrated her new post-war prosperity and freedom by piling on the jewels.

Bare arms and waistless dresses changed fashion's focus from the wide waist-cinching belts, sash and corsage ornaments of the *belle époque* to multiple bracelets, and small plaque brooches or jeweled ornaments worn at the hips and shoulders. There were endless variations of the diamond and platinum bracelet variously referred to as the plaque, flexible link or box, strap, band, or straightline. Some were accented with natural or synthetic sapphires or rubies, or emeralds, or a combination of these. Short hairstyles gave rise to long pendent drop earrings. The screwback finding (called the "French back" by some in the trade) was now the norm, as most women no longer pierced their ears. Large hats, hatpins, tiaras and haircombs disappeared, to be replaced by bandeaux and cloche hats embellished with small hat ornaments.

The sautoir remained, but in modified "modernized" form, becoming more geometric. It was often made entirely of diamonds and platinum, terminating in a diamond-set drop instead of a tassel, and it was convertible, forming bracelets, choker and a pendant. Lorgnettes continued to be fashionably suspended from long chains or cords; in the thirties, they adapted for wear as clips. Tasseled ropes of gemstone beads were also worn.

Pearls remained popular, worn as sautoirs or long ropes, or twisted about the wrist. The recently marketed cultured pearl was affordable to the middle classes, although it caused a furor among natural (oriental) pearl merchants. Dog collars narrowed to become short delicate necklaces, often worn in addition to a sautoir. The bar pin and plaque brooch continued to be worn as transitional jewels in addition to two new forms introduced by Cartier: the circle or ring brooch (Cartier called it *broche de ceinture,* "belt brooch") and jabot pin, or *cliquet*. Both could be worn as hat ornaments. Pierced platinum or white gold and diamond rings retained the elongated outline of the past two decades, but became increasingly geometric in design. New ring shapes were hexagonal or octagonal, with colored gemstones and diamonds set in domed or stepped mounts.

The excesses of the twenties were sharply curtailed by the 1929 stock market crash and the onset of the Great Depression. But even though it was out of reach for most pocketbooks, and production diminished, precious jewelry continued to be made. The elite of Hollywood and New York could still afford it; women of wealth everywhere continued to wear their status symbols. Indeed, jewelry grew larger and more three-dimensional as fashions became less severe. During the early thirties, the waistline returned, sleeves grew longer and/or fuller, and a woman's curves were emphasized by bias-cut gowns in soft and satiny fabrics.

The dress clip became the most important jeweled accessory of the thirties. Usually worn in pairs at the neckline, they were held in place by means of a flat-backed hinged mechanism that snapped shut over the fabric's edge. The story goes that Louis Cartier came up with the idea for the clip while watching a woman use clothespins to hang laundry out to dry. These versatile ornaments could also be worn on jacket lapels, hats, purses, belts, and, with the attachment of an additional pinback mechanism, a pair could be joined for wear as a brooch.

The all-white look of diamonds and platinum that began with the Edwardians at the turn of the century persisted well into the 1930s, with the additional use of colorless rock crystal. Over the years, geometric forms insinuated upon, then replaced the garland style. By the early twenties, diamond cutting had advanced to such a degree that unusual shapes, such as the half-moon, the obus or bullet (a narrow pentagon), the epaulet (a wide pentagon), the trapeze, and the triangle, could be produced for added geometric interest in all-white jewels. At the same time, color was injected into some jewelry designs in the form of rubies, emeralds, sapphires, jade, coral, lapis, onyx, and enamels, as the style which later came to be known as Art Deco exerted its influence.

Art Deco itself was influenced by a number of design sources: Oriental, Persian/Islamic, East Indian, ancient Egyptian and pre-Hispanic Mexican, African, American Indian, and, most directly, by turn-of-the-century Austrian and German Secessionist and *Jugendstil* designs.

While the commonly held view is that the Art Deco style arose as a result of the 1925 Paris exposition from which it derives its name, *L'Exposition Internationale des Arts Décoratifs et Industriels Modernes,* in fact that date is more correctly a culmination of developments that occurred throughout the previous two decades. It should be noted that the outbreak of war forced the exposition's postponement. It was originally planned for 1916, the idea having been discussed since 1907, according to Sylvie Raulet in her book *Art*

Deco Jewelry, cited below. So we see the seeds of modernism being planted at the turn of the century, and reaching full flower after World War I. Still, the popularization of the style was not widely felt in the United States until after the exposition–an event in which the U.S. did *not* participate. (Herbert Hoover, Secretary of Commerce at the time, was noted as saying this country did not have any "modern" decorative arts, and thus could not meet the entry requirements of newness and originality.)

The name Art Deco was not applied to what was then called "modernistic" or "moderne" until 1968, when it appeared in the title of a book by Bevis Hillier, *Art Deco of the Twenties and Thirties.* This probably explains why there are several different interpretations of what the style really is, and why there is debate over the period in which it flourished. For some, it is an all-encompassing label that includes what others separate into Art Deco, Zig-Zag Moderne, Streamline Moderne, and the International Style. Some say the style ended in 1925; others claim it spanned the entire period between the world wars. Mr. Hillier takes the inclusive, evolutionary point of view that although "there was a difference in character between the 'twenties and the 'thirties... Art Deco was a developing style...There was a strong continuity." (From the introduction to *The World of Art Deco*, catalog of an exhibition at the Minneapolis Institute of Arts, 1971).

The credo of the modernists was "form follows function," and all excess ornamentation was to be avoided, on a parallel with the tenets of the Arts and Crafts Movement. Unlike the purists of that movement, however, the modernists espoused and embraced the use of the machine. The style is characterized by the simplification and stylization of motifs from nature, and the introduction of abstract, non-representational, structural and geometric forms. Futuristic and speed-associated motifs were also part of the repertoire. Suffice it to say that whatever the label, there is general agreement that the design developments of the period between the wars were as much a departure from Victorianism as the chemise was from the hoop skirt.

In jewelry, too, one often hears the term Art Deco applied to everything from slight variations on Edwardian pierced platinum-and-diamond plaque brooches to starkly simple abstract metal and enamel pendants or bangles. The tendency is to call any piece from the twenties or thirties Art Deco–a matter of subjective interpretation. In fact, the evolution of the style in jewelry can be traced through several different lineages, from the traditional French *haute joailliers* to the avant-garde artist-designers, continuing to popular adaptations and modifications by American jewelers inspired by French designs.

Cartier is the most famous of the former for its version of Art Deco, which tended toward the figurative and exotic Eastern-influenced designs. Notable were Cartier's use of carved gemstones in circular "belt brooches," jabot pins (called *cliquet* pins by Cartier), multicolored "fruit salad" arrangements of leaves and berries in flexible band bracelets, flower vase brooches, and double clip brooches (patented by Cartier in 1927). Now, just having celebrated its 150th anniversary with a major exhibition in New York and London, and accompanying catalog (see References), the firm is once again in the spotlight, with newly documented pieces and information from the Cartier collection.

Van Cleef and Arpels also contributed a great deal to the genre. They were particularly known for their Egyptian Revival motifs executed in calibré-cut colored gemstones and pavé diamonds on strap bracelets, inspired by the discovery of Tutankhamen's tomb in 1922 (an event that launched a general mania for Egyptian motifs). The firm also excelled at creating convertible diamond and platinum jewels in the prevailing geometric forms, e.g., a sautoir necklace that separated into bracelets and a pendant.

Other famous French houses whose pieces come up for sale at important jewelry auctions include Boucheron, Mauboussin, Chaumet, and Lacloche. Less often seen is the work of the French avant-garde designers: Jean Desprès (1889-1980), Jean Dunand (1877-1942), Georges Fouquet (1862-1957) and son Jean Fouquet (b.1899), Gérard Sandoz (b.1902), and Raymond Templier (1891-1968). When a significant piece by any of these houses or designers is offered, it can realize five or six figures.

Several American firms made and sold noteworthy Art Deco jewels inspired by the French, especially after the 1925 exposition: the manufacturing jewelers William Scheer, Inc., and Oscar Heyman & Bros., Raymond C. Yard, retailers J.E. Caldwell & Co., Black, Starr & Frost, Tiffany & Co., Marcus & Co., C.D. Peacock, and the New York branches of Cartier and Van Cleef & Arpels.

Many anonymous French and unsigned American-made pieces of the period are sold at auction. Price is often determined by the number, size, quantity and quality of the gemstones used, as much as, if not more than the design, which can be repetitious and unoriginal. Less-than-important commercial pieces signed by the famous houses are also auctioned regularly. Their names are often cause for an escalation in price, but astute buyers *always* evaluate a piece on its own merits before taking its marks into consideration.

References: Franco Cologni and Eric Nussbaum, *Platinum by Cartier, Triumph of the Jewelers' Art*, Harry N. Abrams, 1996; J. Mark Ebert, "Art Deco: The Period, The Jewelry," article in *Gems and Gemology,* Spring, 1983; Melissa Gabardi, *Art Deco Jewellery, 1920-1949*, Antique Collectors' Club, 1989; Neil Letson, "Art Deco Jewelry, Its Past, Present and Future," article in *JCK-Heritage*, August, 1988; Sylvie Raulet, *Art Deco Jewelry,* Rizzoli International, 1985 (out of print); Judy Rudoe, *Cartier, 1900-1939*, exhibition catalog, Harry N. Abrams, 1997; Janet Zapata, "Jewelry and Accessories," in *The Encyclopedia of Art Deco,* Alistair Duncan, ed., E.P. Dutton, 1988; exhibition catalog: *The Art of Cartier,* Musée du Petit Palais, 1989.

Museum: *Musée des Arts Décoratifs*, Paris

Reproduction Alert: The Deco revival that began in the early 80s has generated a plethora of knockoffs, and "Deco style" pieces that never existed during the '20s and '30s. Many of these come from Thailand and Hong Kong where the workmanship is rarely as good as the originals, but European and American manufacturers are producing quality repros, some of which defy detection. Among them: Branca de Brito of Portugal, Hermes of Munich, Germany; and Authentic Jewelry in New York City. A quantity of this jewelry is now coming onto the secondary market. Ask questions, read auction catalog warranties, conditions, and descriptions carefully–if a piece is described as "Art Deco *style*," it is not of the period–and examine pieces thoroughly. Be aware that descriptions are the *opinions* of the auction houses.

Advisor: Peter Shemonsky.

Bracelet

Bangle

Diamonds, platinum, c. 1925, geo design of sm oe diamonds set in a pierced and engr plat hoop, 3/8" w, 2-1/2" inside dia .... 8,050 (A)

Charm

Platinum, diamonds, colored stones, c. 1930, fine cable link plat chain suspending eight romantic motif plat charms set with circ-cut and baguette diamonds and colored stones: "I LOVE U," wedding ring set, "MY SWEET," a couple under an umbrella, a cottage, a Scottie dog with "LOVE ME" plaque, a jockey on a racehorse, and a dressing table, padlock clasp, 7-1/2" tl, largest charm 3/4" x 5/8" .... 6,900 (A)

Flexible

Cat's eye chrysoberyls, diamonds, platinum, c. 1925, five grad millegrained collet-set circ cat's eye chrysoberyl cabs, interspersed along a line of carré-set oe diamonds, v-spring and box clasp, safety clasp, 3/8" w x 7-1/4" tl .... 12,650 (A)

Diamonds, emeralds, platinum, c. 1925, four tapered plaques flanking a tapered rect plaque with central lg oe diamond, approx 2.30 cts, pavé-set throughout with one hundred thirty-eight sm oe diamonds, approx 7.00 cts tw, plaques separated by vertical rows of sm calibré-cut emeralds, sgd "TIFFANY & CO.," extra links, 5/8" w x 6-3/4" tl .... 18,400 (A)

Diamonds, platinum, blue stones, c. 1920-25, line of thirty-six oe diamonds and five circ-cut diamonds, approx 4.00 cts tw, central buckle motif set with eleven Fr-cut and calibré-cut blue stones, in engr plat mount, 1/2" w x 7-1/4" .... 3,990 (A)

Diamonds, platinum, c. 1925, pierced equal width strap pavé-set throughout with sm circ-cut diamonds, approx 9.50 cts tw, three pierced quatrefoil motifs collet-set with larger circ-cut diamond centers alternating with three pierced opposed V-shaped motifs enclosing carré-set diamonds, 1/2" w x 7" tl .... 15,525 (A)

Diamonds, onyx, platinum, c. 1925, narrow band centering five oe diamonds, approx 1.50 cts tw, each flanked by triple rows of calibré-cut black onyx forming opposed bullet shapes, pavé-set throughout with two hundred eighty sc diamonds, approx 5.60 cts tw, 3/8" w x 7" ..... 9,200 (A)

Diamonds, sapphires, platinum, c. 1920, five lg sq-cut channel-set blue sapphires, approx 10.00 cts tw, alternating with rect pavé-set diamond plaques, approx 7.25 cts tw, v-spring and box clasp, safety clasp, mkd "CAH" #47606, 3/8" w x 6-1/2" tl .... 18,400 (A)

Diamonds, sapphires, platinum, c. 1925, flexible straightline of thirty-nine circ-cut carré-set diamonds, approx 7.80 cts tw, flanked by rows of channel-set Fr-cut blue sapphires, 3/8" w x 7" .... 14,950 (A)

Diamonds, synthetic sapphires, platinum, c. 1920, line of carré-set oe diamonds, centering a stepped truncated oval, a lg oe diamond bezel-set in center, flanked by four calibré-cut syn blue sapphires in a geo pierced mount accented by sm bc diamonds, v-spring and box clasp, safety chain, 1/2" w (at center), 7" tl .... 2,825 (A)

Sapphires, diamonds, platinum, c. 1925, straightline of twenty oe diamonds, approx 2.00 cts tw, alternating with twenty-five Fr-cut blue sapphires, set in engr plat, 1/4" w x 7" tl .... 4,560 (A)

Bracelet, flexible, diamonds, sapphires, plat, c. 1920, three flexible panels of circ-cut diamonds within a calibré-cut sapphire border joined by open rounded rect diamond-set buckle links, sgd "Cartier No. 10724," 1/2" w x 7", **$18,400** [A]. (Photo courtesy of Christie's Los Angeles, CA, 10/3/96).

Bracelet, flexible, diamonds, platinum, c. 1920, cusped and bracketed oblong openwork central plaque with a central marquise-cut diamond flanked by two baguette-cut diamonds and surrounded by circ-cut and sc diamonds and calibré-cut sapphire detail, joined to a circ-cut diamond box link band, pierced borders, maker's mk for Hayden W. Wheeler & Co. (H W within a lg rounded W), New York, NY, 5/8" w (at center) x 6-3/4", **$6,325** [A]. (Photo courtesy of Christie's Los Angeles, CA, 10/3/96).

Seed pearls, diamonds, onyx, platinum, c. 1925, three latticework panels of seed pearls on plat wire, each centering three entwined open lozenge motifs, one set with calibré-cut black onyx, two with sc diamonds, panels joined by two oe diamond-set spacer bars, Fr hmk (dog's head) for plat, maker's mk of two entwined "C" s, v-spring and box clasp, 1/2" w x 6-3/4" tl .... 3,743 (A)

Link

Diamonds, emeralds, platinum, c. 1920, three short stepped rectangles alternating with two long pierced rect plaques and two short end links forming a third long rectangle, short links centering a baguette diamond flanked by two rect-cut emeralds and pavé-set with sm circ-cut diamonds, longer links pavé-set with rows of sm circ-cut diamonds, approx 9.00 cts tw, 1/2" w x 7-1/4" .... 13, 225 (A)

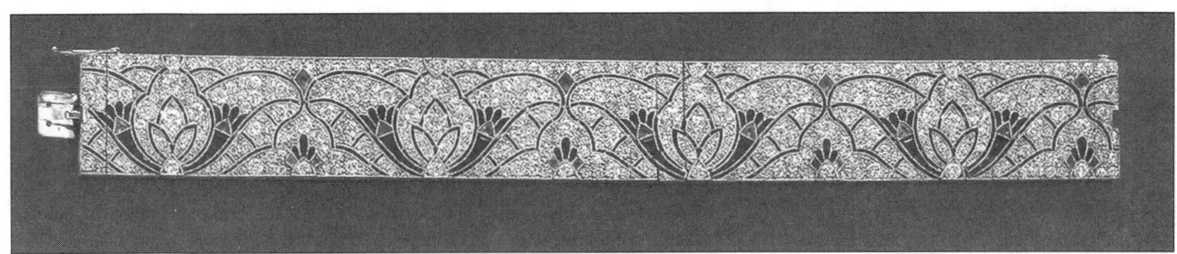

Bracelet, flexible, diamonds, emeralds, sapphires, platinum, c. 1925, flexible strap pavé-set throughout with four hundred eighty-four bead-set sm circ-cut diamonds, approx 24.00 cts tw, continuous panel of pierced stylized lotus motifs, each flanked by stylized foliate motifs set with calibré-cut blue sapphires and emeralds, alternating with sm sapphire and emerald palmette motifs, v-spring and box clasp, safety clasp, 3/4" w x 7" tl, **$29,900** [A]. (Photo courtesy of William Doyle Galleries, Inc. New York, NY, 9/11/97).

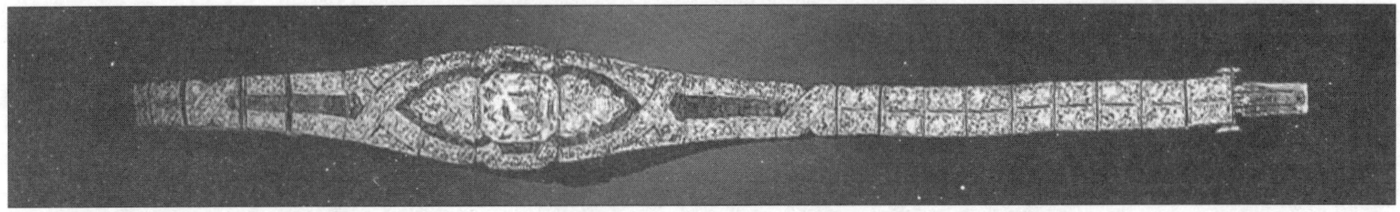

Bracelet, flexible, diamonds, emeralds, platinum, c. 1925, tapered band, center rect-cut diamond, approx 3.00 cts, flanked by calibré-cut emeralds outlining a cusped navette shape with pavé-set circ-cut diamonds in center and outer border, flanked by rows of grad calibré-cut emeralds, continuing to flexible segments set with double rows of circ-cut diamonds, approx 3.55 cts tw, v-spring and box clasp, mkd "PLATINUM," 1/2" w x 6-1/2" tl, **$10,350** [A]. (Photo courtesy of Christie's Los Angeles, CA, 3/13/97).

Bracelet, link, opals, diamonds, enamel, platinum, 18k wg, c. 1925, one lg central flanked by four sm oval black opal cabs, set in black-enameled engr 18k wg rect frames with chamfered corners, evenly spaced between open foliate and geo motif articulated links set in plat with oe, rc, and bc diamonds, approx 5.25 cts tw, Fr hmk for gold and plat mixed, v-spring and box clasp, 1" w (at center), 7-1/2" tl, **$11,400** [A]. (Photo courtesy of Beverly Hills Auctioneers, Inc., CA, 9/21/97).

Bracelet, link, diamonds, platinum, c. 1930, open stepped rectangle centering a rect-cut diamond measuring approx 8.20 x 6.30 x 3.00 mm, framed by baguette, sc, and oe diamonds, flanked by stepped baguettes, joined to semi-cylindrical and open rect links set with oe, sc, and baguette diamonds, leading to tapered open rect links with a center row of baguettes framed by sc and oe diamonds, foldover box clasp, 7/8" w (at center), 6-3/8" tl, **$23,000** [A]. (Photo courtesy of Christie's, New York, NY, 10/23/96).

Diamonds, platinum, c. 1920, three pairs of diamond-set open oval links alternating with narrow pierced rect plaques, pavé-set with three hundred forty-two sm circ-cut diamonds, approx 8.10 cts tw, v-spring and box clasp, fitted case, 1/2" w x 7" .... 12,075 (A)

Diamonds, platinum, c. 1925, flexible openwork band of oe diamonds with pentagon-cut and Fr-cut diamonds set in arrow motifs along both sides pointing toward center, sgd "Cartier" #01442, 1/2" w x 7-1/4" tl .... 23,000 (A)

Diamonds, platinum, c. 1925, four pierced rounded oblong plaques, each center set diagonally with a marquise diamond, approx 1.80 cts tw, alternating with four open cushion-shaped links, joined by oval links, pavé-set throughout with one hundred sixty sm circ-cut diamonds, approx 5.00 cts tw, and seventy-two sc diamonds, approx 2.10 cts tw, v-spring and box clasp, 3/8" w x 7" tl .... 10,062 (A)

Diamonds, platinum, c. 1930-35, three lg open rect geo linked plaques, each centering a lg circ-cut diamond, set throughout with twelve baguette and three hundred fifty-five sm circ, om, and oe diamonds, 1" w x 7" tl .... 12,650 (A)

Diamonds, rubies, platinum, c. 1935, open repeating rect and sq design centering a rect-cut diamond, of approx 2.50 cts, surrounded by baguette diamonds in an open stepped rect frame, flanked by open sq links of calibré-cut rubies with baguette diamond accents, linked to side rows of calibré-cut rubies outlined by two rows of baguette diamonds, foldover box clasp of calibré-cut rubies and baguette diamonds, diamonds approx 22.50 cts tw, rubies approx 20.00 cts tw, 3/4" w at center, 7-1/4" tl .... 77,300 (A)

Diamonds, sapphires, platinum, c. 1920, eleven open-centered navette-shaped links pavé-set with a total of one hundred ten oe diamonds, joined with expandable spring-loaded rect bars set with calibré-cut blue sapphires, 3/8" w .... 5,462 (A)

Diamonds, sapphires, platinum, c. 1920, three rounded rect sections with open ends centering lg marquise-cut diamonds of approx 0.50 ct each, flanked by rows of calibré-cut blue sapphires and surrounded by sm circ-cut diamonds, alternating with open cushion-shaped links and rect interlinks pavé-set with sm circ-cut diamonds, diamonds approx 7.25 cts tw, sgd "TIFFANY & CO.," 3/8" w x 6-3/4" tl .... 11,500 (A)

Bracelets, link, rubies, diamonds, platinum, c. 1930:
T, center link with central emerald-cut prong-set ruby, approx 5.00 cts, framed by two kite-shaped and two half moon-shaped diamonds, surrounded by sm oe diamonds in a pierced scrolling plat plaque, flanked by baguette and oe diamond-set cylinders, joined to open rect links set with sm oe diamonds, to pierced crown-shaped links pavé-set with small oe diamonds, attached to three rows of round ruby beads separated by two rows of sm carré-set diamonds, butterfly-shaped clasp set with one lg baguette and pavé-set sm oe diamonds, diamonds approx 9.75 cts tw, v-spring and box clasp, safety chain, 5/8" w x 6-1/2" tl, **$24,150** [A].
B, open rect links of calibré-cut rubies alternating with opposed buckle-shaped links pavé-set with sm circ-cut diamonds, central tapered rect arch set with baguette diamonds, foldover box clasp set with baguette diamonds, approx 6.40 cts tw, safety chain, (nearly identical to a bracelet illustrated in *Vogue* magazine, Dec. 8, 1930, pictured in *American Jewelry,* Proddow and Healy, p. 120), 5/8" w x 6-1/2", **$10,062** [A].
(Photo courtesy of Sotheby's Beverly Hills, CA, 5/21/96).

Bracelet, link, diamonds, sapphires, platinum, c. 1930, flexible link band of openwork stylized floral/foliate motifs, diagonally opposed, forming an S-curved pattern, six lg collet-set oe diamonds enclosed by curves and brackets set with sm om and sc diamonds, to the edge, breaking the lines of calibré-cut blue sapphire borders, v-spring and box clasp, 7/8" w x 7-1/4" tl, **$13,800** [A]. (Photo courtesy of Christie's, New York, NY, 10/23/96).

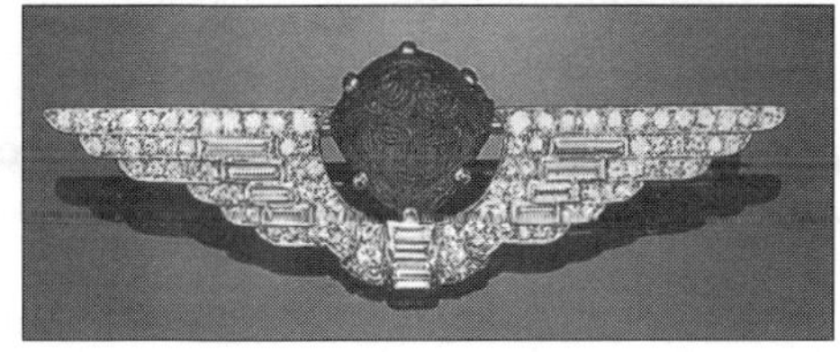

Brooch/Pendant, diamonds, emerald, platinum, c. 1920, a carved prong-set emerald cab, approx 9.40 cts, depicting a female head, partially framed by plat wings pavé-set with sm circ-cut diamonds, a vertical row of baguette diamonds bisecting the wings below head, flanked by a stepped series of four horizontally set baguettes, pendant hoop, provenance: from the Lyn Revson collection, 2-3/4" w x 7/8", **$17,250** [A]. (Photo courtesy of Christie's, New York, NY, 10/23/96).

Onyx, diamonds, platinum, c. 1930, sq black onyx plaques alternating with double open rows of sm circ-cut diamonds, approx 4.80 cts tw, v-spring and box clasp, safety clasp, 1/2" w x 6" tl .... 10,350 (A)

Star sapphires, diamonds, rock crystal, enamel, 18k yg, c. 1927, seven graduated star sapphires alternating with rounded open rect rock crystal links and joined by single-cut diamond bands with blue enamel borders, Fr hmks (for 18k), with letter of authenticity from Cartier that the bracelet is Cartier, made in 1927, #02126, 1/2" w x 7-1/2" .... 10,925 (A)

Synthetic sapphires, diamonds, platinum, c. 1925-30, four rows of syn blue sapphire beads with interspersed cusped rect plat spacer bars set with sm circ-cut diamonds and edged with black enamel, shield-shaped terminals with rect black enamel sections, syn sapphire cabs and sm circ-cut and baguette diamonds, foldover box clasp, two extra beads, 5/8" w x 6-1/4" tl .... 5,750 (A)

Brooch/Pendant

Diamonds, platinum, c. 1935, a central oe diamond measuring approx 7.90 x 4.60 mm, in a rounded rect center plaque and inner frame of pavé and baguette diamonds, within an openwork bombé frame set with oe, baguette, and circ-cut diamonds, (with a bail fitting and screwdriver, converts to be worn as a pendant), 1-3/4" w x 1-3/8" .... 11,500 (A)

Brooch/Pin

Black onyx, diamonds, platinum, emeralds, c. 1920, open rounded black onyx oval, two pierced plat foliate motifs set throughout with circ-cut diamonds with sm calibré-cut emerald centers, mounted diagonally opposed across oval, 1-1/2" w x 1" .... 1,495 (A)

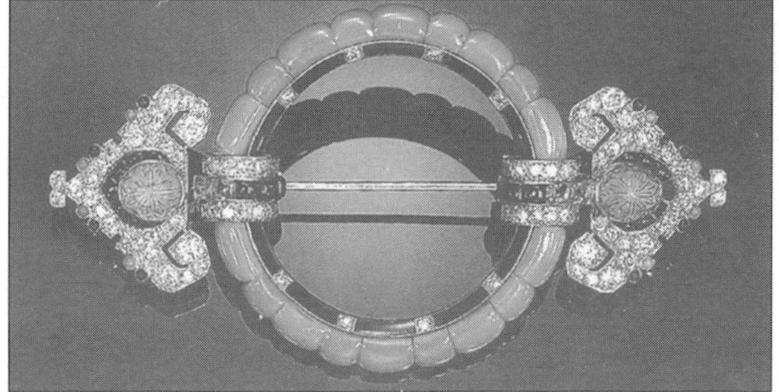

Brooch/Pin, coral, diamonds, onyx, emeralds, plat, 18k yg, enamel, c. 1920, an open circle of sculpted scallop-edged coral, inner ring of black enamel and sc diamonds, flanked by geo scrolled arrow-shaped pierced plat plaques of pavé-set diamonds, each centering a lg circ carved emerald cab partially outlined in calibré-cut black onyx, four pairs of sm circ coral and black onyx cabs at the edges of each, Fr hmks, sgd "Cartier" # 6418, 0520, 3-3/4" w x 2", **$96,000** [A]. (Photo courtesy of Christie's, New York, NY, 10/23/96).

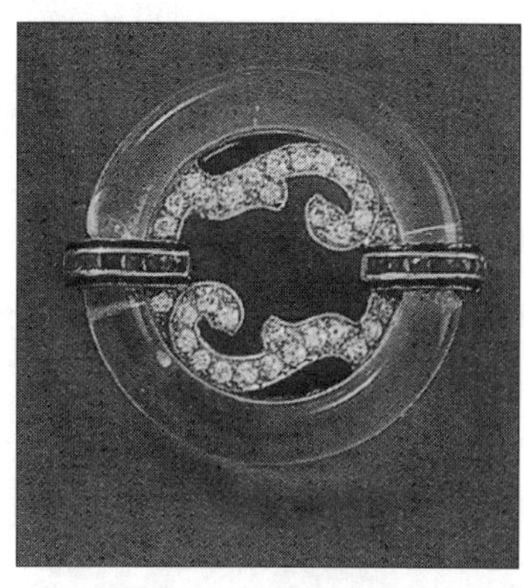

Brooch/Pin, rock crystal quartz, diamonds, sapphires, enamel, platinum, c. 1920, annulus (ring) of rock crystal quartz (damaged), centering an open scroll of plat bead-set with sm oe diamonds, a teardrop-shaped section of black enamel at top and bottom, a plat arch set with calibré-cut blue sapphires outlined in black enamel on each side, sgd "Cartier" #2717019, 1-1/4" dia, **$2,645** [A]. (Photo courtesy of Sotheby's Beverly Hills, CA, 5/21/96).

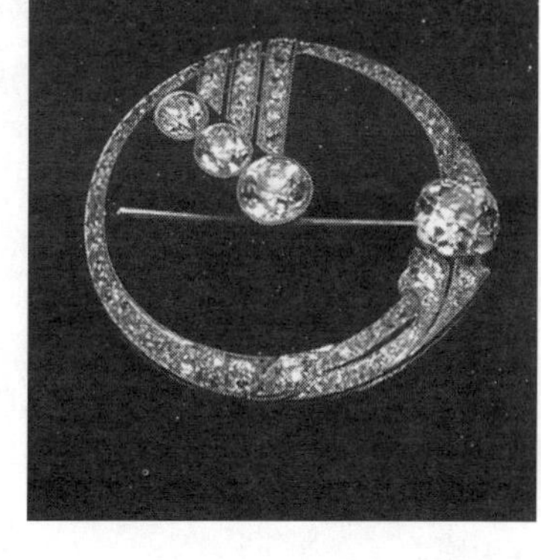

Brooch/Pin, diamonds, platinum, 14k wg, c. 1920, open circle, one lg oe diamond, approx 1.85 cts, surmounting a side scroll, three grad vertical rows of sc diamonds terminating in three oe diamonds, approx 1.60 cts tw, from top to center of circle, pavé-set in plat with a total of sixty-three sm oe and sc diamonds, approx 1.80 cts tw, catch mkd "14k," 1-1/2" dia, **$5,175** [A]. (Photo courtesy of Sotheby's, Beverly Hills, CA, 5/20/97).

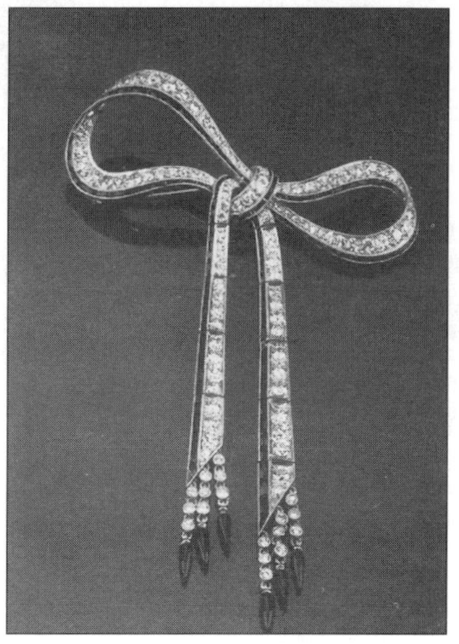

Brooch/Pin, diamonds, black onyx, platinum, c. 1920, open bow shape, asymmetrical loops and articulated ribbon ends pavé-set with circ-cut diamonds, calibré-cut onyx bordering one edge, each ribbon terminating in a fringe of three diamond-set chains with inverted teardrop onyx terminals, 2-1/8" x 3-1/4" tl, **$8,050** [A]. (Photo courtesy of Skinner, Inc., Boston, MA, 6/10/97).

Brooch/Pin, jadeite, diamonds, platinum, c. 1920-25, navette shape centering a scalloped pierced oval green jadeite carved floral and hummingbird motif plaque, total of twenty-two sc diamond accents set at compass points, sm crack in jadeite, 2" w x 1", **$1,083** [A]. (Photo courtesy of Beverly Hills Auctioneers, Inc., CA, 9/21/97).

Brooch/Pin, diamonds, emeralds, platinum, c. 1930, depicting a fountain surmounted by a lg pear-shaped diamond measuring 9.50 x 6.00 x 3.30 mm, staggered and overlapping inverted J-shaped lines of sc and baguette diamonds flanking a central row of trapezoidal, baguette, navette, and half moon-cut diamonds, terminating in a pool of calibré-cut emeralds contained within a baguette and pavé-set diamond pedestaled bowl, 1-3/8" w x 2-1/4", **$52,900** [A]. (Photo courtesy of Christie's, New York, NY, 10/23/96).

Brooch/Pin, diamonds, platinum, c. 1930, "Temple of Love" architectural motif, set with eighteen bc and twenty-two baguette diamonds, approx 3.00 cts tw, Fr, brooch fitting replaced, 3/4" w x 1", **$5,462** [A]. (Photo courtesy of Sotheby's Beverly Hills, CA, 5/21/96).

Brooch/Pin, rubies, emeralds, diamonds, platinum, enamel, c. 1930, depicting a basket of flowers, carved ruby and emerald flowers and leaves interspersed with circ-cut diamonds and accented with black enamel, in a sq and circ-cut diamond-set basket, trombone catch, 2" w x 1-3/8", **$15,525** [A]. (Photo courtesy of Christie's Los Angeles, CA, 3/13/97).

Diamonds, blue stones, platinum, c. 1920, open horizontal oval frame pavé-set with sixty-two sm circ, om, and oe diamonds, a ribbon bow motif to one side, one lg marquise diamond in bow center, diagonal row of sm calibré-cut blue stones on opposite side, 1-3/4" w x 7/8" .... 1,955 (A)

Diamonds, enamel, onyx, platinum, c. 1925, depicting a flying crane of pavé-set sm diamonds with three lg triangular-cut diamonds on one wing, red enamel beak, black enamel wing and tail tips, sm circ black onyx cab eye, sgd "Janesich" #12251, 2-3/4" w x 1-5/8" .... 18,400 (A)

Diamonds, emeralds, onyx, platinum, c. 1919, "*lambrequin*" (literally, valance or drapery), crescent-shaped plat plaque with geo design of calibré-cut emeralds, black onyx and pavé-set sc diamonds, bisected by an articulated lobed plaque extending below crescent, giving the illusion of a draped cloth, set with vertical rows of calibré-cut onyx and emeralds and pavé-set with oe and sc diamonds, a lg oe diamond in the center, suspending a collet-set oe diamond drop, Fr hmks, sgd "Van Cleef & Arpels," 1-5/8" w x 2-1/4" .... 23,000 (A)

Diamonds, platinum, c. 1920, in the shape of a turtle with pierced honeycomb-patterned shell, set throughout with forty-nine om diamonds, 1-3/8" w x 1" .... 2,415 (A)

Diamonds, platinum, c. 1920, triangular shield-shaped open plaque, set throughout with fifty-three om diamonds, approx 5.00 cts tw, 1-5/8" w x 1-1/8" .... 4,025 (A)

Diamonds, platinum, c. 1920, rounded rect cross-hatched pierced plaque centering one oe diamond, approx 2.00 cts, and set throughout with forty-four sm oe diamonds, approx 2.00 cts tw, sgd "Cartier," brooch fitting missing, 1-1/4" w x 5/8" .... 5,750 (A)

Diamonds, platinum, c. 1925, pierced rect plaque with stepped cusped sides, open geo design with two central collet-set oe diamonds, approx 3.25 cts tw, set throughout with one hundred thirteen sm oe diamonds, 2" w x 7/8" .... 6,900 (A)

Diamonds, platinum, c. 1925-30, open lobed rect plaque centering one oe diamond of approx 2.00 cts, flanked top and bottom by two half moon-cut diamonds, two curved rows of baguette diamonds above and below, set throughout with six sm marquise diamonds, sixty oe diamonds, two baguettes at terminals, approx 8.00 cts tw, 1-3/4" w x 1" .... 7,980 (A)

Brooch/Pin, rock crystal, aquamarine, black onyx, wg, c. 1930, cusped rect black onyx base, ridged rock crystal top, prong-set emerald-cut aquamarine in center, lever catch, mkd "14k," 1-3/4" w x 1", **$1,200**. (Courtesy of E. Foxe Harrell Jewelers, Clinton, IA).

Diamonds, platinum, c. 1927, depicting the *Arc de Triomphe* in plat set with sc, baguette, and trapeze-cut diamonds, sgd "Cartier," 3/4" w x 3/4" .... 18,400 (A)

Diamonds, platinum, c. 1930, open circle with floral and ribbon motif, six bead and bezel-set oe diamonds, 3.15 cts tw, eighty bead-set oe diamonds 2.85 cts tw, 1-1/2" w x 1-3/4" .... 3,738 (A)

Diamonds, sapphire, enamel, ruby, red stone, platinum, c. 1925, depicting a goose in flight, pavé-set with sixty-four full and sc diamonds, approx 1.35 cts tw, carved blue sapphire body, red enamel beak, sm ruby eye, red stone tail feathers (slight damage), 1-7/8" w x 3/4" .. 2,850 (A)

Diamonds, sapphires, platinum, c. 1920-25, geo bow of sm circ-cut diamonds with four outer vertical rows of calibré-cut blue sapphires, in a plat mount, in a Shreve, Crump and Low (Boston, MA) leather box, 1-7/8" w x 1/2" .... 9,200 (A)

Diamonds, sapphires, platinum, c. 1925, elongated open hexagon, inner row of French-cut sapphires within an outer row of diamonds, four carré-set diamonds at compass points, 2" w x 1" .... 2,875 (A)

Diamonds, sapphires, red stone, plat, c. 1925, open circ frame centering a bird in flight, with sm circ-cut diamonds throughout, calibré-cut blue sapphires at tail and wings, sm circ-cut red stone eye, 1-1/4" dia .... 2,300 (A)

Diamonds, platinum, black onyx, opal, c. 1930, open stepped rect frame set with grad rows of bc diamonds, central stylized bird motif of pavé-set diamonds, calibré-cut black onyx crest, eye, beak, wing and tail, sm oval opal on chest, flanked by three grad pierced disks, each with lg bc diamond center framed by sm bc diamonds, 2-1/8" w x 1" .... 5,750 (A)

Diamonds, wg, c. 1920, sq plaque, pierced geo cipher set with lines of seventy-six rc diamonds in millegrained wg, later-added brooch fittings, 7/8" w x 7/8" .... 575 (A)

Brooch/Pin, Bar, diamonds, platinum, 14k wg, c. 1920, pierced geo tapered bar with cusped ends, bead-set throughout with twenty-three oe diamonds and twenty sm circ diamonds, approx 3.25 cts tw, lever catch mkd "14k," 3" w x 1", **$2,280** [A]. (Photo courtesy of Beverly Hills Auctioneers, Inc., CA, 2/16/97).

Brooch/Pin, Bar, diamonds, emeralds, platinum, c. 1925, geo ribbon bow motif centering one lg circ-cut diamond flanked by om and oe diamond-set loops and cusped ribbon ends of opposed rows of calibré-cut emeralds and oe diamonds, mkd "J.E.C. & Co." for J. E. Caldwell & Co., Philadelphia, PA, #H9303, 3" w x 1/2", **$3,680** [A]. (Photo courtesy of Christie's Images, New York, NY, 12/11/96).

Pearls, diamonds, plat, 18k wg, c. 1920, pavé-set diamond pierced cut-corner rect plaque flanked by pierced ogival plaques, centering a lg button pearl measuring 10.20 x 7.90 mm, a button pearl in four corners and in ogive centers, in a fitted leather case, sgd with maker's mk for Chaumet, Paris (JC in lozenge with crescent above and star below), with GIA certificate #4265139 stating center pearl is of natural origin, 3-3/4" w x 1-1/2" .... 23,000 (A)

Rock crystal quartz, 14k wg, diamond, c. 1920, octagonal carved rock crystal quartz, in a stamped floral filigree wg frame, one sm circ-cut diamond accent, pierced die-rolled gallery, lever catch, 1-1/8" w x 7/8" ... 399 (A)

Bar

Aquamarine, diamonds, platinum, c. 1925, open narrow rectangle pavé-set with seventy-two rc diamonds, centering a prong-set cushion-cut aquamarine of approx 8.80 cts, 2-3/8" w x 5/8" .... 2,760 (A)

Diamonds, emeralds, platinum, c. 1925, pierced rounded oblong plaque, one lg and two sm oe diamonds in a navette-shaped center, flanked by four sm bc diamonds, two rows of calibré-cut emeralds (one missing, one replaced), and two triangular-cut diamonds forming opposed arrow motifs, and set throughout with sm bc diamonds, 2" w x 1/2" .... 1,955 (A)

Jadeite, diamonds, onyx, platinum, 18k yg, c. 1920-25, pierced oblong green jadeite plaque carved with bird and floral/foliate motifs, flanked by grad overlapping C-scroll plaques, centers set with calibré-cut onyx framed by circ-cut diamonds, Eng, 2" w x 5/8" .... 6,900 (A)

Synthetic sapphires, diamonds, platinum, 14k yg, c. 1920, rect bar, a row of three rect-cut syn blue sapphires alternating with two oe diamonds, eight diamonds and twelve syn sapphires total, bead set in plat-topped yg, approx 1.50 cts tw diamonds, 3" w x 3/16" .... 1,254 (A)

Cuff Links

14k yg, wg, MOP, sapphires, c. 1920, double-sided circ disks, each centering a sapphire cab surmounting a MOP disk within an engr wg-topped yg frame yg bar connectors, mkd "585 XX," pr .... 275 (A)

Double Clip Brooch

Diamonds, emeralds, platinum, c. 1930, each clip a stepped open square centering a rect-cut prong-set emerald measuring approx 6.85 x 6.44 mm and 6.92 x 6.51 mm,

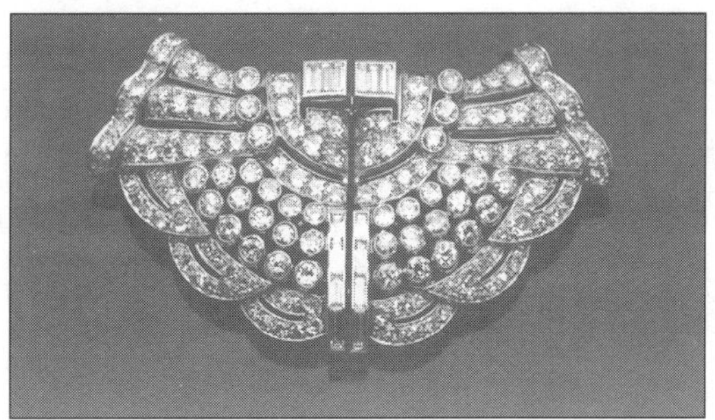

Double Clip Brooch, diamonds, platinum, c. 1935, joined to form a truncated fan shape, pierced scalloped overlapping edges set with lines of oe and sc diamonds, surmounted by curved and tapered sections of bead-set oe and sc diamonds, central rows of baguette diamonds flanked by curved rows of sm oe diamonds, removable brooch mechanism, Fr hmk (dog's head) for plat, 2-1/2" w x 1-3/8" (joined), **$5,750** [A]. (Photo courtesy of Phillips Fine Art Auctioneers, New York, NY, 5/1/97).

Double Clip Brooch, diamonds, rubies, platinum, c. 1930, joined opposing shield shapes centering stepped baguette diamonds flanked by lg prong-set oval ruby cabs, open geo design set with marquise-cut, baguette and sm oe diamonds, outer fringe of oval and pear-shaped carved rubies, diamonds approx 8.40 cts tw, removable brooch mechanism, 3" w x 1-3/8" (joined), **$10,350** [A]. (Photo courtesy of Sotheby's Beverly Hills, CA, 5/21/96).

bisected by a row of channel-set baguette diamond arches, pavé-set with sm circ-cut diamonds, two sm bezel-set emerald cab terminals at top of each, diamonds approx 5.90 cts tw, removable brooch mechanism, 1-5/8" w x 3/4" joined .... 14,375 (A)

Diamonds, enamel, platinum, c. 1930, two opposed triangles, each composed of alternating bands of undulating black enamel and sm circ-cut diamonds, bisected by overlapping rows of diamond baguettes, removable brooch mechanism, 1-7/8" w x 1-1/8" (joined) ... 29,900 (A)

Diamonds, rubies, platinum, c. 1930, joined as an asymmetrical foliated scroll motif pavé-set with sm circ-cut and sc diamonds, ten baguette diamonds, six prong-set carved rubies around one curved end, one lg carved ruby at opposite end, six calibré-cut channel-set rubies around side edge, removable brooch mechanism, 1-5/8" w x 7/8" (joined) .... 5,462 (A)

Dress Clip

Yg, citrine, rock crystal quartz, diamonds, pearl, enamel, c. 1927-30, tapered lobed rect white enameled yg frame enclosing a carved citrine bird, carved rock crystal quartz flower, black enamel branches, a pearl in one corner, surmounted by a bezel-set rect citrine cab (some enamel loss), sgd "Cartier," flat-backed hinged clip mechanism, 7/8" w x 1" .... 2,760 (A)

Dress Clips

Diamonds, platinum, c. 1935, scrolling ribbon cascade motif, forty-seven baguette diamonds, approx 2.00 cts tw, twenty-seven lg circ diamonds, approx 7.00 cts tw, one hundred sixty sm circ-cut diamonds, approx 6.50 cts tw, 1-3/8" w x 1-5/8", pr .... 12,075 (A)

Dress Clip, diamonds, platinum, c. 1935, shield-shaped pierced geo plaque centering one prong-set marquise diamond framed by twenty-one channel-set baguette diamonds, ten bead-set sc diamonds, and twenty full cut diamonds, approx 3.25 cts tw, open-center flat-backed hinged clip on rev, 1" w x 15/16", **$2,052** [A]. (Photo courtesy of Beverly Hills Auctioneers, Inc., CA, 2/16/97).

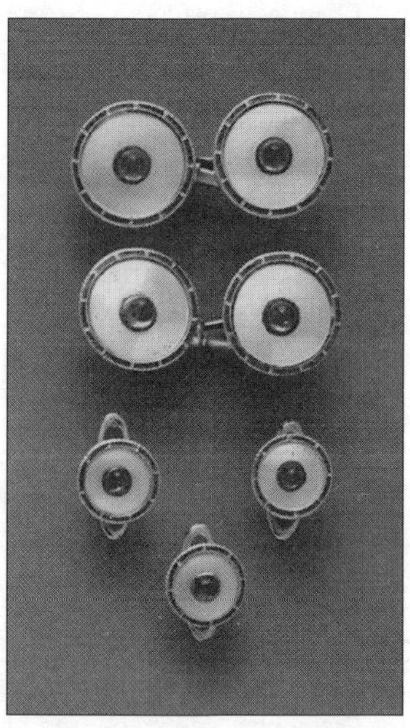

Dress Set, Cuff links and Three Shirt Studs, MOP, emeralds, 14k yg, 18k yg, enamel, c. 1925, double-sided circ cuff links, each side centering a MOP disk with central circ emerald cab, encircled by green enamel on 18k yg, with 14k yg fittings, three matching shirt studs, Fr hmks and sgd fitted box for Lacloche Frères, Paris, cuff links 1/2" dia, studs, 3/8" dia, **$1,824** [A]. (Photo courtesy of Beverly Hills Auctioneers, Inc., CA, 2/16/97).

Dress Set: Cuff Links, Three Shirt Studs, Four Shirt Buttons

MOP, plat, diamonds, 14k yg, c. 1930, octagonal MOP top centering a sm circ-cut diamond in an engr plat frame on a yg base, cuff links 1/2" dia, set .... 2,300 (A)

Dress Set: Cuff Links and Three Shirt Studs

Platinum, onyx, diamonds, 14k yg, c. 1920, each with an octagonal slab of black onyx surmounted by a plat octagonal plaque centering a sm circ-cut diamond, yg backings, cuff links 1/2" dia, studs 3/8" dia, set .... 2,990 (A)

Earrings, pendent

Black onyx, diamonds, platinum, c. 1920-25, inverted lobed trefoil black onyx plaque (sm chip in one), a curved center row of circ-cut diamonds flanked top and bottom by a diamond, diamond-set bottom border, and kite shape at top, suspended from a three collet-set diamond chain, sm circ black onyx disk surmount with diamond center, 3/4" w x 1-1/2", pr .... 805 (A)

Diamonds, cat's eye chrysoberyl, platinum, c. 1925, surmount a round cluster of sm prong-set bc diamonds, suspending an articulated line of collet-set bc diamonds terminating in a drop with circ prong-set cat's eye chrysoberyl cab encircled by prong-set sm bc diamonds, 1/2" w x 1-3/8" tl, pr .... 3,450 (A)

Pendent Earrings, diamonds, emeralds, platinum, c. 1920-25, a cusped and lobed fan-shaped surmount set with a sq-cut emerald surmounted by three rc diamonds, suspending an articulated chain of nine collet-set rc diamonds terminating in an inverted pierced cusped and lobed fan shaped drop with pear-shaped emerald center flanked by two collet-set rc diamonds and six rc diamonds set throughout, 1/2" w x 2-1/4", pr, **$5,175** [A]. (Photo courtesy of Phillips Fine Art Auctioneers, New York, NY, 10/26/97).

Pendent Earrings, jadeite, enamel, diamonds, platinum, yg, c. 1920, circ surmount centering sm sq green jadeite cab, black enameled baton link to black enameled and rc diamond-set bail suspending a lg carved and pierced floral/foliate motif narrow tapered rect green jadeite plaque, yg screwbacks, 1/2" w x 2-3/8", pr, **$2,645** [A]. (Photo courtesy of Sotheby's Beverly Hills, CA, 5/21/96).

Pendent Earrings, pearls, diamonds, platinum, c. 1920, three articulated open triangular links set with single-cut diamonds suspending a sc and rc diamond-set geo pierced cap with drilled natural pearl drop, in fitted box marked "S.J. Phillips, London," 1/2" w x 2-1/4", pr, **$10,925** [A]. (Photo courtesy of Christie's Los Angeles, CA, 10/3/96).

Diamonds, onyx, platinum, c. 1925, oval surmount set with sm oe diamonds, suspending a cusped necktie-shaped plaque with short and long diagonal lines of calibré-cut black onyx and sc diamonds, later-added clipbacks, pr, 1/4" w x 1-1/2" .... 2,070 (A)

Emeralds, diamonds, platinum, enamel, c. 1925-30, a melon-carved oval emerald drop suspended from an articulated collet-set diamond chain with black-enameled center sq bead, kite-shaped surmount with black-enameled lozenge-shaped center enclosed by pavé-set diamonds, screwbacks, 3/8" w x 1-3/4" tl, pr ...... 2,530 (A)

Jabot Pin

Diamonds, onyx, platinum-topped 18k yg, c. 1920, in the shape of an arrow, head with three collet-set oe diamonds and calibré-cut black onyx forming V shape through diamonds, feather at opposite terminal pierced and set with triangular calibré-cut onyx, surmounted by a collet-set oe diamond, four oe diamonds approx 0.61 ct tw, set throughout with sm rc diamonds in millegrained plat on yg, 2" w x 1/2" .... 1,150 (A)

Onyx, coral, diamonds, platinum, 18k wg, c. 1925, each terminal an open U shape centering coral segments outlined in sc diamonds set in plat, flanked by black onyx segments and sc diamond-set terminals, mounted at opposite ends of wg pinstems, provenance: from the collection of Lyn Revson, 3" w x 1" .... 4,600 (A)

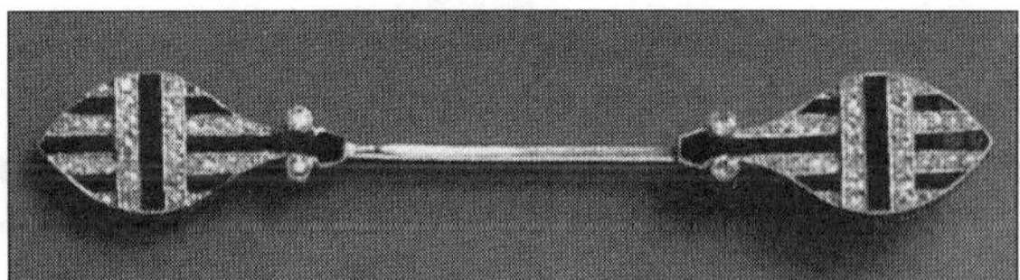

Jabot Pin, diamonds, onyx, platinum, c. 1925, navette-shaped plaques at opposite ends of a plat pinstem, one removable, geo design of perpendicular rows of diamonds and calibré-cut black onyx, seventy-two sm circ bead-set diamonds approx 0.90 ct tw , one terminal removable, Fr hmk (dog's head) for plat, maker's mk in lozenge-shaped reserve, 3-1/8" w x 1/2", **$2,850** [A]. (Photo courtesy of Beverly Hills Auctioneers, Inc., CA, 2/16/97).

Lavalier and Chain

Diamonds, platinum, onyx, c. 1920, rounded kite-shaped plaque, pierced and pavé-set with sm circ-cut diamonds, larger diamond center, crescent and V-shaped outlines of calibré-cut onyx around edges, suspended from a Y-shaped articulated diamond and onyx surmount and platinum fetter link chain, 15" tl, 3/4" w x 2-1/2" tl .... 3,450 (A)

Lorgnette

Diamonds, onyx, platinum, c. 1925, bottle-shaped openwork plat plaque, lg oval onyx cab with lg diamond carré-set in center, surrounded by oe-cut diamonds, pear-shaped onyx cab below bail, two horizontal rows of calibré-cut onyx channel-set above and below a lg single carré-set diamond, diamond-set bail, opening to a pair of rect lenses, suspended from a plat fancy link chain, 3/4" w x 2-1/2" (closed), chain 21" tl .... 6,325 (A)

Necklace

Coral, lapis, diamonds, platinum, c. 1930, carved melon-shaped beads, four clustered strands each of coral on one side and lapis on the other, joined by two pierced tapered rect diamond-set clips, approx 1" x 1/2", sgd "Cartier" #3515380, 15" tl .... 8,050 (A)

Diamonds, platinum, c. 1930, open geo links with central emerald-cut prong-set diamond, 1.00 ct, pavé-set throughout with forty-six baguette, ninety-two sm circ-cut, and forty-four sc diamonds, approx 7.55 cts tw, separates into two bracelets, 5/8" w (at center), 14" tl .... 19,550 (A)

Lavalier, 14k wg, diamonds, c. 1920, tapered rect geo plaque with a vertical row of three sm oe diamonds, approx .20 ct tw, in pierced and millegrained collets and sq frames, Dutch hmk for 14k imp on rev, ridged rect bail, 3/8" w x 1" (with bail), **$300** (Paula Straub collection).

Pendant/Brooch, diamonds, platinum, emeralds, wg, c. 1920, geo pierced cut-corner rect plaque with a hinged cusped bail set throughout with oe and circ-cut diamonds, three larger oe diamonds set vertically in center with two short rows of sm calibré-cut emeralds, curved rows of sm calibré-cut emeralds in corners, at sides and across bail (some missing), suspended from a later-added 18" wg chain, bail folds under for wear as a brooch, 1-1/8" w x 2-3/4" tl with bail, **$5,980** [A]. (Photo courtesy of Christie's Images, New York, NY, 4/8/97).

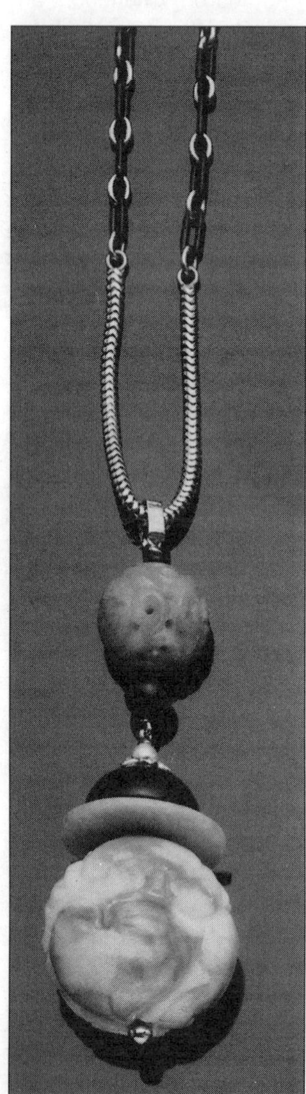

Pendant/Necklace, jadeite, black onyx, platinum, enamel, diamonds, pearl, c. 1930, pendant a lg carved green and white jadeite sphere, 1" dia, surmounted by a jadeite disk and a domed onyx cap set with a pearl and sm diamonds, suspended from a smaller carved jadeite sphere and bail, a plat snake chain interspersed with short chain lengths of black-enameled oval links alternating with lg plain oval plat links, 18" tl, pendant 3" tl, **$1,955** [A]. (Photo courtesy of Phillips Fine Art Auctioneers, New York , NY, 6/10/97).

Diamonds, seed pearls, platinum, c. 1925, central shield-shaped plat plaque of open geo design with pierced and lobed trefoils set with om and oe diamonds, suspending a grad fringe of sm circ collet-set diamonds, each row terminating in an inverted pear-shaped collet-set diamond drop, diamond-set circ bail attached to two diamond-set triangular open geo terminals set with oe and collet-set sm circ-cut diamonds, joined to a woven seed pearl band, Fr hmk (dog's head) for plat, 1-1/8" w x 3", 16-3/8" tl .... 23,000 (A)

Pendant and Cord

Opal, diamonds, platinum, cord, c. 1920, rect black opal plaque, approx 1-3/16" x 1", held by sm diamond-set plat pierced triangular prongs at compass points, suspended from an articulated line of three diamonds linked to a black cord with diamond-set plat caps, 3/4" w x 1-1/4", 20" tl .... 4,313 (A)

Pendant/Locket

Diamonds, plat, c. 1920, rect with chamfered corners, pierced geo design with a diagonal row of marquise-shaped diamonds, six vertical rows of sm sc diamonds and a border of sm rc diamonds, diamond-set bail surmounted by inverted triangular open wire diamond-set plaque, diamonds approx 3.15 cts tw, rev engr with initials "BDM," 1-1/4" w x 1-7/8" tl (with bail) .... 4,600 (A)

Ring

Diamonds, emeralds, platinum, c. 1925, lobed rect plaque, center set with three stepped rect and baguette-cut diamonds flanked top and bottom by calibré-cut emeralds, shoulders set with two baguette diamonds, narrow shank, 1/2" w x 5/8", size 4-3/4 .... 8,050 (A)

Diamonds, emeralds, platinum, c. 1930, sq plaque, central oval-cut emerald flanked top and bottom by two sm rect-cut emeralds, surrounded by twelve oe diamonds, approx 2.75 cts tw, 3/4" w x 5/8", size 6-1/2 .. 2,850 (A)

Diamonds, platinum, c. 1920, circ domed pierced and millegrained mount centering a lg oe diamond, set throughout with sc and oe diamonds, 3/4" w x 1/2", size 3 .... 1,380 (A)

Diamonds, platinum, c. 1920, pierced plat mount centering a natural fancy light greenish-yellow bc diamond, 0.87 ct, with GIA report stating natural color, surrounded by fourteen sm circ-cut diamonds forming flowerhead, 3/4" w x 3/8" .... 2,415 (A)

Diamonds, platinum, c. 1920, pierced oval geo top set with a vertical row of three lg oe diamonds, approx 0.80, 0.75, and 0.70 ct, and set throughout with four sm oe and twenty sc diamonds, approx 2.85 cts tw, tapered shank, 5/8" 2 x 1-1/8", size 5 .... 2,850 (A)

Diamonds, platinum, c. 1925, a lozenge-shaped diamond, approx 2.94 cts, prong-set in a narrow plat band with diamond-set shoulders, engr shank, with GIA certificate, D color, VS1 clarity, 3/8" w x 5/8" .... 34,500 (A)

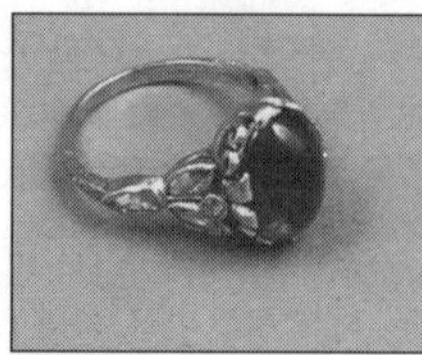

Ring, sapphire, diamonds, platinum, c. 1920, central blue sapphire cab, approx 8 mm by 10 mm, set in cutout and scrolled plat bezel, flanked by three marquise and one oe millegrained collet-set diamonds at shoulders, engr narrow shank, mkd "PLATINUM 5% IRID," 1/2" w, approx size 5-1/2, **$1,500**. (Ellen Borlenghi collection).

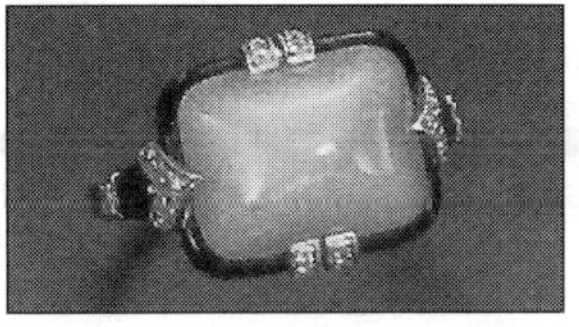

Ring, jadeite, enamel, diamonds, platinum, c. 1925, central rect sugarloaf jade cab framed by a narrow black enameled band, sm sc diamond accents in cusped and bar shapes at compass points, mounted on a narrow shank, Fr, 3/4" w x 1/2", size 7, **$4,312** [A]. (Photo courtesy of Sotheby's Beverly Hills, CA, 5/20/97).

Diamonds, platinum, c. 1925-30, central prong-set oe diamond, approx 1.70 cts, flanked by six sm circ-cut diamonds, in a pierced and engr plat mount, approx size 4-1/2 .... 4,560 (A)

Diamonds, platinum, c. 1925-30, lobed rect plaque, sq center set with one oe diamond, and pavé-set with eighteen om, oe, and circ-cut diamonds, narrow shank, 5/8" w x 1/2", size 6-1/2 .... 1,610 (A)

Diamonds, platinum, c. 1930, rounded rect plaque centering one oe diamond, approx 0.80 ct, flanked by six sm oe diamonds, approx 0.70 ct tw, pierced gallery, narrow shank, mkd "PLATINUM," 7/8" w x 3/8", size 5-1/2 .... 2,565 (A)

Diamonds, platinum, c. 1935, central circ-cut prong-set diamond, approx 1.75 cts, flanked by two tapered baguette diamonds and two trapeze-cut diamonds, approx 0.60 ct tw, maker's mk for W.J. Harber Co. Inc. (H in a circle), New York, NY, 1931-50, 5/8" w x 1/4" .... 9,775 (A)

Diamonds, platinum, c. 1935, navette-shaped cluster of oe and sc diamonds, plat mount worn, 3/4" w x 1/2", size 5-3/4 .... 633 (A)

Diamonds, platinum, green stones, c. 1920, oval pierced plaque flanked by pierced heart shapes, central marquise-cut diamond, approx 0.35 ct, framed by sm calibré-cut green stones, with ten sm sc diamond accents, tapering to a narrow shank, engr plat mount, 5/8" w x 5/8", size 6 .... 855 (A)

Diamonds, rubies, platinum, c. 1925-30, lozenge-shaped geo plat plaque with central om diamond framed by eight sm sugarloaf ruby cabs forming opposed V-shapes surmounted by two oe diamonds top and bottom, surrounded by sixteen sc diamonds, approx 2.00 cts tw, two triangular ruby cabs at each side, 1/2" w x 3/4" .... 2,850 (A)

Diamonds, sapphires, plat, c. 1925, oval plaque, vertical center row of three collet-set diamonds, approx .75 ct tw, flanked by two vertical rows of three calibré-cut sapphires each, one sapphire above and below, and set throughout with circ-cut diamonds in a pierced plat mount, 3/4" w x 1-1/8" .... 2,875 (A)

Diamonds, sapphires, platinum, c. 1925, central collet-set oe diamond, approx 3.10 cts, within a sq calibré-cut blue sapphire frame (missing two), sm oe diamond-set shoulders tapering to a narrow shank, 3/4" w x 1/2" .... 7,475 (A)

Ring, Sapphire, diamonds, platinum, c. 1930, rect geo design with central cushion-cut bezel-set blue sapphire, approx 1.25 cts, flanked by two om bezel-set diamonds, approx 1.50 cts tw, accented with sixty-six sm circ prong-set diamonds, approx 0.75 ct tw, filigree mounting and shoulders, 3/4" w x 3/8", **$26,450** [A]. (Photo courtesy of William Doyle Galleries, Inc., New York, NY, 12/4/96).

Diamonds, synthetic sapphires, platinum-topped 14k wg, c. 1925-30, central bead-set oe diamond, approx 0.80 ct, flanked top and bottom by two triangular bezel-set syn sapphires, shoulders bead-set with six sc diamonds, engr gallery, 3/8" w x 5/8", size 7 .... 1,026 (A)

Jadeite, diamonds, platinum, c. 1925, central oval prong-set green jadeite cab measuring approx 16.22 x 11.20 x 6.76 mm, flanked by stepped geo design of baguette and sm circ-cut diamonds, 3/4" w x 5/8" .... 4,888 (A)

Opal, diamond, platinum, c. 1930, oval black opal measuring 21.00 mm by 15.30 mm, flanked by baguette and round diamonds in a plat mount, 5/8" w x 3/4" .... 13,800 (A)

Opal, diamonds, platinum, c. 1920, circ top centering a lg rounded rect prong-set black opal flanked by sc and baguette diamonds, tapered sides, narrow shank, 3/4" w x 5/8" .... 6,037 (A)

Rubies, diamonds, platinum, c. 1935, rectilinear design centering calibré-cut rubies and baguette diamonds, shoulders of tapered baguettes bordered by calibré-cut rubies, 3/4" w x 1/2" .... 9,200 (A)

Sapphires, diamonds, platinum, c. 1925, central elongated cushion-cut blue sapphire, approx 1.80 cts, flanked by two rows of bezel-set scissors-cut sm sapphires in a tapering band set with a row of circ-cut diamonds, 1/4" w, size 3-1/2 .... 7,475 (A)

Star sapphire, diamonds, platinum, c. 1935, circ prong-set blue star sapphire, approx 30.00 cts, flanked by geo stepped design of forty-two channel-set baguette diamonds, approx 1.00 ct tw, 1" w x 3/4", size 6-1/2 .... 3,450 (A)

Scarf Pin/Stickpin

Diamonds, blue stones, platinum, 14k yg, c. 1925, open shield-shaped plat plaque with one oe diamond surrounded by seven sc diamonds, wg pinstem, 1/2" w x 2-3/4" tl .... 124 (A)

Diamond, rubies, platinum, 14k yg, c. 1920, circ with central collet-set diamond of approx .65 ct encircled by calibré-cut rubies in a plat mount, 14k yg pinstem, maker's mk for Allsopp and Allsopp, Newark, NJ, 3/8" dia .... 1,093 (A)

COSTUME JEWELRY C. 1920-1935

History: When Coco Chanel (1883-1971) reputedly declared in 1924, "It does not matter if they are real, as long as they look like junk!," costume jewels had already begun to enjoy widespread acceptance by women at all social levels. Both Chanel and her arch-rival, Elsa Schiaparelli, were foremost among Parisian couturiers in designing and promoting the wearing of *faux* jewelry as an accessory to clothing, and as a means of self-expression. Today we call it "making a statement."

Because they were made from non-precious materials, costume jewels gave manufacturers and designers a greater freedom to experiment with designs, and the opportunity to cater to fashion's whims, trends, and fads. Consequently we see a far greater diversity in costume jewelry of the period compared to fine jewelry.

To be sure, many directly imitative pieces were made, substituting "paste" or rhinestones, and molded or cut glass, for gemstones, and silver or white "pot" metal (tin alloyed with lead) for platinum. Some of these pieces were remarkably well-made. The metal was often rhodium-plated for an even closer resemblance to platinum (rhodium is one of the six metals in the platinum group). Stones were prong- or bead-set; occasionally, millegrained settings were used. At a short distance, one would find it difficult to discern them from the "real" thing. Verbatim translations of the period style from fine to costume jewelry include flexible and linked plaque bracelets, bead sautoirs (sometimes called "flapper beads"), pendent earrings, geometric brooches and pendants, dress clips and double clip brooches. (Coro's version of the double clip brooch, trade named the "Duette," was patented in 1931.)

As with fine jewelry, Art Deco costume pieces originated in Europe, where the *Jugendstil*, Bauhaus, Wiener Werkstätte and Liberty styles had already made a case for modernism, emphasizing design over intrinsically valuable materials. But even in France, where *haute joaillerie* and Cartier reigned, the more adventurous Art Deco artist-designers turned to silver, chrome, glass, lacquer and enamel, and plastics. Although a separate section on plastic and novelty jewelry is included elsewhere in this book, German and French Deco pieces in chrome and plastic are included here because the modernity of their design classifies them with similar period pieces made of other materials.

Some French Deco costume jewelry is of the *faux* diamond and platinum variety, usually referred to as "French paste," set in silver, extremely well-made. The transitional path of Edwardian to Deco can be followed in these all-white pieces, along the same route as fine jewelry. Similarly styled bracelets, clips, buckles and brooches in rhinestones and white metal were made in the United States, by costume jewelry manufacturers such as Trifari, Krussman and Fishel, later known simply as Trifari (also see section on "Designer/Manufacturer Signed" costume). Ciner Mfg. Co., in business since 1892, made both fine and costume jewelry. They produced rhinestone and sterling pieces in the French mode during the '20s and '30s. The White Metal Casters' Association made inexpensive rhinestone and "pot" metal buckles and clips as dress accessories in the '30s.

The French and the Germans also excelled at designing modern-looking jewelry in sterling set with inexpensive gemstones and marcasites, small faceted bits of iron pyrite. Theodor Fahrner, already famous for its early twentieth-century *Jugendstil* designs (as mentioned in the Arts & Crafts section), kept up with fashion by producing fine quality Deco pieces in high-grade silver set with marcasites combined with amazonite, smoky quartz, rock crystal, onyx, carnelian, chrysoprase, lapis, or coral. Other less well-known German manufacturers also made jewelry in this style, most commonly using dyed blue or green chalcedony (imitating chrysoprase) with marcasites and sterling.

Most accounts of fashion history tend to focus on what was original about the twenties and thirties, but all was not geometry and streamline. The Victorians did not have a monopoly on revivals; in fact, Victorian fashion and historicism itself were revived beginning in the late twenties, and growing in popularity in the thirties and early forties. Period films and their stars helped set the mood: Mae West in "She Done Him Wrong" (1933), Greta Garbo in "Camille" (1936) and "Conquest" (1937), Bette Davis in "Juarez" (1939), and of course, Vivien Leigh in the immortal "Gone With The Wind" (1939). The clothes and the jewelry (much of the latter created by Eugene Joseff, aka Joseff of Hollywood–see section on "Designer/Manufacturer Signed" costume) may not have always been authentically of the period portrayed, but they inspired a 1930s trend for softer, more romantic dresses with longer hems, peplums and puffy sleeves and such Victorian staples as cameos and jet (imitated in glass and plastic), ornate metal filigree, and flower jewelry.

A unique type of collectible jewelry, which appears to be attracting a growing number of collectors, originated in England. However, its primary component, the wings of the Morpho butterfly, came from South America. Several British firms made these pieces, which usually consist of a reverse-painted scene or a white sulfide bas-relief (reminiscent of Wedgwood jasperware) backed with an iridescent blue butterfly wing ground, a domed glass cover, and usually, a sterling silver frame and back. The backs are often marked with a British patent number, granted to Shipton & Co. of Birmingham, England in 1923. Note that the wings can deteriorate, or the iridescence can flake off, if exposed to light, moisture or air, or even excessive movement, especially if the compartments are not air-tight.

The exotic influences of the period that permeated the work of Cartier, Van Cleef and Arpels et al, found widespread expression in costume jewels as well. The "Egyptomania" instigated by the discovery of King Tutankhamun's treasures and sustained by Hollywood films (e.g., *Cleopatra* in 1934), caused Egyptian motifs to be particularly conspicuous. Enameled silver or gold-plated metal winged scarabs, falcons, vultures and other motifs were produced in several European countries and the U.S., as well as in Egypt itself for export or the tourist trade. The "slave" bracelet, of enameled metal links set with glass cabochons or molded scarabs, was an extension of the craze. One of the primary sources for Egyptian-themed pieces was Czechoslovakia. Here, the medium was usually glass, but celluloid and metal pieces, or a combination of materials, were also made.

After World War I, Bohemia, long renowned for its glasswork, beads, and garnet jewelry, became part of the new country called Czechoslovakia, created in 1918. In the period between the wars, quantities of glass beads, faceted and molded glass stones and stamped metalwork were produced and exported, some in the form of finished jewelry, some for use in jewelry manufactured in other countries. The center of this production was a town called Gablonz, now known as Jablonec. Because the country was taken over by the Germans during World War II (exports were curtailed in 1939), the glass and jewelry makers were dispersed to other areas, such as Neugablonz in Germany. Today, the boundaries have been redrawn once again, and Czechoslovakia is now divided into the Czech Republic and Slovakia. Jewelry marked "Czechoslovakia" is easily circa-dated, and has become quite sought-after. Prices have risen accordingly.

Czechoslovakia was the source of several types of costume jewelry. Stamped gilt metal filigree necklaces, bracelets, brooches, buckles, clips, earrings and rings were set with glass cabochons and embellished with enameled foliate motifs, resulting in an ornate look that was more Victorian Revival than Art Deco. The Deco style was not ignored, however. Geometric-cut pieces of glass resembling gemstones were prong-set in short necklaces and pendent earrings. Glass buckles, clasps and clips were made in simple modern designs. Small faceted glass stones were often silver-plated to imitate marcasites. Oriental-inspired pieces were made with molded and pierced glass plaques imitating carved jade and carnelian. Glass bead sautoirs were another Czech product. Some Czech pieces are marked in difficult-to-read places, like the circumference of a jump ring. Other unmarked pieces are so characteristic of Czech glass and metalwork that they are unmistakable. Still others may have Czech components, but were assembled elsewhere, and may be hard to identify.

References: Lillian Baker, *Art Nouveau and Art Deco Jewelry*, Collector Books, 1981, values updated 1992; Stella Blum, *Everyday Fashions of the Twenties*, Dover Publications, 1981, and *Everyday Fashions of the Thirties,* Dover Publications, 1986; Deanna Farneti Cera, *Amazing Gems, An Illustrated Guide to the Worlds' Most Dazzling Costume Jewelry,* Harry N. Abrams, 1997; Deanna Farneti Cera, ed., *Jewels of Fantasy, Costume Jewelry of the 20th Century*, Harry N. Abrams, 1992; Sibylle Jargstorf, *Baubles, Buttons and Beads, The Heritage of Bohemia*, Schiffer Publishing, 1993, *Glass in Jewelry,* Schiffer Publishing, 1991 and *Glass Beads from Europe*, Schiffer Publishing, 1995; Ellie Laubner, *Fashions of the Roaring '20s, with Values*, Schiffer Publishing, 1996 (chapter on jewelry); Ginger Moro, *European Designer Jewelry*, Schiffer Publishing, 1995; Jane Mulvagh, *Costume Jewelry in Vogue,* Thames and Hudson, 1988 (out of print); Penny Proddow, Debra Healy, and Marion Fasel, *Hollywood Jewels*, Harry N. Abrams, 1992; Jody Shields, *All That Glitters, The Glory of Costume Jewelry,* Rizzoli International, 1987; Ulrike von Hase-Schmundt et al, *Theodor Fahrner Jewelry, Between Avant-Garde and Tradition*, Schiffer Publishing, 1991; Robin Walsh, "Butterfly Jewelry: New Finds of an Old Fashion," *Jewelers' Circular-Keystone/Heritage*, May, 1994.

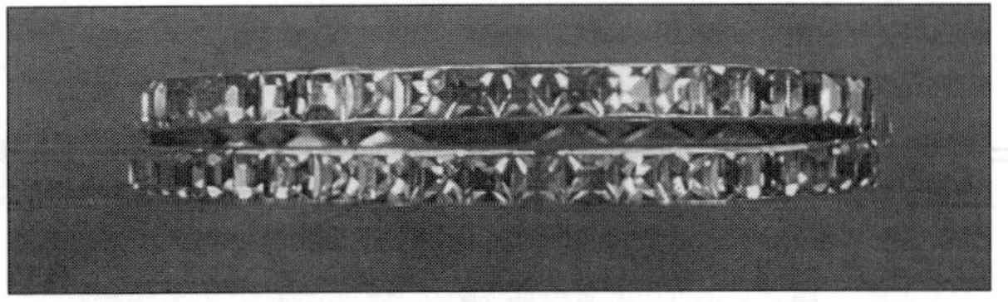

Bracelet, Bangle, hinged, sterling, rhinestones, c. 1920-25, front half a double row of colorless sq-cut r.s. channel-set in engr and pierced ster, continuing to a single back row, mkd "STERLING," v-spring and box clasp with swivel safety lock, 2-1/4" inside dia, 1/2" w, **$185**. (Leigh Leshner collection).

Periodical and Collectors' Club: *Vintage Fashion & Costume Jewelry Newsletter/ Club*, P.O. Box 265, Glen Oaks, NY 11004, published quarterly.

Museums: Glass and Costume Jewelry Museum, Jablonec and Nisou, Czech Republic; Jewelers' Museum, Providence, RI.

Reproduction Alert: The same conditions and caveats apply for costume as for fine jewelry, particularly marcasite and silver, which has been reproduced in mass quantities. Again, quality varies widely. Some British and German exports are very well-made. Wholesalers specializing in repros advertise in antiques trade papers.

Advisor: Ruth Levin Watters (butterfly wing jewelry).

Bracelet

Link

Glass, sp brass, c. 1930, eleven sq green glass cabs prong set in linked sp brass, mkd "CZECHOSLOV." on v-spring and box clasp, 1/2" w x 7" 40

Gp brass, Bakelite, glass, c. 1935, strap of circ reeded gp brass links suspending round textured brass beads linked to round green Bakelite beads with narrow conical brass terminals, turq and white glass cab on circ box clasp with v-spring, 2-1/2" w at center, 7" l 250

Rhinestones, gp brass, enamel, c. 1925-30, six stamped brass filigree oval floral motif links with collet-set red r.s. and blue enamel on sm flowerheads, enamel loss, v-spring and box clasp, 3/4" w x 7" 95

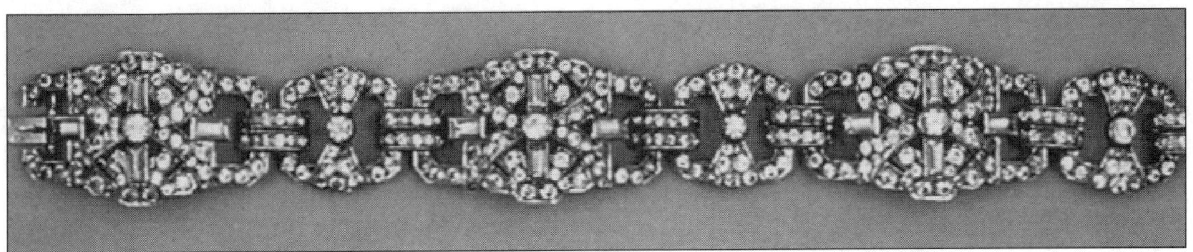

Bracelet, Link, paste, silver, gold, c. 1925, three pierced rect geo design plaques set with lg and sm colorless circ pastes and colorless baguettes alternating with sm sq open links with central bow shapes set with lg and sm colorless pastes, joined by double-rows of arcing links channel-set with sm circ colorless pastes, Fr maker's mk illegible, Fr hmk for mixed metals (conjoined boar's head and eagle's head) for silver and gold on v-spring, box clasp, 1" w x 7-1/2" tl, **$550**. (Connie Parente collection).

Bracelet, Link, gp brass, enamel, c. 1925, Egyptian Revival, six oval enameled links, each depicting a different ancient Egyptian figure or scene, shades of brown, black, blue, yellow and orange on ivory-colored ground, spring ring clasp, 5/8" w x 7", **$245**. (Charles Pinkham collection).

Bracelet, Link, brass, glass, enamel, rhinestones, c. 1935, four sq stamped filigree brass links set with lg central oval green glass cab, each flanked by two green r.s., green enameled leaves in four corners, spring ring closure, unmkd, probably Czech, 1-3/8" w x 7", **$185**. (Leigh Leshner collection).

Bracelet, Link, brass, c. 1935, central arched sections surmounting rect plaques joined by cylindrical hinges, mkd "MADE IN FRANCE," v-spring and box clasp, 1" w x 7-1/2", **$250**. (Al Munir Meghji collection).

Bracelet, Link, glass, lapis, amber, sterling, c. 1930, prong-set sq cabs of colorless glass with engr floral design, alternating with circ prong-set links of opposed semi-circ amber and lapis cabs, mkd "STERLING GERMANY," v-spring and box clasp with safety, 7/8" w x 7-3/4", **$750**. (Charles Pinkham collection).

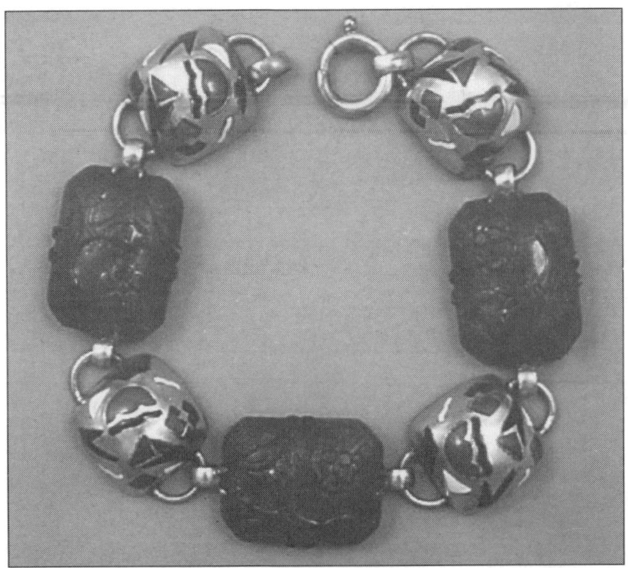

Bracelet, Link, glass, gp brass, enamel, c. 1930-35, three links of prong-set floral/foliate pattern molded green glass rect cabs alternating with four domed sq gp brass with geo design enameled in red, white and black, mkd "GERMANY" and mk M in a triangle, spring ring closure, 3/4" w x 7-1/2", **$300**. (Charles Pinkham collection).

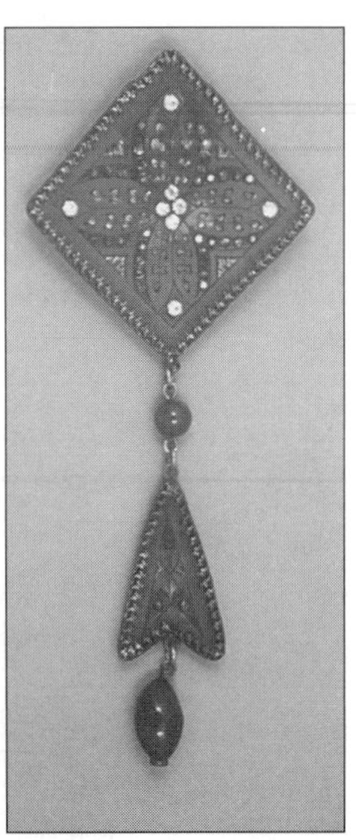

Brooch/Pin, celluloid, glass, enamel, rhinestones, c. 1925, sq turned 45 degrees, translucent amber-colored celluloid plaque in a stamped brass frame, incised, ptd and set with blue and colorless sm circ r.s., suspending a round blue glass bead, and an arrowhead-shaped celluloid plaque set with blue circ r.s. in a brass frame, terminating in an oval blue glass bead, probably Fr, C-catch, 2" w x 4-3/4", **$120**. (Diane White collection).

Silver coins, 835 silver, c. 1920, five Austro-Hungarian silver coins dated from 1896 to 1915 of one Korona denomination, bent to conform to wrist and with appl twisted wire and stamped rect plaques of foliate motif, spring ring closure, mkd "HPB 835" on jump ring, 7/8" w x 7-1/4" tl 125

"Slave," sterling, glass, enamel, c. 1925, alternating links of open rect green enamel and sq green glass cabs, reeded ster link spacers, mkd "STERLING" and "G.G.," spring ring clasp, 1/2" w x 7-1/4" 200

"Slave," sterling, glass, enamel, c. 1925, alternating links of mottled green glass rings and sq dk green glass cabs, lobster clasp, 1/2" w x 7-1/2" 200

Brooch/Pin

Brass, glass, enamel, c. 1920, Egyptian Revival, circ tubular brass frame enclosing brass wire scallops, surmounted by a circ enameled plaque with Egyptian Eye of Horus, wings flanked by two owls, and lotus blossom border, central red glass high-domed cab above a half circle of sm blue glass cabs, enameled in blue, white, green, orange and red, C-catch, tube hinge, extended pinstem, 2" dia 285

Glass, rhinestones, rh pl brass, c. 1930-35, faceted barrel-shaped colorless glass prong-set in center flanked by faceted colorless glass triangles, a row of five faceted colorless lozenges above and below in geo design, bordered with circ and sq r.s., safety catch, 3-3/8" w x 2-3/8" 125

Glass, sterling, Eng., c. 1925, circ shape, rev-painted glass cover over butterfly wing depicting lady in Georgian (18th century) dress, trees and shrubs in bg, ropetwist ster frame, rev stamped "MADE IN ENGLAND STERLING SILVER PT 220213," (1923) C-catch, tube hinge, 1-1/2" dia 65

Glass, rh pl wm, c. 1930, two disks, each with an angled cylinder and semi-circ lt brown glass bezel-set cab and bead details flanking a central circ disk of half glass cab and half wm dome, mkd "CZECHOSLOVAKIA" on rev, 1-1/2" w x 1/2" 75

Brooch/Pin, butterfly wings, paint, glass, sterling, Eng, c. 1925, rect ptd scene of sailboats in the lagoon at Venice, in shades of yellow, orange, blue, white, black, and brown, on a bg of iridescent blue butterfly wing, bezel-set in a beaded ster frame and backing mkd "STERLING SILVER ENGLAND PAT 202213," (1923). C-catch, flanged hinge, 1-1/2" w x 1", **$85**. (Patrick Kapty collection).

Brooch/Pin, butterfly wings, paint, glass, sterling, Eng, c. 1920-25, rounded rect shape with white sulphide (bas-relief clay figure). of Cupid and Psyche in colorless glass with irid blue butterfly wing ground, beaded-edge frame mkd "ENGLAND STERLING," C-catch, tube hinge, 7/8" w x 1", **$125**. (Elaine Sarnoff collection).

Marcasites, sterling, pearls, c. 1935, open quatrefoil frame enclosing central floral and foliate motif, bead-set throughout with marcasites, three grad split cultured pearls set off-center, rev mkd "0.925" in a rectangle, safety catch, 2-1/2" w x 1-3/4" 165

Rhinestones, rh pl wm, c. 1935, lg colorless r.s. ribbon-tied floral spray, lg central circ flowerhead with lg circ r.s. center and sm colorless r.s. encircled by lg pear-shaped and emerald-cut r.s., flanked by pear-shaped r.s-set sprays and lg sq r.s.-set leaves, 2-7/8" w x 5" 475

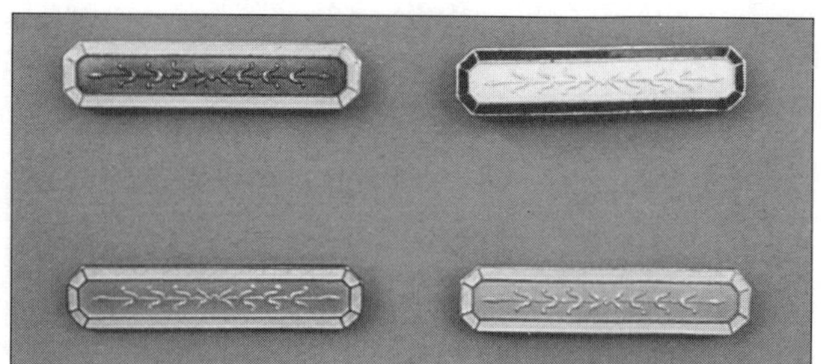

Bar Brooches/Pins, sterling, enamel, c. 1920:
Four rect bars with beveled corners, foliate design under *basse-taille* enamel.
TL, purple center with white border;
TR, white center with black border;
BL, pink center with white border;
BR, blue center with white border, all mkd "STERLING," 2" w x 1/2", each, **$30**. (Sue James collection).

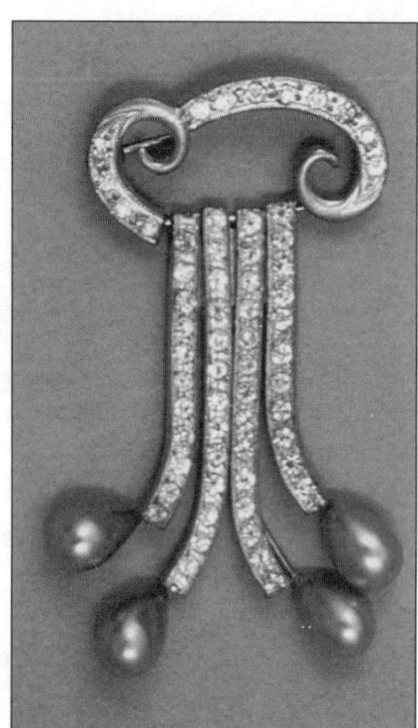

Brooch/Pin, rhinestones, wax pearls, rh pl wm, c. 1925-30, scrolling openwork oval set with sm circ colorless r.s. connected to a wire rod suspending four free-swinging curved bars set with sm circ colorless r.s. each with a lg "wax" faux pearl terminal, 1-5/8" w x 3", **$75**. (Diane White collection).

Rhinestones, ptd enamel, rh pl wm, c. 1935, in the shape of a flamingo with one leg raised, pavé colorless r.s. with red r.s. eye, black and white enameled wings, black feet, yellow and black beak, 1-3/4" w x 2-3/4" 125

Rhinestones, rh pl wm, c, 1935, in the shape of a stylized fuchsia, pavé colorless r.s. throughout, pierced petals, baguette-tipped wire stamens, safety catch, 2-3/8" w x 3-1/4" 175

Rhinestones, rh pl wm, c. 1925-30, chamfered corner rect geo pierced plaque flanked by omega-shaped buckle motifs with baguette r.s. centers, three central lg marquise-cut colorless r.s. and sm circ colorless r.s. throughout, safety catch, 3-1/4" w x 1" 75

Rhinestones, rh pl wm, c. 1925-30, circ dome of alternating blue and white r.s. bands, attached geo shape with framed "fountain" in colorless r.s., later-added safety catch, 3" w x 1-1/2" 155

Rhinestones, rh pl wm, c. 1930, lg and sm colorless r.s. in closely-set flowerheads forming triangle, mkd "DOCTOR DRESS," bead broken off at base, safety catch, 2-1/2" w x 2-1/2 150

Rhinestones, rh pl wm, c. 1930, bow-shaped, lg oval and sm circ colorless r.s. prong-set within a wire frame, mkd "CZECHO" on rev, safety catch, 2-1/2" w x 1-1/2" 120

Rhinestones, rh pl wm, c. 1930-35, depicting a bird of paradise on a branch pavé-set with sm colorless r.s, red r.s. eye, safety catch, 2-1/8" w x 3-1/8" 185

Rhinestones, rh pl wm, c. 1930-35, six-petaled flowerhead with lg central colorless r.s. and pavé r.s. petals surmounting two curving lines of sm r.s. with lg r.s. terminals, mkd "CZECHOSLOVAKIA" and unknown maker's mk, safety catch, 2-7/8" w x 1-3/4" 45

Bar Brooch/Pin, Egyptian Revival, silver gilt, enamel, date letter for 1925, pharaoh's head in profile flanked by wings in green, orange and white *plique à jour* enamel, Egyptian hmks, date letter "A" on pinstem, rev mkd "800" # 5, 2" w x 5/8", **$250**. (Sue James collection).

Bar Brooch/Pin, Egyptian Revival, c. 1925, gp brass, scarab, rhinestones, genuine scarab beetle prong-set in the center of an opposed pr of falcon wings and birds' heads with green r.s. eyes, rev mkd "MADE IN FRANCE," safety-pin catch, 2-7/8" w x 3/4", **$125**. (Author's collection).

Brooch/Pin, silver, marcasites, red stones, c. 1935, in the shape of a Chinese dragon set throughout with marcasites, red faceted stone eyes, unmkd, 4-3/4" w x 1-5/8", **$375**. (Claudette Beaulieu collection).

Brooch/Pin, rhinestones, rh pl wm, ptd enamel, c. 1935, depicting a peacock with scrolled tailfeathers, two rows of lg marquise-cut colorless r.s., two rows of sm colorless r.s., and wm wire terminating in lg pink, blue, yellow and green r.s., body in sm colorless pavé r.s., blue r.s. eye, traces of enamel on feet and crest, safety catch, 2-1/8" w x 3-3/4", **$225**. (Leigh Leshner collection).

Rhinestones, rh pl wm, c. 1935, pavé colorless r.s. lg and sm tulips with leaves, 3-3/8" w x 2" 145

Rhinestones, rh pl wm, c. 1935, pavé colorless r.s. rose with leaves and stem, 2-1/8" w x 3-1/8" 165

Rhinestones, rh pl wm, Lucite, c. 1935-40, lg flowerhead with central lg burgundy-colored moonstone-effect Lucite cab encircled by nine smaller cabs and pavé colorless r.s., surmounting scrolled and figure-8 colorless r.s.-set stylized stems and leaves, safety catch, 2-1/8" w x 4-3/4" 175

Rhinestones, wm, c. 1935, pavé colorless r.s. bird with outstretched wings and tail feathers, red r.s. eye, safety catch, 3-1/8" w x 3-1/4" 135

Rhinestones, wm, c. 1935, pavé-set colorless circ and baguette r.s. in an open geo plaque with opposing "arrows" on each end flanking two rounded bars in center, safety catch, 3-1/2" w x 1-5/8" 135

Rhinestones, wm, c. 1935, colorless r.s. bow, lg oval r.s. center flanked by four loops set with grad oval and cushion-shaped r.s. outlined by sm circ-cut r.s. borders, safety catch, 3-1/2" w x 2" 235

Bar

Rhinestones, rh pl brass, c. 1920, narrow pierced bow shape with central floral cluster of sm colorless r.s., flanked by triangles with comma-shaped cut-outs and colorless sm r.s., pavé r.s. borders, safety catch, 2" w x 1/2" 95

Brooch/Pin, glass, rhinestones, wm, c. 1935, circ and baguette colorless r.s. crown, baguette links suspending pierced heart-shaped pendant with central green glass cab and green glass marquise at top, set throughout with colorless r.s., mkd "AJ," safety catch, 1-3/8" w x 2-1/8", **$175**. (Leigh Leshner collection).

Brooches/Pins, "tremblers," rhinestones, rh pl wm, c. 1930-35:

L, tulip with green ptd enamel leaves, brown ptd enamel stem, pavé colorless r.s. blossom with green baguette r.s. stamens *en tremblant*, 1-1/2" w x 3", **$125**.

C, floral and foliate motif with central flowerhead *en tremblant*, lg green r.s. center encircled by sm green r.s., sm colorless r.s. pavé-set throughout, safety catch, 2" w x 1-1/4", **$45**.

R, floral spray with three flowerheads *en tremblant*, lg green r.s. centers with sm colorless r.s.-set petals and leaves, 2-1/4" w x 2-3/4", **$85**.

(Diane White collection).

Silver gilt, Egyptian Revival, c 1925, postage stamps, glass, enamel, horizontal row of three overlapping glazed red, green and blue Egyptian postage stamps turned at an angle, lotus blossom terminals enameled in red, green and blue, mkd "800," C-catch, tube hinge, 2-1/8" w x 3/4" 125

Earrings, pendent

Brass, glass, c. 1925, Egyptian Revival, pharaoh's head surmounts suspending crescent moon-shaped drops of stamped openwork brass surmounted by red glass beads, screwbacks, 1/2" w x 1-1/2" tl, pr 95

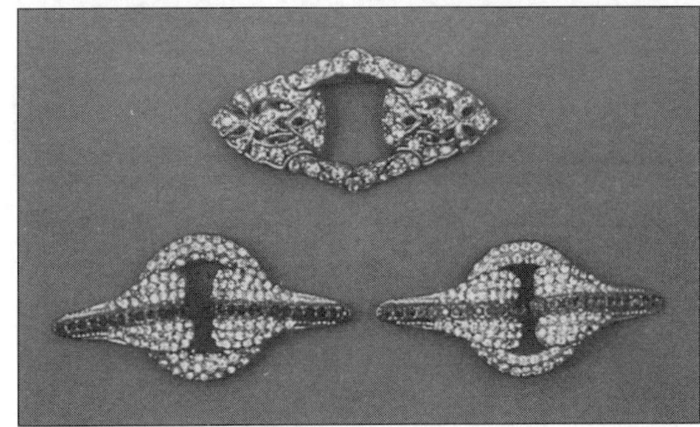

Double Clip Brooches, rhinestones, rh pl wm, c. 1935:

TC, lozenge-shaped, open center flanked by triangular pierced plaques, sm colorless r.s. throughout, flat-backed hinged clips mkd "Pat 1852188" (1932), removable pin back mechanism, 2-1/2" w x 1-1/4 joined, **$95**.

BL, two tapered triangles, each with a row of green r.s. down the center, flat-backed hinged clips enclosing a ring with soldered loops on rev for sew-on attachment, pavé-set colorless r.s. throughout, 2-5/8" w x 1-1/4" joined, **$135**.

BR, two tapered triangles, each with a row of red r.s. down the center, flat-backed hinged clips enclosing ring, colorless r.s. pavé-set throughout, 2-1/2" w x 1" joined, **$125**.

(Sue James collection).

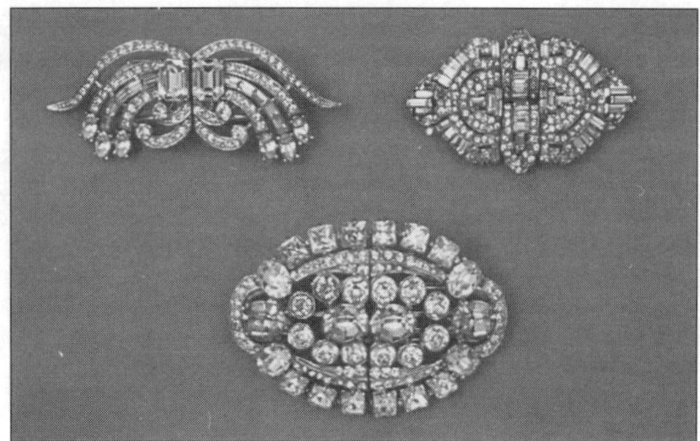

Double Clip Brooches, rhinestones, rh pl wm, c. 1935:

TL, colorless r.s. floral scroll design with two lg central cushion-shaped r.s. flanked by curv rows of sm r.s., three with marquise r.s. terminals, center row of baguette r.s., paired C-scrolls at the base, flat-backed hinged clips with removable sliding pin back mechanism on rev, 3" w x 1-1/4" joined, **$95**.

TR, geo design of colorless baguette and sm circ r.s., removable pin back assembly, converts into two dress clips with flat-backed hinged clips and a pair of clip earrings, 2-1/2" w x 1-1/2" joined, **$125**.

B, pierced geo design, colorless r.s., an outer row of sq r.s. leading to cushion shapes at terminals, surrounding an inner row of circ r.s. and two lg oval r.s., sm r.s. details, appl oval plaque mkd "JOSEPH WIESNER NY" on rev, flat-backed hinged clips with removable sliding pin back assembly for wear as a brooch, 3" w x 2" joined, **$165**.

(Sue James collection).

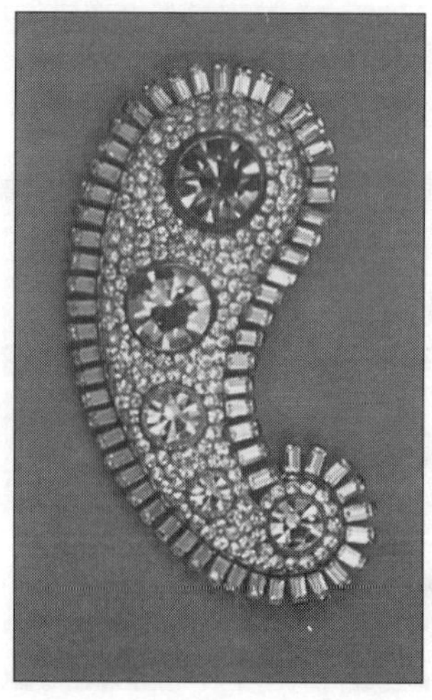

Dress Clip, rhinestones, rh pl wm, c. 1930, *boteh* (paisley) shape with five bezel-set lg colorless r.s. in field of sm pavé-set colorless r.s., border of baguette r.s., flat-backed hinged wm clip on rev, 1-1/4" w x 3", **$180**. (Leigh Leshner collection).

Glass, rhinestones, sp brass, c. 1925, sm circ bezel-set green r.s. surmount suspending a fan-shaped stamped sp brass section with green and colorless r.s. linked to a scalloped pierced oval plaque of scroll and fleur-de-lis motif set with sm circ green and colorless r.s., further suspending a lg shield-shaped pierced plaque set with sm circ green and colorless r.s. terminating in a lg sq-cut green glass bezel-set stone, screwbacks, 5/8" w x 3-5/8" tl, pr 275

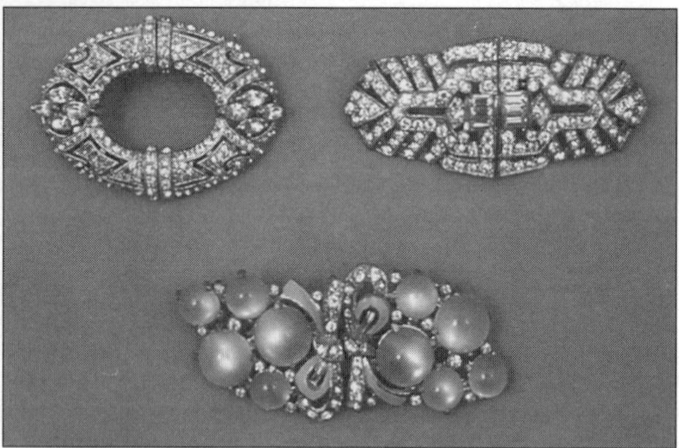

Double Clip Brooches, Coro Duettes, rhinestones, rh pl wm, c. 1932-37:

TL, openwork annular oval with clusters of marquise-shaped colorless r.s. at each end, set throughout with sm colorless r.s., pierced geo design, flat-backed hinged clips mkd "Coro Duette," detachable pin back mechanism mkd "Coro Duette, Pat No 1798867" (1931), 2" w x 1-1/2" joined, **$170**.

TR, openwork geo design, stepped rect shape with cusped ends, central semi-cylinder of colorless r.s. baguettes, sm colorless r.s. throughout, detachable pin back mechanism mkd "Coro Duette Pat No 1798867" (1931), flat-backed hinged clips mkd "Pat No 1852188" (1932), 2-1/2" w x 1-1/8" joined, **$170**.

BC, Lucite, ptd enamel, floral and bow design with lg circ pastel pink cabs of Lucite (DuPont trade name for acrylic introduced in 1937), ptd pink enamel on the bows, and sm colorless r.s. accents, detachable pin back mechanism mkd "Coro Duette" and "Pat No 1798867" (1931), flat-backed hinged clips mkd "Pat No 1852188" (1932), 2-3/4" w x 1-3/8" joined, **$145**.

(Diane White collection).

Pendent Earrings, sterling, marcasites, glass, faux pearls, c. 1920-25, sm triangular surmount with bead-set marcasites suspending an articulated shank of navette-shaped links, each centering a sq with bead-set marcasites, linked to an annular marcasite-set drop surmounted by an arc set with calibré-cut green glass, and bisected by a vertical marcasite-set bar terminating in a lg faux pearl drop, screwbacks, mkd "GERMANY STERLING," 3/4" w x 2-3/4" tl, pr, **$350**. (Connie Parente collection).

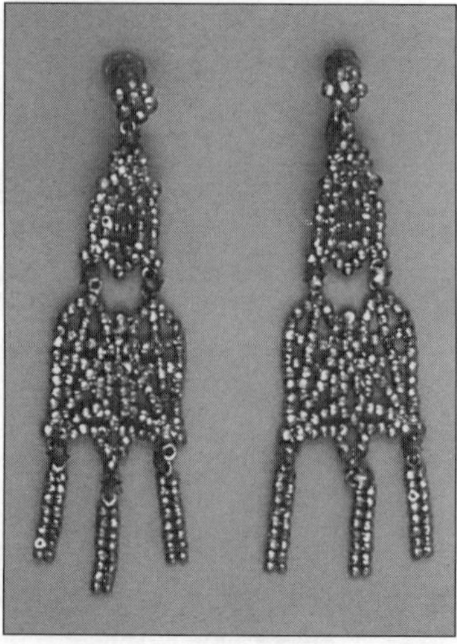

Pendent Earrings, cut steel, c. 1925, circ flowerhead surmount suspending shield-shaped open plaque further suspending lobed rect open plaque and a fringe of three rect drops, riveted throughout with sm faceted cut steel studs, screwbacks, mkd "MADE IN FRANCE" on rev of surmount, 7/8" w x 3" tl, pr, **$400**. (Connie Parente collection).

Pendent Earrings, brass, glass, c. 1925, faceted blue glass briolettes suspended from cable link and bead brass chain and bezel-set blue r.s. surmount, screwbacks, 1/2" w x 2" tl, pr, **$65**. (Sue James collection).

Pendent Earrings, rh pl sterling, rhinestones, c. 1925-30, lg and sm circ colorless collet-set r.s. surmount suspending a line of three sm circ r.s. linked to a r.s.-set scallop-edged open triangle and annular drop with blue r.s. baguette and sm circ colorless r.s. center, screwbacks mkd "GERMANY STERLING," 1/2" w x 1-7/8" tl, pr, **$175**. (Connie Parente collection).

Necklace

Glass, gp brass, c. 1925, central shield-shaped pink and white glass cab flanked by gp brass links each set with two marquise-shaped prong-set pink and white glass stones, spring ring clasp, mkd "CZECHO" on rev of central element, 7/8" w (at center), 15" tl 95

Glass, gp brass, c. 1925, geo stepped blue glass prong-set in gp brass links, spring ring clasp, mkd "CZECHO" on jump ring, 1/2" w x 16" tl 75

Glass, sp brass, c. 1920, central plaque of die-stamped metal leaves set with one lg and three sm purple r.s., continuing to links of stamped filigree metal plaques alternating with purple barbell-shaped glass beads, unmkd, probably Czech, 18" tl x 1" at center plaque 75

Glass, gp brass, beetles, paint, c. 1925, Egyptian Revival, central plaque centering a ptd faux scarab flanked by patinated gp brass wings, suspending two irregular oval green glass beads, further suspending a shield-shaped gp brass plaque centering a prong-set iridescent beetle framed by inverted lotus motifs at sides and bottom, terminating in a green glass bead drop, flanked by beads leading to smaller winged plaques centering beetles and suspending beads, continuing to a chain of beads alternating with circ links, spring ring closure, 4" top to bottom at center, 19" tl .... 546 (A)

Gp brass, glass, c. 1925, stamped geo design plaque with central rect prong-set pink glass, flanked by stepped geo design plaques, continuing to fine link chain, spring ring closure, 1/2" w (at center), 16-1/2" tl 65

Bead

Glass, gp brass, c. 1930, central lg elliptical rust-colored glass bead with stamped gp brass filigree caps, linked to a chain of sm molded rust-colored glass beads in floral, foliate, round and tube shapes, alternating with stamped round gp brass beads, foldover box clasp, probably Czech, 5/8" w (at center), 18" tl 85

Choker

Sp brass, enamel, c. 1920, snakeskin motif with black and white enamel on mesh, mkd "GERMANY DRGM" (*Deutsches Reich Geschmack Muster*, a design patent protection designation), v-spring and box clasp, 1/2" w x 13" tl 175

Sautoir

Glass, brass, enamel, c. 1925, oval, elliptical and sm round orange glass beads with brass links suspending a pendant of stamped gp brass trefoil set with sm orange glass cabs and green enamel paisleys, surmounting a molded horseshoe-shaped glass plaque, a fringe of beaded drops at the base, two outer drops terminating in multiple bugle beads, mkd "CZECHOSLOVAKIA" on attached plate on rev, spring ring closure, 18" tl, pendant 1-5/8" w x 4" tl 185

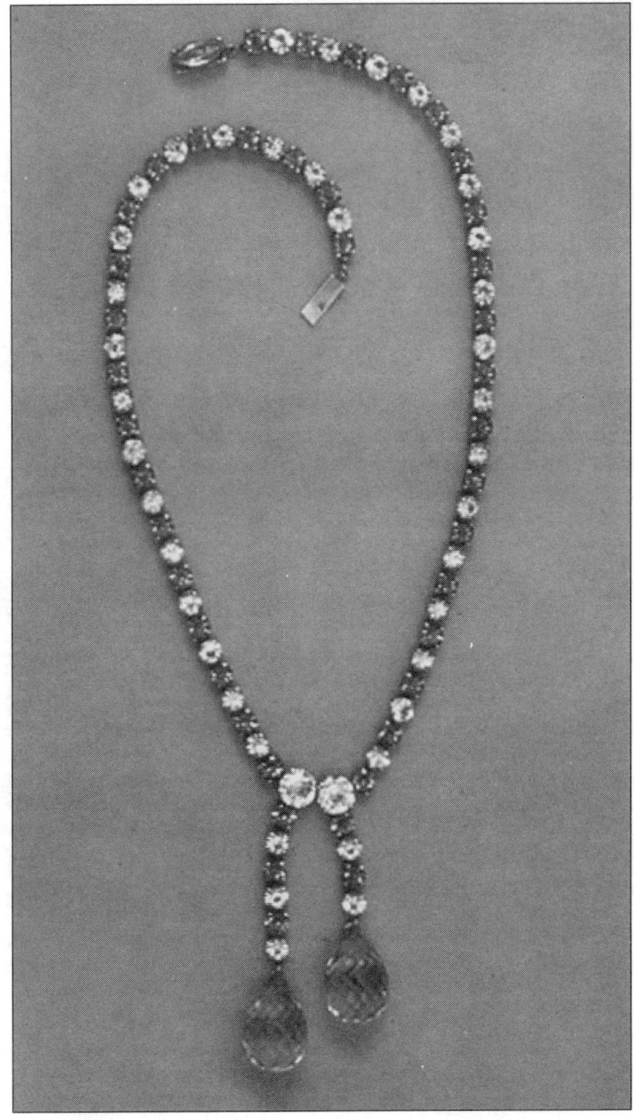

Necklace, rhinestones, sterling, glass, c. 1920, single line necklace of alternating blue and colorless r.s., two central lg colorless r.s. suspending *négligée* drops of blue and white r.s. terminating in lg faceted blue glass briolettes, mkd "STERLING," v-spring and box clasp, 15-1/2" tl, 2-1/2" drops, **$145**. (Leigh Leshner collection).

Necklace, gp brass, enamel, faux seed pearls, c. 1920, three circ stamped and pierced gp brass filigree plaques, beaded scroll and foliate design with central faux pearl surrounded by circ lt green enameled "cabs" and dk green enamel, suspending a similarly decorated triangular drop and flanked by similar rect and oval plaques, continuing to a flat link chain and spring ring closure, unmkd, possibly Czech, 2-1/2" w (at center), 18" tl, **$250**. (Terrance O'Halloran collection).

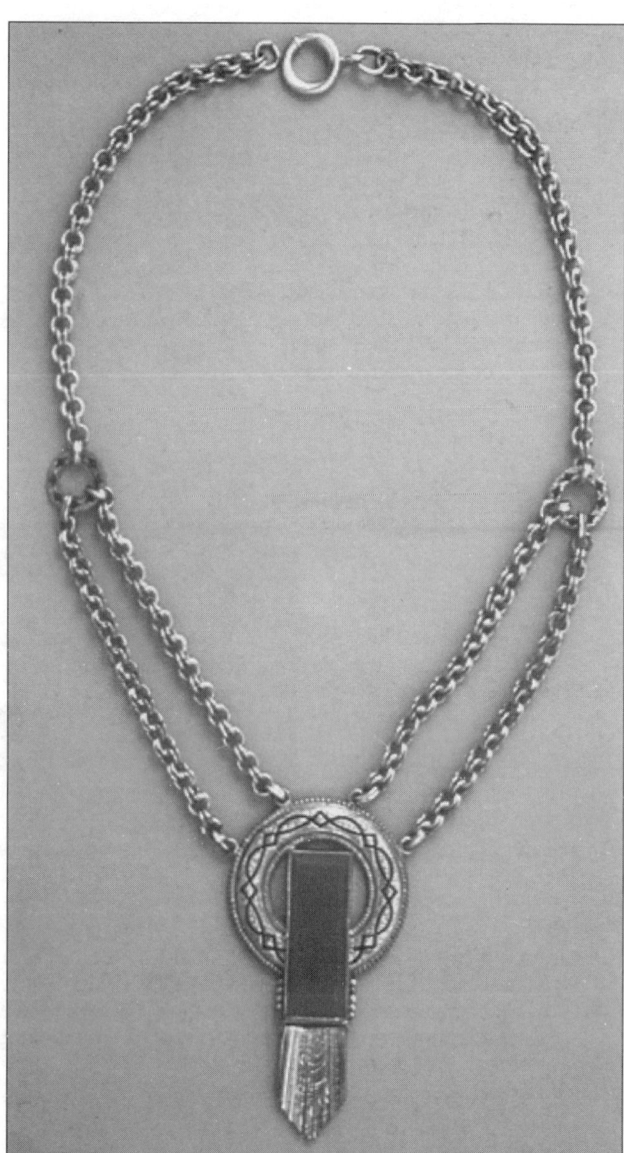

Necklace, brass, glass, c. 1930, bezel-set central rectangle of carnelian-colored glass surmounting stamped brass annular center decorated with black enamel, terminating in brass fringe, suspended from double chain to enameled circ links halfway, single chain to spring ring closure, 16-1/2" tl, 1-1/2" w x 2-3/4" at center, **$95**. (Leigh Leshner collection).

Necklace, sp brass, enamel, c. 1925-30, thirteen stepped triangular linked plaques, five larger flanked by eight smaller, purple, green and black *basse-taille* enameled geo design, mkd "Czechoslovakia" on spring ring , center link 1-1/2" w x 7/8", 16" tl, **$295**. (Charles Pinkham collection).

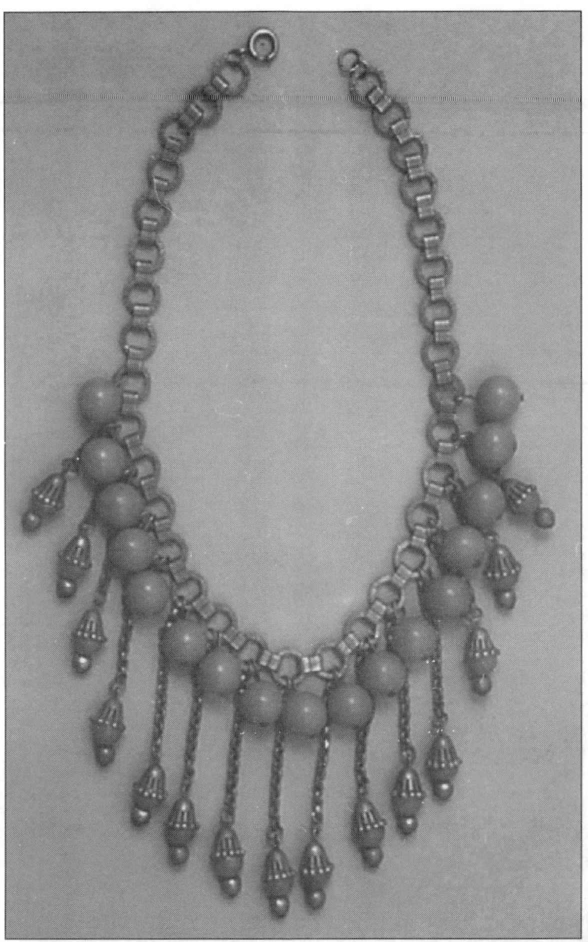

Necklace, Bib, brass, plastic, c. 1935, circ link chain suspending seventeen round red plastic beads alternating with grad fringe of brass chain each terminating in sm red plastic beads with stamped brass caps and brass bead terminals, spring ring closure, 3" w (at center), 16" tl, **$125**. (Sue James collection).

Necklace, glass, rh pl silver, c. 1925, necklace of alternating spiral fluted ellipsoid yellow glass beads and framed faceted rect prong-set yellow glass, suspending a lg faceted oval yellow glass pendant with etched rose motif intaglio in table, prong-set in silver frame, mkd "MADE IN FRANCE" and Fr hmk (boar's head for 800 silver) on jump ring and pendant frame rev, spring ring closure, necklace 1/2" w x 34" tl, pendant 1-3/4" w x 2-1/2", **$500**.

Necklace, glass, brass, c. 1930-40, Ital mosaic, center drop a sq turned forty-five degrees flanked by eight circ, pear-, and heart-shaped drops, set in brass, *tesserae* in shades of blue, green, red, pink and white, suspended from sm circ linked plaques continuing to a foxtail chain, 16" tl x 1-3/8" at center, **$125**. (Elaine Sarnoff collection).

Necklace, Sautoir, glass, gp brass, c. 1920, chain of lg and sm amber-colored glass beads with four die-stamped yellow enameled fan-shaped spacers, suspending a die-stamped enameled pendant with knotted bow motif top and foliate motif conical bottom set with amber-colored r.s., terminating in a large amber-colored glass cab, unmkd, probably Czech, 33" tl, drop 1" w x 3-1/2", **$150**. (Sandra Willard collection).

Necklaces, brass, glass, Egyptian Revival, c. 1925:

L, stamped oval brass rose motif plaque bezel-set with a lg molded red glass scarab, suspended from strand of sm irregular red glass beads and seed beads alternating with molded glass scarab beads, unmkd, probably Czech, plaque 1-5/8" w x 2-1/2", 23" tl, **$125**.

R, sautoir, rect plaque of stamped brass lotus design set with white molded glass pharaoh's head, suspending a molded green glass scarab from a short chain, suspended from two lengths of curb link chain interspersed with molded green glass scarabs, sm oblate and lg elliptical black and green glass beads and twisted brass wire beads, spring ring closure, rev mkd "FN Co." for Fishel Nessler Co, New York, NY, and "CZECHOSLOVAKIA" on jump ring, pendant 1-1/4" w x 2-3/4" tl, 36" tl, **$95**.

(Sue James collection).

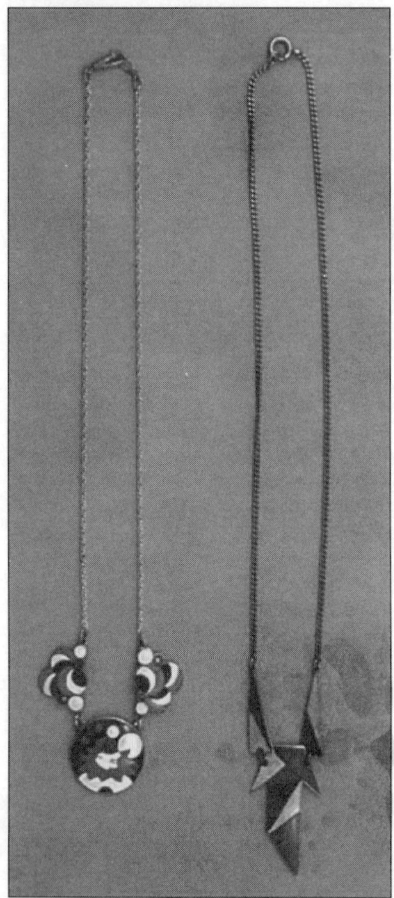

Pendants and Chains, sterling, enamel, Am, c. 1925:

L, central disk of a harlequin enameled in shades of black, yellow, orange, and green flanked by "bubbles" motif plaques in similar shades, mkd "STERLING" on each plaque, suspended from two lengths of curb link chain, spring hook closure, 7/8" w (at center), 15" tl, **$125**.

(Dawn Lowe collection).

R, three linked geo plaques, triangle motif in blue and green enamel suspended from two lengths of curb link chain, mkd "STERLING" with maker's mk for F.A. Hermann Co., Melrose Highlands MA (an "H" in a triangle), spring ring closure, 16" tl, 1-1/2" w at center, **$125**.

(Charles Pinkham collection).

Pendant, silver, marcasites, glass, c. 1920, openwork quatrefoil, circ-cut pink glass center stone, four green glass stones at compass points, set throughout with grad marcasites, Fr hmk (boar's head) for 800 silver, maker' mk in a lozenge imp on rev, 2" w x 2-1/2" tl, **$250**. (Julia Alberts collection).

Sautoir, glass, gp brass, enamel, r.s., c. 1925, chain of alternating fine brass link and elliptical and round yellow glass beads suspending a stamped and enameled trefoil set with one yellow r.s., further suspending a larger rect stamped gp brass pendant with central lg yellow glass cab held by stamped filigree prongs, yellow r.s. at four compass points, blue and green enameled floral and foliate motifs, three drops at bottom, center drop a stamped and enameled cusped triangle, two side drops of round and pear-shaped glass beads, mkd "Czechoslovakia" on rev, 24-3/4" tl, pendant 1" w x 3-1/2" tl 245

Pendant

935 silver, enamel, glass, c. 1925, lt and med blue matte enameled plaque, rounded top, stepped and cusped base, geo design of lines and curves accentuated by corded wire, prong-set elongated oval faceted black glass in the center, stamped wire bail, appl sm plaque on rev imp "935," maker's mk for Theodor Fahrner, Pforzheim (Ger), 1/2" w x 1-7/8" tl 250

Pendant and Chain

Glass, rhinestones, sp brass, c. 1925, central rect bezel-set green glass stone set *à jour* suspending two baguette r.s. drops, surmounted by geo and foliate design with sm colorless r.s. accents and two baguette r.s. suspended from elongated oval link chain, sliding hook clasp, 17" tl, pendant 7/8" w x 2" 115

Gp brass, glass, enamel, rhinestones, c. 1920, sawtooth bezel-set faceted oval amber-colored glass in a stamped cusped and lobed pierced gp plaque with appl sm yellow enameled leaves interspersed with sm circ collet-set faceted amber-colored r.s., suspended from a trace and cable link chain, unmkd, probably Czech, spring ring clasp, 1-1/2" w x 2-1/4", 18" tl 100

Rhinestones, glass, rh pl base metal, c. 1925, rounded rect hinged plaque tapering at top to point, set throughout with sm colorless r.s., lg green faceted oval glass stone set *à jour* at base encircled by colorless r.s., suspended from elongated oval trace chain, 15" tl, pendant 1/2" w x 1-7/8" 65

Rhinestones, wm, c. 1930, single articulated row of colorless r.s. forming an "X" within an open circle of colorless r.s., continuing to uneven terminals, chain and spring ring, mkd "CZECHOSLOVAKIA" on rev plate, 16" tl, pendant 1-3/8" w x 2-5/8" 85

Silver, glass, c. 1920, Egyptian Revival, two opposed vulture heads surmounting an oval bezel-set iridescent art glass scarab flanked by silver wings, suspending a baroque f.w. pearl in a wire cage, suspended from two lengths of cable link chain, 1-3/8" w x 1-3/4", 15" tl 350

Sterling, dyed green chalcedony, c. 1925, bow-shaped ster plaque prong-set with two semi-cylindrical dyed green chalcedony cabs, suspended from sm kite-shaped ster plaques and two lengths of trace chain, mkd "STERLING" on rev and "GERMANY" on spring ring, plaque 1-1/2" w x 5/8", chain 17" tl 100

Pendant/Necklace

Chrome pl wm, Bakelite, c. 1930, central pendant of tapered sq blue Bakelite flanked by stepped chrome pl wm rings, flanked by tapered rect blue bakelite links continuing to tubular chrome pl wm links leading to spring ring, jump ring mkd "GERMANY," 1" (at center), 16" tl 200

Pendant and Chain, silver, marcasites, enamel, amazonite, c. 1927, slightly domed sq plaque, black matte enamel ground, meandering abstract design in appl corded wire, interspersed with marcasites in sm triangles, suspending a grad wire fringe, surmounted by a semi-circ plaque bezel-set with a sq amazonite cab flanked by beading, suspended from an inverted teardrop-shaped marcasite-set enameled bail mkd "935," maker's mk for Theodor Fahrner, Pforzheim (Ger.), 3/4" w x 2-1/2" tl, double fetter and trace link chain mkd "800," 26" tl, **$450**. (Author's collection).

Pendant/Necklace, glass, sp brass, c. 1925-30, navette-shaped pendant with central concave/convex-sided rect green and black glass cab molded to resemble snakeskin, flanked by stamped sp brass snake heads, four sm turquoise-colored glass cabs top and bottom, faux opal glass cabs in ropetwist frames above and below, mounted on a stamped sp brass plaque, triangular bail, suspended from a hollow round mesh chain with snake head terminals, mkd "CZECHOSLOVAKIA" on rev of pendant, 28" tl, pendant 1-1/8" w x 2-1/4", **$300**. (Leigh Leshner collection).

Pendant/Necklace, chalcedony, marcasites, sterling, c. 1925-30, rect cutout plaque set with sq and rect black and blue dyed chalcedony cabs, pierced marcasite-set palmette motifs in opposing corners, bead-set marcasites in vertical parallel rows and in a stepped frame from the sides to the bail, suspended from a marcasite-set chain of linked rect shapes with opposed triangular ends, mkd "STERLING GERMANY," spring ring closure, pendant 1" w x 2-1/8" from bail, chain 15" tl, **$600**. (Elayne Glotzer collection).

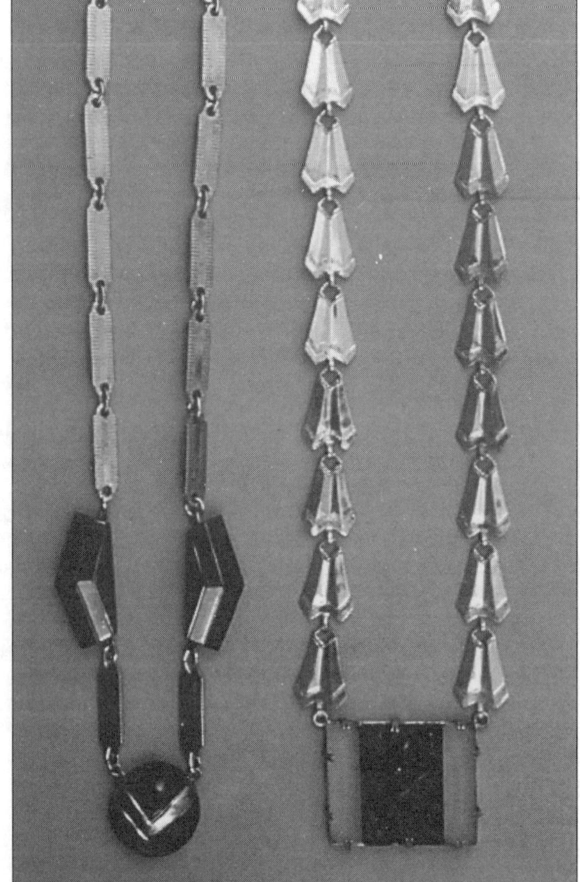

Pendants/Necklaces, glass, wm, c. 1930:

L, central circ glass dome with molded and ptd silver V shape, flanked by two grooved rect links and two chevron-shaped glass links with ptd silver geo design, "*Deposé*" molded into rev, continuing to a chain of grooved rect links and spring ring closure, 3/4" w (at center), 17" tl, **$145.**

R, rect molded black glass in geo design flanked by cylindrical frosted glass cabs, prong-set in wm, suspended from chain of indented triangular flat wm links, spring ring mkd "GERMANY," 1-1/4" w x 1", 16" tl, **$175**. (Sue James collection).

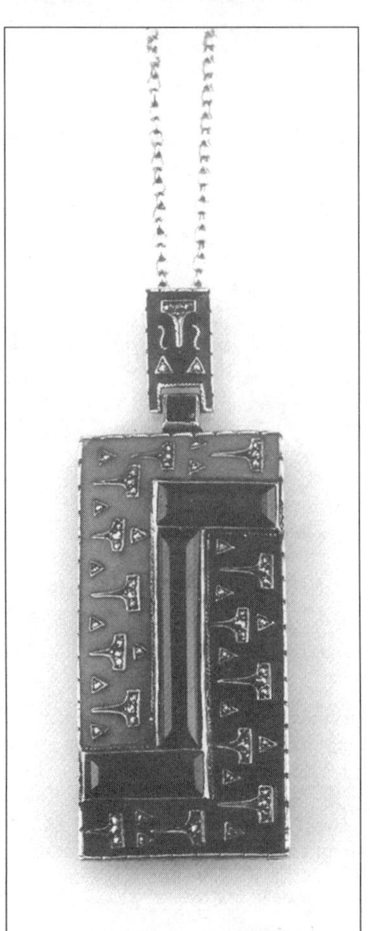

Pendant/Brooch and Chain, 935 silver, onyx, marcasites, enamel, c. 1929, rect shape of opposed L-shaped sections of matte red and black enamel inlaid with sm triangles and larger tapered T-shapes set with marcasites, separated by three rect step-cut bezel-set black onyx bars, surmounted by a sm sq bezel-set black onyx framed by a rect bail of similarly designed black enamel and marcasites, maker's mk for Theodor Fahrner, Pforzheim, Germany, 1-1/8" w x 3" tl, on a trace link silver chain, 20" tl, **$3,105** [A]. (Photo courtesy of Skinner, Inc., Boston, MA, 9/23/97).

Rings, sterling, c. 1925-30:
L, stepped oval shape set with two rows of marcasites concentrically encircling an oval prong-set dyed green chalcedony cab, mkd "STERLING," size 6-1/2, top 7/8" w x 1", **$125**.
R, enamel, elliptical plaque with radiating engr design under green *basse-taille* enamel, white enamel border, mounted on a narrow shank, size 6-1/2, top 1/2" w x 1-1/8", **$75**. (Sue James collection).

Chrome plated wm, Bakelite, c. 1930, rect geo motif plaque surmounting a black Bakelite disk with appl chrome pl wm dome, flanked by two triangular links continuing to box link chain, spring ring clasp mkd "GERMANY," 1-5/8" l, 17" tl 225

Ring

Butterfly wing, sterling, glass, paint, c. 1920-25, circ plaque, ptd tropical sunset scene, butterfly wing ground, domed glass cover, flat back mkd "Hoffman Sterling," mounted on a narrow shank, 1/2", approx size 7 45

Glass, brass, c. 1925-30, rect molded blue glass with ptd green details, a pharaoh's head in relief surrounded by imp hieroglyphic symbols, prong set in hammered textured brass, adjustable shank, probably Czech, 5/8" w x 3/4" 25

Suite: Pendant and Chain, Brooch/Pin

Silver, black onyx, coral, marcasites, c. 1925, pendant a geo stepped rectangle, three sq coral cabs vertically spaced down center flanked by two elongated rect-cut onyx bars, set throughout with marcasites, suspended from marcasite-set bail and 32" beaded scroll motif chain, matching brooch with a horizontal row of three sq coral cabs turned 45 degrees, two marcasites between each, flanked by rect onyx bars top and bottom, two half-cylinders of marcasite-set silver at sides terminating in two diagonally opposed prong-set faceted onyx squares, mkd "TF" for Theodor Fahrner, Pforzheim (Ger), pendant 7/8" w x 2-1/2" tl, brooch 2-1/4" w x 1-1/4", suite .... 4,025 (A)

Suite: Necklace and Pendent Earrings, Rock crystal quartz, sterling, marcasites, c. 1920, fifteen round rock crystal quartz beads in ster wire rings, interspersed along two grad lengths of ster cable and twisted trace chain, spring ring clasp, 38" tl, matching pendent earrings, each a single quartz bead suspended from articulated marcasite-set shank, screwbacks marked "STERLING, Germany," 1-7/8" tl, **$200**. (Paula Straub collection).

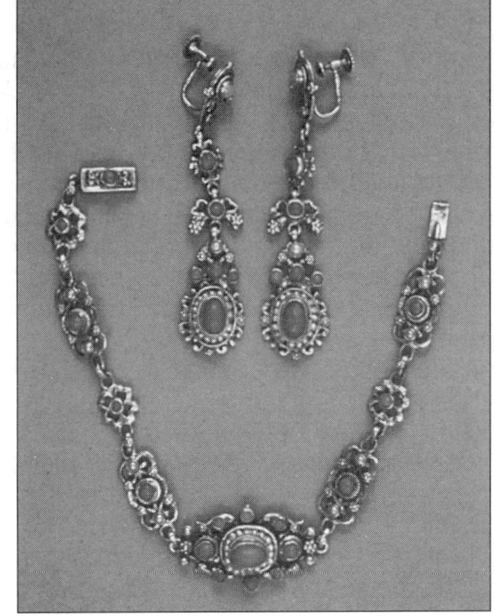

Suite: Link Bracelet and Pendent Earrings, 800 silver gilt, coral, seed pearls, c. 1925, central pierced scrolled plaque, a bezel-set oval coral cab encircled by seed pearls within a gilt frame surrounded by sm circ coral cabs and seed pearls interspersed with gilt flowerheads, continuing to alternating pierced lobed and quatrefoil links set with sm coral cabs and seed pearls, v-spring and box clasp mkd with Hungarian hmks (dog's head, "3 P" in a coffin-shaped reserve) and import mks after 1922 (wing "4 W"), matching articulated pendent earrings with bow and flowerhead motifs, screwbacks similarly mkd, bracelet 7-1/2" tl x 3/4", earrings 5/8" w x 2-1/2" tl, suite, **$400**. (Courtesy of E. Foxe Harrell Jewelers, Clinton, IA).

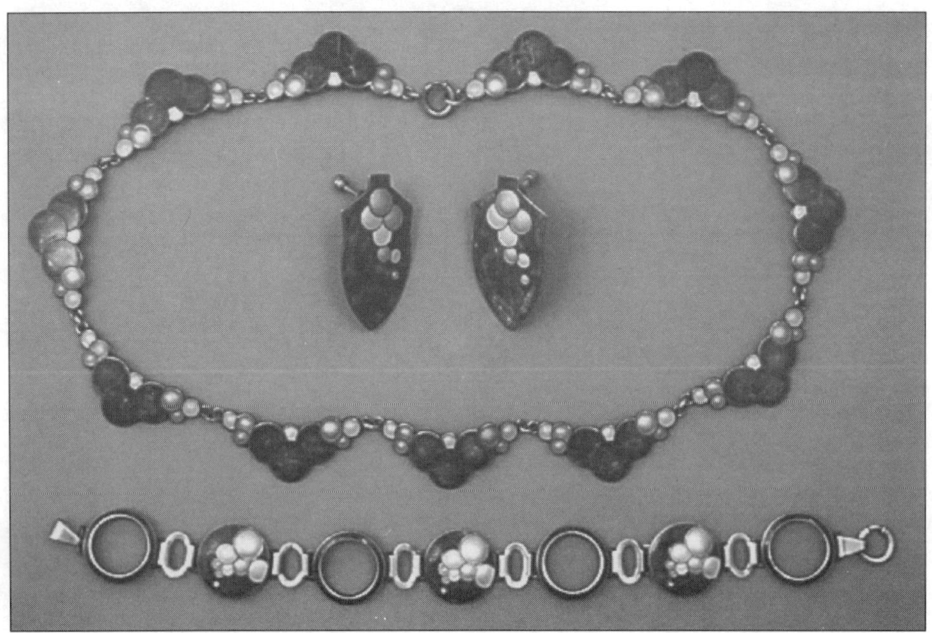

Suite: Necklace, Bracelet and Earrings, sterling, enamel, c. 1925-30, necklace of eleven linked plaques of overlapping "bubbles" motif in green, yellow and white enamel, each plaque imp "STERLING," maker's mark "E" in a sq imp on one link, earrings of shield shape with similar motif, link bracelet of circ enameled plaques of similar motif alternating with green enameled annular links, necklace and bracelet with spring ring clasps, screwback earrings, necklace 1/2" w x 14" tl, bracelet 5/8" w x 7", earrings 3/4" w x 1-1/4", suite, **$600**. (Kerry Holden collection).

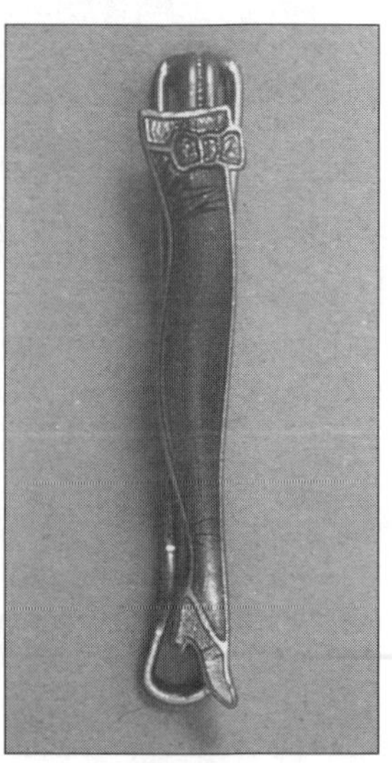

Tie bar, sp wm, enamel, c. 1920, in the shape of a stockinged leg in blue, shoe and bows in violet enamel, 1/4" w x 2", **$85**. (Charles Pinkham collection).

PLASTIC AND OTHER NOVELTY JEWELRY c. 1920-1970

History: In her introduction to the chapter on jewelry in *Art Plastic*, Andrea DiNoto remarks, "If one word were needed to summon up the spirit of the twenties and thirties, 'novelty' would do nicely." For the first time, the idea of wearing jewelry for *fun* caught on. The ideal material for creating this new type of jewelry was plastic–lightweight, inexpensive, and colorful. Although jewelry had been made from celluloid, the earliest semi-synthetic plastic, as far back as 1875, it was limited in style, made mostly in the form of imitation ivory, coral, amber, and tortoiseshell for naturalistic ornamental and utilitarian pieces (see Early Celluloid in Late Victorian section). It was worn primarily by those who could not afford "the real thing." It wasn't until the reckless, lighthearted attitude of the flapper came on the scene that we begin to see whimsical and flamboyant items appear, in decidedly *un*natural colors.

In the first half of the twentieth century, many types of plastic were developed and given trade names by the manufacturers that produced them. Numerous different trade names were given to the same generic substance, as each manufacturer strove for proprietary identification of the material. Over the years, certain names came into generic usage in spite of the fact that they were registered trade names (like Kleenex and Xerox). The three names in most common usage today are celluloid (the word is now seldom capitalized) for pyroxylin-camphor thermoplastic, Bakelite (sometimes written lowercase) for thermosetting phenol formaldehyde resin, and Lucite (seldom lowercase) for thermoplastic polymethacrylates or acrylics. Sometimes these labels are erroneously applied to other, related but not chemically identical, plastics. For example, cellulose acetate (trade name "Lumarith") is often incorrectly called celluloid, and casein plastic, a thermoset (trade name "Galalith"), is commonly confused with Bakelite. Accurately identifying these materials requires a variety of tests, some of which are potentially destructive.

Some collectors believe that a piece of plastic jewelry is collectible and has value because of other factors, such as design and craftsmanship, and that the type of plastic used is of secondary importance. They feel that knowing exactly what a piece is made of is not worth the risks involved in testing. Others consider correct material identification an important part of classifying, circa-dating, and putting a piece in historical context, all of which serves to enhance the value of their collection. The middle ground–the one taken here–is making educated guesses based on *non*-destructive sensory tests, and grouping plastics by generic types–thermoplastics and thermosets–and their related trade names. Although there are now dozens of different plastics on the market, for most collectible jewelry purposes, the ones covered here are celluloid, casein (Galalith), Bakelite, cellulose acetate (Lumarith), and Lucite.

Thermoplastics are those that will soften or melt with the application of heat. Once cooled they will again become solid. Thermosets are liquid (resinous) before they are molded or cast, but once they solidify, they remain solid. Thermoplastic scraps can be recycled. Thermosets cannot. All plastics can be classified in one or the other of these two categories.

Celluloid and cellulose acetate

Celluloid, the first successful *semi*-synthetic thermoplastic, is part natural fiber, or cellulose. Its generic names, pyroxylin-camphor thermoplastic, sometimes referred to as cellulose nitrate, are clues to its makeup: cellulose fiber mixed with nitric acid (nitrated) to which camphor is added, and subjected to heat. Celluloid was first used as a substitute for natural materials, but its versatility, coupled with imaginative designs and new processes, later yielded a variety of forms. In 1902, a patent was granted for a process of setting rhinestones or metal into celluloid, thereby enhancing its decorative potential. In 1923, a synthetic pearl essence was invented, called "H-scale". It replaced the more expensive fish scale type of pearl essence (the coating on simulated pearls) for celluloid, and was used on toilet articles, decorative accessories, and jewelry.

One of the major drawbacks of celluloid was its flammability, due to the nitrocellulose it contained. In 1927, the Celluloid Corporation introduced Lumarith, their trade name for cellulose acetate, which substituted acetic acid (vinegar) for nitric acid and camphor. Except for its bright colors, in appearance and use cellulose acetate is the same as Celluloid, but non-flammable. It is often labeled celluloid, but technically and chemically, this is incorrect. When warmed in hot water, the two materials can be differentiated: Celluloid smells like camphor; cellulose acetate, like vinegar. (This test should not be used on a piece set with rhinestones or other materials susceptible to water damage, nor should any piece be immersed in water for more than a few seconds.) The use of cellulose acetate coincided with the development of the injection-molding process, which made mass-production of inexpensive plastic items possible. In the 1960s and 70s, an extensive line of large and small pins, bangles and "stretchy" bracelets was made from laminated cellulose acetate by Lea Stein of Paris. These colorful figural and geometric pieces now have a large collector following.

Celluloid articles should be stored carefully, in a dry and ventilated place. They are subject to disintegration if exposed to extremes of temperature, constant moisture or corroding metal. Cracks, crystallization, and discoloration are signs of decomposition. Already damaged pieces are "contagious" and should be kept separate from others.

Much of the foregoing information on celluloid was brought to light by Julie P. Robinson, celluloid historian, who is co-author of a book on collectible celluloid and its inventor, John Wesley Hyatt (see References below). She has obtained copies of U.S. patents and perused the archives of the Celluloid Corporation and other pyroxylin plastics manufacturers, and the Smithsonian Institution. Most material on collectible plastics published within the last twelve years has focused on Bakelite and later plastics, with sketchy–and sometimes conflicting–details about plastic's earliest developments. Therefore, the information on celluloid that Ms. Robinson has researched from original archival material has been the primary technical source for this section.

Hair combs and hatpins were among the earliest items of personal adornment made of celluloid, following fashion's currents at the turn of the century. (Leominster, Massachusetts was a center for hair-comb production, first in natural materials, then plastics. It is now the center for a plastics museum, see below). But when fashions changed, these fell by the wayside. Hatpins shrank to become hat ornaments, with a threaded metal pinpoint that was pushed through the hat and secured with a second ornamental "head" (similar to fine jewelry's "jabot" or "*cliquet*" pins).

Famous dancer Irene Castle cut her hair in a "bob" in 1914, prompting thousands of her fans to follow suit, thus signaling the demise of the hair comb. Surprisingly, hair combs didn't completely disappear when "the bob" became the predominant hairstyle. Large and ornate Spanish-style back combs, often embellished with rhinestones and painted enamel, were still occasionally worn, bound to the head, in the late twenties, when the tango was all the rage, and Spanish lace, fringed shawls, and flounced skirts were part of a dancer's costume. A more typical twenties head ornament was the headband, or bandeau. These too, were made of rhinestone-studded celluloid. Because the material is flexible, the headbands are adjustable, held by an ornamental celluloid clasp. Today, these are rare finds. Celluloid bangles, many ivory- or amber-colored, but in other colors as well, were worn from wrist to elbow, in the fashion made popular by heiress Nancy Cunard. The ones most sought-after today have painted designs and/or geometric patterns of pavé rhinestones set into them. Whimsical figural pins, and short chain necklaces with dangling floral or figural motifs were also made of celluloid. Celluloid (pyroxylin plastics) continued to be used for jewelry well into the 1940s (post-WW II molded figural pieces marked "Occupied Japan" can still be found), but with the development of other less flammable and more easily mass-produced plastics, celluloid fell out of favor. After the Celluloid Corp. became part of Celanese in 1947, U.S. production was discontinued. Japan continued to make pyroxylin items during the fifties.

Bakelite and casein

The first entirely synthesized plastic was invented by Leo H. Baekeland in 1908 (patented 1909). As with many inventions, it was accidental. He was searching for a formula for synthetic shellac, at which he failed miserably. Instead, he came up with "the material of a thousand uses," as the advertisers called it: thermosetting phenol formaldehyde resin. He christened it Bakelite. Other companies started manufacturing similar phenolics, and came up with their own trade names, among them: Catalin, Marblette, Durez, and Prystal. Bakelite is the name that has stuck with collectors, although some purists insist upon calling it by the generic name "phenolic" or the trade name "Catalin" (most jewelry made from this material was made by the Catalin Corporation).

Jewelry was not the first of the thousand uses. The Depression created a market for it, because it was cheap to manufacture, colorful, and lent itself to a wide range of styles and manufacturing techniques. It gave women a much-needed lift, to both their outfits and their spirits. Bakelite was well suited to the chunky, heavy jewelry styles of the '30s. It could be laminated into geometric shapes (polka dots were a popular motif), set with rhinestones, clad or inlaid with metal, carved on a lathe, made into the shapes of animals, fruits, or other realistic figurals. Colorless Bakelite (introduced in 1935 by the Catalin Corp., whose trade name for it was Prystal) was carved on the back side with floral or figural designs. The carving was sometimes enhanced with paint. From the front, the designs look three-dimensional. "Reverse-carved" is today's name for this technique. Over time, the pieces have oxidized to a light amber color, which collectors call "apple juice." Reverse-carved fish and aquarium motifs are particularly desirable.

Bracelets of all types–solid and hinged bangles, link, elastic "stretchies," cuffs, and charm bracelets, brooches, dress clips, shoe clips, buckles, earrings, rings, necklaces, beads, and pendants were all made from Bakelite. Bakelite jewelry and objects have been avidly collected for the past fifteen years. Several books and magazine articles have covered the subject quite thoroughly (see references below for some of them). Four books on Bakelite jewelry and related objects were published in 1996 and 1997 alone, an indication of Bakelite's heightened popularity (and escalating prices) in recent years. "Themed" figurals (patriotic, school, sports, animals, people, fruits and vegetables, Mexican motifs, etc.), and multi-colored laminated geometrics (especially bangles, solid and hinged) are among today's most sought-after Bakelite items.

Casein plastic has received relatively little attention compared to Bakelite, the material it is often confused with. Most pieces made of casein plastic generate relatively little collector interest or value, with one exception. Not much plastic jewelry is signed or even attributed, but certain casein plastic pieces are: Auguste Bonaz, whose company is known for its geometric necklaces of the early thirties, which are now rare and sought-after. According to Ginger Moro in *European Designer Jewelry*, cited below, these necklaces were always made of Galalith, the trade name for casein.

Lucite

Although the German manufacturers Röhm and Haas are credited with being the first to formulate acrylic resin (1928), their trade name for it, Plexiglas, seems to be used mainly in reference to utilitarian and decorative objects. Lucite, introduced by DuPont in 1937, is the trade name most often heard in reference to jewelry. Lucite is water clear in its original form, but it is often tinted in a wide range of transparent to opaque colors. Jewelry made entirely of Lucite has only recently been recognized as collectible. Molded, tinted and reverse-carved Lucite figurals are becoming nearly as sought-after as their early '40s Bakelite contemporaries. After the war, Bakelite was no longer cost-effective to produce, but Lucite, a thermoplastic, continued to be manufactured and is still in use today. Post-war jewelry forms, however, are quite different from earlier pieces.

Some circa 1940s novelty jewelry was made of Lucite combined with other materials like Bakelite, wood, leather, and metal. One of the hottest items amongst costume jewelry collectors in recent years, "jelly bellies," have Lucite as the center, or "belly," of sterling animal pins. These were made in the forties by Trifari and other American manufacturers (see "Designer/Manufacturer Signed Costume" section). In the fifties, "pearlized" Lucite bangles and button earclips, often rhinestone-studded, were popular accessories, as were laminated brooches, bracelets and earrings encasing flowers, or embedded with pastel-dyed shells and glitter. In the 1960s, Lucite was often used in colorless form for chunky rings, necklaces and bracelets.

Identifying plastics

Sensory tests can reveal a plastic's identity without being destructive. The aforementioned hot water test works for Bakelite, Lucite and casein as well as celluloid and cellulose acetate. See appendix, Comparison Tests for Plastics, for various sensory tests for each.

As prices of collectible plastics, especially Bakelite, have skyrocketed over the past few years, it is important to remember that plastics, unlike gold and gemstones, are not intrinsically valuable. The material itself is not collectible; what was made from it is. An unimaginative, plain, or downright ugly piece–even though it is "genuine" celluloid, Bakelite, or Lucite–will have little collector interest or value.

Other materials were used concurrently with plastics to produce whimsical novelty articles. In the 1940s, carved wood was a favorite material, alone or in combination with other materials. Western motifs were all the rage in wood as well as plastic, due once again to the movies' influence. Horses' heads are the most prevalent motif.

During wartime shortages, with factories given over to military production and European sources cut off, a kind of "make do" novelty jewelry was made, using readily available non-rationed materials to create amusing pieces. Many of these were hand-constructed. Ceramic or plaster composition, felt, yarn, leather, feathers and sequins were combined to make fashion head brooches, some of them resembling popular movie stars. These have been nicknamed "Victims of Fashion" by collectors. Others had exotic Oriental or African faces, some of which were also carved in wood. Wooden heads were also painted with "politically incorrect" cartoon-like features. The Sears catalog of 1944 advertised "lapel 'pin-ups' in gay hand-painted ceramics"–caricatures of animals and people–with Lucite and yarn details. Once the war was over, this type of jewelry faded into oblivion. In the '50s, "cute" replaced "whimsical," and gold-plated metal and rhinestones were the usual materials of choice.

References: Lillian Baker, *Twentieth Century Fashionable Plastic Jewelry*, Collector Books, 1992; Dee Battle and Alayne Lesser, *The Best of Bakelite and Other Plastic Jewelry*, Schiffer Publishing, 1996; Matthew L. Burkholz, *The Bakelite Collection*, Schiffer Publishing, 1997; "Techniques and Materials" (Chapter 8), in Deanna Farneti Cera, ed., *Jewels of Fantasy, Costume Jewelry of the 20th Century*, Harry N. Abrams, 1992; Corinne Davidov and Ginny Redington Dawes, *The Bakelite Jewelry Book*, Abbeville Press, 1988; Andrea DiNoto, *Art Plastic, Designed for Living*, Abbeville Press, 1984; Stephen Fenichell, *Plastic, The Making of a Synthetic Century*, HarperCollins, 1996 (history of plastics); Tony Grasso, *Bakelite Jewelry, A Collector's Guide*, Chartwell Books, 1996; Sylvia Katz, *Early Plastics*, Shire Publications, Ltd., 1986, and *Plastics, Common Objects, Classic Designs*, Harry N. Abrams, 1984 (Katz' books contain little jewelry, but a great deal of information about plastics, including testing methods); Keith Lauer and Julie Robinson, *Celluloid, A Collectors' Reference and Value Guide*, Collector Books, 1998; Ginger Moro, *European Designer Jewelry*, Schiffer Publishing, 1995; JoAnne Olian, *Everyday Fashions of the Forties As Pictured in Sears Catalogs*, Dover Publications, 1992; Sheryl Shatz, *What's It Made Of? A Jewelry Materials Identification Guide*, 3rd ed., published by the author, 1996; Donna Wasserstrom and Leslie Piña, *Bakelite Jewelry, Good, Better, Best*, Schiffer Publishing, 1997.

Collectors' Clubs: The American Plastics History Association (quarterly newsletter "APHA Notes"), G. Marshall Naul, founder, 534 Stublyn Road, Granville, OH 43023; The Plastics Historical Society (bimonthly PHS newsletter and quarterly journal, "Plastiquarian") 1 Carlton House Terrace, London SW1Y 5DB England

Museums: National Plastics Center and Museum, Leominster, MA; National Museum of American History, Smithsonian Institution, Washington, DC

Reproduction Alert: As with anything that becomes highly collectible and expensive, Bakelite jewelry is now being knocked off. Producing a desirable piece is extremely labor-intensive, and requires a certain amount of craftsmanship. A couple in Florida, the Shultzes, have been making good quality repros for a number of years. Some of it is signed, some is not. Now that their earliest unsigned pieces are in the secondary market, it is more difficult to separate new from old. Marriages of old parts, and "fakelite" imitations (made of plastics other than Bakelite) are also common. Comparing a piece with a known old one, and buying from reputable dealers who stand behind their merchandise are a collector's best protection.

Advisors: Keith Lauer, Julie Robinson (celluloid), Colin Williamson.

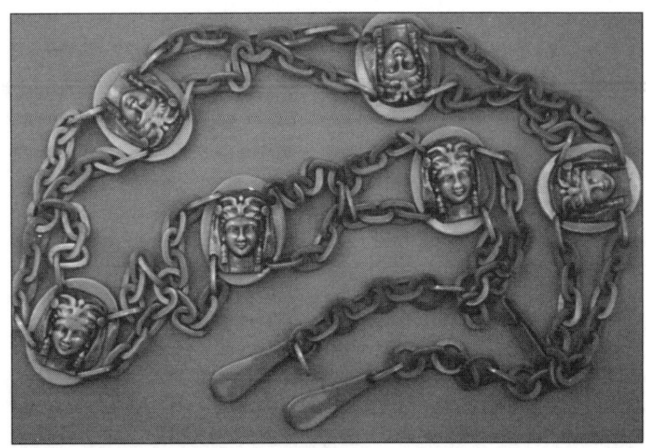

Belt, celluloid, c. 1925, Egyptian Revival, six oval plaques with appl molded pharaoh's heads alternating with double rows of lg link chain, hook closure, pear-shaped drop terminals, plaques 1-1/2" w x 1-3/4", 45" tl, **$145**. (Sue James collection).

Bracelet

Bangle

Bakelite, c. 1935, rounded sq, red inlaid dots on black ground, 1" w, 2-1/2" inside dia 375

Bakelite, c. 1935, rounded sq, black inlaid dots on ivory-colored ground , 5/8" w, 2-1/2" inside dia 350

Bakelite, c. 1940, laminated, striped red, yellow, and dk blue Bakelite (oxidized, was red, white, and blue), 3/4" w, 2-1/2" inside dia 200

Bakelite, c. 1950, multicolor "bowtie" bangle, 1/2" w, 2-1/2" inside dia .... 2,645 (A)

Cellulose acetate, c. 1940, white cellulose acetate bangle with appl carved and dyed alternating red and blue Scottie dogs, 1" w, 2-1/2" inside dia 300

Cellulose acetate, c. 1965, laminated beige, red, green, and black plain band, 3/8" w 50

Cellulose acetate, c. 1965, laminated brown and white plain band, 3/8" w 50

Cellulose acetate, c. 1965, laminated red, white, and orange wraparound design with snake head terminals, paper tag mkd "Made in FRANCE," 1/2" w (at center) ... 125

Cellulose acetate, c. 1965, purple and white patterned laminate in the shape of a snake, 5/8" w (at head), 2-1/2" inside dia 100

Cellulose acetate, c. 1965, red, white, and black laminated band with white bead, paper tag mkd "Made in FRANCE," 3/8" w 50

Cellulose acetate, c. 1965, blue band with white bead, paper tag mkd "Made in FRANCE," 3/8" w 50

Cellulose acetate, c. 1965, pink band with white bead, 3/8" w 50

Cellulose acetate, c. 1965, wraparound black and white checkerboard design, 3/4" w 30

Bangle, hinged

Wood, leather, paint, c. 1940-45, carved wood horse's head with ptd eye and leather bridle surmounting a leather-topped circ wood disk, leather laced through punched holes and wrapped around outside edge, mounted on a hinged shaped wood bangle with leather lacing through holes around center, top 1-3/4" dia, 2-1/8" inside dia 200

Bangle Bracelets, dots, Bakelite, c. 1935:
L, rounded sq, red inlaid dots on black ground, 1" w, 2-1/2" inside dia, **$375**.
C, red and black inlaid dots on ivory-colored ground, 1-5/8" w, 2-1/2" inside dia, **$700**.
R, black inlaid dots on ivory-colored ground, 1" w, 2-1/2" inside dia, **$350**.
(Patrick Kapty collection).

Bangle Bracelets, Bakelite, wood and Bakelite, c. 1935-40:
L, heavily carved marbleized-green Bakelite in ropetwist pattern in center, flanked by two appl brass wires and notched outer edge, 1" w, 2-1/2" inside dia, **$400**.
TC, two outer rings of green Bakelite riveted to two curved inner sections of wood carved in a crosshatch pattern, alternating with open sections, 1-1/2" w, 2-1/2" inside dia, **$250**.
BC, heavily carved marbleized butterscotch Bakelite in a raised textured design, 3/4" w, 2-1/2" inside dia, **$350**.
R, two outer segmented rings of red Bakelite flanking an inner section of carved wood in a ropetwist pattern, 1" w, 2-1/2" inside dia, **$300**.
(Patrick Kapty collection).

Bangle Bracelets, hinged, wood, c. 1940:
L, three-dimensional carved dk brown wood head of an elephant with raised trunk, inset glass eyes and carved bone tusks, tapering to a back hinge joined to a curved tapered section completing the bangle, 2-3/8" inside dia, head 1-7/8" x 1", **$150**.
(Author's collection)
R, three-dimensional carved jockey on a racehorse, ptd green, yellow, beige, black, and red details, red vinyl-coated cord reins, one horse ear chipped, screwed-in hinge mechanism, 1" w, 2-1/2" inside dia, carved section 2-1/2" w x 1-1/4" height, **$125**.
(Patrick Kapty collection).

Cuff

Cellulose acetate, c. 1965, laminated black and pearlized white, tapered to one side, 1-3/4" w 45

Elastic

Cellulose acetate, c. 1965, sq links of multicolored laminated plastic, 5/8" w 90

Cellulose acetate, elastic, c. 1965, laminated sq links in yellow, green, and red on outside, and green with black design on inside, 1" sq links 125

Link

Cellulose acetate, wm, c. 1935-40, open rect red links, hidden hook carved into one center link, 1-1/4" w x 8" tl 275

Brooch/Pin

Bakelite, c. 1935-40, pierced and carved dk amber-colored female stag beetle, inset pin assembly, 1-1/8" w x 2-1/4" 150

Bakelite, c. 1935-40, carved and ptd amber-colored Bakelite seated ethnic figure, ptd red and black details, riveted pin mechanism, 1-3/8" w x 3" 300

Bakelite, c. 1935-40, in the shape of a red heart with dangling cherries, riveted pin mechanism, 2" w x 3" 300

Bakelite, c. 1935-40, in the shape of a wide-brimmed hat, red crown, black brim with appl white plastic-coated string bow, riveted pin mechanism, 2-1/2" dia 550

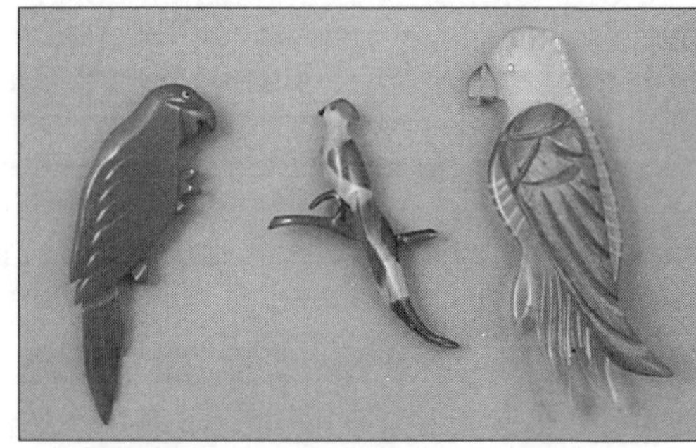

Brooches/Pins, bird motif, c. 1935-40:
L, Bakelite, paint, wm, carved red Bakelite in the shape of a parrot, ptd yellow and black eye, blue-green beak, inset pin back assembly, 1-1/8" w x 3-3/8", **$200**.
(Author's collection).
C, Bakelite, paint, tropical bird on a branch, carved "apple-juice" Bakelite, rev ptd in red, yellow, green, and brown, sm circ blue r.s. eye, pin mechanism inset into rev, 2-3/4" w x 1-5/8", **$250**.
(Patrick Kapty collection).
R, Lucite, wood, paint, parrot with carved colorless Lucite body and rev-ptd orange beak, wing of carved wood, 1-1/4" w x 3-3/4", **$95**.
(Diane White collection).

Bakelite, c. 1935-40, Jai Alai player in carved yellow Bakelite, ptd details in red, black and white, riveted pin mechanism, 1-3/4" w x 2-3/4" 350

Bakelite, c. 1940-45, heart-shaped laminated layers of black, yellow, and red Bakelite (oxidized, was blue, white, and red), riveted pin mechanism, 2" w x 2" .. 150

Bakelite, c. 1940-45, stepped semi-cylindrical bar of black, yellow, and red laminated Bakelite (oxidized, was red, white, and blue), pin mechanism inset into rev, 1-3/4" w x 3/4" 100

Bakelite, brass, paint, c. 1935-40, in the shape of a scimitar, carved orange Bakelite hilt with ptd details and appl brass decoration, carved butterscotch-colored Bakelite blade (surface crack), suspending a brass double-chain swag, riveted safety catch, 4-1/8" w x 1-1/2" 300

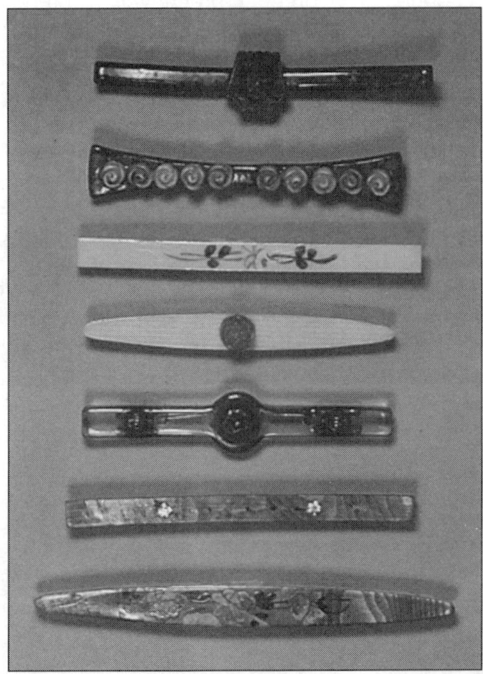

Bar Brooches/Pins, celluloid, paint, c. 1920-25:

T1, rect swirled multicolored bar, central appl molded red pharaoh's head with ptd blue details, C-catch, 3" w x 5/8", **$75**.

T2, black bar with flared terminals, appl pastel pink, blue and yellow flowers and ptd green leaves, C-catch, 2-5/8" w x 5/8", **$40**.

T3, ivory-colored and grained bar with ptd floral and foliate design in pink, red, and green, C-catch, 3" w x 1/2", **$30**.

C, ivory-colored and grained ellipse with central appl molded coral-colored rose, C-catch, 2-3/4" w x 5/8", **$30**.

B1, translucent amber-colored bar with rounded center, three appl blue flowers and green ptd leaves, C-catch, 2-3/4" w x 1/2", **$65**.

B2, laminated rect bar with ivory-colored backing and laminated pearlescent orange and silver front, two circ colorless r.s., pink and green ptd design (worn), C-catch, 3" w x 1/2", **$35**.

B3, tapered bar, laminated orange and silver front with ivory-colored backing, ptd pink roses, C-catch, 3-3/4" w x 5/8", **$45**.

(Photo courtesy of Julie P. Robinson).

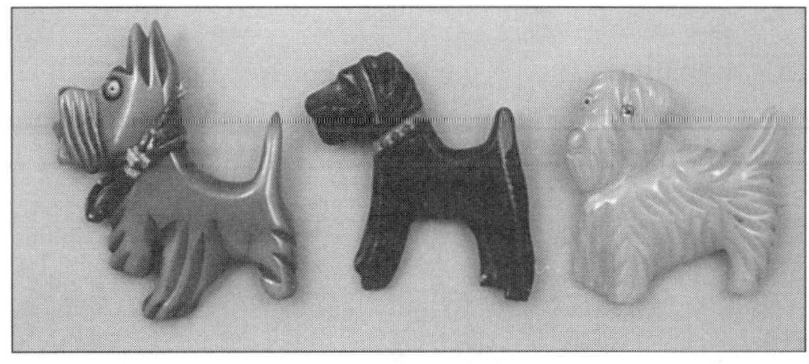

Scottie Dog motif brooches/pins, Bakelite and wood, c. 1935-40:

L, red resin-coated butterscotch Bakelite, ptd black glass eye, vinyl-coated cord tied in a bow at neck, riveted pin assembly, 2-3/4" w x 3-1/4", **$350**.
(Patrick Kapty collection).

C, carved and ptd wood, brass studs at collar, 2-1/4" w x 2-3/8", **$100**.
(Diane White collection).

R, deeply carved butterscotch Bakelite, glass eyes, wm pin back assembly mounted with screws, 2-3/8" w x 2-1/4", **$275**.
(Author's collection).

Brooches/Pins, molded ivory-colored celluloid, paint, flower basket motifs, c. 1920-50:

L, red, pink, and green ptd details, 2-1/4" w x 1-1/2", **$50**.

C, purple, pink, and green ptd details, 1" w x 1-1/4", **$35**.

R, coral-red, pink, and green ptd details, 2-1/4" w x 1-1/2", **$50**.

(Photo courtesy of Julie P. Robinson).

Brooches/Pins, plastic, wood, paint, dog caricatures, c 1935-40:

L, Plastic, wood, brass, paint, c. 1935-40, bulldog of laminated white plastic and wood with carved details, head of carved wood with ptd black and white eyes, brass chain around neck with green plastic dog tag, pin back assembly inset into rev, 2-1/4" w x 3", **$125**.

R, Plastic, wood, paint, c. 1935-40, dog holding an umbrella, laminated white plastic and wood with carved and ptd details in yellow, black, and white, pin back assembly inset into rev, 2-1/2" w x 2-3/4", **$100**.
(Patrick Kapty collection).

Brooch/Pin, Lucite, copper, c. 1940, carved and ptd tortoise with stamped copper shell attached with rivets, rev carved Lucite head and feet, inset safety catch and pin, 3-1/4" w x 2", **$100**. (Gilly Phipps collection).

Bakelite, brass, string, c. 1935-40, in the shape of a violin with resin-coated and carved butterscotch-colored body and carved black neck, replaced brass strings with remnants of plastic-coated string at top, riveted pin mechanism, 1-1/4" w x 3-1/2" 600

Bakelite, brass, c. 1941, "MacArthur Heart," red Bakelite carved key suspending by brass chain a carved red Bakelite heart with central carved-through keyhole, accompanied by a copy of Life magazine, April 28, 1941, with a photograph of a woman wearing the brooch on the cover, 2-1/4" w x 2-3/4" tl .... 2,185 (A)

Bakelite, celluloid, c. 1940-45, laminated red, yellow and black (oxidized, orig red, white and blue) Bakelite heart suspended by two white celluloid rings from a laminated red and yellow Bakelite bar with appl blue plastic star, riveted pin assembly, safety catch, 1-7/8" w x 2-1/2" tl 350

Bakelite, cellulose acetate, c. 1935-40, carved tortoiseshell-colored Bakelite in the shape of a log suspending three carved tortoise Bakelite leaves and three carved amber-colored Bakelite logs from a cellulose chain, riveted pin mechanism, 3" w x 4" tl 350

Bakelite, paint, brass, c. 1935-40, figure of a man with movable arms and legs attached with sm circ brass rings, carved dk red body, amber-colored legs, red face with ptd black and white details, green hat, incised on rev "1941," approx 2" w x 3-1/2" .... 345 (A)

Bakelite, paint, c. 1938-42, stylized walking African figure of black Bakelite with red and white ptd details, designed by Martha Sleeper, safety catch mechanism inset into rev, 1-1/2" w x 2-1/2" 650

Bakelite, vinyl-coated cord, c. 1935-40, red resin-coated butterscotch Bakelite bowling ball suspending nine yellow bowling pins (one missing) with ptd red stripe, on vinyl-coated cord (some worn off), riveted pin mechanism, 2-1/4" w x 3-1/4" 350

Celluloid, c. 1920, pseudo cameo, oval black molded bust of a woman appl to black disk, 1-1/8" w x 1-1/4" 25

Celluloid, c. 1920, pseudo cameo, oval cream-colored molded bust of a woman appl to amber-colored disk, 1-5/8" w x 2" 50

Celluloid, c. 1925, oval laminated gray and black plaque with appl gray pharaoh's head, 1-3/4" w x 2-1/4" 65

Celluloid, cord, c. 1950, cream and purple-colored molded bone shape suspending molded ivory-colored dove appl to a rect plaque, from knotted brown silk cord, mkd "Made in Japan," 1-3/8" w x 2" 15

Celluloid, cord, c. 1950, molded ivory colored tusk suspending an elephant by a lt gray cord, mkd "Japan," 1-5/8" w x 2-3/4" 15

Celluloid, cord, c. 1950, molded ivory-colored bone suspending a Scottie dog ptd red, white, and blue, on a red cord, mkd "Japan," 1-3/8" w x 2-1/4" 20

Celluloid, gp brass, c. 1935-40, bow of extruded round strands of green celluloid suspending three heart-shaped drops on gp brass chain, outer two hearts green, center heart white, 1-7/8" w 60

Celluloid, paint, c. 1920, pseudo cameo, oval cream-colored molded bust of a woman in scallop-edged frame, brown ptd trim, 1" w x 1-3/8" 30

Celluloid, paint, c. 1925, oval base of laminated black and tan with appl ivory-colored pharaoh's head ptd silver, 1-1/2" w 65

Celluloid, paint, c. 1925-30, ivory-colored pearlescent domed oval with ptd scene of a house, trees, and a road, in shades of dk green, lt green, yellow, orange, brown, red, and black, pearlescent clouds, 1-1/2" w x 2" 35

Celluloid, paint, c. 1925-30, purple pearlescent domed rectangle with ptd white swan, flanked by a row of sm circ purple r.s., colorless r.s. above, 1-3/4" w x 1-1/2" 35

Celluloid, paint, c. 1925-30, amber-colored pearlescent domed celluloid oval, with ptd black swan, lily pads, and vines in silhouette effect, 1-1/2" w x 2" 45

Celluloid, paint, c. 1930, marbleized red domed oval with appl band of molded cream-colored roses with ptd details in pink, blue, and green, C-catch, 2" w x 5/8" 35

Celluloid, paint, c. 1930-40, molded cream-colored floral motif with pearlescent ptd details in pink, yellow and green, mkd "Made in Japan," 2" w x 1-1/4" 25

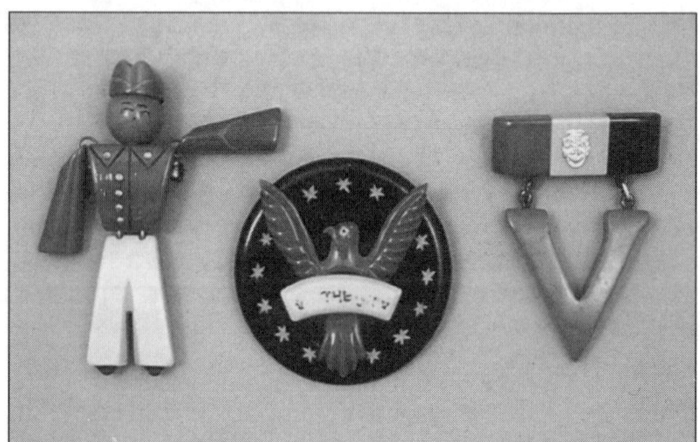

Brooches/Pins, Bakelite, paint, brass, patriotic motifs, c. World War II:

L, articulated soldier of red resin-coated butterscotch Bakelite torso, arms, and cap, yellow Bakelite legs, and lt brown Bakelite face, all attached by brass rings, ptd red, white, blue, and black details and sm brass stud buttons, riveted pin mechanism, 2" w x 3-3/8", **$700**.

C, circ plaque of dk blue resin-coated yellow Bakelite carved-through on front in a ring of stars design, appl carved red Bakelite eagle with wings spread, glass eye, surmounted by appl yellow curved bar with the words "WIN THE WAR" ptd on front (partially worn off), riveted pin assembly, 2-1/2" dia, **$500**.

R, rect laminated red, yellow, and black bar (oxidized, was red, white and blue) with appl wm U.S. naval insignia, suspending a carved red Bakelite letter "V" (for Victory), riveted pin mechanism, 2" w x 2-3/4", **$350**.
(Patrick Kapty collection).

Celluloid, paint, c. 1950, pierced rounded rect plaque of stylized Japanese symbols surmounted by a three-dimensional molded cream-colored floral motif with ptd pink details, mkd "Occupied Japan," 2-1/4" w x 1-5/8" 30

Celluloid, paint, c. 1945-50, chatelaine pin, in the shape of a molded bluebird ptd blue and white, attached with a brass chain to circ stamped brass souvenir pin reading "Fort McHenry/Baltimore," mkd "Made in Japan," 1-1/2" w x 1-1/2" 20

Celluloid, paint, c. 1935-40, two long-necked geese, an ivory-colored one overlapping a dk brown one with ptd details in black, blue, green, white, ivory one's tail with red cross-hatching, 1-1/4" w x 1" 40

Celluloid, paint, c. 1945-50, mottled red, blue, off-white, green, and purple molded bird, 1-1/2" w x 1" 15

Celluloid, paint, c. 1945-50, molded ruby-throated hummingbird on a branch with ptd details in black, brown, purple, and silver, mkd "Made in Japan," 2-1/4" w x 1-1/2 30

Celluloid, rhinestones, c. 1930, in the shape of a skull and crossbones of pale amber-colored celluloid with red r.s. eyes and rows of sm circ yellow r.s. on crossbones, 1-5/8" w x 1-1/2" 50

Celluloid, rhinestones, c. 1935-40, tortoiseshell-colored celluloid bow with sm colorless r.s. in center knot, 2-1/4" w x 1-7/8" 35

Celluloid, rhinestones, glitter, c. 1930, in the shape of an elephant of amber-colored celluloid with gold glitter-covered surface pavé-set with sm colorless r.s, green r.s. eye, 2-1/4" w x 2-1/4" 35

Celluloid, rhinestones, paint, c. 1930, in the shape of a parrot's head, lt pink celluloid with incised line details ptd black, black ptd beak, sm green r.s. eye and row of sm colorless r.s. across crest, 1-3/4" w x 2-3/4" 45

Celluloid, wm, c. 1925 oval molded green scarab beetle in wm bezel, 3/4" w x 2" 45

Celluloid, wm, c. 1930, two side-by-side domed disks in pressed-together "end of day" chunks of red, cream, brown, and black, a wm collar at joined center, probably Japanese, 1-3/4" w x 3/4" 25

Brooches/Pins, wood, Bakelite, plastic, nautical motifs, c. 1940-45:

L, in the shaped of an anchor, wood top laminated to carved butterscotch-colored Bakelite back, inset pin back assembly, 1-3/4" w x 2-7/8", **$125**.

C, carved wood sailor with ptd details in blue, white, black, and red, hanging out his carved yellow Bakelite shirt on a green vinyl-coated cord clothesline attached to a red plastic rod, pin assembly inset into rev, 2-7/8" w x 3", **$300**. (Patrick Kapty collection).

R, cutout wood plaque in the shape of a cartoon-like sailor's head, painted white, red, brown and blue features, movable "googly" eyes, glued-on pinback assembly, 1-5/8" w x 2-1/8", **$65**. (Author's collection).

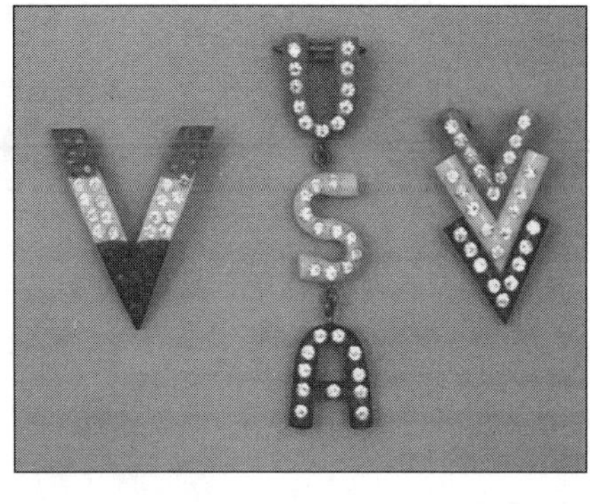

Brooches/Pins, celluloid, rhinestones, patriotic motifs, c. World War II:

L, "V for Victory" shape, three horizontal red, white and blue stripes set with red, colorless and blue r.s., glued-on pin mechanism, 1-3/4" w x 2", **$85**.

C, vertical row of linked letters "USA" in red, white and blue extruded celluloid with sm colorless r.s., glued-on pin mechanism, 3/4" w x 3-3/4", **$95**.

R, fused vertical row of three "Vs for Victory" in red, white and blue set with sm colorless r.s, glued-on safety pin on rev, 1" w x 2-1/8", **$75**.
(Patrick Kapty collection).

Celluloid, ym, c. 1925, swirled multicolored surface appl to oval black plaque with appl stamped ym Egyptian woman's head, C-catch, 1-1/4" w x 1" 65

Cellulose acetate, wm, c. 1965, "candy cane" twisted laminated cylinder shape in shades of yellow, red, white and green, paper label mkd "Made in FRANCE," 1-3/4" w x 1/4" 45

Cellulose acetate, wm, c. 1965, "candy cane" twisted laminated cylinder in shades of green, red, white and yellow, paper label mkd "Made in FRANCE," 1-3/4" w x 1/4" .. 45

Cellulose acetate, wm, c. 1965, black bird with white patterned wings and beak, pin back mkd "LEA STEIN PARIS," paper label mkd "Made in FRANCE," 1-3/4" w x 1" 75

Cellulose acetate, wm, c. 1965, foliate motif in red plastic with clear berries, pin back mkd "LEA STEIN PARIS," 2-1/2" w x 1-1/2" 65

Cellulose acetate, wm, c. 1965, laminated, in the shape of a female figure with black hair, white arms, legs and face, pearlized red dress, pin back mkd "LEA STEIN PARIS," 1-1/2" w x 2-1/4" 75

Cellulose acetate, wm, c. 1965, navette-shaped, geo design in black and pearlized white, pin back mkd "LEA STEIN PARIS," 2-1/2" w x 1-1/2" 40

Cellulose acetate, wm, c. 1965, navette-shaped, geo design in laminated yellow, blue, and purple, pin back mkd "LEA STEIN PARIS," paper label mkd "Made in FRANCE," 1-3/4" w x 1" 40

Cellulose acetate, wm, c. 1965, V-shaped laminated layers in red, green, yellow, white and pink, pin back mkd "LEA STEIN PARIS," paper label mkd "Made in FRANCE," 1-1/2" w x 3/4" 65

Ceramic, fabric, paint, c. 1940-45, molded green ceramic dog's head with ptd black and red features surmounted by an orange fabric bow, multi-colored embroidered fabric collar below, glued-on C-catch pin back, 2-1/4" w x 2" 75

Gp wm, c. World War II, in the shape of a bow with red, white and blue ptd enamel ribbons, sm colorless rhinestone border, mkd "Coro," 3" w x 2-1/8" 95

Gp wm, c. World War II, die-stamped female skater in movement over a "V" for Victory, ptd red, white and blue enamel, 2" w x 2-1/4" 45

Leather, paint, c. 1940-45, cut and sewn leather cowboy with beige leather head and body, black hat, belt, and shoes, and red scarf, ptd black and white features on face, 2" w x 3-1/4" 45

Novelty Brooches/Pins, "make-do" materials, c. 1940-45:
L, Beads, fabric, circ beaded hat with beaded decoration around crown of hat in beige, dk green, lt green, and red, 2" dia, **$45**.
C, Fabric, ribbon, plastic, crocheted hat suspending crocheted pocketbook in shades of orange, white, yellow, and dk green, applied red ribbon on hat, red plastic closure on pocketbook, 2-1/2' w x 4", **$45**.
R, Felt, thread, white felt pocketbook suspending mittens, red thread trim whip-stitched around edges, 1-1/2" w x 1-3/4", **$25**.
(Diane White collection).

Mexican motif brooches/pins:
TL, c. 1935-40, Mexican sombrero of carved dk wood with four appl gp brass studs, ptd yellow, green, and red stripes, dangling green vinyl-coated cord with ptd red wood bead, pin back assembly inset into rev, 2-1/2" w x 4" tl, **$150**.
TC, c. 1935-40, carved marbleized orange Bakelite Mexican jug with ptd blue, gold, and yellow geo design, suspending four carved and ptd wood sombreros with blue, green, and red details, on vinyl-coated cotton cord (vinyl worn off), pin mechanism inset into rev, 2" w x 3-1/8", **$325**.
BL, c. 1955, carved wood Mexican man wearing a sombrero, astride a burro with ptd yellow, black, and red details, pin mechanism inset into rev, 1-1/2" w x 1-1/4", **$50**.
(Patrick Kapty collection).
TR, c. 1935-40, carved butterscotch-colored Bakelite Mexican sombrero, ridged to simulate straw texture, painted red and green decoration on brim and crown, suspending a fringe of red, green, and yellow ptd glass beads from brass jump rings around front edge, riveted pin back assembly on rev, 2-5/8" dia, crown 1-3/8" h, **$500**.
BR, c. 1940, depicting a sleeping Mexican wearing a sombrero and a serape, carved butterscotch Bakelite with red, black, and green ptd details, wood sombrero with red, yellow, green, and blue irregular stripes, inset pin back assembly, 7/8" w x 2-1/8", **$125**.
(Author's collection).

Lucite, glass, c. 1940, carved Lucite horse's head, colorless with red-tinted mane, collar and bridle, rev-carved parallel grooves, yellow glass eye, inset pin back, 2-3/8" w x 3" 100

Lucite, paint, c. 1940-45, colorless Lucite, rect shape with beveled edges and chamfered corners, rev-carved and ptd scene of two goldfish and a plant in yellow, white, and green paint, 2-1/4" w x 1-3/8" 75

Lucite, sterling, c. 1940, in the shape of a three-dimensional carved horse of dk green Lucite, appl ster mane, saddle, tail, and backplate, mkd "STERLING," 2" w x 1-1/2" .. 400

Lucite, wood, c. 1935-40, butterfly with carved dk wood body and carved green Lucite wing, pin back assembly inset into rev, 3" w x 3-3/4" 200

Plastic, c. World War II, bow shape of lacy red and white molded thermoplastic with solid blue center, pin back glued on, 1-7/8" w x 1-1/2" 25

Brooches/Pins, ceramic, fabric, paint, Chinese figures, c. 1940-45:
L, female in traditional costume and orange and black woven fiber hat with black braided fiber hair, blue glaze body with red ptd details, red, black, and white ptd details on face, 1-3/4" w x 2-3/4", **$60**.
R, male in traditional Mandarin dress, head mounted on a spring ("nodder"), ptd details in red, yellow, and black on white bg, 1" w x 3-1/4", **$70**.
(Diane White collection).

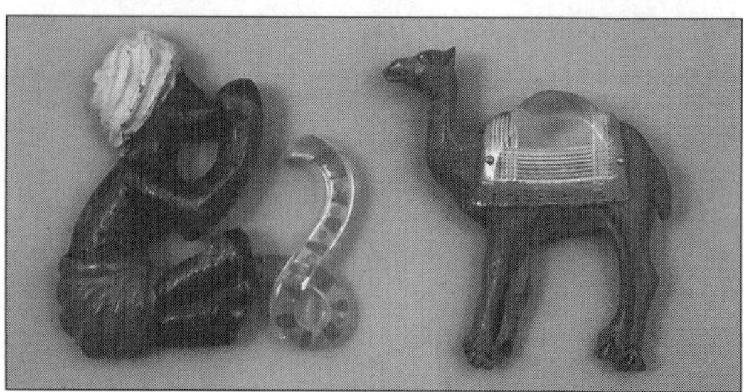

Brooches/Pins, wood, Lucite, paint, c. 1940-45:
L, deeply-carved dk wood figure of a snake charmer playing a musical instrument with ptd yellow turban and red loin-cloth, charming a carved coiling Lucite snake with ptd red stripes and blue dots, pin mechanism inset into rev, 2-3/4" w x 3", **$300**.
(Sue James collection).
R, carved wood camel with appl rev-carved Lucite saddle, ptd green border, riveted pin back assembly, 2-3/4" w x 3", **$135**.
(Patrick Kapty collection).

Brooch/Pin, Bakelite, plastic, metal, c. 1935-40, carved yellow Bakelite carnival hawker with ptd features, red and white hat and green and white bow tie holding molded heart-shaped red plastic balloons on metal strings, riveted pin mechanism, 1-5/8" w x 3-3/4", **$600**. (Courtesy of Morning Glory Antiques & Jewelry).

Patriotic motifs, Bakelite and white plastic (probably urea formaldehyde), laminated red, white and blue layers carved as one, c. World War II:

TL, spread-winged eagle with painted black eye and beak, inset safety catch, 3-3/8" w x 1-5/8", **$350**.

C, anchor, appl brown globe with carved and painted details, red, white, and blue fiber cord wound from top to bottom, inset safety catch, 1-3/4" w x 2-1/4", **$450**.

TR, winged anchor with shield center, painted red and blue details on shield, red, white, and blue cord and tassel, 3-5/8" w x 2-1/2" tl **$350**.

(Patrick Kapty collection)

Novelty brooches/pins, plastic, c. 1950-60:

L, red plastic heart with photo compartment, compartment cover on swiveling rivet imprinted with "Be My Valentine," on original card, 1-1/2" w x 1-3/4", **$45**.

R, red confetti Lucite in the shape of a lollipop with ears, ptd face in green, black, and white, 1-3/4" w x 3-3/4", **$100**.

(Diane White collection).

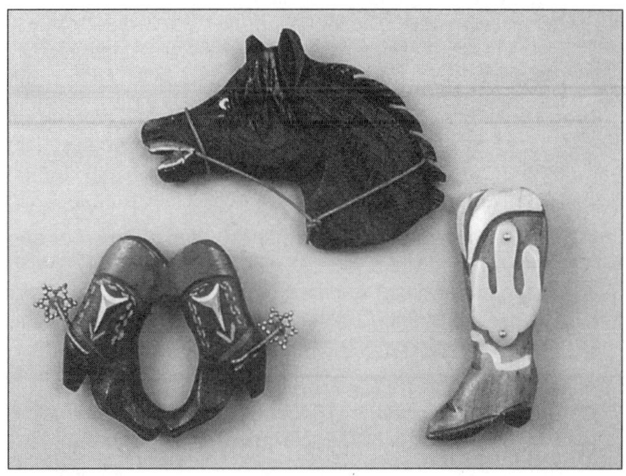

Western motif brooches/pins, wood, c. 1940:

TC, carved and ptd dk brown wood horse's head with attached red bridle, glued-on C-catch, 3-7/8" w x 2-5/8", **$75**.

BL, opposed carved dk brown wood cowboy boots with red, black and white ptd details, appl cut steel triangular studs and cut steel spurs, six-pointed stars attached with brass wire, inset safety catch and hinge, 3-1/4" w x 2-3/8", **$65**.

BR, carved lt brown wood cowboy boot, yellow and black ptd details, with appl beige cutout plastic cactus, riveted pin back, 1-1/4" w x 3" tall, **$50**.

(Gilly Phipps collection).

"Politically incorrect" cartoon-like "head" pins, wood, paint, c. 1940:

L, head of an African native, half-round black, red and white ptd wood with brass rings through nose and ears, topknot of black fiber wrapped with gold braid surmounted by a yellow Bakelite "bone," glued-on pin back assembly, 1-1/2" w x 3-1/2" tl, **$125**.

C, head of an island native girl, half round brown, black, white and red ptd wood, black fiber braids with red and beige ties, carved flowers at top (one damaged), glue-on pin back assembly, 1-1/2" w x 3-1/2" tl, **$65**.

(Author's collection).

R, depicting an African native of carved and ptd red, yellow, black and white wood with applied white plastic nose and hair-bone, green vinyl-coated cord necklace, 1-1/2" w x 3", **$125**.

(Diane White collection).

Wood, Bakelite, glass, paint, c. 1935-40, carved wood flamingo with ptd glass eye appl to carved tortoiseshell Bakelite foliate bg, pin back assembly inset into rev, 2" w x 4-1/4" 200

Wood, Bakelite, c. 1935-40, depicting a Scottie dog begging on a chair, intricately carved red Bakelite Scottie with a bow around neck on a carved wood chair, pin back assembly inset into rev, 3" w x 3" 250

Wood, Bakelite, paint, glass, c. 1940, depicting a cat and a fishbowl, carved wood cat with ptd glass eyes, ptd red mouth and paws, rev-carved and ptd red, blue and black fish in "apple juice" Bakelite bowl (oxidized, was colorless), inset pin back assembly, 2-3/8" w x 2-3/4" .... 660 (A)

Wood, Bakelite, paint, c. 1940, carved wood elephant head with ptd features on "apple juice" Bakelite center, inset safety catch and hinge, 2-1/2" w x 2-1/8" 175

Wood, Lucite, glass, paint, c. 1935-40, carved lt brown wood elephant's head with ears spread, ptd glass eyes, colorless Lucite tusks, riveted pin back assembly, 5" w x 3-1/2" 100

Wood, Lucite, wm, c. 1935-40, carved dk brown wood swan with appl wm studs and eye and carved colorless Lucite wing, pin back assembly inset into rev, 3" w x 3-3/4" 175

Wood, brass, c. 1940-45, bucking bronco, carved and ptd wood with brass wire reins, 2" w x 3" 100

Buckle

Celluloid, c. 1925, oval laminated base of tan, dk brown and blue with appl ivory-colored pharaoh's head ptd silver, 2-1/2" w 65

Double Clip Brooch

Bakelite, rh pl wm, c. 1935, elongated oval, lt brown carved floral motif, flat-backed hinged wm clips joined with a detachable wm pin back mechanism mkd "Pat No 1798867 Reg US Pat Off" (1931), "Pat 1852188" (1932) mkd on clips, 2" w x 3/4" joined 125

Brooch/Pin, wood, paint, plastic, c. 1940-45, carved and ptd wood scarecrow-on-a-stake with plastic moveable "googly" eyes, ptd details in yellow, green, red, and brown, pin back assembly inset into rev, 2" w x 3-3/4", **$300**. (Patrick Kapty collection).

Brooches/Pins, carved resin-coated yellow Bakelite, paint, wm, Walt Disney's "Bambi" characters, c. 1940:

TL, in the shape of an owl with slightly spread wings, ptd features and details in black, white, and red, pin mechanism inset into rev, 2-1/4" w x 2-1/4", **$300**.

TR, in the shape of Bambi with ptd features in black, white, and red, pin mechanism inset into rev, 2-1/8" w x 3-1/4", **$400**.

BC, deer jumping over a carved wood log, ptd features and details in black, white, and red, pin mechanism inset into rev, 3" w x 2", **$200**.

(Terrance O'Halloran collection).

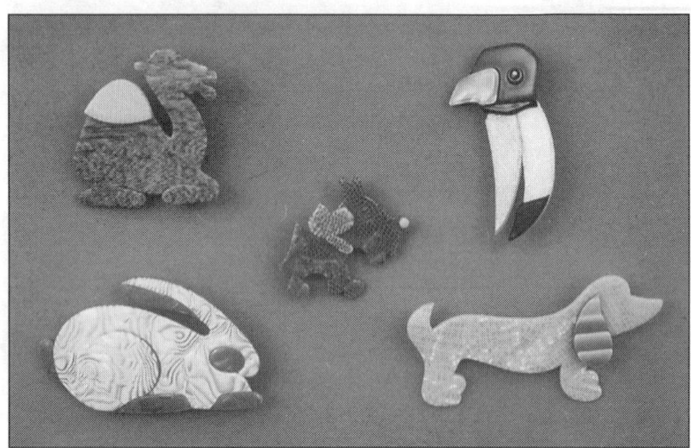

Brooches/Pins, Cellulose acetate, wm, Lea Stein, c. 1965:

TL, gray patterned camel with cream-colored saddle, pin back mkd "LEA STEIN PARIS," 1-3/4" w x 1-3/4", **$75**.

TR, toucan head in laminated blue, white, yellow, and black with glass cab eye (two different birds when viewed horizontally or vertically), pin back mkd "LEA STEIN PARIS," 2-1/8" w x 1", **$75**.

C, Scottie dog in violet checkered pattern with black and white checkered bow and white bead nose, pin back mkd "LEA STEIN PARIS," paper label mkd "Made in FRANCE," 1-1/2" w x 1-1/2", **$85**.

(Sue James collection).

BL, in the shape of a rabbit with pearlized white body and red accents, pin back mkd "LEA STEIN PARIS," 2-3/8" w x 1-1/2", **$75**.

BR, in the shape of a dachshund with a white pearlized body and laminated yellow, red, orange, and purple ear, pin back mkd "LEA STEIN PARIS," 2-3/4" w x 1-1/2", **$75**.

(Mary Williamson collection).

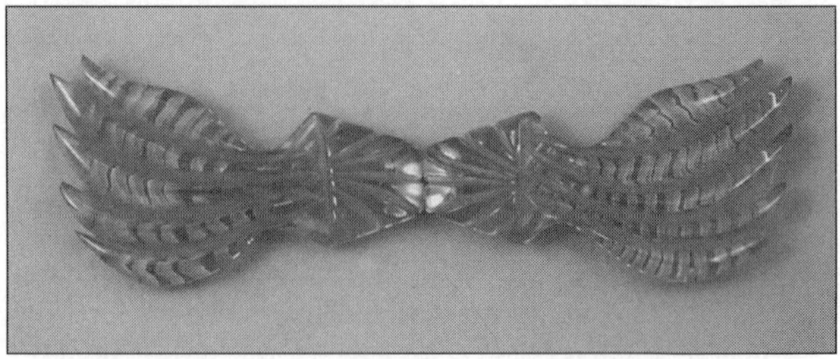

Buckle, Bakelite, c. 1935, two opposed stylized fan shapes of rev-carved lt amber-colored Bakelite, metal eye screws for sew-on attachment and hook and eye closure on rev, 6-1/4" w x 1-1/4", **$65**. (Richard Levey collection).

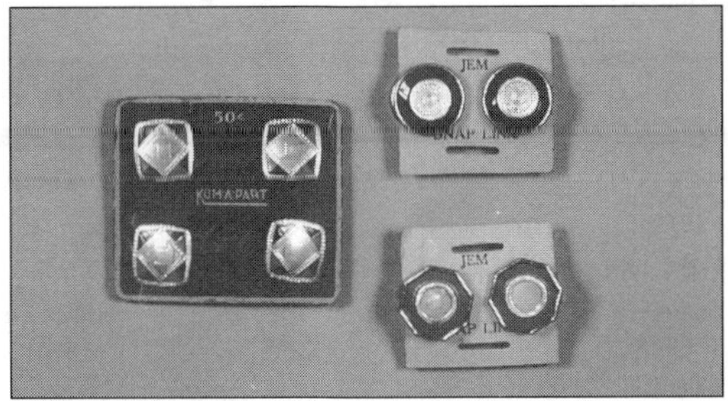

Cuff Links, celluloid, wm, on original cards, c. 1920-25:

L, purple and black celluloid in triangular geo pattern set in sq wm frame, stamped wm sq turned 45 degrees in center, four pcs on original card mkd "50 ¢" and "Kum-A-Part," trade name for snap links developed by Baer & Wilde (later known as Swank) in 1914, 1/2" dia, pr, **$60**.

R, two pr on original cards, one pr green octagonal celluloid plaque in octagonal wm frame, MOP disk in central wm frame, other pr circ black celluloid with stamped ym center in wm frame, cards mkd "Jem Snap Links," 1/2" dia, each pr, **$40**. (Photo courtesy of Julie P. Robinson).

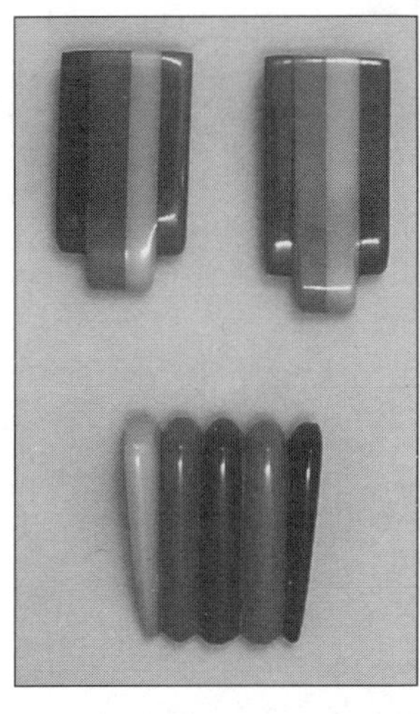

Dress Clips, Bakelite, wm, c. 1935:

T, geo stepped design in green, yellow, red and brown laminated Bakelite, riveted flat-backed hinged wm clips, 1" w x 1-7/8", pr, **$175**.

B, "Philadelphia" style, serrated design with rounded segments in black, orange, green, red and yellow laminated Bakelite, riveted flat-backed hinged wm clip, 1-1/2" w x 1-5/8", **$300**.
(Courtesy of Morning Glory Antiques & Jewelry).

Dress Clip

Bakelite, brass, paint, wm, c. 1935-40, laminated red and black Bakelite in the shape of a ladybug with brass trim and ptd black dots, riveted flat-backed hinged wm clip, 1" w x 2" 75

Dress Clips

Bakelite, wm, c. 1935-40, leaves and berries motif in deeply carved green Bakelite, riveted flat-backed hinged wm clips, 1" w x 1-1/4", pr 50

Earrings

Wood, paint, c. 1940, carved wood in the shape of cowboy boots, ptd red and yellow, screwbacks, 5/8" w x 1", pr 30

Hair Comb

Celluloid, rhinestones, paint, c. 1915-20, lg open asymmetrical overlapping scroll design set with rows of blue r.s. on blue ptd ground, lt amber-colored celluloid four-pronged comb, 4-1/2" w x 6" 65

Necklace

Bakelite, cellulose acetate, brass, c. 1940, twenty-eight cut-out five-pointed Bakelite stars, mix of red, yellow and black (oxidized, were red, white and blue) on brass jump rings suspended from double strand of off-white cellulose acetate chain, continuing to single strand and brass spring ring clasp, 15-1/2" tl, 2" at center 300

Bakelite, cellulose acetate, c. 1935-40, brown cellulose acetate chain suspending five Bakelite oranges, 3/4" dia, and six green cellulose acetate leaves, 17" tl 400

Galalith (casein), c. 1930, central oval plaque, half red, half black, overlapping two smaller oval plaques flanked by grad rounded rect links, one side red, the other side black, Fr, sgd "Auguste Bonaz," metal barrel clasp; provenance: worn by Barbra Streisand in the movie "The Main Event," approx 16" tl .... 3,450 (A)

Wood, leather, wm, c. 1940, eight brown leather-topped wood horseshoe-shaped charms suspended from a wm chain, spring ring closure, charms 1" w x 1", chain 16" tl 80

Bead

Casein, c. 1935, grad beads, round, floral, bullet, cylinder and elliptical shapes, carved-through red-to-ivory curved fluted centers with sawtooth edges, segmented cylinder ivory-colored spacers, barrel clasp, 5/8" (at center), 18" tl 45

Dress Clip, Bakelite, leather, paint, c. 1935-40, Tyrolean hat of carved black Bakelite with ptd yellow feather and green leather hatband tied at one side, flat-backed hinged clip riveted on rev, 1-3/4" w x 1-1/2", **$125**. (Patrick Kapty collection).

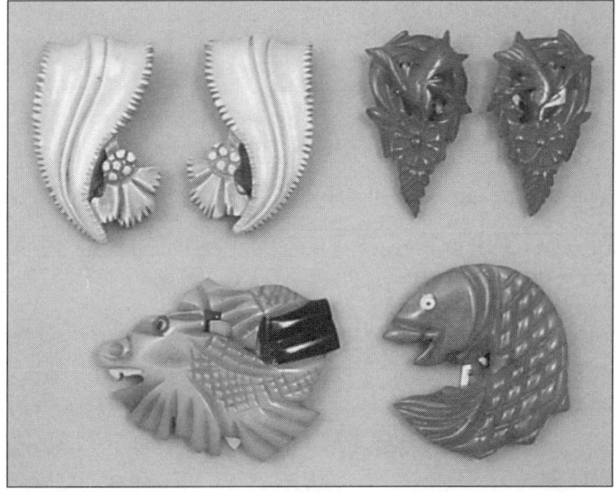

Dress Clips, Bakelite, riveted flat-backed hinged clip findings, c. 1935:

TL, carved and pierced yellow scrolled leaf and flower motifs, 1-1/4" w x 2-1/4", pr, **$200**.

TR, rounded triangular carved-through red, depicting a hummingbird sipping at a flower, 1" w x 1-7/8", pr, **$200**.

BL, carved butterscotch dragon with ptd black and white details, 2" w x 1-3/4", **$175**.
(Patrick Kapty collection).

BR, carved green fish with carved and ptd yellow and black eye, 2" w x 2", **$145**.
(Diane White collection).

Pendant

Celluloid, rhinestones, c. 1925, amber-colored rectangle, cusped at the top, chamfered bottom corners, two rows of yellow r.s. bordering laminated pearlescent green center, 1-1/4" w x 2-1/4" 60

Necklace, plastic, wood, metal, c. 1940, Western motif necklace with seven charms: gun, two whiskey jugs, two cowboy boots, accordion, and hat, suspended from brown celluloid chain, brass spring ring closure, 16-1/4" tl, boot charm 3/4" w x 1-3/8", **$70**. (Gilly Phipps collection).

Pendent Earrings, celluloid, brass, glass, c. 1925, Egyptian Revival, ornate brass links alternating with black glass beads and rings suspending molded black celluloid drops depicting the Sphinx with red and yellow ptd details, screwbacks, 3/4" w x 2-1/2" tl, pr, **$95**. (Sue James collection).

Suite: Brooch/Pin and Earrings

Bakelite, cellulose acetate, vinyl-coated string, c. 1935-40, brooch a cut brown Bakelite log suspending five Bakelite oranges from green vinyl-coated string, 2-3/4" w x 3" tl, screwback earrings each a Bakelite half-orange, 3/4" dia, suite 450

Suite: Cuff Links and Tie Pin

Celluloid, rh pl wm, rhinestones, c. 1915-20, cuff links each a circ ivory-colored and grained disk with central sm circ colorless r.s. set in rh pl wm octagonal frame with stamped design, wm disk back, tie pin with similarly designed head, cuff links 1/2" dia, tie pin 2-1/4" w x 1/2", suite 55

Pendant, celluloid, paint, c. 1920, kite-shaped ivory-colored and grained celluloid layered with black celluloid, ptd scroll, foliate, and geo design in black and gold, 2" w x 3-1/4", **$125**. (Photo courtesy of Julie P. Robinson).

Pendant and Chain, Bakelite, cellulose acetate, c. 1935-40, rect "apple juice" rev- and front-carved plaque with appl black plastic woman's face with ptd red hair and features, suspended from a black cellulose acetate chain, pendant 1-7/8" w x 2-1/4", chain 22" tl, **$300**. (Courtesy of Morning Glory Antiques & Jewelry).

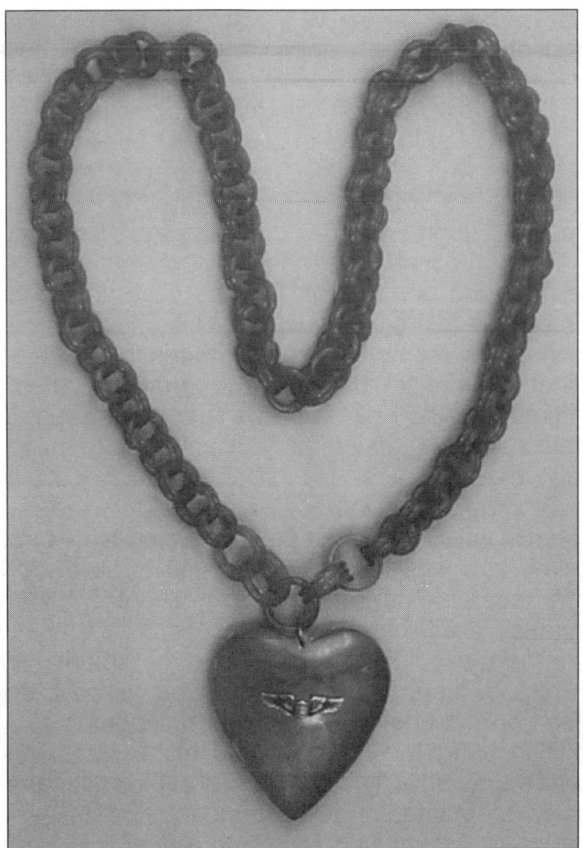

Pendant and Chain, Lucite, celluloid, sterling, c. 1945, red Lucite heart pendant surmounted by appl ster Air Force emblem, suspended from red celluloid chain, pendant 1-3/4" w x 1-3/4", chain 19" tl, **$145**. (Patrick Kapty collection).

Ivory-colored molded celluloid, c. 1930:

TL, Bangle bracelet, floral and foliate motif with pierced sections, 3/4" w, 3" inside dia, **$35**.

TR, Bangle bracelet, molded floral/foliate motif, 5/8" w, 2-3/4" inside dia, **$35**.

BL, Dress clip, inverted pear shape, molded floral and foliate motif, flat-backed hinged wm clip on rev, mkd "Japan," 1-3/4" w x 2", **$25**.

BC, Ring, oval molded floral motif, mkd "Made in Japan," 1-1/2" w, **$30**.

BR, Dress clip, oval molded lily motif, "Japan" molded on rev, flat-backed hinged clip mkd "Made in USA," 1-1/8" w x 1-7/8", **$25**.

(Photo courtesy of Julie P. Robinson).

Suite: Bar Pin and Cuff Links, leather, brass, c. 1935, equestrian motif, brass bar with lozenge-shaped sewn leather surmounted by a brass stirrup, C-catch; sq sewn leather cuff links, each surmounted by a brass stirrup, leather strap and button, pin 2-3/4" w x 1", cuff links 3/4" sq, suite, **$38**. (Gilly Phipps collection).

Suite: Necklace and Bracelet, wood, felt, cellulose acetate, glass, c. 1940, nine hollow wood bead flowers with felt petals and glass bead centers in alternating colors of yellow, red, and green, on a cellulose acetate chain of alternating yellow, red, and green links, matching bracelet with eight flowers, molded red plastic hook clasps, necklace 1" w x 16" tl, bracelet 1" w x 7" tl, suite, **$150**. (Patrick Kapty collection).

FINE JEWELRY c. 1935-1945

History: The stylistic developments of the 1930s started taking a markedly different path about half-way through the decade. By the mid-'30s, the all-white look of diamonds and platinum that had been a mainstay of fine jewelry fashion since the turn of the century began to fade. Colored gold and gemstones gradually became more prominent, encouraged by changes in clothing styles and later, by wartime shortages and restrictions. The repeal of Prohibition and the abandonment of the gold standard in 1933 may have precipitated the change.

Although the Depression had the Nation, and Europe as well, in its grip for the duration of the decade, these two events could have sparked hope for better days ahead. Nightclubs were once again in business and gold jewelry was once again in fashion, as publicized by Hollywood and its stars, the epitome of glamour. Jewelry was still desirable to own in hard times, not only as personal adornment, but also as portable wealth, a concept that remained viable throughout the war years. In the "make-do" spirit of the period, however, fewer and less expensive gemstones were used, including synthetic rubies and sapphires, and less expensive gold took the place of platinum, which became totally unavailable for jewelry during the war.

A resurgence of romanticism in the mid- to late-'30s generated a desire for femininity in fashion and a return to "old-fashioned" Victorian sentimentality. There was even a reprise of British royal influence, which nearly upstaged all of Hollywood. The abdication of King Edward VIII in 1936, and his subsequent marriage to Wallis Simpson, was called the "the most famous love story of modern times." Jewelry played a well-publicized, prominent and sentimental role in that story. (Not to be outdone, Margaret Mitchell and Hollywood gave us "Gone With The Wind," the most famous love story of Victorian times.*)* The Duke and Duchess of Windsor, as they became known, were the equal of Victoria in their influence on the jewelry-buying public. The most famous of the Duchess' jewels were made by Cartier and Van Cleef & Arpels, but designs by Suzanne Belperron, Harry Winston, Verdura, David Webb, and Seaman Schepps were also part of her collection. (All of these were sold by Sotheby's in Geneva at its renowned record-breaking auction of April, 1987.)

Retro Modern is the somewhat controversial name recently coined for the fluid forties jewelry style that began to emerge around 1935. It is an appropriately contradictory term, carrying the suggestion of looking back and forward at the same time. The style's characteristics were truly an infusion of past and futuristic themes. The Machine Age, streamlined look of the late twenties and early thirties continued to evolve, becoming larger and more three-dimensional. But geometric severity was tempered by curvilinear softness, asymmetry, and a return to naturalistic motifs, usually interpreted on a larger scale and in more stylized forms than their Victorian counterparts. In the gradual move away from abstraction, flowers, animals and birds became increasingly popular. Buckles, bows, ribbons, and fabric-like folds were often executed in combined contrasting colors of gold alloys in overtones of pink (rose) and green as well as yellow (called bicolor and tricolor gold). Pieces were massive-looking, but hollow and, especially during wartime, the gold was of a thin gauge. In German-occupied France, the customer supplied the gold and gemstones, and the government took a percentage of the gold's value. While the U.S. was under no such restriction on gold, patriotism dictated restraint. Patriotism itself was a prevalent theme in wartime jewelry, both in colors (rubies and sapphires, often synthetic, accented with small diamonds) and motifs (flags, eagles, and military insignia).

Elements of the Machine Age style were reinterpreted in yellow and rose gold, including large geometric link and wide strap bracelets in "tank track" and other repeating patterns. In 1934, Van Cleef & Arpels designed a flexible strap of honeycomb or brickwork patterned segments with a large ornamental buckle-shaped clasp. They christened it the "Ludo" bracelet, after Louis "Ludovic" Arpels, but it appears to have been inspired by Victorian gold mesh *jarretières*, or "garter" bracelets. The design was copied by many others, and remained popular throughout the forties. Bangles were wide and three-dimensional, often with a single large rectangular-cut gemstone (aquamarine and citrine were favored) in the center of a scroll or bow of gold with small colored stone accents. Sentiment was expressed in charms of personal significance, some suspended from the traditional link bracelet, others mounted on wide hinged bangles or cuffs. Charms were also fine jewelry's form of whimsy. Disney cartoon characters became popular, especially after the appearance of the first feature length animated film, "Snow White and the Seven Dwarfs," in 1937.

Dress clips, the ornamental mainstay of the early thirties, became even more versatile as the central removable decoration of bangle bracelets, and as the "*passe-partout*"–another Van Cleef & Arpels invention (introduced in 1938), an enhancer for a snakechain necklace. The ubiquitous double clip brooch also continued to be worn through the forties. Early '30s pairs of clips were flat, geometric, symmetrical twins; later they became more three-dimensional and asymmetrical mirror images, or figurals. The double-pronged hinged clip finding took the place of the flat-backed clip by the end of the '30s. This type of fastening continued to be used on fine jewelry, often with the addition of a safety catch for one or both prongs.

During the war years, clothing fashions grew more severe and masculine, but jewelry, especially brooches, became more feminine. Large floral sprays were prevalent, worn high on a square-shouldered jacket, like a corsage of real flowers. Bicolor gold ribbon bows were another favorite, as were gem-set birds and butterflies. Necklaces became a focal point, shortened to collarbone or choker length. The flexible, slinky flattened gold tube, known variously as snake chain, gas pipe, or mouse tail, first exhibited in 1934, remained popular throughout the forties. Earrings became earclips with the introduction of the clipback finding, patented in 1934. The emphasis was on the lobe rather than below it. Multi-petaled flowerheads, scrolls and cornucopia were popular motifs. Pendent earrings continued to be worn at night, but were usually wider at the top, narrower at the bottom. Rings were massive, generally set with a large central colored gemstone flanked by scrolls of gold or small gemstones of contrasting color. Suites and demi-parures returned to favor after a hiatus of several decades, in matched brooches and earrings, clips and earrings, and necklaces, bracelets and earrings.

French jewelers continued to be innovative and influential designers until 1940, when France fell under German occupation. Suzanne Belperron (1900-1983) was a celebrated French artist-jeweler whose distinctive style must be studied to be recognized, because she seldom signed her work. She favored inexpensive gemstones like citrine and rock crystal, often sculpturally carved or set in clusters. She worked briefly for Cartier, and also ran her own shop; her longest association was with Jean Herz, with whom she formed the partnership Herz-Belperron in 1945.

Van Cleef & Arpels was one famous firm whose designs came to prominence during the prewar period. In addition to the aforementioned creations, they are credited with the invention of the "invisible setting" of calibré-cut gemstones, used primarily for sapphires and rubies. Another of their well-known designs was the ballerina clip or brooch. This design actually originated in the U.S., executed in the early forties by John Rubel Co. for Van Cleef & Arpels, New York. It inspired a host of female figurals, which remained popular through the fifties.

Cartier, long renowned for their impeccably crafted original designs, continued to produce distinctive, mostly figural pieces before the war. They even managed to create some new designs during wartime. Their famous "Bird in a Cage" and "Liberated Bird" brooches, executed in 1942 and 1944 respectively, symbolized the Occupation and the Liberation of Paris.

After 1940, most European jewelry production was curtailed, although the large French houses managed to stay afloat with a limited output of mostly prewar designs. By contrast, having been cut off from Europe during World War II, and with no Paris fashions to emulate, American jewelers and their designs came to the fore. Some of these jewelers were transplanted Europeans, others were "homegrown." One house, which became particularly well-known for their Retro Modern designs, was a merger of American and French firms: Trabert & Hoeffer-Mauboussin. Joining forces just after the stock market crash in 1929, the company became famous for their line of Retro-styled jewels, named "Reflection" in 1938. Their slogan was "Reflection–your personality in a jewel." The unique feature of this line was a standardized array of elements that the customer could arrange and combine to suit her fancy. Trabert & Hoeffer-Mauboussin were among the first to take advantage of the recently developed method of mass-production using lost-wax casting with vulcanized rubber molds, which facilitated the making of interchangeable components for the Reflection line. While the firm of Trabert & Hoeffer, Inc. continues today, the association with Mauboussin was terminated in the 1950s.

Texas-born Paul Flato (b.1900) opened his first salon in New York in the late '20s. His fame and fortune seemed assured when he opened a second establishment in Los Angeles in 1937, catering to Hollywood's elite. He was known for a wide variety of original, whimsical, naturalistic and surrealistic designs. Fame and fortune were fleeting, however. His business closed in the early 1940s. Flato was recently "rediscovered" in Texas, where he now resides. Consequently, more information about him and his work is now available. Portfolios of his designs were auctioned by Christie's Los Angeles in November, 1995.

One of Flato's designers, a European émigré who had already made a name for himself working for Chanel in Paris, was Fulco Santostefano della Cerda, duc di Verdura (1898-1978), known simply as Verdura. After leaving Flato in 1939, he opened his own shop in New York. He was known for his bold and imaginative designs and figural conceits. He emphasized design rather than large gemstones, the importance of which he dismissed, reputedly saying that "mineralogy is not jewelry." He occasionally incorporated shells and pebbles in his work. The firm founded by Verdura is still in business, under the ownership of Edward J. Landrigan, who continues to produce original Verdura designs.

Seaman Schepps (1881-1972), a native American, opened his first shops in California, but he moved to New York in 1921, where his establishment remained, except for a five-year hiatus from 1929 to 1934. His work reflects influences by Belperron, Flato, and Verdura in his sculptural and figural pieces. His most-often seen design is for clip earrings, a pair of gem-set turbo (snail-shaped) shells, inspired by Verdura.

Less well-publicized perhaps than their prestigious New York competitors, manufacturers in Newark, New Jersey, continued to produce well-made and affordable gold jewelry in the prevailing style of the period. Geared to conservative tastes, the pieces were more restrained examples of the "tailored" look that was popularly worn with suits at the time.

References: Annella Brown, "The Mysterious Madame Belperron," *Jewelers' Circular-Keystone/Heritage*, May 1992; John Culme and Nicholas Rayner, *The Jewels of the Duchess of Windsor*, Vendome Press/Sotheby's London, 1987; Ulysses G. Dietz, ed. *The Glitter & the Gold, Fashioning American's Jewelry*, The Newark Museum, 1997; Melissa Gabardi, *Art Deco Jewellery, 1920-1949*, Antique Collectors' Club, 1989; Lael Hagan, "The Retro Revival," *Jewelers' Circular-Keystone/Heritage*, May, 1994; George E. Harlow, *The Nature of Diamonds*, exhibition catalog, American Museum of Natural History, Cambridge University Press, 1998; Eileen Michaelis, "Reflection Jewelry: The Style of Trabert & Hoeffer-Mauboussin," *Jewelers' Circular-Keystone/Heritage*, February 1998; Sylvie Raulet, *Jewelry of the 1940s and 1950s,* and *Van Cleef & Arpels*, Rizzoli International, 1987 (both out of print); Christie Romero, "Dates to Remember," *Jewelers' Circular-Keystone/Heritage,* February, 1997; Kenneth Snowman, ed., *The Master Jewelers*, Harry N. Abrams, 1990; Sally A. Thomas, "'Modern' Jewelry: Retro to Abstract," *Gems and Gemology,* Spring 1987; Janet Zapata, "The Legacy of Value from Newark Jewelers," *Jewelers' Circular-Keystone/Heritage*, November, 1993; auction catalog: "American Jewelry," Christie's New York, October 21, 1992 (biographies and background information on American jewelers and jewelry by Janet Zapata).

Advisor: Janet Zapata.

Bracelet

Cultured pearls, 18k yg, amethysts, c. 1940-45, clasp of open opposed yg scrolls with fan-shaped sections set with baguette and sm circ amethyst cabs and seed pearls, joining four strands of cultured pearls, v-spring and box clasp, 1" w (at clasp), 6" tl .... 1,093 (A)

Bangle, hinged

Yg, diamonds, c. 1940, open loop rope-twist design with circ-cut diamond polka dots throughout and a center row of circ and sc diamonds, sgd "FLATO" for Paul Flato, Los Angeles, CA and New York, NY, provenance: from the estate of Ginger Rogers, 1-1/8" w .... 16,100 (A)

Charm

14k yg, c. 1935-40, fourteen charms, including two dogs, a typewriter, a thimble, an airplane, a red enameled ring, spring ring closure, all charms and chain mkd "14K," 7-1/2" tl 500

Sterling, c. 1943-45, fifteen World War II motif charms including an airplane, a tank, an artillery gun, binoculars, several coin charms of allied nations, spring ring closure, all charms and chain mkd "STERLING," 8" tl 250

Flexible

18k rose gold, diamonds, rubies, c. 1940, honeycomb-patterned wide strap, appl buckle set with five sm circ-cut diamonds in simulated hasp, approx .20 ct tw, two sm circ bezel-set ruby cab "grommets," 1" w x 7" tl .... 1,320 (A)

Link

14k yg, rose gold, rubies, diamonds, platinum, c. 1940, interlocking repeating bicone-shaped yg links, front clasp a central oval set with a row of grad prong-set ruby cabs bordered by rows of sm circ-cut diamonds mounted in plat, flanked by one long stepped cylinder and one short barrel, both with borders of channel-set calibré-cut rubies, sgd "Cartier" #1339, 1-1/8" w, 6-1/4" tl .. 5,175 (A)

14k red and yg, c. 1940, "tank track" style, ridged hollow bicolor links, cusped box shape, foldover box clasp, 32.0 dwt, 3/4" w x 6-1/2" tl .... 632 (A)

14k yg, c. 1945, "tank track" design, textured rounded rect links alternating with and flanked by outer ridged semi-cylindrical polished links, sgd "TIFFANY & CO.," 51.0 dwt, 1-1/4" w x 7-1/2" tl .... 1,824 (A)

Aquamarines, 18k rose gold, diamonds, c. 1945, nine oval bezel-set aquamarine cabs alternating with sq links, four central sq links each with a sm bezel-set oe diamond, mkd "18K," 1/2" w x 7-1/2" tl .... 2,990 (A)

Pearls, rock crystal quartz, paint, yg, c. 1940, six circ bezel-set reverse-painted crystal intaglios depicting various breeds of hunting dogs painted in multicolors, evenly spaced along a double strand of pearls of approx 4 mm each, gold spacers, mkd "14K," "Lucien Piccard," orig box, 3/8" w x 7" .... 690 (A)

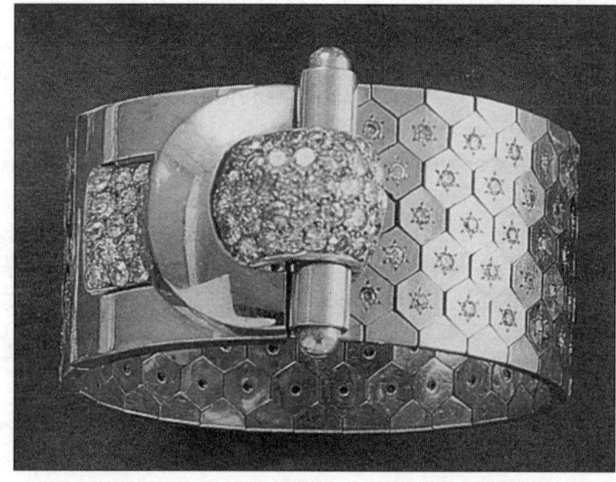

Bracelet, flexible, yg, diamonds, c. 1935-40, variation of the "Ludo," wide strap and buckle motif, clasp center pavé-set with om and oe diamonds, the strap of interlocking hexagons, each with a star gypsy-set sm circ-cut diamond, diamonds approx 7.25 cts tw, one extra link, sgd "VAN CLEEF & ARPELS," #48835, 1-3/8" w, 6-1/4" tl, **$13,800** [A]. (Photo courtesy of Sotheby's Beverly Hills, CA, 5/21/96).

Bracelet, flexible, 18k yg, diamonds, platinum, c. 1945, articulated band of engine-turned engr yg, allover pattern of polished yg daisies with pavé-set diamond centers, long edges flanked by pavé-set diamond and plat S-scrolled-edge ("ruffled") plaques, sgd "VAN CLEEF & ARPELS" #62589, Fr hmks, 1-1/2" w x 7-1/2" tl, **$32,200** [A]. (Photo courtesy of Christie's New York, NY, 10-23-96).

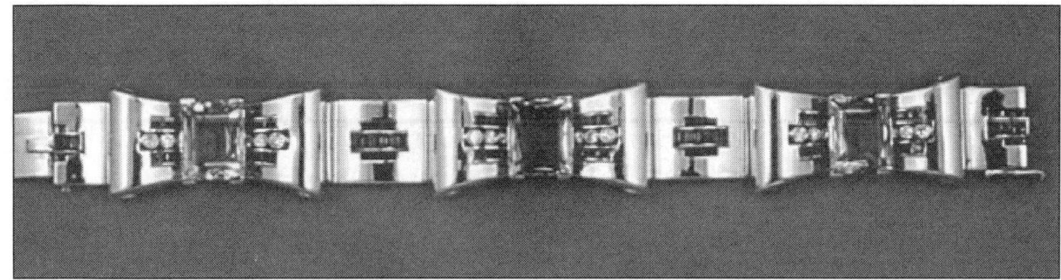

Bracelet, Link, 14k rose gold, citrines, rubies, diamonds, c. 1940-45, scrolled stylized bow-shaped links, each centering a lg emerald-cut prong-set citrine, flanked by a row of sm circ-cut diamonds bordered by two rows of channel-set calibré-cut rubies, alternating with slightly domed open sq links with channel-set ruby centers, mkd "TIFFANY & CO. 14K" on rev, v-spring and box clasp, 7/8" w x 7" tl, **$46,500**. (Ellen Borlenghi collection).

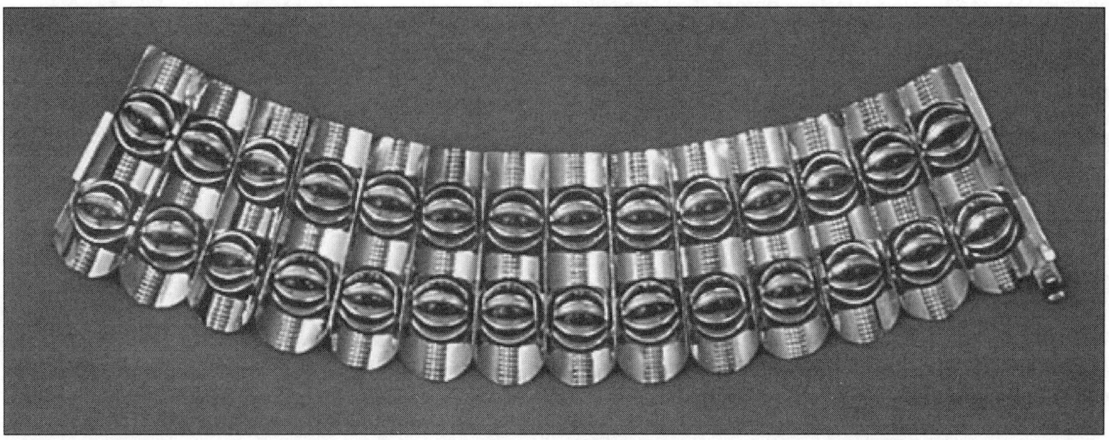

Bracelet, Link, 14k yg, enamel, c. 1940-45, slightly tapered concave rect plaques, hinged together, rounded outside edges forming scallop, each plaque vertically bisected by a ridged split tube surmounted by two circ domes, each with stripes of foiled red enamel in melon pattern, sliding hingepin closure, forms flared cuff when closed, provenance: from the estate of Joan Crawford, 1-3/4" w x 7", **$2,200**. (Ellen Borlenghi collection).

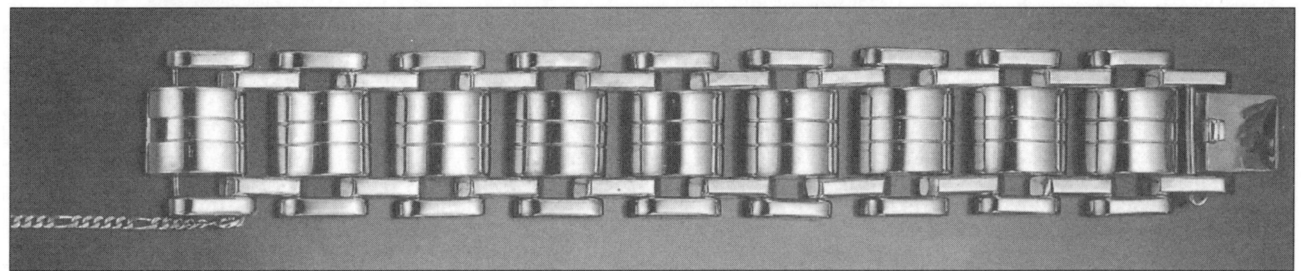

Link Bracelet, yg, "tank track" style, c. 1940: Overlapping rect bars flanking rounded sq links with incised parallel lines, Fr hmks for 18k, v-spring and box clasp, safety chain, 3.73 oz, 1-1/8" w x 7-1/2" tl, **$1,840** [A]. (Photo courtesy of Christie's Images, New York, NY, 12/11/96).

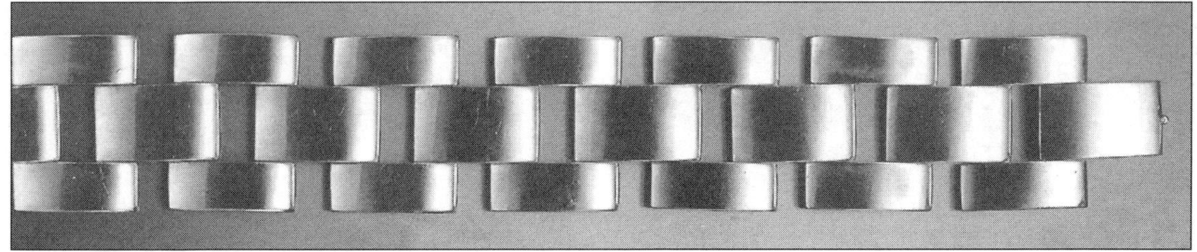

Link Bracelet, yg, "tank track" style, c. 1940: Wide polished staggered rect bar links, 3.74 oz, foldover box clasp, 1" w x 7-1/4", **$2,185** [A]. (Photo courtesy of Christie's Images, New York, NY, 12/11/96).

Rubies, 18k yg, diamonds, sapphires, c. 1945, central floral scroll clasp, bands of pavé-set diamonds bisecting three yg scrolls, sm circ-cut diamonds surrounded by lg prong-set ruby cabs, one central flowerhead of a domed diamond-set cluster encircled by lg prong-set blue sapphires, double tubular link band, foldover box clasp, sgd "BOUCHERON," Fr hmk (eagle's head) for 18k gold, clasp 2-3/8" w x 1-3/8", 6-1/4" tl .... 8,050 (A)

Yg, amethysts, c. 1940, lg central octagonal prong-set amethyst, sixteen sm circ prong-set amethysts clustered on four sides, flanked by grad rounded chevron-shaped yg links to two lg octagonal prong-set amethysts, continuing to chevron-shaped yg links, foldover box clasp, safety chain, 1" w (at center), 7-1/4" tl .... 1,150 (A)

Yg, rubies, c. 1940, seven lg links, each of opposed semi-circ plaques flanking inverted ribbed V shape, center set with two rows of sm ruby cabs, joined by prs of arched links flanked by elongated sm domes, 6.98 oz tw, 1-5/8" w x 7-7/8" tl .... 5,175 (A)

Yg, rubies, diamonds, c. 1940, horseshoe-shaped yg links joined with inverted V-shaped links, one side of V with star-cut set diamonds, the other side with ruby baguettes, 5/8" w x 8" tl .... 3,450 (A)

Brooch/Clip

Yg, tourmaline, c. 1935-40, stylized Athena's helmet with lg circ-cut green tourmaline in center, clip and brooch findings, Am, sgd "FLATO" for Paul Flato, 2-1/2" w x 1-1/2" .... 5,750 (A)

Brooch/Pin

14k yg, amethyst, c. 1940, open scrolling ribbon bow design with central prong-set oval amethyst, 2-1/8" w x 3-1/4" .... 575 (A)

14k yg, peridots, ruby, c. 1940, stylized flower of open circ loops of tubular yg forming petals, six prong-set oval-cut yellow peridots encircling a central sm circ prong-set ruby, two flattened wires forming stem, 2" w x 2-3/4" .... 542 (A)

14k yg, rose gold, diamonds, rubies, c. 1945, rose gold ribbon gathered by a yg center with an appl row of collet-set sm circ-cut diamonds and rubies, 2-1/2" w x 1-5/8" .... 460 (A)

14k yg, rubies, c. 1940, tubular yg wire forming an open heart diagonally surmounted by a key prong-set with eight sm circ-cut rubies, 8.5 dwt, 1-1/2" w x 1-1/2" .... 288 (A)

14k yg, rubies, c. 1940, yg bow of three ribbon loops, two ribbon ends, center knot set with eight calibré-cut rubies, lever catch, 12.00 dwt, 2" w x 1-7/8" .... 825 (A)

Brooch/Pin, aquamarine, diamonds, rubies, 10k yg and wg, c. 1940, scrolling bicolor gold ribbon motif centering a lg emerald-cut prong-set aquamarine surrounded by eight rows of prong-set circ ruby cabs and forty-two sm circ-cut diamond accents, 2-1/2" w x 2-1/2", **$3,680** [A]. (Photo courtesy of Christie's Images, New York, NY, 12/11/96).

14k yg, tourmaline, moonstone, c. 1945, in the shape of a flower on a foliated stem, a sm circ bezel-set moonstone cab encircled by six lg faceted oval prong-set green tourmalines, three polished yg leaves and a flower bud of a single prong-set pear-shaped green tourmaline, mkd "994," 1-1/4" w x 2-3/4" .... 403 (A)

18k yg, sapphires, rubies, diamonds, c. 1940, stylized floral spray, three cushion-cut sapphires prong-set at the terminals of grad wire stems, flanked by wire volutes with collet-set ruby centers, lg yg leaf, diamond-set ribbon tie, 1-5/8" w x 2" .... 1,035 (A)

Rock crystal quartz, diamonds, platinum, c. 1935, semi-circle with U-shaped center of fluted rock crystal quartz with an inside border of circ-cut diamonds, terminating in pavé-set diamond scrolls with baguette diamond borders, set in plat, by Suzanne Belperron, 2" w x 1-1/4" .... 61,900 (A)

Brooch/pin, 18k rose gold, diamonds, platinum, ruby, c. 1935-40, in the shape of the stylized figure of a woman in rose gold wearing hat and muff in plat set with sm circ-cut diamonds, coat with diamond-set plat collar and hem, diamond eye, sm ruby cab mouth, mkd "LACLOCHE FRÈRES, MADE IN FRANCE," Fr hmk (eagle's head) for 18k, Paris hmk, 1/2" w x 1-3/4", **$1,850**. (Photo courtesy of Lovejoy's Estate Jewelry, Bellingham, WA).

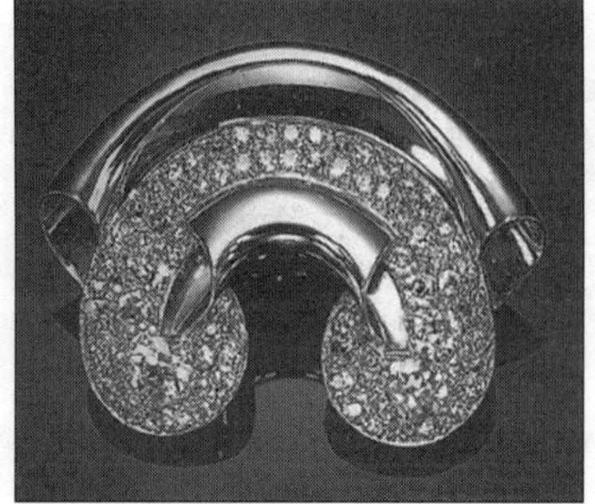

Brooch/Pin, diamonds, platinum, c. 1935, draped crescent and scroll motif of folded platinum enclosing a pavé-set diamond inverted U-shaped plaque, two lg oe diamonds within terminals, in a suede case, sgd "RAYMOND TEMPLIER," 2-1/4" w x 1-5/8", **$29,900** [A]. (Photo courtesy of Christie's New York, NY, 10/23/96).

Brooch/Pin, 14k rose and yg, rubies, c. 1940, two open ovals, outlined on opposing sides with eight circ prong-set rubies and bisected by two bicolor gold tapered cylinders in opposing directions, flanking pierced bicolor gold scrolling ribbon motifs, lever catch, appl plate mkd "14K" on rev, 2-3/4" w x 2", **$1,600**. (Ellen Borlenghi collection).

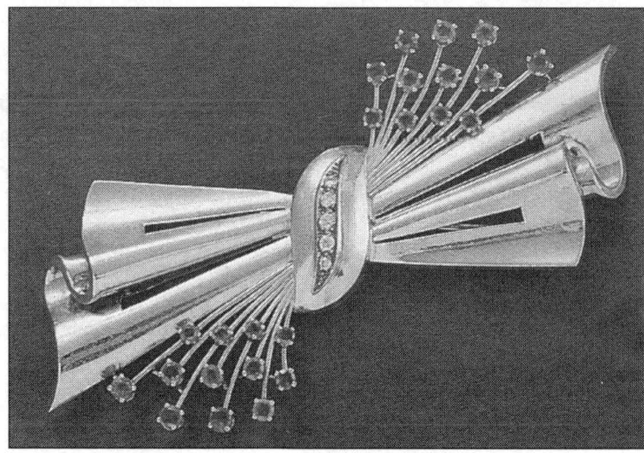

Brooch/Pin, rose gold, rubies, diamonds, c. 1940, folded rose gold ribbon motif gathered in center, surmounted by curved navette-shaped knot set with a center row of five sm circ-cut diamonds, flanked by sprays of twenty-four sm circ-cut prong-set rubies on gold wires in opposing directions, 3" w x 2-1/8", **$690** [A]. (Photo courtesy of Sotheby's Beverly Hills, CA, 5/21/96).

Rose and yg, rubies, diamonds, c. 1940, three-dimensional bi-colored gold ribbon bow central knot set with sm bc diamonds and calibré-cut rubies, 2-1/2" w x 1-1/4" .... 1,380 (A)

Yg, diamonds, rubies, c. 1940, stylized three-flower spray, three-dimensional curved yg leaves, flower centers prong-set with numerous circ-cut rubies, circ-cut diamond-set stems, ribbon tie with diamond-set border, 1-3/4" w x 2-3/4" .... 2,990 (A)

Yg, rubies, diamonds, c. 1940, three-dimensional five-petaled flower, leaves and ribbon bow design in polished yg, center and edges set with twenty-nine sm circ-cut and oe diamonds, circ-cut and calibré-cut rubies, 1-1/2" w x 2-1/2" .... 978 (A)

Yg, topaz, diamonds, wg, c. 1945, single flower with petals and leaves of polished yg, flower center a lg circ-cut prong-set yellow topaz surrounded by seven oval topaz, stem of twelve sm circ-cut diamonds mounted in wg, 1-3/4" w x 2-3/4" .... 2,645 (A)

Brooches/Pins

14k rose and yg, amethysts, rubies, c. 1940, three overlapping bicolor gold scrolls backing a grad fanned-out row of five sm circ-cut ruby-tipped wires surmounting a prong-set rect-cut lg amethyst, mkd "14K," 7/8" w x 1-7/8", pr .... 315 (A)

Brooch/Pin, moonstones, diamonds, 18k pink gold, c. 1940-45, three floral clusters of oval and circ rainbow moonstones with bc diamond centers, interspersed with bc diamonds, enclosed on one side by a polished pink gold convex arc, a row of bc diamonds along one edge, 1-3/4" dia, **$2,300** [A]. (Photo courtesy of Phillips Fine Art Auctioneers, New York, NY, 6/10/97).

Brooch/Pin, yg, wg, rose gold, rubies, sapphires, moonstones, c. 1945, depicting a three-color gold horse and carriage with two wirework figures, horse with a sm circ ruby cab eye, wheels with sm circ ruby cab hubs, a grad row of sm circ sapphires at the front of the carriage, two ruby beads as the heads of the figures, a row of grad circ moonstones along the crescent-shaped back of the carriage, 2-1/2" w x 1-1/2", **$1,610** [A]. (Photo courtesy of Sotheby's Beverly Hills, CA, 5/20/97).

Clip

Amethyst, yg, platinum, diamonds, c. 1945, stylized sunflower design, flowerhead centering a lg oval prong-set amethyst within satin-finished yg petals, satin-finished plat leaves, tips set with sm circ-cut diamonds, double-pronged hinged clip on rev, 1-3/4" w x 2-3/4" .... 2,300 (A)

Diamonds, yg, c. 1940, in the shape of a classical man's profile in brushed gold with pavé-set diamond hair, sgd "FLATO" for Paul Flato, provenance: from the estate of Ginger Rogers, 1-1/4" w x 1-1/2" .... 13,800 (A)

Emeralds, rubies, yg, diamonds, c. 1945, stylized flower motif, flowerhead a cluster of lg circ prong-set emerald cabs interspersed with sm circ collet-set diamonds, three leaves of half polished yg and half pavé-set sm circ rubies, sgd "TRABERT & HOEFFER-MAUBOUSSIN, Reflection," double-pronged hinged clip, 2" w x 3" .... 6,900 (A)

Clips

Diamonds, yg, platinum, c. 1939, in the shape of a pr of three-dimensional feathers, one a yg shaft and diamond-set plat barbs, the other diamond-set plat shaft with yg barbs, featured in a Paul Flato advertisement in *Vogue* Magazine, page 33, Oct. 15, 1939, provenance: from the estate of Ginger Rogers, each 1-3/4" w x 2-3/4", pr .... 43,700 (A)

Clip, 18k yg, diamonds, enamel, platinum, ruby, c. 1940, depicting Donald Duck hanging from four yg balloons, plat hands, face and body set with twenty-eight sm circ bead-set diamonds and one sm circ prong-set ruby eye, blue enamel sleeves and cap, red enamel bowtie, hmks, double-pronged hinged clip, 1-1/4" w x 2-3/4", **$1,710** [A]. (Photo courtesy of Beverly Hills Auctioneers, Inc., CA, 2/16/97).

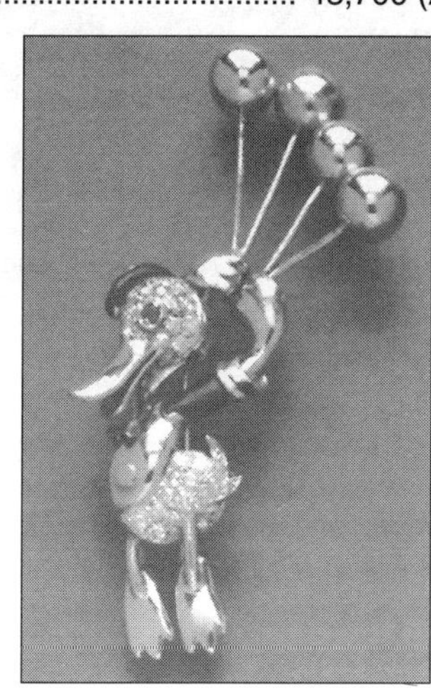

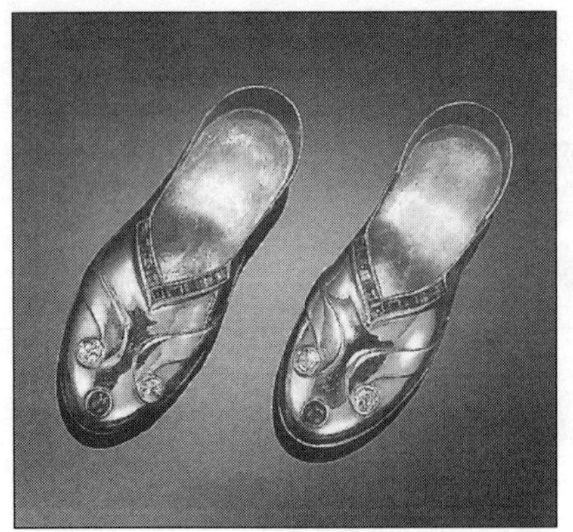

Clips, yg, diamonds, rubies, sapphires, c. 1940, depicting slipper-style shoes with collet-set diamonds, ruby cabs, and calibré-cut sapphire details, Am, sgd "FLATO" for Paul Flato, provenance: from the estate of Ginger Rogers, 3/4" w x 2", pr, **$8,050** [A]. (Photo courtesy of Christie's Los Angeles, CA, 10/3/96).

Double Clip Brooch, 18k rose gold, diamonds, platinum, rubies, c. 1935-40, stylized opposed feather and scroll motif with central line of eleven sc diamonds bead-set in plat-topped rose gold, approx 0.75 ct tw, cluster of three sm circ-cut prong-set rubies at the end of each clip, double-pronged hinged clips, removable pinback mechanism, 3-3/4" w x 1-1/2" (joined), **$2,280** [A]. (Photo courtesy of Beverly Hills Auctioneers, Inc., CA, 2/16/97).

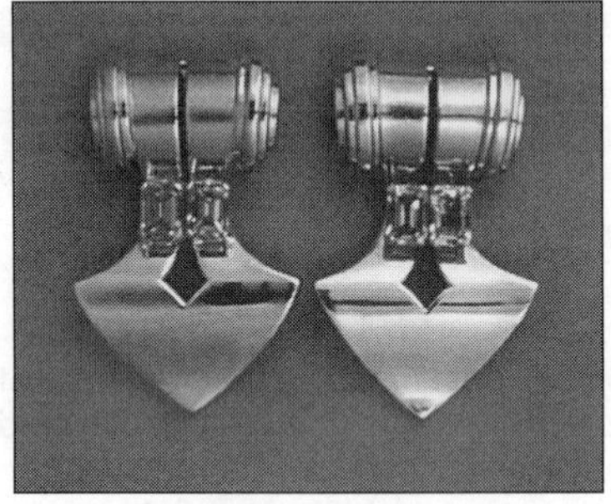

Clips, 14k rose and yg, aquamarines, c. 1940, each a convex/concave cusped yg kite shape with cutout center surmounted by a stepped rose gold cylinder, center prong-set with two emerald-cut aquamarines (one chipped), double-pronged hinged clip, mkd "14K" on rev, 1-1/8" w x 1-3/4", pr, **$2,800**. (Ellen Borlenghi collection).

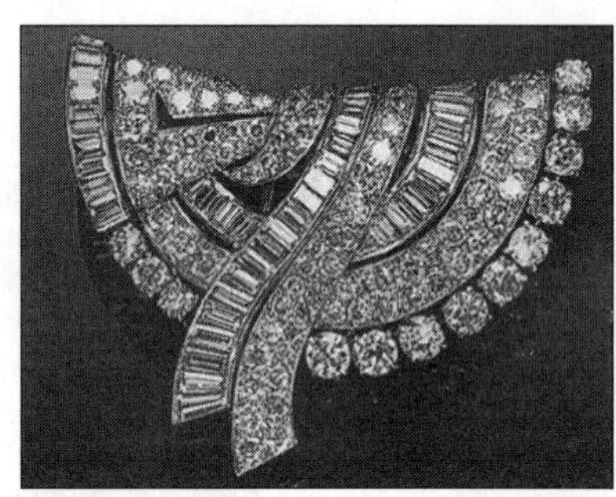

Double Clip Brooch, diamonds, platinum, c. 1938, two asymmetrical sectors join to form a semi-circle with pavé-set and baguette diamond ribbon motif center, and concentric semi-circ rows of baguette and circ-cut diamonds, sgd "BOUCHERON, PARIS," removable brooch mechanism, 2-1/4" w x 1-7/8" (joined), **$20,700** [A]. (Photo courtesy of Christie's New York, NY, 10/23/96).

Double Clip Brooch, 14k yg, c. 1940-45, opposed three-dimensional scroll and fan motifs, removable brooch mechanism, maker's mk for Larter & Sons, Newark NJ, 2-1/2" w x 1" (joined), **$1,265** [A]. (Photo courtesy of Skinner, Inc., Boston, MA, 6/10/97).

Earrings, 14k yg, rubies, diamonds, c. 1940, each a yg bow of four ribbon loops, three ribbon ends, center prong-set with a cluster of five circ-cut rubies around a bc diamond, five circ-cut rubies prong-set at the ends of five yg wires between the bow loops, mkd "14k", clipback findings, 1" w x 1-1/4", pr, **$770** [A]. (Photo courtesy of Beverly Hills Auctioneers, Inc.), CA, 6/22/97).

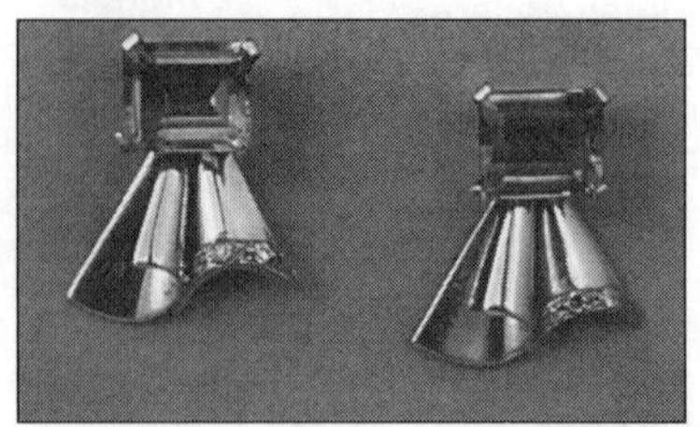

Earrings, amethysts, yg, diamonds, wg, c. 1940, each earring a prong-set emerald-cut amethyst surmounting a scrolled fan shape with two sm diamonds bead-set in engr wg along half of bottom edge, clip backs, 3/4" w x 1", pr, **$385**. (Courtesy of E. Foxe Harrell Jewelers, Clinton, IA).

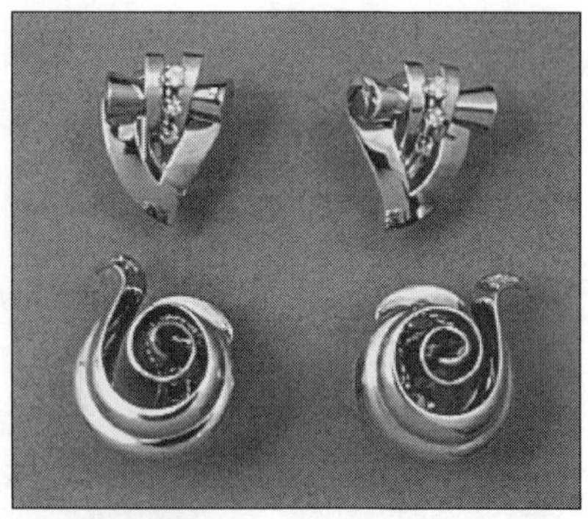

Earrings, c. 1940:

T, 14k yg scrolled leaf motif, each cutout center pierced by a V-shaped strip set with three sm bc diamonds, screwbacks mkd "14K," one mkd "Cartier," 3/4" w x 1", pr, **$1,250**.

B, rose gold volutes with curved tips, each set with three sm bc diamonds (one missing), clipbacks, 7/8" w x 1-1/4", pr, **$1,000**.

(Ellen Borlenghi collection).

Cuff Links

14k yg, c. 1940, each in the shape of a threaded bolt with slotted head and a screw-on nut, attributed to Paul Flato, 5/8" dia, pr .... 1,150 (A)

Earrings/Earclips

14k yg, c. 1940, V-shape with cutout center and scrolled top centering a stepped cylinder, screwbacks, sgd "TIFFANY & CO.," 7/8" w x 7/8", pr .... 518 (A)

Aquamarines, diamonds, platinum, yg, c. 1945, each with three prong-set rect-cut aquamarines surmounting a pierced diamond-set scroll motif, clipbacks, 1" w x 1-1/4" .... 1,840 (A)

Citrine, diamonds, platinum, c. 1940, circ clips, central oe and om diamond cluster encircled by calibré-cut citrines, sm circ-cut diamonds spaced around the rim, wearable as dress clips, sgd "V.C.A." for Van Cleef & Arpels, New York, #15287, 1-1/8" dia, pr .... 32,200 (A)

Yg, sapphires, rubies, diamonds, c. 1940, floral and foliate motif, each with three lg faceted oval prong-set yellow sapphires accented with six prong-set sm circ-cut rubies and a single sm circ-cut prong-set diamond, clipbacks, 3/4" w x 1-1/4" .... 633 (A)

Neckchain

14k yg, c. 1940, snake chain, foldover box clasp, 24.2 dwt, 1/4" w x 15-1/2" tl .... 690 (A)

Necklace

14k yg, diamonds, c. 1945, yg snake chain terminating in a cross-hatched textured snake's head, bc diamond eyes, prong-set oe diamond on mouth, crossing over opposite terminal with a fringe of five bead-tipped chains, 17-3/4" tl, approx 34 dwt .... 1,490 (A)

18k yg, diamonds, c. 1940, double strand of flexible yg tubes, reeded alternating with polished segments, dome-shaped front terminals with circ-cut diamond borders suspending an open pear-shaped drop, scalloped edges set with a row of circ-cut diamonds, two intertwined yg flexible loops of polished yg tubular segments interspersed with diamond-set rings suspended from open center, Fr hmks, sgd "Regner, Paris," 15" tl, center 1" w x 3-1/8" top to bottom .... 6,325 (A)

Pendant

Yg, turquoise, diamonds, platinum, c. 1945, scalloped circ flowerhead, overlapping polished yg loops centering a circ prong-set turq cab within a bombé mount of pavé-set diamonds, encircled by eight circ turq cabs and eight sm circ-cut diamonds in triangular plat mounts, bail on rev, 1-1/2" dia .... 920 (A)

Pendant and Chain

10k yg, shell, f.w. pearl, c. 1940, Victorian Revival, openwork quatrefoil with central navette-shaped cameo of a woman suspending f.w. pearl drop, mkd "OB 10k" on bail for Otsby & Barton, Providence, RI, suspended from fine curb link chain, spring ring closure, pendant 1/2" w x 1-5/8" tl, chain 14-1/2" tl 100

Ring

Aquamarine, diamonds, rubies, yg, platinum, c. 1940, lg central emerald-cut prong-set aquamarine of approx 42.50 cts, flanked by domed shoulders of pavé-set sm circ diamonds each bordered by rows of calibré-cut rubies, plat and yg shank, 1-1/4" w x 1" .... 6,900 (A)

Diamonds, 14k wg, c. 1945, wide band with foliate scroll motif centering one oe diamond of approx 0.40 ct, with eight sc and three sm circ-cut diamonds, approx 0.40 ct tw, 1/2" w (at top), approx size 6 .... 627 (A)

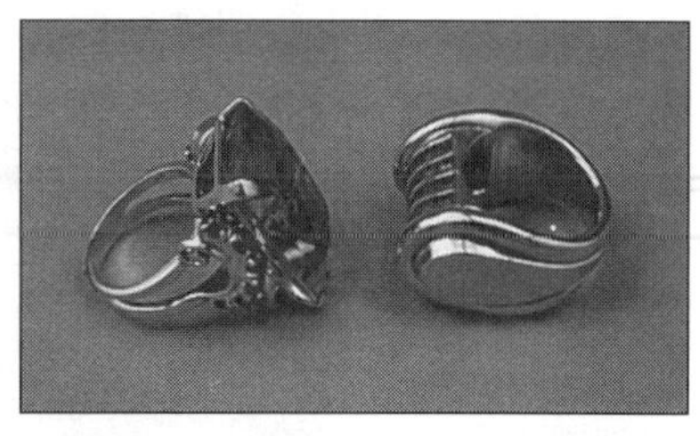

Rings, c. 1940: **L**, citrine, rubies, yg, central step-cut prong-set citrine, approx 24 mm by 16 mm, flanked by scrolled yg wire shoulders each set with six sm ruby cabs, on a tapered split shank, approx size 6-1/2, **$1,800**.
R, rose gold, rubies, half cylinder top with four rows of channel-set sq-cut rubies (one missing, three damaged), flanked by rounded stepped shoulders tapering to shank, 7/8" w x 5/8", **$3,500**.
(Ellen Borlenghi collection).

Rings, 14k, c. 1940: **L**, wg, emerald-cut aquamarine, approx 28.00 cts, prong-set in narrow shank, mkd "14k," approx size 5-1/2, 5/8" w x 7/8", **$2,500**.
R, yg, step-cut citrine, approx 29.00 cts, prong-set in scrolled shoulders, narrow shank, mkd "CKG 14k," approx size 6, 3/4" w x 7/8", **$500**.
(Ron Belkin collection).

Rock crystal quartz, rubies, diamonds, platinum, c. 1935, sculpted rock crystal quartz domed mount set with rows of calibré-cut rubies and sc diamonds, by Suzanne Belperron, 1" w x 1", size 6-1/4 .... 19,550 (A)

Rock crystal quartz, emeralds, platinum, c. 1935, cushion-shaped rock crystal quartz mount, set with a lg sq-cut emerald surrounded by calibré-cut sm emeralds in a plat frame, formerly the property of Vera Zorin, famous ballerina and first wife of George Balanchine, purchased directly from Suzanne Belperron, 1" w x 7/8", size 6-1/2 .... 51,750 (A)

Suite: Bracelet and Clips

Diamonds, rubies, platinum, c. 1935, "machine age" design, bracelet of pavé-set and baguette diamond scroll design, centering a rotating cylinder, one side of calibré-cut rubies, the other of pavé-set diamonds, matching pair of clips, scrolled and pierced rounded plaques with similar design features, diamonds approx 94.00 cts tw, rubies approx 25.00 cts tw, bracelet 1-1/2" w, clips 1-5/8" w x 1-7/8", suite .... 156,500 (A)

Suite: Bracelet, Pendant/Brooch, Earrings, and Ring

Aquamarines, 18k yg, sapphires, diamonds, palladium, c. 1940, bracelet top of pierced scrolled lozenge shape centering a prong-set emerald-cut aquamarine of approx 50.00 cts, with sm prong-set blue sapphire trefoils at compass points and rows of sm circ-cut diamonds set in palladium bisecting four yg scrolls, mounted on a flexible snake chain band, pendant/brooch a shield shape of similar design with central aquamarine of 56.00 cts, detachable yg snake chain, matching clipback earrings and ring, sgd "TIFFANY & CO.," bracelet 1-3/4" w (at center), 6-1/2" tl, brooch/pendant 2-1/8" w x 2-1/2", earrings 1" w x 1-1/8", ring 3/4" w x 1-1/8", suite .... 17,250 (A)

Suite: Double Clip Brooch, Earrings, and Ring

Rose gold, diamonds, rubies, c. 1940, pr of clips of opposed scrolling ribbon motif in polished rose gold with prong and bead-set diamond borders, rays of diamonds and

Suite: Brooch/Pin and Earrings, 14k yg, sapphires, rubies, diamonds, c. 1940, brooch an open-centered circ frame with scalloped petal-like edge, flanked on one side by an arc, surmounted by a lg stylized bow motif set with lg cushion-cut sapphires, sm circ-cut rubies and diamonds, 1-1/2" w x 1-3/4" matching bow-shaped earclips 3/4" w x 1-1/4", suite, **$3,220** [A]. (Photo courtesy of Christie's New York, 4/8/97).

calibré-cut rubies, removable pinback mechanism, matching ring and clipback earrings, one hundred twenty circ-cut and oe diamonds total, brooch 3" w x 1-1/4", earrings 1/2" w x 3/4", ring 1" w x 1/2", size 6, suite .... 4,600 (A)

Suite: Three Brooches/Pins and Earrings

18k yg, rubies, diamonds, c. 1940, each brooch a ruffled circ yg disk randomly set with thirteen sm circ-cut diamonds, centering a cluster of prong-set circ and oval ruby cabs, matching clipback earrings, sgd "TRABERT & HOEFFER-MAUBOUSSIN, Reflection," brooches 1-5/8" dia, earrings 3/4" dia, suite .... 13,800 (A)

Suite: Bracelet, Clip, and Earrings

Yg, moonstones, citrines, rubies, sapphires, c.1940, bracelet a double snake chain centering a flowerhead of a lg circ-cut citrine surrounded by sm circ-cut rubies and eight lg oval moonstones flanked by sm circ-cut ruby and sapphire accents, clip with watch mounted on rev, a similar flowerhead with ten lg oval moonstones flanked by yg sculptural leaves, clipback earrings, each a bouquet with three lg oval moonstones accented by sm circ-cut rubies and sapphires, bracelet 2" w x 1", 2-1/4" inside dia, clip/watch 2" w x 1-1/4", earrings 1/2" w x 3/4", suite .... 2,875 (A)

Suite: Brooch/Pendant and Earrings

14k yg, rubies, diamonds, platinum, c. 1945, starburst design of radiating yg conical rays, alternating with yg ruby-tipped wire rays, central sm bc diamond set in plat encircled by sm circ-cut rubies, matching clipback earrings, brooch 1" dia, earrings 1/2" dia, suite ...... 805 (A)

Suite: Brooch/Pin and Earrings

14k yg, diamonds, rubies, c. 1945, brooch of two eccentric tubular circles surmounted by a notched concave disk with radiating yg wire rays set with sm bc diamonds and rubies, clipback earrings of similar design, brooch 1-1/2" dia, earrings 5/8" w x 1-1/4", suite .... 748 (A)

Suite: Hinged Bangle, Brooch/Pin, Ring, Earrings

14k yg, emeralds, diamonds, c. 1945, a three-dimensional yg conch shell design, circ-cut diamonds set in a spiraling row, suspending a fringe of articulated pear-shaped emerald bead drops with collet-set diamond caps, appl to a similar yg and diamond rope-twist hinged bangle, central element can be detached and worn as a clip, *en suite* with similar brooch, ring, earrings, sgd "FLATO" for Paul Flato, provenance: from the estate of Ginger Rogers, bangle 1-1/2" w x 3-1/2", brooch 1-7/8" w x 2-1/2", earrings 1" w x 1-1/4", ring 1" x 1-1/8", suite .... 43,700 (A)

MID-CENTURY MODERN AMERICAN STUDIO JEWELRY, c. 1945-1965

History: Just as the adherents of the Arts & Crafts movement rebelled against mainstream tradition at the turn of the century, so too did studio artists of the mid-century follow a path of their own. They reinterpreted the earlier movement's guiding principles in new forms, with new approaches to design, creating a new definition of the word "modern," with which the 1950s came to be identified.

True to the Arts & Crafts philosophy, the emphasis was on design, hand-craftsmanship and accessibility to the public. Gold and precious stones were used on occasion, but sterling was the preferred metal, alone or in combination, most often with stones of the quartz family, cultured pearls, wood, brass, copper, and enamels. Although the jewelry was meant to be affordable for most people, the audience for these pieces was not wide. As was also the case at the turn of the century, this was not jewelry for the masses, but rather for an intellectual elite–the "Beat Generation"–that congregated primarily in urban centers on the East and West coasts. The "beatniks" were more ready and willing to accept the "far-out" designs that artist-jewelers produced than the average suburban housewife.

Still, as the crafts movement gathered momentum, demand did grow, and some jewelers attempted to manufacture more commercialized production pieces. Many of their hand-crafted designs were not well-suited to mass production, however, and when demand increased, prices for one-of-a-kind pieces by well-known artists went up. Today these pieces–by important designers such as Sam Kramer and Margaret De Patta -command thousands.

The mid-century modernist movement had its roots in pre-war Europe, under the influence of the Bauhaus and fine and applied arts "isms" such as Dadaism and Surrealism, Cubism, Biomorphism and Constructivism. Several European painters and sculptors of these artistic schools also designed jewelry, among them: Salvador Dalí, Pablo Picasso, Jean Cocteau, and Georges Braque. In crossing the Atlantic, however, these influences were translated into a uniquely American idiom by artists who were jewelry *makers* as well as designers. This was the case even when the European influences were more direct. Some American metalsmiths studied under leaders of the movement who had come to the United States just before the war and set up schools of design, or became directors of design programs at established schools and universities. Among them were Walter Gropius, Marcel Breuer, and László Moholy-Nagy of the Bauhaus. Other influences came from Scandinavia, where modernism flourished under the auspices of several important designers and their companies (see Scandinavian section under Special Collectibles).

Still another source of education came, surprisingly, from the U.S. government. After World War II, returning veterans entered into government-sponsored "rehab" programs. Workshops were led by metalsmith Margret Craver Withers (b.1907) from 1947 to 1951. These helped to generate interest in pursuing the study of crafts further through the G.I. Bill. In response to this growing interest, a number of "how-to" books on jewelry-making were published from the late '40s through the '60s. Today these books are invaluable resources for the historian, because they picture and give information about the work of modernist jewelers (see References below).

The overriding concepts characterizing the modernists' work were abstraction and nonobjective form, but each of them interpreted these concepts in different ways with a variety of techniques. Artist-jeweler Philip Morton, author of a "how-to" book, *Contemporary Jewelry, a Studio Handbook*, in evaluating the work of mid-century metalsmiths, divides design into two groups, or "expressive modes": "rational" and "nonrational." Within each mode he names several forms and techniques: "plate-shape," "linear," "strip-plate," "constructed," "fused," "forged," and "cast." Each approach yielded a unique design, and yet for all their differences, there is an identifiable cohesiveness uniting the overall body of work by these artists. Space does not permit discussing the finer points of the work of every one of them here. Mention should be made, however, of the seminal, influential, and important American studio jewelers whose work is collected today. Pieces by some of them are included in this section. A longer, but of necessity still incomplete, list can be found in the appendix, Mid-century Modern American Studio Jewelers.

Harry Bertoia (1915-1978) was born in Italy, and came to the United States in 1930. He made his first pieces of jewelry in Detroit, at the age of twenty-one. He attended Cranbrook Academy of Art beginning in 1937, and emerged a multimedia artist, particularly fluent in metalworking. His jewelry, mostly executed in hammered brass, became something of a sideline to his primary focus on furniture, and later, sculpture. It is never signed. The earrings on page 186 bear a striking resemblance to a documented c. 1948 pair that is part of the "Messengers of Modernism" exhibition (see References and Museums, below). Bertoia lived in Los Angeles CA for a while in the forties, where he worked with Charles and Ray Eames before moving to Bally PA in 1950 to design furniture for Knoll Associates.

Sam Kramer (1913-1964), another one of the first, and perhaps the most avant-garde studio artist of them all, also began making jewelry in 1936, a full decade before the crafts movement was truly established. He opened a shop in New York City's Greenwich Village in 1939. His work, and his personality, were a decided departure from the ordinary, a fact that he emphasized in advertising his wares as "fantastic jewelry for people who are slightly mad." He was called a "surrealistic jeweler" by *New Yorker* magazine. Kramer was known for incorporating bizarre materials like taxidermists' glass eyes and found objects into even more bizarre biomorphic fused, cast and constructed designs that have been given such names as "Creature Brooch," "Skeletal Cuff," and "Pterodactyl Brooch." He trained his wife Carol to design and make jewelry, which she continued to do after his death until 1970. His mark, a mushroom inside a lobed circle, gave him the nickname "Mushroom Sam"; like some of his pieces, the mushroom had erotic implications. Not all of Kramer's work was one-of-a-kind oddities. He did make some multiples of designs in a constructivist mode. Perhaps they were meant for his slightly less mad customers, but today these pieces bring slightly less money.

Several other studio artists set up shop in Greenwich Village in the 1940s and 1950s, taking advantage of the favorable intellectual climate there. Among them, Paul Lobel (1900-1983) successfully maintained a commercial production operation from about 1945 to 1964, making large cuff bracelets and brooches from cutout silver sheet and soldered forged wire. He was known for both nonobjective designs and abstract figurals such as musical instruments, animals, fruit and leaf forms, all of which were given names in his catalogs. Art Smith (1917-1982), also worked in sheet and forged silver wire (as well as brass and copper), and although he was influenced by Lobel, his work was more sculptural and biomorphic; he used the human body as a point of departure or supportive armature for his designs. In 1948, Smith opened a shop in the Village, a few doors down from Lobel's. He signed his name in script on some, but not all, of his pieces.

Ed Wiener (1918-1991), began working in his own shop in 1946, in Provincetown, MA, but opened a store in New York City soon after, in 1947, called "Arts and Ends." His long career, ending only with his death, encompassed a succession of stylistic approaches, wrought or cast in silver and gold, often with the addition of gemstones. His signature is his name in lowercase print or block letters, but his jewelry is not always signed. Some later pieces are marked "E.W." His earlier work (1940s-50s) is generally more sought-after than his later pieces. He didn't start working in materials of high intrinsic value until the mid-1960s.

Ronald H. Pearson (1924-1996) was one of the founding fathers of Shop I in Rochester NY. Opened in 1952, Shop I was the first independent gallery to exhibit and sell modern crafts exclusively. Pearson's work in forged or cast silver or gold is characterized by graceful simplicity of form, reminiscent of Scandinavian design. Pearson resided and worked in Deer Isle, Maine until his recent death.

Other East coast artist-jewelers of note (New York City unless otherwise specified): Jules Brenner, Alexander Calder, Betty Cooke (Baltimore, MD), Ed Levin (also Bennington, VT), Earl Pardon (Saratoga Springs, NY), Frank Rebajes, Olaf Skoogfors (Philadelphia, PA), Henry Steig, Bill Tendler.

On the opposite coast, in Northern California, Margaret De Patta's "rational" approach was the opposite of Sam Kramer's "nonrational" one, but her influence on others was seminal, and possibly greater than his. A modernist pioneer, De Patta (1903-1964) began jewelry-making in 1930, and had her own workshop by 1935. She established a studio in the San Francisco Bay Area in 1941, after studying with László Moholy-Nagy at his Bauhaus-oriented School of Design in Chicago. In 1946, disturbed by the fact that demand had driven up prices so that her jewelry was becoming inaccessible to the average person, De Patta and husband Eugene Bielawski responded by going into limited production of some of her designs using lost-wax casting methods. Each piece sold for under fifty dollars. One of these, the brooch on page 183, is shown in a 1948 photograph of De Patta in the act of mounting the pearl. The energy and time-consuming tasks required to run the business caused the couple to abandon this endeavor in 1958.

De Patta's constructivist techniques yielded jewelry with optical effects achieved by combining specially cut or faceted transparent stones with metal rods, wire, sheet, or textured surfaces. Her pieces were three-dimensional spatial studies. She worked in both silver and gold, occasionally using diamonds, more often rock crystal and rutilated quartz and other inexpensive gemstones. In the late '50s, she began incorporating pebbles picked up during walks on the beach, foreshadowing the "found object" trend of the late '60s and '70s. Her mark is a stylized M surmounted by a dot; she sometimes used her last name, with or without her mark.

In 1951, De Patta initiated the organization of the Metal Arts Guild in San Francisco, a resource, information, and support network for local metalsmiths. Joining this group were several artists who made names for themselves in the fifties and sixties. All of them give credit to De Patta as an inspirational and influential mentor. Some of them are still living and working today. Irena Brynner (b. 1917), who lived in San Francisco until 1956, started making jewelry in 1950. Her work there was constructivist and geometric. In 1956, she moved to New York, where she changed her techniques to lost-wax casting and welding, and her style became looser and more organic. She signs her pieces with her first initial and last name, alternately spelled with one or two n's.

One of Irena Brynner's early influences was Claire Falkenstein (1908-1997). While not a member of M.A.G., Ms. Falkenstein was an inspiration to several members of that group (she lived in San Francisco before moving to Paris in 1950). She was a painter, and a metal sculptor who utilized the same linear forging techniques applied to her larger works for her jewelry. Her work was exhibited at the Louvre in Paris, as well as several galleries and museums in the U.S. She made her first piece of jewelry in the mid-'40s. During the 1950s, she made a series of large neckpieces of forged silver or gold wire, including unusual inverted U-shaped and C-shaped pieces with undulating organic lines. Her mark is a superimposed "CF." In 1997, at the age of 89, Ms. Falkenstein died in Venice California, where she had worked and lived since 1965.

Peter Macchiarini (b. 1909) made his first piece of jewelry in 1937, but it wasn't until after the war that he was able to set up a studio and workshop. He was one of the founding members of the Metal Arts Guild, and worked in the constructivist mode with a variety of materials, including ivory, ebony, brass and copper. He signed his pieces with his first initial and last name, or last name alone. Smaller items, like rings, are sometimes signed MACC. Macchiarini still lives and works in San Francisco's North Beach.

Merry Renk (b. 1921), another Metal Arts Guild founding member, has explored a number of techniques and forms, including *plique à jour* enamel, forged wire, lost-wax cast folded fabric, and solderless interlocking shapes. In 1947, she studied at the Institute of Design in Chicago, where she first exhibited in a gallery opened with two other students. Ms. Renk moved to San Francisco in 1948, where she still lives and works as a watercolorist, but she is no longer making jewelry. She signed her work with her last name in lowercase script.

Other West coast artist-jewelers whose work can be found pictured or listed here include Franz Bergmann, Milton Cavagnaro, Lois E. Franke, Arnold Frew, Robert Lasnier, Esther Lewittes, Everett MacDonald, and Byron Wilson.

Because the concentration of studio artists is on the East and West coasts, Midwesterners are often overlooked. Three that are represented here: Philip Morton (St. Paul, MN), Ruth Roach (Plainfield, IA), and Christian Schmidt (Minneapolis, MN). Of the three, Roach (b. 1913) is the least well-known today, although during the 1950s her work was in a number of exhibitions, was awarded prizes, and is owned by several museums. A 1964 local newspaper review of an exhibit at the State College of Iowa enthused: "Anyone who has seen her work longs to own some." Perhaps the articulated pendant on page 188 will inspire other collectors to "long to own some."

In 1956, H. Fred Skaggs (d. 1983) moved from Kansas City, MO, where he made traditional fine jewelry, to Scottsdale, AZ. He opened a shop with his wife at the Lloyd Kiva Craft Center, a prestigious collection of shops, which included prominent Native American artists such as Charles Loloma. (In fact, it is to Skaggs that Loloma gave credit for inspiring and teaching him to make jewelry.) He turned to handcrafting silver upon his arrival because, according to his wife, "this is silver country...He loved working in silver and he loved working with wire. He was very good and fast." Even though he loved silver, he also made many designs in gold. He usually incorporated a variety of gemstones into his designs. His wife still runs the shop they opened in 1966, across the street from the Kiva Craft Center, which is where Advisor Shari Miller conducted an interview with her. Skaggs' work is known to a few discriminating collectors, but perhaps because he shunned publicity while he was alive, not many are aware of his accomplishments.

There are many other lesser-known and unknown studio artists whose work has found its way into the collectibles marketplace. Because many studio artists supplemented their income by teaching classes in jewelry-making, their students' work, much of it unsigned, has also filtered into the secondary market. Some unsigned pieces are very well-made and designed, others are quite amateurish and imitative. A practiced eye will separate the wheat from the chaff.

Modernist mid-century jewelry is a specialized genre that does not appeal to everyone. But a dedicated and burgeoning corps of astute collectors, who, like the makers themselves, tend to be outside the mainstream, have caused interest to grow and prices to rise. Because the jewelry was mostly hand-made and one or few of a kind, a limited quantity is available for sale today. Pieces by the most sought-after artists occasionally come up at twentieth-century decorative arts, rather than fine jewelry, auctions (Skinner's in Boston is the exception). Dealers who sell this type of jewelry are most often found at twentieth-century design shows and galleries in large cities.

Reproduction Alert: According to Steven Cabella, owner of The Modern i Gallery in San Anselmo, CA, plagiarism does exist in modernist jewelry; there are some outright fraudulent copies being made. There are also "authentic limited reproductions" which are openly advertised as such, as well as newly made pieces by the original artist being sold as old ones. These are not fakes, but most collectors prefer pieces to have the "historical patina" (Cabella's words) of the artist's earlier work. The usual caveats apply: when paying a substantial price for a piece, make sure there is substantial documentation for it as well, or that the dealer from whom the piece is purchased is reputable and knowledgeable enough to guarantee the authenticity and circa date of his or her merchandise.

References: Marcia Chamberlain, *Metal Jewelry Techniques*, Watson-Guptill Publications, 1976 (out of print); Jeannine Falino and Yvonne Markowitz, "Margret Craver, A Foremost 20th Century Jeweler and Educator," *Jewelry, The Journal of the American Society of Jewelry Historians*, Vol. One, 1996-1997; Toni Greenbaum, *Messengers of Modernism*, exhibition catalog, Montreal Museum of Decorative Arts, Flammarion, 1996; Graham Hughes, *Modern Jewelry, an International Survey, 1890-1967*, Crown Publishers, 1968 (out of print); Susan Grant Lewin, *One of a Kind, American Art Jewelry Today*, Harry N. Abrams, 1994; Charles J. Martin, *How to Make Modern Jewelry*, Musuem of Modern Art, 1949 (out of print); Philip Morton, *Contemporary Jewelry, A Studio Handbook*, Holt, Rinehart and Winston, 1970 (out of print); Robert von Neumann, *The Design and Creation of Jewelry*, revised ed., Chilton Book Co., 1972; Sylvie Raulet, *Jewelry of the 1940s and 1950s,* Rizzoli International, 1987; Nancy Schiffer, *Silver Jewelry Designs, Evaluating Quality*, Schiffer Publishing, 1996 (chapter on "modern abstract"); Ralph Turner, *Contemporary Jewelry, a Critical Assessment, 1945-1975,* Van Nostrand Reinhold, 1976 (out of print), and *Jewelry in Europe and America, New Times, New Thinking*, exhibition catalog, Thames and Hudson, 1996; Oppi Untracht, *Jewelry Concepts and Technology*, Doubleday, 1985; exhibition catalogs: Martin Eidelberg, ed., *Design 1935-1965, What Modern Was* (multimedia), Harry N. Abrams, 1991; Lee Nordness, *Objects: USA* (multimedia), Viking Press, 1970 (out of print); Camille Billops, *Arthur Smith, A Jeweler's Retrospective*, Jamaica Arts Center, 1990; The *Jewelry of Margaret De Patta*, The Oakland Museum, 1976; *Jewelry By Ed Wiener, Retrospective Exhibition*, Fifty-50 Gallery, New York, 1988; *Structure and Ornament, American Modernist Jewelry, 1940-1960,* Fifty-50 Gallery, New York, 1984.

Periodical: *Metalsmith*, quarterly journal of the Society of North American Goldsmiths, 5009 Londonderry Drive, Tampa, FL 33647. Past issues have published monographic articles on many noted mid-century and later metalsmiths, as well as more general articles on the history of metalsmithing in the U.S. and abroad. A great deal of the information for this section was obtained from these articles. From 1987 to 1992, monographs on Betty Cooke, Clarie Falkenstein, Ed Levin, Paul Lobel, Peter Macchiarini, Art Smith, Ed Wiener, and Byron Wilson were authored by Toni Lesser Wolf (now known as Toni Greenbaum). Back issues are available at the above address.

Museums: The American Craft Museum, New York City; The Renwick Gallery at the Smithsonian Institution, Washington, D.C.; The Oakland Museum, Oakland, CA, houses an extensive collection of jewelry by Margaret De Patta; *Schmuckmuseum*, Pforzheim, Germany; *Le Musée des Arts Décoratifs de Montréal,* Québec, Canada, maintains a collection of modern decorative arts, including jewelry, that was part of the touring exhibit, "Design 1935-1965, What Modern Was," 1991-1993. The museum is also the sponsor of the "Messengers of Modernism" exhibition currently touring the United States and Canada, through the year 2000.

Advisors: Steven Cabella, Ellen Hoffs, Al-Munir Meghji, Shari Miller.

Bracelet

Cuff

Sterling, c. 1950-55, tapered and angled cuff with off-center circ cutout, appl sq wire curving from center of cutout around to one end of cuff, mkd "TENDLER STERLING" for Bill Tendler, New York NY, 1-1/4" w (at center), 2-1/2" inside dia 300

Link

18k yg, colored gemstones, c. 1970, eight textured matte finish yg geo plaques of varying shape, each center bezel-set with a faceted colored gemstone of a different type and shape (amethyst, chrome tourmaline, citrine, peridot, garnet), irregular granulation on surface around bezels, imp "E.W." for Ed Wiener, "18k," 3/4" w x 7" .... 1,725 (A)

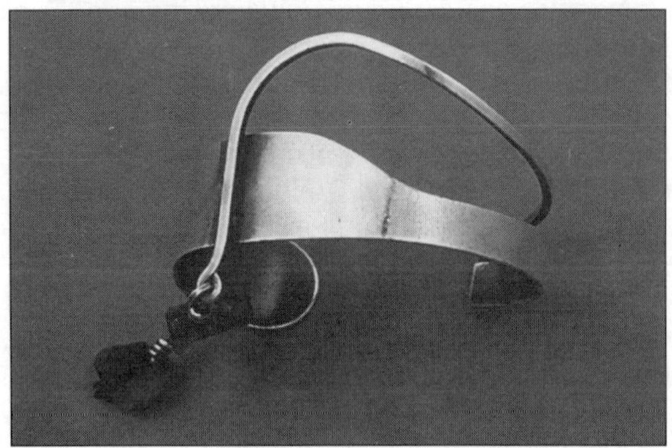

Cuff Bracelet, sterling, agates, c. 1955-60, irreg-cut sheet silver forming cuff with appl sq wire suspending a drop of linked wire and rough-cut agates, sgd "LOBEL STERLING" for Paul Lobel, New York, NY, drop with agates 2-1/4", cuff 3/4" w tapering to 1/4", 2-1/4" inside dia, **$750**. (Shari and Jeff Miller collection).

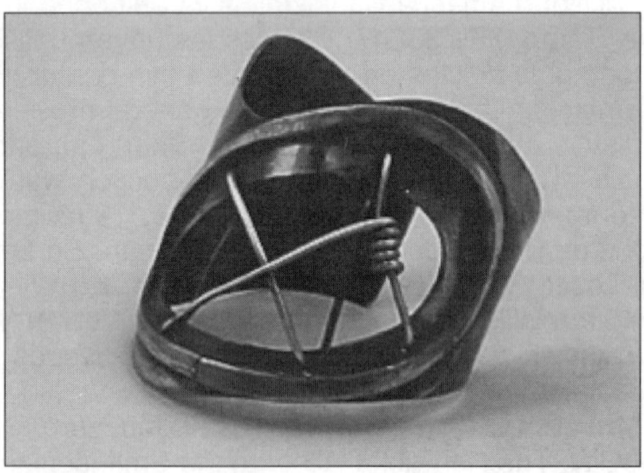

Cuff Bracelet, copper, brass, c. 1955, copper sheet cuff with off-center oval cutout, framed by an appl copper strip (sm crack to one side), brass wire passed through drilled holes around cutout and crisscrossing with ends wrapped at one side, sgd "Art Smith" in script, 2-1/4" w (at center), 2-3/4" inside dia, **$700**. (Patrick Kapty collection).

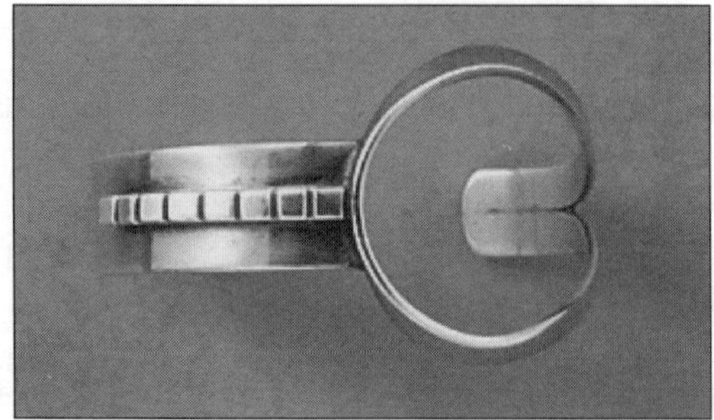

Cuff Bracelet, sterling, c. 1950, one half a flat curved 1/2" w band partially surmounted by a notched rect bar, the other half a looped and shaped cutout band designed to fit over the wrist-bone, mkd "HENRY STEIG STERLING," 1-1/4" w (loop), 2-1/4" inside dia, **$400**. (Author's collection).

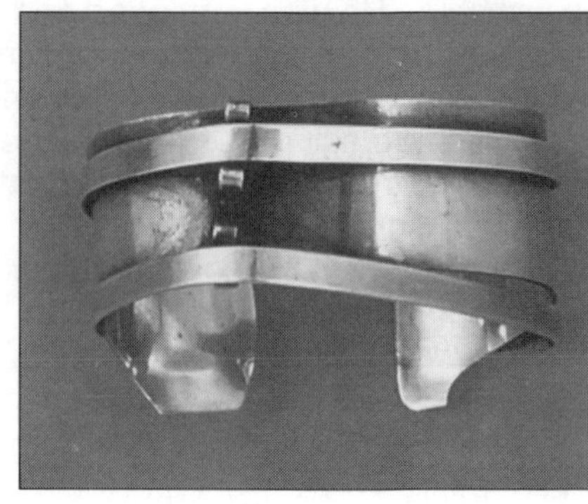

Cuff Bracelet, sterling, c. 1950, flat band tapering out to irregular terminals, surmounted by two appl horizontal strips over a vertical undulating strip, rev imp "LEWITTES HANDMADE STERLING" for Esther Lewittes, Los Angeles, CA, 1" at center, 1-3/8" at terminals, 2-1/2" inside dia, **$350**. (Shari and Jeff Miller collection).

Brooch/Pin

Dioptase, 18k yg, diamonds, c. 1970, an irregular cluster of dioptase crystals mounted in the center of a textured asymmetrical yg frame, projecting spikes with sm diamond-set terminals, sgd "WIENER" for Ed Wiener, New York, NY, 2-1/2" w x 2-1/4" .... 920 (A)

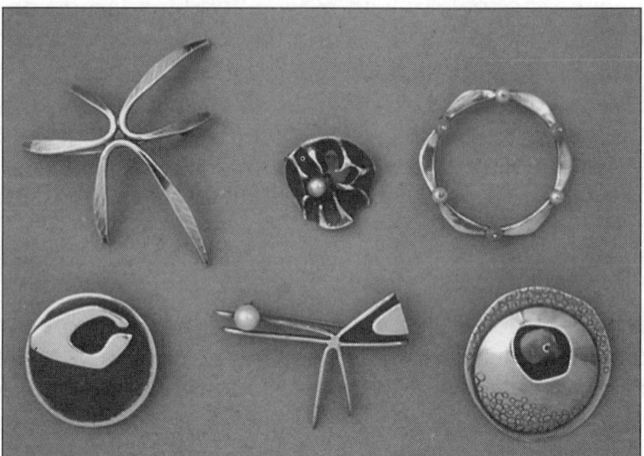

Brooches/Pins, sterling, c. 1955-65:

TL, c. 1955, three uneven U-shaped hammered flat ster wires attached at the bases forming a design of radiating ellipses, mkd "CHRISTIAN SCHMIDT STERLING," 1-7/8" w x 2-1/4", **$200**.

TC, c. 1955, circ shape, deeply indented organic design with a cultured pearl slightly off center, mkd "STERLING PEARSON" for Ronald Pearson, 1" dia, **$150**.
(Shari and Jeff Miller collection).

TR, c. 1960, open circle, hammered scalloped edge set with three pearls alternating with three coral beads, mkd "LEVIN STERLING" for Ed Levin, 1-1/2" dia, **$250**.

BL, c. 1955, concave oxidized ster disk with off-center appl cutout stylized "C," mkd "phyllis" and abstract maker's mk, 1-1/4" dia, **$250**.

BC, c. 1960, linear design of six paired rays, two rays centering an oxidized plaque with an applied ster triangle, a cultured pearl mounted between two opposite rays, rev imp "phyllis" possibly for Phyllis W. Jacobs, 1-3/4" w x 1-1/4", **$350**.

BR, c. 1965, slightly concave ster circ disk, stamped overlapping circles around edge, with appl domed ster disk with cutout off center, turq bead set in center of cutout, stamped overlapping circles around opposite side, mkd "Herrold" for Clifford Herrold, 1-3/8" w x 1-1/2", **$250**.
(Al Munir Meghji collection).

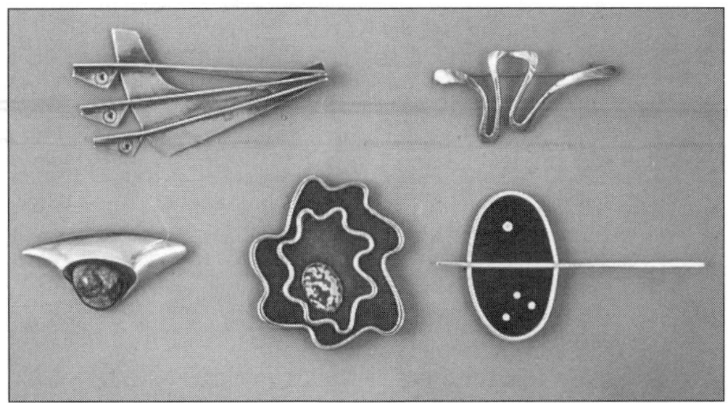

Brooches/Pins, sterling and other materials:

TL, c. 1950, truncated boomerang-shaped plaque surmounted by three strips mounted on edge, each terminating in a "blade" stamped with an imp dot within a circle, rev imp "LEWITTES HAND MADE STERLING" for Esther Lewittes, Los Angeles, CA, 3-1/4" w x 1-5/8", **$235**.

TR, c. 1950, hammered flat wire, undulating W-shaped freeform, rev imp "STERLING, CHRISTIAN SCHMIDT," Minneapolis, MN, 2-3/8" w x 7/8", **$225**.

BL, c. 1960-70, rounded domed triangular shape with cutout center enclosing a bezel-set irregular ovoid Mexican matrix opal cab in shades of beige, brown and yellow, rev imp "STERLING PEARSON" for Ronald H. Pearson, Rochester, NY, 2-1/8" w x 1", **$275**.

BC, c. 1950, biomorphic freeform concentric wire shapes mounted on cut-to-shape oxidized ster plaque, oval agate cab bezel-set off-center, shades of dk brown and pale green, rev imp "BYRON" for Byron Wilson, Oakland, CA, 2-1/8" w x 2-1/4", **$250**.

BR, c. 1955, two semi-elliptical ebony plaques set within an elliptical ster frame bisected by a ster baton extending unevenly, three inlaid ster dots, one dot on opposing side, baton rev imp "COOKE STERLING" for Betty Cooke, Baltimore, MD, "1955 circa" inscribed on wood, 3-3/8" w x 1-7/8", **$350**.
(Shari and Jeff Miller collection).

Jadeite, 18k yg, c. 1970, a jagged, spiked, abstract asymmetrical textured yg casting projecting from one corner of a rounded rect carved apple green jadeite bezel-set in a frame of irregular yg cubed and step-cut diamonds in rect bezels, imp "E.W." for Ed Wiener, New York, NY, "18k," 2-1/8" w x 2-1/2" .... 12,650 (A)

Sterling, c. 1950, boomerang-shaped, tapered ends, rev imp "COOKE STERLING" for Betty Cooke, Baltimore, MD, 3" w x 1/4" 150

Sterling, c. 1950, stylized cutout fish with appl triangular plaque for head, notched for mouth, raised bead for eye, stamped scales, rev sgd "ED. WIENER," 1-1/2" w x 1-1/2" .... 546 (A)

Sterling, c. 1950-60, hand constructed, in the shape of a fish, repoussé body with chased and engr features and scales, flanked by bead-tipped wire fringe fins at top and bottom and forming tail-fin, hand-engr mks, sgd "Emaus 0.925," 2-1/4" w x 2-1/8" 150

Sterling, c. 1955, in the shape of a stylized fish, partially oxidized plaque, one end fringed for dorsal fin, flattened sq ster wire loop appl from tailfin to pierced eye, mkd "phyllis STERLING," 1-3/4" w x 1" 100

Sterling, c. 1955, in the shape of a stylized snail with appl domed head, bead-tipped wire antennae and coiled flattened wire for shell, mkd "TENDLER STERLING" for Bill Tendler, New York, NY, 1-1/2" w x 1" 150

Sterling, ceramic bead, c. 1965, rounded arrow-shaped concave plaque, oxidized center surmounted by a ceramic bead strung on an appl ster wire, imp "phyllis STERLING" possibly for Phyllis W. Jacobs, 2" w x 1" 275

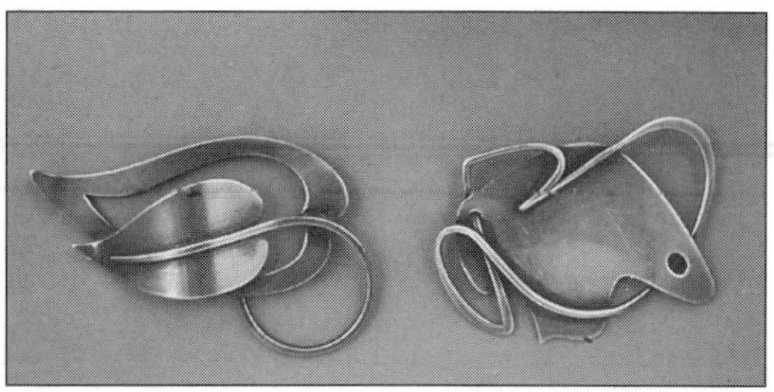

Brooches/Pins, sterling, c. 1945-50:

L, stylized leaf of cutout and appl ster sheet and sq wire, mkd "LOBEL STERLING," 2-3/4" w x 1-3/4", **$400**.
(Patrick Kapty collection).

R, cutout and pierced biomorphic plaque with appl bent freeform sq ster wire around and through it, mkd "HENRY STEIG STERLING," 2-1/2" w x 2", **$250**.
(Courtesy of Before Antiques, Santa Monica, CA).

Sterling, fine silver, enamel, c. 1955, bezel-set domed pear-shaped plaque enameled in an abstract design of short curved lines perpendicular to a long straight line, black to green on a green to rust-colored ground, plaque flanked by a lg and a sm cusped C-shaped silver plaques mounted on short sq wire bars, lg plaque surmounted by lg silver bead, rev sgd in script "Ackerman" in two places, for Paul H. Ackerman, Phillipsburg, NJ, "STERLING" on one plaque and "PURE SILVER" on the other, 1-3/8" w x 2-5/8" 300

Sterling, c. 1955, cutout triangular oxidized plaque with three grad lengths of sq wire appl at one end, mkd "I. BRYNNER STERLING" for Irena Brynner, San Francisco, CA, 1-1/4" w x 2-3/4" 500

Sterling, c. 1950, abstract fish of heavy gauge round wire hammered flat at ends, one end notched, forming long narrow tapered arrow shape, surmounting a triangular plaque (forming "fins") at end with incised circ eye, mkd "STERLING STEIG" for Henry Steig, New York, NY, 1/2" w x 3" 300

Sterling, c. 1960, abstract bird design, two ster split bars diverging at one end, converging at the other end, a cultured pearl post-set "eye" at one end, hand-inscribed "COOKE 1960 STERLING" for Betty Cooke, Baltimore, MD, 4" w x 1/2" 450

Sterling, glass, c. 1950, six-lobed amorphous plaque, irregular cutout in one lobe and bezel-set glass cab in another, maker's mk for Sam Kramer (mushroom within a lobed circle), New York, NY, on rev, 2-3/4" w x 2-3/4" .... 546 (A)

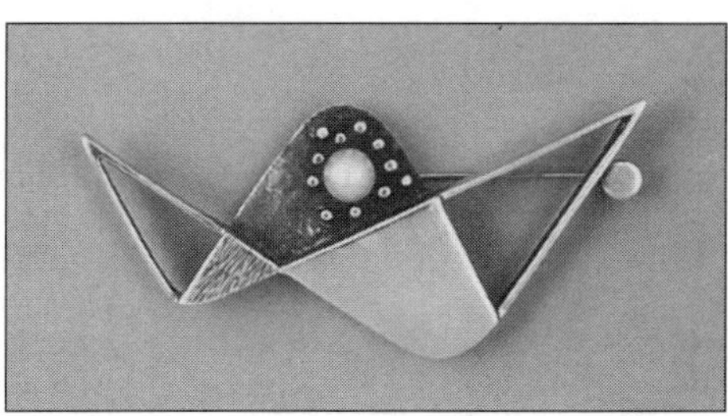

Brooch/Pin, sterling, cultured pearl, c. 1948, conjoined rounded triangular shapes, open frames partly covered with one polished, one textured segment surmounted by flat oxidized textured-surface plaque, eleven short rods soldered perpendicularly around a cultured pearl (approx 7.5 mm), safety catch appl on circ disk mounted outside frame, rev imp "de patta," maker's mk for Margaret De Patta, San Francisco, CA, 3-1/4" w x 1-5/8", **$1,500**.
(Shari and Jeff Miller collection).

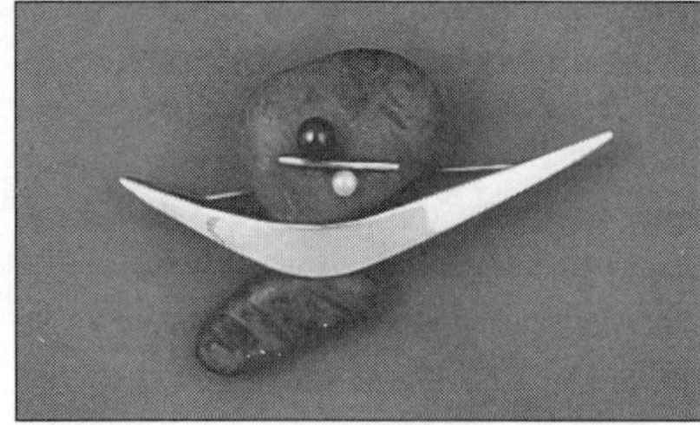

Brooch/Pin, beach pebbles, sterling, cultured pearls, c. 1958-60, boomerang-shaped ster trough flanked top and bottom by irregular rounded oval lt and dk brown mottled beach pebbles, top stone resting within trough and surmounted by a black and smaller white cultured pearl on either side of an appl ster "fin" mounted on edge, rev imp "STERLING de patta," and maker's mk for Margaret De Patta, San Francisco, CA, 3" w x 2", **$1,800**. (Sue James collection).

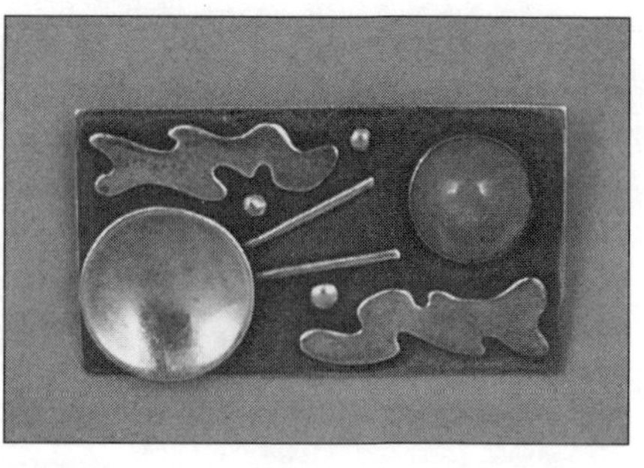

Brooch/Pin, sterling, rose quartz, c. 1950-55, rect plaque with appl design of a circ concave disk with appl cloud shapes, appl radiating wire and beads, and a circ bezel-set rose quartz cab to one side, mkd "FB STERLING" for Franz Bergmann, San Francisco, CA, 2-1/8" w x 1-1/4", **$400**. (Courtesy of Before Antiques, Santa Monica, CA).

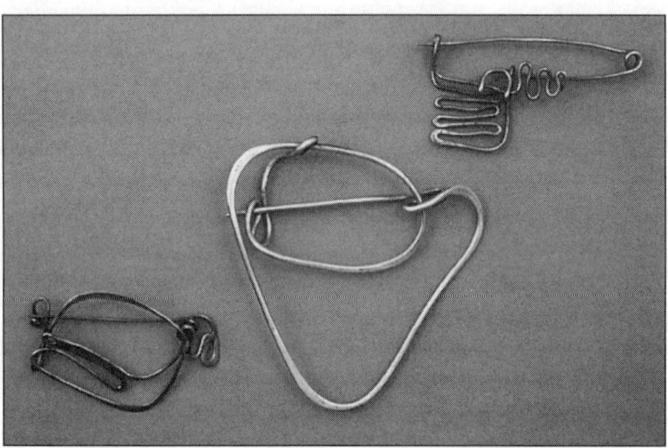

Brooches/Pins by Claire Falkenstein, Venice, CA:

BL, c. 1955, a single piece of brass wire hammered and shaped into a looping oval shape with one end forming the pinstem and the other end looping to form a catch, imp with maker's mk (conjoined CF), and ©, 2-3/4" w x 2", **$250**.

C, c. 1965, a single piece of silver wire hammered and shaped into an open design of looped irregular shape, one end the pinstem, the other end looped to form a lg C-catch and wrapped at the top, imp with maker's mk (conjoined CF) and ©, 3-3/4" w x 4", **$750**.

TR, c. 1955, a single piece of brass wire hammered and shaped into an irregular L-shape with looped sections, one end forming the pinstem, the other end looping to form a catch, mkd "© C. FALKENSTEIN," 3-1/2" w x 1-5/8", **$350**.
(Courtesy of Before Antiques, Santa Monica, CA).

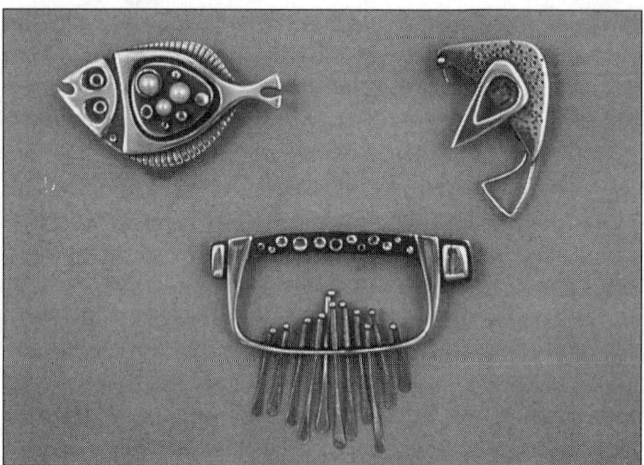

Brooches/Pins, sterling, unmkd, c. 1950-55:

TL, stylized fish, cutout and layered appl tubes and short rods, three cultured pearls in body center, safety catch, 2" w x 1-1/8", **$150**.

TR, stylized bird, cutout textured plaque and appl wire, surmounted by cutout wing, 1-5/8" x 1-1/8", **$125**.

BC, open rounded rect frame, appl circ and rect decoration across top, bottom portion pierced with varying lengths of kinetic wire, each flattened on bottom end, tube collar and bead on top end, 2-3/8" w x 2" tl, **$200**.
(David Skelley collection).

Cuff Links, sterling, c. 1950, cutout lg biomorphic plaque with appl sm irregular quatrefoil plaque and appl dimpled dome encircled by dimples, joined with lg oval link to cutout sm biomorphic plaque with appl center bead, rev imp "STERLING," maker's mk for Sam Kramer, 7/8" w x 1-1/8", **$1,000**. (Richard Levey collection).

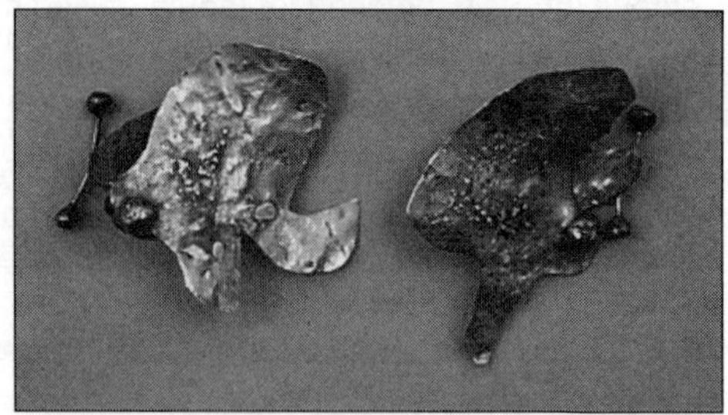

Cuff Links, brass, c. 1965-75, cutout irregular freeform plaque with layered and textured silver plating, circ brass bead on one edge, hinged back with bead-tipped wires on smaller amoeboid plaques, maker's mk for Claire Falkenstein (conjoined CF), Venice, Calif., and copyright symbol, 2-1/2" w x 1-3/4", pr, **$600**. (Courtesy of Before Antiques, Santa Monica, CA).

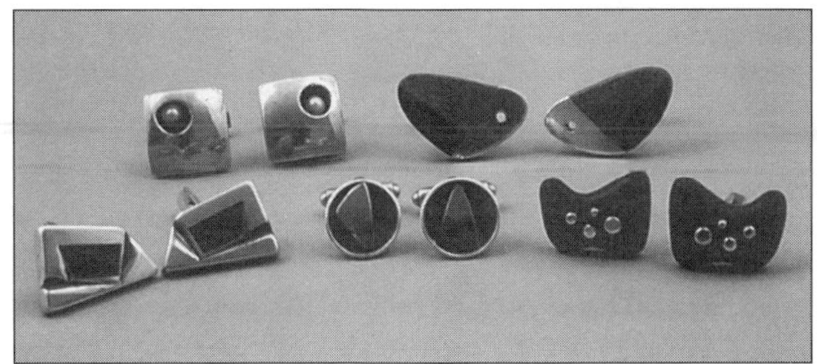

Cuff Links, sterling and other materials, c. 1950-60:

TL, each a concave oxidized sq bottom ster plaque surmounted by a sq convex ster plaque with a pearl set off-center in a circ cutout, mkd "LASNIER STERLING," for Robert Lasnier, San Francisco, CA, hinged bar findings, 3/4" w x 3/4", pr, **$150**.

TR, rounded triangular shape with sections of inlaid dk and lt wood and a polished ster section with a cutout sm circ hole, mkd "LEWITTES HANDMADE STERLING" for Esther Lewittes, Los Angeles, CA, 1-1/8" w x 3/4", pr, **$150**.

BL, ster quadrangle with inlaid wood quadrangle in raised center outlined by oxidized groove, mkd "LOIS SILVER" for Lois E. Franke, Los Angeles, CA, hinged bar findings, 1" w x 5/8", pr, **$150**.

BC, circ ster disks with raised edges surmounted by appl yg triangles over oxidized surface, mkd "LEVIN STERLING" for Ed Levin, Bennington, VT, hinged bar findings, 5/8" dia, pr, **$150**.

BR, bow-shaped wood, each with four inlaid ster disks of varying size mounted on cut-to-shape ster plaques mkd "MACDONALD STERLING" for Everett MacDonald, Laguna Beach, CA, hinged bar findings, 1/2" w x 1", pr, **$200**.
(Al Munir Meghji collection).

Tiger's eye, sterling, c. 1940, in the shape of a bumblebee with tiger's eye head and abdomen, assembled and engr ster body, legs and wings, mkd "STERLING HANDMADE RUSSELL," safety catch, 1-5/8" w x 1-3/8" 400

Yg, c. 1965-70, abstract design of varying lengths of textured yg sq bars mounted at various angles to one another, sgd "ED WIENER," 3-1/8" x 2" .... 1,093 (A)

Buckle

Beach pebble, sterling, c. 1955, irregular oval black textured stone mounted on rect ster plaque, loop and hook for belt, rev imp with maker's mark for Margaret De Patta (stylized "M"), mkd "STERLING," 2-1/8" w x 1-1/2" 750

Cuff Links

Sterling, cultured pearls, c. 1950-55, circ disk with recessed oxidized and textured center, appl polished freeform design and a single cultured pearl mounted off-center, hinged bar mechanism on rev, mkd "FREW" for Arnold Frew, Los Angeles, CA, 3/4" dia, pr 175

Earrings

Brass, c. 1965, rect plaque appl perpendicular to surmount, mounted with vertical bead-tipped patinated wires, screwbacks, unmkd, by Claire Falkenstein, Venice, CA (purchased from artist), 1/4" w x 7/8", pr 250

Sterling, c. 1950, semi-circ plaque, raised frame around curved edge, appl disk and short tubes in oxidized center, screwbacks, 1" w x 5/8", pr 45

Sterling, c. 1955, three-dimensional scrolled triangles with appl flattened wire borders, clipbacks, mkd "SALO STERLING" for George K. Salo, Sutton, NH, 3/4" w x 1-1/4", pr 95

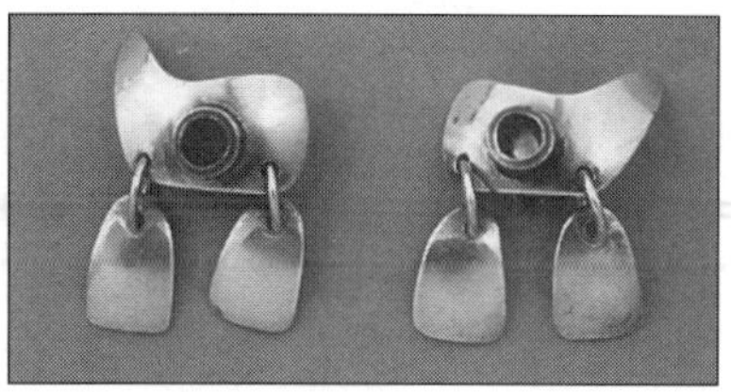

Earrings, sterling, copper, c. 1940-45, slightly convex cusped and angled plaques, each surmounted by a short copper tube and suspending two slightly convex rounded triangular plaques from oversized jump rings, rev of one mkd "STERLING," maker's mk for Sam Kramer (lobed mushroom in a circle), New York, NY, clipbacks mkd "Pat. 1967965" (1934), 7/8" w x 1-1/2", **$450**. (Anne Eichner collection).

Sterling, coral, c. 1955, U-shaped ster bars on oxidized ster plaque, pierced at the bottom with ster wire and two coral beads mounted in the hollow, mkd "STERLING" and illegible mark for Ed Wiener, New York, NY, screwbacks, 1/2" w x 7/8" 250

Sterling, cultured pearls, c. 1954, cupped oxidized disks, a cultured pearl mounted on post in center, mkd "LEVIN STERLING" for Ed Levin, New York, NY, screwbacks, 5/8" dia, pr 150

Sterling, glass, c. 1955-60, each a concave rounded triangular ster plaque mounted off center with a purple glass bead, mkd "LEWITTES STERLING" for Esther Lewittes, Los Angeles, CA, clipbacks, 1" w x 3/4", pr 200

Pendent

Silver, bone, c. 1960, flattened wire open vertical rect with central mobile wire suspending a bone bead and boomerang-shaped terminals, kidney earwires, 3/4" w x 2-1/4", pr 100

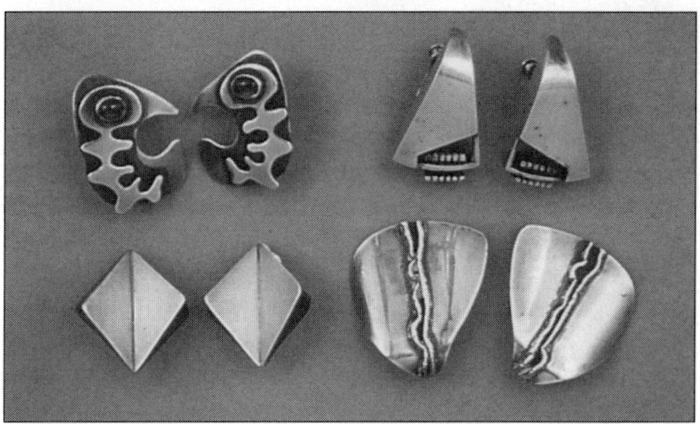

Earrings, sterling:

TL, c. 1948, opposed cutout C-shaped plaques, partially oxidized ground, each surmounted by an appl cutout biomorphic abstract design set with a garnet cab, rev mkd "ED. WIENER STERLING," screwbacks, 7/8" w x 1-1/4", **$350**.
(Author's collection).

TR, c. 1950, hollow three-dimensional triangle, bent at the apex, with a slightly curved L-shaped cutout at the base, cut ends of sq wire forming two rows flanking long edge, screwbacks, mkd "de patta" and maker's mk for Margaret De Patta, San Francisco, CA, 3/4" w x 1-1/8", pr, **$600**.

BL, c. 1955, sq ster plaque turned 45 degrees with vertically folded center, flat back, inlaid wood segments in side openings, clipbacks, mkd "STERLING LEWITTES" for Esther Lewittes, Los Angeles, CA, 7/8" w x 1", pr, **$250**.

BR, c. 1960-65, bent rounded triangular plaques, vertically split down the middle, irregularly undulating lengths of wire appl to oxidized edges, clipbacks, mkd "STERLING HANDMADE H. FRED SKAGGS," Scottsdale, AZ, 1-1/4" w x 1-1/4", pr, **$65**.
(Courtesy of Before Antiques, Santa Monica, CA).

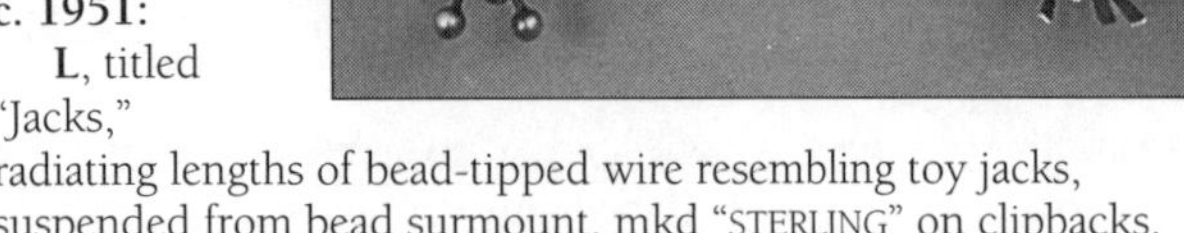

Earrings, sterling, by Merry Renk, San Francisco, CA, c. 1951:

L, titled "Jacks," radiating lengths of bead-tipped wire resembling toy jacks, suspended from bead surmount, mkd "STERLING" on clipbacks, unmkd (purchased from artist), 1" dia, pr, **$400**.

R, titled "Starburst," bead-tipped and hammered flat wires radiating from a central bead, screwbacks, mkd "STERLING," sgd "renk" in lowercase script, 1" dia, pr, **$400**. (Courtesy of Before Antiques, Santa Monica, CA).

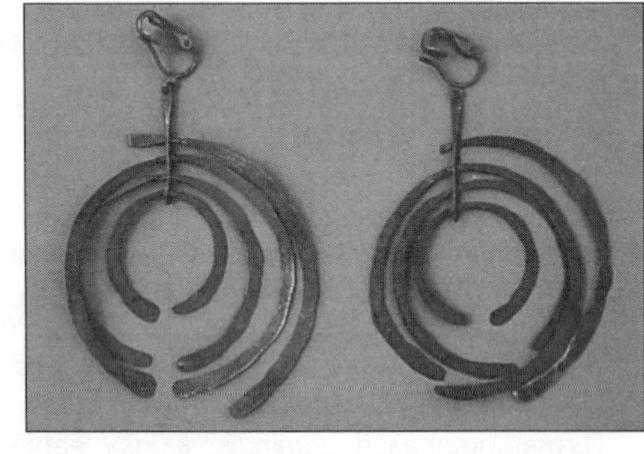

Pendent Earrings, brass, wm, c. 1948, each with three patinated hammered brass concentric penannular segments and one crescent-shaped segment piercing a narrow hammered plaque, suspended from wm earclips, attributed to Harry Bertoia (similar to pr in "Messengers of Modernism" exhibition), 2-1/8" w x 2-3/4" tl, pr, **$1,500**. (Al Munir Meghji collection).

Pendent Earrings, 14k yg, syn sapphire, c. 1960, each a rounded triangular C-shaped drop, raised edge, oxidized center, prong-set oval blue syn sapphire cab in opening, suspended by bead-tipped wire from *boteh*-shaped (paisley) surmount, screwbacks mkd "14k," "ED WIENER" imp on rev of each drop, 2" tl x 7/8", pr, **$900**. (David Skelley collection).

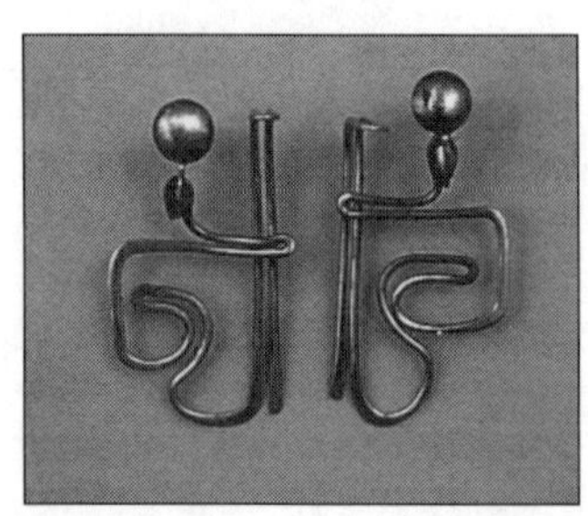

Pendent Earrings, brass, c. 1965, circ domed surmount suspending a forged brass wire forming a geo curv three-dimensional abstract design, screwbacks, unmkd, by Claire Falkenstein (purchased from the artist), 1" w x 1-3/4" tl, pr, **$400**. (Courtesy of Before Antiques, Santa Monica, CA).

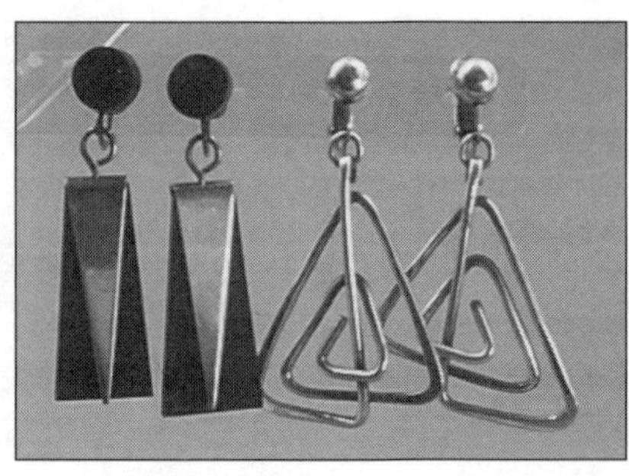

Pendent Earrings, sterling, c. 1955-60:

L, tapered rect wood plaques with overlaid ster inverted triangles suspended from wood disk surmounts, screwbacks, sgd on wood "CAVAGNARO" for Milton Cavagnaro, Mill Valley, CA, 1/2" w x 2", pr, **$200**.

R, bent wire forming concentric triangles suspended from clipbacks with bead surmounts, mkd "STEIG" for Henry Steig, New York, NY, 1-1/4" w x 2" tl, pr, **$250**. (Al Munir Meghji collection).

Silver, wood, c. 1960, each a hammered silver wire suspended from a kidney earwire, surmounted by a mobile elongated wood triangle with an incised crosshatch pattern, turning on a circ silver disk mounted in triangle center, 1/2" w x 2-1/2", pr 125

Sterling, c. 1950, inverted triangular surmounts vertically bisected by appl wire, suspending triangular bent wire open drops, mkd "LOBEL STERLING" for Paul Lobel, New York, NY, 7/8" w x 2-1/2" 300

Sterling, copper, c. 1960, concave disk with polished rim and oxidized inner surface suspending a larger concave disk with appl copper bead center, screwback findings, rev mkd "HURST AND KINGSBURY STERLING," 3/4" w x 1-3/8", pr 300

Sterling, cultured pearls, c. 1955-60, flattened ster wire forming a spiraling S shape, mounted with a cultured pearl on central vertical rod, screwbacks, bead surmounts, mkd "MENZIN STERLING," 3/4" w x 2-1/4", pr 200

Sterling, cultured pearls, c. 1960, each an undulating tapered ster strip, curved cutout base with cultured pearl terminal, surmounted by another cultured pearl, suspended from domed surmounts, screwbacks, mkd "LEWITTES STERLING" for Esther Lewittes, 1/4" w x 2-1/8" tl, pr 200

Hair Ornament

Brass, onyx, c. 1965, rect brass plaque pierced by four vertical wires, one tipped with an onyx bead, one with a brass ring, one with a triangle, one with a circ disk, unmkd, attributed to Leonard Edmondsen (Southern CA artist), 1-1/4" w x 2-5/8" 75

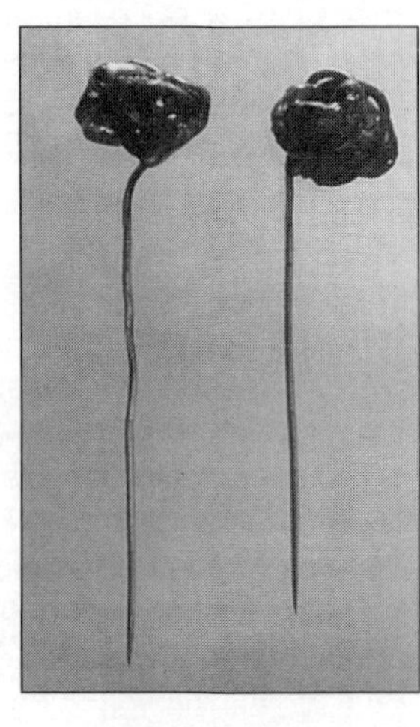

Hatpins, glass, copper, c. 1960, each an irregularly-shaped fused red, blue, and yellow glass bead with copper wire wrapped and through the glass, continuing to a patinated copper wire pin stem, unmkd, by Claire Falkenstein, Venice, CA (purchased from the artist), 3/4" w, pinstems 2-3/4" tl and 3-1/4" tl, each, **$300**. (Courtesy of Before Antiques, Santa Monica, CA).

Money Clip, sterling, onyx, c. 1950, rect bar, bent under to form clip, appl oval bezel-set off-center with oval onyx cab, mkd "HURST AND KINGSBURY STERLING," New York, NY, 1" w x 2", **$175**. (Courtesy of Before Antiques, Santa Monica, CA).

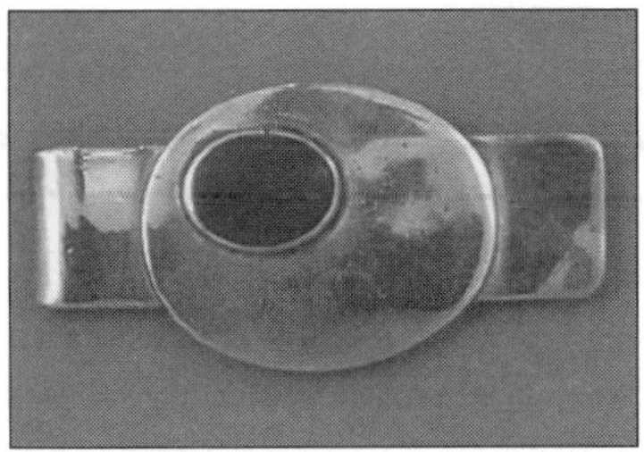

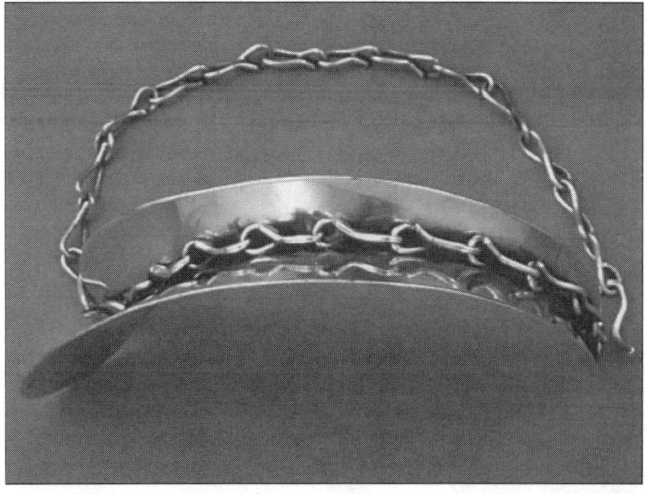

Necklace, sterling, c. 1950, tapered rounded triangular plaque folded toward the front, lg curb link chain appl at fold, bg oxidized behind chain, continuing to a side hook clasp, mkd "Art Smith" in script, plaque tapers from 1/2" at one end to 1-1/2" at the other end, 15-3/4" tl, **$1,800**. (Shari and Jeff Miller collection).

Money Clip

Sterling, c. 1947, top a crenelated rect oxidized plaque with raised edge, center bar incised with parallel lines, rev imp "ED. WIENER STERLING," 1-1/2" w x 3/8" 250

Sterling, c. 1955, rect with irregularly spaced polished ster strips over oxidized ground, mkd "gs" in a shield for George K. Salo, Sutton, NH, "STERLING HANDWROUGHT," 2-1/2" w x 3/4" 150

Necklace

Sterling, c. 1950, a collar of four curved tapered oblong plaques, each surmounted and linked by appl flat L-shaped wire turned on edge, attached by rings through pierced openings at end of each plaque, hook and ring closure, mkd "ED. WIENER STERLING," 1-1/8" w (at center), 13-1/2" tl 600

Sterling, c. 1950, circ links of scrolling sq ster wire, attached by tapered rect interlinks, sgd "LOBEL" for Paul Lobel, New York, NY, hook clasp, 3/4" w x 16" tl .... 575 (A)

Sterling, amethyst, c. 1960, concave ster disk with central bezel-set amethyst cab, suspending a fringe of three uneven flattened wires and domed disks, suspended from riveted flattened wire segments and hook clasp, mkd "KOLODNY STERLING," 3-1/4" (at center), 18" tl 175

Sterling, cultured pearl, c. 1950, in three sections, bracket-shaped front section set with a cultured pearl in center indentation, flanked by two hammered flat tapering back sections attached with bead-tipped U-shaped links, hook and eye closure, sgd "ED. WIENER," 14" tl .... 288 (A)

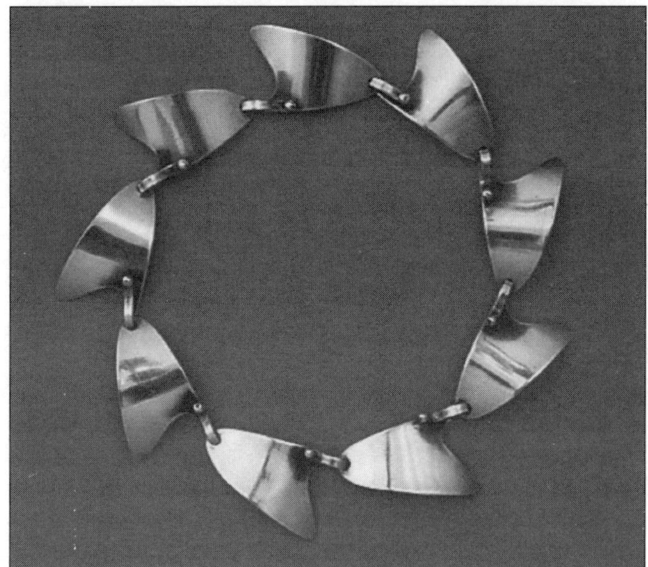

Necklace, collar, sterling, c. 1950, nine convex lobed triangular plaques joined with bead-tipped hooks, oxidized at base, any one functions as closure, rev imp "ED. WIENER STERLING," 1" w x 15-1/4" tl, **$1,000**. (Al Munir Meghji collection).

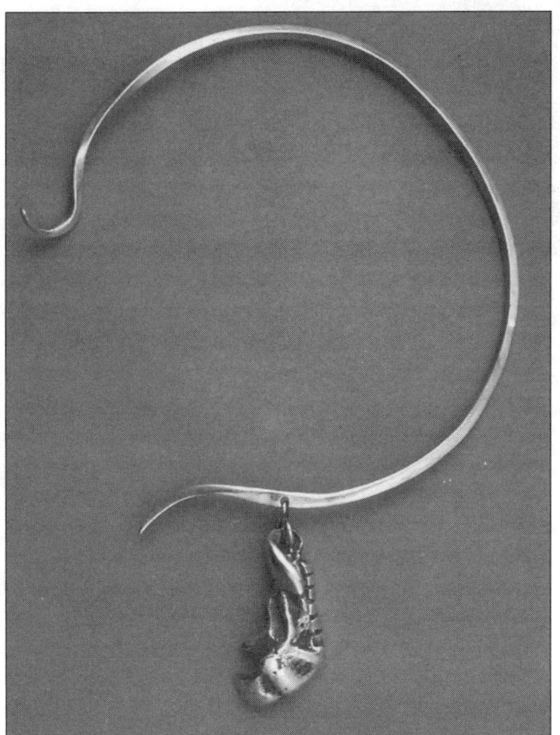

Neckpiece, sterling, c. 1950-55, cast textured freeform pendant suspended from an open forged C-shaped hammered sq wire neckring with curved terminals, maker's mk for Claire Falkenstein (conjoined CF), Venice, CA, and "© C. FALKENSTEIN" on neckring, pendant 1" w x 2-1/4", neckring 5" inside dia, **$1,500**. (Courtesy of Before Antiques, Santa Monica, CA).

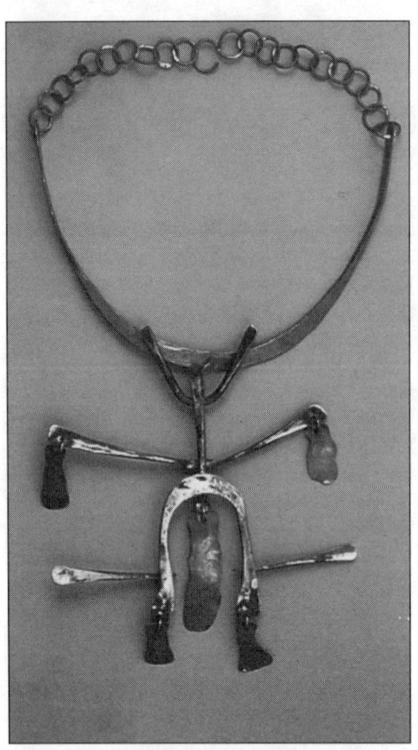

Neckpiece and Pendant, copper, steel, c. 1960, hammered steel rods with flattened ends forming an abstract male stick figure suspending cutout and hammered copper hands, feet, and genitalia, suspended from a hammered copper U-shaped bar and circ link copper chain, one end link open for clasp, maker's mk for Claire Falkenstein (conjoined CF), Venice, CA on rev, pendant 4" w x 5" tl, neckpiece 4-3/4" inside dia, **$1,500**. (Courtesy of Before Antiques, Santa Monica, CA).

Pendant

Sterling, c. 1955, stylized Star of David, two rounded triangular ster plaques, oxidized triangle surmounted by inverted cutout triangle, mkd "gs" in a shield for George K. Salo, Sutton, NH, 3/4" w x 1-1/2" with bail 100

Sterling, c. 1955-60, cusped oval plaque with central polished cutout boomerang-shaped plaque surmounting larger similar plaque with wirebrushed finish, oxidized outlines, bail for chain, mkd "LUSTIG STERLING," 1-1/2" w x 2-5/8" tl 100

Sterling, c. 1960, hammered flat circ disk with cutout abstract figures, mkd "LEVIN STER. BENN VT" for Ed Levin, 1-3/4" dia 150

Ring

14k wg, c. 1955, wedding band with appl joined, opposing abstract male/female figures, mkd "14k," maker's mk for Sam or Carol Kramer (mushroom in circle without lobes), approx size 9-1/2, 3/8" w 300

14k yg, sterling, c. 1960, plain domed shape divided by incised and oxidized undulating horizontal line separating polished ster section from polished yg section, mkd "14k STERLING" and maker's mk for Byron Wilson, Oakland, CA (a flower with "BYRON"), 1/2" w, size 8 250

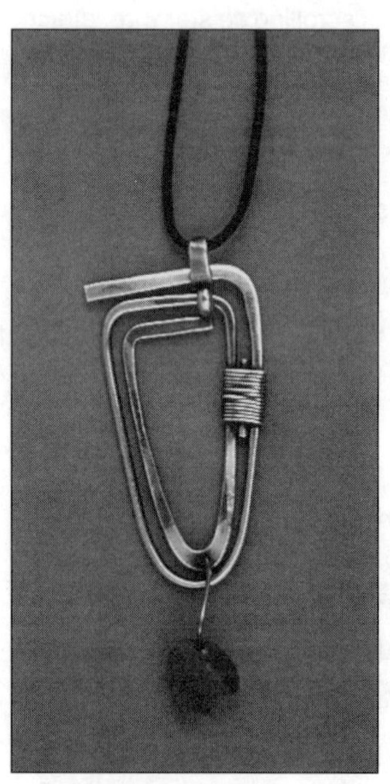

Pendant and Cord, sterling, tourmaline, c. 1955-60, flattened wire forming concentric inverted rounded triangles, side section wire-wrapped, terminating in a bead-tipped ster wire suspending a tumble-polished watermelon tourmaline drop from inner apex, suspended from a 27" silk cord through an off-center bail, mkd "STEIG STERLING" for Henry Steig, New York, NY, 1-1/2" w x 3-3/4" tl, **$500**. (Al Munir Meghji collection).

Pendant and Cord, sterling, leather, c. 1960, articulated linked shapes, disks, open ovoid, and berry-like bead-tipped wire clusters, each with textured surface and appl granulation, suspended from 15" leather cord, ster hook clasp, bail imp "ROACH STERLING" for Ruth Roach, Plainfield, IA, pendant 1/2" w x 8-1/4" tl, **$650**. (Shari and Jeff Miller collection).

Ring, sterling, taxidermy eye, c. 1950, stylized eye design, bezel-set yellow taxidermy eye surmounted by an inverted U-shaped plaque incised with radiating lines, enclosed underneath by undulating ster wire, mounted on a wide shank imp with maker's mk for Sam Kramer, New York, NY (mushroom within double-lobed circle), 1" w x 1-3/8", **$1,200**. (Al Munir Meghji collection).

Black opal, yg, c. 1970, a lg circ black opal bezel-set in the center of a concave closed-back rounded sq frame, upper edge turned outward, a bc diamond prong-set to one side, accompanied by a bill of sale from Ed Wiener Jewelry reading "round opal gem 11.50 ct, full black mounted in 18K yg with one .25 round diamond," 1-1/8" x 1-1/8" .... 3,450 (A)

Bloodstone (jasper), sterling, brass, c. 1955-60, circ bloodstone cab set in wide brass bezel, flanked by short lengths of alternating ster and brass wire appl to shoulders, mounted on plain ster band, mkd "MACC" for Peter Macchiarini, San Francisco, CA, 7/8" dia, approx size 9 475

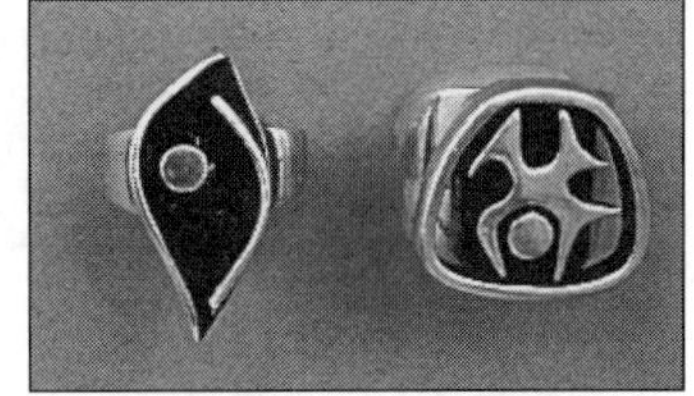

Rings, sterling, Ed Wiener, c. 1950:
L, stylized eye with outline and pupil of polished raised silver on oxidized plaque, imp "ED. WIENER" inside shank, approx size 6, 1/2" w x 1", **$500**.
R, cutout abstract bird motif enclosing circ peg on one side, within an open rounded trapezoidal frame, mounted on tapered shank, inside imp "ED. WIENER," approx size 5-1/2, 3/4" dia, **$600**. (Private collection).

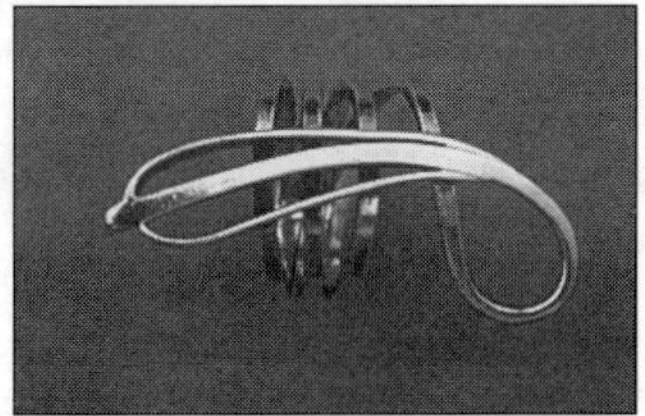

Ring, sterling, c. 1950, looped stylized leaf motif continuing to a spiraling sq wire shank, mkd "LOBEL" for Paul Lobel, New York, NY, approx size 8, 1/2" w x 1-3/4" at top, **$600**. (Private collection).

Ring, sterling, by Frank Rebajes, New York, NY, c. 1950, irregular oval tumble-polished quartz cab with wire-wrapped bezel mounted on adjustable tapered shank, mkd "STERLING ORIGINAL Hand Wrought DESIGN REbajEs" for Frank Rebajes, New York, NY, top 3/4" w x 1/2", **$225**. (Courtesy of Before Antiques).

Rings, sterling, by Frank Rebajes, New York, NY:
L, c. 1950, oval moonstone cab with wire-wrapped bezel mounted on adjustable tapered shank, mkd "STERLING ORIGINAL Hand Wrought DESIGN REbajEs" for Frank Rebajes, New York, NY, top 3/4" w x 7/8", **$225**.
R, c. 1975, high relief cast organic shape enclosing an irregular tumble-polished malachite and a gray cultured pearl, mkd "REBAJES STERLING," provenance: purchased in Spain from the artist, size 8, 1" w x 1-1/2", **$150**.
(Shari and Jeff Miller collection).

Rings by H. Fred Skaggs, Scottsdale, AZ, c. 1960:
L, bezel-set oval aquamarine cab framed by two undulating ster wires continuing to narrow shank, rev mkd "STERLING, H. FRED SKAGGS, HAND MADE" and designer's mk, conjoined and superimposed HFS, 3/4" x 5/8", approx size 5-1/2, **$150**.
C, lg oval bezel-set nephrite plaque mounted on a ster wire "cage," four oval carnelian cabs set perpendicular to nephrite at compass points, horizontally at top and bottom, vertically at sides, vertical ster wire bars piercing sm ster disks between cabs, continuing to a narrow shank, bezel rev mkd "STERLING, HAND MADE, H. FRED SKAGGS," 1-1/8" w x 1-3/8", approx size 7, **$225**.
(Author's collection).
R, high-domed circ turq cab set in a frame of corded and ropetwisted wire, continuing to corded and twisted wire shank flanked by plain ster wires, rev mkd "STERLING, H. FRED SKAGGS, HAND MADE" and designer's mk, conjoined and superimposed HFS, 7/8" dia, approx size 6-1/2", **$175**.
(Shari and Jeff Miller collection).

Sterling, c. 1950, lozenge-shaped plaque with appl incised pyramidal shapes at each end flanking two beads, creating mask-like effect, mounted on tapered shank, maker's mk for Margaret De Patta imp on rev (stylized "M"), approx size 8, 5/8" w x 1-1/2" 1,200

Sterling, c. 1955, open sq box, oxidized inner surface with appl sq bead set off-center, mounted on narrow shank, mkd "LOBEL STERLING" for Paul Lobel, New York, NY, 1/2" w, size 6 300

Sterling, c. 1965, wide barrel-shaped band, maker's mk for H. Fred Skaggs, approx size 5, 3/4" w 50

Sterling, amethyst, MOP, c. 1950, cutout and bent biomorphic shape with central bezel-set MOP, bezel-set amethyst on one lobed end, mkd "J. NELSON STERLING," 3/4" w, adjustable shank 150

Sterling, tourmaline, c. 1950, biomorphic pierced plaque, narrow section wrapped with ster wire, sm green tourmaline cab on shoulder, mkd "STERLING," maker's mk for Sam Kramer (mushroom within double-lobed circle), approx size 7-1/2, top 3/4" w x 1-1/8" 1,100

Sterling, dome surmounted by two small domes appl to overlapping bands extending from wide shank, imp with maker's mk for Sam Kramer (mushroom within a lobed circle), "STERLING," approx size 5-1/2, top 3/4" w x 1" 800

Sterling, c. 1955-60, cutout curvilinear indented "swoosh" surmounted by a capsule-shaped amethyst within yg wire "cage" of grad loops, imp "Art Smith" in script, "14k STERLING," approx size 4-1/2, 1-1/2" w x 3/4" 1,200

Suite: Cuff Links and Tie Bar

Sterling, wood, c. 1950, tie bar a tapered rect ster plaque with inlaid wood bisected by a horizontal silver bar, a dot of silver on one side, cufflinks ster rectangles with rect wood inlay, tie bar mkd "ED WIENER STERLING," cuff links mkd "ED" with remainder of signature illegible, alligator clip on tie bar, 1-3/4" w x 3/8", hinged bars on cuff links, 3/4" w x 3/8" 300

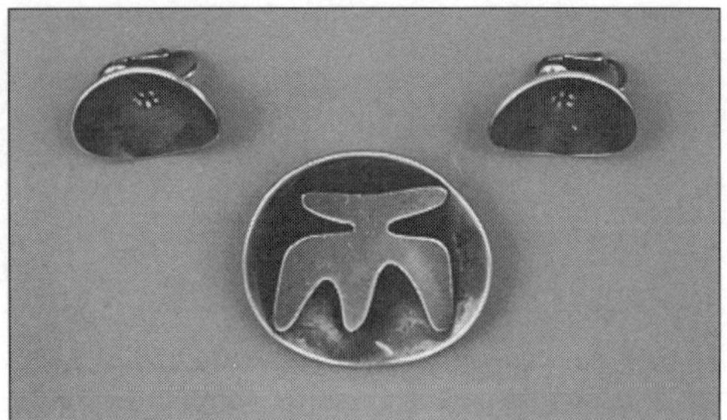

Suite: Brooch and Earrings, sterling, c. 1955, concave oval ster disk with cutout polished biomorphic plaque mounted on post on oxidized ground, earrings concave ovals with sm raised bead centers on oxidized ground, all pieces mkd "PM" over "STERLING" in a rect shape for Philip Morton, St. Paul, MN, brooch 1-1/2" w x 1-3/8", earrings 3/4" w x 1", **$450**. (Al Munir Meghji collection).

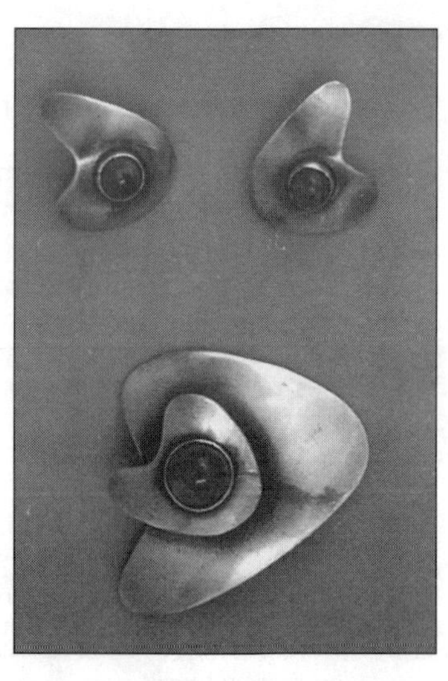

Suite: Brooch/Pin and Earclips, sterling, amethyst, c. 1950, slightly convex rounded lobed triangular plaque surmounted by smaller lobed plaque mounted on a raised collar, bezel-set with round amethyst cab, matching earclips each set with amethyst cab, each piece imp with maker's mark for Sam Kramer, New York, NY (mushroom within double-lobed circle), "STERLING," brooch/pin 1-3/4" w x 2", earclips 7/8" w x 1" (old style triangular clips with 1934 pat No), suite, **$1,150**. (Shari and Jeff Miller collection).

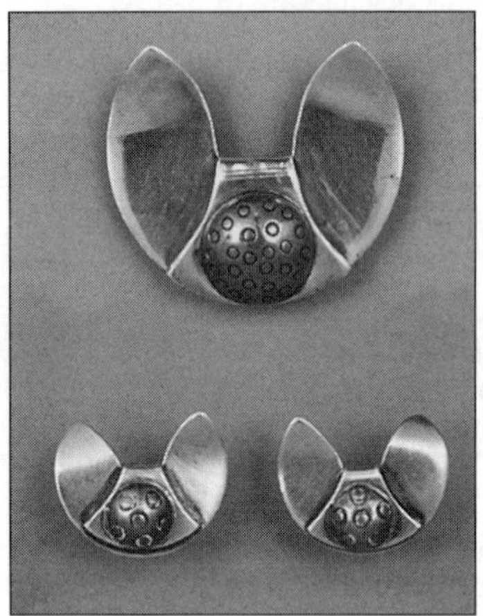

Suite: Brooch/Pin and Earrings, sterling, copper, Sam Kramer, c. 1950:

T, Brooch a cutout stylized bat's head, ears bent forward, appl copper domed disk "face" with allover stamped sm circles, imp with maker's mk for Sam Kramer (mushroom within double-lobed circle), "STERLING," 1-7/8" w x 1-5/8", **$600**. (Richard Levey collection).

B, Earrings each a cutout and bent ster plaque in the shape of a bat's head, one ear forward, the other back, appl circ domed copper disk stamped with sm open circles, mkd "STERLING," maker's mk for Sam Kramer, New York, NY, screwback findings, 1" w x 3/4", pr, **$450**. (Courtesy of Before Antiques).

Tie bar, sterling, amethyst, c. 1950, central sm oval amethyst cab flanked by appl and incised ster rod and cutout and notched hook shape appl to oxidized ground, imp "STERLING," maker's mk for Sam Kramer (mushroom within double-lobed circle), 3/8" w x 2-1/2", **$350**. (Richard Levey collection).

FINE JEWELRY c. 1945-1975

History: History records wars as lines of demarcation. What happens after them is usually a radical departure from what was happening before and during wartime. World War II was no exception. Post-war prosperity unleashed an indulgence in luxury long frustrated by deprivation. All aspects of popular culture changed, including a marked change in fashion. Christian Dior introduced his "New Look" in 1947: long full skirts, nipped-in waist, unpadded, sloping shoulders, tight bodices and décolleté necklines. Femininity was back in style. To complement the look, jewelry had to change, too. In fact, jewelry design took off in two divergent directions, that of the "traditionalists" of fine jewelry, including the large houses and those who designed for them, and that of the new modernist designs of avant-garde studio artists (see preceding section on Mid-Century Modern American Studio Jewelry). Among the former group, there was a return to an extravagant display of all kinds of gemstones, but especially, diamonds were a girl's best friend once again. In 1948, De Beers Corporation set the tone for the era with their now-famous slogan, "a diamond is forever." A nearly imperceptible flexible platinum wire setting (said to have been inspired by a holly wreath), pioneered by diamond magnate Harry Winston around 1946, allowed clusters of stones to dominate a jewel. Fancy cuts, such as marquise and pear, were particularly favored in diamond jewelry.

The motifs and forms of traditional jewelry in the fifties and early sixties were not a radical departure from those of the forties, but their execution was decidedly different. Where forties pieces had a heavy, solid, and smooth polished look (even though they may have been hollow and light in terms of actual weight), fifties pieces were open and airy with textured surfaces such as Florentine (brushed metal), ropetwisted or braided wire, mesh, reeding, fluting and piercing. Yellow gold was predominant except for all-diamond jewels, for which the preferred metal was once again platinum.

Following the trend for matching accessories, the suite returned in force as a full parure of necklace, bracelet, earrings and brooch. Floral motifs were still in vogue, as well as a variety of leaf shapes, with increasing emphasis on gemstones and texture. Necklaces remained short as chokers, collars or bibs. These could be draped, swirled, or fringed, in gold or entirely gem-set. Diamond necklaces typically featured a row or fringe of baguette and/or marquise diamonds flanked by scrolled or draped side elements. Bracelets were primarily of the flexible sort, often gemstone-encrusted. Charm bracelets also maintained their popularity. Earrings were usually circular, floral, or foliate yellow gold clips for day, long fringes of gemstones, usually diamonds, for evening wear. Upswept styles that enveloped the ear were also common. Brooches in the forms of animals and people continued to amuse, more often as cartoon-like caricatures than realistic portrayals. Stylized foliate sprays entirely set with numerous baguette, marquise and pear-shaped stones were another often-seen form. Modernism exerted its influence in the form of starburst and "atomic" shapes. Rings were domed clusters of gemstones, or one large stone surrounded by smaller stones, usually marquise or other fancy-cut diamonds.

The famous *haute joaillerie* houses–Cartier, Van Cleef & Arpels, et al–continued to produce opulent jewels in new designs as well as reprising pre-war "classics" which were finding a wider audience among the newly prosperous. One French house that began making its mark in the early 1950s was Sterlé, founded by Pierre Sterlé in 1934. Most famous among his designs is a fantastic "Bird of Paradise" brooch–a bird, not a plant, with a carved amethyst head, textured yellow gold body, fringes of foxtail chain for tail and wings, set with turquoise, with diamond-set edges and beak. The company closed its doors in the early 1960s.

American jewelry firms began achieving greater recognition in the 1950s. Harry Winston (1896-1978), a retailer, broker and manufacturer since the 1930s, made an even bigger name for himself with his touring "Court of Jewels" exhibit, which opened in 1949, the same year he purchased the Hope Diamond. (He donated it to the Smithsonian Institution in 1958.) For obvious reasons, Winston became known as the "King of Diamonds." Beginning in 1955 under Walter Hoving's directorship, Tiffany & Co. gained new distinction with designs by Jean Schlumberger (1907-1987), a former associate of Elsa Schiaparelli. Known for his use of colored gemstones, enamels, and animals and other motifs inspired by nature, Schlumberger became the first Tiffany designer whose jewels bore his signature. American-born Donald Claflin (d.1979), noted for his whimsical animal designs, joined Tiffany's in 1965. Claflin had previously worked for David Webb.

After opening an office in New York in 1946, and a salon in 1963, David Webb (1925-1975) came to prominence in the mid-1960s, when both clothing and jewelry styles were undergoing a significant change. He fostered, if not initiated, a trend for wearing quantities of large-scale, flamboyant jewels of Renaissance and fantasy-inspired design. Webb's animal motifs were influenced by Jeanne Toussaint of Cartier, creator of the famous panther jewels for the Duchess of Windsor and other wealthy clients. Today, pieces by Webb come up for sale regularly at auction, and generally do very well. This is no doubt partly due to the fact that Webb's "make a statement" jewels are so readily identifiable as his.

Designers Verdura, Seaman Schepps and Suzanne Belperron remained active through the sixties. Companies founded by Verdura, Schepps, Herz-Belperron, and Webb continue in business today.

In the late fifties and sixties, the fashion world turned its eyes to Italy, where clothing designers like Emilio Pucci were garnering attention. Italian jewelers were also creating a stir. The fashion for yellow gold created a new demand for Italian goldsmiths' talents. Foremost among Italian jewelers are the two family-run houses of Bulgari and Buccellati. The former house is famous for its Renaissance-inspired colored gemstone pieces, and classical designs incorporating ancient coins with heavy gold chains. Buccellati is known for its patterned textured engraving using a *bulino* graver, a technique also inspired by Renaissance goldwork, particularly that of Benvenuto Cellini. Both firms expanded to international branches, including the United States in 1952 (Buccellati) and 1970 (Bulgari).

The 1960s were indeed a time of extreme changes, in fashion and in society at large. "Flower power" and the "sexual revolution" were watchwords of the day. There was a rejection of "the establishment" in favor of radical ideas and behavior. The mid-1960s also signaled the beginning of a renaissance of international style and multi-cultural consciousness, incorporating American, French, English, Italian, Islamic and East Indian motifs, materials and artistry. "Ethnic" looks became fashionable. New trends in art also inspired fashion and jewelry design: the black-and-white geometry of "Op Art" and the colorful irreverence of "Pop Art" found expression in jewelry and fabrics.

New practitioners of a new jewelry style emerged in the mid-1960s as well. Although conventional precious materials continued to be used, the designs themselves were decidedly *un*conventional, and large in scale. Abstract, textured, jagged-edged, and amorphous organic forms took shape in yellow gold, sometimes accented with diamonds and/or pearls. Other more unusual stones were also used, including clusters of rough crystals, nodules and irregularly polished colored stones, and organic materials. In England, the master of this style is Andrew Grima (b. 1921), who opened his own business in 1965. His company now has shops all over the world. Arthur King (1921-1986), based in New York, also worked in a similar vein, as did Gilbert Albert in Switzerland. Like the Modernists of the 1950s, these and other designers of the period all followed a similar path, but each had his own individual mode of expression.

One designer who made pieces with a more geometric, polished look was Jean Dinh Van, a Frenchman of Vietnamese parentage, who worked for Cartier for ten years before striking out on his own in Paris. He specialized in square rings, some with added devices such as rotating gemstones or suspended gold jump rings. He also designed geometric chains with unusual clasps.

More traditionally designed jewels of the late sixties and early seventies also display a unique period twist: the setting of diamonds in yellow gold, rather than a white metal (platinum, white gold, or silver). Diamonds were often combined with colored gemstones, especially turquoise and rubies, or emeralds and rubies, typically framed in textured yellow gold or corded yellow gold wire. These stone combinations were also worked into Mogul-inspired pendants, necklaces and suites.

A few auction houses are beginning to recognize the 1950s as a "period," including circa dates in their descriptions; others do not. Most 1960s and 1970s jewelry is still described as contemporary, or simply not dated. Auction house catalogs of "important" or "magnificent" (i.e., very high-end) jewelry usually include biographical information on designers and manufacturers, which can be quite helpful. The second edition of *Understanding Jewellery* includes an additional chapter on 1960s and 1970s jewelry. Daniela Mascetti's and Amanda Triossi's *Earrings* and the recently published *The Necklace* both cover styles up to the present, as does Proddow and Fasel's *Diamonds, A Century of Spectacular Jewels.* Now that the twenty-first century is nearly upon us, historians will undoubtedly acquire a clearer perspective on later twentieth century styles (perhaps someone will even come up with names for them), and more reference material will continue to be published.

References: David Bennett and Daniela Mascetti, *Understanding Jewellery,* 2nd ed., Antique Collectors' Club, 1994; Graham Hughes, *Modern Jewelry, an International Survey, 1890-1967*, Crown Publishers, 1968 (out of print); Penny Proddow and Debra Healy, *American Jewelry*, Rizzoli International, 1987; Penny Proddow, Debra Healy and Marion Fasel, *Hollywood Jewels,* Harry N. Abrams, 1992; Penny Proddow and Marion Fasel, *Diamonds, A Century of Spectacular Jewels,* Harry N. Abrams, 1996; Daniela Mascetti and Amanda Triossi, *Earrings from Antiquity to the Present*, Rizzoli International, 1990; *The Necklace from Antiquity to the Present*, Harry N. Abrams, 1997, and *Bvlgari,* Abbeville, 1996; Sylvie Raulet, *Jewelry of the 1940s and 1950s,* Rizzoli International, 1987; Kenneth Snowman, ed., *The Master Jewelers*, Harry N. Abrams, 1990; Luisa Somaini and Claudio Cerritelli, *Jewelry by Artists in Italy, 1945-1995,* Electa/Gingko, 1995; *Janet* Zapata, "American Jewelry Gains Ground at Auction," article in *JCK-Heritage*, March, 1993.

Advisors: Bruce Healy, Amanda Triossi, Janet Zapata.

Bracelet

Charm

14k yg, c. 1954, seventeen charms on braided chain, including sunglasses, map of Africa, two rings with prong-set gemstones, a scroll, a horse, from the estate of Bebe Daniels, was retailed by Marchal of NY for the television program, "This is Your Life," v-spring and box clasp, all charms and chain mkd "14K," 8" tl .. 2,070 (A)

Sterling, c. 1950, five charms on a dog bone link bracelet, including sq and circ plaques with dogs' heads, a Scottie dog, a three-dimensional dog's head, and a dog in a dog house, bracelet and charms all mkd "STERLING," 7-1/4" tl 200

Flexible

Diamonds, platinum, c. 1955, central panel of fourteen emerald-cut diamonds, ranging from approx .75 ct to 1.85 cts each, approx 16.55 cts tw, flanked by an S-curved ribbon of thirty-eight marquise diamonds, approx 9.50 cts tw, intertwined with a tapering undulating ribbon of forty-nine baguette and thirty-one tapered baguette diamonds, continuing to two flexible baguette-set tapered bands, all baguettes approx 16.30 cts tw, total diamond weight approx 42.35 cts, attributed to Harry Winston, 1-1/2" w x 6-3/4" tl .... 62,700 (A)

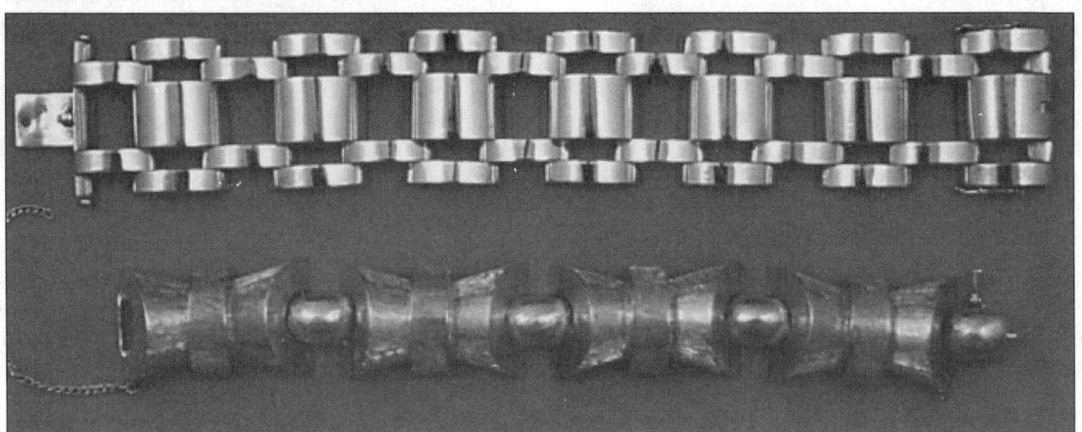

Link Bracelets, 14k yg:

T, c. 1949-54, slightly domed open rect links alternating with double bars, v-spring and box clasp, Romanian hmk for 14k (in use 1949-1954), 1-1/4" w x 7-1/4", **$850**.

B, c. 1950, four bow-shaped reeded textured links alternating with sm domed oval textured links, fold-over box clasp, safety chain, mkd "14K" on clasp, 7/8" w x 6-3/4", **$800**.

(Ellen Borlenghi collection).

Link

18k yg, c. 1950, two adjacent rows of crescent-shaped links with round bead terminals, 1-3/8" w x 7-1/2" tl .... 1,035 (A)

Diamonds, 18k yg, platinum, c. 1965, links a row of rope-textured yg loops, open centers surmounted by flowerhead clusters of bc diamonds in plat, flanked by prs of marquise-cut diamonds, 60 bc, 39 marquise diamonds, 15.35 cts tw, 3/4" w x 7" tl .... 10,780 (A)

Diamonds, platinum, c. 1950, six open navette-shaped links set with circ-cut diamonds with central sq-cut diamonds, baguette terminals, joined to links of a circ-cut diamond flanked by four marquise-cut diamonds, sgd "Cartier," in a leather Cartier box, 1/2" w x 7-1/4" .... 20,700 (A)

Diamonds, sapphires, emeralds, 18k yg, c. 1955, flexible openwork band of circ-cut diamond flowerheads flanked by lg and sm leaves alternately set with circ-cut emeralds or sapphires, outlined by twisted yg wire, sgd "VAN CLEEF & ARPELS" #78671, Fr hmk (eagle's head) for 18k gold, v-spring and box clasp, 1" w x 6-3/4" tl .... 36,800 (A)

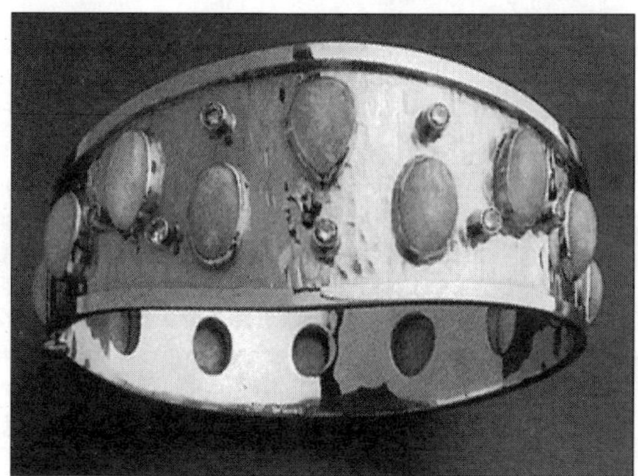

Bangle Bracelet, hinged, 18k yg, opals, diamonds, c. 1960, tapered band with raised edges, textured yg surface set irregularly with one pear and thirteen oval bezel-set opal cabs, seven bezel-set sm circ-cut diamonds, sgd "BROOKS," v-spring and box clasp, 1-1/8" w (at center), 2-1/4" inside dia, **$1,824** [A]. (Photo courtesy of Beverly Hills Auctioneers, Inc., CA, 9/21/97).

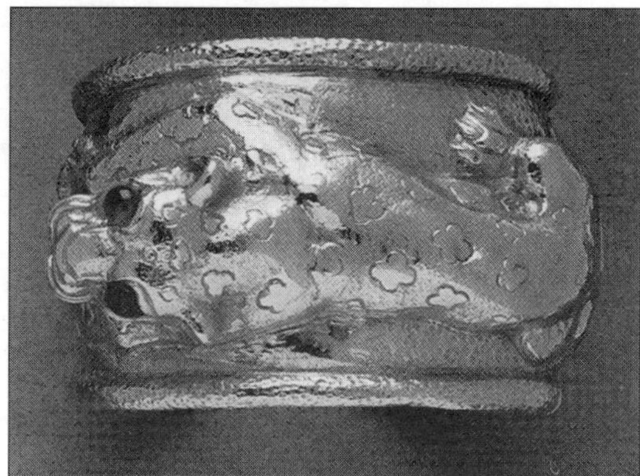

Cuff Bracelet, hinged, 18k yg, emeralds, c. 1965-70, repoussé design, depicting the body of a leopard as viewed from the top, emerald cab eyes, curving around a textured band with raised rounded edges, hinged at the sides, sgd "WEBB" for David Webb, New York, NY, 1-3/4" w, **$7,410** [A]. (Photo courtesy of Beverly Hills Auctioneers, Inc., CA, 6/22/97).

Brooch/Clip, 18k yg, rose gold, sterling, c. 1950-60, two thistles with 18k yg leaves, 18k rose gold buds, ster stem and thistledown, double pinstem with trombone catch, leaves and buds with *bulino* engraving, mkd "BUCCELLATI ITALY 18K," 1-1/2" w x 3-3/8", **$2,565** [A]. (Photo courtesy of Beverly Hills Auctioneers, Inc., CA, 9/21/97).

Silver, MOP, enamel, silver, c. 1970, a lg bezel-set MOP disk with black enamel optical art design suggesting movement, flanked by six repeating overlapping circ links of black enamel and polished silver "op art" design, centering sgd "VASARELY" for Victor Vasarely, #39/250, produced by CFA, double hook spring and polished silver box clasp, 1-1/2" w (at center), 6" tl .... 2,300 (A)

Brooch/Clip

18k yg, c. 1965, stylized textured yg dragon, sgd "© DAVID WEBB" on hinge, "® WEBB 18K" on appl plaque on rev, double-pronged hinged clip with trombone safety catch, with sgd "David Webb" box, 4" w x 3-1/4" ...... 3,420 (A)

Brooch/Pendant

Diamonds, 18k yg, platinum, c. 1965, open heart shape formed of ropetwist yg bordered on each side with a row of seventy bc diamonds, approx 5.50 cts tw, set in plat, suspending an inverted pear-shaped diamond, approx .50 ct, in open center, 1-1/2" w x 1-3/4" .... 5,130 (A)

Brooch/Pendant, diamonds, 18k yg, platinum, enamel, emeralds, c. 1965, titled *"Poissons"* (Fish), a bow of baguette diamonds outlined in yg, suspending two fish, one from the mouth, the other from the tail , with pavé-set diamond bodies, red enamel fins and tails outlined in yg, sm circ emerald cab eyes set in yg bezels, sgd "SCHLUMBERGER TIFFANY," provenance: from the Lyn Revson collection, 2-1/8" w x 3-1/2", **$40,250** [A]. (Photo courtesy of Christie's New York, NY, 10/23/96).

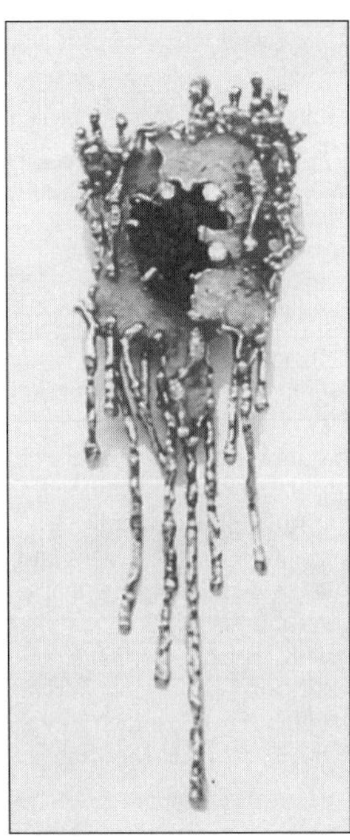

Brooch/Pendant, 18k yg, wg, dioptase crystals, diamonds, c. 1975, two amorphous, textured yg plaques, one overlapping the other, flanking and enclosing a prong-set dioptase crystal cluster accented with sm diamonds and wg, framed in projecting and cascading irregular yg strands of uneven lengths, Italian, mkd "750," sgd "MOAWAD," retailer, 4" w x 5" tl, chain (not shown), 27" tl, **$3,000**. (Private collection, photo courtesy of Amanda Triossi, © John Quinn, London).

Brooch/Pin, smoky quartz, yg, syn rubies, c. 1945-50, lg central emerald-cut prong-set smoky quartz flanked by pierced Florentine finish yg scroll motifs and scrolled yg wire set with two sm circ-cut syn rubies, C-catch, 1-3/4" w x 1-1/4", **$600**. (Ellen Borlenghi collection).

Brooch/Pin

14k yg, pearls, coral, sapphires, ruby, c. 1965, stick figure of a woman golfer with coral bead body, standing on two f.w. pearls, mabé pearl head with two sm circ-cut blue sapphire eyes and a sm circ-cut ruby mouth, mkd "LJ 14K," 7/8" w x 2-7/8" .... 200 (A)

18k yg, c. 1971, rect with appl letters "LOVE" with the "O" designed as a screw head, sgd "A. CIPULLO" #22385, 1" w x 1/2" .... 259 (A)

18k yg, diamonds, sapphires, c. 1960, flowerhead of textured yg petals centering a prong-set bc diamond encircled by five sm circ-cut blue sapphires, five sm bc diamonds interspersed between petals, 1-3/4" w x 1-7/8" .... 805 (A)

18k yg, enamel, rubies, diamonds, platinum, c. 1965, caricature of a seated monkey wearing a diamond bracelet, white enameled face (sm chips) with sm bezel-set circ ruby cab eyes, body and tail with green enameled stripes and dots, bracelet of sm circ prong-set diamonds set in plat banded in twisted yg wire, sgd "WEBB" for David Webb, provenance: from the Lyn Revson collection, 1-5/8" w x 2-1/4" .... 5,175 (A)

18k yg, green stones, c. 1970, three-dimensional cat's head with green stone eyes, textured yg, Fr hmk (eagle's head) for 18k gold, maker's mk for Cartier, France, 17.1 dwt, 1" w x 1-1/2" .... 1,610 (A)

Amethysts, diamonds, emeralds, yg, platinum, c. 1950, depicting a bouquet of violets, clusters of circ amethyst cabs interspersed with sm circ-cut prong-set diamonds, sm and lg circ and pear-shaped emerald cabs along lower edge bordered by an open textured yg doily, terminating in a pavé-set diamond and plat cone-shaped holder, sgd "VERDURA," provenance: from the Lyn Revson collection, 2" w x 2-1/4" .... 9,775 (A)

Coral, diamonds, yg, platinum, emeralds, c. 1965, stylized fox with fluted red coral body, textured yg head with sm marquise-cut emerald eyes, pavé-set diamond and plat ruff and tail, sgd "VERDURA," in a suede case, provenance: from the Lyn Revson collection, 7/8" w x 2-1/2" .... 10,925 (A)

Diamonds, emeralds, rubies, platinum, c. 1945-50, openwork scroll plat frame set with sc and circ-cut diamonds, centering a detachable floral spray clip of lg oval and circ emerald cabs and circ-cut, sc, and baguette diamonds, and an interchangeable ruby cab and diamond clip of similar design (with a bracelet attachment), sgd "TRABERT & HOEFFER-MAUBOUSSIN, Reflection," 2-1/8" w x 2-5/8" .... 20,700 (A)

Brooch/Pin, rubies, sapphires, diamonds, platinum-topped yg, c. 1945-50, stylized floral spray of grad paired oval and circ prong-set ruby cabs on one stem and blue sapphire cabs on the other, the lower stems set with lines of sc diamonds, 2-3/8" w x 2-3/4", **$2,760** [A]. (Photo courtesy of Phillips Fine Art Auctioneers, New York, NY, 5/1/97).

Brooch/Pin, 14k yg, wg, diamonds, emeralds, c. 1950, in the shape of a peacock, body of pavé-set diamonds, yg beak and crest, marquise emerald eye, on a yg branch, body wrapped in yg foxtail chain continuing to a fringe of uneven lengths forming tail, with thirteen bc diamonds and eleven circ-cut emeralds prong-set on chain terminals, total of 76 bc, 25 sc diamonds, approx 4.00 cts tw, 1-1/2" w x 4-1/4" tl, **$5,130** [A]. (Photo courtesy of Beverly Hills Auctioneers, Inc., CA, 6/22/97).

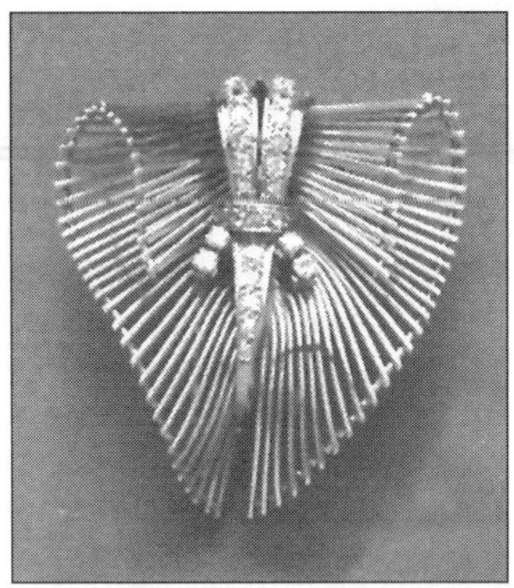

Brooch/Pin, 18k rose gold, diamonds, platinum-topped rose gold, c. 1945-50, heart-shaped open folded ribbon motif of radiating wires, plat-topped rose gold center set with twenty-four sm circ diamonds, approx 0.80 ct tw, 1-3/8" w x 1-1/2", **$1,100** [A]. (Photo courtesy of Beverly Hills Auctioneers, Inc., CA, 2/16/97).

Diamonds, emeralds, rubies, platinum, c. 1945-50, openwork scroll plat frame set with sc and circ-cut diamonds, centering a detachable floral spray clip of sm and lg emerald cabs, and circ-cut, sc, and baguette diamonds, and an interchangeable ruby cab and diamond clip of similar design, sgd "TRABERT & HOEFFER-MAUBOUSSIN," 3-1/8" w x 3-5/8" .... 41,400 (A)

Diamonds, platinum, c. 1950, three-dimensional scroll of pavé-set and baguette diamonds, with four lines of baguette diamonds of varied widths forming a curv spray through open center of scroll, terminating in pear-shaped and triangular-cut diamonds, 2-1/8" w x 2-1/2" .... 50,600 (A)

Diamonds, sapphires, emeralds, 18k yg, c. 1955, floral/foliate spray of circ-cut emeralds, sapphires and diamonds, outlined by yg twisted wire, sgd "VAN CLEEF & ARPELS, NY" #31381, 2-1/8" w x 2-7/8" .... 17,250 (A)

Moonstones, diamonds, platinum, c. 1950, depicting two pussy willow stalks of sc and sm circ-cut diamonds with lg oval prong-set moonstone cab catkins, gathered by a spiraling baguette diamond ribbon, sgd "TIFFANY & CO.," 6-1/4" w x 2" .... 112,500 (A)

Platinum, 14k yg, seed pearl, diamonds, blue stones, c. 1960, golf club with a seed pearl ball, the handle of plat set with four sm circ-cut diamonds and three rect blue stones, maker's mk, "14K," 1/4" w x 2" .... 200 (A)

Turquoise, 18k yg, wg, diamonds, c. 1960, floral spray, three round clusters of yg-tipped turq beads (one missing), mounted on textured yg branches, three pavé diamond-set wg leaves, fifty-three sc diamonds, approx 1.10 cts tw, 2" w x 2-1/2" .... 991 (A)

Yg, c. 1955, open wirework yg flowerhead, 1-5/8" w x 1-5/8" 300

Brooch/Pin, rubies, sapphires, diamonds, platinum-topped yg, c. 1945-50, stylized floral spray of grad paired oval and circ prong-set ruby cabs on one stem and blue sapphire cabs on the other, the lower stems set with lines of sc diamonds, 2-3/8" w x 2-3/4", **$2,760** [A]. (Photo courtesy of Phillips Fine Art Auctioneers, New York, NY, 5/1/97).

Brooch/Pin, 18k yg, diamonds, enamel, pearl, amethyst, c. 1965, in the shape of a three-dimensional textured yg camel with blue enameled hump, sm circ diamond accents on saddle and harness, pearl plume on head, gypsy-set oval amethyst on rear leg, sgd "TIFFANY SCHLUMBERGER," 2" w x 2-1/2, **$13,800** [A]. (Photo courtesy of Christie's Images, New York, NY, 12/11/96).

Brooch/Pin, diamonds, platinum, c. 1950, stylized spray centering one oe diamond, approx. 1.70 cts, flanked by two oe diamonds, approx 1.00 ct tw, seventy-four circ-cut and sc diamonds, nine baguette, one bullet, six marquise, and four sq diamonds, all prong-set, approx 6.15 cts tw, 1-1/2" x 2-1/4", **$4,560** [A].

Charms

14k yg, c. 1955, two, one a martini shaker that opens to reveal a pop-up red enameled devil, the other a martini glass with an olive, both mkd "14K," shaker 1/2" w x 3/4", glass 1/4" w x 3/4", each 70

14k yg, c. 1955, musical TV that plays "Happy Birthday," slot for photo to be inserted behind glass screen, mkd "14K," 1/2" w x 1-1/8" 350

14k yg, c. 1955, TV with glass screen flanked by two cultured pearls, slot for photo to be inserted behind screen, mkd "14K," 1/2" w x 1-1/8" 120

14k yg, c. 1955, cuckoo clock that releases a bird on a spring when pressed, mkd "14K," 3/4" w x 1-1/8" 125

Clip

Diamonds, turquoise, 18k yg and wg, c. 1960, design of two crossed berries and leaves, open yg wirework berries set with sm circ-cut diamonds alternating with sm turq

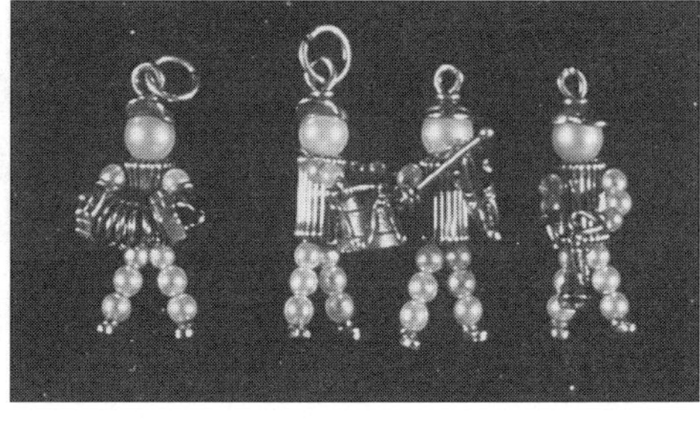

Charms, cultured pearls, 14k yg, c. 1955, four charms representing musicians with pearl heads, legs, and arms, and yg bead bodies playing yg musical instruments, one playing an accordion, bells, a fiddle, and a trumpet, each with a yg cap on head, all mkd "14K," 1/2" w x 1-1/8", each, **$100**. (Private collection, photo by John Neister).

cabs, pavé-set diamond leaves, sgd "TIFFANY SCHLUMBERGER" for Jean Schlumberger, Fr hmks, double-pronged hinged clip on rev, 1-1/4" w x 2"....... 7,475 (A)

Cuff Links

14k yg, c. 1950, designed as two-sided hinges with engr screws, sgd "BROCK & CO.," 16.40 dwt, 1/2" w x 1-1/4", pr .... 805 (A)

14k yg, ruby, topaz, c. 1950, each in the shape of a three-dimensional airplane with ruby and topaz accents, approx 5.00 dwt, 1" w x 1-1/4, pr .... 690 (A)

Onyx, 14k yg, c. 1950, green onyx cylinders with yg centers and terminals, sgd "TIFFANY & CO., FRANCE," #9918, 1-1/4" w x 1/4", pr .... 633 (A)

14k yg, blue stones, c. 1960, seated three-dimensional poodles with blue stone eyes, rect backs, sgd "RUSER" for William Ruser, Los Angeles, CA, 1/2" w x 7/8", pr .... 228 (A)

Sterling, c. 1975, three-dimensional design of The Little Mermaid seated on a rock, Am, mkd "ALLAN ADLER STERLING," 3/4" w x 1", pr 100

Dress Set: Cuff Links and Studs

18k yg, c. 1960, double-sided textured figure-eight design cufflinks with appl ropetwist around centers, three textured spherical studs with sm polished semi-circ disks appl to top and around sides, sgd "SCHLUMBERGER, TIFFANY," with Tiffany box, cufflinks 1-1/4" w x 3/8", studs 1/2" dia, set .... 2,185 (A)

Cuff Links, sterling, glass, c. 1950, each in the shape of an owl's head with lg red and black glass eyes, hinged swiveling bar finding mkd "STER PAT 2472958" (1949), 7/8" w x 3/4", pr, **$125**. (Richard Levey collection).

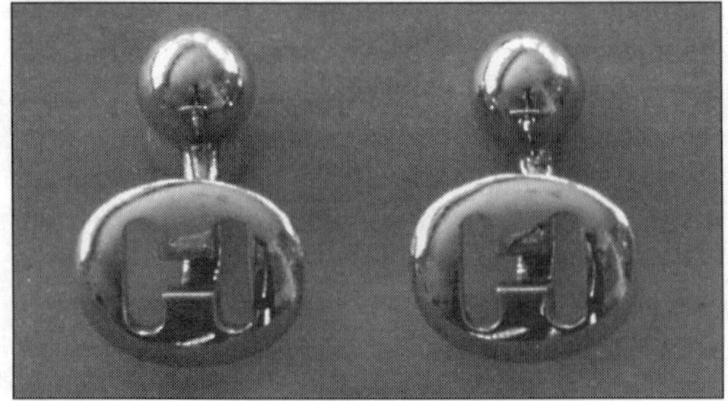

Cuff Links, silver, c. 1977, design titled "*Vulcain,*" oval with a cutout "H" center, appl curved shank and ball on rev, Fr hmk (crab), mkd "Hermès," Paris, 1-2/8" w x 1-1/8", pr, **$175**. (Photo courtesy of Bruce Healy).

Earrings

Diamonds, 14k wg, c. 1945-50, ribbon and floral motif, with forty-two sm circ diamonds in bead and bezel setting, approx 0.75 ct tw, clip/post backs, 3/4" w x 1-1/4" .... 627 (A)

Diamonds, sapphires, emeralds, 18k yg, c. 1955, double leaf design of circ-cut diamonds, sapphires, and emeralds, with textured yg accents, sgd "V.C.A." #82457 for Van Cleef & Arpels, Fr hmk (eagle's head) for 18k gold, 3/4" w x 1-1/8", pr .... 9,775 (A)

18k yg, garnets, c. 1965, rounded yg triangle with Florentine finish, centering bezel-set carved rect garnet cab, sgd "BURLE MARX," clipbacks, 1" w x 1-1/2" .... 920 (A)

Pendent

Yg, c. 1950, Victorian Revival, tapered shield-shape of five interlocking plaques with appl bead and scrollwork in the Etruscan style, grad fringe of five navette-shaped drops, hmks, locking kidney wires, approx 10.5 dwt, 5/8" w x 2" tl, pr .... 633 (A)

Emeralds, 18k yg, diamonds, c. 1965, chandelier design, flowerhead surmount centering an oval emerald cab surrounded by sm circ-cut diamonds in a serrated yg frame, suspending a detachable pendant with five oval emerald cabs in a double-tiered diamond-set floral/foliate yg-frame, terminating in an emerald cab drop in a scallop-edged pear-shaped diamond-set frame, emeralds approx 37.00 cts tw, diamonds approx 5.00 cts tw, sgd "WEBB" for David Webb, New York, NY, 1" w x 2-3/4" tl, pr .... 17,250 (A)

Jadeite, rubies, diamonds, onyx, 18k yg, c. 1969, hexagonal surmount centering a circ carved floral motif green jadeite cab on a sm circ-cut diamond ground outlined by calibré-cut channel-set rubies, surmounting a sm triangle of three sm circ-cut diamonds surrounded by two sm

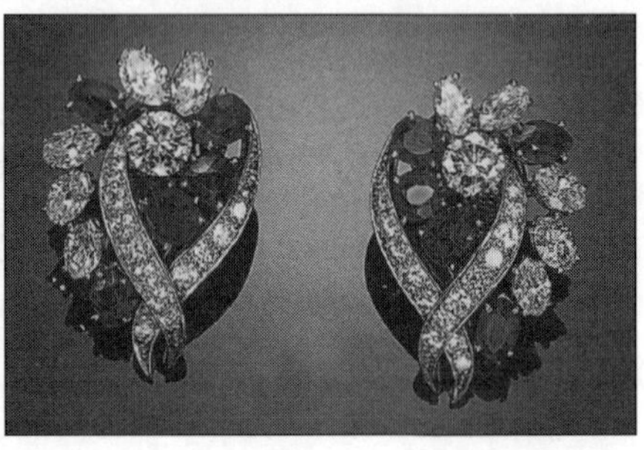

Earrings, diamonds, rubies, platinum, c. 1954, each an open scrolling ribbon motif centering a lg prong-set circ-cut diamond of approx 2.04 cts, surrounded by three pear-shaped and two marquise-cut rubies and five marquise-cut diamonds, and two scrolling plat plaques pavé-set with sm circ-cut diamonds, sgd "BELLOCCHIO," rubies approx 8.00 cts tw, clipbacks, 1" w x 1-3/8", pr, **$17,250** [A]. (Photo courtesy of Christie's New York, NY, 10/23/96).

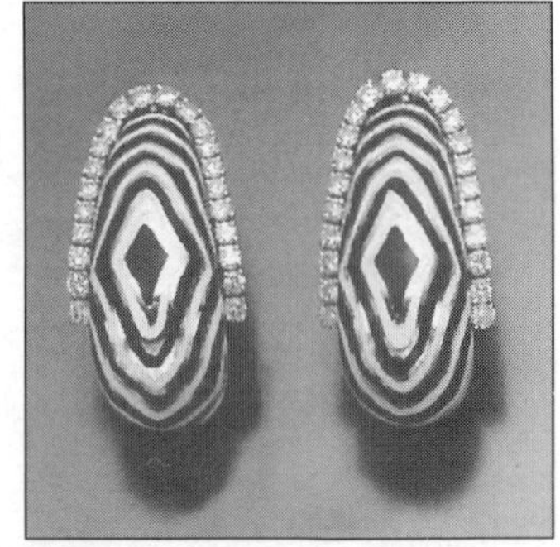

Earrings, enamel, diamonds, 18k yg, c. 1965, oval dome of black and white zebra-striped enamel outlined by a row of sm circ-cut prong-set diamonds, clipbacks, sgd "WEBB" for David Webb, New York, NY, 3/4" w x 1-3/8", pr, **$3,450** [A]. (Photo courtesy of Christie's Images, New York, NY, 12/11/96).

triangles and one trapezoid of black onyx suspending a lg tapered rect plaque centering an oval floral carved and pierced green jadeite plaque, surrounded by sm circ-cut prong-set diamonds, two triangular bezel-set black onyx cabs in the lower corners, all outlined by calibré-cut channel-set rubies, a horizontal row of calibré-cut black onyx cabs and a row of sm circ-cut diamonds across the base, sgd "BVLGARI," Fr hmk (eagle's head) for 18k gold, provenance: from the Lyn Revson collection, 1-1/8" w x 3-1/2", pr .... 18,400 (A)

Necklace

Amethysts, jade, 18k yg, diamonds, rubies, plat, c. 1965, central carved green nephrite jade Mayan mask with oval-cut bezel-set ruby eyes encircled by sm circ-cut diamonds, sculpted hammered yg headdress with appl diamond-set plat plaques and nine grad cushion-shaped amethyst cabs, flanked by five strands of grad round amethyst beads, sgd "WEBB" for David Webb, New York, NY, central plaque 4" w x 4-1/8", 17" tl .... 50,600 (A)

Diamonds, 14k wg, c. 1950, central cluster of pear, marquise, oval and heart-shaped diamonds flanked by three rows of pears and ovals tapering to two rows of oval and marquise diamonds, continuing to a single row of pear-shaped diamonds and v-spring and box clasp, stones prong-set on a wire frame, approx 60.00 cts tw, 1-3/4" w (at center), 18" tl .... 57,000 (A)

Diamonds, platinum, c. 1950, double-looped row of grad channel-set baguette diamonds capped by baguette-set curved bars at sides, surmounting a row of bc diamonds and suspending a fringe of grad pear-shaped diamonds each with a sm circ-cut diamond surmount, continuing to a single line of baguette diamonds, diamond-set foldover box clasp joining two U-shaped terminals set with sm circ-cut diamonds, 1-1/8" w (at center), 14-1/2" tl .... 57,500 (A)

Diamonds, platinum, c. 1950, a flexible line of seventy baguette diamonds, approx 16.50 cts tw, suspending a fringe of pear-shaped diamonds, approx 13.50 cts tw, terminating in side scrolling ribbon motifs set with thirty-four

Necklace, diamonds, sapphires, emeralds,18k yg, c. 1955-60, cascading foliate motifs set with circ-cut diamonds alternating with emeralds and sapphires, each within a twisted gold wirework frame, joined to an articulated back chain of circ-cut diamonds, sgd "V.C.A," for Van Cleef & Arpels, #31055, 3" w (at center), 14-3/4" tl, **$39,100** [A]. (Photo courtesy of Christie's New York, NY, 10/23/96).

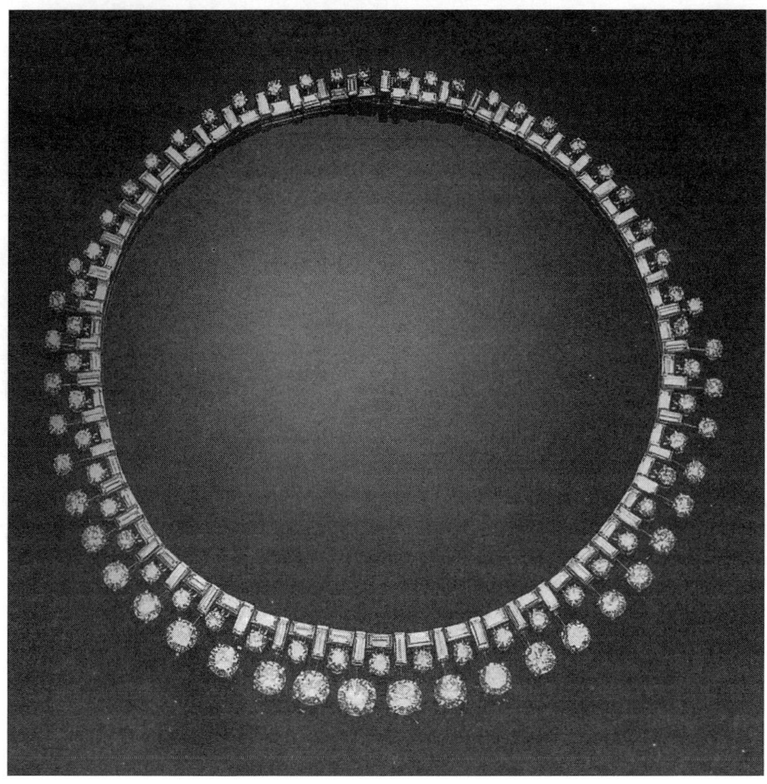

Necklace, diamonds, platinum, c. 1948, grad repeating design of alternating vertical and horizontal baguette diamonds, each horizontal baguette suspending a sm circ-cut diamond drop, each vertical baguette suspending a lg circ-cut diamond drop, baguette diamond-set clasp, sgd "Cartier," v-spring and box clasp, 3/4" w (at center), 13-7/8" tl, **$123,500** (A). (Photo courtesy of Christie's New York, NY, 10/23/96).

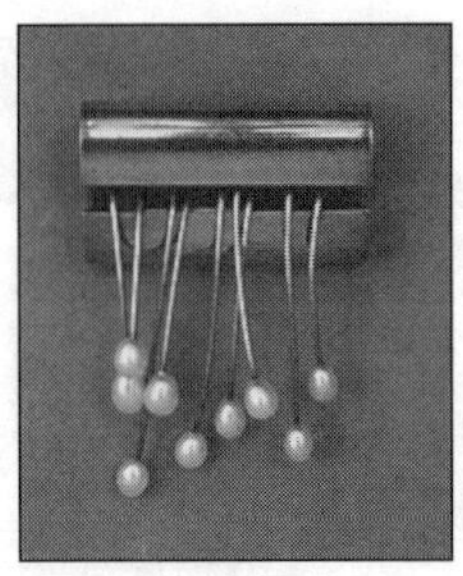

Pendant, sterling, cultured pearls, c. 1960, tubular rect ster plaque horizontally split through the center, nine pearl-tipped movable ster wires suspended from opening, mkd "STERLING ARIE OFER ISRAEL," also mkd in Hebrew, 1-1/4" w x 1-1/2" tl, **$275**. (Al Munir Meghji collection).

baguette and eight marquise-cut diamonds, approx 3.75 cts tw, spiraling around baguette line, attributed to Harry Winston, 1/2" w x approx 15" tl .... 42,750 (A)

18k wg and yg, c. 1970, bicolor gold torque suspending an octagonal plaque pendant with geo surface design, 67.5 dwt, sgd "BVLGARI," pendant 1-1/4" w x 2-1/2" .... 2,530 (A)

Emeralds, 18k yg, diamonds, platinum, c. 1965, articulated tapering band of grad cusped open leaf shapes of yg wire, each center prong-set with a lg oval emerald cab, the front interspersed with sm circ-cut diamonds, sgd "WEBB" for David Webb, emeralds approx 158.00 cts tw, diamonds approx 6.00 cts tw, 1-7/8" w (at center), 15-3/4" tl .... 29,900 (A)

Pendant

18k yg, dated 1969, circ medallion, abstract male profile with a pattern of spoons for "hair," "Dali" in script across the man's chin for Salvador Dalí, a floral design of teaspoon shapes on rev, mkd "1969," #7, 1-3/8" dia .... 1,840 (A)

Pendant and Chain

Agate, 18k yg, c. 1970, inverted truncated pear-shaped banded blue agate with circ pierced center, suspended from a textured dendritic organic motif yg mount with similar bail, handmade chain of figure-eight links convertible to form a bracelet and shorter necklace, sgd "KING" for Arthur King, New York, NY, original suede pouch, pendant 2" w x 2-3/4" (with bail), chain 36" tl .... 1,495 (A)

Ring

18k yg, diamonds, rubies, c. 1970, domed oval with rows of diamonds alternating with rubies separated by braided yg wire, twenty-five prong-set bc diamonds, 1.25 cts tw, thirty-nine prong-set mixed-cut rubies, 1-1/4" w x 3/4", size 9 .... 920 (A)

18k yg, lapis diamonds, c. 1970, cast freeform yg mount set with a lg oval lapis cab surmounted by an irregular cluster of eight sm bc diamonds, mono for Arthur King, New York, NY, 3/4" w x 1-1/2", size 6 .... 633 (A)

18k yg,emeralds, pearls, diamonds, c. 1970, cast freeform centering a gray cultured pearl of 10.8 mm, flanked top and bottom by two prong-set pear-shaped emeralds, five sm bc diamonds at sides, sgd "KING" for Arthur King, New York, NY 3/4" w x 1" .... 920 (A)

18k yg, malachite, c. 1970, cast textured freeform mount, irregular cusped prongs centering a lg malachite cab, sgd "KING" for Arthur King, New York NY, 7/8" w x 1", size 4 .... 403 (A)

Amethyst, 18k yg, c. 1965, oval amethyst cab approx 24 mm x 18 mm, bezel-set in a hand hammered yg oval frame, wide shank, sgd "JANIYE," 1" w x 1-3/8" .... 1,150 (A)

Rubellite, diamonds, platinum, c. 1955, rect plaque prong-set with a step-cut rubellite tourmaline (pink),

Ring, diamonds, wg, c. 1945-50, scroll and cylinder motif with four rows of pavé-set sc diamonds surmounted by one prong-set bc diamond, approx 1.00 ct, set in grooved and pierced bezel above channel-set baguettes in scroll at one side, 7/8" w x 1/2" (at top), approx size 7, **$2,700**. (Ellen Borlenghi collection).

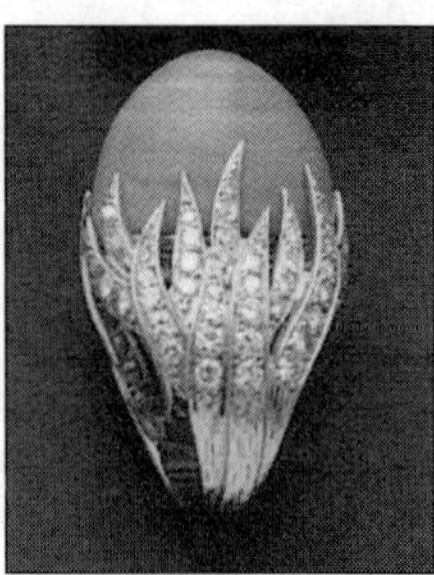

Ring, coral, diamonds, 18k yg, c. 1955-60, circ high-domed central pink coral cab held by multiple flamelike yg prongs set with seventy-seven full and sixteen sc diamonds, sgd "STERLÉ, PARIS," Fr hmk (eagle's head) for 18k gold, cab 1/2" thick, 7/8" w, size 5-1/2, **$2,280** [A]. (Photo courtesy of Beverly Hills Auctioneers, Inc., CA, 9/21/97).

framed by fourteen channel-set baguette diamonds, split tapered shank, 5/8" w x 3/4", size 6 .... 1,380 (A)

Sapphires, diamonds, 18k yg, c. 1970, domed circ floral motif, six flowerheads each centering a sm circ-cut prong-set diamond surrounded by six sm circ-cut prong-set blue sapphires, sgd "TIFFANY & CO.," 1" w x 1", size 6-1/2 .... 2,185 (A)

Star ruby, rubies, platinum, c. 1955, domed plat mount centering lg oval star ruby cab (damaged), flanked by two sm ruby sugarloaf cabs, sgd "RUSER" for Wm Ruser, Los Angeles, CA, mkd "10% IRID. PLAT," 1/2" w, size 8-3/4 .... 3,135 (A)

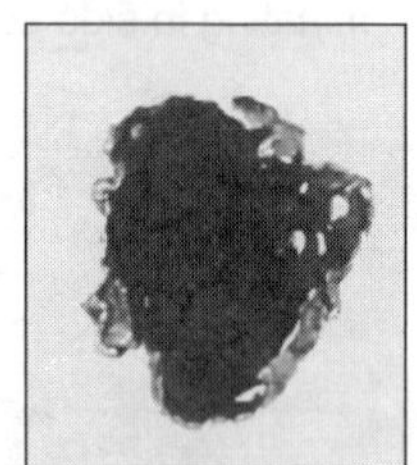

Ring, dioptase crystals, 18k yg, c. 1965, an irregular cluster of dioptase crystals mounted in a textured, pierced asymmetrical frame on a narrow shank, Fr hmk, **$1,500**. (Private collection, photo courtesy of Amanda Triossi, © John Quinn, London).

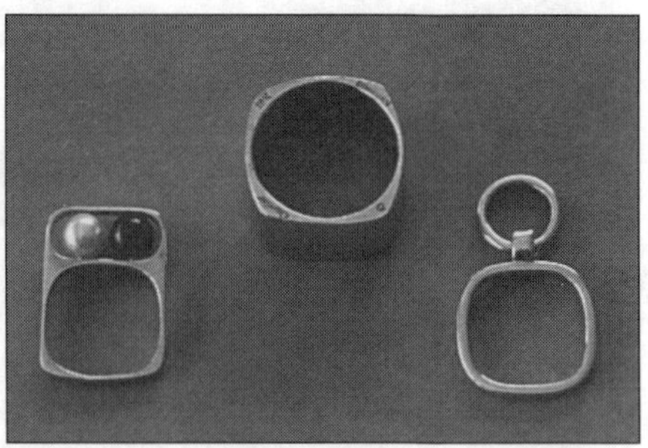

Rings, 18k, by Jean Dinh Van, Paris, France, Fr hmks:

L, wg, c. 1968, squared shank supporting an open rect cage holding two post-set freely rotating drilled cultured pearls, one white and one black, mkd "18K DINH VAN," 5/8" w, **$700**.

C, wg, c. 1968, slightly squared plain band, mkd "18K DINH VAN," illegible maker's mk in lozenge, 7/8" sq, 1/2" w, **$400**.

R, c. 1975, sq wg shank with appl yg loop at top holding a yg ring, mkd "18K DINH VAN," illegible maker's mk in lozenge, 3/4" sq, **$650**.

(Alice Healy collection, photo by Bruce Healy).

Suite: Bracelet and Ring

18k yg, rubies, turquoise, diamonds, c. 1955, bracelet of domed oval textured links, each with a central row of four turq cabs flanked by rows of three sm circ-cut rubies, v-spring and box clasp, ring a domed oval framed in sm cir turq cabs enclosing rows of sm bc diamonds, two rows of grad sm rubies, central row of sm bezel-set bc diamonds, bracelet 1/2" w x 6-1/2" tl, ring size 6-1/4, suite .... 1,150 (A)

Suite: Pendant/Necklace and Pendent Earrings

Diamonds, rubies, platinum, c. 1956, necklace a line of baguette diamonds flanked by S-curved rows of oval, cushion, and circ-cut rubies with interspersed baguette diamond accents, centering a detachable cascading pendant of articulated baguette diamond fringe, each strand terminating in a pear-shaped diamond drop, the largest approx 4.01 cts, pavé-set diamond bail, pr of matching pendent earrings, necklace with maker's mk for Harry Winston, in a suede case, with GIA certificate stating that the 4.01 cts pear-shaped diamond is D color and clarity SI1, 3-1/4" top to bottom at center, 15-1/4" tl, suite .... 266,500 (A)

Suite: Necklace, Bracelet, Earrings, Ring, 18k yg, chalcedony nodules, cultured pearls, diamonds, c. 1970, a lg chalcedony nodule, surface encrusted with drusy quartz crystals, set within an irregular three-dimensionally textured openwork yg frame with lg baroque cultured pearls and sm diamonds mounted around the edges, flanked by four smaller nodules similarly set, the frames tapering to an articulated back section set with pearls and diamonds, and a nodule in the clasp, matching bracelet with one nodule and three pearls, sm diamond accents, earrings and ring each of one nodule and pearl with diamond accents, sgd "Gilbert Albert," Geneva, Switzerland, necklace approx 21" tl, bracelet, approx 9", ring 1" dia, earrings 3/4" dia, suite, **$15,000**. (Private collection, photo courtesy of Amanda Triossi, © John Quinn, London).

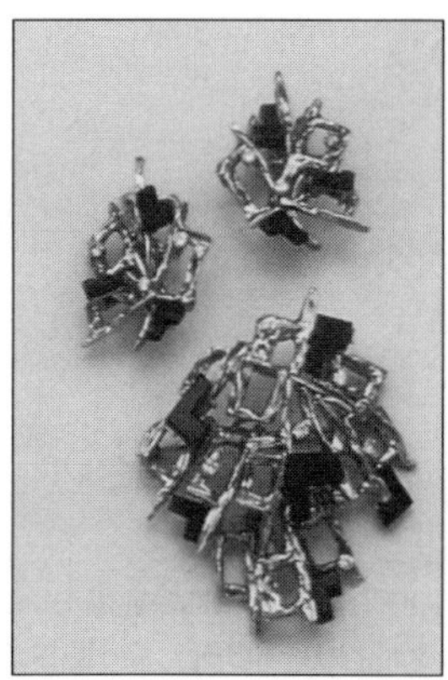

Suite: Brooch/Pin and Earrings, 18k yg, lapis, diamonds, c. 1970, brooch a stepped series of irregular openwork textured yg rectangles set randomly with six L-shaped lapis plaques and five sm diamonds, matching earrings each a cluster of yg rectangles with three L-shaped lapis plaques and three diamonds, sgd "Kutchinsky," London, England mfr, brooch 2-1/4" w x 2-1/2", earrings, 1"w x 1-1/2", suite, **$2,500**. (Private collection, photo courtesy of Amanda Triossi, © John Quinn, London).

Suite: Brooch/Pin and Earrings, 18k yg, cultured pearls, diamonds, c. 1975, brooch a roughly circ three-dimensional open network of textured yg set throughout with elongated baroque cultured pearls, a cluster of five sm diamonds prong-set off-center, matching ring with a central cluster of four sm diamonds encircled by pearls, earrings each with five elongated pearls, sgd "Gilbert Albert," Geneva, Switzerland **$3,000**. (Private collection, photo courtesy of Amanda Triossi, © John Quinn, London).

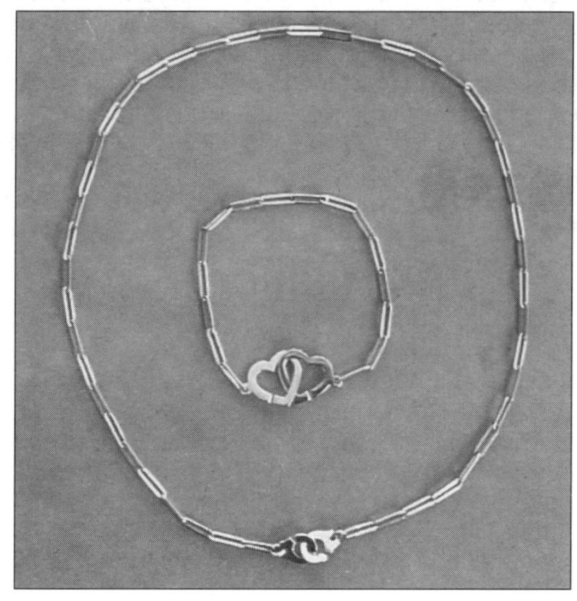

Suite: Necklace and Bracelet, 18k yg, c. 1975, necklace a chain of open rect links with lg interlocking hook clasp worn at the front, similar bracelet with interlocking hearts clasp, mkd "18K DINH VAN" for Jean Dinh Van, Paris, France, Fr hmk (eagle's head). for 18k, necklace 15-1/2" tl, bracelet 6-1/2" tl, **$1,700**. (Alice Healy collection, photo by Bruce Healy).

Suite: Necklace and Earrings, diamonds, emeralds, amethysts, turquoise, 18k yg, platinum, c. 1965, flexible V-shaped bib necklace prong-set with circ emerald, amethyst, and turq cabs, each within a circ-cut diamond and yg inverted pear-shaped frame, suspended from and interspersed with alternating bc diamonds and sm turq cabs, matching lg clipback pendent earrings of inverted kite-shaped outline, approx tw: emeralds 63.00 cts tw, amethysts 51.00 cts tw, diamonds 38.50 cts tw, turq 35.00 cts tw, Fr hmks, sgd "BVLGARI," provenance: from the Lyn Revson collection, necklace 2-1/2" top to bottom at center, 15-3/4" tl, earrings 1-1/2" w x 2-1/2" tl, suite, **$134,500** [A]. (Photo courtesy of Christie's New York, NY, 10/23/96).

COSTUME JEWELRY c. 1935-1975

(DESIGNER/MANUFACTURER SIGNED AND OTHER)

History: A few years ago, no one would have believed that a brooch made of rhinestones and base metal could be worth more than one made of diamonds and platinum. Up until about ten or fifteen years ago, that same old rhinestone brooch probably would have been tossed in a drawer or thrown away. That was before costume jewelry collectors, and price guides, entered the picture. Now, it seems that everyone knows and recognizes the "name" pieces–and knows their value, or at least knows better than to throw them away. Costume jewelry was elevated to an even higher level with the opening of an exhibition that toured museums in Europe and the U.S., from 1991 to 1993, called "Jewels of Fantasy, Costume Jewelry of the 20th Century." The exhibit's accompanying catalog (see References) has become an important reference resource.

Expanded though it may be, it is not possible to go into great detail in one section of this book about the many manufacturers and designers whose history and product have already been amply documented by a plethora of entire books on signed, and unsigned, costume jewelry. New books on the topic in general as well as monographs on specific makers continue to be published. The References below list some of them. While these are recommended for the examples, marks, and information they contain, readers should be aware that it is not uncommon to find conflicting information about the same makers in different sources.

It is not likely, however, that the "true story" will ever be known. Most companies did not keep detailed records of their jewelry lines that, at the time they were produced, were thought to be as ephemeral and disposable as the fashions they were meant to complement. Much of the recent research on costume jewelry has of necessity been based on recollections of company executives, patent and trademark searches, advertising and articles in consumer and trade periodicals of the times.

A listing of American costume jewelry manufacturers, including dates of operation if documented, can be found in an appendix at the end of this book. Since the first edition of *Warman's Jewelry*, dates have been added, and revised in some cases, because of information recently discovered by researchers in the field, including the Advisors named below.

Even though much has already been written by others, a few salient points should be made here, especially as they relate to the specific listings that follow.

The bulk of the "name" jewelry that collectors seek was produced from circa 1935 through the 1960s (1970s costume jewelry is beginning to generate collector interest as well). The few manufacturers who were making costume jewelry before 1935, e.g., Ciner, Coro, Miriam Haskell, Hobé, Napier, Trifari, and designer/couturiers Chanel, Hattie Carnegie, and Schiaparelli, did not consistently mark their pieces, if they signed them at all (the collector terminology for manufacturers' markings is "signed"). Their attributable circa 1920s (and some early 1930s) designs are rare and usually expensive.

As mentioned in the introduction, attribution of unsigned pieces and circa-dating of any piece should be backed up by printed evidence, or provenance. Because they assist in circa-dating, patent numbers found on the backs of pieces are given in the listings and captions, with the year the numbers were issued in parentheses, which is the *earliest* year the piece could have been made. Other aspects of a piece, such as style and other elements, may date it later. For example, Coro patented the *mechanism* for the double clip brooch with Coro's tradename Duette in 1931, when the clips were flat-backed and the motifs were geometric (see Costume Jewelry c. 1920-1935 for examples), but figural motif Duettes with double-pronged hinged clips (often called "fur clips") bearing this same patent number were made in the late thirties and early forties.

Aside from novelty items, covered in the previous section on plastics, most costume, or fashion jewelry continued to follow fine jewelry trends until the late '50s, when "fabulous fake" pieces became more exaggerated and glitzier than their fine jewelry counterparts. Hollywood had perhaps even more influence on non-precious jewelry than on fine jewelry. Joseff of Hollywood outfitted many stars with fabulous fakery for their roles in "period" films, and Marilyn Monroe's "diamonds are a girl's best friend" jewels were really rhinestones, as were Audrey Hepburn's "Breakfast at Tiffany's" baubles. It was also a profitable and common practice for manufacturers to produce costume jewels imitating the precious ones worn by the stars, so that even a woman of modest means could afford to emulate her favorite glamour queen. Mid- to late-'30s and early '40s Retro Modern costume pieces made of rhinestones and gold-plated or rhodium-plated white metal or sterling silver were often larger in scale than precious stone, gold and platinum equivalents, but many of the overall designs were quite similar. Some costume jewelry designers, such as Miram Haskell, also took inspiration from earlier styles, especially during the Victorian Revival of the late thirties and early forties.

During World War II, base metals were restricted for the war effort, as was platinum. Costume jewelry factories were called into service to make munitions and other military equipment. Jewelry production was diminished, but not curtailed. Sterling silver was used as a substitute for other metals. Fewer rhinestones were used because supplies from Czechoslovakia and Austria were cut off, as were simulated ("faux") pearls from Japan. Manufacturers made do with existing stock and with "stones" of Lucite and other plastics. Although base metal restrictions were lifted after the war, some manufacturers continued to use sterling for their higher-end lines until the mid-'50s.

Fashion jewelry *forms* also paralleled those of precious jewels. In the '30s and '40s, clips were just as stylish in rhinestones and white metal as they were in diamonds and platinum, moving to gold-plating and colored glass stones as fine jewelry changed to colored gold and gemstones. Gold-plated costume pieces of the late thirties and early forties were often bi-colored rose and yellow. As with fine jewelry, the late forties and fifties saw the return of the parure, or suite of necklace, bracelet, earrings, and brooch, or two or three of these. (It should be noted that only one or two components of a suite may be marked with a manufacturer's name. If the pieces are separated, identification may prove difficult.) In the fifties, the crafts movement influenced commercial production of modernist copper and enameled copper designs, notably by Rebajes of New York and Renoir/Matisse of California. Though mass-produced and inexpensive, this "copper art" jewelry was usually hand-made or hand-finished. Frank Rebajes' status has recently been elevated to that of "studio artist," his work having been included in the "Messengers of Modernism" exhibition of studio artists' jewelry (see Mid-Century Modern section above). Some of his limited production sterling pieces (on which a special stamped mark was used) are shown in that section. Fifties modernism is also evident in sterling figurals by Beaucraft of Providence RI.

Although the majority of the jewelry in this section is American-made, two of the genre's most important influences came from Europe, in the persons of designers Gabrielle "Coco" Chanel (1883-1971) and Elsa Schiaparelli (1896-1973). While their influence was felt in the early years of costume jewelry manufacture (see Costume Jewelry c. 1920-1935), their early pieces, many of which are not signed, are rarely seen today. Chanel closed her business in Paris in 1939 with the advent of World War II, and reopened in 1954, coming out of retirement at the age of seventy-one and working until she died. It is during this later period that the multi-colored glass, faux pearl, and gold-plated metal necklaces, bracelets, brooches and pendants most familiar to collectors were made. Chanel's company, under Karl Lagerfeld's supervision, continues producing costume jewelry designs today.

Elsa Schiaparelli's avant-garde and surrealistic touch is evident in her early thirties jewelry designs (usually unsigned). She opened an office in New York in 1949 and licensed her name for mass production of costume jewelry and accessories. Her pieces were still bold and imaginative, but they lacked the "off-the-wall" look of her earlier work. Chunky suites set with molded iridescent glass stones (sometimes called "watermelon" or "oil-slick") and "aurora borealis" rhinestones (developed by Swarovski in 1955), or large faceted colored glass stones, were mid-fifties Schiaparelli trademarks, signed with her famous script signature. Schiaparelli retired in 1954, but American manufacturers continued producing her designs through the remainder of the decade.

Chanel and Schiaparelli also helped launch the careers of fine jewelry designers Verdura and Schlumberger, both of whom designed costume pieces for their respective employers in the thirties (see Fine Jewelry sections).

Some European designs included here are not signed, but merely marked with country of origin, France or Germany. One known German maker is Perli, which specialized in matte enamels with modernistic tendencies.

Other currently sought-after designs include circa 1940s sterling vermeil (gold-plated) figural brooches and clips by Marcel Boucher, Coro (including sterling and white metal figural Duettes, although demand for these has fallen off a bit) and Corocraft, Eisenberg Original, Hobé, Mazer Bros., Pennino, Réja, Staret and Trifari, and well-made unsigned examples. Among these are the now-famous animal "jelly bellies" with clear Lucite centers (most signed Trifari, Coro, or unsigned). Knockoffs and fakes have now cooled the jelly belly market considerably. Genuine rarities still command a premium, however. Vintage forties and fifties Miriam Haskell necklaces, bracelets, and suites continue to have a following, particularly the designer's more elaborate creations. The demand for Haskell is likely to increase now that a book devoted solely to her jewelry has been published. High quality "real-looking" rhinestone pieces by Boucher, Trifari, and others are also marketable.

In 1930, Trifari hired their most celebrated designer, Alfred Philippe, who designed their most sought-after pieces until 1968. A Frenchman trained in fine jewelry design (he produced designs made by William Scheer for Cartier and Van Cleef & Arpels), Philippe was known for creating molded glass and rhinestone pieces for Trifari which resembled Cartier's "fruit salad" or "tutti frutti" carved gemstone and diamond jewels from the late twenties and early thirties.

Some c. 1960s and later pieces, by Boucher, Stanley Hagler, Jomaz, Kenneth Jay Lane, Schreiner, and couturiers Christian Dior, Givenchy, Nettie Rosenstein, Yves St. Laurent, Pauline Trigère, as well as Carnegie, Chanel, and Schiaparelli, have a collector following. Sixties and early seventies designs tended toward the large and the dramatic. The more "over the top" it is, the more desirable to collectors.

Belt, rhinestones, gp wm, c. 1965-70, lobed rect buckle with a lg emerald-cut colorless r.s. prong-set in center of open lacy scrolled design set throughout with lg and sm colorless r.s., continuing to a belt of braided gp metal cable bordering four rows of med and sm colorless r.s., central row of r.s.-set scrolled wire flanked by two rows of sm r.s., rev mkd "© KJL" on appl oval, for Kenneth J. Lane, 2-3/4" w x 32-1/4" tl, **$350**. (Sue James collection).

Today, many collectors and dealers tend to focus on the name of the manufacturer or designer rather than on the jewelry itself. Novice dealers often price a piece high because it is "signed," not because of its overall design and craftsmanship. It is true that certain manufacturers and designers have reputations for high-quality production and innovative design, and their names do make an upward difference in price compared to similar unsigned pieces. However, the same caveats apply to this genre of jewelry as to any other: A maker's mark is not a guarantee of quality. Be sure to evaluate a piece on its own merits *before* you turn it over to look for a mark.

Condition is an especially important factor in costume jewelry, because costume pieces are more easily damaged than fine jewelry, and difficult to repair well. Major damage *or* major repairs lower value considerably. Replaced rhinestones and some wear are acceptable to most collectors, but replating, re-enameling and soldering often are not. If badly done, the piece is ruined, and even if done well, it may end up not looking "right." Proper restoration of a worn or broken piece is a job for a skilled professional who specializes in costume jewelry.

Note on prices in this section: this is one area of jewelry collecting that is comparable to other collectibles, e.g. dolls or glassware, because the pieces were mass produced, and many of them are well-known, identifiable designs by recognized manufacturers and/or designers. A collector can say "Corocraft Siamese Fighting Fish" or "Trifari jelly belly turtle," and another collector will know exactly what he or she is talking about. Some pieces are common and some are rare; rarity and demand drive this segment of the market in particular, as reflected by four-figure prices for the most sought-after rarities. However, prices are less stable than for collectibles like depression glass, for example. Regional differences affect prices, and what's hot and what's not is constantly changing in different parts of the country. In urban areas where the market is strong for particular designs by certain "names," prices will undoubtedly be higher than those listed here. Outside of these markets, however, prices will be comparable or lower. Readers should keep in mind that the values given here are *average* retail. Most of the listings in this section are in the three-figure range or lower. Four-figure pieces assuredly do exist, but mostly in the collections of an elite few. The majority of readily *available* pieces on the market today are priced in the tens and hundreds, not thousands.

References: Lillian Baker, *Fifty Years of Collectible Fashion Jewelry, 1925-1975*, Collector Books, 1986, values updated 1992; Joann Dubbs Ball, *Costume Jewelers: The Golden Age of Design,* and *Jewelry of the Stars, Creations from Joseff of Hollywood,* Schiffer Publishing, 1990 and 1991; Joann Dubbs Ball and Dorothy Hehl Torem, *Masterpieces of Costume Jewelry*, Schiffer Publishing, 1996; Vivienne Becker, *Fabulous Costume Jewelry*, Schiffer Publishing, 1993; Matthew Burkholz and Linda L. Kaplan, *Copper Art Jewelry, A Different Lustre*, Schiffer Publishing, 1992;

Deanna Farneti Cera, *Amazing Gems, An Illustrated Guide to the Worlds' Most Dazzling Costume Jewelry,* Harry N. Abrams, 1997, and *The Jewels of Miriam Haskell,* Antique Collectors' Club, 1997; Deanna Farneti Cera, ed., *Jewels of Fantasy*, Harry N. Abrams, 1992; Maryanne Dolan, *Collecting Rhinestone & Colored Jewelry*, 3rd ed., Books Americana, 1993 (large section on makers' marks); Lyngerda Kelley and Nancy Schiffer, *Costume Jewelry, The Great Pretenders*, Schiffer Publishing, 1987, values updated 1990; Roseann Ettinger, *Popular Jewelry 1840-1940,* Schiffer Publishing, values updated 1993, *Forties & Fifties Popular Jewelry*, Schiffer Publishing, 1994, and *Popular Jewelry of the 60s, 70s, and 80s*, Schiffer Publishing, 1997; Jill Gallina, *Christmas Pins, Past & Present,* Collector Books, 1996; Angie Gordon, *Twentieth Century Costume Jewelry*, Adasia International, 1990; Gabriele Greindl, *Gems of Costume Jewelry*, Abbeville Press, 1990; Kenneth J. Lane, *Faking It,* Harry N. Abrams, 1996; Gabriella Mariotti, *All My Baskets, American Costume Jewelry, 1930-1960,* FMR, 1996; Patrick Mauriès, *Jewelry By Chanel,* Bullfinch Press, Little, Brown & Co., 1993; Harrice Simons Miller, *Costume Jewelry Identification and Price Guide,* 2nd ed., Avon Books, 1994; Ginger Moro, *European Designer Jewelry*, Schiffer Publishing, 1995; Jane Mulvagh, *Costume Jewelry in Vogue,* Thames and Hudson, 1988 (out of print); Dorothy Rainwater, *American Jewelry Manufacturers,* Schiffer Publishing, 1988; Fred Rezazadeh, *Costume Jewelry, A Practical Handbook & Value Guide*, Collector Books, 1998; Nancy Schiffer, *Fun Jewelry*, Schiffer Publishing, 1991, values updated 1996; Jody Shields, *All That Glitters, The Glory of Costume Jewelry*, Rizzoli International, 1987 (out of print); Cherri Simonds, *Collectible Costume Jewelry*, Collector Books, 1997; Nick Snider, *Sweetheart Jewelry and Collectibles*, Schiffer Publishing, 1995.

Periodical and Collectors' Club: *Vintage Fashion & Costume Jewelry Newsletter/Club*, PO Box 265, Glen Oaks, NY 11004, e-mail: VFCJ@aol.com, published quarterly.

Internet: Jewelcollect online discussion group (e-mail list) on costume jewelry. Go to http://www.lizjewel.com/jc.html for information on how to subscribe.

Museums: Glass and Costume Jewelry Museum, Jablonec nad Nisou, Czech Republic; Jewelers' Museum, Providence, RI; *Schmuckmuseum*, Pforzheim, Germany.

Charm Bracelets, sterling and wm:

T, c. 1950-55, nine charms, including a ster suitcase that opens, a lobster, a telephone, a boat, a locomotive, a Native American figure, and a coffee shop scene with swiveling chairs, all pieces mkd "sterling" except Native American figure, spring ring closure, chain 7" tl, **$100**.

C, c. 1950-76, ten ster U.S. patriotic motif charms, including a politician, a scroll of the U.S. Constitution, two enameled U.S. flags, a scene of planting the flag at Iwo Jima, a Liberty Bell, a red blue and yellow enameled sampler reading "God Bless Our Home," a red, white and blue enameled Revolutionary soldier, a Statue of Liberty, and an enameled Bicentennial charm, on a double-linked ster chain, all pieces mkd "sterling," v-spring and box clasp mkd "ELCO STERLING" for Miglo Jewelry Co., New York, NY (on identification bracelets), chain 6-3/4" tl, **$115**.

B, c. 1950-55, six Asian motif charms including a seated Buddha, two pagodas, a Japanese-style sandal, Japanese mks, on a silver chain with spring ring closure, 6-3/4" tl, **$75**.
(Sue James collection).

Reproduction Alert: Knockoffs of Eisenberg Originals, Trifari jellybellies (the frog, turtle, stork, fish, and pig), and other big-name and pricey pieces have been infiltrating the market for the past several years. The most problematic are the ones which have been cast from the original pieces or molds, signatures intact. Some manufacturers, notably Cini, Eisenberg, Miriam Haskell and Trifari, are "reissuing" their vintage designs, now that they are so collectible. In some cases, only a side-by-side comparison of old with new will reveal subtle differences. Other repros are clearly marked, sometimes with dates. Many designers/manufacturers, such as Kenneth Jay Lane, never discontinue a line or design as long as it sells, which can be many years. As usual, the best defense is a buyer's knowledge and a seller's reputation.

Advisors: Charles Pinkham, Pat Seal, Lucille Tempesta.

Bracelet

Charm

Sterling, c. 1950-55, six ster charms of Cub Scout emblems, labeled "CUB SCOUTS BSA" (one also reading "DEN MOTHER," another "BOBCAT") in circ, sq, and rect shapes on a ster chain, spring ring closure, all pieces mkd "STERLING," chain 7-3/4" tl 75

Sterling, wm, enamel, c. 1950-55, twenty charms of travel-related themes, including a nut that opens to become a boat with a man pushing a pole, a UN Building, a U.S. Capitol Building, a cruise ship, a submarine, a razor, an enameled maple leaf, a plaque reading "MADE IT PIKE' PEAK, COLO.," ice skates, a statue, etc., some pieces mkd "STERLING," ster chain with spring ring closure 7" tl 200

Cuff

MOP, plastic, glass, gp brass, c. 1950, double row of spring wire strung with round red plastic faceted beads, oval black plastic beads set with colorless r.s., r.s. beads and rondels, irregular MOP beads and disks, r.s.-set gp bars and gp filigree caps, oval tag mkd "MIRIAM HASKELL," 1-1/4" w 140

Link

Brass, c. 1937-40, four rounded triangular links, each pierced by three short grad tubes, spring ring closure, unsgd, attributed to Monet, 3/4" w x 7" 150

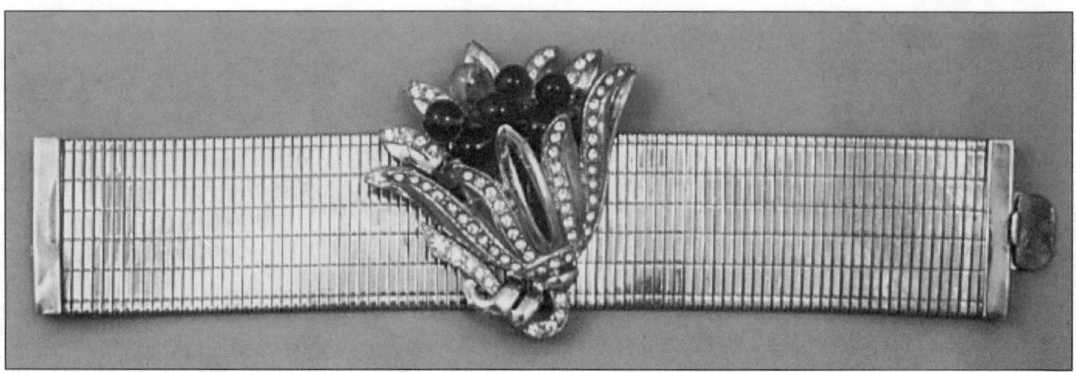

Bracelet, flexible, gp brass, rhinestones, glass, c. 1940, Retro Modern, gp strap with central floral ornament soldered in place, sm colorless r.s. petals with green, blue, yellow and red glass bead-tipped wire stamens, v-spring and box clasp, 2" w at center, 7" l, **$140**. (Leigh Leshner collection).

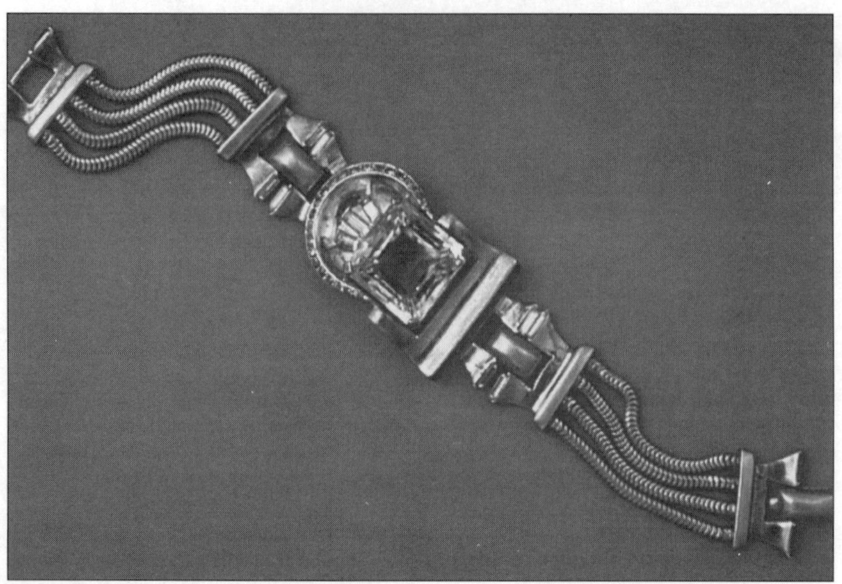

Bracelet, flexible, sterling vermeil, glass, rhinestones, c. 1940, Retro Modern, central buckle motif, lg sq-cut lt blue glass stone set *à jour* with three radiating colorless r.s. baguettes, encircled on one side by a row of sm colorless r.s. bordering a concave gp horseshoe shape, enclosed on the other side by gp open concave rectangle set with sq red r.s. along edge, flanked by lg shaped gp hinges topped with colorless baguette r.s., continuing to four strands of snake chain and foldover clasp, mkd "MAZER STERLING" and "62," 1" w (at center) x 6-1/2", **$400**. (Terrance O'Halloran collection).

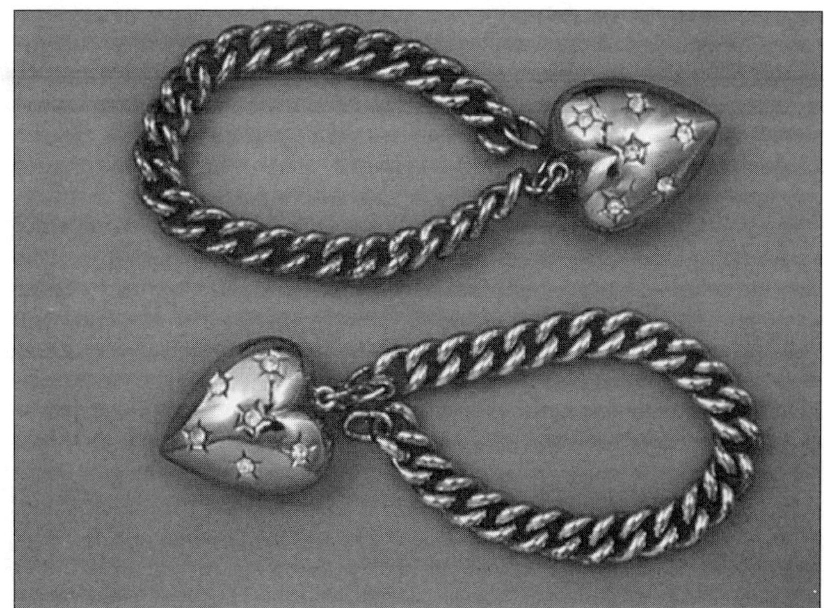

Link Bracelets, rose gp brass, rhinestones, c. 1940, each with a lg puffed-heart charm suspended from a curb link chain, set with sm colorless r.s. in star motif centers, foldover hook closure, charm 1" w x 1-1/8", chain 3/8" w x 7", pr, **$90**. (Charles Pinkham collection).

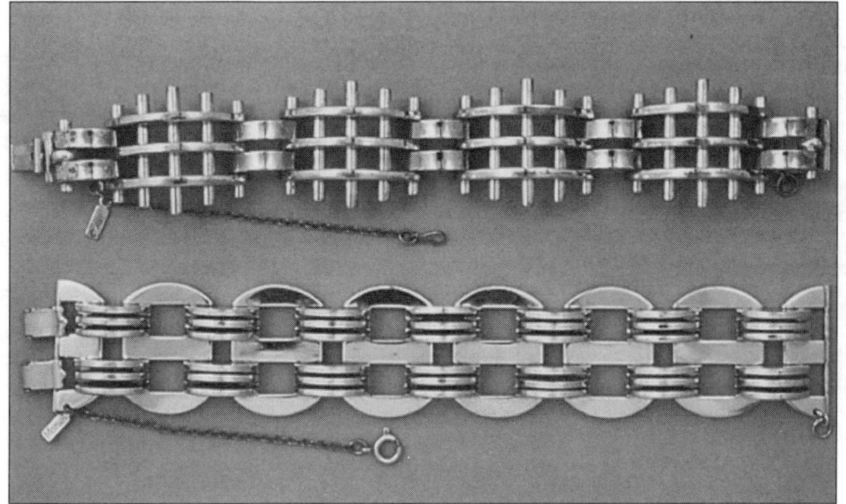

Link Bracelets, Monet, c. 1937-40:

T, gp brass, four geo links, each composed of three arches and five tubular crossbars grad from center, hanging metal tag mkd "Monet Jewelers," safety chain, 1-1/8" w x 7-1/2" tl, **$175**.

B, chrome pl wm, flat rounded rect links, each with two central cutouts, joined with prs of three-layered semi-circ hinges, hanging tag and double clasps mkd "Monet," safety chain, 1-1/8" w x 7-1/2" tl, **$100**.
(Richard Levey collection).

Link Bracelets, enamel, Germany, c. 1945-50:

T, four rect linked wm plaques with lg and sm circ design of *cloisonné* enamel in shades of black, brown, maroon, blue on white ground, unmkd, probably Ger, v-spring and box clasp, 1-1/8" w x 6-1/4", **$650**.

C, six rect linked gp brass plaques, abstract floral/geo motif of matte *champlevé* enamel in shades of lt blue, dk blue, brown and yellow, mkd "Germany" on box clasp, 1" w x 7-1/4", **$195**.

B, six rect linked ster plaques, each with a different horse or other Western motif in *cloisonné* enamel in shades of yellow, black, white and gray on mottled orange ground, mkd on rev "MADE IN GERMANY US ZONE" and "925," v-spring and box clasp, 3/4" w x 6-1/2", **$575**.
(Charles Pinkham collection).

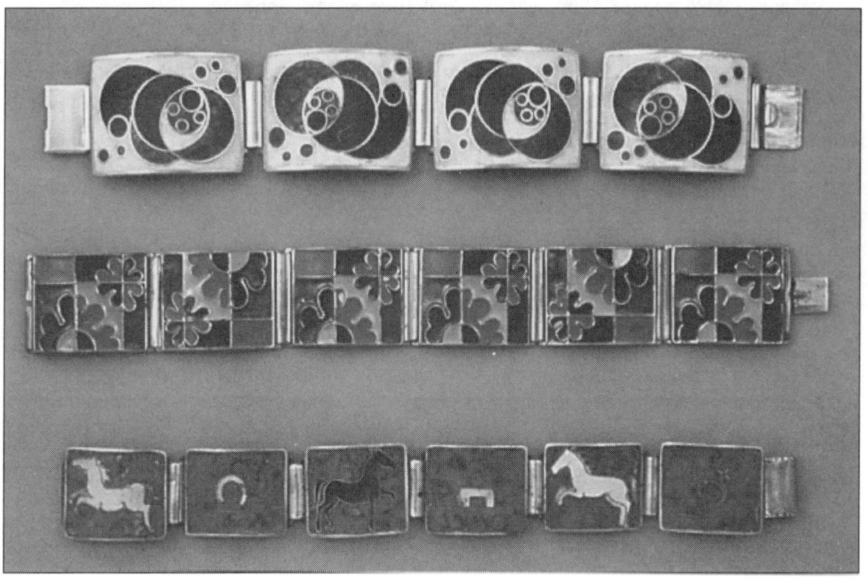

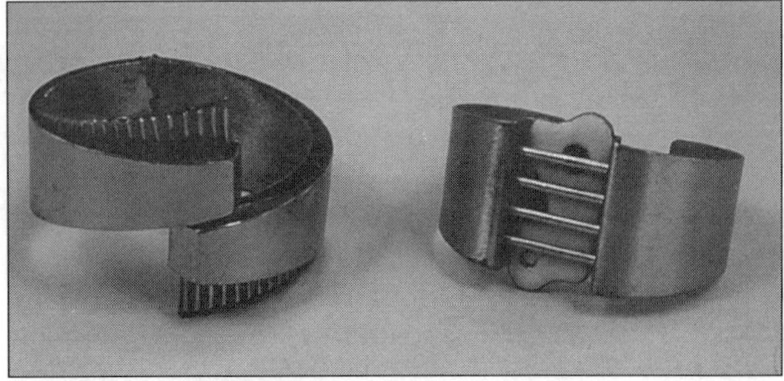

Bracelets, copper, enamel, c. 1955:
L, Bangle, hinged, crossover tapered boxed polished copper sections enclosing red-enameled triangular plaques with parallel appl copper wire segments , mkd "© Matisse" in script, 1-5/8" w (at center), 2-1/2" inside dia, **$100**.
R, Cuff, tapered with indented center holding a cutout opaque yellow-enameled biomorphic plaque on oxidized bg surmounted by four horizontally parallel polished copper tubes, mkd "Matisse" in script on outside at bottom, 1-3/4" w, 2-1/2" inside dia, **$100**. (Patrick Kapty collection).

Bangle Bracelets, hinged, ptd enamel, gp wm, c. 1965-70:
L, domed oval hinged at the sides, with irregularly-shaped cells of translucent blue and green ptd enamel within gp raised edges, central crossover design pavé-set with sm colorless r.s., r.s.-set thumbpiece on V-spring, mkd "JOMAZ," 2-1/4" inside dia, **$165**. (Brett Benson collection).
R, one terminal in the shape of a leopard's head clasping the other terminal in its mouth, gp leopard with blue glass cab eye and sm red and turq glass cab accents, continuing to alternating white enameled ropetwist sections and gp with red and turq glass cab-set sections, appl plate on rev mkd "PAULINE RADER," leopard 1-1/4" w, 2-3/8" inside dia, **$225**.
(Sue James collection).

Copper, enamel, c. 1950-55, speckled blue and white enameled open-centered truncated triangles, alternating upright and inverted, joined with prs of leaf-shaped copper hinged links, hook closure, 2-3/4" inside dia, 2" w x 7-1/4" 95

Copper, c. 1950, seven appl die-struck leaves, mkd "REbajEs," for Frank Rebajes, New York, NY, v-spring and box clasp, 1" w x 6-1/2" 65

Copper, c. 1950, sp, seven slightly domed rect links surmounted by four-petal flowerhead motifs, mkd "REbajEs" for Frank Rebajes, New York, NY, on outside terminal, v-spring and box clasp, 1-5/8" w x 6-7/8" tl 125

Enamel, sterling, c. 1950, enameled plaque in the shape of a fox, shades of orange, yellow, brown, black and white joined to oval link chain, "925 218F" mkd on plaque rev, "925 133AR" on jump ring joined to spring ring clasp, possibly Ger, center plaque 1-1/4" w x 3/4", 6-1/2" tl 225

Faux pearls, gp metal, c. 1960, floral links in goldtone and lg and sm faux pearls, foldover clasp, safety chain, imp "Tortolani" in script on rev, 1-1/8" w x 8" tl 50

Sp brass, glass, c. 1940, seven links of double-layered six-petaled flowerheads with central blue glass cabs, spring ring closure, mkd "JOSEFF HOLLYWOOD," 1" w x 7-1/2" 195

Sterling, plastic, c. 1960, stepped rect ster plaque with sq bezel-set tortoise-colored plastic center, flanked by slightly domed hinged rect links terminating in fold-over box clasp, mkd "STERLING LDV #1987," 1" w (at center), 7" tl 125

Brooch/Pin

Copper, c. 1950, stamped cartoon-like design, man's head with cutout and appl features wearing a rakish top hat and a bowtie, 1-3/8" w x 2" 50

Copper, c. 1955, cutout stylized violin motif surmounting an abstract keyboard, 2" w x 2-3/8" 35

Glass, gp brass, c. 1960, three-dimensional molded coral-colored glass pseudo cameo of a woman's head encircled by coral-colored glass seed beads, set in gp brass frame, mkd "MIRIAM HASKELL" on appl oval plate, 1-2/3" w x 2-1/3" 345

Glass, gp metal, ptd enamel, stylized geo rooster with lg faceted rect red glass center, ptd tail and features in red, green, black and white, mkd "Coro," 2-1/4" w x 2-1/8" 185

Bangle Bracelet, hinged, gp wm, c. 1960, three-dimensional stamped metal with appl astrological motifs: a nude woman (Virgo), a goat (Capricorn), a lion (Leo), a fish (Pisces), a bull (Taurus), a ram (Aries), etc., and stars, sgd "© Tortolani" in script, snap clasp at center opening, 2-1/2" w (at center), 2-1/4" inside dia, **$200**. (Terrance O'Halloran collection).

Brooch/Pendant, glass, rhinestones, gp brass, c. 1965, overlapping gp scallop shells forming equilateral cross, with central lg oval bezel-set orange glass cab encircled by flowerheads of sm circ green glass cabs and sm colorless r.s., with sm circ and oval green and orange glass cab clusters at terminals, mkd "© CHANEL ®," "MADE IN FRANCE" and overlapping opposed double "C" trademark, 3-1/4" w x 3-1/2", **$750**. (Brett Benson collection).

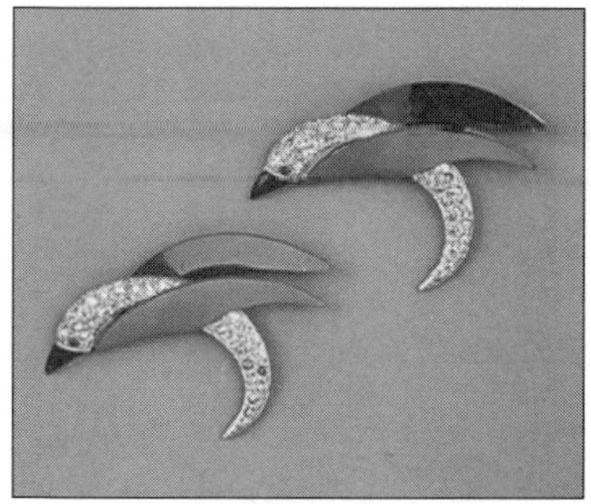

Brooches/Pins, gp brass, rhinestones, wm, enamel, c. 1935-40, stylized birds, crescent-shaped wm bodies pavé -set with sm colorless r.s., gp brass wings, black enamel beaks, red r.s. eyes, 2-1/2" w x 1-3/4", pr, **$120**. (Leigh Leshner collection).

Glass, rhinestones, gp metal, c. 1945-50, scrolled feather shape set with molded floral/foliate pink glass cabs with colorless r.s. accents in gp frame, two prong clip mechanism with one prong removed, remaining with safety catch, mkd "TRIFARI" (with crown), 1-3/4" w x 3-1/2" 250

Glass, rhinestones, sterling vermeil, c. 1945, sachet pin, circle of molded green glass flowers, each set with a sm colorless r.s., encircling a sm colorless r.s. cluster and gp center, sm colorless r.s. clusters around outside edge, removable compartment on rev holds perfume-soaked pad, mkd "TRIFARI" (crown mk), "PAT PEND, STERLING," 1-3/4" dia 245

Glass, rhinestones, sterling vermeil, c. 1945, circle of molded red glass flowers, each set with a sm colorless r.s., encircling a sm colorless r.s. cluster and gp center, sm colorless r.s. clusters around outside edge, mkd "TRIFARI (crown mk), PAT PEND, STERLING," 1-3/4" dia 195

Gp base wm, rhinestones, c. 1950, depicting a ballerina *à point*, as seen from behind, angled with arms outstretched, pierced rose gp skirt, sm colorless r.s. borders, mkd "BOUCHER" #3052, safety catch, 2-1/8" w x 1-1/2", 3/4" height (from top of head) 125

Gp metal, ptd enamel, c. 1950, open sq frame surrounding a stick figure bongo player enameled in metallic red and green, upper torso *en tremblant*, 1-3/4" sq 25

Gp metal, ptd enamel, Retro Modern, stylized crested bird's head, red, white, blue feathers, black and green eye, 2-1/2" w x 3" 125

Pewter, c. 1959, rect cast plaque with design of a reclining smiling cartoon-like man holding a cane, flanked by clock motifs, with the words "*Fasnacht* 59" below, mkd "FELIX MULLER BASEL," Swiss, 2" w x 1" 45

Brooch/Pin, ptd enamel, rhinestones, gp wm, c. 1940, in the shape of a hand holding a Liberty Torch, sm colorless r.s. pavé -set throughout, three oval red r.s. and blue enamel bands around torch, a circ red r.s. terminal, red and orange ptd enamel flame, lt skintone ptd enamel hand with pink fingernails, brown cuff, rev mkd "Staret," 1-1/8" w x 3-7/8", **$1,200**. (Kerry Holden collection).

Brooch/Pin, rhinestones, rh pl metal, c. 1940, cascading ribbon bow set with rows of lg lt blue marquise, pink and colorless oval r.s. within sm colorless r.s. borders, surmounted by fan-shaped rows of sm and lg oval colorless, lg circ pink, and sm circ lt blue r.s., rev mkd "Eisenberg ORIGINAL" on appl plate, and imp "D," 3" w x 4", **$600**. (Private collection).

Rhinestones, glass, rh pl wm, c. 1935-40, lg floral spray tied with bow, two lg faceted oval colorless glass flowerhead centers framed by colorless marquise-shaped r.s., sm colorless r.s. pavé-set throughout, 3-1/4" w x 3-3/4" 235

Rhinestones, enamel, gp wm, c. 1955-60, floral and foliate cluster, orange r.s.-set flowerheads, brown enamel leaves, gp wm, 2-1/2" w x 2-1/8" 35

Rhinestones, faux pearls, wm, c. 1945, floral spray with ribbon, nine faux pearl flower buds, three with colorless baguette r.s. stems, sm colorless r.s. throughout, all stones replaced, mkd "ARTISAN N.Y.," safety catch, 3-7/8" w x 2-3/4" 100

Rhinestones, gp brass, c. 1935, guitar shape set with round, cushion and marquise r.s. in green, amber, lavender and purple with twisted wirework strings, wirework and bead decoration, unmkd, in the style of 1930s Hobé, 3-3/4" w x 1-1/4" 195

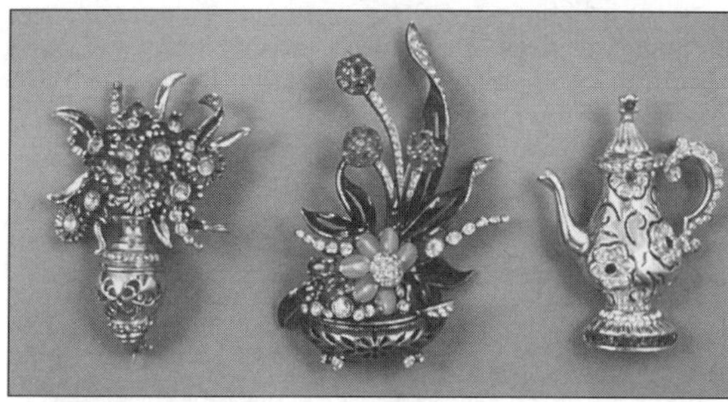

Brooches/Pins, gp wm or sterling, rhinestones, Retro Modern, c. 1940-45:

L, pierced gp wm vase surmounted by a floral bouquet, sm colorless r.s. centers and red r.s. petals, green ptd enamel leaves, blue petals (some enamel loss), rh pl back, 1-5/8" w x 2-1/4", **$235**.

C, sterling vermeil, three-dimensional bowl of flowers, green ptd enamel curling leaves with pavé r.s. undersides, lg central flower with colorless r.s. center and blue chatoyant glass cab petals, cluster of three lg blue r.s. to the left, surmounted by three lines of colorless r.s. terminating in red r.s. clusters, grad colorless r.s. accents throughout, pierced floral pattern on r.s.-footed ster bowl, unmkd, 2" w x 2-7/8", **$275**.

R, in the shape of a coffee pot, pierced gp wm with floral decoration in red, green, blue and colorless r.s., colorless r.s.-set handle, red r.s.-set base, mkd "Coro," 1-1/2" w x 2-1/8", **$235**.

(Leigh Leshner collection).

Brooches/Pins, basket of flowers motif, rhinestones, rh pl wm, ptd enamel, c. 1935-40:

L, basket pavé -set with sm circ and baguette colorless r.s., flowers ptd in shades of red, pink, blue and green and interspersed with colorless r.s., 2-3/4" w x 2-1/8", **$65**. (Author's collection).

R, basket of flowers motif in lt and dk blue, yellow, green, pink and white ptd enamel, one flowerhead of lg pink glass oval cabs, sm colorless r.s. accents, safety catch, 2-1/8" w x 2-1/8", **$50**.
(Sandra Willard collection).

Rhinestones, gp wm, c. 1940, heart shape, central lg colorless r.s. surrounded by sm red and colorless r.s., encircled by radiating twisted gp wm spikes tipped with sm colorless r.s., 1-3/8" w x 1-5/8" 125

Rhinestones, gp wm, c. 1940, Retro Modern, floral spray tied with a bow, scrolled ribbons at sides, flower centers set with circ yellow r.s., sm colorless r.s. accents throughout, 2-5/8" w x 3-3/4" 125

Rhinestones, gp wm, c. 1975, cruciform, pierced and cusped layers, cusped terminals pavé -set with sm colorless r.s., center cluster of five lg colorless r.s., rev mkd "KJL" on appl oval for Kenneth J. Lane, 2-1/4" w x 2-3/4" 225

Rhinestones, rh pl wm, c. 1935, single flowerhead spray tied with bow, sm colorless r.s. pavé-set throughout, safety catch, 2" w x 3-1/4" 145

Rhinestones, rh pl wm, c. 1955, sm circ lt blue r.s. prong-set in rh pl wm spelling out the words "Dear John," in open script, safety catch, 4-3/4" w x 2-1/2 75

Brooches/Pins, sterling vermeil, glass, rhinestones, Retro Modern, c. 1940-45:

L, stylized floral spray with two lg prong-set faceted lozenge-shaped pink glass blossoms and sm colorless r.s. pavé-set in gp stems and leaves, rev mkd "CoroCraft STERLING," 2-1/4" w x 4", **$250**.

R, stylized rose gp ster floral spray with lg central prong-set faceted cushion-shaped blue glass blossom, a fringed gp scroll with dk blue rect r.s. tips wrapped around sm colorless r.s.-set leaves, rev mkd "STERLING," 1-1/2" w x 3-1/4", **$150**.
(Diane White collection).

Brooch/Pin, rhinestones, rh pl wm, c. 1940, colorless r.s. daffodil spray, flowerhead *en tremblant*, mkd "STARET," safety catch, 1-5/8" w x 2-5/8", **$150**. (Leigh Leshner collection).

Rhinestones, rh pl wm, c. 1935-40, Retro Modern, three flower heads with lg colorless r.s. centers, sm colorless r.s. throughout, scrolled wm stems and leaves with scrolled ribbon tie, 1-3/4" w x 3-1/2" 165

Rhinestones, rh pl wm, c. 1935-40, Retro Modern, four-stem floral spray tied with bow, lg marquise colorless r.s. flower centers, colorless pavé r.s. throughout, mkd "Coro," 3-1/2" w x 2-1/4" 195

Rhinestones, rh pl wm, c. 1935-40, Retro Modern, prong-set faceted oval purple glass stones set *à jour* as flower petals and buds, sm colorless r.s. accents, ptd brown and green enamel stems, lg colorless r.s. flower centers , sm colorless r.s.-set leaves and bowknot, 3" w x 4" 120

Sp brass, c. 1940, scalloped circ openwork flowerhead motif with overlapping scrolled petals and bead-tipped wire stamens, safety catch, mkd "JOSEFF HOLLYWOOD," 1-7/8" dia 150

Brooches/Pins, "tremblers," rhinestones, gp wm, c. 1955-65:

TL, flowerhead with brushed finish gp metal petals encircling a ring of alternating lg oval orange r.s. and sm circ brown r.s, a brushed finish gp metal center with orange circ r.s. cluster *en tremblant*, looped wire stem, and two marquise yellow and brown r.s. buds, rev mkd "Coro," 2" w x 2-1/2", **$80**.

BC, depicting a frog *en tremblant* on a textured gp lily pad, frog with mottled green glass cab body, sm colorless r.s. accents and red r.s. eyes, rev mkd "ART©," 1-1/2" w x 2", **$60**.

TR, insect with wings *en tremblant*, white ptd enameled wings, sm circ green r.s. pavé-set on body, rev mkd "FLORENZA ©," 2" w x 1-1/2", **$75**.
(Diane White collection).

Brooch/Pin, plastic, sterling, sterling vermeil, c. 1940, ivory-colored molded plastic Chinese fisherman mounted on a back plate surmounted by an openwork oval with ster vermeil foliate motifs and ster bead and wirework, smaller similar design at the base, mkd "Hobé 1/20 14K ON STERLING DES PAT'D," 1-3/4" w x 2-3/4", **$250**. (Patrick Kapty collection).

Brooch/Pin, enamel, gp brass, c. 1940, in the shape of a squirrel holding a nut, *basse-taille* and *champlevé* enameled in shades of red, white, blue, brown, rev mkd "Eole Made in France *Deposé*," C-catch, 1-3/4" w x 1-3/8", **$95**. (Charles Pinkham collection).

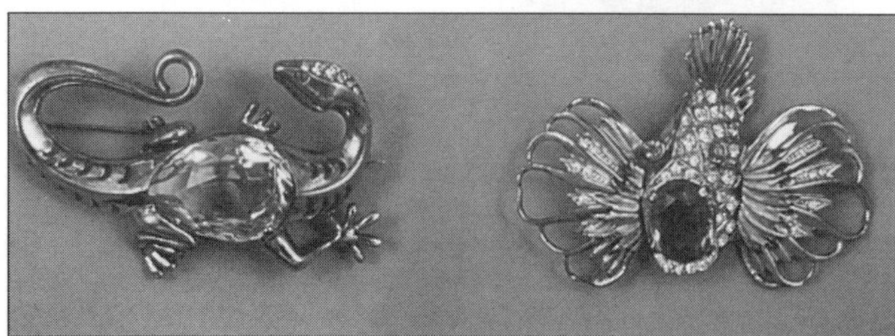

Brooches/Pins, sterling vermeil, glass, rhinestones, animal motifs, Am, c. 1940-45:

L, depicting a lizard with curv head and curling tail, lg pear-shaped faceted blue glass center set *à jour* in rose gp sterling, two rows of cut-out slits on neck and tail, red r.s. eye and colorless r.s. crest, mkd "STERLING Réja," safety catch, 2-3/8" w x 1-3/8", **$225**. (Leigh Leshner collection).

R, "Siamese Fighting Fish," faceted oval blue glass prong-set '*à jour* in mouth, sm pink r.s. eyes, black, pink, lt and dk blue, green and white ptd enamel on outstretched fins, sm colorless r.s. pavé -set on body and fins, rev mkd "STERLING Corocraft" with Pegasus on appl plate, 2-3/4" w x 1-3/4", **$575**. (Maureen Stuart collection).

Sterling vermeil, glass, rhinestones, c. 1945, lg fancy key shape, top center prong-set with a lg blue glass cab flanked by two smaller red glass cabs, sm colorless r.s.-set heart-shaped frame entwined with gp ster snakes, red r.s. eyes, surmounted by a blue glass cab, key terminal prong-set with red glass cab (missing two others), sm colorless r.s., rev mkd "STERLING CoroCraft" with Pegasus trademark, 4-3/8" w x 1-1/2" 350

Sterling vermeil, Lucite, plastic, rhinestones, c. 1940, depicting a ster cat hovering over a rose gp ster goldfish mounted on the back of a Lucite fishbowl, a row of colorless r.s. on rim and base of bowl, a half-cylinder of blue plastic under cat, appl plate on rev mkd "Anthony, PAT PEND STERLING," probably for Anthony Novelty Co., Providence, RI, 2-1/2" w x 2" 1,200

Sterling, c. 1940, depicting a bird of paradise flower, mkd "Ming's STERLING" for Ming's of Honolulu, Hawaii, 3" w x 2" 250

Sterling, c. 1940, depicting a breadfruit and leaves, mkd "Ming's STERLING" for Ming's of Honolulu, Hawaii, 1-1/2" w x 2-1/2" 300

Sterling, c. 1940, depicting a gardenia blossom, bud and leaves, mkd "Ming's STERLING" for Ming's of Honolulu, Hawaii, 1-7/8" w x 2-1/2" 250

Sterling, c. 1940, depicting a hibiscus flower with leaves, mkd "Ming's STERLING" for Ming's of Honolulu, Hawaii, 2-1/8" w x 2-3/4 225

Sterling, c. 1940, depicting a sugarcane plant with tassel, mkd "Ming's STERLING" for Ming's of Honolulu, Hawaii, 2-7/8" w x 3-1/2" 350

Brooches/Pins, enamel, wm, Ger, c. 1940-45:

L, rounded lozenge-shaped plaque, two stylized fish in *cloisonné* enamel, mottled shades of blue, green and white, "Made in Germany" etched on rev, safety catch, 1-5/8" sq, **$350**.

R, sq plaque with five ym thread volutes laid out in domino pattern, mottled enamel ground of blue, green, orange and black, mkd "Perli Metall" on rev under counter-enamel, C-catch, 1-1/4" sq, **$275**. (Charles Pinkham collection).

Brooch/Pin, rhinestones, rh pl wm, c. 1940, stylized female face of pavé colorless r.s. surmounted by a semi-circ row of colorless baguette r.s. forming hair, sq red r.s. turned 45 degrees in forehead, red, blue, and green pear-shaped r.s. clusters at ears, pierced mouth, eyes and eyebrows, unmkd, safety catch, 2-3/8" w x 2-5/8", **$300**. (Leigh Leshner collection).

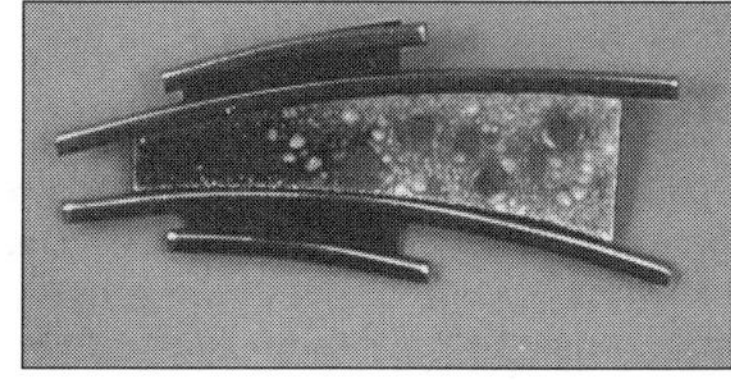

Brooch/Pin, enamel, copper, c. 1955, four curving parallel lengths of sq copper wire, longer inner pair framing a copper plaque with mottled blue and white shading to blue and black enamel, mounted on smaller enameled copper plaque framed by pr of shorter wires, mkd "© Matisse," 1-1/4" w x 2-3/4", **$40**. (Terrance O'Halloran collection).

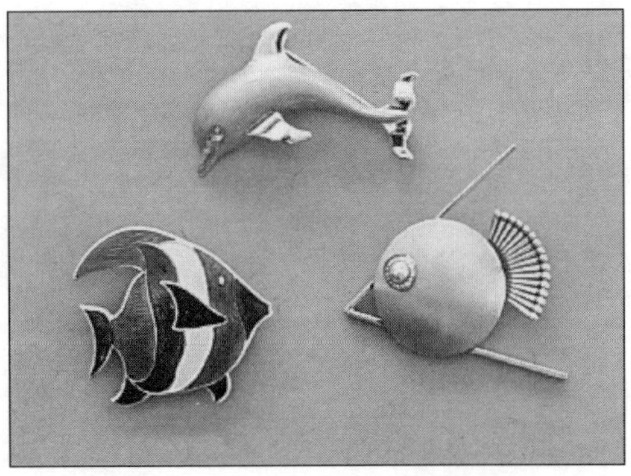

Brooches/Pins, sterling fish motifs by Beaucraft, Inc., Providence RI, c. 1950-60:

T, c. 1960, in the shape of a dolphin, brushed textured body, polished fins and tail, mkd "BEAU STERLING," 1-5/8" w x 7/8", **$40**.

BL, c. 1955, a stylized angelfish, *basse-taille* enameled in sections of red, white, blue and black, mkd "BEAU STERLING," 1-3/8" x 1-3/8", **$50**.

BR, c. 1950, a stylized fish, convex circ disk with appl domed "eye," and fan-shaped cluster of bead-tipped wire, forming head and tail, surmounting sideways V-shaped sq wire forming mouth and fins, rev mkd "BEAU STERLING," 1-1/2" w x 1-5/8", **$45**.

(Charlotte Healy collection, photo by Bruce Healy).

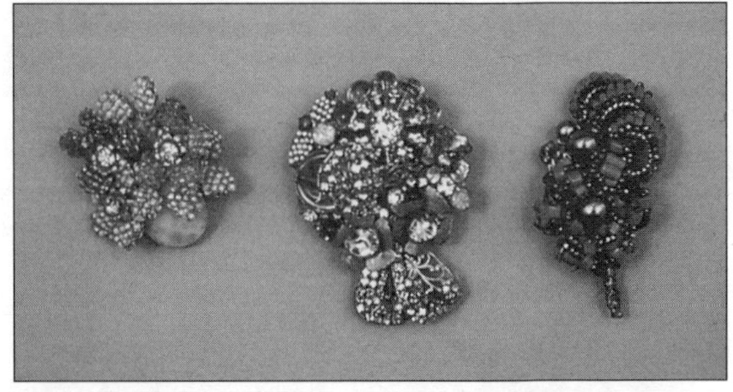

Brooches/Pins, glass, rhinestones, faux pearls, gp brass, Miriam Haskell, c. 1955-60:

L, floral design with green, yellow, and pink lg circ r.s. centers and beaded glass petals, above a mottled pink, blue, and white glass cab, appl oval plaque on rev mkd "MIRIAM HASKELL," safety catch, 1-5/8" w x 1-7/8", **$175**.

C, floral and foliate design with lg colorless and pink r.s. centers with faux seed pearl, faux opal, and sm r.s. accents and molded glass leaves, appl oval plaque on rev mkd "MIRIAM HASKELL," safety catch, 1-3/4" w x 2-5/8", **$225**.

R, floral and foliate design with dk gray metallic faux pearls centers with red glass beads and dk gray metallic beads strung on wires, appl oval plaque on rev mkd "MIRIAM HASKELL" safety catch, 2-1/4" w x 1-3/4", **$100**.

(Sue James collection).

Brooch/Pin, glass, rhinestones, faux pearls, gp brass, c. 1965, oval open-centered floral wreath, lg faux pearl cab at the bottom surmounted by pink molded glass flowers with sm colorless r.s. centers, pink glass beads and seedbeads, faux pearl seedbeads, "*roses montées*" (sm colorless flat-backed r.s.) on brass wires, mkd "MIRIAM HASKELL" on appl oval plate, 3-1/3" w x 3-1/4", **$445**. (Photo courtesy of Morning Glory Antiques, Albuquerque, NM).

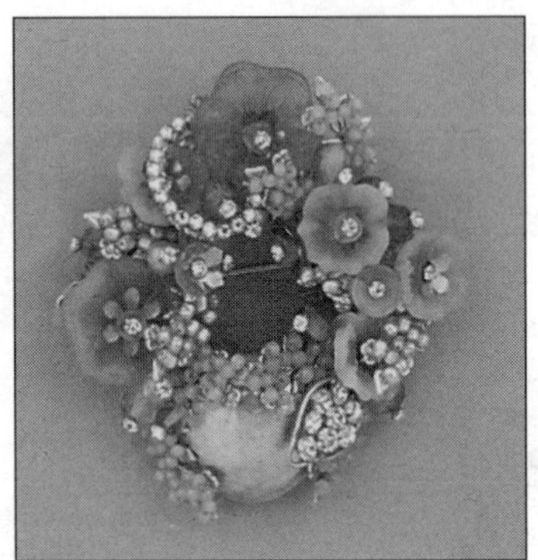

Christmas tree Brooches/Pins, gp wm, c. 1955-60:

TL, red, yellow, green and pink circ r.s., colorless baguettes, textured goldtone finish, mkd "HOLLYCRAFT ©," 1-1/2" w x 2-1/2", **$100**.

TR, red glass beads suspended from green ptd enamel leaves, rev mkd "Original by Robért" encircling ©, 1-1/4" w x 2-1/2", **$100**.

C, prong-set green r.s. branches, colorless baguette and circ yellow r.s. candles, circ red r.s. ornaments, surmounted by colorless pear-shaped r.s. top, amber r.s. base, rev mkd "WEISS," 1-1/4" w x 2-1/8", **$175**.

BL, "Marguerite," asymmetrical pierced textured gp wm set with blue, red, and green glass scallop-edge rondels ("marguerites") interspersed with aurora borealis r.s., rev mkd "WEISS," 1-3/8" w x 2-3/8", **$150**.

(Mary Williamson collection).

BR, brushed gp finish, set with varying sizes of blue, green, red, colorless, and yellow r.s. in cushion, sq, circ, marquise and pear shapes, rev mkd "WEISS," 2" w x 2-3/4", **$125**.

(Sue James collection).

Brooches/Pins and Earrings, glass, rhinestones, gp wm, Trifari, from the "Allure" line, c. 1960:

L, owl set with lg and sm circ turq-colored glass cabs, pavé colorless r.s. on head, wings, and tail, textured gp wm, mkd "© TRIFARI," 2-1/3" w x 2-1/4", **$120**.

TC, lg and sm mushroom, caps set with sm circ turq-colored glass cabs, cluster of lg oval cabs at base, colorless r.s.-set blades of grass, textured gp wm, mkd "© TRIFARI," orig tags, 1-1/3" w x 1-5/8", **$120**.

BC, Earrings, volute with sm circ turq-colored glass cabs on textured gp wm, lg turq-colored glass cab center, row of colorless r.s. at one end, mkd "© TRIFARI," orig tags, on orig card, 7/8" dia, pr, **$45**.

R, butterfly set with lg pear-shaped and sm circ turq-colored glass cabs, sm colorless r.s. accents, textured gp wm, mkd "© TRIFARI," orig tags, 1-7/8" w x 1-1/2", **$120**.
(Photo courtesy of Morning Glory Antiques).

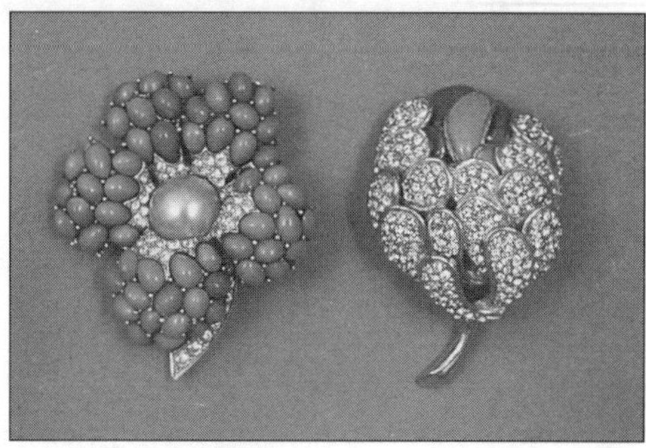

Brooches/Pins, c. 1965-70:

L, five-petal flowerhead, turq-colored glass cab petals encircling lg faux pearl center with sm colorless pavé r.s. accents in rh pl wm, rev mkd "© BOUCHER," 1-3/4" dia, **$200**.
(Diane White collection).

R, in the shape of a flower, faux coral and turq plastic cab center, pavé-set sm colorless r.s. overlapping petals, gp wm stem, rev mkd "KJL" on appl oval for Kenneth J. Lane, 1-1/2" w x 2", **$225**.
(Sue James collection).

Brooch/Pin, glass, gp brass, faux pearls, rhinestones, print on paper, paint, c. 1974, foliate gp brass double-layered frame centering an oval portrait of an officer in military dress, transfer print with white hp details, under glass dome, accented with "*rose montée*" colorless r.s. on brass wires, suspending a double swag of grad baroque faux pearls and brass bead spacers suspending and flanking a lg faux pearl in a gp brass foliate and r.s. frame and a lg pear-shaped drop with r.s.-set filigree cap, designed and made by Larry Vrba for the Broadway play "Crown Matrimonial," worn by the actress playing Queen Mary, portrait from the estate of Nettie Rosenstein, one-of-a-kind piece, mkd "MIRIAM HASKELL" on rev in appl oval, safety catch, 3-1/4" w x 5-1/2", **$1,400**.
(Photo courtesy of Morning Glory Antiques, Albuquerque, NM).

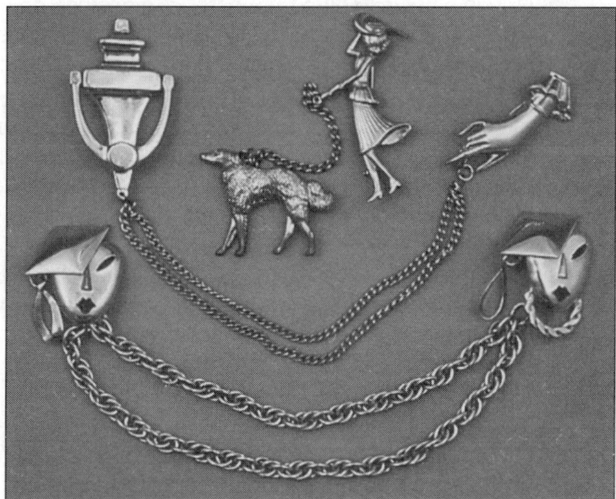

Chatelaine Pins, c. 1940-45:

T, stamped rh pl wm plaques depicting a woman holding her hat on her head attached by a wm chain to a walking dog, mkd "Coro" with winged horse (Pegasus) on rev, woman 1-1/4" w x 3-5/8", dog 2-7/8" w x 1-1/2", chain 4-3/4", **$45**.

C, stylized woman's hand attached by a double-strand chain to a door knocker, mkd "Coro" with Pegasus on rev, hand 1-3/4" w x 1-3/8", door knocker 1-1/2" w x 2-1/2", chain 6-1/2" (each strand), **$45**.

B, two die-stamped stylized gp wm women's heads, each wearing a graduation cap with a lg loop at opposite ends of a double-strand chain, one head wearing a necklace, head 1-3/8" w x 1-3/4", chain 8-1/2" (each strand), **$45**.
(Sue James collection).

Chatelaine pins, sterling vermeil, c. 1940, two floral spray and bow motif brooches joined by a triple swag chain, mkd "Hobé 1/20 14k ON STERLING DESIGN PAT'D," brooches 1-1/4" w x 2-3/4", chains 6", **$350**. (Martha Exline collection).

Clip, rhinestones, wm, c. 1940, floral bouquet with lg green r.s. in centers of flowerheads and leaves, sm colorless r.s. throughout, dk green ptd enamel on stems, double-pronged hinged clip on rev mkd "TRIFARI" (crown mark), 2-1/8" w x 3-1/2", **$195**. (Leigh Leshner collection).

Chatelaine Pins

Gp wm, rhinestones, c. 1940, two stylized horse's heads with sm circ colorless r.s. accents and sm red r.s. eyes at opposite ends of a double chain, each head 3/4" w x 2", chain 6" (each strand) 25

Clip

Glass, rh pl wm, ptd enamel, c. 1935, in the shape of a penguin in a tux with blue "moonstone" glass cab belly, pavé colorless r.s. accents, black and red ptd details, double-pronged hinged clip on rev, 3/4" w x 1-1/2" 30

Glass, rhinestones, gp wm, c. 1945-50, depicting a gp flower pot with r.s. accents and rim, a scrolled gp vine set with molded floral/foliate pink glass cabs and sm circ colorless r.s. twining up and down one side, double-pronged hinged clip on rev mkd "TRIFARI" (crown mk), 1-1/3" w x 2-1/4" 325

Gp wm, rhinestones, c. 1940-43, stylized swirled floral bouquet set with buff-top and faceted oval, circ, and cushion-shaped amber-colored glass, gp wm stems and leaves with four sm colorless r.s. accents, double-pronged hinged clip on rev mkd "Eisenberg ORIGINAL," 2-1/4" w x 4" 250

Ptd enamel, gp wm, c. 1940, circ multi-looped bow ptd red, white and blue stripes, surmounting three ptd white notched ribbons inscribed with the words "*Liberté, Egalité, Fraternité*" (Fr Revolutionary motto: Liberty, Equality, Brotherhood) in raised script, Am, rev mkd "SILSON Pat. 120967" (design patent, 1940), double-pronged hinged clip, 1-1/2" w x 2-3/4" 35

Ptd enamel, rhinestones, rh pl wm, c. 1940, Retro Modern scrolled floral/foliate motif, white and green ptd enamel, red and colorless r.s. accents, mkd "Coro," double-pronged hinged clip on rev, 1-1/4" w x 3-1/8" 75

Ptd enamel, rhinestones, sterling vermeil, c. 1940, in the shape of a carnation with white-enameled petals and green-enameled leaves and sm colorless r.s. accents, mkd "STERLING CoroCraft," double-pronged hinged clip on rev, 1-1/4" w x 2-1/2" 150

Rhinestones, gp wm, c. 1945-50, rose gp scrolled feather center set with row of colorless baguette r.s., double-pronged hinged clip on rev, mkd "TRIFARI" (with crown), 2-3/8" w x 2-1/2" 75

Rhinestones, wm, c. 1935, lg stylized floral motif, colorless r.s. of mixed cuts, spray of lg and sm oval r.s. surmounted by oval flowerhead of central lg emerald-cut encircled by pear-shaped r.s. forming petals, constructed in two parts, attached with screws, double-pronged hinged clip on rev mkd "Eisenberg ORIGINAL," additional mark illegible, 2" w x 4-1/4" 225

Clip, glass, rhinestones, gp wm, c. 1940, Retro Modern, lg stylized flower, gp wm stamens encircled by concentric rows of pavé -set sm colorless r.s., prong-set lozenge-shaped blue and red glass stones, sm colorless r.s. tips, sm colorless r.s.-set gp leaves, some plating wear, double-pronged hinged clip on rev, mkd "R. DE ROSA," 2-1/4" w x 4", **$300**. (Diane White collection).

Clip, gp wm, rhinestones, c. 1940-43, red, lt blue, dk blue, green, purple, pink, yellow, and colorless r.s. of various shapes mounted on gp wire forming a floral spray with gp leaves, tied with a gp bow, double-pronged hinged clip on rev mkd "Eisenberg ORIGINAL" and "N," 2-3/4" w x 4", **$600**. (Private collection).

Clips, glass, rhinestones, wm, Trifari, c. 1935-40:
L, circ dome with red glass molded in the shape of five-petaled flowers prong-set *à jour* with sm colorless r.s. centers, surmounted by two gp circ volutes set with sm colorless r.s., double-pronged hinged clip on rev mkd "TRIFARI" (crown mark) and "PAT PEND," 1-3/8" dia, **$150**.
R, rh pl geo basket set with sm circ and baguette colorless r.s. with molded floral/foliate lt blue and frosted clear glass, sm colorless r.s. stems, double-pronged hinged clip on rev, mkd "TRIFARI" (crown mark) and "PAT PEND," 1-1/4" w x 2", **$250**. (Diane White collection).

Double Clip Brooch, rhinestones, rh pl and gp wm, ptd enamel, c. 1940, double flower design in rh pl and gp metal with red and colorless r.s. and green ptd enamel leaves, red baguette r.s. stamens *en tremblant*, mkd "Coro Duette" and "Pat No 1798867" (1931) on removable pin back frame, open flat-backed hinged clips unmkd, 2-1/4" w x 3-1/4" joined, **$275**. (Sue James collection).

Rhinestones, wm, c. 1945, floral with bow design, central marquise-shaped colorless r.s. and three stems with lg round r.s. buds, sm colorless r.s. details, double-pronged hinged clip on rev mkd "Coro" and "PAT NO 125982" (1941), 2-1/4" w x 3" 175

Gp wm, rhinestones, c. 1940-43, floral motif, three-, four- and five-petaled flowerheads of lg faceted oval amber-colored r.s., single circ-cut amber r.s. in center, sm colorless r.s. accents, green ptd enamel leaves, curv gp stems, double-pronged hinged clip on rev mkd "Eisenberg ORIGINAL" and "X" (in a circle), 2-3/4" w x 4" 400

Dress Clips, rhinestones, wm, Eisenberg, c. 1935:
T, each a curv triangle prong-set with lg colorless rect, oval and marquise colorless r.s., branchlike rows of sm circ colorless r.s. bordering top edge, joined by a swivel hinge with circ r.s. cap, flat-backed hinged wm clips on rev mkd "Eisenberg ORIGINAL," 2" w x 1-1/2", pr, **$175**.
B, horizontally opposed stylized floral motifs prong-set with lg oval, marquise, and emerald-cut colorless r.s. interspersed with sm circ r.s., flat-backed hinged clips mkd "Eisenberg ORIGINAL" and "N," 2-1/2" w x 1-3/8", pr, **$150**. (Private collection).

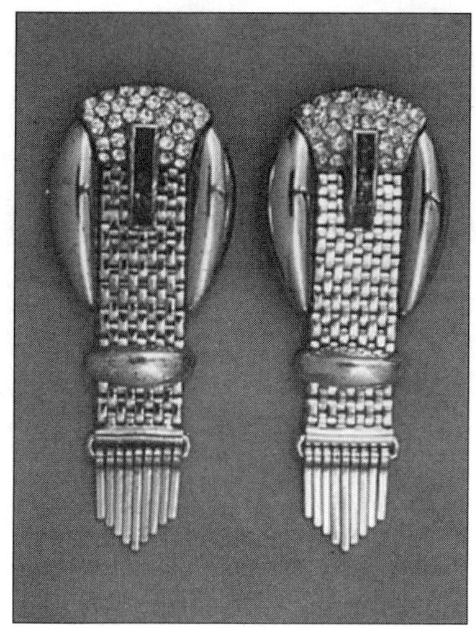

Clips, sterling vermeil, rhinestones, c. 1940, Retro Modern, rose gp brickwork strap and buckle motif, sm red and colorless r.s. accents, terminating in grad fringe, double-pronged hinged clips on rev, mkd "STERLING Kreisler USA" for Kreisler Mfg. Corp., North Bergen NJ, 1-1/8" w x 2-3/4", pr, **$225**. (Charles Pinkham collection).

Dress Clips, glass, rhinestones, rh pl wm, c. 1935, pentagonal with molded green and coral-colored glass floral and foliate shapes with sm r.s. centers, surmounted by rows of sm colorless r.s. surrounding pierced V, flat-backed hinged wm clips on rev, mkd "TKF" for Trifari, Krussman and Fishel, each 3/4" w x 1", pr, **$175**. (Private collection).

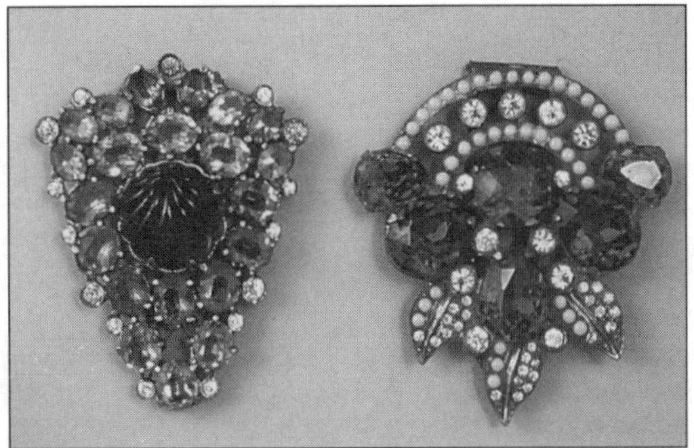

Dress Clips, rhinestones, glass, rh pl wm, Eisenberg, c. 1935:

L, shield-shaped, lg central molded dk blue glass circ domed shell shape surrounded by lg oval cobalt blue and pink r.s., sm colorless r.s. interspersed around outside edge, flat-backed hinged wm clip mkd "Eisenberg ORIGINAL" and "S," 2-1/8" w x 2-3/4", **$275**.

R, a central triangular cluster of lg faceted oval red r.s. surmounted by an arc of circ colorless r.s. with sm turq-colored glass cab borders, three leaves set with colorless r.s. and turq-colored glass at the base, flat-backed hinged wm clip mkd "Eisenberg ORIGINAL" and "D," 2-1/2" w x 2-3/4", **$275** (Private collection).

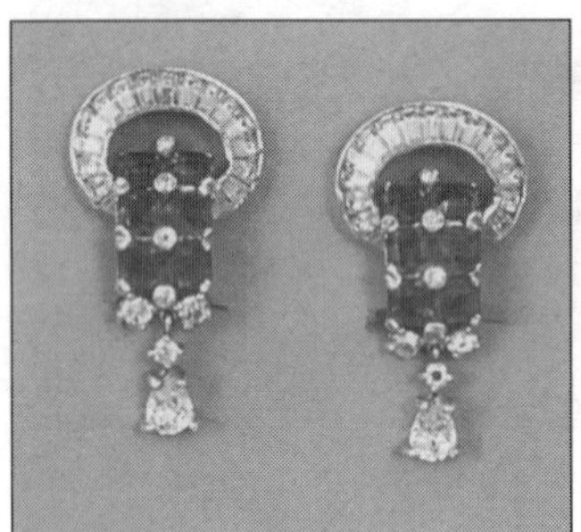

Earrings, rhinestones, rh pl wm, c. 1950, each a ring of colorless calibré-cut r.s. enclosing six red sq-cut r.s. in two rows forming central rectangle, suspending a lg pear-shaped colorless r.s. drop, mkd "JOMAZ," clipbacks, 3/4" w x 1-1/2" tl, pr, **$125**. (Leigh Leshner collection).

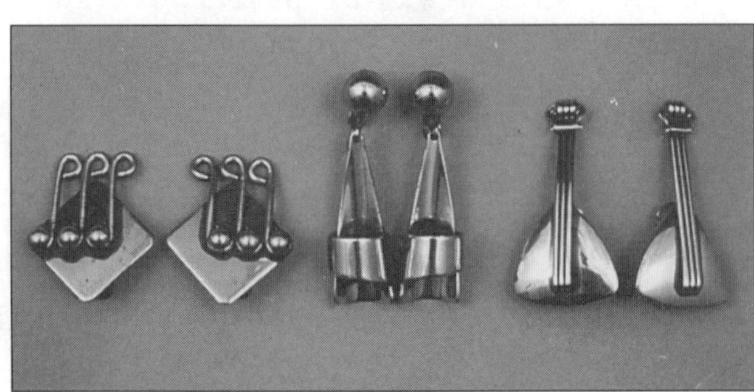

Earrings, copper, Renoir, c. 1950-55:

L, sq plaques with appl wire and beads forming musical notes, clipback earrings mkd "Renoir" in script, 1" w x 1-1/4", pr, **$15**.

C, circ domed surmounts suspending cutout concave triangles with appl tapered convex rectangles, clipbacks, mkd "© RENOIR," 1/2" w x 1-3/4", pr, **$20**.

R, cutout sheet with appl wire in the shape of a lute, clipbacks, mkd "Renoir" in script, 3/4" w x 1-5/8", pr, **$25**. (Terrance O'Halloran collection).

Sterling vermeil, rhinestones, ptd enamel, depicting a bird on a branch with pavé colorless r.s. breast, branch and leaf tips, red r.s. eye, ptd details in green, yellow, orange, brown, black and red, mkd "Corocraft STERLING" on appl plaque, double-pronged hinged clip on rev, 2-3/8" w x 2-3/8" 175

Double Clip Brooch

Sp brass, glass, c. 1936-40, rounded triangles of sp brass openwork floral scroll design, each with a central green, red, blue and purple r.s. flowerhead, flat-backed hinged clips with removable sliding pin assembly mkd "Pat 2045385" (1936), 2-1/4" w x 1-1/2" joined 125

Earrings

Copper, c. 1940, cutout sheet with appl wire and bead design and oxidized outlines forming masks for comedy and tragedy, screwbacks, unmkd, attributed to Frank Rebajes, New York, NY, 1" w x 1", pr 60

Copper, c. 1950, stamped masks of comedy and tragedy, clipbacks, one clip mkd "Renoir" in script, 5/8" w x 1", pr 45

Pendent Earrings, plastic, rhinestones, gp wm, c. 1965-70, circ floral motif surmount with central circ translucent dk green plastic cab surrounded by sm circ colorless r.s. suspending shield-shaped ornate central section of oval and circ green cabs encircled and framed by sm circ colorless r.s., terminating in a drop of a pear-shaped green plastic cab encircled by r.s. and sm r.s. cluster, mkd "K.J.L." for Kenneth J. Lane on rev of clipbacks, 1-3/8" w x 4-3/8" tl, pr, **$295**. (Brett Benson collection).

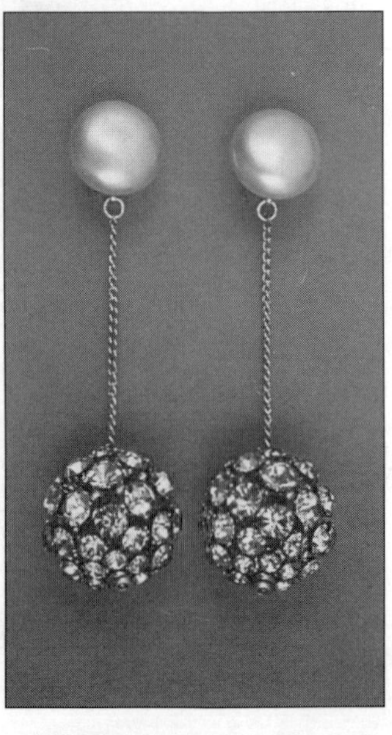

Pendent Earrings, rhinestones, faux pearls, gp wm, c. 1970, lg faux pearl button surmounts, gp curb link chain suspending gp spheres encrusted with lg prong-set colorless r.s., clipbacks, mkd "MADE IN FRANCE," "CHANEL" flanked by © and ® above overlapping opposed double "C" trademark, #2 and 8, 1" dia (drop), 3-3/4" tl, pr, **$225**. (Brett Benson collection).

Hair Comb, rhinestones, gp metal, c. 1955, floral/foliate branch with elements mounted on springs (*en tremblant*), prong-set with lg circ colorless r.s. and sm circ colorless r.s. accents, mounted on gp hair comb, sm bird motif with sm colorless r.s. pavé-set body mounted *en tremblant* to one side, rev mkd "Hattie Carnegie" on appl plate, 2-3/4" w x 2-3/4", **$180**. (Diane White collection).

Enamel, copper, c. 1952, circ domed red-enameled disk with appl copper dome at bottom and appl copper wires at top forming an abstract eye, one clipback mkd "Matisse" in script, 3/4" dia, pr, ... 20

Plastic, gp wm, c. 1970, "shrimp," split ribbed shell shape, half in faux coral plastic, other half polished gp wm, clip backs, mkd "KJL" on appl oval for Kenneth J. Lane, 1/2" w x 1", pr 75

Necklace

Enamel, copper, c. 1955, slightly tapered rect links, folded edges top and bottom enclosing red oval enamel cab centers on oxidized bg, chain and hook clasp, mkd "© MATISSE" on rev, 7/8" w x 18-3/4" tl 125

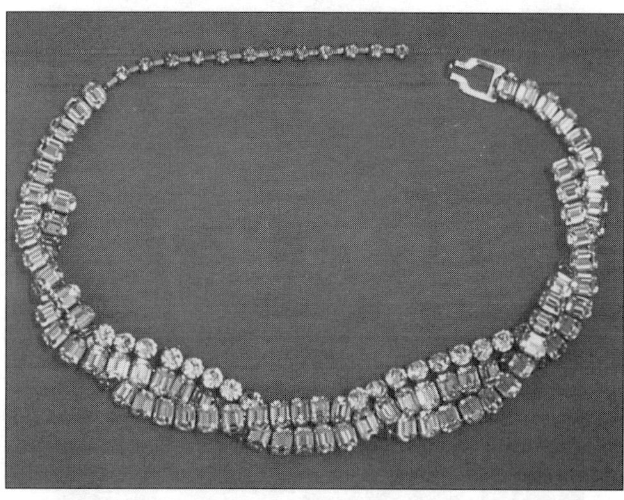

Necklace, rhinestones, rh pl metal, c. 1950, double row torsade of emerald-cut colorless r.s. surmounted by two short rows of circ colorless r.s. at center, continuing to a sm r.s.-set chain and keyhole clasp mkd "EISENBERG," 1" w (at center), 17-1/4" tl, **$250**. (Private collection).

Necklace, glass, rhinestones, wm, c. 1950, double strand slightly curved black glass tubes, bicone faceted fuchsia glass beads, colorless and black r.s-set round metal beads, adjustable hook closure, wm terminal mkd "Hobé," approx 22" tl including strand of beads for closure, 1" at center, **$75**. (Sandra Willard collection).

Necklace, copper, c. 1945-50, flexible interlocking flattened-link copper chain with appl cutout and stamped copper leaves at terminals, mushroom-shaped appl catch at one side, mkd "REbajEs" for Frank Rebajes, New York, NY, leaves 1-1/4" w x 1-3/4", necklace 19" tl, **$125**. (Sue James collection).

Bib Necklace, glass, rhinestones, rh pl wm, c. 1960, a row of three above a row of four lg prong-set faceted and foiled opalescent glass ovals alternating with sm circ aurora borealis r.s., suspended from a rh pl wm chain terminating in a hook clasp, mkd "Schiaparelli" in script on rev of two lg stone settings, 3" w (at center), 16" tl, **$650**. (Brett Benson collection).

Bib Necklace, rhinestones, glass, plastic, faux pearls, gp wm, c. 1968, three linked openwork panels, each set with a vertical row of three grad plastic faux moonstone cabs in scrolled gp wirework frames, flanked by bezel-set faux pearls, surrounded by rows of prong-set opalescent glass cabs and r.s., linked with scrolled gp wirework, suspending a fringe of lg round faux pearls, continuing to a wide band of similar design, v-spring and box clasp, clasp mkd "K.J.L." in an appl oval for Kenneth J. Lane, New York, NY, 5-1/2" w (at center), 2-5/8" w (at sides and back), 12-1/4" across (at front), **$1,000**. (Patrick Kapty collection).

Pendant and Chain, gp brass, faux pearls, glass, c. 1950, chain composed of alternating segments of lg foxtail chain and red glass beads and faux pearls with gp spacers, suspending a semi-circ stamped openwork plaque with scroll and bead design linked by two outside chains and one inside beaded segment to another larger semi-circ stamped plaque of similar design further suspending a chain, faux pearls and re glass bead fringe, terminating in pear-shaped faux pearl drops, mkd "Joseff" in script on appl circ plaque on rev for Joseff of Hollywood, spring ring clasp, pendant 2-1/4" w x 7-1/2" tl, chain 16" tl, **$1,200**. (Charles Pinkham collection).

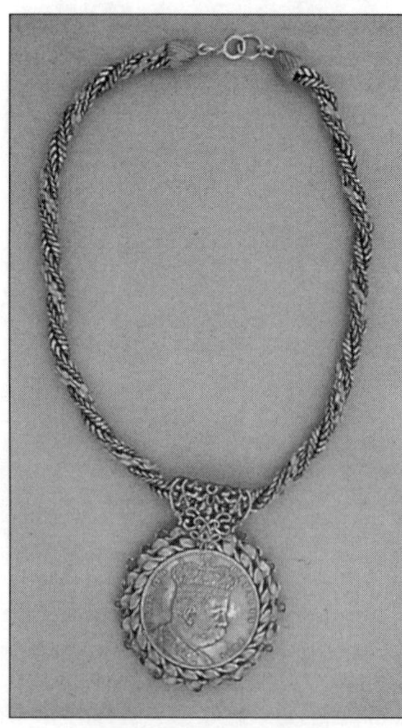

Pendant and Chain, gp and sp brass, coin, c. 1960, pendant a coin mkd "UMBERTO, I RE D'ITALIA, 1891" encircling a crowned profile of a mustachioed monarch, set in a double ropetwist gp frame with filigree back and open sp foliate motif bail, suspended from a gp and sp brass chain torsade, mkd "MIRIAM HASKELL" on attached oval plate, pendant 2-1/4" dia, chain 15-1/2" tl, **$195**. (Photo courtesy of Morning Glory Antiques, Albuquerque, NM).

Glass, rhinestones, gp brass, c. 1960, clusters of three molded red glass and brass bead flowerheads with red r.s. centers, suspended from red molded flowerhead beads, brass and colorless faceted glass rondels, alternating with red faceted glass beads, continuing to a hook clasp, mkd "MIRIAM HASKELL" on attached oval hang tag, 20" tl 420

Gp brass, plastic, faux pearls, rhinestones, c. 1960, central triangular plaque of three gp dragon's heads, each set with a pink r.s. and a sm faux pearl, alternating with three lg irregular black plastic beads, central faux pearl, suspended from a pair of gp winged gargoyle's heads with a pink r.s. at the base, continuing to a double strand flat link chain, foldover clasp, 15" tl, central plaque 1-3/4" w x 1-3/4" 45

Rhinestones, gp metal, c. 1950, undulating crossover design, two rows of double snake chain with lg blue marquise r.s. centers and sm circ blue r.s. accents, continuing to single row of sm blue r.s., hook and chain closure, mkd "ALICE CAVINESS," 1" w (at center), 16" tl 70

Rhinestones, wm, c. 1960, a row of paired circ-cut aurora borealis alternating with single circ-cut amber-colored r.s., suspending clusters of sm and lg circ-cut and emerald-cut green, orange, aurora borealis and amber-colored r.s., fancy pronged wm settings, terminating in a r.s.-set chain and hook clasp mkd "© VENDOME," appl plaque rev center mkd "Vendôme," 1-7/8" w x 18" tl 115

Pendant and Chain

Gp brass, c. 1940, stamped gp brass in a design of three overlapping circ disks with open scroll and geo motif, suspending by two outside and two inside crossing chains a lg circ disk with geo design, appl plate on rev mkd "Joseff," hook and ring clasp on gp brass foxtail chain, pendant 3" w x 5", chain 16" tl 200

Lucite, rh pl wm, c. 1970-75, Lucite "ice cube" held by rh pl wm tongs on a matching lg curb link chain, pendant 1-3/4" w x 4", chain 30" tl 75

Pendant and Chain, rh pl wm, gp wm, c. 1970-75, starburst design, stamped rh pl wm with lg central domed gp disk encircled by ten rh pl rays terminating in sm domed disks, suspended from a linked domed rh pl disk chain, hinged hook clasp on sm link chain, mkd "GIVENCHY MADE IN FRANCE," pendant 5" dia, chain 30" tl, **$125**. (Terrance O'Halloran collection).

Ring

Faux pearl, glass, rhinestones, gp wm, c. 1960, triangular cluster, one lg half-round faux pearl, two flowerheads, each center set with five colorless r.s. encircled by glass cabs, one streaked turq-colored and the other mottled green, mkd "VOGUE," adjustable shank, 1-7/8" w x 1-5/8" 50

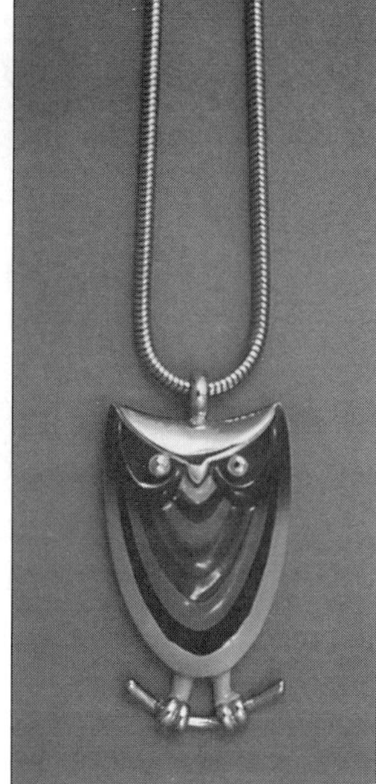

Pendant and Chain, gp wm, ptd enamel, c. 1970, owl on a branch in dk, medium, and lt green, and black ptd enamel, suspended from a gp wm snake chain, pendant rev mkd "EISENBERG," pendant 1-1/4" w x 2-1/2" (with bail), chain 20-1/22" tl, **$50**. (Diane White collection).

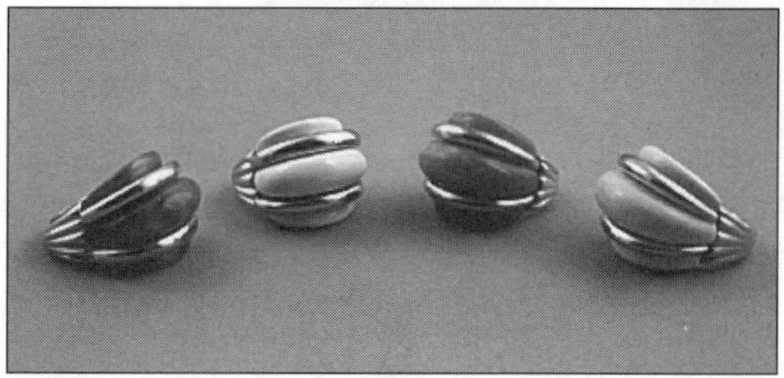

Rings, plastic, wm, Kenneth J. Lane, mkd "KJL ©," c. 1970-75:

TL, two wm bands holding ridged and domed white plastic cab, mounted in wm, size 7, **$75**.

TR, faux coral plastic, mounted in gp wm, size 7, **$75**.

BL, faux jade plastic, gp wm, size 9, **$75**.

BR, faux ivory plastic, gp wm, size 7, **$75**.

(Sue James collection).

Glass, rhinestones, gp wm, c. 1935, lg circ collet-set blue glass stone with ropetwist frame, encircled by eight smaller circ colorless collet-set r.s. with bead and wire-work decoration, mounted on a narrow double wire shank, unmkd, attributed to Hobé, top 1" dia 200

Suite: Bracelet and Earrings

Enamel, rh pl wm, c. 1950, six rounded rect plaques, each with blended bands of lacquered enamel in shades of yellow, green, blue, purple and red, paper label on rev mkd "KUNSTHANDW. EMAIL-LACK MADE IN GERMANY" in outer band of lozenge shape surrounding maker "CYRKO-MAIL," v-spring and box clasp, matching circ disk clipback earrings, bracelet 5/8" w x 7", earrings 7/8" dia, suite 150

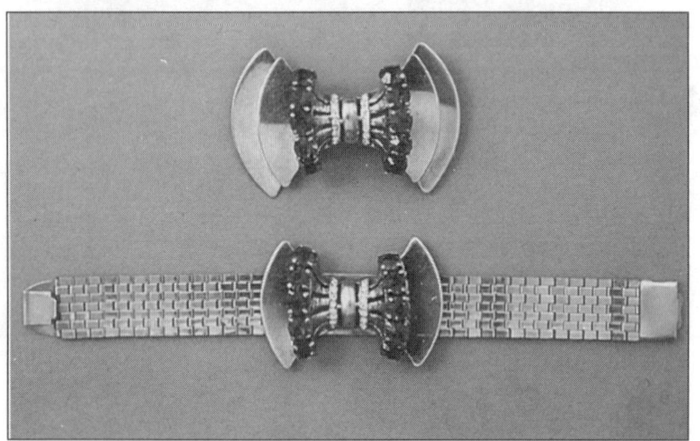

Suite: Bracelet and Brooch/Pin, sterling vermeil, gf, rhinestones, c. 1945, Retro Modern, stylized bow motif with two rows each side of sm colorless r.s. flanked by rows of lg blue r.s. on overlapping plates of highly polished gp ster, repeated as central element of gf brickwork mesh strap bracelet, brooch mkd "SCEPTRON STERLING" (for Sceptron Jewelry Creations, a partnership with Reinad Novelty Co., New York, NY, mk in use from 1944), bracelet band mkd "1/20-12K" at v-spring and box clasp, brooch 2-3/8" w x 1-5/8", bracelet 1-3/8" w, 6-1/2" l, suite, **$450**. (Leigh Leshner collection).

Suite: Bracelet, Earrings and Ring, sterling, 14k rose and yg, c. 1940, bracelet of five rect links, openwork floral, ribbon bow and scrolled wire design, layered rose and yg and ster, mkd "STERLING 14kt Hobé," safety chain; ring of smaller similar design mounted on narrow shank, screwback earrings in the shape of flowerheads, gp petals, ster centers, mkd "STERLING," bracelet 1-3/4" w x 7-1/4", earrings 3/4" dia, ring 5/8" w x 1", suite, **$550**. (Mary Williamson collection).

Suite: Bracelet and Pendent Earrings

Rhinestones, faux pearls, gp metal, c. 1951-53, pastel blue r.s. and faux seed pearl linked clusters, gp base metal, foldover clasp, safety chain, mkd "HOLLYCRAFT COPR. 1953," 5/8" w x 7" tl, matching pendent earrings, mkd "HOLLYCRAFT COPR. 1951," screwbacks, 3/4" w x 1-3/4" tl, suite 125

Suite: Bracelet, Brooch/Pin, and Earrings

Glass, enamel, gp brass, c. 1960-65, floral clusters of pastel pink and blue glass beads, pale blue seed beads, and pale blue enameled petals on brooch and earrings,

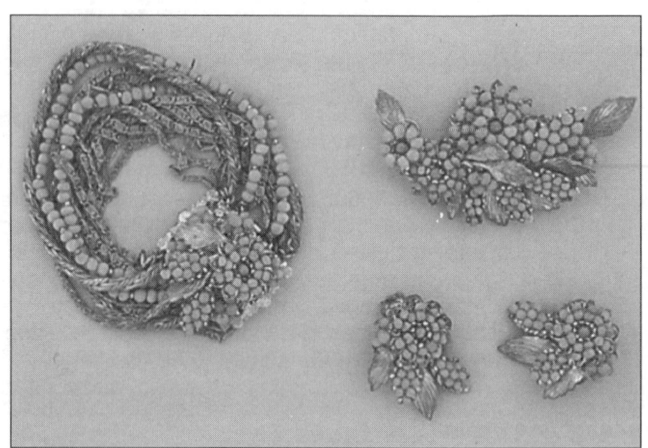

Suite: Bracelet, Brooch/Pin, and Earrings, glass, gp brass, c. 1950, multi-strand bracelet of loop-in-loop and S-link gp chains and two strands of coral-colored glass beads and brass beads spacers strung on wires, terminating in a floral cluster front clasp with stamped gp brass leaves and coral-colored glass beads, brooch and clipback earrings of floral motif of coral-colored glass beads and gp brass leaves, mkd "DE MARIO" on appl oval tag on rev, bracelet 1-1/3" w x 7-1/4", brooch 1-1/2" w x 3", earrings 1-1/3", suite, **$345**. (Photo courtesy of Morning Glory Antiques, Albuquerque, NM).

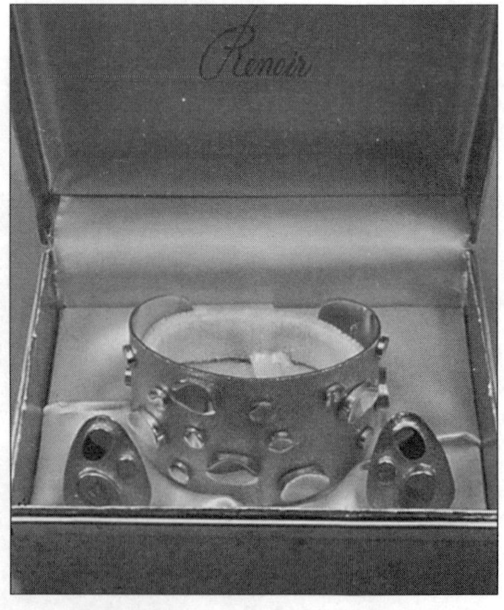

Suite: Bracelet and Earrings, gp wm, c. 1960, tapered cuff with randomly scattered lg and sm polished concave oval and circ disks riveted to a textured bg, cast clipback earrings, each a rounded triangle with polished ovals riveted to textured bg, all pieces mkd "SAUTEUR © RENOIR," in orig box mkd "Renoir" in script on the inside, bracelet 1-1/2" w (at center), 2-3/8" inside dia, earrings 3/4" w x 1", suite, **$125**. (Patrick Kapty collection).

bracelet a floral cluster at the top of a double-hinged gp bangle, clipback earrings a single flowerhead, all pieces mkd "MIRIAM HASKELL" on appl oval plate, bracelet 1-1/3" w x 2" (at top), 2-1/2" inside dia, brooch 2-3/4" w x 1-1/2", earrings 3/4" dia, suite 335

Sterling vermeil, rhinestones, c. 1940-45, brooch in the shape of a key with an open circle of colorless r.s around domed gp center disk, surmounted by a crown motif, sm colorless r.s. accents along key shaft, matching clipback earrings, domed disks with a border of sm colorless r.s., brooch mkd "TRIFARI" (crown mark), "STERLING" and "PAT PEND," earrings mkd "TRIFARI" (crown mark), brooch 2-1/2" w x 3/4", earrings 3/4" dia, suite 250

Suite: Brooch/Pin and Earrings

Faux pearls, rh pl wm, c. 1955-60, floral spray of faux pearls on textured wm stems, tied with a wm bow, mkd "TRIFARI ©.," brooch 2" w x 1-7/8", matching clip earrings 3/4" w x 1", suite 75

Glass, rhinestones, gp brass, faux pearls, c. 1945-50, circ floral motif, floral center with faux pearls, faceted green glass beads, sm circ colorless r.s., and powder blue molded glass flowers encircled by purple glass briolettes, joined by a frame of seed pearls and gp brass beads, mounted on gp brass stamped filigree backing, matching clipback earrings, each a fan-shape with three purple glass briolette beads surmounted by a multi-colored bead floral/foliate cluster, mkd "MIRIAM HASKELL" in appl horseshoe-shaped plate, brooch 2" dia, earrings 1-1/3" w 345

Gp, wm, glass, rhinestones, c. 1970, brooches in the shape of lg and sm birds with oval blue or white faux moonstone bodies, red r.s. eyes and pavé-set sm circ colorless r.s., Florentine finish gp wings and tails, matching oval swirl clipback earrings, mkd "© TRIFARI" (crown mk), lg bird 2" w x 2-3/4", sm 1-7/8" w x 2-1/2, earrings 1" 225

Rhinestones, gp metal, c. 1955-60, triangular openwork Christmas tree of intersecting ropetwist textured lines forming lozenge pattern, set with red, blue, yellow and green circ r.s. in centers, surmounted by a r.s.-set star, matching clipback earrings, mkd "© HOLLYCRAFT," brooch 1-1/4" w x 2-3/8", earrings 3/4" w x 1-1/8", suite 150

Suites: Hinged Bangles and Earrings, copper, c. 1955:
L, hinged crossover bangle flared from the sides to form two opposed triangles framing inlaid triangular wood plaques, clipback earrings, each a convex triangle surmounting a tapered rect, both with inlaid wood, all pieces mkd "© Renoir" in script, bracelet 1-1/2" w (at center), 2-1/4" inside dia, earrings 3/4" w x 1-1/4", suite, **$75**.
R, slightly tapered bangle of sq copper wire framing four conforming enamel plaques of abstract geo design in black and turq opaque enamel, appl polished copper opposed tapered rectangles at center opening, each with an appl bead rivet, matching tapered rect earrings, all pieces mkd "© Matisse" in script, bracelet 1-1/2" w (at center), 2-1/8" inside dia, clipback earrings 3/4" w x 1", suite, **$175**.
(Patrick Kapty collection).

Suite: Brooches/Pins and Earrings, Lucite, sterling vermeil, rhinestones, c. 1943, "jelly belly" turtles, one sm and one lg brooch, and matching earrings, all with Lucite bellies and gp ster frames, lg turtle brooch with green r.s. eyes, sm with red r.s. eyes, and earrings with colorless r.s., lg brooch mkd "TRIFARI" (crown mk), and "Des. Pat. No. 185170" (1943) and "STERLING," sm brooch mkd "TRIFARI" (crown mk), and "STERLING," earrings mkd "STERLING," lg 1-1/2" w x 2-1/4", sm 1-1/4" w x 1-1/2", screwback earrings 5/8" w x 3/4", suite, **$500**. (Elaine Sarnoff collection).

Suite: Hinged Bangle and Earclips, gp wm, faux pearls, c. 1960, wraparound gp foliate motif terminating in prs of pear-shaped faux pearls, matching earclips, appl plate imp "Tortolani" in script, bangle 2" w at center, 2-1/4" inside diameter, earclips 1" w x 1-1/8", suite, **$70**. (Sandra Willard collection).

Suite: Brooch and Earclips, glass, rhinestones, gp brass, c. 1950, six-petaled flowerhead brooch, tapered elliptical yellow glass beads, circ colorless r.s., stamped gp filigree, appl oval plate on rev stamped "MIRIAM HASKELL," matching earclips mkd in block letters, brooch 2-3/8" w x 2", earclips 7/8" w x 7/8", suite, **$275**. (Sandra Willard collection).

Rhinestones, plastic, faux pearls, gp brass, c. 1960, floral foliate wreath brooch set with green and brown plastic cabs on die-stamped gp brass accented with faux pearls and green aurora borealis r.s., brooch 2-1/8" w x 2-3/8", earrings 1-1/8" w x 1-3/4", suite 50

Sterling, c. 1950, brooch in the shape of a stylized owl on a branch constructed with cutout and stamped geo shapes and sq and round wire, mkd "BEAU STERLING," for Beaucraft, Inc., Providence, RI, 1-3/8" w x 1-5/8", matching screwback earrings, each an owl's head, 7/8" dia, suite 75

Suite: Brooch/Pendant, Bracelet, Earclips

Wm, plastic, rhinestones, c. 1960, brooch/pendant a stylized floral and foliate motif in a circ pierced plaque, ropetwist border, green and orange plastic pear-shaped cabs alternating around a central orange plastic marquise shape flanked by six orange r.s. at compass points, bracelet of similar links alternating green and orange plastic marquise-shaped cabs, matching earclips, all mkd "© EMMONS," brooch 2-1/2" dia, foldover clasp bracelet 1" w x 7-1/2" tl, earclips 1" dia, suite 45

Suite: Chatelaine Pins and Earrings

Gp wm, rhinestones, c. 1940, two flying geese in rose gp wm with red r.s. eyes, green r.s. accents on wings, and sm colorless r.s. star gypsy-set on body, attached by a double strand chain, screwback earrings a pr of wings with green r.s. accents, geese 2" w x 2", chain 6" (each strand), earrings 3/4" w x 1-1/4", suite 65

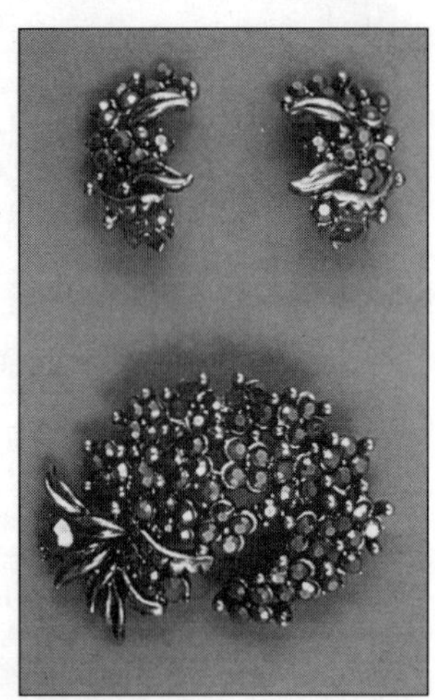

Suite: Brooch and Earclips, glass, rhinestones, gp wm, c. 1954, floral and foliate design, metallic gold-colored r.s., gp wm, imp "HOLLYCRAFT COPR. 1954" on rev brooch and earclips, brooch 2-1/8" w x 1-1/2", earclips 3/4" w x 1-1/8", suite, **$65**. (Sandra Willard collection).

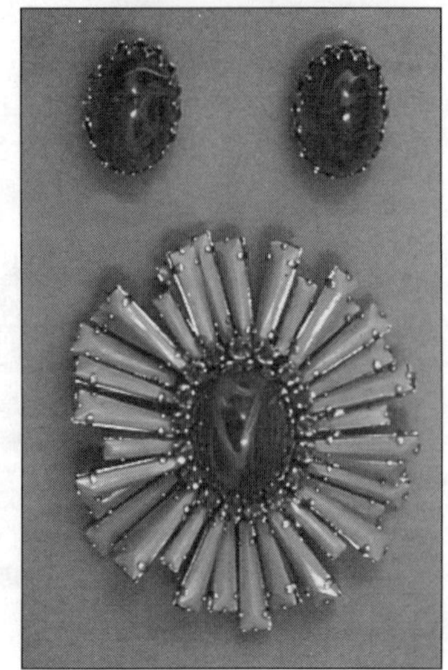

Suite: Brooch and Earrings, glass, rhinestones, gp wm, c. 1960, central bezel-set oval marbled translucent green and white glass cab encircled by prong-set sm circ hot pink r.s. and a radiating row of alternating short and long tapered rect-shaped opaque powder blue prong-set glass cabs, clipback earrings each an oval marbleized green glass cab bezel-set in gp wm, unmkd, attributed to Schreiner, brooch 2-3/4" w x 3", earrings 3/4" w x 1-1/8", suite, **$295**. (Brett Benson collection).

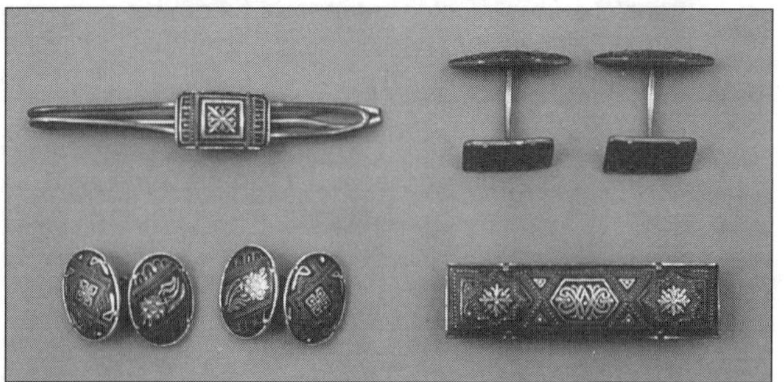

Suites: Cuff Links and Tie Bars, iron, silver, gold, gp brass, damascening, Toledo, Spain, c. 1965:
L, double-sided cuff links, each a pr of oval patinated iron plaques with damascened geo motif design of silver and gold, floral design on rev, prong-set in gp brass frames and linked by a chain, tie bar a rect plaque of similar geo design, all pieces mkd "SPAIN," cuff links 1/2" w x 3/4", tie bar 3" w x 1/2", suite, **$50**.
R, cuff links a pair of oval patinated iron plaques with damascened geo motif in silver and gold, prong-set in gp brass frames and attached by rigid bars to rect backs of similar design, tie bar a rect plaque of similar geo design, all pieces mkd "SPAIN," cuff links 1" w x 1/2", tie bar 2-3/4" w x 5/8", suite, **$60**.
(Patrick Kapty collection).

Suite: Clip and Earrings

Sterling vermeil, glass, rhinestones, c. 1945-50, clip a sunburst with radiating gp rays interspersed with sm colorless r.s., center prong-set with unfoiled faceted pink glass ovals encircled by sm colorless r.s., double-pronged hinged clip on rev, matching clipback earrings, mkd "TRIFARI" (crown mk), "STERLING," "Des Pat 142666" (1945), brooch 2-1/2" dia, earrings 1-1/4" dia, suite 165

Suite: Link Bracelet and Brooch/Pin

Enamel, rhinestones, gp wm, c. 1960, foliate motif, bracelet of paired translucent green enameled leaves flanked by sm colorless r.s.-set blades, brushed gp finish, v-spring and box clasp with safety chain, matching brooch an asymmetrical spray, both pcs mkd "© TRIFARI," bracelet 5/8" w x 7-1/4", brooch 2-3/4" w x 1-1/2", suite 145

Suite: Necklace and Earclips

Glass, rhinestones, gp wm, c. 1955-60, a row of oval coral-colored cabs in fancy stamped bezels alternating with aurora borealis r.s., hook and chain closure, earclips a cluster of r.s. encircling coral-colored cabs, mkd "SELRO," 1/2" w x 17" tl, earclips 1" w x 1-1/2", suite 55

Glass, gp metal, c. 1955-60, double strand round turquoise-green white-flecked glass beads, central stamped gp metal floral cluster set with aurora borealis, faux seed pearls, and turquoise-green beads, hook closure, 18" tl including six beads for closure, 1-1/2" at center, matching earclips 1-1/8" w x 1-1/2", suite 80

Suite: Necklace, Bracelet and Earclips

Glass, rhinestones, plastic, gp wm, c. 1960, round white glass beads with gold-colored textured coating (much of it flaked off), round black plastic beads with textured iridescent metallic coating, faceted round aurora borealis glass beads, molded black glass disks with gold-coated floral design, smoky gray and amber-colored circ r.s. mounted on gp wm, necklace 15" tl, 1-3/4" at center, bracelet 7-1/8" tl x 1-1/8" w (some beads missing), earclips 7/8" w x 1-1/4, suite 70

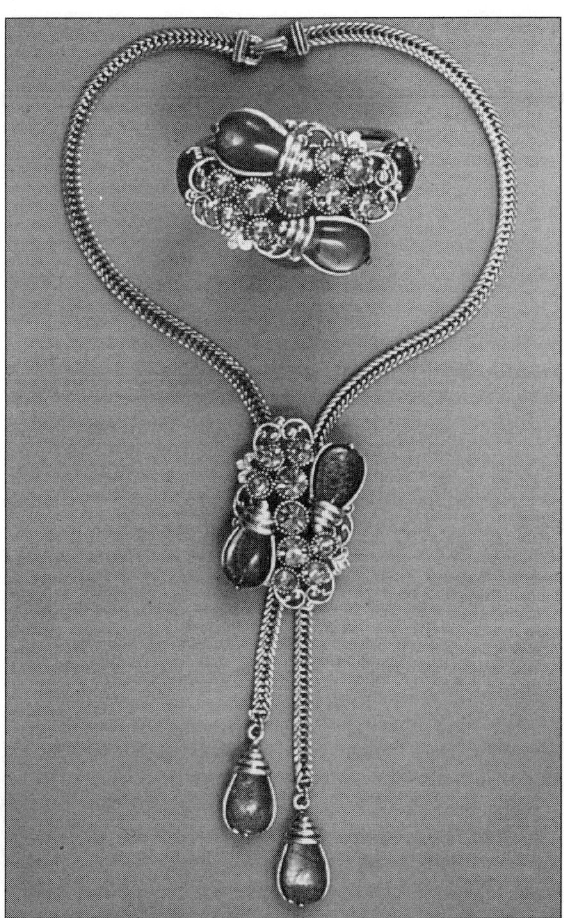

Suite: Necklace and Bracelet, gp metal, glass, rhinestones, c. 1960, lariat style necklace with slide on herringbone chain, slide with lg pear-shaped amber-colored glass cabs and cluster of brown r.s., terminating in two amber-colored cab drops, foldover clasp, mkd "SELRO," matching double-hinged crossover bangle with amber-colored glass cabs and brown r.s. on top appl plaque and on sides, unmkd, necklace 1/4" w x 20-1/2" tl, slide 1-1/2" w x 2-1/4", bracelet 2" inside dia, top 1-1/2" w x 2-1/4", suite, **$75**. (Sandra Willard collection).

Rhinestones, glass, rh pl wm, c. 1955-60, necklace in purple, lavender and aurora borealis circ and marquise r.s. linked clusters, sm purple r.s. chain, hook clasp, oval plate mkd "REGENCY" appl to rev center, 16" tl, 1-1/8" w at center, matching flexible bracelet, linked r.s. clusters, mkd on rev, box and v-spring clasp, safety chain, 7-1/8" tl x 1" w, matching earclips with lg center circ faceted purple glass encircled by circ lavender and marquise aurora borealis r.s., unmkd, 1-1/4" dia, suite 175

Suite: Necklace, Brooches/Pins, Ring

Rhinestones, gp metal, c. 1950, cluster of multi-colored r.s. in lavender, pink, turquoise, blue, green and yellow around lg pink oval center r.s., suspended from "antiqued" goldtone rope chain, r.s.-set clasp, matching pr of sm brooches, lg cluster ring, all pcs mkd "HOLLYCRAFT COPR. 1950," necklace 16-1/2" tl, pendant 1-1/2" w x 1-1/2", brooches, each 7/8" w x 3/4", adjustable ring 1" w x 1-1/8", suite 200

Suite: Necklace, Clip, and Earrings

Glass, gp wm, rhinestones, c. 1950, necklace of lg and sm molded blue glass leaf-shaped cabs with sm circ colorless r.s. accents in gp frames, joined with rect gp links, hook clasp mkd "©TRIFARI," 1/2" w x 17-1/2" tl, matching circ clipback earrings, each a cluster of molded blue glass leaves, 1" dia, clip a leaf shape with molded blue glass leaf-shaped cabs and sm circ colorless r.s. on one half bisected by r.s.-set stem, polished r.s.-set gp wm on the other side, double-pronged hinged clip on rev, 1-3/8" w x 2", matching leaf-shaped clipback earrings, 1" x 1", mkd "TRIFARI" (crown mk) on rev of clip and earrings, suite 445

Suite: Necklace and Link Bracelet

Glass, gp metal, r.s., c. 1940, Retro Modern, open gp links alternating with colorless r.s.-set links suspending a central gp and r.s.-set scrolled ribbon bow with two lg molded clear glass cherries and three grad clear glass cabs, mkd "Z" on rev, matching bracelet of linked molded glass cherries alternating with clear glass cab and r.s.-set scrolls, mkd "K" on rev, both pcs mkd "MAZER," fold-over clasps, necklace 16" tl, center 2-1/4" w x 2-1/2, bracelet 1" w x 7-1/2", suite 175

Suite: Necklace and Bracelet, gp brass, glass, rhinestones, c. 1940, necklace composed of multi-strand foxtail chain sections with stamped foliate terminals alternating with circ stamped elements set with topaz-colored r.s., suspending a foliate motif pendant with lg faceted oval glass stone in beaded frame flanked and surmounted by marquise-cut topaz-colored r.s., terminating in a r.s.-capped multi-strand tassel, unmkd, attributed to Joseff of Hollywood, hook closure, 21" tl, central drop 2-1/4" w at top x 6-3/4" tl, foxtail chain bracelet with front clasp matching necklace pendant, 1-3/4" w x 6-3/4", suite, **$350**. (Leigh Leshner collection).

Suite: Necklace, Brooch/Pin, and Clip, gp wm, glass, rhinestones, enamel, c. 1935-40, three-dimensional floral/foliate motif, gp wm flowerheads prong-set with faceted oval glass, sm circ colorless r.s. accents, intertwined with navy blue ptd enameled ribbon, necklace with two red glass, brooch with two green glass, clip with one purple glass faceted ovals, necklace with fold-over box clasp, mkd "TKF" for Trifari, Krussman, and Fishel, double-pronged hinged clip mkd "TRIFARI" (crown mk), brooch unmkd, necklace 3-1/4" w x 15" tl, brooch 3-1/4" w x 1-3/4", clip 2-1/3" w x 1-1/3", suite, **$600**. (Photo courtesy of Morning Glory Antiques, Albuquerque, NM).

Suite: Necklace and Earrings, copper, c. 1955, necklace with a central element of bent and soldered wire in a looping and overlapping open design, flanked by two smaller similar elements leading to a chain terminating in a hook and ball closure, screwback earrings with bent and soldered wire in ring-shaped drops, all pieces mkd "REbajEs" for Frank Rebajes, New York, NY, necklace 1-3/4" w (at center), 14-1/2" tl, earrings 1-1/8" dia, suite, **$175**. (Sue James collection).

Suite: Necklace and Earclips, glass, rhinestones, gp wm, c. 1950, grad purple and swirled white pear-shaped glass beads with foliate gp caps suspended from clusters of marquise lavender r.s. continuing to a sm lavender r.s. chain, hook clasp, appl oval plate on rev of necklace link terminal mkd "REGENCY," matching earclips not mkd, 1-3/4" w at center, 16" tl, earclips 7/8" w x 1-1/8", suite, **$150**. (Sandra Willard collection).

Suite: Necklace and Earrings, gp brass, glass, rhinestones, c. 1955, necklace with a vertical center row of red glass and r.s. rondels linked to sm fluted gp beads and five strands of gp brass box-link chain joining at each side two lg open trefoils with lg emerald-cut colorless r.s. centers, prong-set red pear-shaped r.s., stamped gp leaves and sm colorless r.s. within surrounding frames, continuing to five strands of box link chain and rect v-spring and box clasp, appl oval plate on rev mkd "MIRIAM HASKELL," 18" tl, matching circ button earrings with faceted red glass bead centers, sm colorless r.s. borders, clipbacks, 3/4" dia, suite, **$425**. (Photo courtesy of Morning Glory Antiques, Albuquerque, NM).

Late Georgian, garnet jewelry, late 18th and early 19th century:
Suite: Necklace and Pendent Earrings, c. 1820, necklace a five-petaled flowerhead center of oval-cut garnets flanked by grad links of paired foliate motif pear-shaped foil-backed garnets, v-spring and box clasp, matching earrings of paired pear-shaped foil-backed garnets, closed-back gilt metal settings, probably Eng, necklace 16″ tl, earrings 2-1/4″ tl, suite, **$1,300**
TC, Brooch/Pin, c. 1780, circ multi-petaled flowerhead set with cut-to-shape foil-backed garnets in closed silver mount, probably Portuguese, 1-1/2″ dia, **$650**
BC, Brooch/Pin, c. 1820-30, floral/foliate spray set throughout with foil-backed garnets in closed-back silver mount, probably Eng, 2″ w x 7/8″, **$330** (Photo courtesy of Sharen and Nicholas Wood, London)

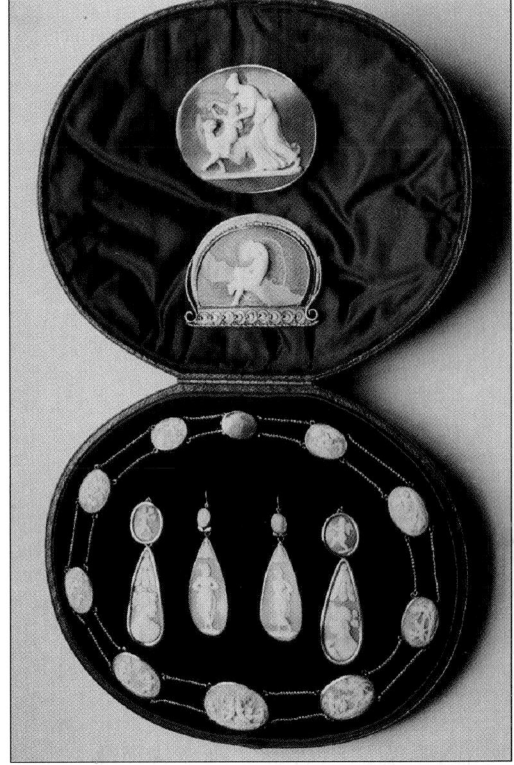

Late Georgian, shell cameos, early 19th century:
T, Brooch/Pin, c. 1800-20, high relief carving of classical scene, woman holding child on back of a lioness, mounted in plain yg frame, stress marks on right side of shell, 2-1/4″ w x 2″, **$750**
C, Brooch/Pin, c. 1830, depicting Ariel (from Shakespeare's *The Tempest*) on a bat's back, holding a peacock feather, possibly taken from an 1826 painting by Joseph Servern, bezel-set, mounted in arcing gilt metal frame terminating in C-scrolls flanking concentric disk and bead decoration on horizontal base, 2-1/4″ x 1-3/4″, **$750**
BC, Pendent Earrings, c. 1820, sm cameo surmounts of butterflies suspending pear-shaped drop cameos of full-figure women in classical dress surmounted by palmette motifs, mounted in plain yg frames, Fr hmks on earwires, 3/4″ w x 2″ tl, pr, **$500**
BLR, Pendent Earrings, c. 1810, cameo surmounts depicting *putti* playing cymbals and trumpet, suspending pear-shaped drop cameos of women's profiles with classical drapery, surmounted by palmette motifs, mounted in plain yg frames, Fr hmks on earwires, 3/4″ w x 2-1/2″ tl, pr, **$640**
B, Suite, c. 1810, necklace of grad oval cameos depicting *putti* (cherubs) engaged in various activities: playing instruments, feeding and riding animals, drinking wine, backed with agate-colored glass, mounted in plain yg frames linked with double strands of handmade fine box link chain, goldwork probably Fr, matching earrings (not pictured), sm oval cameos of putti on chariots suspended from cameo surmounts of butterflies, plain yg frames, back-hinged yg earwires, 1/2″ w x 1″ tl, necklace 1″ w at center, 17″ tl, suite, **$3,200** (Photo courtesy of Sharen and Nicholas Wood)

Late Georgian, brooches and pendants, late 18th and early 19th century:
T, Brooch/Pin, c. 1820, in the shape of a wheat stalk, 15k yg set with alternating prs of rect-cut emeralds and natural pearls, C-catch, tube hinge, 3-1/4″ x 1/2″, **$785**
TC, Brooch/Pin, c. 1790, *girandole* form set throughout with foil-backed colorless pastes, black spot on culets, closed-back silver mount, three lg pear-shaped pastes framed by sm circ-cut colorless pastes suspended from central bow motif, C-catch, tube hinge, 1-3/4″ w x 1-1/8″, **$330**
CL, Brooch/Pendant, c. 1790, rock crystal-covered navette-shaped painting on ivory, depicting a pastoral scene of a young girl with her arm around a flower-garlanded lamb, plain yg frame and back, C-catch, tube hinge, pendant bail, 1″ w x 1-1/2″, **$495**
C, Pendant, c. 1800-10, rounded oblong, central silver urn motif set with and encircled by foiled colorless pastes, black spot on culets, on a blue-enameled ground, white enamel border, enameled bail, domed silver back, 1″ w x 1-1/2″ l, **$620**
CR, Brooch/Pin, c. 1790-1800, converted from a bracelet clasp, central triangular-faceted domed rect amethyst framed by cushion-cut chrysoberyls set in cut-down collets, 18k yg mount, 3/4″ x 1″, **$580**
BL, Brooch/Pin, c. 1820, in the shape of a butterfly, set with foiled chrysoberyls, top wings foiled in dark green, 18k yg mount, beaded border, C-catch, tube hinge, **$620**
BR, Brooch/Pin, c. 1790, glass-covered navette-shaped painting on ivory, mourning scene of a young man gazing at three urns on a pedestal inscribed "AFFECTON WEEPS, HEAVEN REJOICES," 18k yg mount, beaded frame, C-catch, tube hinge, 7/8″ w x 1-3/8″, **$420**
(Photo courtesy of Sharen and Nicholas Wood)

Early Victorian, c. 1830-1860:
TL, Brooch/Pin, c. 1840, floral motif, seed pearls strung with horsehair, mounted on cut-to-shape MOP backing, yg pin back, C-catch, tube hinge, 2″ w x 1-1/8″, **$325**
TC, Brooch/Pin, c. 1860, Scottish, open circle, scalloped edge, eight segments set with banded agate and jasper in engr silver mount, C-catch, tube hinge, 2-1/8″ dia, **$350**
TR, Brooch/Pin, c. 1830-40, rect raised and engr gp frame, faceted oval foiled yellow paste center, convex back, C-catch, tube hinge (repaired), 1-1/8″ w x 1″, **$175**
CL, Ring, c. 1840-60, woven patterned brown hair channel-recessed in a yg band surmounted by a rounded rect engr yg name plate with plain central ribbon motif (blank), 3/8″, approx size ten, **$275**
CR, Charm, c. 1840-60, in the shape of an urn, yg with hollow hairwork center, 5/8″ w x 1″, **$185**
BL, Pendent Earrings, c. 1830-40, yg "top and drop," flowerhead surmount and detachable torpedo-shaped drop with raised stippled textured surface, appl yg disks, beaded foliate motifs and bead terminal, hinged earwire inserts through back of lobe, 3/8″ w x 2-5/8″ tl, pr, **$1,250**
BC, Brooch/Pin, c. 1840-50, oval glazed compartment containing a daguerreotype of a gentleman's painted portrait mounted in plain gf frame and back, within an independent gf frame with stamped raised scrollwork at compass points, sm oval glazed compartment on rev, containing braided gray-brown hair on cloth ground, C-catch, tube hinge, extended pinstem, loop for safety chain, 2-1/8″ w x 2-3/8″, **$650**
BR, Pendent Earrings, c. 1830-40, "top and drop," circ carnelian cab in yg flowerhead surmount, detachable torpedo-shaped carnelian drop, hinged earwire inserts through back, 3/8″ w x 2-1/2″ tl, pr, **$650**
B, Brooch/Pin, c. 1830, cruciform, rect-cut green pastes set in pronged yg bezels, engr yg frame around center stone, cutout yg scrollwork between arms, 1-1/2″ x 1-3/8″, **$285**
(Courtesy of E. Foxe Harrell Jewelers, Clinton, IA)

Early Victorian, c. 1830-1860:
T, Link Bracelet, c. 1840, Berlin iron, six cast and black-lacquered Gothic and foliate motif openwork links, each a rectangle surmounting a cusped triangle and branched foliate terminal, v-spring and box clasp, rev imp "GEISS A BERLIN," 6-1/8″ x 1-1/2″ w, **$1,000**
CL, Brooch/Pin, c. 1830-35, rect miniature portrait on ivory of a young girl, narrow engr yg frame, flat back, Am, C-catch, tube hinge, 1″ w x 1-1/8″, **$475**
C, Brooch/Pin, c. 1840, domed oval center, *en grisaille* enameled rose motif, set in a black lacquered metal frame with wire mesh and scroll decoration, C-catch, tube hinge, 1-7/8″ w x 1-1/2″, **$300**
CR, Brooch/Pin, c. 1830-40, oval Swiss ptd enamel pastoral scene of a young shepherdess tending three sheep, carrying a basket, a dog at her side, a young man watching from behind a tree, a lion statue on a pedestal in the background, mounted in an engr yg frame, replaced pin back assembly, 1-3/8″ x 1-5/8″, **$700**
BL, Fob Seal, c. 1850, engr gp brass with beveled rect foiled colorless paste set in base, engr with mono in rev for seal, 1″ w x 1-3/8″, $195
BC, Brooch/Pendant, c. 1850-60, six domed 18k yg navette shapes with emerald cab centers, ropetwist frames, forming scalloped circ outline, spaced with seed pearls in trefoil clusters around outside edge, encircling a raised yg star shape with engr sides and ropetwist border, central flowerhead with blue enameled petals around seed pearl cluster with emerald cab center, C-catch, tube hinge, hinged pendant bail, 2″ dia, **$2,500**
BR, Fob, c. 1850, engr gp wm, plain beveled rect chalcedony plaque set in base, 1″ w x 1-1/4″, **$175**
(courtesy of E. Foxe Harrell Jewelers, Clinton, IA; BC, P. Tonge and D. Usher Collection)

Brooches/Pins, yg and gemstones, c. 1860-1870:
TL, Floral/foliate engr 14k buckle motif set with cushion-cut garnets and pale yellow-green chrysoberyls, mounted on a ring-shaped frame with wiretwist decoration, C-catch, tube hinge, extended pin stem, safety chain and pin, 1-1/2″ w x 1-3/4″, **$1,250**
TR, Snake motif, 18k, stamped zigzag patterned overlapping segments on body, scrolled design on head set with two garnet cabs, rc diamond eyes, flat backing, suspending a heart-shaped locket with garnet cab center, rock crystal-covered compartment containing braided brown hair on rev, C-catch, tube hinge, extended pinstem, safety chain and pin, 1-3/4″ w x 2-1/4″ tl, **$1,850**
BC, Knot motif, two almandite carbuncles (garnets) enclosed in rc-diamond-set foliate frames flanking engr 14k leaves and notched ribbons, C-catch with added hinged safety, tube hinge, extended pinstem, 2-1/2″ w x 2-3/8″, **$3,500** (Gail Freeman collection)

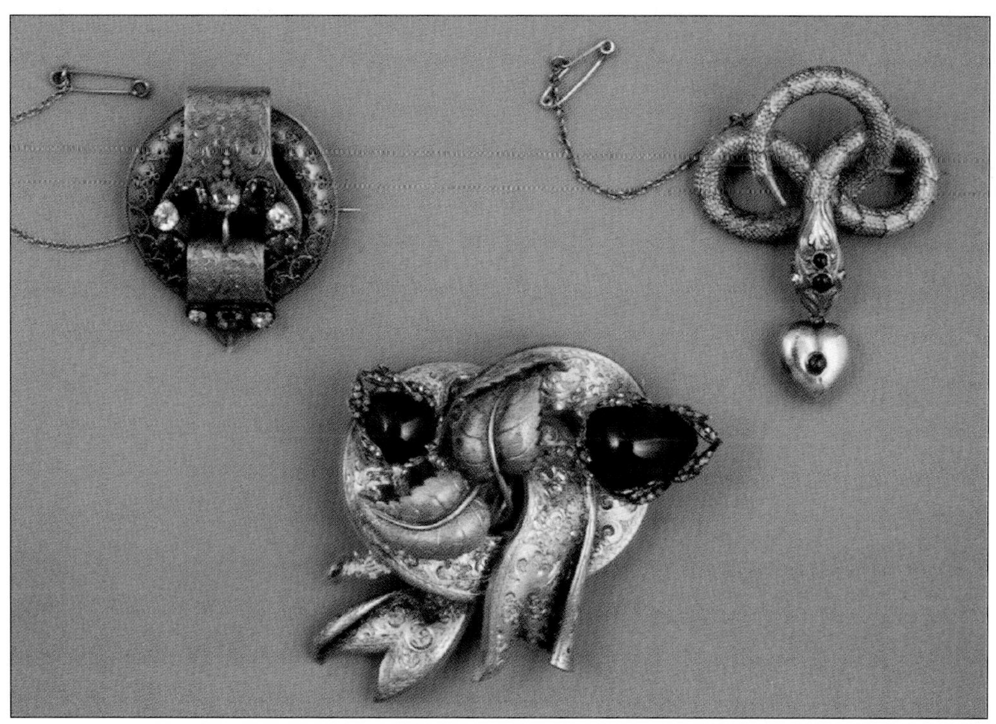

Mid-Victorian, Revivals, Mosaics, and Cameos, c. 1860-1880:
TL, Pendent Earrings, c. 1870, bow-shaped silver surmounts and chains set throughout with seed pearls, suspending navette-shaped drops, hp porcelain depictions of young women in regional dress with seed pearl frames and drops, garnets flanking drops and in bow centers, Fr hmks (boar's heads) and illegible maker's mk, shepherd's hook earwires, 7/8″ w x 2-1/2″ tl, pr, **$1,250**
TC, Pendant/Brooch, c. 1860-70 *pietra dura*, rect black marble plaque with mosaic of carnations and forget-me-nots, set in Archeological Revival-style 18k yg frame with scrolled wirework and beading, scalloped shell-shaped terminal, removable wiretwist-decorated bail, enclosed C-catch, tube hinge, 1-3/8″ w x 3″ tl, **$2,250**
TR, Pendent Earrings, c. 1870, mosaic and gilded silver, circ disk surmount suspending mosaic-decorated plaques and disks, central disk with iridescent scarab motif center, chain and disk terminal, shepherd's hook earwires, 3/4″ w x 2″ tl, pr, **$1,150**
(Gail Freeman collection)

BL, Bar Brooch/Pin, c. 1880, mosaic and enamel on silver gilt, mosaic disks depicting St. Mark's lions flanking central black-enameled bar with raised letters "VENEZIA" C-catch, 2-5/8″ w x 5/8″, **$350**
BC, Brooch/Pendant, three-dimensional coral carving of the head of a bacchante with grapes and leaves in her hair and around her neck, flanked by carved goat's heads, mounted on a yg armature with later-added yg grape leaf and vine motif frame and pendant bail, enclosed C-catch, tube hinge, 2-1/8″ x 2-1/8″, **$1,200**
CR, Brooch/Pin, c. 1880, circ sp brass disk with polychrome mosaic scarab on a white ground, illegible mark on rev, C-catch, 3/4″ dia, **$100**
BR, Brooch/Pin, lava cameo of winged cherub's head (putto), silver pin back assembly, C-catch, tube hinge, 1-5/8″ w x 7/8″, **$300**
(P. Tonge and D. Usher collection)

Late Victorian, gold and gemstones, c. 1880-1900:
T, Bracelet, c. 1890, hinged open tubular yg links forming bangle, convex center surmounted by a cluster of om and oe diamonds flanked by pavé diamond-set foliate motifs outlined in green enamel, v-spring and box clasp, 6-5/8" l x 7/8" w, **$6,500**
TC, Bar Brooch/Pin, c. 1890-1900, narrow yg bar with circ-cut sapphire terminals, surmounted by a swan motif with oval opal body, ruby cab eye, set throughout with rc diamonds in st yg mount, 2-1/4" w x 3/4", **$3,950**
BC, Fringe Necklace and Charm Pendant, c. 1890-1900, yg set throughout with seed pearls, three flowerheads with oe diamond centers, central hook on rev suspending removable bow-topped heart pendant pavé-set with seed pearls, circ cut rubies and oe diamond flowerhead in center, glazed compartment on rev, with orig fitted box stamped "To the Queen, J. W. Benson Ltd, 25 Old Bond St, London," 15" tl x 7/8" at center, pendant 1" x 1", **$6,900**

B, Necklace and Pendant/Brooch, c. 1880, central floral/foliate ornament prong-set with a cushion-cut and an emerald-cut emerald, sm pearls and set throughout with rc diamonds in st yg, mounted on a scrolled yg link and knife-edge swag necklace, flanked by four rc diamond-set florets with circ-cut emerald centers, pearl, diamond, and emerald-set drops and swags, center detaches for wear as a brooch with additional brooch fitting, Fr hmks, 15" tl, 1-5/8" at center, **$7,000**
(Courtesy of Neil Lane Jewelry, Los Angeles, CA)

Late Victorian, gold-filled, silver, c. 1880-1905:
TL, Hinged Bangle, c. 1900, tapered hollow gf tubing, stamped open scrolled front surmounted by a faceted oval purple glass stone, 2-3/8" inside dia, 1" at center, **$200**
TC, Expansion Bracelet, gf, engr mono on oval center, stamped oblong links strung on spring-hinged wire, "A.A.G. Co. Pat. '05" on inside two links, in orig box mkd "THE GREENE ADJUSTABLE BRACELET, PATENTED 1905, A.A. Greene & Co., PROVIDENCE, R.I.," 7/8" w, **$150**
TR, Love Token Bangle, adjustable notched silver band with keeper, suspending eight engr coins or tokens, U.S. silver coins dated 1876 and 1886 with various ciphers, names and monos, one 1" silver disk with engr rose gold ciphers on both sides, seven 3/4" dia disks, 2-1/4" to 2-1/2" inside dia, **$285**
CL, 1, Chatelaine Hook, three grad stamped and engr sp wm owl's heads with glass eyes, joined with horizontal and vertical articulated bars, bead terminals, hinged wide hook waist clasp on rev of largest owl, hinged snap closure on rev of smallest owl, 1-3/8" w x 3", **$300**
(Kirsten Olson collection)
CL, 2, Brooch/Pin, c. 1900, curved foliate spray with bow motif at one end, set throughout with pear-shaped and circ rc pyrope garnets in silver mount, C-catch, tube hinge, 1-7/8" x 1/2", **$275**
C, Brooch/Pin, c. 1880, lg oval ptd porcelain portrait of a lady in Renaissance costume, in plain gf frame with ropetwist border, C-catch, tube hinge, 2-1/8" w x 2-1/2", **$200**
CR, 1, Bar Brooch/Pin, stamped gf scrollwork with faceted oval fuchsia-colored glass center, later-added trombone catch, 2-1/8" x 5/8", **$65**
CR, 2, Locket Fob, gf, hinged oval locket base suspended from scrolled wire top and ropetwist ring, 7/8" w x 1-1/4" tl, **$200**
B, Longchain and Slide, gf cable link chain with six-pointed star-shaped slide set with seed pearls and pink rhinestones, opal center, 7/8" dia, 48" tl, **$400**
(Courtesy of E. Foxe Harrell Jewelers, Clinton, IA)

Art & Crafts, English sterling and unmarked silver, c. 1900-1910:
L, Pendant and Chain, lozenge-shaped openwork silver pendant, six lg circ moonstones forming triangles above and below a central circ lapis cab, two smaller circ moonstones at side terminals, smaller circ lapis cab drop, suspended from two lengths of fine cable link chain, T-bar clasp, 19″ tl, pendant 1-3/4″ w x 2-1/2″ tl, **$750**
CL, Pendant and Chain, date letter for 1909, inverted lobed triangular ster plaque with heart-shaped silver leaves on mingled blue and green enameled ground outlined in silver, terminating in an enameled pear-shaped drop, suspended from two short lengths of chain joined to a sm enameled disk and bail, 15″ cable link chain, makerís mk "CH" for Charles Horner, Chester (Eng) hmks, 1-1/8″ w x 2-3/4″ tl from bail, **$475**
C, Festoon Necklace, a central oval pale green chalcedony cab set in a sawtooth bezel, flanked by two circ blister pearls joined with swagged chains to two blue-green enameled figure 8 motifs continuing to a cable link chain and T-bar clasp, suspending a narrow rect enameled plaque, a blister pearl, and a smaller oval green chalcedony cab drop, 16″ tl, 3″ top to bottom at center, **$1,400**
CR, Pendant and Chain, domed heart shaped plaque, center oval blister pearl encircled by green and white enameled C-scrolls outlined in silver on a blue enameled ground, rev counter-enameled, suspended from two lengths of silver trace chain, spring ring clasp, 18″ tl, 1-1/8″ w x 1-3/8″, **$350**
R, Pendant and Chain, open lozenge-shaped silver plaque bezel-set with three oval and one larger pear-shaped pink tourmaline (rubellite) cabs, interspersed with sm bead clusters and scrolled wire, suspending a similarly decorated oval pink tourmaline cab drop, suspended from two lengths of fetter and trace chain, v-spring and tubular clasp, 16-1/2″ tl, 1″ w x 2″ tl, **$450**
B, Buckle, two piece, date letter for 1911, two opposed bird motifs within pierced openwork interlocking scrolls in ster bordered with mingled blue and green enamel, central hook and eye, bars for belt attachment on rev, maker's mk for Liberty & Co ("L & Co" in adjacent lozenges), Birmingham (Eng) hmks on one pc, lion hmk and date letter on the other, 4-1/4″ w x 2-1/4″, **$1,200** (Gail Gerretsen collection)

Arts & Crafts, American, c. 1910-1940:
TL, Ring, c. 1910-15, oval gray opal within a navette-shaped pierced foliate motif yg frame interspersed with six sm circ-cut Montana blue sapphires, continuing to a narrow shank, 1/2″ w x 1″, approx size 7-1/2, **$900**
T, Cuff Bracelet, c. 1930-40, domed and engr lg and sm lily pad motifs interspersed with sm beads and wire tendrils, rev imp "MARY GAGE STERLING," 2-1/8″ inside dia, 1-7/8″ w, **$600**
TCL, Penannular Pin Brooch, of Celtic Iron Age inspiration, c. 1910-20, hammered raised and engr floral/foliate motifs, rev imp "STERLING," maker's mk "SGP" in a triangle, 2″ dia, 2-3/8″ with pin, **$300**
TC, Brooch/Pin, c. 1910-15, three overlapping patinated brass disks depicting ancient coins with Roman heads, one labeled "CICERO," another "ROMA," 2-7/8″ w x 1-1/8″, wide C-catch, flanged hinge, **$85**
BCL, Ring, c. 1935-40, lg circ carnelian cab within a floral/foliate motif ster mount, adjustable split shank, mkd "HAND MADE STERLING," maker's mk for The Art Metal Studios, Chicago, IL (T above M flanked by A and S), successors in 1934 to The Art Silver Shop (to present), 3/4″ w x 7/8″, **$250**
BC, Brooch/Pin, c. 1935-40, lg spray of daffodils, appl oval plate on rev imp "FRIEDELL PASADENA STERLING HAND WROUGHT" for Clemens Friedell, Pasadena, CA, 2-5/8″ x 4-1/8″, **$800**
BCR, Pendant and Chain, c. 1920, cusped shield-shaped ster plaque bezel-set with a lg circ carnelian cab, rev imp with maker's mk for The Art Silver Shop, Chicago, IL, flanked by "HAND MADE" and "STERLING," 1″ w x 1-1/2″ tl, suspended from a fetter and trace chain, spring ring clasp, 15-1/2″ tl, **$200**
B, Festoon Necklace, c. 1910-15, central oval pendant bezel-set with an oval amethyst cab encircled by ster foliate motifs, beading and scrolled wire, suspending a trefoil drop, swagged cable link chains joined to similarly designed trefoil side elements and bead clusters, continuing to a single cable link chain, spring ring clasp, 16-1/2″ tl, pendant rev imp "STERLING," 2″ top to bottom at center, **$650**
(TL, TCL, B, Gail Gerretsen collection; T, BCL, Kirsten Olson collection; TC, BCR, courtesy of E. Foxe Harrell Jewelers; BC, Maranda Blackwelder collection)

Costume jewelry, silver, brass, enamel, marcasites and paste, c. 1915-1935:
L, Pendant Necklace, c. 1920, pendant i the shape of a draped handkerchief, a prong-set triangular black onyx plaque in the center, borders pavé-set with marcasit surmounted by rigid sq ster links in an open V-shape joined to four pierced navette-shaped links with marcasite cente flanking two sq links set with sq onyx plaques and marcasites, continuing to a g and floral ster link chain, spring ring clasp 16-1/2″ tl, pendant rev mkd "STERLING," 7 w x 2-1/4″ tl, **$350**
TC, Brooch/Pin, c. 1935, cut-corner keystone-shaped brass plaque, beveled borders enclosing two raised die-stamped stylized Greek figures with red and blue p enamel drapery on black enameled groun rev imp "E. Bouillot, PARIS MADE IN FRANCE tubular C-catch, 2″ w x 2-1/8″, **$300**
BC, Necklace, c. 1925-30, enamel on brass, curved rect linked plaques, each wi opposed triangle design in dk green, flank ing a central circ plaque with stepped geo design in red and green, on lt green grour approx 16″ tl, 1″ top to bottom at center, **$325**
R, Suite: Pendent Earrings, Brooch/Pin, and Pendant, c. 1925-30, brooch a truncated lozenge shape with lg sq faceted purple glass center, rows of four red glass baguettes at terminals, pierced ster plaque set throughout with marcasites, earrings and pendant with cut-corner rect faceted purple glass in similarly decorated conformir mounts tapering to trefoil surmounts and bail, pendant and brooch mkd "STERLING GERMANY," earrings unmkd, post backs (probably later-added), brooch 2″ w x 1″, earrings 3/8″ w x 2″ tl, pendant 7/8″ w x 2-1/2″ tl (added chain), suite, **$600**
B, Suite: Dog Collar Necklace and Link Bracelet, c. 1915-20, heavy textured sq silver links, each with a circ-cut colorless paste center, four circ-cut blue glass stones in corners, both pieces mkd "830," v-spring and box clasps, safety chains, necklace 12-1/2″ tl x 5/8″, bracelet 6-3/4″ l, suite, **$1,000**
(L, author's collection; TC, BC, B, Kirsten Olson collection; R, P. Tonge and D. Usher collection)

Costume Jewelry, Czechoslovakian glass, c. 1925-35:
L, Bead Sautoir, c. 1925, two two-sided molded mottled green glass Billiken motifs and two four-sided rect beads with Egyptian figures on brickwork and hieroglyphic ground, hand-knotted on a strand of sm irregular round faceted mottled green glass beads joined to an oval plaque with molded relief Asian figure and a Billiken motif drop, 30″ tl, plaque 1-1/8″ w x 1-3/8″, 4″ top to bottom of drop, **$200**
CL, Bead Sautoir, c. 1925, Egyptian Revival, two-sided molded yellow glass scarab beads with cobalt blue rondelle spacers suspending a rounded triangular cobalt blue plaque pendant with molded relief design of an Egyptian falcon god, painted green accented details, 26″ tl, pendant 1-1/8″ x 1-1/8″, **$175**
TR, Drop Earrings, c. 1925, Egyptian Revival, two-sided molded cobalt blue glass pear-shaped plaques with painted green-accented relief design of an Egyptian goddess, later-added shepherd's hook earwires, 1″ w x 1-3/4″, pr, **$50**
TCR, Pendant, c. 1925, Egyptian Revival, triangular molded two-sided plaque with a central relief figure of a pharaoh flanked by hieroglyphics and brick-pattern design, red glass with painted green accented details, ym pendant bail, 1-1/2″ w x 2-1/4″, **$50**
BCR, Dress Clip, c. 1930, Egyptian Revival, molded in the shape of a sphinx, green glass with painted orange accented details, set in a flat-backed gp bezel, engr flat-backed hinged clip on rev, 1-1/4″ w x 1-3/4″, **$65**
BR, Pendant, c. 1925, Egyptian Revival, two-sided, molded in the shape of a sarcophagus, red glass with painted green accented details, 5/8″ w x 1-3/4″, **$30**
B, Buckle, c. 1935, two-piece stamped pierced sp "pot" metal, fancy scrollwork design with braided design border, set with two lg navette-shaped and two circ faux lapis glass cabs, eight lg mottled green circ glass cabs, and four sm yellow, twelve red glass cabs, two center hooks and eyes on rev imp "CHECHOSLOV," #230, bars for belt attachment, 4″ w x 3-1/4″, **$100**
R, Bead Sautoir, c. 1925, Egyptian Revival, two Assyrian figures in two-sided molded relief, cobalt blue with painted green accented details, hand-knotted with green thread on a strand of sm round cobalt beads joined to an octagonal one-sided molded relief plaque of a pharaoh's head, rev mkd "Registered," continuing to a short strand of sm beads terminating in a molded two-sided relief pendant of an Assyrian head, 35-3/4″ tl, pendant 7/8″ w x 1-5/8″, **$225**
(Author's collection)

Novelty jewelry, c. 1935-45:
Top row, "Victims of Fashion" brooches/pins:
L, Two painted ceramic faces, one with Lucite hat and fur trim, the other with woven straw hat, 3-1/2″ w, pr, **$132 (A)**
C, Two painted ceramic faces, one with a leather hat, the other with fur hat and scarf, 3-1/2″ w, pr, **$99 (A)**
R, Two painted ceramic faces, one a Swiss girl with embroidered hat and bow, the other with felt turban and brass necklace, 3-1/2″ w, pr, **$22 (A)**
Center row, carved and painted wood brooches/pins:
L, American Indian profile with Bakelite pipe, and cowboy on bucking bronco, 4″ h, pr, **$275 (A)**
C, A pair of birds on a branch, and a Mexican playing violin with hinged arm, 4″ h, pr, **$187 (A)**
R, Head of a sailor smoking a cigarette, with leather hat, and googly-eyed and jointed soldier, 5″ h, **$330 (A)**
Bottom row, Bakelite and wood brooches/pins:
L, Wood hand with red Bakelite ball and brass jacks, 4-1/2″ w, **$209 (A)**
LC, Bakelite hand, butterscotch-colored with brass bracelet and red ptd fingernails, 4″ w, **$1,100 (A)**
RC, Black Bakelite hand holding black Bakelite cherries on vinyl-coated string stems, 3″ w, **$403 (A)**
R, Two dogs, one a carved wood cocker spaniel's head, the other a wood bulldog with metal chain collar and red plastic heart, white plastic laminated on legs, pr, **$143 (A)**
(Photo courtesy of Dan Ripley/Treadway/Toomey Galleries, 2/15/98)

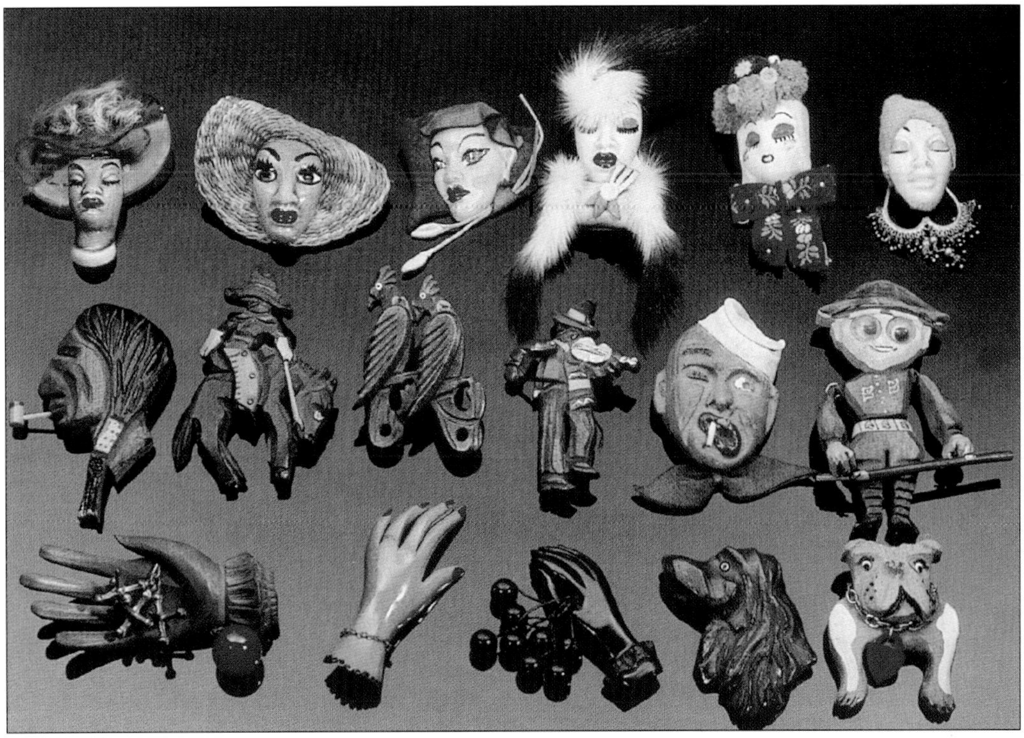

Bakelite Brooches/Pins, c. 1935-45:
Top Row:
L, Butterscotch-colored Bakelite cruise ship suspending two wood and Bakelite suitcase charms, ptd details, 3″ w, **$2,200 (A)**
CL, Depicting a school girl reading her "ABC" book, resin-coated ivory-colored Bakelite, black yarn ribbon-tied hair, 4″ w, **$4,950 (A)**
CR, Depicting a serenading frog playing a stringed instrument, red Bakelite with pivoting "arm," ptd details, 2-1/2″ x 3″, **$2,420 (A)**
R, Depicting a mother and baby penguin on an iceberg, baby pivots on metal spring, ptd details, 3″ h, **$4,675 (A)**
Center row:
L, "School Days" motifs, a ruler suspending a globe, pen, wooden slate, and book charms from a celluloid chain, ptd details, 4″ w, **$3,575 (A)**
CL, Red resin-coated butterscotch-colored Bakelite caricature of a bear with pivoting arm holding a sword, ptd details, 3″ h, **$2,530 (A)**
CR, "Moon over Miami," carved butterscotch-colored Bakelite crescent "man in the moon" with carved palm tree, 3″ w, **$4,950 (A)**
R, Marbled green cat, back view with pivoting tail, ptd red bow, 4″ h, **$6,050 (A)**
Bottom row:
L, Marbled green dagger with carved and gilt details, brass bands, 4″ w, **$187 (A)**
C, Christmas motifs, a candy cane suspending snowman and teddy bear charms, ptd details, designed by Martha Sleeper, 3″ w, **$1,430 (A)**
R, Western motifs, rust resin-coated butterscotch-colored Bakelite six-gun with hat and lasso charms, 3″ w, **$264 (A)**
(Photo courtesy of Dan Ripley/Treadway/Toomey Galleries, 2/15/98)

American Studio Artists, California, c. 1945-1955:
Top row:
L, Brooch/Pin, 1947, a single piece of hammered brass wire forming undulating loops and pinstem, strung with a red Lucite bead with one facet, sgd "Claire 47," for Claire Falkenstein, Venice, CA, 5″ x 4-1/2″, **$950**
CL, Brooch/Pin, 1946, a circ walnut plaque with a squared extension, inlaid with a sq malachite plaque and two vertical sterling wires, sgd "46 D PARK" for David Park, California painter, 3″ w x 2-1/2″, **$750**

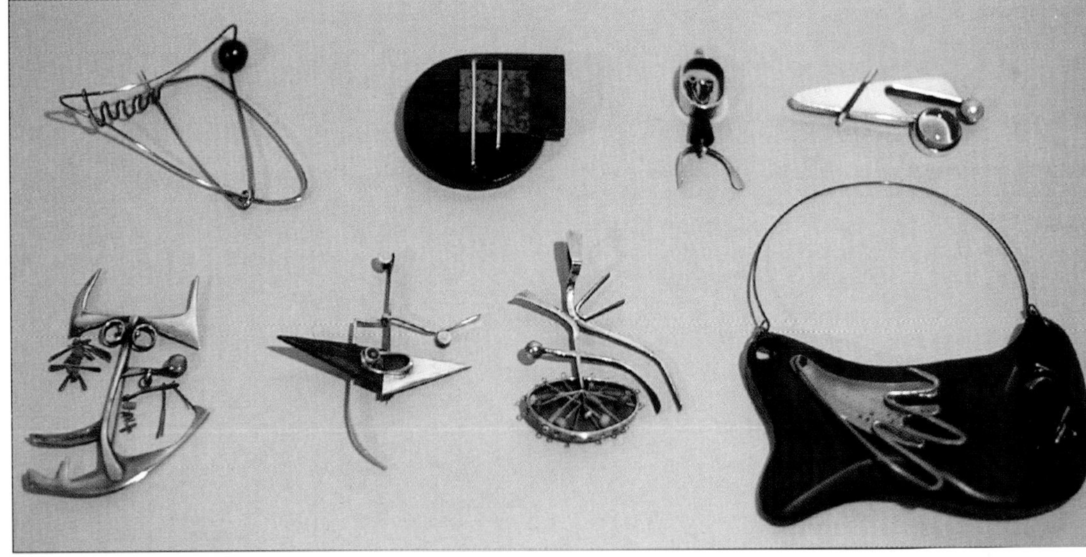

CR, Pendant, c. 1952, a stylized human figure of forged sterling, walnut, brass and gold, by sculptor/jeweler Keith Monroe, unsgd, 1-1/2″ w x 2-1/2″, **$250**
R, Brooch/Pin, c. 1950, abstract rounded triangular ster plaque with cutout section, circ rock crystal cab and baroque pearl bezel-set at one end, sgd "de patta" with maker's mk for Margaret De Patta, San Francisco, 4" w x 2", **$1,500**
Bottom row:
L, Pendant/Brooch, 1953, stylized "cat mobile" of cast and etched sterling and coral beads, sgd "Coleman 53" (script), 4″ x 4″, **$450**
CL, Brooch/Pin, c. 1950, abstract design with triangles of ster and wood, copper and ster wire, brass disks, sgd "MACCHIARINI" for Peter Macchiarini, San Francisco, 3-1/4″ w x 4-1/2″, **$950**
CR, Pendant/Brooch, 1956, abstract design of hammered ster wire and disk with coral, shell, and steel wire, sgd "S-P GEE" for Sammy Gee, San Francisco, 3" w x 4", **$850**
R, Neckpiece, c. 1945, rounded, lobed and shaped carved mahogany plaque surmounted by punched and scored brass sheet, brass wire and black glass, suspended from a brass wire neckring, by Claire Falkenstein, unsgd, 7-1/2″ w x 6-1/2″, **$1,200**
(Photo courtesy of the Modern i Gallery, San Anselmo, CA, Steven Cabella collection)

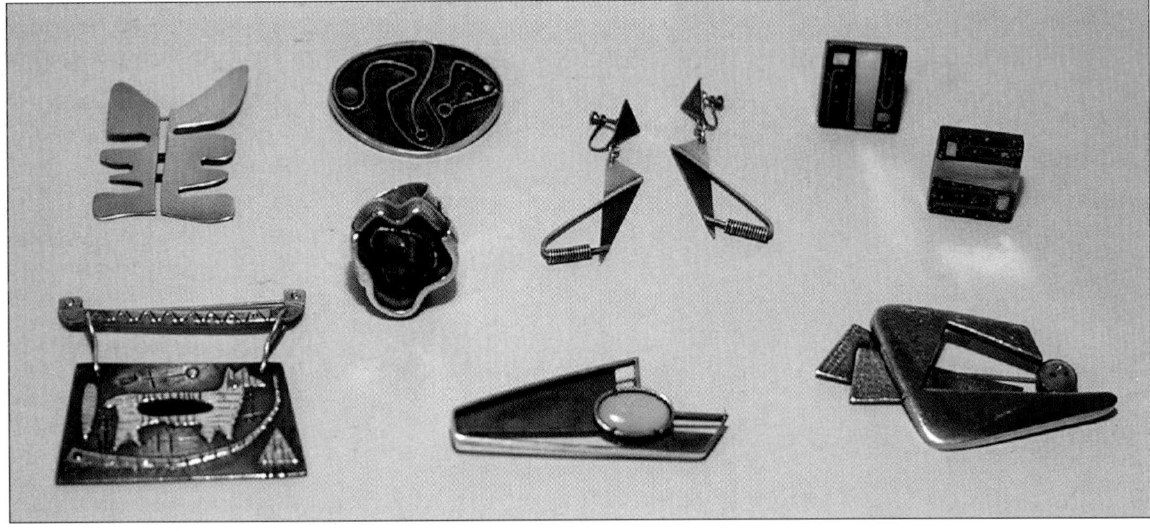

American Studio Artists, c. 1945-1960:
TL, Brooch/Pin, c. 1947, cutout ster plaque, abstract design, unsgd, by Robert Howard, San Francisco sculptor/painter, 2-1/2″ x 2-1/4″, **$350**
TC, Brooch/Pin, 1960, oxidized ster oval disk with appl ster wire and brass rings, sgd "MACCHIARINI 1960" for Peter Macchiarini, 2-1/4″ x 2″, **$950**
TR, Cuff Links, 1953, wood squares inlaid with ster quadrangles and plastic resin lines and dots, sgd "CAVAGNARO" for Milton Cavagnaro, California, 1″ sq, pr, **$200**
CL, Ring, c. 1950, biomorphic freeform design, silver and copper undulating outline enclosing a bezel-set irregular piece of California jadeite, mounted on a wide shank imp with maker's mark for Sam Kramer, New York, NY, 1-1/2″ x 1-1/2″, **$1,500**
CR, Pendent Earrings, c. 1950, partially oxidized ster triangular plaques and wire suspended from oxidized triangular surmounts, screwbacks, sgd "ALLISON" for Vera Allison, Mill Valley, CA, 1″ x 2″, **$275**
BL, Brooch/Pin, 1955, rect copper plaque with engr designs, appl ster cutouts, a stylized animal with enameled accents, suspended by ster wire from a stylized canoe-shaped and decorated ster bar with pin assembly on rev, sgd "H.R. Schleeter 55" (script) for Herbert Schleeter, Arizona and New Mexico, 2-1/4″ w x 2-3/4″, **$550**
BC, Brooch/Pin, 1953, cutout and oxidized angular ster plaque bezel-set off-center with an oval turquoise cab, mkd with conjoined "JN" for Jack Nutting, San Francisco, 3″ w x 1-1/2″, **$750**
BR, Brooch/Pin, 1945, textured ster plaques, a lg rounded-edge angular cutout surmounting two smaller overlapping triangles, a bezel-set circ jade cab mounted at the end of a wire at open end of top plaque, sgd "de patta" for Margaret De Patta, 3-1/4″ x 1-3/4″, **$1,100**
(Photo courtesy of the Modern i Gallery, Steven Cabella collection)

An assortment of costume jewelry by Trifari, c. 1935-1960:
TL, 1, Earclips, c. 1950, each with a lg oval green glass cab center, gp wm S-scroll with sm red r.s. accents, clip-backs mkd "TRIFARI," 3/4″ x 1″, **$95**
TL, 2, Brooch/Pin, gp wm, glass, rhinestones, c. 1955, crown set with faux-moonstone and red glass cabs, and sm circ red, blue, and green r.s. accents, pave-set sm circ colorless r.s. sections, mkd "TRIFARI" (crown mk), "Des Pat 137542" (1944), 1-7/8″ w x 2″, **$195**
TR, Brooch/Pin, rhinestones, glass, enamel, rh pl wm, c. 1935-40, lyre with lg red and blue oval cabs, red and blue ptd enamel, pavé-set with sm circ colorless r.s., mkd "TRIFARI," 1-1/3″ w x 2″, **$195**
CL, Brooch/Pin, glass, rhinestones, gp wm, c. 1955, crown set with faux-moonstone and red glass cabs, and sm circ red and green r.s. accents, blue baguette-cut r.s., and pavé-set sm circ colorless r.s. sections, mkd "TRIFARI" (crown mk), "Des Pat 137542" (1944), 1-1/3″ w x 1-3/8″, **$145**
C, Necklace, glass, rhinestones, gp wm, c. 1940, central gp and pavé-set r.s. hooked and foliated motif, suspending *négligée* two articulated drops set with blue pear-shaped r.s., two lg molded melon pattern red glass oval cabs surmounting smaller circ blue glass cabs, terminating in sm colorless r.s-set *pampilles* (inverted teardrops), continuing to a chain of polished gp ropetwist links, mkd "TRIFARI" (crown mk), "Pat Pend," 3-1/4″ w (at center), 15″ tl, **$425**
BL, Brooches/Pins, gp wm, glass, enamel, faux pearls, c. 1960, pair of crowns with red, green, and blue glass cabs and enamel, faux pearl accents, brushed finish, mkd "© TRIFARI," orig tags, 1″ w x 7/8″, each, **$85**
BR, Suite: Clip and Earrings, sterling vermeil, glass, rhinestones, c. 1945, clip an open scrolled heart shape surmounted by a crown, tapered rod at the base, earrings cornucopia-shaped, set with red glass cabs, green marquise-shaped r.s., blue emerald-cut r.s. and pavé-set sm colorless r.s. accents, double-pronged hinged clip, clipback earrings, mkd "TRIFARI" (crown mk) "STERLING" clip 1-3/8″ w x 3-1/4″, earrings 1″ w, suite, **$325**
(Photo courtesy of Morning Glory Antiques, Albuquerque, NM)

Costume Jewelry, Brooches/Pins and Clips, American Manufacturers, c. 1935-45:
Top row, from left: Suite: Clip and Earrings, bicolor gp wm, clip a floral/foliate cascading spray set throughout with lg aqua and pink faceted glass and colorless r.s., matching button-style clip earrings, each with two oval aqua stones flanking a pavé r.s.-set V shape, mkd "TRIFARI," clip 2″ w x 3″, suite **$550 (A)**
Brooch/Pin, sterling vermeil, exotic bird with swirled red ptd enamel and pavé colorless r.s. plumage, pavé colorless r.s. head mounted *en tremblant*, ptd enamel beak, red r.s. eye, mkd "Coro Craft," 3-1/2″ w, **$1,100 (A) Clip,** depicting a jester, an animated marionette with jointed arms and legs which move when chain is pulled, rh pl wm, pink and turq ptd enamel costume with colorless r.s. stripes and ruffles, red ptd enamel pompons, black shoes, circ opalescent glass cab face, maker's mk for Boucher, 3″ h, **$1,760 (A) Clip,** rh pl wm, grape cluster of faux pearls, leaves ptd green enamel on one half, pavé colorless r.s. on the other, mkd "TRIFARI," 2″ x 3″, **$358 (A) Brooch/Pin,** sterling vermeil, in the shape of a parrot, colorless r.s. crest and tail, lg faceted lt blue glass body, faceted oval lt blue stones on perch terminals, red glass cab eye, ptd enamel details, mkd "Coro," 2-1/2″ h, **$99 (A)**
Center row, from left: Brooch/Pin, sterling vermeil, in the shape of a fly, pear-shaped aqua faceted glass body, pavé colorless r.s. center, red r.s. eyes, mkd "Réja," 1″ w x 1-1/2″, **$275 (A) Brooch/Pin,** rh pl wm, in the shape of a gourd, pearlized ptd enamel leaves, wm borders and tendrils, pavé r.s. striping on gourd, maker's mk for Boucher, 3", **$935 (A) Brooch/Pin,** rh pl wm, red and green ptd enamel chili peppers and leaves with colorless r.s. tips, maker's mk for Boucher, 3", **$880 (A) Brooch/Pin,** rh pl wm, in the shape of a praying mantis, pavé colorless r.s. throughout, black ptd enamel eyes, maker's mk for Boucher, 4″ w, **$825 (A) Brooch/Pin,** rh pl and gp wm, depicting a squirrel in a tree, pavé colorless r.s. squirrel with a line of green baguette r.s. on tail, red eye, gp tree branch, mkd "TRIFARI," 2″ h, **$198 (A)**
Bottom row, from left: Brooch/Pin, sterling vermeil, in the shape of a fly with lg purple faceted glass body, colorless r.s. eyes, ptd enamel wings, mkd "Coro," 2-1/2″ w, **$165 (A) Clip,** rh pl wm, a lily with blue ptd enamel petals, yellow stamen, with green ptd enamel leaves, pavé colorless r.s. accents, mkd "TRIFARI,"2-3/4″, **$121 (A) Brooch/Pin,** rh pl wm, a lily with yellow and red pearlized ptd enamel petals, grn ptd enamel leaves, colorless r.s. accents, maker's mk for Boucher, 3-1/4″, **$231 (A) Clip,** rh pl wm, a flower basket, ptd yellow enamel with multicolored ptd enamel flowers, colorless r.s. accents, mkd "Trifari," 1-1/4″ w, **$154 (A)** (Photo courtesy of Dan Ripley/Treadway/Toomey Galleries, 2/15/98)

Native American:
T, Cuff Bracelet, Navajo, c. 1965-70, bow-shape with geo border design of crushed turq inlay and stampwork, recessed oxidized cente bezel-set with a tapered coral baton flanked by two irregular oval turq cabs, rev imp "HAND MADE, B. NEZ," 1-3/4" w, 2-1/2" inside dia, **$200**
TL, Cuff Bracelet, Fred Harvey style, central circ turq cab flanked by horseshoe shapes surmounting a scallop-edged plaque with stampwork, sun, feather and arrow symbols continuing around sides, 1/2" w, 2-1/4" inside dia,**$85**
C, Cuff Bracelet, Hopi, c. 1960, overlay design of dancing figures, textured and oxidized inside layer, rev imp with maker's mark (snow cloud symbol) for Bernard Dawahoya (working since 1956), 1-1/2" w, 2-1/2" inside dia, **$225** (Patrick Kapty collection)
TR, Cuff Bracelet, Zuni, c. 1950, a row of sawtooth bezel-set sm oval turq cabs bordered by raised silver beads, stamped terminals, 3/8" w, 2-3/8" inside dia, **$125**
B, Squash Blossom Necklace, Zuni, c. 1940, "box bow" style, twenty-two blossoms, each bezel-set with an oval turq cab surmounting a stamped bow-shaped silver plaque, strung on double rows of silver beads, suspending a tufa-cast naja with fleur-de-lis center bezel-set with an oval turq cab, 26-1/4" tl, naja 2" dia, **$750**
(P. Tonge and D. Usher collection)

Native American Cuff Bracelet:
Sterling, turquoise, red coral, jet, MOP, abalone, c.1968, Hopi/Mission, tufa cast, two horizontal channels inlaid with varying rect widths of turq, coral, jet, MOP, and abalone, flanking central design, a horizontal row of paired opposed crescents on oxidized textured ground, maker's mk for Preston Monongye (Peyote Rain Bird incorporating initial P) on raised octagonal plaque on rev, 1-1/2" w, 2-1/4" inside dia, **$1,800**.
(Shari and Jeff Miller collection).

Mexican, Taxco School, c. 1940-1950:
Г, **Link Bracelet,** each hinged link a stamped raised silver stylized seated female figure with a sm turq cab "earring," upraised hands, holding an ear of corn, v-spring and box clasp imp with unknown maker's mk and "MEXICO SILVER" 1-3/8″ w x 7″ **$250**
CL, **Brooch/Pin,** floral spray, four blossoms on wire stems with pear-shaped amethyst cab centers, imp with conjoined ìHAî in a circ reserve for Héctor Aguilar, "TAXCO 940," designed by Valentín Vidaurreta, 3-1/2″ w x 2-1/2″, **$750**
C, **Brooch/Pin,** circ disk, oxidized center with appl wirework quatrefoil and raised beads, a carved navette-shaped amethyst cab bezel-set in center, polished frame, rounded edge, rev imp "MEXICO STERLING BECK-MANN" for Carmen Beckmann, C-catch with hinged wire safety, 1-1/2″ dia, **$175** (Author's collection)
CR, **Brooch/Pin,** raised and incised cornucopia with floral spray, three pear-shaped amethyst cabs on ster wire stems, rev imp "STERLING MADE IN MEXICO" #2002, 2″ x 3-1/8″, **$200**
BC, **Earrings,** projecting horn-shaped amethyst cabs enclosed by an incised ster volute and bead-tipped wire, screwbacks, one imp with 1940-45 maker's mk for William Spratling, the other with "SPRATLING SILVER," 7/8″ w x 1-3/8″, pr, **$400**

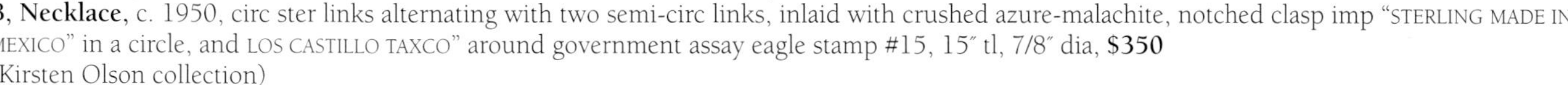

B, **Necklace,** c. 1950, circ ster links alternating with two semi-circ links, inlaid with crushed azure-malachite, notched clasp imp "STERLING MADE IN MEXICO" in a circle, and LOS CASTILLO TAXCO" around government assay eagle stamp #15, 15″ tl, 7/8″ dia, **$350**
(Kirsten Olson collection)

Mexican, Taxco School, c. 1930-60:
TL, **Drop Earrings,** c. 1955, rounded domed triangular drops partially inlaid with green turquoise, suspended from hemi-spherical surmounts, rev imp "STERLING 925, LOPEZ TAXCO, HECHO EN MEXICO," for Gerardo López, government assay eagle #26, screwbacks, 3/4″ w x 1-1/2″ tl, pr, **$50**
TC, **Pendant/Brooch,** c. 1955, biomorphic freeform design set with an obsidian, green turq matrix, and Mexican fire opal cab enveloped by undulating ster bezels, flanking by radiating wires, detachable freeform bail for wear as a brooch, rev imp "STERLING MEXICO" "Salvador" (script) for Salvador Terán, #124, 1-5/8″ w x 2-3/4″, **$650**
TR, **Suite: Pendant and Pendent Earrings,** c. 1950, pendant an elongated rounded triangular ster plaque with triangular and circ cutouts, brass and crushed stone inlay and overlay on a cut-to-shape layer of obsidian backed with a sterling plaque imp "STERLING HECHO EN MEXICO D.F. 0.925," sgd "popowski," government assay eagle #33, triangular bail, 1-3/8″ w x 4″ tl, matching pendent earrings, triangular surmounts, screwbacks, same marks, 5/8″ w x 2-1/4″ tl, suite, **$300**
C, **Link Bracelet,** c. 1940-45, each link a carved hematite stylized frog mounted on a pronged ster plaque, one plaque imp "STERLING SILVER TAXCO," another with an appl disk imp with 1940-45 maker's mk for William Spratling, v-spring and box clasp, 3/4″ w x 7-1/4″, **$4,000**
BC, **Pendant,** c. 1960, a stylized sun face with appl ster features over azure-malachite crushed stone inlay encircled by undulating ster rays, rev imp with maker's mk for Miguel Melendez (script M enclosed in a circle), "TAXCO," "STERLING HECHO EN MEXICO" in a circle, government assay eagle #3, open hook bail, 3-5/8″ w x 3-3/8″, **$150**
B, **Necklace,** c. 1930, rounded triangular obsidian, shaped and cut as a stylized face, bezel-set, flanked by six slightly convex grad shaped silver plaques joined with reeded links, continuing to an open rect and reeded link chain, hook closure, rev imp "MADE IN MEXICO SILVER," maker's mk for Frederick Davis (conjoined FD), chip on rev of obsidian, 18″ tl, 1-1/4″ top to bottom at center, **$1,200**
(Author's collection)

Danish silver brooches/pins, skønvirke, c. 1900-1935
TL, c. 1905, pierced and raised scrolled plaque with a central bezel-set oval moonstone, suspending a similarly designed lobed triangular drop set with a sm circ moonstone, flanked by scrolled wires, each suspending an oval moonstone in a bead-tipped bezel, flat backing imp "830S (in two places), WmF," possibly for William Fuglede, 1-3/4" w x 2-1/2" tl, **$350**
TR, c. 1900, a rect chalcedony plaque bezel-set in the center of an open silver bow shape with C- and S-scrolls at the base suspending a chain swag and four drops bezel-set with carnelian and tourmaline cabs, rev imp with maker's mk for Mogens Ballin (conjoined MB), 1-5/8" w x 1-3/8" tl, **$1,800**
BL, c. 1910, a raised and incised stylized flowerhead, lobed lozenge shape, center bezel-set with an oval amber cab encircled by a beaded frame, rev imp "826 S," maker's mk for C. M. Cohr (C M [reverse] C), 1-3/8" w x 1-3/4", **$100**
BR, c. 1935, circ stamped relief depicting a bird eating berries suspended from a foliate branch, rev imp with 1933-44 maker's mk for Georg Jensen, "STERLING DENMARK," #53, 2-1/4" dia, **$425**
(Photo courtesy of Gail Roeshman Selig)

Scandinavian, c. 1955-1975:
TL, Brooch/Pin, c. 1955, sterling vermeil in the shape of a hummingbird in flight, in shades of aqua, yellow, black and white basse taille enamel, rev imp "VB" probably for Volmer Bahner, "STERLING DENMARK" 1-1/2" x 1-1/2", **$50**
TR, Ring, date letter for 1969, cast freeform oblong, textured and ridged surface with a raised knob in one corner, mounted on a wide shank, designed by Björn Weckström, inside imp with Finnish hmks, date letter Q7, maker's mk for Lapponia, "STERLING FINLAND," 7/8" w x 1-1/4", approx size 5, **$200**
CL, Suite: Hinged Bangle and Ring, date letters for 1967, each with a decorative notched and punched bezel set with high-domed cabs, an amethyst in the ring mounted on a narrow shank, a labradorite in bangle mounted on open rect hinged front spring-hook closure, both imp with Finnish hmks, "813H" for 830 silver, date letter O7, designer's initials "MV," ring 1/2" x 3/4", approx size 5-1/2, bangle 1/2" w, 2-1/2" inside dia, suite, **$150**
C, Pendant, sterling, c. 1965, textured jagged edge sunburst design with polished tapered bars radiating from open center, suspended from tapered textured bail, appl plaque on rev mkd "DANMARK" (Danish spelling of Denmark), designer's initials "KVA," maker's mk for A. Michelsen (AM surmounted by crown inside triangle), "925S," 2-3/8" w x 2-1/2" tl, **$100**
CR, Pendant, c. 1960, a rose quartz sphere upheld in a tapered four-prong ster mount inside an open circ frame with tapered sides, bead terminals top and bottom, suspended from three lg circ jump rings, one imp with maker's mk for Kupitaan Kulta (anvil), Finland, "925S," 1-1/8" w x 1-3/4" tl, **$50**
BL, Ring, c, 1960, 14k yg, side-by-side triangles, angled apexes, tapering to continuous shank, imp "HANDMADE DENMARK, 585," maker's and designer's initials "JA" and "CFH," possibly for Christian Frederik Heise, 3/4" x 3/8", approx size 5, **$225**
BC, Necklace, sterling, date letter for 1976, shaped tapered triangular segmented front section, center set with a triangular spectrolite plaque, joined with jump rings to a sq wire neck ring, side hook closure, rev imp with maker's mk for Kaunis Koru (adorsed k's), Finnish hmks, "925," date letter Y7, designer's conjoined initials HN, approx 15" tl, 1" top to bottom at center, **$200**
BR, Brooch/Pendant, c. 1960-70, stamped sterling vermeil cartoon-like bumblebee, *basse-taille* enameled in shades of yellow and orange, red eye, rev mkd "DAVID-ANDERSEN, NORWAY STERLING 925s," designer's initial "W" in a circle, 2" w x 1-3/4", **$65**
B, Link Bracelet, c. 1960, sterling, rounded lozenge-shaped links outlined in matte black enamel, hook closure, mkd "WARMIND STERLING DENMARK," for Poul Warmind, #39, 1-1/8" w x 7-1/2" tl, **$175**
(Author's collection)

Part IV

SPECIAL COLLECTIBLE JEWELRY

INTRODUCTION

Certain types of jewelry do not fall neatly into period or style categories. While space does not permit exploring all of these special types of jewelry, the references below direct readers to other categories that could not be included here, e.g., folk and ethnic jewelry, and beads.

The three special collectibles categories in this section, Native American, Mexican, and Scandinavian, are based on country of origin. While jewelry-making traditions date back to earlier periods in all three areas, availability and collector interest are concentrated in the twentieth century. Most examples are from the 1920s or later. It is interesting to note that the three have certain features in common: the metal most often used is silver, the work is most often done by hand, and there was a certain amount of cross-cultural exchange of ideas and techniques between them. During the 1940s and 1950s, all three enjoyed a period of popularity in the U.S., brought about in part by World War II.

References (for other categories not included in this section): Martha Boyer, *Mongol Jewelry*, Thames and Hudson, 1995; Janet Coles and Robert Budwig, *The Book of Beads*, Simon and Schuster, 1990; Lois Sher Dubin, *The History of Beads, from 30,000 B.C. to the Present*, Harry N. Abrams, 1987; Peter Francis, Jr., *Beads of the World*, Schiffer Publishing, 1994; James J. Kellner, *Siam Sterling Nielloware*, self-published by the author, 1993; Robert O. Kinsey, *Ojime: Magical Jewels of Japan*, Harry N. Abrams, 1991; John Mack, ed., *Ethnic Jewelry*, Harry N. Abrams, 1988; Dona Z. Meilach, *Ethnic Jewelry, Design & Inspiration for Collectors and Craftsmen*, Crown Publishers, 1981 (out of print); Jane Casey Singer, *Gold Jewelry from Tibet and Nepal,* Thames and Hudson, 1996; Susan Stronge, Nima Smith and J.C. Harle, *A Golden Treasury, Jewellery from the Indian Subcontinent* (Victoria and Albert Museum Indian Art Series), Rizzoli, 1988; Oppi Untracht, *Jewelry Concepts and Technology*, Doubleday, 1985, and *Traditional Jewelry of India*, Harry N. Abrams, 1997.

Periodical: *Ornament*, the Art of Personal Adornment, articles on ancient, antique and contemporary beadwork, contemporary art jewelry and fiber arts; P.O. Box 2349, San Marcos, CA 92079; (619) 599-0222, fax (619) 599-0228.

NATIVE AMERICAN JEWELRY

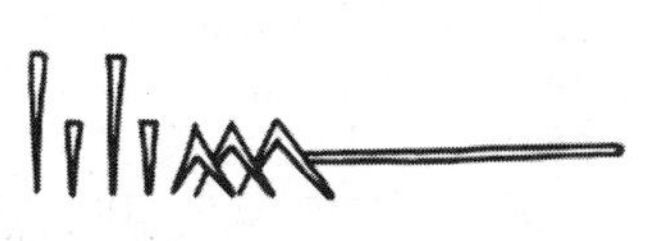

Charles Loloma

STERLING HAND MADE

White Hogan-Allen Kee

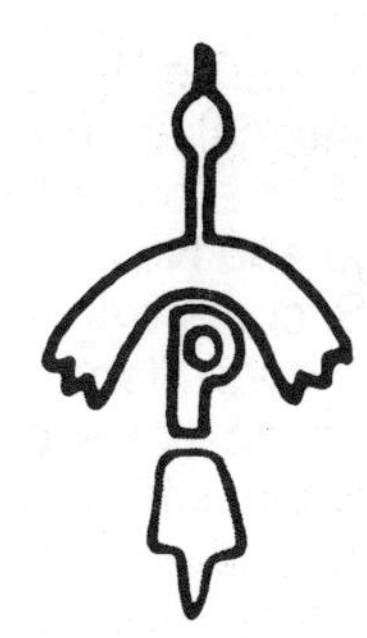

Preston Monongye

History: In the late 1960s and early 1970s, the booming popularity of Southwestern American Indian jewelry was at its peak. The volume of poor quality machine-made knockoffs, imported fakes, and "white man's work" had become so great that potential collector interest soured; most people were afraid to buy for fear a piece was not "authentic."

As a result, over the past twenty-five years, the market for Indian jewelry, both old and new, has changed considerably. Today, there are two kinds of collectors: those who collect only traditional old pieces, preferably dating before World War II, and those who buy the traditional and contemporary work of recognized "name" artists.

The first type of collector makes a distinction between jewelry made for tribal wear and jewelry made for the tourist trade, although old examples of both are considered collectible. The second type is primarily concerned with quality of workmanship and originality of design. The following section concentrates on older, traditional Native American pieces. However, the work of some post-World War II artists is now considered "period," and is certainly collectible.

The pioneers of the "new Indian art"–a phrase coined by one of its practitioners, Preston Monongye–are for the most part no longer living, including

Monongye, Charles Loloma, and Kenneth Begay. The individual styles they developed are considered the "turning point" in Native American art, and it is to them that contemporary Native American artists give credit for inspiration. Consequently, a few examples of these seminal artists' work are included here.

For readers interested in the work of today's Native American artists, Dexter Cirillo's *Southwestern Indian Jewelry* (see references below), which also includes a substantial amount of historical background, is recommended. As there are many caveats to be aware of, and much study required in order to fully understand the differences between old and new, authentic and imitation, readers are also directed to a number of other reliable resources on traditional and old Indian jewelry.

Although other tribes in other parts of the U.S. made jewelry, the work of the silversmiths and lapidaries of the Southwest–the Navajo, and the Santo Domingo, Zuni, and Hopi Pueblo tribes–is the best known and most sought-after. What follows here is a basic introductory summary of the history, materials, techniques, and identifiable characteristics of typical traditional jewelry made by the major Southwest Native American tribes.

Many people are surprised to learn that silversmithing is a relatively new development in Native American arts, first practiced by the Navajo during the last quarter of the nineteenth century. However, other jewelry forms and materials, such as beads made from stone or shell, date to prehistoric times. Today, most of the oldest pieces are in museum collections. Ancient jewelry, and silver jewelry made before 1900 (the period 1868-1900 is known as "first phase") rarely comes up for sale, and is usually priced in the five-figure range when it does.

The earliest silverwork was made strictly for tribal use as symbols of status, portable wealth and for ceremonial purposes. During lean times, the Indians would take some of their jewelry to the trading post and pawn it for credit. There are common misconceptions about the term "old pawn," one being that pawn jewelry is somehow more valuable because it has been pawned. In fact, the opposite is true. The Indians would pawn only expendable less-important pieces that they were willing to risk losing. The pawn system is still is use today, but only pieces made before 1900 are correctly called "old" pawn.

The influence of the trader and burgeoning tourism should not be underestimated. Traders mentored many a tribal silversmith and encouraged the development of distinctive styles, providing designs as well as an outlet for the selling of finished goods. In addition to tools, the traders also brought in otherwise unavailable materials.

The building of the railroad (the Atchison, Topeka & Santa Fe, which ran from Chicago to Southern California via Albuquerque, New Mexico, was completed in 1880) led to the appearance of Harvey Houses–restaurants and rest stops constructed along the rail routes during the late nineteenth century. The commercialization of American Indian jewelry began in 1899, when the Fred Harvey Company placed its first order for silver jewelry to be made for the general public and sold in Harvey House "curio shops."

The company provided the silversmiths with sheet silver, machine-drawn wire and precut stones. To appeal to tourists, they required the jewelry to be lighter in weight and decorated with stampings of arrows and other "symbols" that they thought souvenir buyers would associate with American Indian culture. Many of these "symbols" had no actual meaning to the silversmiths themselves. One symbol, however, the swastika, was taken from Navajo sand paintings. Although this ancient sign, representing the sun and infinity, had nothing to do with Nazism, its use was discontinued around 1930. Today, pieces stamped with swastikas are understandably a "tough sell."

Turquoise is a gemstone which has been used since ancient times in Southwest Native American cultures, as the mines are indigenous to the area. Highly prized turquoise is often labeled with the name of the mine from which it came, and turquoise from an identifiable mine raises the value of a piece set with it. Most of these mines are not active today. The cost of extracting the turquoise from some of them has become prohibitive, and others have been exhausted. High-quality turquoise has also been imported from Persia since the turn of the century, and is now coming from China.

Porous and soft low-grade turquoise is often subjected to one of several alterations to enhance its appearance: it can be stabilized with the injection of polymer resin (plastic) to increase hardness, treated with dyes to alter its color, or completely reconstituted and formed into shaped "stones" from turquoise powder and particles mixed with resin. Stabilized turquoise is considered acceptable if identified as such, but its value is not as high as natural turquoise. Other types of treated turquoise, along with synthetics and dyed substitutes such as howlite, are usually found in lesser quality jewelry, imitations and foreign imports of low value.

Other than turquoise, materials used in Native American jewelry, such as coral and shell, have been obtained through traders and imported. Several varieties of shell, brought in from the Gulf of California and the Pacific, have been used since prehistoric times. Coral, called "red gold," was first brought to the Zuni by traders around 1938 and later used by the Santo Domingo and Navajo. Silver was never mined by the tribes. U.S. coins were used until they were prohibited in 1890 (although illegal use since that time is not unheard of). Mexican coins continued to be used until the 1920s. Sterling silver sheet and wire were then purchased from traders.

The Navajo were the first to use turquoise in combination with silver, in the late nineteenth century. However, most of their early work was all silver, with the occasional addition of a stone or two. The Navajo traded with Mexican *plateros* (silversmiths), from whom they learned silversmithing beginning in the 1870s.

In the first phase period, prior to commercialization, the Navajo forged their own ingots from coin silver, which they then hammered into sheets and rods and drew into wire. They preferred making heavy pieces of simple design for tribal wear, and continued to do so after they began using pre-formed sheet silver and machine-drawn wire for commercial tourist production. Therefore, Navajo jewelry from the so-called transitional or second phase period, 1900-1930, is a mixture of first phase style and early tourist pieces.

Certain forms and techniques are associated with Navajo silver jewelry. The "squash blossom" necklace with "naja" pendant is one of the most familiar forms (other tribes also made them). The squash blossom is actually a pomegranate motif taken from Spanish and Mexican clothing ornaments, and the crescent-shaped or penannular naja was a bridle ornament for horses copied from the Spanish, who copied it from a Moorish amulet. Early squash blossom necklaces are heavy and simple with little if any turquoise, and entirely handmade from ingot coin silver. "Squashes" from the '60s and '70s are larger and gaudier, often composed of machine-made elements and elaborately decorated with turquoise.

Concha belts are another early Navajo ornament. Simple circular disks with lozenge-shaped cutout centers, minimally decorated and threaded on leather straps, date from the first phase period. Later conchas are oval with more stamping and other decorative elements, including turquoise. Concha belts were also made by Zuni and Hopi silversmiths.

Some jewelry forms are relative newcomers to the Native American idiom. Brooches did not appear until the 1930s. Bola ties and slides (the correct word is bol*a,* not bol*o*) were "invented" and popularized by an Anglo Arizonan, Vic Cedarstaff, in 1949, although Indian antecedents from the twenties are known but rare. The Bola Tie Society of Phoenix was formed in 1966, and bolas became the official Arizona state neckwear in 1971.

Tufa casting is a Navajo technique used since the first phase period to make najas, "ketohs" (ornamental wrist bowguards), buckles, rings, and bracelets. Sometimes referred to as sand casting, the technique involves carving a pattern for a mold in tufa, a porous rock formed from volcanic ash (more correctly known as "tuff"), then pouring molten metal into the mold. The hardened piece is then shaped, decorated and polished.

Early decoration techniques included "rocker engraving" with a short-bladed chisel, and stamped designs similar to those used by Mexican leather workers, using a hand-held punch. In general, the early pieces had simple decorations; pieces made for tourists were more elaborately stamped and embellished. The Navajo taught silversmithing to other tribes, who copied their designs, so it is often difficult to determine tribal origins of earlier pieces.

The Pueblo tribes, particularly the Santo Domingo, are known for their bead, shell, and mosaic work. The disk-shaped shell beads strung on string known as "heishi" (alternately spelled "heishe"), are a Santo Domingo specialty and a fifteen-hundred-year tradition. The shells are individually cut into squares, drilled, strung, and then rolled by hand or machine to make thin circular disks. The word "heishi" is also erroneously used to refer to a similar type of bead made of turquoise or other stone. The Santo Domingo are also known for their mosaics, patterns of stone, jet, coral and shell applied to a shell, wood, or bone base. During the 1930s and '40s, the Depression and the war forced artisans to use car battery casings and 78 rpm phonograph records for bases and as jet substitutes. Pieces of old plastic toothbrush handles were used as substitutes for coral and turquoise. Depression-era necklaces strung with tubular shell beads interspersed with tabs and suspending thunderbird motif pendants, battery-backed with mosaic overlay, are now collectible. Prices range from $100 to $1,000, depending on quality. The necklace is the most common form of jewelry made by the Santo Domingo, but they also produce pendants, earrings, rings and bracelets.

The ancient tradition of fetish-carving is still carried on by the Santo Domingo and the Zuni. Fetishes are animals and birds carved from stone or shell. Small ones are strung on necklaces, often in combination with shell heishi.

The Zuni are another Pueblo tribe known for their lapidary work, but early Zuni silver jewelry is difficult to distinguish from that of the Navajo. Zuni began establishing their own style of jewelry-making around 1915. They are noted for bezel-setting stones in clusters and patterns, and channel inlay of stone into silver. Numerous small, narrow navette-shaped turquoise slivers set in patterns are called needlepoint; somewhat larger pear-shaped or oval stones are called petit point. Zuni cluster work evolved during the 1920s, petit point and needlepoint were developed in the 1940s. Channel inlay is a technique that the Zuni began using just prior to World War II. All of these techniques were made possible by the introduction of more sophisticated tools and equipment, supplied by traders.

The Hopi were the last tribe to develop their own identifiable style, beginning in the late 1930s. Until that time, the jewelry they made was copied from Navajo and Zuni designs. The all-silver layered technique that the Hopi are now noted for is called overlay, introduced by the founders of the Museum of Northern Arizona in 1938, using Hopi pottery and textile patterns. Abstract and/or figural designs are cut out from a piece of silver, which is then soldered to another piece. The background is oxidized and textured to bring out the design. The earliest Hopi overlay was not signed, but later silversmiths began using marks, either symbols or their names. (In general, pre-World War II Native American jewelry is not signed; since the '60s, many artists have been marking their work.)

World War II was a turning point in the history of Native American jewelry-making. For the first time, Native Americans were drafted into the armed forces and sent overseas. They were exposed to cultures other than their own, and returned with a broader view of the world, cash in their pockets, and an opportunity to further their education through the GI Bill. Like many other American veterans, they attended classes in jewelry making, learning new techniques using modern equipment. They formed guilds that enabled them to market their own goods. For some Native Americans, making jewelry became more than a traditional tribal occupation. They became *artist-jewelers.*

A paragraph in the article "American Expressions" by Lane Coulter, cited below, sums it up nicely:

"A few artists had established fresh directions for jewelry at mid-century. The Navajo metalsmith Kenneth Begay (1913-1977), working out of the White Hogan Shop in Scottsdale, Arizona, in the late 1940s, created strong, simple forms utilizing the Navajo techniques of stamped and chased silver...The best-known modern Native American jeweler, the Hopi artist Charles Loloma (1921-1991) served in the armed forces during World War II and trained as a ceramist in the 1950s on the GI Bill at the School for American Craftsmen in Alfred, New York. He pioneered the use of gold, ivory, lapis lazuli and other materials while teaching at the Institute of American Indian Arts in Santa Fe in the 1960s. He also created new imagery and textures and a distinctive sense of scale in his jewelry designs. Loloma's work was widely published, particularly in the 1970s, influencing a generation of Native American jewelers. A third artist who opened up avenues for today's jewelers was Preston Monongye (1927-1987), who was of California Mission ancestry, but was raised on the Hopi Reservation. His small cast containers and jewelry emphasized line drawings and retained the coarse texture of the tufa stone molds while incorporating beautiful colored stone and shell inlays. The importance of these innovators cannot be overstated. Both Begay and Loloma taught and Monongye was often quoted and his work reproduced in numerous articles. Their efforts at individualizing designs while retaining the 'Indianness' of their work has given other Native jewelers the impetus to experiment further with materials, techniques and forms."

Another artist whose work is sold through The White Hogan Shop (still in business) is Allen Kee (d. 1976). His silver designs are sleek, simple, and polished, appealing to modernists as well as Native American jewelry collectors.

Today, Native American silversmiths' work, both traditional and contemporary, is sought-after for its unique designs and superb quality. The best pieces can be priced in the thousands to ten thousands. Many artists exhibit and sell at the annual Indian Market, a tradition since 1922, held every August in Santa Fe, New Mexico.

References: John Adair, *The Navajo and Pueblo Silversmiths*, University of Oklahoma Press, 1944 (out of print); Theda Bassman, *The Beauty of Hopi Jewelry*, Kiva Publications, 1993; Theda and Michael Bassman, *Zuni Jewelry*, Schiffer Publishing, 1992; Dexter Cirillo, *Southwestern Indian Jewelry*, Abbeville Press, 1992; Kathleen Conroy, *What You Should Know about Authentic Indian Jewelry*, Gro-Pub, 1975 (out of print); Lane Coulter, "American Expressions," *American Craft* magazine, October/November, 1997; Larry Frank and Millard J. Holbrook, *Indian Silver Jewelry of the Southwest, 1868-1930*, Schiffer Publishing, 1990; Lois Essary Jacka, *Navajo Jewelry, A Legacy of Silver and Stone*, Northland Publishing, 1995; Preston Monongye, "The New Indian Jewelry Art of the Southwest," *Arizona Highways*, 1972; J. Ostler et al, *Zuni, A Village of Silversmiths*, Shiwi Publications, 1996; Nancy Schiffer, *Silver Jewelry Designs, Evaluating Quality*, Schiffer Publishing, 1996 (chapter on Native American); Peter Schiffer, *Indian Jewelry on the Market*, Schiffer Publishing, 1996; William A. and Sarah P. Turnbaugh, *Indian Jewelry of the American Southwest*, Schiffer Publishing, 1988; Barton Wright, *Hallmarks of the Southwest*, Schiffer Publishing, 1989; Margaret N. Wright, *Hopi Silver, the History and Hallmarks of Hopi Silversmithing*, fourth ed., Northland Publishing, 1989; exhibition catalogs: Diana Pardue, *The Cutting Edge,* The Heard Museum, 1997; *Native American Jewelry and Metalwork: Cotemporary Expressions*, Institute of American Indian Arts Museum, 1997.

Periodical: *Arizona Highways,* issues with articles on Native American jewelry: July 1971, January 1974, August 1974, March 1975, August 1976, October 1976, April 1979; reprints of articles also in *Turquoise Blue Book and Indian Jewelry Digest*, published by *Arizona Highways*, 1975.

Museums: Museum of Northern Arizona, Flagstaff, AZ; The Heard Museum, Phoenix, AZ; Southwest Museum, Los Angeles, CA; Field Museum of Natural History, Chicago, IL; Wheelwright Museum of the American Indian, Santa Fe, NM; Millicent Rogers Museum, Taos, NM; National Museum of the American Indian, New York, NY; Smithsonian Institution, Washington, D.C.

Auction House: R. G. Munn Native American Art Auctions, PO Box 705, Cloudcroft, NM 88317, (505) 687-3676, (505) 687-3592 FAX.

Reproduction Alert: Low quality imitation Indian jewelry is mass produced in Taiwan and the Philippines. Some skilled Anglo craftspeople copy old techniques and designs well enough to fool the experts. "Old pawn" may be neither old nor pawn (fake pawn tickets can be easily attached to any piece). Treated turquoise and simulants may be difficult to identify. *Caveat emptor*: know your source, and obtain written documentation.

Advisors: Shari and Jeff Miller, Steve Nelson.

Bola Tie

MOP, turq, spiny oyster, jet, silver, leather, c. 1950, Zuni, Rainbow Man motif slide, stone-to-stone inlay in geo patterns of MOP, spiny oyster, jet, and turq, silver mount, on a braided leather thong tie, 1" w x 2-1/4" .... 188 (A)

Silver, turquoise, leather, c. 1940-50, Navajo, slide a three-dimensional kachina-like figure with circ disk spiderweb turq eyes, ropetwist-framed oval spiderweb turq on torso, stampwork decoration, on braided leather thong, sunface motifs stamped on silver disk tips, maker's mk an arrow over a fan, for silversmith Art Lewis, slide 1-1/2" w x 2-3/4" .... 248 (A)

Bracelet

Cuff

Silver, c. 1930-40, Navajo, forged ingot equal width band, oval and lozenge-shaped patterned stampwork, rev imp "U.S. Navajo," 1-1/2" w....................................... 770 (A)

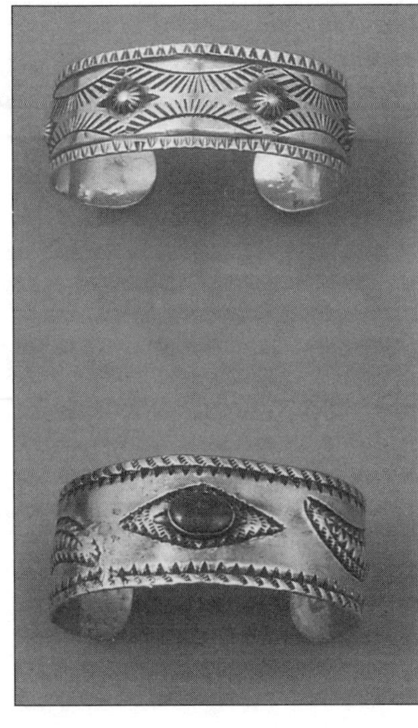

Cuff Bracelets, silver, c. 1925, Navajo, forged ingot:
T, silver band with repoussé "bumps" and stamped geo decoration, 1" w, 2-1/4" inside dia, **$450**.
B, silver band with central bezel-set oval turq cab and stamped lozenge-shaped decoration, flanked by stamped feather design, 1-1/4" w, 2-3/8" inside dia, **$500**. (Courtesy of Mountain Lion Trading Post, Redondo Beach, CA).

Silver, c. 1960-70, wide equal width cuff with central incised circ design flanked by stamp work, mkd "J.Y" in a rect, 1-3/4" w at center, 2-3/8" inside dia 125

Silver, turquoise, Navajo, c. 1930-40, equal width band with elaborate stampwork, rounded ends, central flowerhead motif with circ turq cab center, flanked by curved tapering rows of stamped crescent motifs, central row of chevron pattern, 1-1/4" w .... 523 (A)

Silver, turquoise, Navajo, c. 1960-70, seven bezel-set turq cabs with bead decoration, 7/8" w at center, 2-1/4" inside dia 175

Silver, turquoise, c. 1970, vertical row of three sm oval green turq cabs flanked by vertical rows of ropetwist wire and raised silver beads, three horizontal parallel incised grooves around cuff, 1" w at center, 2-3/8" inside dia 100

Sterling, turquoise, Navajo, c. 1945, heavy ster bar with seven irregularly-shaped bezel-set matrix turq stones and appl ster balls, sgd "CHEE" in a bird shape for Mark Chee, mkd "STERLING HANDMADE," 2-1/8" inside dia, 1/2" w at center.. 150

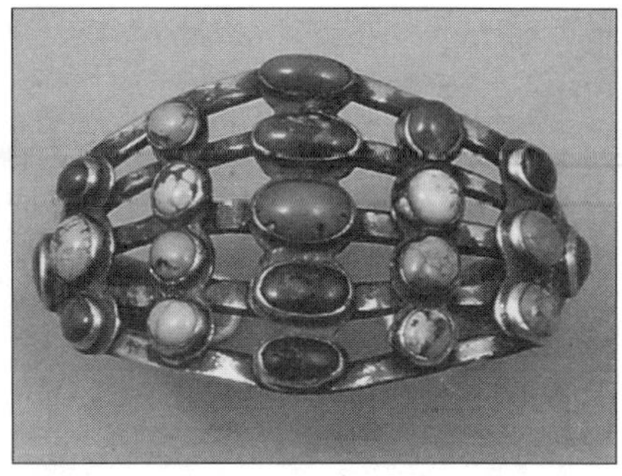

Cuff Bracelet, turquoise, silver, c. 1935, Navajo, six vertical rows of bezel-set oval turq cabs, center row of five, flanked by four, then three, then one, mounted on split silver band of five strips tapering to solid terminals with stamped decoration, 2-1/4" w (at center), 2-1/4" inside dia, **$475**. (Courtesy of Mountain Lion Trading Post, Redondo Beach, CA).

Turquoise, silver, c. 1930-40, Navajo, large rounded oblong natural green turq cab with brown matrix set in a ropetwist bezel with sawtooth stamped frame, mounted on an elaborately stamped tapered four shank bracelet with four stamped rosettes on each shoulder, 2-1/2" w x 3"... 578 (A)

Turquoise, silver, c. 1935, Navajo, split band, three lengths of forged ingot wire tapering to join at back, a row of seven bezel-set grad oval turq cabs with appl silver beads between each cab, 1" w, 2-3/8" inside dia 500

Turquoise, silver, c. 1940, Navajo, a row of seven grad oval turq cabs, two raised beads between each, mounted on ridged wire shanks with ropetwist wire center, scalloped stampwork, 1/2" w.. 275 (A)

Turquoise, silver, c. 1940, Zuni, four rows of thirteen circ turq cabs, silver stampwork terminals, 1" w....... 330 (A)

Turquoise, silver, c. 1940, Zuni, lg cluster setting, blue and green stones, central oval turq cab encircled by sm circ cabs, repoussé crescent motifs alternating with circ cabs, outer row of pear-shaped turq cabs, rows separated by ropetwist wire, shoulders similarly set semi-circles, three-wire shank, 2-3/4" w................................ 220 (A)

Turquoise, silver, c. 1955, Navajo, five grad oval bezel-set turq cabs with wiretwist frames mounted on split band, three silver strips tapering to solid stampwork ends, appl silver beads top and bottom between bezels, 2" w, 2-1/4" inside dia 475

Cuff Bracelet, silver, turquoise, coral, MOP, jet, c. 1935, Zuni, triple band of cabled and beaded wire, central appl moth motif with inlaid turq, coral, MOP, and jet, wiretwist antennae, flanked by appl silver bead grape cluster motifs, 1-1/4" w, 2-1/4" inside dia, **$400**. (Courtesy of Mountain Lion Trading Post, Redondo Beach, CA).

Cuff Bracelet, turquoise, silver, c. 1945, Navajo, split silver band with three clusters of eight oval bezel-set turq cabs forming flowerheads, sm incised appl silver disks in between at top and bottom, 1-1/2" w, 2-3/8" inside dia, **$450**. (Courtesy of Mountain Lion Trading Post, Redondo Beach, CA).

Cuff Bracelet, sterling, c. 1950, "Fred Harvey" style, tapered cuff with appl thunderbird motif flanked by dogs and arrows, stamped decoration, mkd "STERLING," 1" w, 2-1/8" inside dia, **$150**. (Sue James collection).

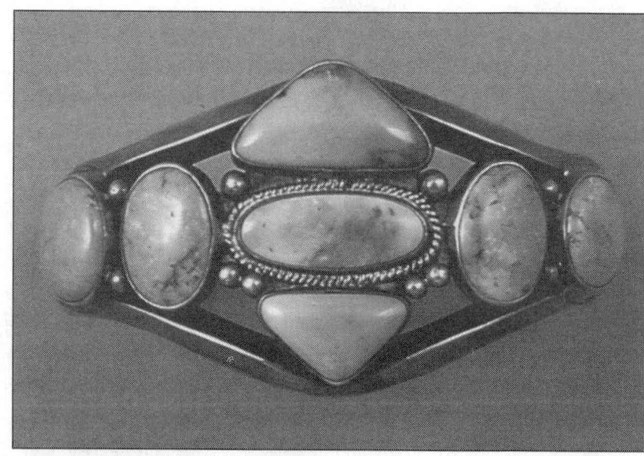

Cuff Bracelet, turquoise, silver, c. 1955, open lozenge-shaped frame enclosing seven bezel-set turq cabs: central elongated oval cab with ropetwist and bead decoration, a triangular cab at top and bottom, flanked by two oval cabs at either side, appl ster bead decoration, 2-1/2" inside dia, 1-1/2" at center, **$225**. (Richard Levey collection).

Cuff Bracelet, turquoise, silver, c. 1960, Navajo, lg central oval turq bezel-set cab with appl wiretwist and bead decoration flanked by a row of appl circ beads, two oval beads, and a lg high-domed appl hollow bead at each side, 2" w, 2-1/4" inside dia, **$200**. (Sue James collection).

Cuff Bracelet, turquoise, sterling, c. 1958, Navajo, lg irregularly-shaped Morenci turq cab bezel-set in a central depression, encircled by radiating incised lines at top of depression, three parallel incised lines from center down sides of cuff, mk for White Hogan, maker's mk "KB" for Kenneth Begay, 1-5/8" w, 2-3/8" inside dia, **$750**. (Jon Bonnell collection).

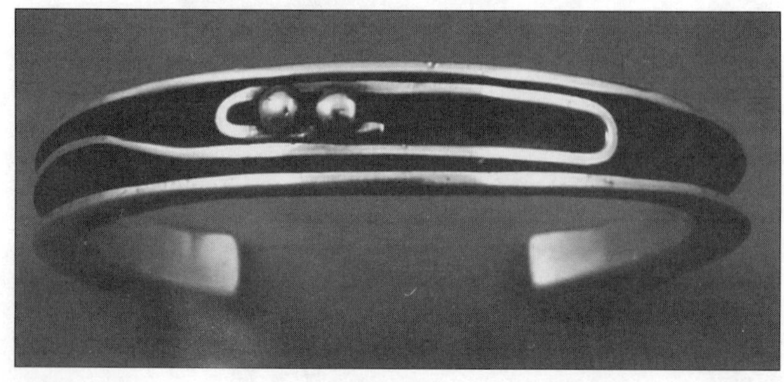

Cuff Bracelet, sterling, c. 1959, Hopi, raised edge ster bar, oxidized ground surmounted by appl looping wire and two raised beads at top, maker's mk for Charles Loloma incised on rev, mkd "STERLING," 1/2" w, 2-7/8" inside dia, **$1,600**. (Shari and Jeff Miller collection).

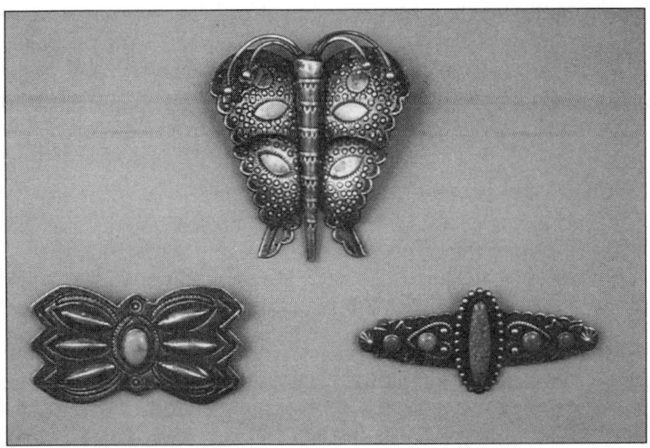

Brooches/Pins, Navajo:

TC, c. 1935, silver, in the shape of a three-dimensional butterfly, central tapered cylinder with stamped decoration surmounted by radiating curv bead-tipped wire antennae, flanked by appl cutout wings with allover stamped decoration, 2-1/2" w x 2-3/4", **$350**.

BL, c. 1925, butterfly-shaped cut and stamped silver plaque with central oval bezel-set turq cab, 2-5/8" w x 1-1/2", **$250**.

BR, c. 1935, Fred Harvey style, tapered horizontal oval plaque with central vertically appl oval plaque with beaded edge centering an elliptical turq cab , flanked by four sm circ turq cabs, appl wire and bead decoration and appl stamped arrows, stars, and hearts, 2-7/8" w x 1-3/8", **$250**.
(Courtesy of Mountain Lion Trading Post, Redondo Beach, CA).

Brooch/Pendant

Jet, silver, c. 1940-50, Zuni knifewing god in all-black jet channel inlay, silver mount, pendant loop, 2" w x 1-1/2" .... 83 (A)

Brooch/Pin

Silver, c. 1930-40, Navajo, Fred Harvey style, thunderbird motif in heavy gauge silver, arrow, rain cloud, bracket and crescent stampwork, 4" w x 1-1/4" .... 165 (A)

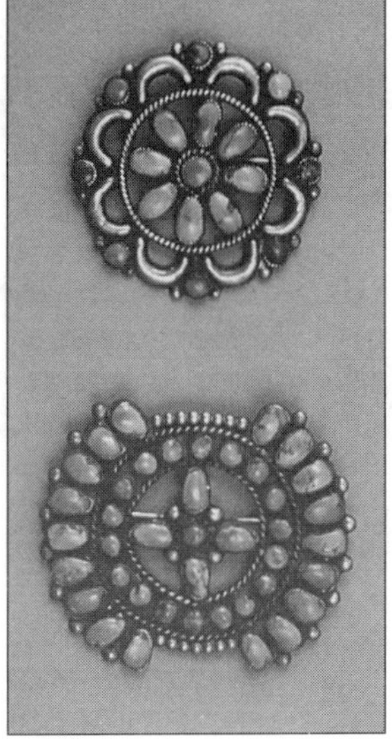

Brooches/Pins, turquoise, silver, c. 1940, Zuni:

T, scalloped open circle, bezel-set circ turq cab encircled by eight oval turq cabs further encircled by twisted silver wire and crescent shapes alternating with circ turq cabs and appl silver beads, 2" dia, **$250**.

B, open circle with central equilateral cross formed by four oval turq cabs alternating with silver beads, sm center turq cab, encircled by circ turq cabs and twisted wire, flanked by fan shapes of oval turq cabs alternating with silver beads, top and bottom center edges bordered with curved rows of silver beads, 2-1/2" w x 2-1/4", **$275**.
(Courtesy of Mountain Lion Trading Post, Redondo Beach, CA).

Brooch/Pin, sterling, c. 1959, Navajo, S-scroll ster plaque with incised and oxidized scrolled design following plaque shape, mkd "STERLING HAND MADE," mk for White Hogan, maker's mk, conjoined "AK" for Allen Kee, 2-1/2" w x 1-1/2", **$350**. (Shari and Jeff Miller collection).

Silver, c. 1940-50, Zuni, cast silver knifewing god, attributed to the silversmith Iule, 1-3/4" w x 2" .... 187 (A)

Silver, turquoise, c. 1940, butterfly motif, cutout domed plaque wings with elaborate stampwork, tapered tubular body set with an elliptical turq cab, scrolled wire antennae, 2" w x 2-1/2" .... 248 (A)

Silver, turquoise, c. 1950, Navajo, Fred Harvey style, navette-shaped eye motif with elliptical center turq cab in a beaded edge frame, mounted on a silver plaque stamped with sun symbols, thunderbirds, arrows, etc., 2-1/2" w x 1-1/2" .... 138 (A)

Buckles:

T, silver, turquoise, c. 1960, stylized fish shape with lg triangular and narrow rect turq cabs, stamped decoration throughout, bar and hook for belt attachment, 1-1/4" w x 1-3/4", **$125**.

B, silver, c. 1940, Navajo, circ disk, central indented dome, raised center bead, incised radiating lines, scalloped border encircled by stamped feather motifs, stamped scalloped decorations around rim, soldered bar and hook for belt attachment on rev, 2" dia, **$65**.
(Richard Levey collection).

Buckle, ironwood, sterling, c. 1959, Navajo, oval silver plaque with raised border and central silver scrolling motif with off-center incised volute separating two sections of inlaid ironwood, mkd "STERLING HAND MADE," mk for White Hogan, maker's mk, conjoined "AK" for Allen Kee, 3-1/8" w x 1-3/4", **$500**. (Shari and Jeff Miller collection).

Buckle, ironwood, turquoise, lapis, coral, ivory, sterling, c. 1982, Hopi, rect slightly convex silver plaque with inlaid lt and dk ironwood plaques bisected by horizontal silver bar, top section inlaid with geo design of turq and one section of coral, lapis, and bone, rect wire loop on one end, hook on rev for belt, incised maker's mk for Charles Loloma (last name in stylized letters), 3-1/4" w x 1-5/8", **$3,900**. (Bill Faust collection).

Turquoise, jet, MOP, spiny oyster, sterling, c. 1980, Zuni, knifewing god of stone-to-stone inlay, geo sections of turq, jet, MOP, spiny oyster in sterling mount, imp "STERLING" on rev, 2-1/2" w x 2" .... 77 (A)

Turquoise, jet, spiny oyster, shell, silver, c. 1950, Zuni, thunderbird motif, channel inlay, geo sections of turquoise, jet, spiny oyster and shell, 1-1/2" w x 1-1/4" .... 66 (A)

Concha Belt

Silver, c. 1940-50, Navajo, six oval conchas alternating with seven butterfly slides, stamped and raised decorations, on a leather belt, open rect buckle with similar decoration, each concha 3-1/4" x 2-3/4", 44-1/2" tl .... 578 (A)

Silver, turquoise, c. 1940, linked stamped conchas, larger ovals with oval turq cab centers alternating with sm lozenge shapes, 36" tl .... 275 (A)

Turquoise (stabilized and treated), silver, leather, brass, c. 1960-70, seven oval conchas each centering a rect turq cab flanked by half-circ turq cabs within ropetwist wire frame, encircled by a row of pear-shaped turq cabs and appl ropetwist wire decoration, framed by stamped silver crescents alternating with beads, brass bars on rev, rect open-centered buckle of similar design, strung on a leather belt, mkd "VMB," buckle 2-3/4" w x 2-1/4", conchas 2-3/8" w x 1-7/8", 37" tl 400

Turquoise, silver, leather, c. 1940, Zuni/Navajo, circ medallions, 2" dia, channel inlay turq in an open snowflake pattern, sm circ inlay border, by Roger Skeet and Lambert Homer .... 1,650 (A)

Earrings, Pendent

Turquoise, silver, c. 1930, Zuni, flowerhead cluster surmount of circ turq cabs, suspending a horizontal row of four circ turq cabs and a fringe of bead-tipped silver wire, fishhook earwires, 7/8" w x 2" tl .... 138 (A)

Money Clip

Silver, c. 1965, Hopi, rect with overlay design of arching figure (rainbow god), oxidized inner surfaces, 1-3/4" w x 3/4" 30

Necklace

Bead

Coral, turquoise, c. 1940-50, Pueblo, three strands of rolled coral beads, suspending two turquoise bead *joclas*, restrung, 21" tl .... 220 (A)

Squash blossom

Silver, c. 1950, Navajo, all-silver, tufa-cast naja, fourteen squash blossoms on double row of spherical beads, continuing to a single row, hook closure, from Yellow Horse collection, approx 26" tl .... 198 (A)

Turquoise, silver, c. 1940, Zuni, twenty "box bow" blossoms, each set with an oval natural turq cab, strung on a double row of spherical beads, continuing to a single row, suspending an open naja with ropetwist center, three oval turq cabs, one at each terminal and in center, 28" tl .... 770 (A)

Ring

Coral, silver, c. 1960, rounded rect bezel-set coral cab flanked by appl and incised silver fan shapes, approx size 11, 3/4" w x 1-1/4" 75

Turquoise, silver, c. 1970, domed rect top inlaid with half disks of turq separated with narrow strips of silver, three parallel incised lines on each side of shank, approx size 10-1/2 110

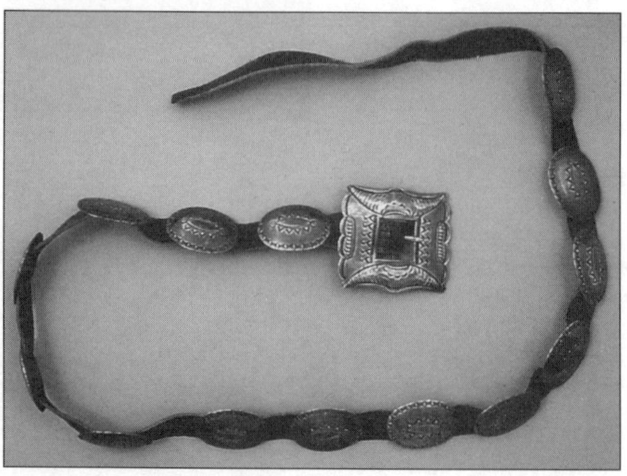

Concha belt, silver, leather, c. 1940, Navajo, fourteen oval conchas with stamped design, rect with cusped sides buckle with open center and stamped decoration, strung on a leather belt, possibly worn as a hatband, conchas 1-1/4" w x 7/8", buckle 2" w x 1-5/8", belt 31-3/4" tl, **$400**. (Sue James collection).

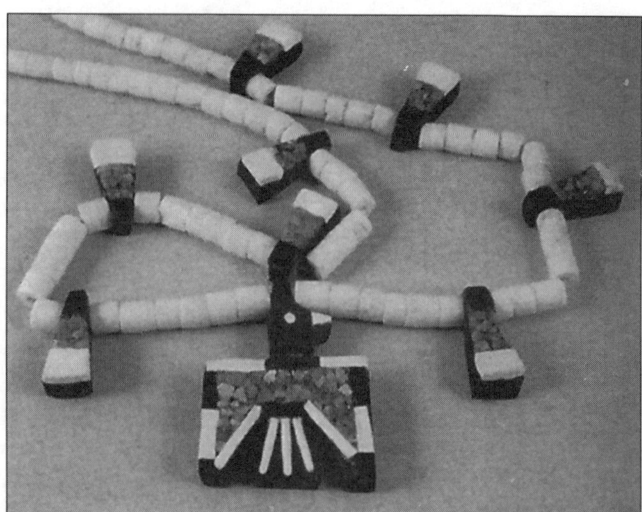

Necklace, gypsum, turquoise, plastic, shell, c. 1940, Santo Domingo, thunderbird motif pendant, battery case back overlaid with crushed turq and shell, strung with tubular gypsum beads interspersed with tabs of similar construction, 28" tl, **$132** [A]. (Photo courtesy of R.G. Munn Indian Art Auctions, Albuquerque, NM, 1/31/97).

Necklace, sterling, c. 1955, Navajo, domed tapered U-shaped polished plaque with incised and oxidized ropetwist design, suspended from a curb link chain, hook closure, mkd "STERLING HAND MADE," mk for White Hogan, maker's mk "KB" for Kenneth Begay on rev, hand engraved in script "Mrs E. Nutt" and "Eloy, Arizona," 7/8" w, 16" tl, **$900**. (Shari and Jeff Miller collection).

Necklace, squash blossom, turquoise, silver, c. 1970, Zuni petit point, flowerhead turq cluster surmounting the naja set with an inside row of circ turq cabs, outside row of teardrop-shaped cabs, flanked by eight squash blossoms surmounted by flowerhead clusters, terminating in a double row of machine-stamped silver beads, **$248** [A]. (Photo courtesy of R.G. Munn Indian Art Auctions, 1/31/97).

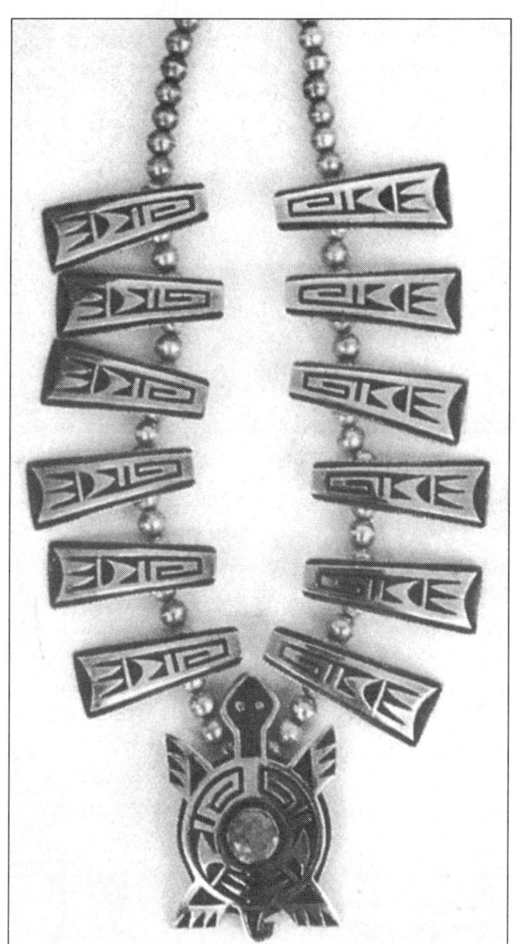

Pendants, sterling, turquoise, coral, MOP, badger-paw motif, tufa cast, by Preston Monongye, c. 1970:

L, inlaid geo design of red coral, turq, and MOP, imp with maker's mark (Peyote Rain Bird symbol incorporating initial P) on rev, 1" w x 2-1/4", **$800**.

R, inlaid geo design of red and white coral, turq, imp with maker's mark on rev, 1" w x 2-1/4", **$800**. (Courtesy of the Old Territorial Shop, Scottsdale, AZ).

Necklace, sterling, turquoise, c. 1977, Hopi, traditional overlay in squash blossom style, with turtle motif pendant, center set with a circ turq cab, twelve side tabs interspersed with hollow spherical ster beads, by Manuel Hayuagawa, first place winner at 1977 New Mexico State Fair, Albuquerque, pendant approx 1-1/2" w x 2-1/2", 26" tl, **$495** [A]. (Photo courtesy of R.G. Munn Indian Art Auctions, 10/11/96).

Ring, turquoise, silver, c. 1970, Zuni, in the shape of a kachina doll with irregular pear-shaped bezel-set turq cab in headdress, two sm bezel-set turq cab eyes, irregular oval bezel-set turq cab in body, rev engr "Coerz," 3/4" w x 2", **$85**. (Richard Levey collection).

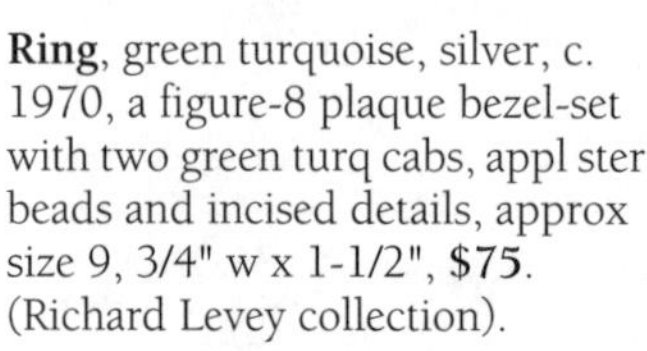

Ring, green turquoise, silver, c. 1970, a figure-8 plaque bezel-set with two green turq cabs, appl ster beads and incised details, approx size 9, 3/4" w x 1-1/2", **$75**. (Richard Levey collection).

Suite: Necklace and Earrings

Bone, turq, old phonograph records, silver, c. 1930-40, Santo Domingo, necklace with thunderbird pendant flanked by six triangular side tabs overlaid with crushed turquoise on plaques made from black phonograph records, spaced by tubular bone beads, conical silver terminals, hook closure, matching earrings each a triangular plaque of similar construction, new earwires, pendant approx 1-1/2" w x 2", 24" tl, earrings 3/4" x 1-1/2" tl, suite.. 175 (A)

Rings, turquoise, silver, Navajo:

L, c. 1950, oval turq cab bezel set and mounted on a flat navette-shaped frame with appl bead decoration at compass points, stamped split shank, 3/4" w x 3/4", size 6-1/2, **$65**.

C, c. 1970, triangular bezel-set turq cab with wiretwist frame encircled by round rod with appl bead and leaf decoration, 1-1/4" w x 1", size 8, **$55**.

R, c. 1970, oval bezel-set turq cab with appl bead decoration, stamped split shank, 3/4" w x 1-1/8", size 7-1/2, **$50**.

(Sue James collection).

Rings, sterling, turquoise, by Charles Loloma, Hopi:

L, c. 1965, cast openwork, irregular pierced design with turq bead bezel-set at top edge, 3/4" w (at stone), 1/2" w (at back), size 5-1/2, **$950**.

R, c. 1975, triangular, tapering to narrow shank, irregular triangular turq cab bezel-set on textured and oxidized ground, raised edges, maker's mk, 1-1/4" w at center tapering to 1/4" w shank, size 9, **$1,400**.

(Bill Faust collection).

MEXICAN JEWELRY (TAXCO SCHOOL, c. 1930-1970)

History: Metalsmithing is a centuries-old Mexican tradition. Mexican *plateros* had already been practicing their craft for generations when they taught silversmithing to the Navajo in the 1870s. There are those who collect the traditional, regional, religious and "folk art" jewelry of Mexico, which fall into the category of true "ethnic" jewelry, a subject covered in the first six chapters of Davis' and Pack's *Mexican Jewelry* (referenced below). The last chapter, which up until recently was virtually the sole source of information for collectors, is on the product of a unique, twentieth-century multicultural amalgam of Mexican, U.S., and European cultures, centered in the town of Taxco (pronounced TAHS-co). This is the place where one man and a serendipitous combination of events founded an industry in 1931.

The story really begins in the 1920s in Mexico City, where another man, an American named Frederick Davis, began designing jewelry and small objects as a sideline to his main occupation as manager of the Sonora News Company. His designs were based on ancient pre-Hispanic motifs, which he had made up in silver, sometimes adding obsidian, a native volcanic glass, or amethyst quartz, a stone which is also indigenous to Mexico. Some of Davis' designs reflect the modernity of the period in smooth shaped plaques which were quite compatible with his use of the geometric motifs found in the clay stamps of pre-Conquest (before 1520) native Mexican tribes.

During a time when most Mexican jewelry was based on colonial, religious or regional designs, and usually made of gold, Davis' work was unique, and seminal to later developments in Taxco. His simple, stylized obsidian face design, which he set into necklaces, bracelets, brooches and clips, was the precursor to what would become ubiquitous tourist-souvenir carved stone face jewelry in the forties and fifties.

In 1933, Davis went to work for Sanborn's as the manager of the antiques and handcrafts shop housed in the restaurant-cum-gift store in downtown Mexico City that still operates today in the historic House of Blue Tile. He continued designing jewelry, which was made and sold alongside Sanborn's own more conventional line of silver articles. Perhaps catering to the burgeoning tourist trade of the time, some Davis designs are of traditional Mexican motifs, like bullfighters and sombrero-clad *paisanos;* others are of then-popular floral sprays. Davis was not a prolific designer, so his pieces are relatively scarce, and important to collectors because they were the first of their kind.

Meanwhile, in 1929, in a little mining village in the mountains southwest of Mexico City, another American had arrived. As an architect from Tulane University in New Orleans, he had come to Taxco to study Spanish Colonial architecture. As a writer, he was to write a book about Mexico (*Little Mexico,* published in 1932). As an artist, he made sketches of the local scenery. But in fact it was as a designer and the proprietor of a little shop selling trinkets to tourists that this twentieth-century Renaissance man, William Spratling (1900-1967), became most famous. Responding to a comment from a friend, U.S. Ambassador Dwight Morrow, Spratling conceived the idea of working the silver that had been mined in the area for centuries, along with other native materials, such as amethyst, obsidian, and rosewood. He created jewelry and objects that were a strikingly original synthesis of Mexican and cosmopolitan design.

When Spratling opened his shop, later called *Taller Las Delicias* (the Delights Workshop), in 1931, he had one master silversmith executing his ideas, and a few young local boys as apprentices. They made pieces entirely by hand with the crudest of implements. Spratling's earliest designs were necessarily simple: the plainest of button earrings, traditional buckles with incised decoration, and plaque brooches based on pre-Hispanic and *ranchero* motifs, all made of heavy gauge, high grade silver (early Spratling pieces are sometimes marked "980"–containing only 2% alloy). These were offered for sale, along with other regional handicrafts such as textiles, tinware, and furniture, in the old abandoned customs house that became Taxco's first workshop.

In 1927, the road from Mexico City to the popular resort of Acapulco had reached Taxco, which was conveniently located half-way between the two cities. With the growth of auto travel and tourism, Spratling's timing was perfect. His shop became a favorite tourist stop, his pieces sold well, and his business grew. By 1940, he had more than 300 artisans working for him. He had made Taxco a major tourist destination, famous for its silverwork. It became a single-industry town, with successive generations carrying on the work of their predecessors.

Today there are more than 10,000 silversmiths working in the area. While the craftsmanship of some of them rivals that found in any other country, many continue to make the cheap tourist trinkets known as *chácharas*, or they merely copy the designs of others, a common practice since the 1940s. Only a few of the best and most original designers and workshops have survived the test of time. Their work, marks and names have become well-known to collectors. Identification of marks is especially important with Mexican silver in determining values, which have escalated as interest has grown over the past few years (see appendix, Marks and Names on Mexican Silver). This is because plagiarism of original designs was (and is) rampant. Spratling's work is understandably the most widely copied. Spratling used a number of different marks, most of them incorporating a conjoined WS (one notorious copyist, Serafín Montezuma, used his own conjoined initials, which look like WS upside down). He took his first mark from his ranch's brand for his horses.

Around 1940, Victor Silson, a businessman with whom Spratling had been in partnership, "appropriated" and patented some of his designs and manufactured them in the U.S., in pewter and silverplate. He used Spratling's conjoined WS mark with "Silson, Inc." under it. These have limited collector interest and do not bring the high prices of Spratling originals.

During World War II, business in Taxco was booming. Spratling exported quantities of silver to U.S. stores cut off from European trade, including Neiman Marcus, Saks Fifth Avenue, Macy's, Lord & Taylor, and Montgomery Ward. Even Ward's catalogs pictured Spratling silver objects and jewelry with hefty pricetags for the time. A 980 silver and carved amethyst Spratling cuff bracelet was originally priced at $45.95 in 1943. The mark found most often on Spratling pieces from the early 1940s was used for those that were sold through Ward's.

Spratling changed his mark in 1949, after he had moved his shop to his ranch outside of town, where he lived and worked until his accidental death in 1967. The jewelry of Spratling's later period is more refined and stylized than his early work. He was influenced, as were many others, by abstract modernism and Scandinavian design. Some later pieces were also made in 18 karat gold.

Spratling established a hierarchical training system still in use today. As his apprentices moved through the ranks to become master silversmiths, some of them showed a talent for creativity as well as skill in executing Spratling's ideas. Their *patrón* (boss) encouraged them to open their own shops and produce their own designs. Many of them did; some were very successful at making names for themselves and establishing individual styles. They are recognized today as the innovators of the Taxco School begun and inspired by William Spratling.

The four brothers Castillo were among the first to go out on their own, opening their shop, Los Castillo, in

1939. The family business became one of the largest, expanding to stores in Mexico City as well as Taxco. They are still in operation today, with second and third generations turning out both old and new designs (of the brothers, only Antonio Castillo is still living). The Castillos' contributions include innovative metalworking techniques and many original designs. Their most famous design, *Perfil de Perico* (profile of parrot) incorporates the techniques of *metales casados* (married metals) and *mosaico azteca* (stone inlay), which are actually refinements of ancient Mexican Indian methods.

Héctor Aguilar (1905-1986) was the manager of the Spratling shop until 1939, when he opened his own *Taller Borda* in the center of town. Aguilar was influenced by Spratling's early work with *ranchero* motifs. He usually used 940 silver without stones, but his earliest work was almost pure silver (980 or 990), as were the decorative elements on some of his later belts and bracelets in leather. In the mid-1960s, Aguilar closed the *taller* and moved with his wife to the resort town of Zihuatanejo. Always sought-after, Aguilar's pieces are in even greater demand now that a book focusing primarily on his work has been published, *Silver Masters of Mexico* (see References below).

Antonio Pineda, another early Spratling apprentice, opened his shop in 1941. His mark, "Antonio Taxco" in the shape of a crown, first used circa 1950, is an important one to know, as his work is sought-after and often copied. He is a favorite among modernists, because of the sleek simplicity and superior craftsmanship of his designs. He preferred to use high-grade (970) silver and often incorporated gemstones in his work, some not usually found in Mexican silver, such as moonstones, chrysocolla, and topaz. Antonio lives in Taxco in semi-retirement.

Margot van Voorhies Carr Castillo, whose mark was "Margot de Taxco," was one of the few women who owned their own shops. She was married to Antonio Castillo and designed for Los Castillo before opening her shop in 1948. Margot was an artist and world traveler who is known for a wide variety of styles and motifs inspired by Art Deco, Egyptian, Arts and Crafts, Art Nouveau and Mexican designs. She is most noted for the use of polychromatic *champlevé* and *basse-taille* enamels, which allowed the painterly expression of her love of color. Margot died in 1985.

Another woman whose work is unmistakably distinctive (and often copied) is Matilde Poulat. She began working in Mexico City in 1934, and opened a retail shop in 1950. Her pieces are typically repoussé silver set with amethysts, turquoise, or coral (or a combination). Her motifs are often figural - birds, fish, butterflies, or religious figures and crosses. Her larger items tend to be quite ornately decorated. Matilde (mark: "Matl") died in 1960, but her nephew, Ricardo Salas Poulat (mark: "Matl" over "Salas") continues to make jewelry in a similar style.

In the 1950s, the next generation of silversmiths began opening their own shops. These were silversmiths who had trained under Spratling and also worked for his first protégés. Each of the ones whose jewelry and objects are collected today had a distinctive approach to design, but the influence of 1950s modernism can be clearly seen throughout their work.

Enrique Ledesma was the first of this generation to have his own establishment, which he opened in 1950. Until then, he had worked for Spratling and Los Castillo. One of Ledesma's signature techniques was to inlay stone into silver and shape the two materials together as a unit. The units were then linked for bracelets and necklaces, or used singly for a brooch or an earring. Ledesma also used silver alone in shaped and oxidized hinged bangles and brooches. His mark is his last name with an elongated L underlining it. Ledesma died in 1979.

Felipe Martinez was another Fifties Generation silversmith whose shop, also opened in 1950, was called *Piedra y Plata* (stone and silver). True to the name, most of Martinez' designs are combinations of silver and turquoise, obsidian, azurmalachite, or other opaque stone inlaid in smooth geometric patterns, or bezel-set and joined to silver shapes. Martinez also made stone carvings which Hubert Harmon and others in Taxco incorporated into their jewelry designs.

Salvador Terán was a cousin of the Castillos, for whom he worked until the opening of his own shop in Mexico City in 1952 (he was also one of Spratling's apprentices in the thirties). Davis and Pack called him "original, inventive, and versatile" (*Mexican Jewelry*, p.213), and indeed his imagination seemed to know no bounds. He designed some strikingly modern pieces, and others that display a fanciful sense of humor. One of his trademarks was creating a three-dimensional effect with cutout motifs mounted on pegs above an oxidized surface. He signed his pieces "Salvador" in script. Salvador died in 1974.

The sole survivor of the Fifties Generation of silversmiths is Sigi (pronounced SEE-hee, b.1929), who opened his shop in Taxco in 1953, after working for Los Castillo and for Margot as her shop foreman. Sigi was the only Mexican silversmith out of the twenty-two who were awarded prizes in a flatware design contest sponsored by International Silver in Connecticut in 1960. His designs reflect both American and Scandinavian modernist influence, yet they are identifiably his own. Sigi recently resumed designing and making new pieces, which are crafted with the same careful attention to detail and finishing as his earlier work. His signature is "Sigi Tasco" (the alternate spelling of Taxco).

Hubert Harmon (b. 1913) is an eccentric American artist who lived and worked in Taxco, where his *taller* produced his designs from c.1943 to 1948. He was recently "rediscovered" living in Mexico, where he was interviewed by Penny Morrill for her article, cited below. He designed out of the ordinary pieces which are scarce and highly collectible today. He had a bizarre sense of humor as well as an imaginative eye. Whimsical motifs were his specialty - including his mark, a pair of winged feet.

Many other Taxco designers and silversmiths have worked in relative obscurity. Only their output and their marks are known. Of the literally hundreds, and at present, thousands, who have worked or are working there, only a few, in addition to the ones mentioned above, have been identified and referenced in any book or catalog. These include: Carmen Beckmann, Ana Nuñez Brilanti (shop name and mark "Victoria"), Isidro García (shop name and mark, "Maricela"), Bernice Goodspeed, Los Ballesteros, Gerardo López, Emma Melendez and Miguel Melendez.

Virtually no written documentation is available on those whose pieces surface repeatedly, which are well-made, with distinctive maker's marks, and others whose initials are all that is known. In addition, there are many pieces of excellent quality with no identifying marks at all, other than "sterling, *Hecho en* (or) Made in Mexico" (or variations). Because of this lack of documentation, attribution, and name recognition, values are comparatively low. As with any jewelry, however, both signed pieces by known makers and unsigned or unknown work should be evaluated with the same criteria. Even some Spratling pieces are less than exemplary, and certainly there is a great quantity of Taxco silver made by unknowns who deserve to remain so.

References: Forrest Colburn, "Silversmith Maestro Tomás Vega," *Ornament*, Autumn, 1994; Mary L. Davis and Greta Pack, *Mexican Jewelry*, University of Texas Press, 1963, reprinted 1982, 1991; Jorge Enciso, *Design Motifs of Ancient Mexico*, Dover Publications, 1953; Penny Chittim Morrill and Carole A. Berk, *Mexican Silver, 20th Century Handwrought Jewelry & Metalwork,* Schiffer Publishing, 1994; Penny C. Morrill, *Silver Masters of Mexico,* Schiffer Publishing, 1996, and "Hubert Harmon: Whimsy and Humor in Mexican Silver," *Jewelry, The Journal of the American Society of Jewelry Historians*, Vol. One, 1996-1997; Christie Romero, "William Spratling and the Taxco School: Mexican Silver Jewelry, 1930-1970," *Jewelers; Circular-Keystone/Heritage*, March 1993; Nancy Schiffer, *Silver Jewelry Designs, Evaluating Quality*, Schiffer Publishing, 1996 (chapter on Mexican); William Spratling, *File on Spratling* (autobiography), Little, Brown & Co., 1967; exhibition catalogs: Sandraline Cedarwall and Hal Riney with Barnaby Conrad, *Spratling Silver*, Chronicle Books, 1990; Centro Cultural/Arte Contemporaneo, *William Spratling/Plata* (Spanish text), Mexico City, 1987; Karen Davidov, *Mexican Silver Jewelry: The American School, 1930-1960,* Muriel Karasik Gallery, 1985; Penny Chittim Morrill, *Hecho en Mexico*, Carole A. Berk Ltd. Gallery, 1990.

Reproduction Alert: Between 1946 (or thereabouts) and 1979, the Mexican government required the stamping of a "spread eagle" assay mark on any piece that was made of 925 (sterling) silver or above. In 1979, the eagle mark was abandoned, and since then all workshops have been required to use individually assigned registry marks of two letters and two or three numbers, separated by a hyphen. Although some pieces escape marking, any item taken out or exported from Mexico should be marked. This is one way to differentiate new from old pieces by the same workshop. Since Spratling's death in 1967, his designs have been produced by the current owner of his estate. The recently-made pieces bear the later WS maker's mark along with the registry number TS-24. Copies of Spratling designs, unsigned or signed by others, were also commonly made during Spratling's lifetime, as they continue to be today. Antonio Pineda and Margot de Taxco fakes regularly appear on the market. Unsigned Frederick Davis designs are common. Los Castillo and Héctor Aguilar designs are reproduced somewhat less frequently. Of the Fifties Generation, Salvador and Ledesma are seldom copied, but Sigi's pieces often are.

Advisor: Jill Crawford.

Bracelet

Bangle, hinged

Sterling, brass, copper, hardstone, c. 1955, tapered hinged band of copper and brass stripes overlaid on ster, centering a circ hardstone post-set disk surmounted by two rotating triangular silver pendants with copper and brass stripe overlay on ster in the "*metales casados*" (married metals) technique, each with a fringe of lg ster beads suspended from bead-tipped soldered rings along bottom edge, sgd "LOS CASTILLO," Mexican government assay mk, 1-3/4" w (at center), 2-1/4" inside dia.... 288 (A)

Cuff

Ebony, sterling, c. 1940-45, central circ ebony cab flanked by a row of alternating ebony and ster crescents forming cuff, 1940-1945 maker's mk for William Spratling, 3/4" w........ 2,800

Sterling, 18k yg, c. 1945, incised and shaped ster bar with appl 18k yg alternating truncated pyramids and S-scrolls, 1940-1945 maker's mk for William Spratling, mkd "STERLING" and "18K," 5/8" w........ 2,500

Bangle Bracelets, hinged, sterling, by Enrique Ledesma, c. 1955:

L, tapered band with smooth concave center, a cultured pearl at each side on an oxidized surface, v-spring and box clasp, mkd "LEDESMA TAXCO *HECHO EN MEXICO* 925," Mexican government assay mark #3, 2-1/8" inside dia, 2" w, $385. (Al Munir Meghji collection).

R, tapered band with polished concave center, appl cutout abstract design of two opposed angelfish and waves, mkd "LEDESMA TAXCO *HECHO EN MEXICO* 925," Mexican government assay mark #3, v-spring and box clasp, safety chain, 2-1/8" inside dia, 2" w, $385. (Author's collection).

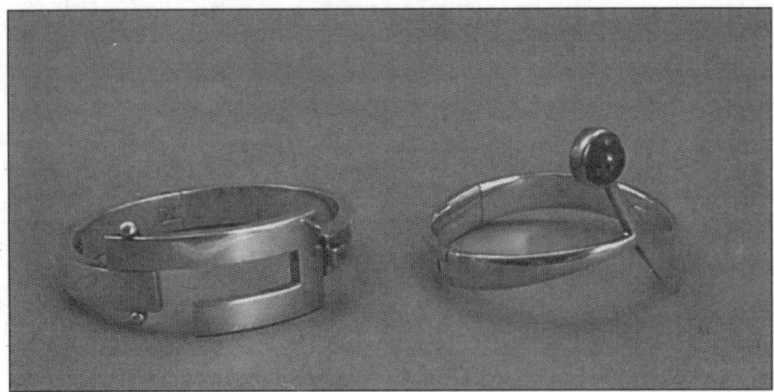

Bangle Bracelets, hinged, sterling, by Sigi, c. 1955-60:

L, top a horizontal rect J shape with bead caps on one hinge, continuing to plain hinged band, v-spring and box clasp, mkd "*HECHO EN MEXICO* STERLING Sigi TASCO" #12, Mexican government assay mark #36, 1-1/4" w, 2-1/8" inside dia, **$325**. (Al Munir Meghji collection).

R, curved and tapered L shape terminating in a bezel-set circ amethyst cab, joined to tapered segment completing bangle to side hinges, back segments and v-spring and box clasp, mkd "Sigi, TASCO" in conjoined ovals, "STERLING *HECHO EN MEXICO*" #610, Mexican assay mark (eagle) #36, 1/2" w, 2" top to bottom, 2-1/8" inside dia, **$350**. (Author's collection).

Link

Green stones, sterling, c. 1945, high-domed circ green stone cabs enclosed within stamped fish motif bezels, sgd "LOS CASTILLO, TAXCO, MEXICO," 3/4" w x 7" tl .... 374 (A)

Sterling, c. 1940-45, alternating circ and ribbed domed oval links, suspending a lg heart-shaped charm at one end, final circ link a spring ring closure, sgd "LOS CASTILLO STERLING MEXICO," 1" w x 7-7/8" tl .... 259 (A)

Sterling, enamel, c. 1950, six domed circ disks, pierced centers, with overlapping Y shape within an arc, concentric bands of black and polychrome *champlevé* enamel, mkd "MARGOT DE TAXCO STERLING *HECHO EN MEXICO,*" government assay mark #16, 1" w x 7-1/4" tl .... 489 (A)

Sterling, enamel, c. 1955, nine overlapping tapered rect open-centered links of black *champlevé* enamel and silver dots, sgd "MARGOT DE TAXCO," Mexican government assay mk, v-spring and box clasp, 7/8" w x 7-3/8" tl .... 575 (A)

Tortoiseshell, sterling, c. 1955, hand-shaped plaques inlaid with cut-to-shape tortoiseshell surmounted by appl circ ster disks, fold-over box clasp, safety chain, rev imp with post-1949 maker's mk for William Spratling, 3/4" w x 7". 2,200

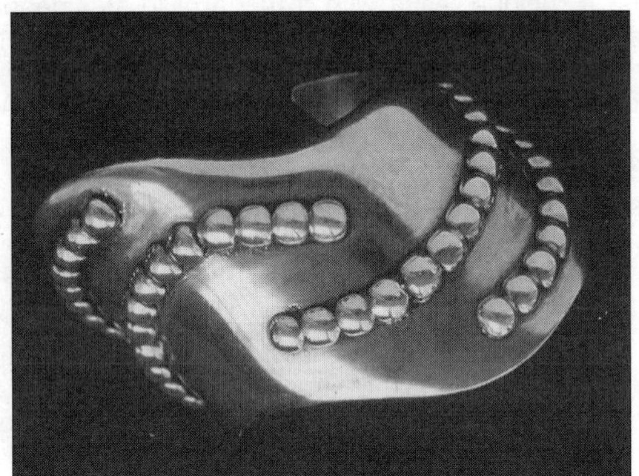

Cuff Bracelet, sterling, c. 1950, S-curved cuff with two opposed pairs of parallel C-curved rows of raised beads, maker's mk for Héctor Aguilar (conjoined HA), 2-1/2" w, **$1,800**. (Jill Crawford collection, photo by Spencer L. McDonald).

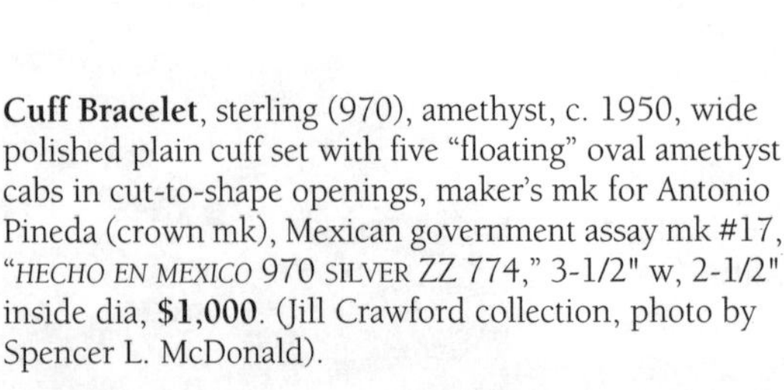

Cuff Bracelet, sterling (970), amethyst, c. 1950, wide polished plain cuff set with five "floating" oval amethyst cabs in cut-to-shape openings, maker's mk for Antonio Pineda (crown mk), Mexican government assay mk #17, "*HECHO EN MEXICO* 970 SILVER ZZ 774," 3-1/2" w, 2-1/2" inside dia, **$1,000**. (Jill Crawford collection, photo by Spencer L. McDonald).

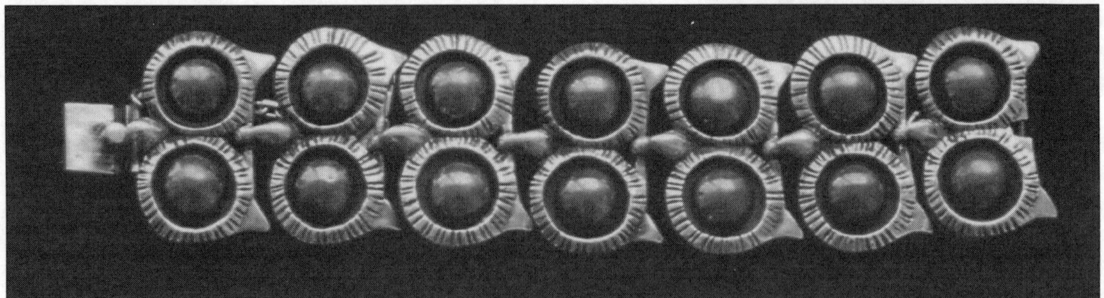

Link Bracelet, sterling, bronze, c. 1945, seven links in the shape of stylized owls' heads with appl bronze domed disks for eyes, v-spring and box clasp, 1940-1945 maker's mk for William Spratling, 2" w x 7-1/2" tl, **$2,500**. (Jill Crawford collection, photo by Spencer L. McDonald).

Link Bracelet, sterling, c. 1950, scroll links surmounted by appl X-shapes and bar with bead terminals, mkd "TAXCO *HECHO EN MEXICO* 925 #138," maker's mk for Pedro Castillo (superimposed PC), Mexican government eagle assay mark, safety chain, 1-3/8" w x 7" tl, **$250**. (Richard Levey collection).

Brooch/Pin

Sterling, c. 1940, cutout and incised pre-Hispanic bird motif, maker's mk for William Spratling, Taxco, 2-3/8" x 1-3/4" .... 374 (A)

Sterling, c. 1955, rounded lozenge-shaped polished plaque with pierced fish design and astrological symbol for Pisces, mkd "LOS CASTILLO TAXCO" (circ mk), 2-1/8" w x 2-1/2" 450

Sterling, amethyst, c. 1945, six-pointed star with amethyst cabs at three points and an amethyst cab center, sgd "SPRATLING MEXICO," 2" dia .... 690 (A)

Sterling, obsidian, c. 1955, two overlapping elongated L shapes surmounted by a bezel-set rect obsidian cab at one end, mkd "Sigi TASCO" in adjacent ovals for Sigi Pineda, "STERLING," #417, government spread eagle assay mk, 2-1/2" w x 7/8" 95

Brooch/Pin, sterling, c. 1940, stylized pre-Hispanic butterfly motif with appl bead decoration, scrolled terminals, rev mkd "SPRATLING SILVER," 1940-1945 maker's mk for William Spratling, 3-1/2" w x 2-1/2", **$2,000**. (Jill Crawford collection, photo by Spencer L. McDonald).

Brooch/Pin, azurmalachite, sterling, c. 1940-45, three-lobed leaf motif tied with a bow, azurmalachite inlay in overlapping elongated oval leaf sections, imp with 1940-45 maker's mk for William Spratling, and "STERLING," converted from double-pronged hinged clip, 1-3/4" w x 3-3/8", **$1,800**. (Charles Pinkham collection).

Brooch/Pin, sterling, c. 1940, pre-Hispanic motif, a scrolled lyre-shaped plaque, domed disk center, with incised line decoration, three radiating scalloped segments around outside edge, maker's mk for Héctor Aguilar (conjoined HA), 1-1/2" w x 1-1/4", **$350**. (Jill Crawford collection, photo by Spencer L. McDonald).

Brooch/Pin, sterling, c. 1940, in the shape of a piggy bank, three articulated grad disk "coins" with raised $ and cent marks overlapping to slot in bank, raised floral design on pig's body, pin back assembly mounted on rev of top coin, rev of pig mkd "LOS CASTILLO, TAXCO STERLING MADE IN MEXICO" #526, design attributed to Margot Van Voorhies Carr Castillo, 2-7/8" w x 3-3/4", **$900**. (Author's collection).

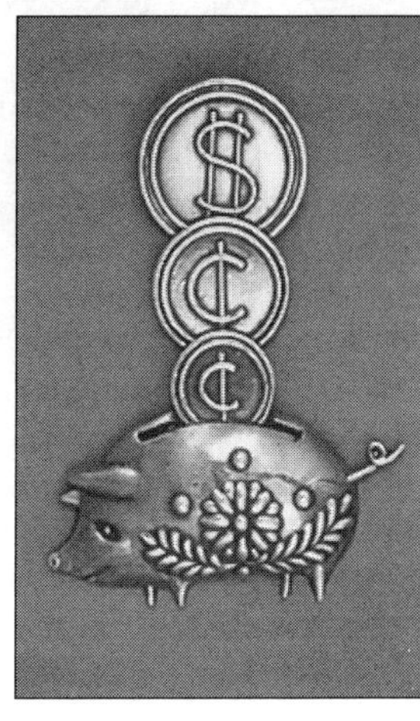

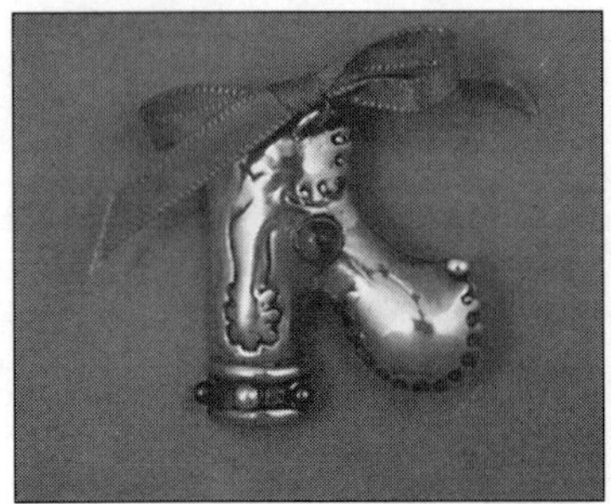

Brooch/Pin, sterling, amethyst, copper, c. 1940-45, depicting the stylized head of a female poodle, amethyst eye, copper and silver studded collar, soldered loop with added ribbon bow at top of head, mkd "STERLING HUBERT HARMON, MADE IN MEXICO," maker's mark (winged feet), 1-1/2" x 1-1/4", **$350**. (Author's collection).

Brooch/Pin, sterling, nephrite jade, c. 1940, central pre-Hispanic carved nephrite jade figure surrounded by a row of appl ster beads with incised circ decoration, enclosed by a scrolled shield-shaped ster frame outlined with three appl parallel wires, mkd "MATL" for Matilde Poulat, 2-1/2" w x 2", **$600**. (Jill Crawford collection, photo by Spencer L. McDonald).

Brooches/Pins, sterling and gemstones:

T, c. 1940, pre-Hispanic butterfly motif, body a pear-shaped amethyst cab held by four voluted prongs, wings with recessed oxidized segmented centers, rev mkd "TAXCO B MEXICO, STERLING" for Bernice Goodspeed, 2-1/4" w x 1-1/4", **$200**.

BL, c. 1960-65, in the shape of a slightly convex palmately lobed and serrate leaf with appl wire veins, surmounted by a prong-set carved amethyst frog, rev mkd "BEKMANN STERLING MEXICO," for Carmen Beckmann, 2" w x 3", **$275**.

BR, Brooch/Pin, sterling, turquoise, c. 1935-40, in the shape of a stylized fish, chased and repoussé details, bezel-set circ turq cab eye, rev mkd "Mat'l" in script on an applied plate for Matilde Poulat, handmade trombone catch, 2" w x 1-5/8", **$175**.
(Author's collection).

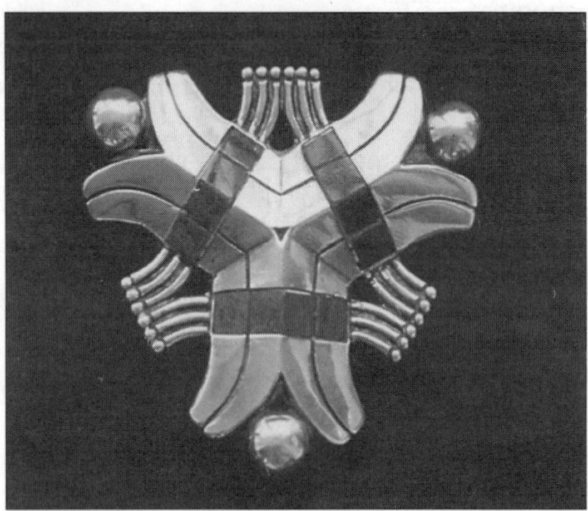

Brooch/Pin, obsidian, sterling, c. 1955, three concave U-shapes joined at their bases, forming a radiating motif inlaid with obsidian rectangles, incised lines running through centers, a lg bead between each paired terminal, surmounting an open triangle of bead-tipped wire, rev imp with post-1949 maker's mk for William Spratling, 3-1/2" w x 3-1/2", **$3,200**. (Jill Crawford collection, photo by Spencer L. McDonald).

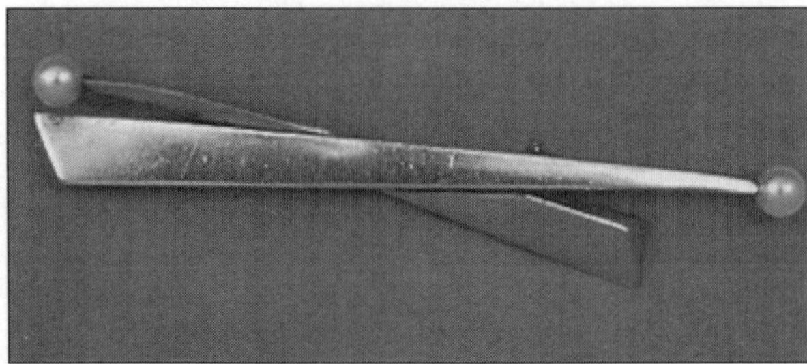

Brooch/Pin, Bar, sterling, cultured pearls, c. 1955-60, two elongated opposed concave triangles, joined at the sides, each with a cultured pearl post-mounted at the apex, maker's mk for Antonio Pineda (crown), "970 Silver" Mexican government assay mark #17, 3-1/2" w x 3/4", **$350**. (Al Munir Meghji collection).

Brooches/Pins, sterling, by Sigi, c. 1955:

L, biomorphic design of an upper polished elongated C shape and a lower textured and oxidized irregular rounded crescent and mushroom shape, mkd "Sigi Tasco" in conjoined ovals, #356, "HECHO EN MEXICO STERLING" and Mexican government assay mark #36, 2-1/4" w x 1-1/8", **$250**.
(Al Munir Meghji collection).

R, conjoined overlapping ellipses, cutout and shaped centers, Florentine finish, mkd "Sigi, Tasco" in conjoined ovals, "STERLING HECHO EN MEXICO" #32, Mexican assay mark (eagle) #36, 2-3/8" w x 1", **$200**.
(Author's collection).

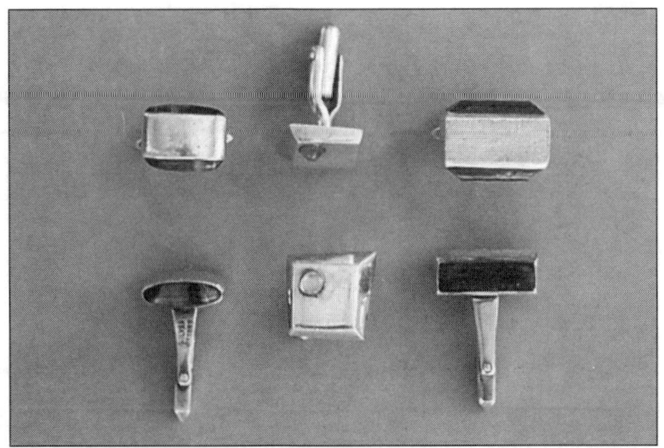

Cuff Links, sterling and gemstones, by Antonio Pineda, c. 1950:

L, tubular oval bezel set with an oval tiger's eye quartz cab on both sides, appl swiveling hinged back, mkd "SILVER BY Toño," Mexican government assay mk #17, 5/8" w x 3/4", pr, **$200**.

C, sq with one elongated corner, circ bezel-set moonstone cab in adjacent corner, swiveling hinged backs, mkd "STERLING **silver**, MEXICO 970" maker's mk (crown), Mexican government assay mk #17, 3/4" x 3/4", pr, **$200**.

R, rect beveled bezel set with beveled rect amethyst cabs on both sides, appl swiveling hinged back, maker's mk (crown), "*HECHO EN MEXICO*," Mexican government assay mk #17, 5/8" w x 7/8", pr, **$175**.
(Photo courtesy of Bruce Healy).

Buckle

Tortoiseshell, sterling, c. 1955, each half a rounded tortoiseshell triangle inlaid with central raised triangular ster plaque within a carved out triangular depression, mounted on ster plaque with three incised ster prongs, hook and ring center closure, rev imp with post-1949 maker's mk for William Spratling, 3-3/4" w x 1-3/4" 2,500

Cuff Links

970 silver, c. 1955, concave polished ovals, mkd with crown mk for Antonio Pineda and "*HECHO EN MEXICO* 970," 1-1/8" w x 3/4" 150

Sterling (970), c. 1950-60, irregular polished ovals with cut-out figures over oxidized bg, mkd with crown for Antonio Pineda and "970 SILVER," 3/4" w x 1-7/8" 350

Cuff Links, sterling, c. 1955:

L, rounded rect oxidized plaques with appl sq volute, hinged back plate, mkd "LEDESMA TAXCO HECHO EN MEXICO 925" for Enrique Ledesma, 7/8" w x 5/8", pr, **$125**.

R, rect ster plaques, 3/4 of each covered by a rect dk wood plaque pierced with one lg and three sm silver-lined "grommets," one link mkd "Sigi TASCO" and Mexican government assay mk, other link mkd "*HECHO EN MEXICO* STERLING #54," 1" w x 3/4", pr, **$125**.
(Patrick Kapty collection).

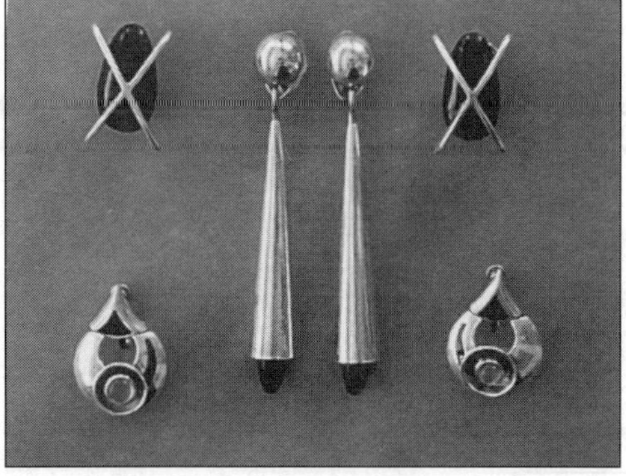

Earrings, sterling (970), by Antonio Pineda, c. 1955:

T, pear-shaped obsidian double cabs in a cage of intersecting open-centered disks forming an X, screwbacks, maker's mk (crown mk), Mexican government assay mk #17, 3/4" w x 1-1/8" tl, pr, **$275**.

C, domed circ surmount suspending an elongated cone drop terminating in an inverted conical obsidian cab suspended freely from within cone, screwbacks, maker's mk (crown mk), Mexican government assay mk #17, "970," 1/2" W X 3-1/4" tl, pr, **$325**.

B, cusped triangular surmount with black enameled center, suspending a hinged rounded tapered U-shaped drop surmounted by a bezel-set circ moonstone within an oxidized concave disk, black enameled tapered band on one side, screwbacks, maker's mk (crown mk) and "970" on one, Mexican government assay mk #17, "*HECHO EN MEXICO*" on the other, 1-1/4" x 1-1/4", pr, **$300**.
(Alice Healy collection, photo by Bruce Healy).

Earrings

Enamel, sterling, c. 1955-60, circ doorknocker shape covered with brickwork geo design of dk blue, lt blue, and black *champlevé* enamel, screwbacks, mkd "MARGOT DE TAXCO," #5689, Mexican government assay mk #16, "STERLING, *HECHO EN MEXICO*," 1" dia, pr 125

Sterling, enamel, c. 1955, circ polished disk with central stylized eye design in black *champlevé* and teal *basse-taille* enamel, screwbacks, mkd "MARGOT DE TAXCO," #5414, 7/8" dia, pr 125

Necklace

Sterling, c. 1948, repeating design of crossover X-shaped links alternating with triple bead clusters at either side of hinges, v-spring and box clasp, maker's mk for Héctor Aguilar (conjoined HA), 1" w x 13" tl 1,200

Sterling, c. 1955, sq concave links, maker's mark for Antonio Pineda, v-spring and box clasp, 5/8" w x 16" tl .... 978 (A)

Sterling, onyx, c. 1955, necklace of stylized scalloped rect links, eleven center front links with appl sq onyx cubes, maker's mk for Antonio Pineda, Taxco, v-spring and box clasp, 3/4" w x 14" tl .... 805 (A)

Pendant and Chain

Sterling, amethyst, c. 1940, heavy curb link chain suspending two ropetwist wire loops surmounted by a sq ster plaque with incised top and bottom flanking a rect amethyst cab center, continuing to three ropetwist wire segments suspending three pear-shaped amethyst drops, 1940-1945 maker's mk for William Spratling, pendant 1" w x 2" tl, 18" tl.. 4,000

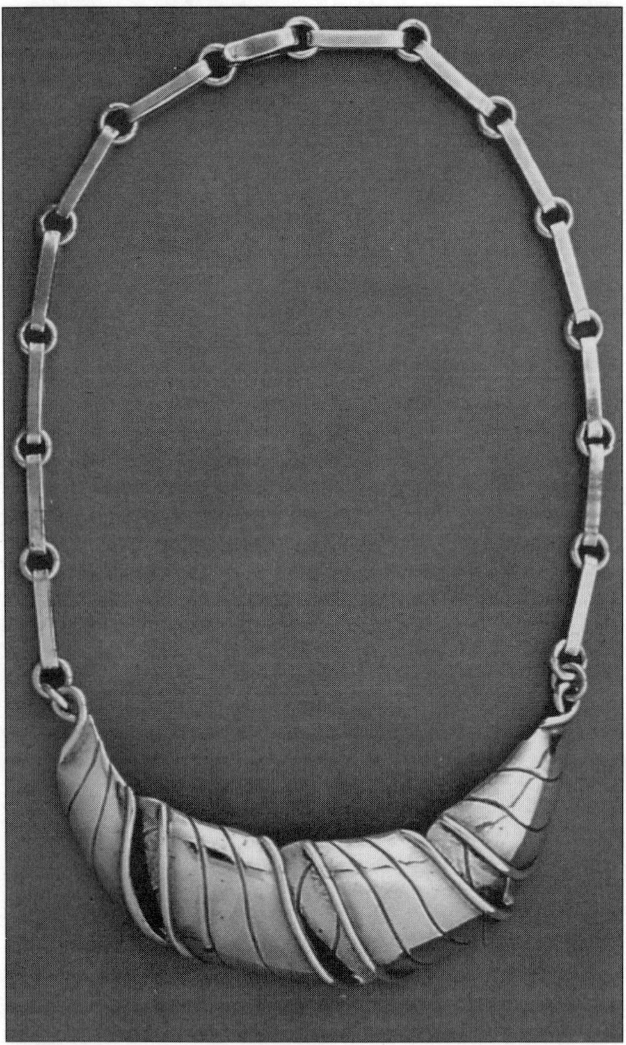

Necklace, sterling, sterling vermeil, c. 1950, convex central plaque of a tapered, twisted segmented crescent (collectors' name: "The Croissant"), each segment with incised lines and raised rolled edges, gp inner surfaces, suspended from elongated flat oval and circ link chain, hook clasp, rev imp with post-1949 maker's mk for William Spratling, "925," 16-1/2" tl, 1-1/4" top to bottom, **$1,600**. (Author's collection).

Sterling, azur-malachite, c. 1951, central carved shell-shaped azur-malachite flanked by shell-shaped ster plaques leading to incised rect links alternating with circ rings, hook clasp, safety chain, rev imp with post-1949 maker's mk for William Spratling, pendant 3" w x 2", chain 16" tl 2,500

Stone, sterling, c. 1945, pre-Hispanic carved black stone disk mounted in a collar within an annular open frame on post, suspended from a rod and ring chain, mkd "LOS CASTILLO" on clasp, pendant 1-1/4" dia, chain 18" tl 450

Suite: Bracelet and Earrings

Enamel, sterling, c. 1955, links of interlocking Greek key design in dk blue, lt blue, and black *champlevé* enamel, v-spring and box clasp, screwback earrings a single link, mkd "MARGOT DE TAXCO," #5542, "STERLING, MADE IN MEXICO," Mexican government assay mk #16, bracelet 7/8" w x 6-3/8" tl, earrings 7/8" w x 5/8", suite.......... 350

Pendant/Brooch, sterling, enamel, c. 1955-60, depicting the head of a Chinese dancer with elaborate headdress and movable drop earrings, *basse-taille* enameled in shades of turq, dk green, lt green, purple, orange, yellow, black, and white, bail for chain, safety catch, mkd "MARGOT DE TAXCO MEXICO STERLING," #5670, Mexican government assay mark (eagle) #16, 2-1/2" w x 4-1/4" tl, **$1,000**. (Patrick Kapty collection).

Suite: Necklace and Cuff Bracelet

Sterling, turquoise, c. 1940-45, necklace of three grad rows of hemispherical beads, inner and middle hemispheres with incised circles, bead-tipped inner row of sm hemispheres strung on chain, joined to larger middle row suspending outer row of bead-tipped larger hemispheres from jump rings, each outer bead set with a sm circ turq cab, hingepin closure, cuff bracelet with a central rounded rect plaque flanked by overlapping D-shaped plates of bezel-set green turq alternating with silver plates, riveted through centers to a flat tapering cuff, both pcs imp with pre-1945 maker's mks for William Spratling, Taxco Mexico, necklace 17-1/2" tl, cuff 1-1/4" w, 2-1/2" inside dia, suite.. 6,325 (A)

Suite: Necklace and Earrings

Sterling (970), obsidian, c. 1955, concave *boteh* (paisley) motif ster links, hollow with flat backs, curved around bezel-set obsidian disks, hook clasp, screwback earrings each a single link, necklace with maker's mk for Antonio Pineda (crown mk), Mexican government assay mk #17, "*HECHO EN MEXICO* 970 Silver YY439" on necklace 5/8" w x 14" tl, crown mk and "silver" on one earring, "*HECHO EN MEXICO*" and assay mk on other, 5/8" w x 1-1/4", suite 1,200

Suite: Necklace, Bracelet, Earrings

Sterling, enamel, c. 1950, necklace in the shape of a snake with articulated scale links enameled in predominantly green polychrome *champlevé*, head with black-enameled eyes and blue-green enameled collar attached to the tail with a spade-shaped tip at front center, v-spring and box clasp in back, matching articulated bracelet, clipback earrings each an undulating enameled snake, all pieces mkd "MARGOT DE TAXCO, STERLING MEXICO," #5554, necklace 15" tl, head 7/8" w, suite ...... 2,012 (A)

Ring, amethyst, silver, c. 1950, scrolled and cusped wire frame surrounding a bezel-set amethyst cab mounted on a plain narrow shank, mkd "Matl" in script on appl plaque, for Matilde Poulat, approx size 7, 1" w x 1", **$350**. (Charles Pinkham collection).

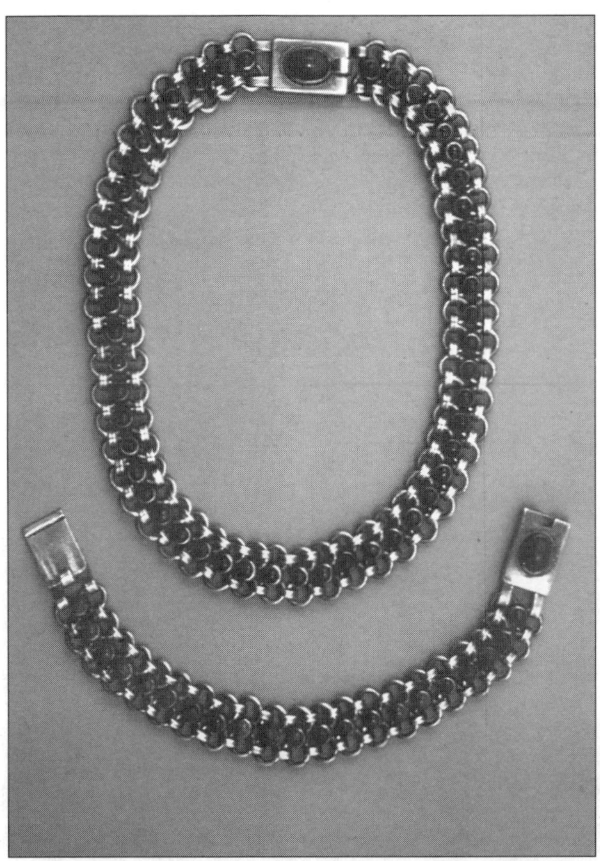

Suite: Necklace and Bracelet, sterling (940), turquoise, c. 1950, oval open links centering circ bezel-set green turq cabs, matching bracelet, box clasps set with oval bezel-set green turq cabs, imp "HA" for Héctor Aguilar, Mexican government assay mark, "940 Taxco," provenance: given to the present owner's mother by Héctor Aguilar (her brother-in-law), necklace 5/8" w x 16" tl, bracelet 5/8" w x 7-1/2" tl, **$1,200**. (Marisela Doria collection).

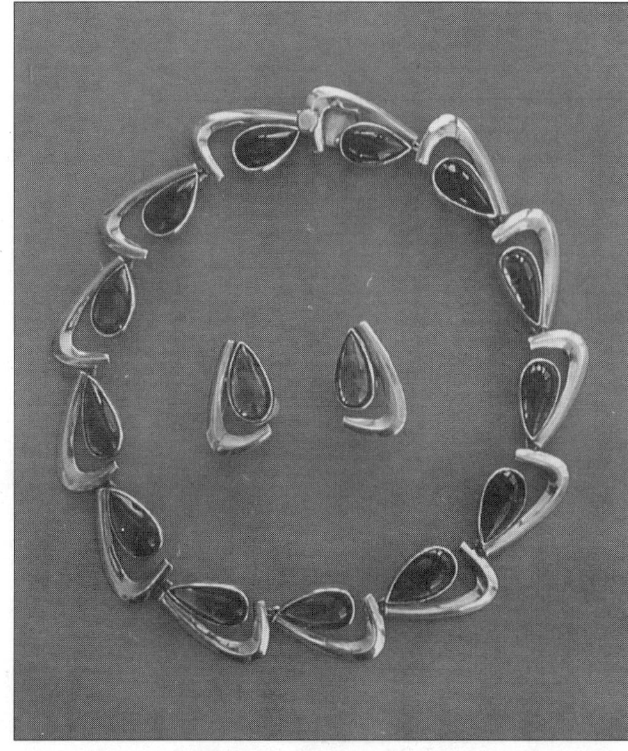

Suite: Necklace and Earrings, amethysts, sterling (970), c. 1955, collar necklace of boomerang-shaped links with a bezel-set pear-shaped amethyst cab mounted inside each, v-spring and box clasp, matching screwback earrings, each a single link, maker's mk for Antonio Pineda (crown mk), Mexican government assay mk #17, "970 SILVER" on necklace 3/4" w x 15-3/4" tl, earrings, crown mk on one, "970" and assay mark on the other, 3/4" w x 1-1/4", suite, **$1,200**. (Alice Healy collection, photo by Bruce Healy).

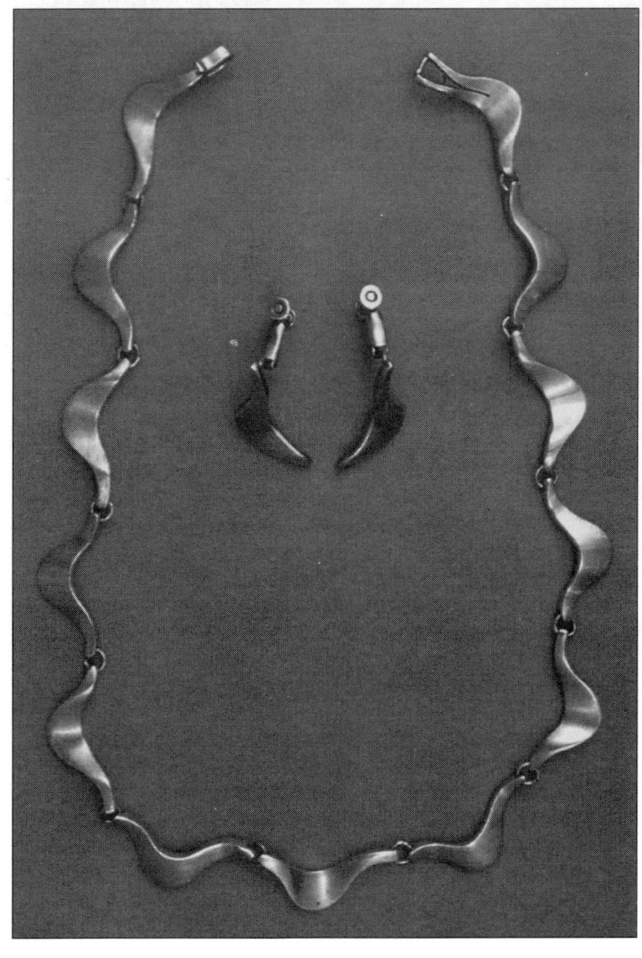

Suite: Necklace and earrings, sterling, c. 1955, necklace of thirteen links, undulating tapered U shapes joined by jump rings, earrings a single link of same design, necklace mkd "Sigi TASCO STERLING" #68 and Mexican government assay mark #36, screw/clipback earrings mkd #68 "STERLING" on one and "Sigi TASCO" on the other, necklace 1/2" w x 14-1/2" tl, earrings 1/2" w x 1-1/8", suite, **$450**. (Al Munir Meghji collection).

Suite: Necklace, Link Bracelet, Earrings, sterling, c. 1950, necklace of twelve linked curved rect plaques, each plaque a raised Roman numeral I through XII on oxidized ground, round bead spacers and short tubes completing to v-spring and box clasp, bracelet of six hinged slightly convex rect plaques, alternating raised letters "AM" and "PM" on oxidized ground, suspending a lg cast hourglass charm, v-spring and box clasp, safety chain, screwback earrings each a rect plaque, one with "AM," the other with "PM" raised letters, all pcs mkd "MARGOT DE TAXCO" #5201, "STERLING MADE IN MEXICO," bracelet also with Mexican assay mk #16, necklace 16" tl x 3/4", bracelet 6-1/2" tl x 5/8" w, charm 7/8" w x 1-5/8", earrings 1-1/8" x 5/8", suite, **$2,000**. (Author's collection).

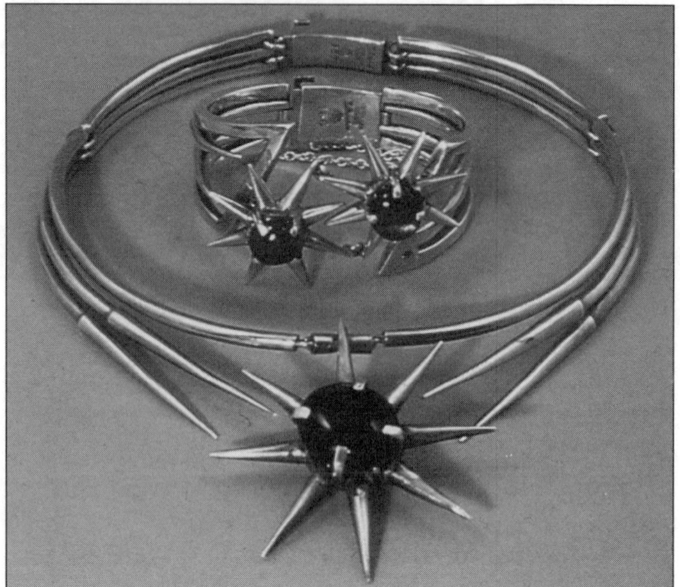

Suite: Pendant/Necklace and Hinged Bangle, sterling, obsidian, c. 1960, necklace of three tubular segments fused side-by-side in four linked sections, two tubes terminating in spikes flanking a removable starburst pendant suspended from the third by an articulated short tube, a circ obsidian double cab prong-set in center of starburst, v-spring and box clasp, matching hinged bangle with two linked starbursts, each prong-set with a circ obsidian cab, joined to side sections of tubular spikes enclosed by angled open frames, v-spring and box clasp, safety chain, both pcs sgd "Salvador" for Salvador Terán, "STERLING MEXICO" #156, Mexican assay mk #36, necklace 16" tl, pendant 2-1/4" dia, bangle, 2-1/4" w x 1-7/8" top to bottom, 2-1/4" inside dia, suite, **$1,500**. (Author's collection).

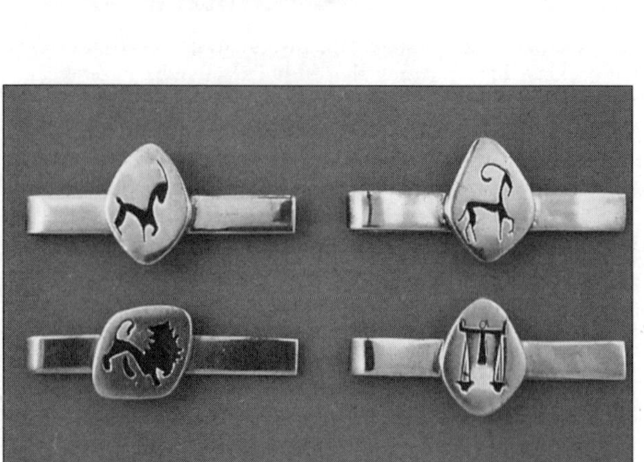

Tie bars, silver, astrological motifs, mkd "LOS CASTILLO TAXCO" (circ mk), c. 1955:

TL, plain narrow rectangle surmounted by an irregular navette-shaped appl plaque with cutout shape of a goat over oxidized bg, astrological motif for Capricorn, 2-1/8" w x 1", $75.

TR, with cutout figure of a ram over oxidized bg, astrological motif for Aries, 2-1/4" w x 1", **$75**.

BL, with cutout figure of a lion over oxidized bg, astrological motif for Leo, 2-1/8" w x 3/4", **$75**.

BR, with cutout figure of a scale over oxidized bg, astrological motif for Libra, 2-1/4" w x 1", **$75**.
(Charles Pinkham collection)

SCANDINAVIAN JEWELRY

History: Scandinavians have approached design in a way that differs from all other European countries, perhaps because of a culture that is rooted in a separate and unique Nordic tradition. Prior to the turn of the century, when historicism was rampant everywhere in the Western world, jewelry designs were derived from direct copies of ancient pieces from the Bronze, Iron, and Viking Ages.

Each of the four Scandinavian countries–Denmark, Finland, Norway, and Sweden–have also produced regional "folk" jewelry which has remained virtually unchanged in appearance and technique for several centuries. During the nineteenth century, too, Danish fine jewelry often had a British-influenced Victorian look, no doubt coming from the fact that the Princess of Wales, Alexandra, was a Dane. The art of hair jewelry-making, another Victorian tradition, is said to have originated in Denmark and Sweden.

Scandinavians are noted for their metalwork, and silversmithing in particular has given expression to original design, most fully realized by twentieth century Scandinavian designers and manufacturers. Many of these designers applied their talents to more than jewelry. Some, like Georg Jensen (1866-1935) of Denmark, began as sculptors, transferring the three-dimensional art form to silver hollow ware, flatware, and jewelry. Others, like Tapio Wirkkala (1915-1985) of Finland, were multimedia artists: they designed glass, porcelain, and wood decorative objects as well as silver.

Denmark

At the turn of the century, the Arts and Crafts Movement found its way to Denmark, where it was called *skønvirke,* or, literally translated, "aesthetic activities." The word was coined in 1907, but the style and movement had earlier roots, as it did in other parts of Europe and Britain. (There is little published documentation in English about jewelry of this period from other Scandinavian countries, but evidence exists of similar work being done in Norway–see below.)

Though similar in form and inspiration to other European Arts and Crafts work, one of the unique qualities of *skønvirke* jewelry is its sculptural three-dimensionality, achieved with repoussage and chasing. Silver, of varying fineness (usually 826 or 830), was the most often-used material, sometimes set with cabochon gemstones such as amber, chrysoprase (or dyed green chalcedony), carnelian, lapis, or moonstones. *Skønvirke* jewelry enjoyed widespread appreciation in Denmark, thanks in part to large-scale production by several manufacturing silversmithies, such as Bernhard Hertz. Like Liberty in Britain and Fahrner in Germany (see Arts & Crafts section), Danish manufacturers commissioned designs from independent artists and also made their own versions of others' work.

Mogens Ballin (1871-1914) was a pioneer of the *skønvirke* style. Inspired by the philosophy of the founders of the English Arts & Crafts movement, William Morris and John Ruskin, his desire was to create "everyday objects with a lovely form of...cheap metals...things which even the smallest purse can afford." However, his style was not influenced as much by the English as by his fellow countrymen, and by German silversmiths. In 1900, he opened a workshop that produced decorative objects and jewelry. From the beginning, he employed a sculptor, Siegfried Wagner, as a designer. In 1901, another sculptor joined the firm, by the name of Georg Jensen–now the most recognized and widely collected name in Scandinavian silver in the United States.

Even though his name recognition in the United States is not that of Jensen's, the work of Evald Nielsen (1879-1958) is very well known in Denmark. He is admired as one of the best of the *skønvirke* designers. Nielsen opened his own shop in 1907. Nielsen's characteristic style of setting stones was to place them within a floral motif in an irregular bezel, so they looked as if they were "bursting forth" from the floral bud. Those who do know Nielsen's work in the U.S. recognize its value. There are many who may recognize the quality, but not the name.

In 1904, Georg Jensen opened his own silversmithy and began designing and making the jewelry and silverware the company is now famous for. Over the past ninety-plus years, a number of noted designers have created jewelry designs for the Jensen firm, many of which are familiar to today's collectors, including those by Sigvard Bernadotte (b. 1907), Torun Bülow-Hübe (b. 1927), Nanna (b. 1923) and Jørgen (1921-1961) Ditzel, Bent Gabrielsen (b. 1928), Henning Koppel (1918-1981), Arno Malinowski (1899-1976), and Harald Nielsen (1892-1977).

A designer's initials are sometimes added to the company marks on a piece, which can raise its value. Many early designs are still produced today, although production methods have changed, in some cases, from die-stamping to casting. Shop marks have changed as well. The mark currently in use, "GEORG JENSEN" inside a dotted oval, has been the same since 1945, but a number of different marks were used prior to that date. The earliest Jensen pieces, c. 1904 to 1914, are made of 826 silver. The grade of silver in pieces dating from the mid-teens through the twenties is 830 or 925; after 1933, the company went to the sterling standard of 925 exclusively. It should be noted that some jewelry designs were also made in 18 karat gold.

In spite of a long tradition in its native countries, Scandinavian design was not well-known in the United States until Frederik Lunning opened a shop and agency for Georg Jensen in New York in 1924. The shop helped to popularize Scandinavian design in general, and Jensen designs in particular. Lunning was an important figure in promoting awareness and appreciation of Nordic decorative and applied arts. From 1951

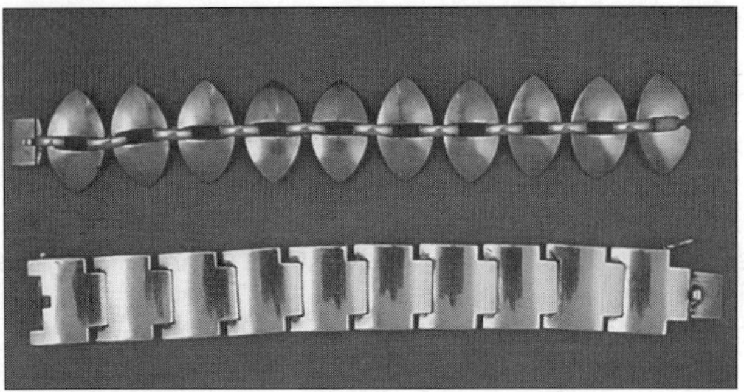

Link Bracelets, sterling, Georg Jensen, Denmark:
T, c. 1955, ten slightly convex navette-shaped plaques with open rect cutout centers joined with oval jump rings, rev imp with post-1945 mark for Georg Jensen "STERLING DENMARK" #106, Swedish import mks (three crowns in an oval), design attributed to Nanna and Jørgen Ditzel, 1" w x 7", **$900**.
B, c. 1938, ten slightly convex rect plaques, hinged with sq-notched terminals inserted into slot in adjacent plaque, v-spring and box clasp, safety clasp, sgd "Sigvard" for designer Sigvard Bernadotte, 1933-44 mk for Georg Jensen, "STERLING DENMARK 925," #73, 7/8" w x 7-1/4", **$1,000**.
(Author's collection).

to 1970, he funded the Lunning Prize, awarded each year to two outstanding Scandinavian designers working in various media.

Among the prizewinners were jewelry and silverware designers and metalsmiths Grete Prytz-Kittelsen (b. 1917), Norway; Henning Koppel, Denmark; Nanna and Jørgen Ditzel, Denmark; Torun Bülow-Hübe, Sweden; Bertel Gardberg (b. 1916), Finland; Börje Rajalin (b. 1933), Finland; Bent Gabrielsen, Denmark; Björn Weckström (b. 1935), Finland; and Helga (b. 1939) and Bent (b. 1932) Exner, Denmark. Tapio Wirkkala was one of the first two prizewinners in 1951. All of these designers are well-known in their own countries; some have achieved world-wide recognition. A number of them maintained their own studios and workshops. Most of them also designed for large manufacturing firms (see appendix, 20th Century Jewelry Designers and Manufacturers in Scandinavia).

The Nordic countries were hard-hit by World War II, which brought shortages of both workers and materials along with the anxiety of invasion and occupation. Remarkably, the arts communities in each country sustained themselves through the hard times. Gold and silver were restricted to mostly settings and inlays. Silversmiths and jewelers began adding other more readily available materials, like glass and ceramics, and substituting other metals, such as iron and bronze. Georg Jensen's designers created a line known as *jernsølv* (iron silver), using patinated iron as a base with silver and gold inlay, similar to damascening or Japanese inlay. The designs themselves, first made by Arno Malinowski and then by others, were inspired by Japanese technique and tradition.

In the United States, when war came and supplies from Europe were cut off, Frederik Lunning turned to American manufacturers and produced a line for Jensen on his own, marked Georg Jensen, U.S.A. There was some controversy after the war concerning the U.S. production. The Copenhagen company disavowed any association with the U.S. designs. A special mark for the Copenhagen shop only, "Georg Jensen & Wendel A/S Denmark," was used for the period 1945-1951. Production of Jensen U.S.A. pieces ended around 1950. Today, they don't bring the prices that the Danish ones do, but they are still of interest to collectors.

The post-war years gave Nordic artists the opportunity to display their talents as never before. For the first time, Scandinavian design was setting the pace for others to follow. Their work was highly influential in Europe and North America. Simplicity of line, adventurous abstract form, and flawlessness of execution were trademarks of Nordic products. For those used to seeing repetitious, derivative "traditional" styles, these designs were an exciting revelation.

The designers at Georg Jensen did not merely keep up with changing times, they were at the forefront of innovation. Collectors of modernist jewelry seek out their work, particularly that of Henning Koppel, Sigvard Bernadotte, and the Ditzels. But they were not alone. Others, too, produced sleek and bold pieces that were the epitome of what came to be known as Scandinavian Modern. Although Jensen is the most well-known in the U.S., several other Danish manufacturers are just as well-known in their own country, including A. Michelsen, A. Dragsted, and Hans Hansen. Hans Hansen's silversmithy has manufactured the work of several highly regarded modernist designers, among them Bent Gabrielsen, Karl Gustav Hansen (b. 1914), the founder's son (who designed a line called "Future" at the age of eighteen), and Anni (b. 1926) and Bent (b. 1924) Knudsen. The company's mark is their name in script, or a superimposed double H (see appendix). Individual designers are not identified on their pieces. Hans Hansen is now under the ownership of the Royal Copenhagen Group, as is Georg Jensen.

N.E. From, first opened in 1931 as a repair shop, began wholesale production in the late forties and are still in business. The firm must have exported a quantity of jewelry to the United States in the fifties and sixties; sterling pieces bearing the name, with modern lines or stylized floral and foliate motifs typical of the period, turn up frequently on the secondary market. Collectors in the U.S. and England are beginning to take notice of From pieces, although price levels continue to be moderate.

Another familiar name, one that confuses dealers and collectors, is Jørgen Jensen (b. 1931), found on modern-looking Danish pewter pieces. The mark is a script signature (see appendix), totally different from but often mistaken for Georg Jensen, who is no relation, although Georg had a son Jørgen who worked for the company (both Jørgen and Jensen are common names in Denmark). The values on these pewter pieces are nowhere near the levels of Georg Jensen silver.

Norway

Very little early twentieth century (or earlier) Norwegian jewelry is found on the market today, other than the traditional filigree brooches with dangling concave disks known as *sølje* (see p. 251), which continue to be made. Other early jewelry that does turn up is usually enameled on silver. At the end of the nineteenth century, a variety of enameling techniques came to be closely associated with Norwegian decorative arts, especially *basse-taille* and *plique à jour*, which several firms were known for, among them: Marius Hammer, J. Tostrup, and David-Andersen. *Plique à jour* fell out of favor concurrently with the demise of Art Nouveau, before World War I, but transparent *basse-taille* and *guilloché,* and opaque *champlevé* enamels were adapted to changing styles throughout the twentieth century. J. Tostrup and David-Andersen continue in business today; Marius Hammer went out of business, but the years of the firm's operation are not documented.

A few examples of enamel and silver jewelry by Marius Hammer (1847-1927) of Bergen have surfaced. Hammer founded his company in the western Norwegian city in the late nineteenth century, specializing in *basse-taille* and *plique à jour* enamels on silver. They were particularly known for their elaborately wrought and enameled souvenir spoons. The firm sold spoons through Liberty of London in the 1890s, and also jewelry, most likely, since examples are found more frequently in England than in the United States.

J. Tostrup, the oldest of the three firms (founded 1832), also produced some enameled jewelry in the early twentieth century, although at that time the firm was better known for its decorative objects. Later, more jewelry was produced, much of it designed (after World War II) by Grete Prytz (now Kittelsen), the granddaughter of Torolf Prytz, the company's production manager at the turn of the century.

The biggest and most well-known Norwegian silver manufacturer is David-Andersen, established in 1876. Famous for their hollowware and flatware enameled in jewel-toned *basse-taille*, the company has also been making jewelry since the turn of the century, both with and without enamel. David-Andersen is still in business, and has been quite prolific (they might be called the Norwegian Georg Jensen), but relatively little information about the history of their production, especially their jewelry, has been recorded in English. (Information on turn-of-the-century Art Nouveau *objects* by Marius Hammer, J. Tostrup, and David-Andersen can be found in *Art Nouveau and Art Deco Silver*, cited below. I thank Didier of Didier Antiques in London for calling the information on Hammer to my attention.)

Early David-Andersen jewelry is relatively scarce. It is also difficult to identify, because one of the early company marks (used c. 1888-1924) does not use its initials or name (see appendix). Two of the pieces illustrated in this section, see photo at right and page 254, eluded identification until a 75th anniversary retrospective catalog (in Norwegian) of the company, showing the marks, was discovered by Advisor Bruce Healy (see appendix).

Later (post-World War II) David-Andersen jewelry is much more commonly available, as the company began exporting to the U.S. in quantity after the war. Designs from this period fall into two categories: modernist abstract and figural.

In the 1950s and 1960s, David-Andersen had several recognized designers in their employ, who are best known for their flatware and hollowware Two of them are Harry Sørby (b. 1905) and Bjørn Sigurd Østern (b. 1935), both of whom also designed jewelry. Sørby worked for the company from 1929-1970, Østern began in 1961 (end date unknown). The latter often used the *basse-taille* enamel the company is famous for in his smoothly-cast and sleekly simple modern pendants and brooches. Both designers also set stones such as amazonite and rhodochrosite in their pieces. The company's marks usually include their initials after the abbreviation "INV," meaning "designer."

Basse-taille enamel is also predominant in the David-Andersen sterling vermeil production pieces most often seen today: long slender curved leaves made into suites of necklace, bracelet, brooch and earrings, die-stamped figural pins in a wide assortment of animals, birds, and fish, and "Viking Revival" scenes. The leaves are usually enameled in a single color, while the other pieces may be in subtle shades of a single color or multicolored. Circa 1950s abstract modern plaques and 1960s lost-wax cast biomorphic shapes are also enameled sterling vermeil. Marks are varied, sometimes with "David-Andersen" written out, sometimes "D-A" with the company logo (in use since 1939), a pair of scales.

Like Georg Jensen, Hans Hansen and many other Scandinavian silversmithies, David-Andersen is a family-run business, handed down from generation to generation. The current president is the founder's great-grandson. His sister, Uni (b. 1930), worked as a designer for the firm until 1959, when she opened her own business.

Tone Vigeland (b. 1938) is the most celebrated Norwegian designer of the 20th century. Her work is in a number of museum collections, including the Museum of Modern Art and the Cooper-Hewitt National Design Museum in New York. A retrospective exhibition was held in 1995, with accompanying catalog (see References, Monographs). Vigeland's earliest work was made at Plus, an arts and crafts center established in Fredrikstad, Norway in 1958, where she apprenticed from 1958 to 1961. Vigeland and other budding young designers created pieces that were then put into production. The artist's initials are stamped on the pieces, along with the marks for Plus (see appendix for Tone Vigeland and Plus). Other artists who worked for Plus include Anna Greta Eker and Erling Christoffersen, some of whose designs are shown or listed in this section, which are very much a part of the Scandinavian minimalist style of the late 50s and early 60s.

Sweden

Wiwen Nilsson (1897-1974) was the first Swedish modernist, designing, in fact defining, the very essence of simplified form with impeccable precision. He

Brooch/Pin, 830 silver, crystal opals, glass, c. 1900-1910, stamped and engr shield-shaped open scroll and interlace plaque, center bezel-set with a lg navette-shaped transparent lt yellow-green glass cab, wiretwist frame, surmounted by two sm bezel-set circ crystal opals in cusped corners, suspending three long articulated filigree drops, center drop set with three, side drops each set with one circ crystal opals, linked triangular, trefoil, quatrefoil and three-dimensional tear-drop motifs terminating in sm filigree rosettes, appl sm plaque on rev of central design imp "830 S" and c. 1900 maker's mark for David-Andersen, Norway, C-catch, tube hinge, 2" w x 5" tl, **$1,000**. (Author's collection).

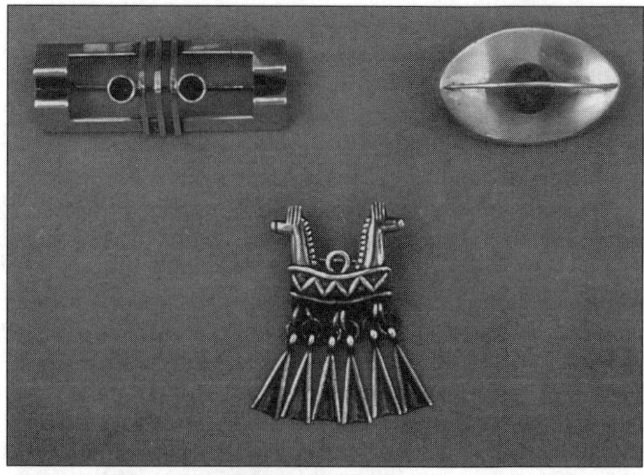

Brooches/Pins, silver, Finnish, 1960s:

TL, 830 silver, smoky quartz, date letter for 1966, open rect frame with V-shaped bend in side centers, angled top and bottom, three inverted V-shaped sq wires surmounting open center, flanked by bezel-set circ-cut smoky quartz, imp with maker's mk for Kupitaan Kulta (anvil), Finnish hmks, date letter N7, "813H," trombone catch, 2" w 3/4", **$200**.
(Kirsten Olson collection).

TR, 830 silver, date letter for 1962, abstract eye motif, concave navette-shaped plaque, center set with a moss agate sphere held in place by a crescent-shaped arc mounted perpendicular to plaque, safety pin style catch, pinstem imp with Finnish hmks, unknown maker's mk, date letter I7, "813H," 1-5/8" w x 1", **$75**.

B, 935 silver, date letter for 1967, die-struck ancient motif, adorsed stylized horses' heads surmounting a zig-zag band, suspending a fringe of triangular plaques with raised edges, Finnish hmks on rev, maker's mk for Kalevala Koru (kk), designer's initials "HGL," date letter O7, "916H," C-catch, 1-1/8" w x 1-7/8" tl, **$50**. (Author's collection).

worked briefly for Georg Jensen in Jensen's Paris studio before returning to Sweden to open his own shop in 1927. He was appointed a court jeweler in 1928. He is well-known in Europe, but has limited name recognition in the U.S., perhaps because so little of his work ever reaches our shores. In Europe, his designs in silver sell in the four figure range.

Sigurd Persson (b. 1914) is the most well-known Swedish metalsmith and jeweler of the mid-twentieth century. His widely lauded designs are noted for their strength, simplicity and innovative concepts. Most of them are one of a kind or limited production. In 1953, Persson designed a series for Atelier Stigbert, a Swedish production company, called "Bowl and Cube."

Very little Swedish jewelry has crossed the Atlantic, judging by its scarcity in the secondary market. There is also a paucity of information about it in print in English. The few pieces that do turn up are as well-made and designed as other Scandinavian work. Swedish jewelry is often hallmarked (see Marks on Metals appendix), with assay marks and date letters (see Tardy, *International Hallmarks on Silver,* cited below).

Finland

Mid-century Finnish silversmiths and jewelers were particularly adept at creating new, fresh concepts in both form and function. Although the Finns' silversmithing legacy goes back to the fourteenth century, Finnish jewelry design is a mid-twentieth century development. Shortage of silver during World War II led to the making of jewelry instead of larger objects from what little reclaimed metal was available. But forms remained traditional. A nationalistic revival of the ancient Iron Age epic, the Kalevala (c. 500-1100 A.D.), during the war yielded replicas of ornaments from ancient tombs, made and sold in a display of national solidarity. The company that made it, Kalevala Koru, went on to become one of the largest jewelry manufacturers in the country. After the war, the search for new ideas began in earnest, and it was then that talented artists began to emerge. But the Finns were slow to accept avant-garde design. It wasn't until 1958, at an exhibition at the Galerie Artek in Helsinki, that the works of a quartet of designers were finally appreciated: Bertel Gardberg (b. 1916, now referred to as the "father of modern silverworking in Finland"), Elis Kauppi, Börje Rajalin, and Eero Rislakki.

Elis Kauppi (b. 1921) was the second of the Finnish avant-gardists to achieve recognition. He helped establish the company Kupitaan Kulta in 1945, but the initial output lacked originality. In 1952, Kauppi began designing original pieces incorporating the native Finnish gemstone spectrolite, also known as labradorite, a dark stone with an iridescent shimmering rainbow of color. Simplicity of form and innovative function, as well as the use of native stones, characterize Kauppi's and the others' work.

By this time, Finnish manufacturers and designers were beginning to venture into promoting Finnish products abroad. The Milan Triennale in 1951 was the first postwar international exhibition to display Finnish (as well as Danish and Swedish) decorative art. The modern designs found a receptive audience in Europe and the U.S. soon after. Triennales of 1954, 1957, and 1960 were likewise successful. Because of this warm reception, Finland began exporting in volume.

Other Finnish designers and manufacturers were established in the fifties and sixties. They found a ready market for their wares overseas. Kaunis Koru, opened in 1954, is known for their sleekly modern, deceptively simple designs. Springy silver bangles with unusual closure mechanisms seem to be a uniquely Finnish concept, which Kaunis Koru excelled at producing. Kaija Aarikka (b. 1929), a textile designer turned jewelry-maker, founded her own company in 1959, making wood and silver jewelry, as it continues to do today. The tradition of using bronze for jewelry was popularized by Kalelevala Koru in their wartime iron age reproductions. Pennti Sarpaneva (1925-1978) was known for his work in cast bronze in the '60s and '70s, which was made by Kalevala Koru and Turun Hopea.

Björn Weckström (b. 1935) is considered one of the most innovative Finnish designers of the 1960s, and is still working today. He was one of the founders and the first designer for the well-known Finnish firm, Lapponia. He was a Lunning prizewinner in 1968. Cast jewelry was the new wrinkle of the '60s, and in fact wrinkled is what some of Weckström's gold and silver jewelry looked like, sometimes combined with acrylic. When Yoko Ono wore one of his silver and acrylic ring designs on the Dick Cavett television show in 1972, Weckström's international fame was assured. In 1977, Carrie Fisher wore a necklace of his in her role as Princess Leia in the movie "Star Wars."

In the early seventies, a company called Kultateollisuus made a series of pendants and chains, all variations on a circular form, the centers set with a variety of native Finnish stones.

It is possible to find pieces from the late fifties through the seventies on the secondary market in the U.S. made by the aforementioned makers as well as several others (see appendix for Finnish makers' marks). The names may seem strange and difficult to pronounce, but the quality of Finnish design and craftsmanship speaks for itself. The Finnish hallmark for local manufacture is a crown inside a heart (see Marks on Metals appendix). They use assay marks, date letters, and manufacturers' marks in a manner similar to the British, but unfortunately, some Finnish pieces are not fully hallmarked.

Mid-century Scandinavian jewelry made by manufacturers other than Georg Jensen has gained the attention of a small coterie of collectors, but there is still a great deal of it that goes unrecognized and underpriced in the marketplace. Numerous books have been published in their native languages on the designers and makers in each of the Scandinavian countries (see list of monographs in References). Some have English translations; however, the books themselves have been somewhat difficult to find in this country. Information in English has only recently become readily available, and is just beginning to have an effect on the general collecting public in the United States. Will Scandinavian jewelry become the next "hot" collectible? Only time will tell.

References: Eileene Harrison Beer, *Scandinavian Design, Objects of a Lifestyle*, The American-Scandinavian Foundation, 1975 (chapter on jewelry & metals); Lars Dybdahl et al, *Nordisk Smykkekunst/Nordic Jewellery*, Nyt Nordisk Forlag Arnold Busck, Denmark, 1995 (text in all Scandinavian languages and English); Janet Drucker, *Georg Jensen, A Tradition of Splendid Silver*, Schiffer Publishing, 1997; Donna Gustafson, "Tone Vigeland, A Physical Pleasure," *Ornament*, Winter, 1995; John Haycraft, *Finnish Jewelry and Silverware*, Otava, 1962 (out of print); Graham Hughes, *Modern Jewelry, An International Survey, 1890-1967,* Crown Publishers, 1968 (out of print); Annalies Krekel-Aalberse, *Art Nouveau and Art Deco Silver,* Harry N. Abrams, New York NY, 1989 (chapter on Scandinavian silversmithies, appendix of makers' marks); Ole Lachmann, "Danish Silver Marks," *Silver* magazine, March-April 1983; Jørgen E. R. Møller, *Georg Jensen The Danish Silversmith,* Georg Jensen & Wendel A/S, 1984; Ginger Moro, *European Designer Jewelry*, Schiffer Publishing, 1995, and "Scandinavian Modern Jewelry," *Jewelers' Circular-Keystone/Heritage*, August and November, 1996; Tuula Poutasuo, ed., Michael Wynne-Ellis, English text, *Finnish Silver*, Teema Oy, 1989; Nancy Schiffer, *Silver Jewelry Designs, Evaluating Quality*, Schiffer Publishing, 1996 (Scandinavian included in several chapters); Jacob Thage, *Danske Smykker/Danish Jewelry* (Danish and English text), Komma & Clausen, 1990; Tardy, *International Hallmarks on Silver* (translated from the French), Paris, 1985; Oppi Untracht, *Jewelry Concepts and Technology*, Doubleday, 1985 (many photographs of work by Scandinavian designers, especially Finns); Donald Willcox, *New Design in Jewelry*, Van Nostrand Reinhold, New York, NY, 1970 (out of print, all Scandinavian); exhibition catalogs: Martin Eidelberg, ed., *Design 1935-1965, What Modern Was*, Harry N. Abrams, 1991(multinational, multimedia); *Georg Jensen Silversmithy, 77 Artists, 75 Years*, Renwick Gallery, Smithsonian Institution Press, 1980; *The Lunning Prize* (multilingual text), Nationalmuseum, Stockholm, 1986; *Scandinavian Modern Design 1880-1980,* Cooper-Hewitt Museum, 1983 (an all-media exhibition, including some jewelry).

Monographs (books on individual designers): *Nanna Ditzel*, catalog of exhibition at Munkeruphus, Denmark, 1992 (Danish/English text); *Bent Gabrielsen, 40 År Med Smykker (40 Years with Jewelry),* Sven Jørn Andersen, catalog of an exhibition at Trapholt Museum of Modern Art, Kolding, Denmark, 1994 (Danish/English text); *Bertel Gardberg,* catalog of an exhibition in Helsinki,1985 (Finnish/Swedish captions); *Karl Gustav Hansen, Sølv/Silber 1930-1994*, Poul-Dedenroth-Schou, ed., Kolding Museum, Denmark, 1994 (Danish/German text); *Saara Hopea-Untracht, Elämä Ja Työ, Life and Work*, Oppi Untracht, Porvoo, Finland, 1988 (Finnish/English text); *Grete Prytz Kittelsen, Emaljekunst og Design (Enamel Art & Design),* Jan-Lauritz Opstad, Norway, 1978 (Norwegian/English text); *Wiwen Nilsson, Silversmeden*, Kersti Holmquist, Sweden, 1990 (Swedish text); *Sigurd Persson, en Mästare I Form (A Master of Design),* Dag Widman,

Carlsson Bokförlag, Sweden, 1994 (Swedish text, English summary); *Torun, Samtal med Vivianna Torun Bülow-Hübe (Conversation with...),* Ann Westin, Carlsson Bokförlag, Sweden, 1993 (Swedish/English text); *(The Jewelry of) Tone Vigeland, 1958-1995,* catalog of exhibition, Anniken Thue, ed., Oslo Museum of Applied Art, Norway, 1995 (English text).

Museums: The Georg Jensen Museum and The Museum of Decorative Art, Copenhagen, Denmark; Museum of Applied Arts, Helsinki, Finland; The Nationalmuseum, Stockholm, Sweden; The Oslo Museum of Applied Art, Oslo, Norway.

Reproduction Alert: Die-stamped copies of Georg Jensen and Jensen-inspired designs were made by Coro, Danecraft and other American companies in the 1940s, but they are usually marked and easily identified because they are not backed with a flat plate as Jensen pieces are. Trade names like "Vikingcraft" and "Norseland" were used to evoke association with Scandinavian design. Pieces marked "Georg Jensen U.S.A." were first made and marketed by Frederik Lunning during World War II when sterling was in short supply in Denmark and trade routes were cut off. Lunning turned to American manufacturers and produced the Jensen line on his own, hence the U.S.A. mark. Values tend to be lower for these items. According to Jensen dealer Caryl Unger of Imagination Unltd in Miami, FL, an Israeli firm was making knockoffs of Jensen jewelry about fifteen years ago, taking molds of original pieces and leaving the marks intact. When purchasing on the secondary market, it's advisable to know your Jensen or know your sources.

Advisors: Bruce Healy, Ginger Moro, Gail Selig, Caryl Unger (Georg Jensen).

Bracelet

Bangle

Sterling, amethyst, date letter for 1973, flat band curving up and widening to a circ concave disk front terminal and a lg oval amethyst cab mounted in the opposing terminal, front closure on underside of amethyst hooks into underside of disk, inside imp with Finnish hmks, "925," maker's mk for Kaunis Koru (adorned k's), date letter U7, designer's initials "OLW" for Olavi L. Wehmersuo, outside imp with Dutch import mks, 1-3/4" top to bottom at center, 2-5/8" w when closed, 2-3/8" inside dia 400

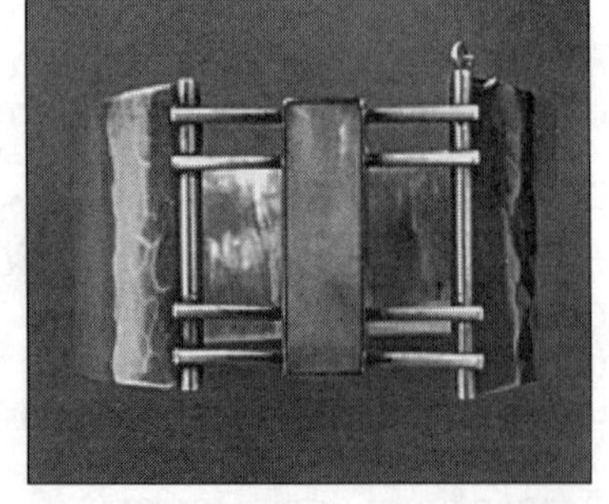

Bangle Bracelet, 930 silver, quartz, date letter for 1962, wide hammered band, tapering to the back, open ornamental front clasp, center bezel-set with a rect pale gray-pink quartz cab surmounting 2 pairs of curved-inward bars in hinged mounting, slotted tube with hingepin closure linked to safety chain, imp on outside back with maker's mk for Tillander, Finnish hmks, "916H," date letter I7, conjoined script "MH" for designer Mauno Honkanen, "K'A'SITY'O" (handwrought), 1-3/8" w, 2-3/8" inside dia, **$250**. (Author's collection).

Link Bracelet with charm, sterling, c. 1945, alternating plain and ropetwist-decorated lg curb links, hook clasp mkd "La Paglia sterling" (for Alphonse La Paglia), #130, suspending a circ disk charm with raised design depicting a pr of scales tossed by thunderclouds and lightning, a flowering plant and three stars around edge, probably an astrological symbol for Libra, possible wartime connotation, rev mkd "STERLING, GEORG JENSEN, INC U.S.A." #310, 7" tl x 1/2", charm 1-1/4" dia, **$200**. (Author's collection).

Bangle, hinged

Sterling, date letter for 1973, tapered band with hinged ornamental rounded rect top clasp with openwork design of intersecting bars and beads , mkd "E. Granit & Co. MADE IN FINLAND 925," date letter U7, top 1-1/4" w x 3/4", 2-1/4" inside dia... 225

Sterling, c. 1965-70, tapered band with hinged ring ornamental top clasp, mkd "Hans Hansen (script mark) 925S Denmark," top 1-1/2" w x 3/4", 2-1/2" inside dia....... 250

Link

18k yg, diamonds, c. 1943, links of alternating floral and foliate scroll motif, each floral link centering a sm bc diamond, approx 0.60 ct tw, sgd "GEORG JENSEN," v-spring and box clasp, 3/8" w, 7" tl .... 2,300 (A)

830 Silver, date letter for 1972, seven geo links of a sq on a line joined by sm circ rings, spring ring closure, mkd "830 S FINLAND," attributed to Kultateollisuus Ky, 3/8" w x 7-3/8" tl 100

Sterling, post-1945 mark, alternating floral and dove motif plaques joined with oval links, sgd "GEORG JENSEN, STERLING DENMARK," #14, 7/8" w x 8"......................... 690 (A)

Sterling, labradorite, c. 1930, alternating links of quatrefoils with scrolled centers and flowerheads with labradorite centers flanked by paired stylized leaves, imp with mk for Georg Jensen, "STERLING DENMARK" #18, v-spring and box clasp, 1/2" w x 7"....................................... 575 (A)

Sterling, lapis lazuli, post-1945 mark, eight links of alternating foliate and floral motif, each foliate link with an oval bezel-set lapis cab to one side, each floral link with a central bezel-set sm circ lapis cab, sgd "GEORG JENSEN STERLING DENMARK," # 3, v-spring and box clasp, 1/2" w x 6-1/2" tl .... 1,380 (A)

Sterling, date letter for 1957, nine open-backed box-shaped links with concave tops joined with triangular wire loops, hook closure, mkd "STERLING SWEDEN," Swedish hmks, date letter G9, mfr's signature "Atelier Stigbert" imp on outside of two links, "Cube" design by Sigurd Persson, 1953, 1/2" w x 8" tl 150

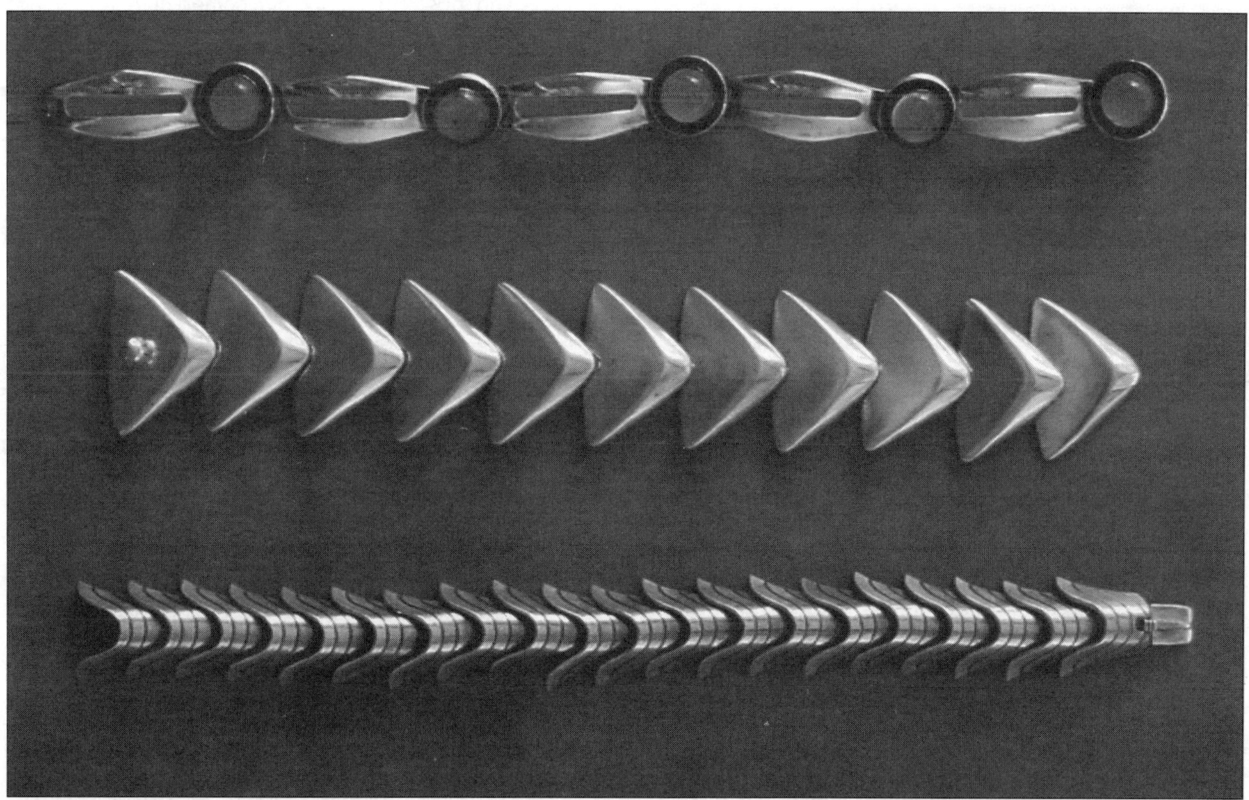

Link Bracelets, sterling, Danish:

T, c. 1960-65, five bezel-set circ rose quartz cabs on oxidized circ disks alternating with open concave center, convex-sided rect ster links, hook clasp, mkd "NE FROM STERLING 925S DANMARK," 1/2" w x 7-1/2" tl, **$125**.

C, c. 1955, ten overlapping shaped triangles, raised at the apexes, appl post and bead at end link, hook clasp, designed by Bent Gabrielsen, mkd "Hans Hansen" (script mark), "925 S Denmark," 1-1/8" w x 6-1/2" tl, **$250**.

B, c. 1950, overlapping convex cusped U-shaped ster links with parallel incised line decoration, v-spring and box clasp, mkd "STERLING DENMARK," Swedish import mks (three crowns in an oval), maker's mk for A. Michelsen (triangular reserve with AM surmounted by a crown), 3/4" w x 7-1/8" tl, **$250**.

(Alice Healy collection, photo by Bruce Healy).

Brooch/Pin

826 silver, amber, c. 1910, Danish *skønvirke*, a lg oval amber cab flanked by two repoussé silver flowerheads, surmounted by four stylized buds, two open lobes and oval links suspending a smaller oval amber cab and flowerhead drop flanked by open lobes, unbacked, rev imp "826S," 2-1/2" w x 3-1/4" tl 650

830 silver, c. 1940, scalloped lozenge shape, interlocking scrolling quatrefoil surrounding spheres, incised lines, oxidized bg, mkd "830 S," maker's mk for David-Andersen (scales), Norway, 1-5/8" w x 1-1/4" 245

830 Silver, date letter for 1972, geo design of repeating sq shapes on a line each terminating in a pendent ring, mkd "MADE IN FINLAND" and mfr's mk for Kultateollisuus Ky, date letter T7, Finnish hmk (crown within a heart), "830 H" and city mk for Turku, C-catch, 1-5/8" w x 1" 100

830 silver, dyed green chalcedony, c.1910, Danish *skønvirke*, repoussé stylized flowerhead bezel-set with a circ dyed green chalcedony cab center, flanked by scrolled foliate motifs surmounting a horizontal C-scroll, suspending a circ scrolled repoussé drop bezel-set with a smaller circ dyed green chalcedony cab, flat backing imp "C.A.C., 830S," C-catch, tube hinge, 2" w x 2-3/4" tl 350

830 silver, moonstone, c. 1920-25, flowerhead and paired leaves flanking central bezel-set circ moonstone, rev mkd "GI" and "830" in dotted ovals flanking "DENMARK" #107, trombone catch, tube hinge, 1-3/8" x 1-1/8"... 300

Gp 835 silver, marcasites, c. 1940, in the shape of a three-dimensional stylized masked jester's head, mask encrusted with bead-set marcasites, rose gp (worn), mkd "835 S," 1-3/4" w x 1" 185

Iron, silver, c. 1940-45, *jernsølv*, slightly convex quatrefoil iron plaque inlaid with dolphin, plant and water motifs, rev imp with an "A" over an "M" for designer Arno Malinowski, "GEORG JENSEN," #5002, 2" x 2" 400

Silver, lapis lazuli, c. 1920, three-part stylized floral motif pierced plaque, center with overlapping petals, suspending three elongated pear-shaped lapis drops with flowerhead caps, early maker's mk for Georg Jensen, #112, 1-1/2" w x 2" .... 1,265 (A)

Sterling vermeil, enamel, c. 1960, shaped oval with cutout center, blue *basse-taille* enamel with studs encircling the cutout and forming rays at the bottom, mkd "BALLE 925S STERLING NORWAY," 1-1/4" w x 2"............................. 100

Sterling, c. 1915-20, rect repoussé design of foliate blossoms, C-catch, mkd "GI" and "830" both in dotted ovals, "DENMARK" #66, 1-1/8" w x 3/4" 400

Sterling, c. 1940, die-stamped dove within a circ foliate wreath, 1933-44 mk for Georg Jensen, #70, 2-1/8" dia .... 431 (A)

Sterling, Danish, c. 1940-50, open rounded rectangle with central oval amber cab, cutout and appl engr fish motifs

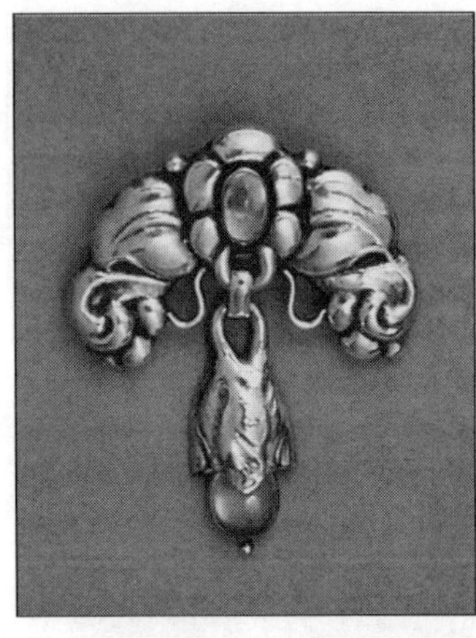

Brooch/Pin, 830 silver, moonstones, c. 1910, Danish *skønvirke*, arching raised floral/foliate motif with central pendent drop, bezel-set moonstone in central flowerhead and at bottom of drop, mkd "Wm F 830S" probably for William Fuglede, 1-7/8" w x 2-1/4", **$600**. (Courtesy of Dawn Lowe, Xcentricities, Beverly Hills, CA),

at four corners, beaded wire frame, mkd "HANDMADE STERLING DENMARK DAURUP," safety catch, 1-3/4" w x 1-1/4" 275

Sterling, Danish, c. 1940-50, circ open design of off center circ bezel-set dyed-green chalcedony cab and appl and engr ster fish, starfish, and bubbles, mkd "STERLING DENMARK N.E. FROM 925S," 1-5/8" dia 175

Sterling, c. 1950, Viking ship motif of scrolled sq ster wire, appl coiled ster wire "waves," cutout ster sheet sail, mkd "STERLING DENMARK," maker's mk for A. Michelsen (AM surmounted by a crown in a triangle), 1-1/4" w x 1-1/8" 55

Sterling, c. 1960, stylized open-center sunburst with alternating short and long rays in two layers, mkd "STERLING NORWAY," designer's mk for Tone Vigeland (T within V), flanked by a lg "N" and "+" for applied arts workshop PLUS, Fredrikstad, Norway , 2-1/4" dia 250

Sterling, post-1945 mark, a cutout incised floral and foliate design with two butterflies, enclosed in an open circ frame, designed by Arno Malinowski, sgd "GEORG JENSEN" in a dotted oval, "STERLING DENMARK" #283, 2" dia .... 489 (A)

Sterling, post-1945 mark, c. 1950, open biomorphic freeform, five-lobed, designed by Henning Koppel, imp "GEORG JENSEN STERLING DENMARK" (post-1945 mark), 1-7/8" w x 1-1/2" 250

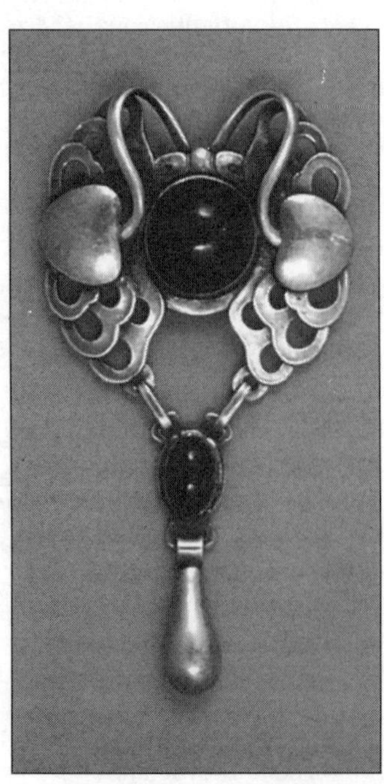

Brooch/Pin, sterling, dyed green chalecedony, c. 1920, later version of a c. 1905 design, a cutout stylized wreath motif with undulating vines terminating in heart-shaped leaves flanking a lg circ green cab bezel-set in the center, suspending an oval green chalcedony cab and a pear-shaped ster drop, rev imp with superimposed "GJ" for Georg Jensen, "925 STERLING DENMARK," #2, trombone catch, tube hinge, 2" w 3-3/8" tl, **$1,200**. (Courtesy of Dawn Lowe, Xcentricities, Beverly Hills, CA).

Sterling, post-1945 mark, circ domed plaque with V-shaped deep indentations at both sides, rev imp "GEORG JENSEN" in a dotted oval, mkd "HK" for designer Henning Koppel, "STERLING DENMARK," 2" dia 275

Sterling, post-1945 mark, circ with open center, entwined foliate motif with rows of raised beads, scallop edge, rev imp "GEORG JENSEN" in a dotted oval, "STERLING DENMARK," 1-1/2" dia 195

Sterling, post-1945 mark, open circ frame enclosing cutout butterfly and floral/foliate motifs, designed by Arno Malinowski, maker's mk for Georg Jensen, #283, 2-1/8" dia. .... 403 (A)

Sterling, amethyst, c. 1933-44, oval pierced ster plaque of floral and foliate motif with a central bezel-set circ amethyst cab, 1933-44 maker's mk for Georg Jensen, "STERLING DENMARK," #13, trombone catch, 1-7/8" w x 1-1/4" .... 633 (A)

Brooches/Pins, sterling, by Evald Nielsen, Denmark:

T, c. 1930, lg and sm pr, each with a floral bud center set with a dyed green chalcedony cab, the larger with three concentric ster wire rings, the smaller with two eccentric rings, both with ster bead decoration, rev mkd "EN," "925 S," trombone catches, tube hinges, lg 1-5/8" dia, sm 1" dia, pr, **$400**.
(Sue James collection).

C, c. 1915, open repoussé floral/foliate design set with two coral cabs in bud-like settings, suspending an elongated teardrop-shaped coral drop from three flat oval links, flat backing mkd "Evald Nielsen, STERLING SILVER, 925 SØLV," C-catch, tube hinge, 1-3/4" w x 3-1/2", **$800**.

B, c. 1925, oval pierced repoussé berry/foliate design with scrolling vines flanking central motif, flat backing mkd "EN," "STERLING SILVER, DENMARK," trombone catch, tube hinge, 2-1/8" w x 1-5/8", **$350**. (Author's collection).

Brooch/Pin, 830 silver, silver vermeil, c. 1950, traditional Norwegian *sølje*, circ wirework with appl beads, six silver vermeil concave disks suspended around outer border and further suspending wirework trefoils with appl beads, mkd "KJS 830 S MADE IN NORWAY," 2-1/2" w x 3-3/8", **$125**. (Diane White collection).

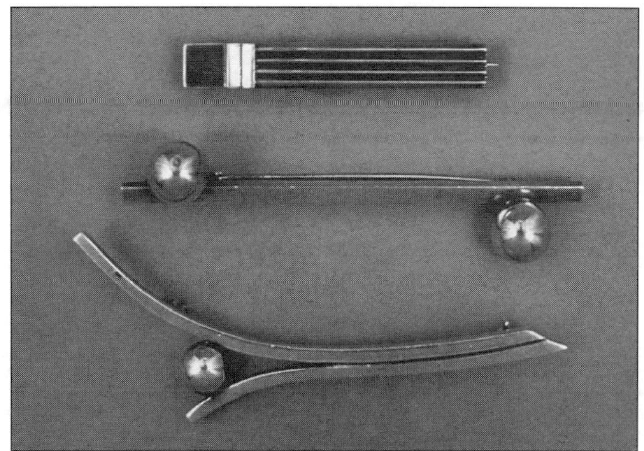

Bar Brooches/Pins, sterling, by Karl Gustav Hansen for Hans Hansen, Denmark, c. 1935:

T, parallel horizontal grooves, joined at one end to an angled rect polished plaque, maker's mk (conjoined Hs), "925 S" on appl rect on rev, 2" w x 1/4", **$95**.

C, sq wire bar balancing a sphere at each end on opposite sides, trombone catch, mkd "HaH," one of "Future" series, designed in 1932, "925 S," 3-1/4" w x 1/2", **$200**. (Patrick Kapty collection).

B, two uneven lengths of sq bar, splayed ends flanking a sphere, sgd "Hans Hansen (early script mark), 925 S DENMARK" #105, one of "Future" series, 3-3/8" w x 1-3/8", **$200**. (Author's collection).

Sterling, enamel, c. 1950, in the shape of a stylized owl, one eye with red and yellow mottled enamel, three diagonal appl parallel sq wire bars at the base, rev imp "JoPol STERLING" for Joan Polsdorfer, New York, NY, #113, 1-1/8" w x 2" 75

Sterling, enamel, post-1945 mark, c. 1947, abstract biomorphic figure-eight design, dk green enameled center outline, mkd "GEORG JENSEN" in a dotted oval, mkd "HK" in a solid oval, "925S DENMARK" #315, safety catch, 1-3/4" w x 1" 450

Sterling, enamel, post-1945 mark, c. 1947, arrowhead shape, freeform translucent dk purple and violet enamel in center, mkd on raised oval on rev "GEORG JENSEN" in a dotted oval, "HK" in a solid oval, "STERLING DENMARK" #307, safety catch, 2-3/8" w x 1-1/4" 475

Sterling, enamel, post-1945 mark, c. 1947, cast biomorphic abstract trefoil, three open cusped lobes, black opaque enameled concave stem, mkd "GEORG JENSEN" in a dotted oval, "HK" in a solid oval for designer Henning Koppel, "STERLING DENMARK" #323, safety catch, 2-1/2" w x 2-1/4" 500

Sterling, lapis lazuli, c. 1933-44, quatrefoil floral motif centering a lg oval bezel-set lapis cab, surrounded by four stamped floral motifs each with three sm circ bezel-set lapis cabs, maker's mk for Georg Jensen, 1933-44, "STERLING DENMARK," #173, 1-7/8" w x 1-5/8"..... 978 (A)

Sterling, moonstone, post-1945 mark, circ design of a magnolia blossom centering one sm bezel-set circ moonstone cab surmounted by five sm appl ster beads, sgd "GEORG JENSEN" in a dotted oval, "STERLING DENMARK," # 113, 1-1/2" dia .... 374 (A)

Brooch/Pin, iron, sterling, c. 1940-45, *jernsølv*, circ convex iron disk with inlaid silver design of a dove on a branch, inlaid silver border, imp "GEORG JENSEN," #5014, "HN" for designer Harald Nielsen, 1-1/2" dia, **$450**. (Mary Williamson collection).

Brooch/Pin, sterling vermeil, enamel, c. 1910-15, lobed oblong, raised mask design in orange, yellow, brown and black *basse-taille* and *cabochonnerie* enamel, segmented border, mkd "J.TOSTRUP 925S" (Norway) and "MØNSTER BESKYTTET" (lit., "design protected"), C-catch, flanged hinge, 1-1/2" w x 1-1/4, **$400**. (Terrance O'Halloran collection).

Brooch/Pin, sterling, c. 1965, cutout design depicting Viking ships at sail with dragon's head prows repeated in profile on either side and at the front, mkd "D-A" for David-Andersen, "925S Norway sterling," and "INV. B.S.Ø." for designer Bjørn Sigurd Østern, 1-3/4" w x 2", **$150**. (Gianna Cagliano collection).

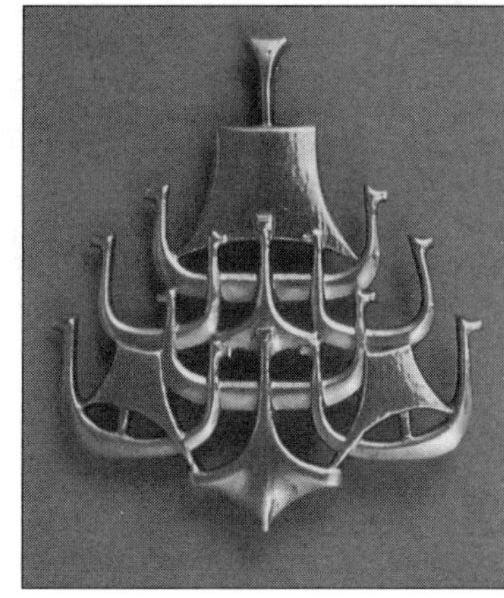

Brooch/Pin, sterling, enamel, c. 1955-60, rect ster plaque with inlaid ster pre-Columbian motif in brownish-green enameled ground, mkd "UNI D-A STERLING NORWAY" for Uni David-Andersen, 1-5/8" w x 1-1/4", **$150**. (Shari and Jeff Miller collection).

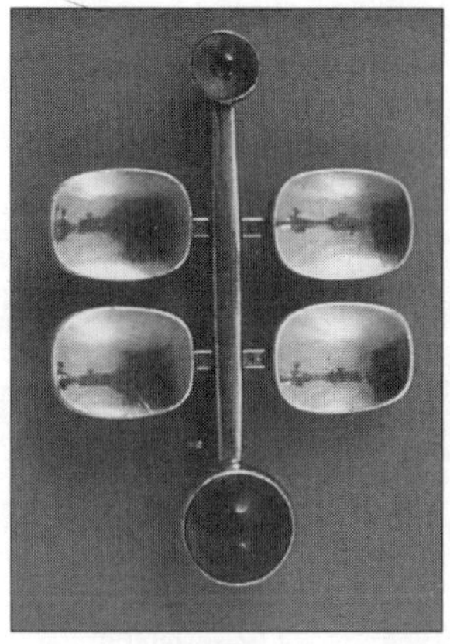

Brooch/Pin, 830 silver, amethysts, date letter for 1963, four rounded rect concave plaques mounted on short sq wire bars flanking a longer sq wire bar, bezel-set with a lg and a sm circ amethyst cab at each end, rev imp with Swedish hmks, date letter N9, initials "AMS" and "JP," unknown designer and maker, 1-1/4" w x 2", **$200**. (Author's collection).

Silver and Enamel Jewelry by Marius Hammer, Bergen Norway, c. 1900-1910:

C, Brooch/Pin, kelly green *basse-taille* enameled open bow-shaped interlace with inverted heart-shaped center, three sm enameled tear-drop shaped drops suspended from base, further suspending an enameled open oval interlace from two lengths of cable link chain, a filigree rosette in center opening and at the base, terminating in three sm enameled tear-drop shaped drops at sides and bottom, rev imp "935 S," maker's mark (capital M with superimposed hammer symbol), C-catch, tube hinge, 1-1/2" w x 3" tl, **$450**.

B, Festoon Necklace, teal blue *basse-taille* enameled navette-shaped links alternating with sm filigree quatrefoils with white enameled centers, swagged chains suspending five open pear-shaped blue *plique à jour* enameled drops with filigree rosette centers, tear-drop shaped *basse-taille* enameled terminals, three from center, one from each side drop and one between each, continuing to a cable link chain, v-spring and tube clasp, rev imp "935 S," maker's mark, 17-1/2" tl, 2" at center, **$650**. (Author's collection).

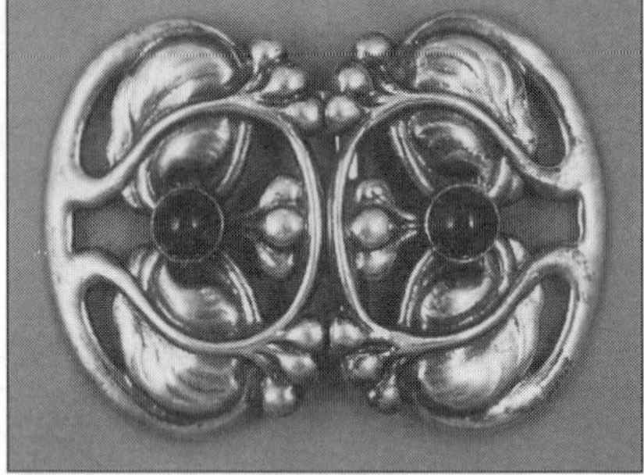

Buckle, Danish *skønvirke,* 826 silver, dyed green chalcedony, c. 1910, two-pc stamped raised undulating vine, berry and leaf motifs, each pc set with a circ green chalcedony cab, unbacked, mkd "BH" for mfr Bernhard Hertz, "826 S," hook and eye closure, bars for belt attachment, 3-3/8" w x 2-3/8", **$400**. (Courtesy of Dawn Lowe, Xcentricities, Beverly Hills, CA).

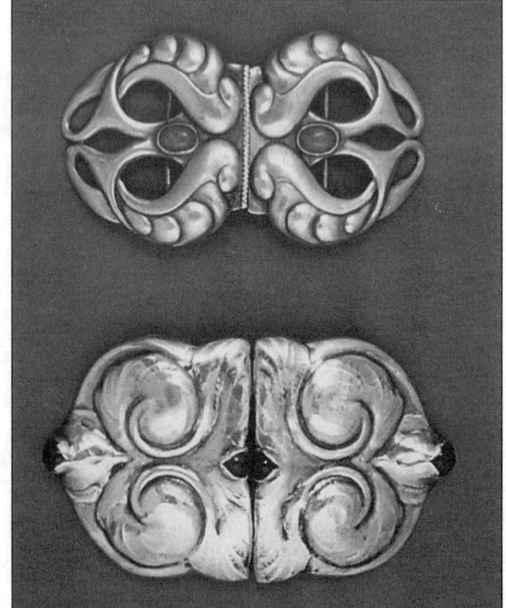

Buckles, two-piece, 826 silver, Danish *skønvirke*, c. 1910:

T, each pc stamped with opposed stylized plumes flanking a bezel-set oval amber cab within open center, tapering to curv vine-like design, unbacked, rev imp "826 S," 3-3/4" w x 2", **$475**.

B, each pc a repoussé design of opposed volutes flanking two floral bud-like settings for circ carnelian cabs, unbacked, rev imp "826 S" and maker's initials "S(?)J," possibly for S.L. Jacobsen, design attributed to Evald Nielsen, hook and eye closure, appl bars for belt attachment, 4" w x 2-1/2", **$850**.

Circle

Sterling, post-1945 mark, open foliate wreath motif, rev imp "GEORG JENSEN" in a dotted oval, "Sigvard" in stylized script for designer Sigvard Bernadotte, and "STERLING DENMARK," 1-1/4" dia 185

Lapel

Sterling, post-1945 mark, rounded bar in the shape of a torch, flared and surmounted by a flame at one end, with appl spiraling vine motif running the length of the bar, rev imp "GEORG JENSEN" in a dotted oval, "STERLING DENMARK," 1/4" w x 2-1/2" 225

Cuff Links

Enamel, sterling, c. 1955-60, open rect plaques with geo design of open rect and enamel sections in lt blue, dk blue, and purple, hinged back plate, maker's mk for David-Andersen, "925 S Sterling Norway," illegible mk on rev of front plate, 1" w x 3/4", pr 100

Sterling, c. 1935, circ plaque with scene of a Viking ship at sail, 1933-44 mk for Georg Jensen, #50, 3/4" dia .... 374 (A)

Sterling, c. 1915, oval bezel-set turquoise cab in segmented oval frame, hinged elliptical back plate with similar repoussé design, designed by Georg Jensen, mkd "GI" in a dotted circle and "830" in a dotted circle, 5/8" w x 1/2", pr 400

Sterling, post-1945 mark, concave shaped oval disks with flat backing, hinged backs of smaller similar shape, designed by Nanna Ditzel, shank imp "GEORG JENSEN" in a dotted oval, #74C, "STERLING DENMARK, 925S," 3/4" dia, pr 200

Sterling, post-1945 mark, sq bars with evenly spaced parallel incised lines, hinged to stepped geo backs, designed by Henry Pilstrup in 1937, imp "GEORG JENSEN" in a dotted oval, # 64, "STERLING DENMARK," Fr import mk, 3/4" w x 3/8", pr 250

Sterling, c. 1950, elongated oval ster plaques with incised and oxidized zigzag and dot design, hinged oval back, maker's mk for Hans Hansen (superimposed lg and sm Hs), and "925S DENMARK #638," 1-1/4" w x 3/8" 75

Sterling, c. 1950, rounded triangular plaque, shaped and tapered from thick to thin edge, navette-shaped hinged back mounted on curved bar mkd "925 S DENMARK," maker's mk for Hans Hansen Silversmithy (superimposed lg and sm Hs), #640, design attributed to Bent Gabrielsen, 1" w x 3/4" 75

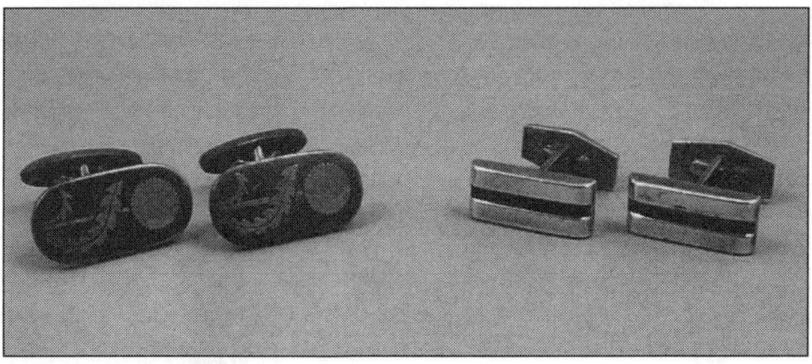

Cuff Links, Danish:

L, c. 1940-45, *"jernsølv,"* rounded oblong iron plaque with inlaid silver in a nettle design, mkd "GEORG JENSEN," design by Arno Malinowski, elliptical hinged backs on curved bars, 1-1/4" w x 1/2", pr, **$175**.

R, c. 1935-40, rounded rectangles with oxidized center groove, hinged back plate, mkd "DENMARK 925 S," "HaH" for Hans Hansen, designed by Karl Gustav Hansen, 3/4" w x 3/8", pr, **$100**. (Patrick Kapty collection).

Dress Set, sterling, post-1945 mark, semi-cylindrical cuff links with recessed threaded center, hinged back plates, three matching studs, designed by Sigvard Bernadotte, mkd "GEORG JENSEN" in a dotted oval, "STERLING DENMARK," cuff links 1" w x 3/8", studs 1/2" w x 3/8", suite, **$450**. (Photo courtesy of Bruce Healy).

Sterling, date letter for 1966, four indented disks with rounded sides, oxidized centers, appl in pairs to rounded sq plaque, hinged bar findings, mkd "AARIKKA STERLING," mfr's mk, Finnish hmk (crown within a heart), "916 H," date letter N7, and Helsinki city assay mk, 1/2" sq, pr 95

Tiger's eye quartz, sterling, date letter for 1971, open rectangle with central dyed-blue tiger's eye quartz bezel-set sq cab, hinged back plate, makers mk for Kupitaan Kulta, Finnish hmk (crown within a heart), "925 H" in a rect reserve, date letter S7, and Turku city assay mk, 7/8" w x 5/8", pr 75

Wood, 800 silver, date letter for 1960, dk wood rectangle mounted on ster plaque, framed on two sides, hinged backs, maker's mk for Eric Granit (stylized EG), Finnish hmk (crown within a heart), "813 H," Helsinki city assay mark, date letter G7, hinged bar findings, 1" w x 3/8", pr 85

Earrings

Sterling, c. 1925-30, oval foliate motif, maker's mk for Georg Jensen, 1/2" w x 3/4", pr 185

Earrings, 830 silver, dyed green chalcedony, c. 1940, oval cabs, bezels surmounted by scrolled wire and bead clusters, maker's mk "EN" for Evald Nielsen, Denmark, screwback findings, 5/8" w x 7/8", **$250**. (Gail Gerretsen collection).

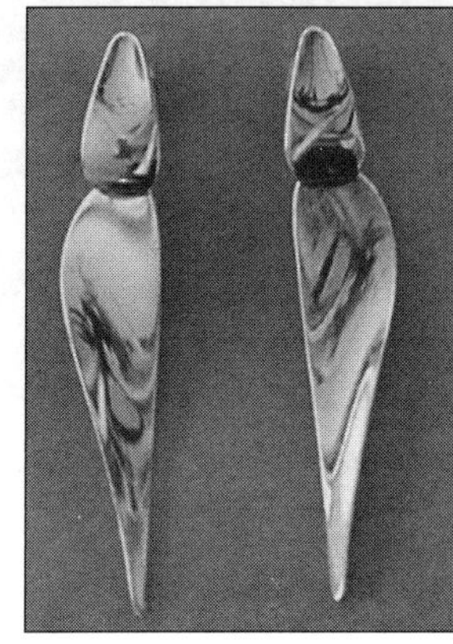

Pendent Earrings, sterling, c. 1957, slightly concave rounded triangular surmounts suspending slightly torqued and elongated inverted teardrop pendants, screwbacks, designed by Nanna and Jørgen Ditzel, mkd "GEORG JENSEN" in a dotted oval, "STERLING DENMARK," #125, 1/2" w x 3", pr, **$450**. (Alice Healy collection, photo by Bruce Healy).

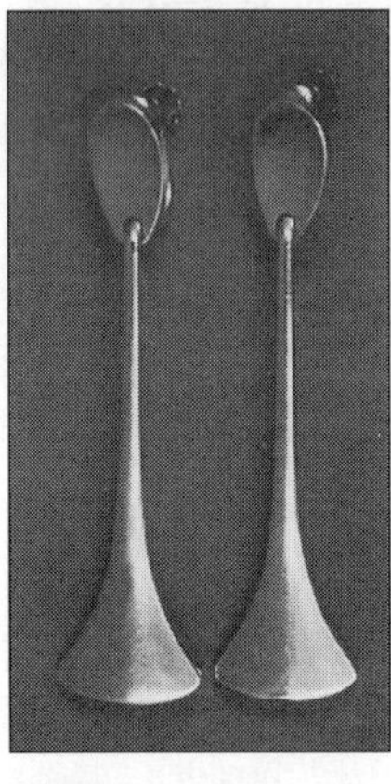

Pendent Earrings, sterling, c. 1955-60, slightly concave ovoid surmount suspending an elongated tapered and flared drop, surmount rev mkd "925 S DENMARK," superimposed lg and sm H for Hans Hansen Silversmithy, #444, design attributed to Bent Gabrielsen, 5/8" x 2-1/2" tl, **$250**. (Author's collection).

Necklace

Sterling, dyed green chalcedony, post-1945 mark, links of quatrefoils with green chalcedony centers alternating with links of paired ovals flanked by stylized foliate motifs, each bezel-set with two green chalcedony cabs, imp "GEORG JENSEN" in a dotted oval, "STERLING DENMARK" #25, 7/8" w x 16-1/2 tl .... 2,645 (A)

Sterling, c. 1950-60, three large shaped and tapered crescent-shaped bars linked with oversize jump rings, hook closure, rev imp "Hans Hansen (script mark), 925 S DENMARK," #320, design attributed to Bent Gabrielsen, 14" tl, 3/8" w 300

Pendant and Chain

Amber, sterling, c. 1960, circ bezel-set amber cab framed by sq ster wire splayed at the top, forming double-sided bail continuing to a sq wire rod and round link ster chain, spring ring clasp, mkd "STERLING DENMARK NE FROM 925 S," pendant 1-1/4" dia, 16-1/2" tl 250

Pewter, c. 1970, cast abstract design of an open rectangle divided by vertical and horizontal bars with irregularly placed appl sm circles interspersed throughout, suspended from cable link chain, rev mkd "JHULL DENMARK" and "B&D" in a rectangle below a circle, pendant 1-1/2" w x 3-1/2" tl, chain 28" tl 50

Sterling, c. 1972, geo design of repeating squares turned 45 degrees continuing to single lines, rows of one, two and three motifs suspended from bead-tipped bars, third row terminating in three pendent jump rings, mkd "830 S Finland" on pendant, mkd "830 S" on chain, attributed to Kultateollisuus Ky, 1-3/8" w x 2-3/4" including bail, chain 23" tl 100

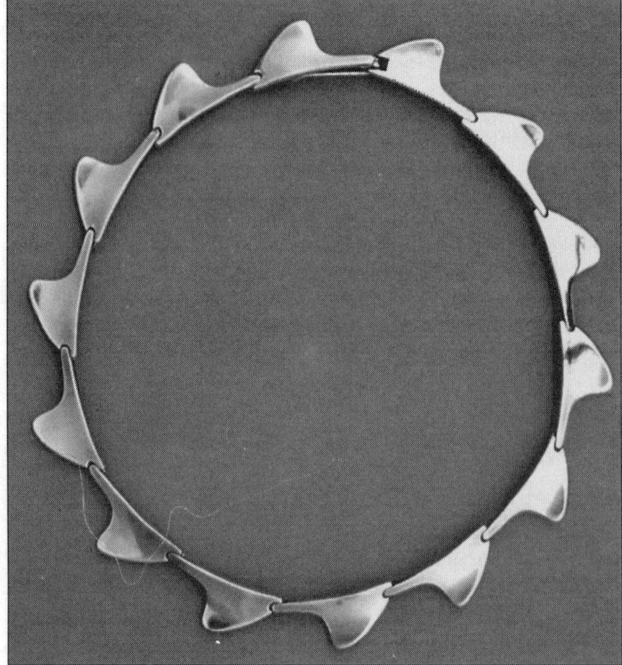

Necklace, sterling, c. 1956, flexible collar of slightly concave rounded fin-shaped links, hook clasp, rev mkd "HANDMADE, STERLING DENMARK, BENT K" for Anni and Bent Knudsen, #2, 5/8" w x 16" tl, **$500**. (Author's collection).

Necklace, wood, wm, c. 1960, paper clip chain suspending a fringe of lg and sm lt wood beads on wire, sgd "KAIJA AARIKKA FINLAND" on metal tag at hook clasp, 2-1/2" w (at center), 17" tl, **$85**. (Sue James collection).

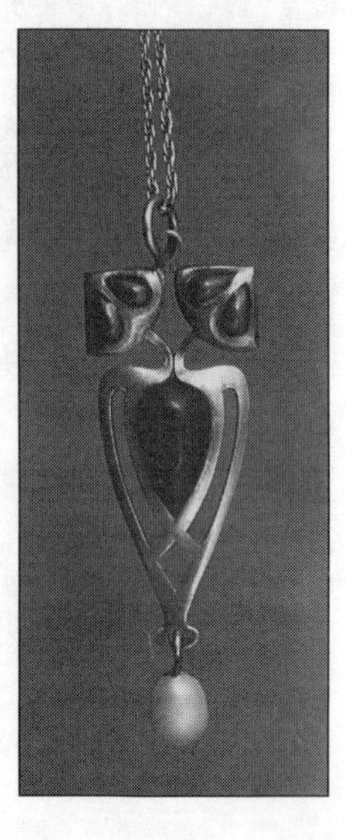

Pendant, sterling vermeil, enamel, c. 1925, pierced and domed tapered shield-shaped plaque, inverted pear-shaped center enameled cobalt blue, surmounted by two stylized cusped buds, each with two pear-shaped centers enameled green, terminating in a white-enameled oval drop, mkd "925," c. 1924 maker's mk for David-Andersen, Norway ("S" above a three-pronged forked motif), 3/4" w x 2", replaced chain 20" tl, **$600**. (Ann Tidwell collection).

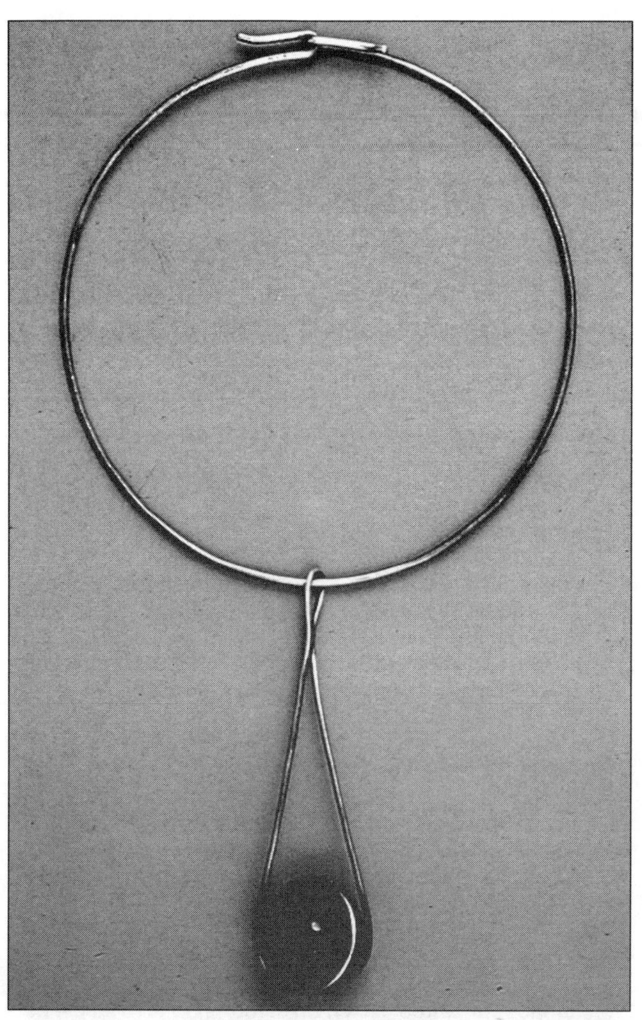

Pendant and Neckring, sterling, glass, c. 1960, elongated teardrop-shaped bent wire looped over a 1" dia blue glass sphere, suspended from a wire neckring, hook clasp, mkd "BENT K STERLING DENMARK" for Bent Knudsen, pendant 1" w x 3 1/2", neckring 4 1/2" dia, **$375**. (Elayne Glotzer collection).

Pendant and Neckring, sterling, red jasper, date letter for 1977, cast ster hummingbird in flight with engr details, suspending a wire-wrapped round red jasper double cab, suspended from a plain ster neckring by lg jump ring, pendant with unknown Finnish maker's mk, Finnish hmk (crown within a heart), date letter Z7, Turku city assay mark, sgd "GARDBERG" for Bertel Gardberg, designer, pendant 2-1/4" w x 3-1/2" tl, neckring 4-3/4" inside dia, **$450**. (Courtesy of Before Antiques).

Pendants and Chains, 830 silver and gemstones, by Kultateollisuus Ky, Turku, Finland, early 1970s:

L, date letter for 1973, central bezel-set spectrolite circ disk encircled by sm silver disks and radiating short silver rods terminating in lg C-scrolls, rev imp "FINLAND, 830" Finnish hmks, date letter U7, maker's mk (winged hammer), 1-7/8" dia, suspended from a flat cable link 830 silver chain, 23" tl, **$150**.
(Author's collection).

R, date letter for 1972, equilateral cross, bezel set circ flat amethyst disk encircled by sm polished disks, pr of disks at each terminal and surmounting bail, suspended from orig cable link chain, 24" tl, Finnish hmk, date letter T7, Turku assay mk, "830 H," maker's mk, "MADE IN FINLAND," 1-3/4" w x 2-1/4", **$150**.
(Gilly Phipps collection).

Pendant, sterling, c. 1960, stylized sunburst motif with two layers of rays around open ring, designer's mk for Tone Vigeland (T within V), flanked by a lg "N" and "+" for applied-arts workshop PLUS, Fredrikstad, Norway, also mkd "JLM 925S," a triangle in a circle and a "T" in a square on pendant and neckring, 2-1/2" w x 3-5/8" tl, **$300**. (Al Munir Meghji collection).

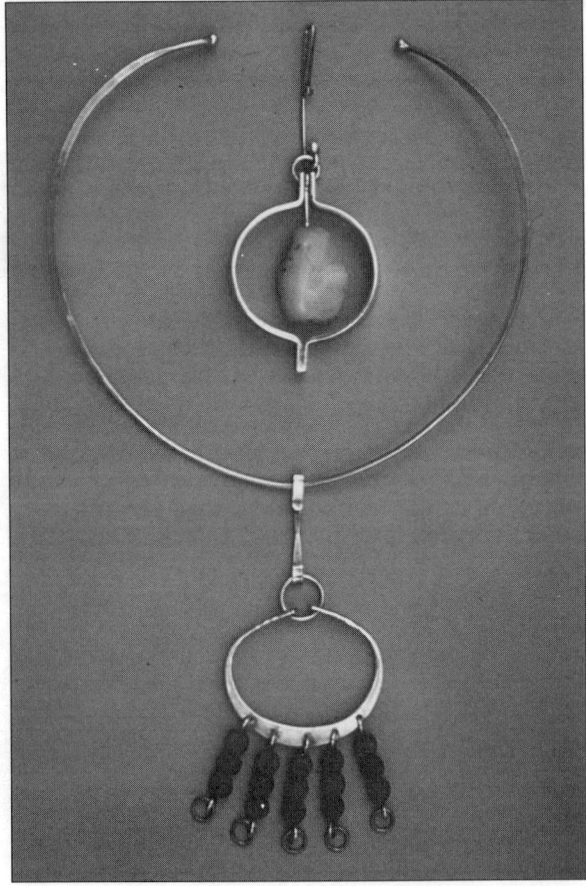

Pendants, sterling, designed by Anna Greta Eker for PLUS applied arts workshop, Frederikstad, Norway, c 1960:

TC, annular cusped oval frame with flat tapered sides, suspending an irregular tumble-polished lavender, gray and white lace agate from elongated open bead-tipped bent wire hook bail, inside frame mkd "N AGE +" and "STERLING 925 S NORWAY," 1-7/8" w x 4" tl, **$150**.
(Author's collection).

B, Pendant and Neckring, hammered penannular oval suspending five rows of circ wood disk beads, each terminating in a ster ring, terminals joined at top by a lg jump ring suspended by an elongated hook bail from a hammered penannular neckring, mkd "STERLING 925 S NORWAY" and "N AGE +," pendant 1-3/4" w x 4-1/2" (with bail), neckring 5-1/2" inside dia, **$300**.
(Al Munir Meghji collection).

Rings, sterling and gemstones, mkd "MOLTKE DENMARK 925 S," **c. 1973:**

L, two sodalite cylinders in conforming setting in elevated mount, shank cusped at the base, 5/8" w x 5/8", **$100**.

C, penannular shank flared to top rect ends inlaid with rect lapis lazuli plaques , 3/8" w x 5/8", $150.

R, turq cube in inverted U-shaped ster cage mounted on plain shank, 1/2" w x 5/8", **$125**.
(Alice Healey collection, photo by Bruce Healey).

Sterling, tiger's eye quartz, c. 1970, two overlapping sq U-shaped ster bars enclosing a post-mounted irregular navette-shaped tiger's eye quartz, suspended from lg link trace chain attached with jump rings to U terminals, mkd with stylized initials EC for designer Erling Christoffersen, flanked by lg "N" and + sign for applied-arts workshop PLUS, Frederikstad, Norway, pendant 1-1/4" w x 2-1/8", chain 27" tl 200

Pendant and Neckring

Sterling, enamel, c. 1955-60, rounded hatchet shape with off-center black enameled oval dot, designed by Bent Gabrielsen, mkd "925S Hans Hansen (script mark) DENMARK" on pendant, "HaH 925" on neckring, pendant 1-7/8" w x 2" tl 350

Ring

830 silver, enamel, c. 1970, flattened hollow sphere, top surface with three circ cutouts, red-enameled inside bottom surface, mounted on plain band, inside imp "830 S, MADE IN FINLAND," top 7/8" dia, approx size 6-1/2 50

Rings, sterling, adjustable designs, made at PLUS, Frederikstad, Norway, c. 1960:

L, wide band divided into three and two interlaced bead-tipped front terminals, mks for PLUS, "AGE" for designer Anna Greta Eker, 3/4" w, **$50**.

CL, concentric pennannular tapered bands, smooth polished surface, rev mkd for PLUS, designer's mk for Tone Vigeland (T inside V), "STERLING 925 S NORWAY," 1/2" w, **$75**.

CR, continuous triple-wrapped strip, wide scored terminals in front flanking narrow center section, rev mkd for PLUS, designer's mk for Tone Vigeland, "STERLING 925 S NORWAY," 1/2" w, **$75**.
(Author's collection).

R, single ster bar bent in a U shape with scrolled terminals, mkd "N NORWAY STERLING 925S," **$50**.
(Terrance O'Halloran collection).

830 silver, date letter for 1972, four grad openbacked cylinders with cutout vertical openings, mounted at angles to one another, interspersed with three flattened beads, mounted on an adjustable shank, mkd "FINLAND" and "JL," unknown Finnish maker's mk, Finnish hmk (crown within a heart), "830 H," Turku city assay mark, and date letter T7, 1-1/4" w x 1-3/8"....................................... 125

Porcelain, sterling, c. 1960-65, circ white porcelain disk bisected by a line of textured cast ster, mounted on plain band, mkd "925 S" and maker's mk for A. Michelsen, DENMARK, 1-1/4" dia, size 6-1/2................................ 125

Sterling, c. 1935-40, rounded rect plaque with oxidized vertical center groove, flanked by two tapered half-crescents mounted on each side of and perpendicular to narrow shank, oxidized shoulders, inside mkd "HaH 925 S DENMARK" for Hans Hansen, design by Karl Gustav Hansen, plaque 1/4" w x 3/4", approx size 6............ 125

Sterling, Danish, c. 1940-50, circ amber bezel-set cab to one side with appl and engr design of fish, starfish, and bubbles, mkd "STERLING DENMARK N.E. FROM 925S," 1" w, size 6-1/2... 125

Sterling, c. 1965, "Saga" design, rect plaque with three stamped raised horizontal bars with domed disks and rows of incised lines and circles, adjustable shank, imp in script on rev "COPY ORIG. YEAR 300," mkd "DAVID-ANDERSEN NORWAY STERLING 925 S," 5/8" w x 1"... 50

Sterling, c. 1970, concave disk with oxidized bg and appl cluster of lg and sm ster beads, mk for Kupitaan Kulta and "925S FINLAND," adjustable shank, 3/4" dia......... 60

Sterling, date letter for 1968, designed by Björn Weckström, irregular ridged, creased and folded cast plaque, a raised knob in one corner, mounted on a plain wide band, inside imp "STERLING FINLAND," maker's mk for Lapponia, "925H," Finnish hmks, date letter Q7, 7/8" w x 1-1/4", approx size 5 200

Sterling, date letter for 1974, penannular, one cusped front terminal opposing other convex double-lobed terminal, tapering to a narrow shank, rev imp "LAPPONIA" with maker's mark, Finnish hmks, V7 date letter, "925," 7/8" top to bottom, size 6... 65

Sterling, aventurine quartz, c. 1968, open cube oxidized interior, a projecting tapered cylinder of green aventurine quartz inserted into center, mounted on a plain wide band, mkd "HaH 925 S DENMARK," for Hans Hansen, design attributed to Karl Gustav Hansen, cube 5/8" sq, 3/8" h, cylinder 5/8" h, approx size 6-1/2......................... 150

Sterling, green agate, c. 1960, cast curv three-dimensional biomorphic shape enclosing a green agate sphere, mkd "FINLAND 925 S," maker's mk for Kupitaan Kulta, 1" w x 1" at top, size 8.. 75

Suite: Brooch and Earrings

Sterling vermeil, enamel, c. 1960, shaped oval with cutout center, red *basse-taille* enamel with studs encircling the cutout and forming rays at the bottom, mkd "BALLE 925S STERLING NORWAY," brooch 1-1/4" w x 2", clipback earrings 5/8" w x 7/8", suite.. 150

Rings, sterling, made by Kupitaan Kulta, Finland, c. 1973:

L, four inverted domes, adorsed at an angle in prs, each with a bead mounted inside oxidized inner surface, mkd "925 S FINLAND," mfr mk (anvil), 5/8" w x 3/4", **$75**.

C, two opposed open clamshell forms, a freely moving carnelian bead inserted into each, mounted on plain adjustable shank, mkd "925 S FINLAND," mfr's mk, 7/8" w x 4/8", **$125**.

R, top resembling a three-dimensional grid of five cubes in domino formation, intersected by an oxidized horizontal plane, mounted on plain adjustable shank, mkd "925 S FINLAND," mfr's mk, 5/8" x 5/8", **$75**. (Alice Healey collection, photo by Bruce Healy).

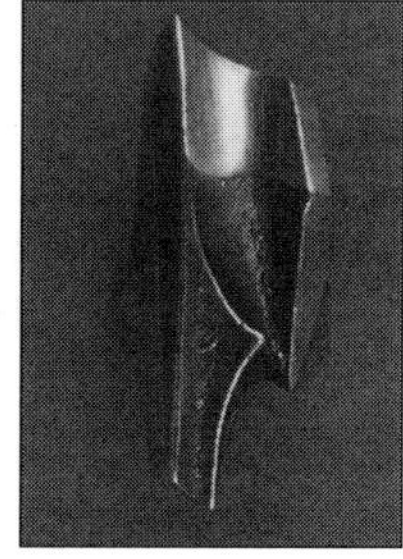

Ring, bronze, c. 1970, cast bronze, elongated irregular "craggy" raised surface, mkd "BW" for Björn Weckström for Lapponia, Finland, adjustable band shank, 3/4" w x 1-3/4", **$155**. (Shari and Jeff Miller collection).

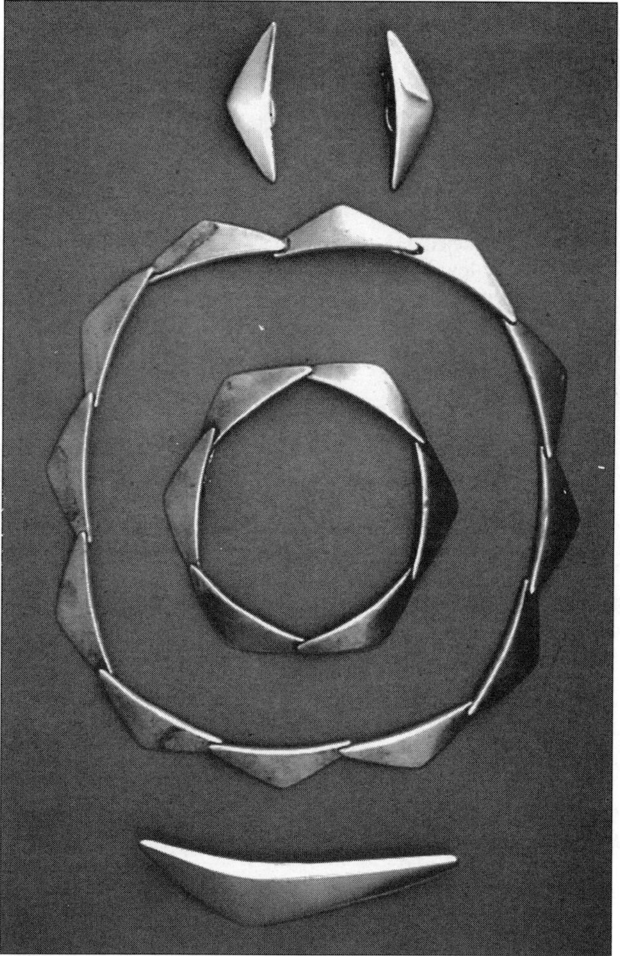

Suite: Necklace, Bracelet, Brooch and Earrings, sterling, c. 1955, boomerang-shaped link necklace and bracelet, earrings single boomerangs of same size, brooch a single lg boomerang, design by Bent Gabrielsen, all pieces mkd "Hans Hansen (script mark) 925S DENMARK," necklace # 315, 3/8" w x 14" tl, earrings #432", 3/8" w x 1-3/8", bracelet mkd #238, 3/8" w x 7-1/2", and brooch # 113, 5/8" w x 2-7/8", suite, **$500**. (Al Munir Meghji collection).

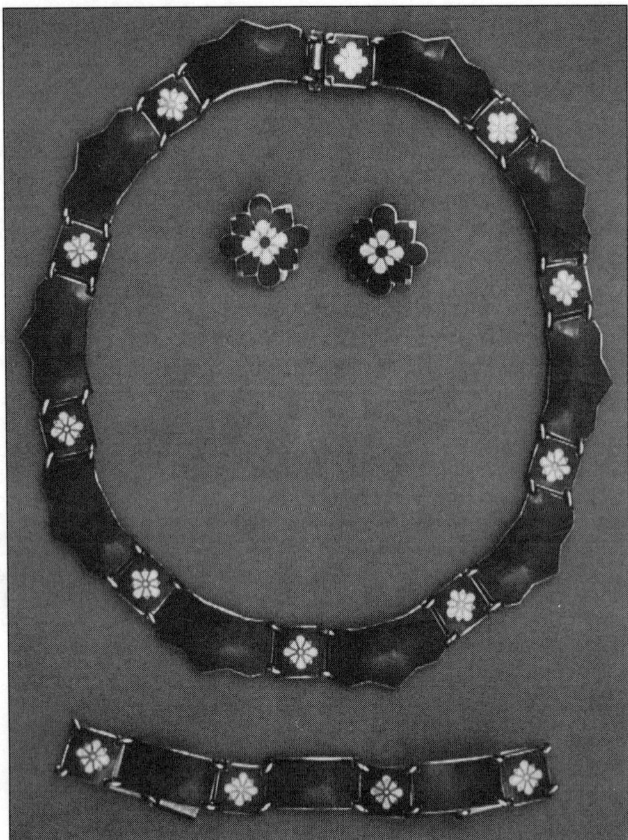

Suite: Necklace, Link Bracelet, Earrings, sterling vermeil, enamel, c. 1950-60, necklace of alternating cusped rect and sq cobalt blue *basse-taille* enameled linked plaques, each square with white enameled geo flowerhead, matching bracelet of plain rect alternating with sq flowerhead links, clip earrings, each a geo blue and white enameled flowerhead, all pcs mkd "STERLING NORWAY," necklace 5/8" w x 17-1/2" tl, bracelet 7/8" x 7-1/4" tl, earrings 7/8" x 7/8", suite, **$250**. (Diane White collection).

Sterling vermeil, enamel, c. 1960, elongated tapering boomerang shape, white *basse-taille* enamel, mkd "925S STERLING NORWAY" and an "H" in a circle, brooch 1" w x 1-3/4", clipback earrings 5/8" w x 7/8", suite 135

Suite: Brooch/Pin and Earrings

Sterling, enamel, c. 1940-41, brooch entitled "Five Wild Swans," white *champlevé* enamel on ster plaque, two swans with red and blue stripes on bodies, one with blue and yellow stripes, one with red, and one with blue, matching earrings with red stripes, sgd "ERIK MAGNUSSEN," with designer's mark (stylized overlapping initials EM), "930S, sterling, MADE IN DENMARK, ENERET," #1, brooch 2-1/4" w x 1", screwback earrings 1" w x 5/8", suite.. 450

Suite: Link Bracelet and Earrings

Silver, moonstones, c. 1920-30, bracelet of alternating foliate and flowerhead links, each bezel-set with a circ or oval moonstone, mkd "GEORG JENSEN," #3, double leaf motif earrings #108, bracelet 1/2" w x 7" tl, screwback earrings 3/4" x 3/8", suite .... 920 (A)

Sterling, white stones, c. 1935-40, realistic floral/foliate circ links, each set with a lg circ white cab, flowerhead surmounting foldover clasp, sgd "NE FROM, DENMARK," 7/8" w x 7-1/4", matching earrings, 7/8" dia.............. 173 (A)

Suite: Pendant and Chain, Pendent Earrings, bronze, amethysts, c. 1965, pendant a rect cast bronze plaque with textured irregular ridges, bezel-set with a cushion-shaped rough-cut amethyst, suspended from a wire-wrapped circ bail and cable link chain, hook closure, rev mkd "BRONZE, P. SARPANEVA, FINLAND" for Pennti Sarpaneva, matching pendent earrings, sm cut-corner squares turned 45 degrees, each set with a sm cushion-shaped rough-cut amethyst suspended from two oval links, screwbacks, pendant 1-1/8" w x 2-3/4", chain 24-1/2" tl, earrings 5/8" w x 1-1/2" tl, suite, **$100**. (Author's collection).

Suite: Necklace and Link Bracelet

Sterling, c. 1960, necklace of three vertically linked domed rect polished plaques suspended from a baton link chain, sgd "GEORG JENSEN DENMARK" #127, bracelet of four linked domed rect plaques, sgd "GEORG JENSEN DENMARK" #220, v-spring and box clasp, necklace 1-3/4" w x 4-1/2" at center, 16" tl , bracelet 1" w x 7-1/2", suite .... 1,610 (A)

Suite: Necklace, Brooch/Pin, and Earrings

Sterling, enamel, c. 1945-50, necklace of eighteen stylized angel-fish shaped ster links, each with two bands of black opaque enamel, clipback earrings a single link of identical design, brooch a larger version with safety catch, all pieces mkd "STERLING MEKA DENMARK," necklace 7/8" w x 15" tl, earrings 7/8" w x 3/4", brooch 2" w x 1-3/4", suite 350

Tie Bars, sterling, Danish:

T, c. 1935-40, rect plaque with rounded ends, three parallel horizontal incised oxidized grooves, mkd "Hans Hansen" (early script mark), "925 S DENMARK #727," 1-1/2" w x 1/4", **$50**.

C, post-1945 mark, plain polished bar surmounted by a stepped rect plaque stamped with a recessed oval flowerhead with overlapping scalloped petals, mkd "GEORG JENSEN" in a dotted oval, "STERLING DENMARK #76," 2-1/4" w x 3/8", **$175**.

B, post-1945 mark, rect with geo design of triangles and parallel zig-zag grooves of varying widths, mkd "GEORG JENSEN" in a dotted oval, "STERLING DENMARK #77," 2-3/8" w x 3/8", **$150**. (Patrick Kapty collection).

APPENDICES

MARKS ON METALS

Marks listed shown larger than actual size

GOLD:

Solid karats:

9c/ct (Brit.)	15c/ct (Brit.)
10k	18k or 18c/ct
12k or 12c/ct	20k
14k	22k or 22c/ct

14KP = plumb (exact) [not used until c. 1980]

375 = 9c/ct

583 or 585 = 14k

750 = 18k

Eagle's head (French) = 18k

Eagle's Head

1/20 14k (or 12k) GF = gold-filled

RGP = rolled gold plate

HGE = heavy gold electroplate

PLATINUM:

900 Plat - 100 Irid

(alloyed with 10% iridium)

Dog's head (French after 1912)

Dog's Head

SILVER:

925 = sterling (92.5% silver)

British: lion passant = sterling

Lion Passant

French: boar's head or crab = 800

Boar's Head

Crab

Swedish: three crowns = 830 or higher (S after 1912, oval reserve for imports)

Sweden

Finnish: **813H** = 830; **916H** = 935

Finland

Austro-Hungarian: dog's or lion's head = 750 or higher (1866-1937)

.800 Dog's Head

.750 Lion's Head

800, **825**, **830**, **850** (European or continental), **900**, **standard** or **coin** (American before 1906) marked on silver = lower silver content than sterling or 925 (92.5% silver, 7.5% copper)

EPNS = electroplated nickel silver

German silver, **nickel silver** = NO silver content (copper, nickel, zinc alloy)

Alpaca = copper, zinc, nickel, 2% silver

COMPARISON TESTS FOR PLASTICS: FOUR SENSES

Trade and generic name, year patented, type of plastic

	Celluloid (cellulose nitrate) [1870] *Thermoplastic*	**Galalith (casein) [1897]** *Thermoset*	**Bakelite (phenolic) [1909]** *Thermoset*	**Lumarith (cellulose acetate) [1927]** *Thermoplastic*	**Lucite (acrylic) [1937]** *Thermoplastic*
SIGHT	opaque, translucent, or transparent with yellowish oxidation, can imitate natural materials (amber, coral, ivory, pearl, tortoiseshell); also pastels, red, blue, green, black	opaque, can imitate natural materials (amber, coral, horn, ivory, tortoiseshell), also many other colors, no chalk white or colorless	opaque or translucent, limited color range: reds, orange, yellows, "butterscotch," greens, browns, black, no chalk white, pastels or colorless, can imitate natural materials (amber, tortoiseshell), no mold marks	same as Celluloid, also bright colors	colorless or tinted transparent, also opaque, laminated, "adularescent" (moonstone-like sheen), all colors, usually no mold marks
TOUCH	lightweight, slightly flexible, brittle, can have mold marks, can be solid, hollow, or laminated	hard, light to medium weight, no mold marks, solid or laminated	hard, heavy, dense, no mold marks, solid or laminated	similar to Celluloid	soft surface feel, lighter than Bakelite, heavier than Celluloid, no mold marks, solid or laminated
SOUND	"click"	"clack"	"clunk" (drumstick on a coconut shell)	"click"	"clunk" (higher pitch than Bakelite)
SMELL (use hot water)	camphor ("Campho-phenique")	"wet wool" (protein)	carbolic acid (formaldehyde)	sour (acetic acid [vinegar])	"fruity" sweet or floral under hot point or *very* hot water, otherwise odorless

AMERICAN MANUFACTURERS' MARKS

NEWARK NJ

ALLING & CO.

ALLSOPP & ALLSOPP

BIPPART, GRISCOM & OSBORN

CARTER, HOWE (after 1915, GOUGH) & CO.

CRANE & THEURER

A. J. HEDGES & CO.

WILLIAM B. KERR & CO.

KREMENTZ & CO.

LARTER & SONS

ENOS RICHARDSON & CO.

RIKER BROS.

SLOAN & CO.

TAYLOR & CO. (for 10K)

UNGER BROS.

WHITESIDE & BLANK (HENRY

BLANK, CRESARROW)

WORDLEY, ALLSOPP & BLISS

GEORGE W. SHIEBLER & CO., NEW YORK, NY

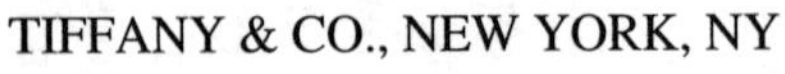

TIFFANY & CO., NEW YORK, NY

GORHAM MANUFACTURING CO., PROVIDENCE, RI

MID-CENTURY MODERN AMERICAN STUDIO JEWELERS

(Dates of birth/death where known)

PAUL ACKERMAN

CARLTON BALL 1911-1992

WARD BENNETT

FRANZ BERGMANN 1898-1977

HARRY BERTOIA 1915-1978

JULES BRENNER 1917-1991

IRENA BRYNNER 1917-

ALEXANDER CALDER 1898-1976

MILTON CAVAGNARO 1915-1993

BETTY COOKE 1924-

MARGRET CRAVER (WITHERS) 1907-

MARGARET DE PATTA 1903-1964

JOSÉ DE RIVERA 1904-1985

CLAIRE FALKENSTEIN 1908-1997

FRED FARR 1914-

LOIS FRANKE

ELSA FREUND 1912-

ARNOLD FREW 1922-

RICHARD GOMPF 1928-

CLIFFORD HERROLD

HURST & KINGSBURY

ADDA HUSTED-ANDERSEN 1900-1990

PHYLLIS W. JACOBS

MICHAEL JERRY 1937-

SAM KRAMER 1913-1964

MARY KRETSINGER 1915-

ROBERT LASNIER

ED LEVIN 1921-

ESTHER LEWITTES

PAUL LOBEL 1900-1983

PETER MACCHIARINI 1909-

EVERETT MAC DONALD 1924-1991

PHYLLIS MALDONADO

FRANK MIRAGLIA

PHILIP MORTON 1911-

HARRY OSAKI

EARL PARDON 1926-1991

RONALD H. PEARSON 1924-1996

CORALYNN PENCE

SVETOZAR & RUTH RADAKOVITCH
1918- 1920-

FRANCISCO (FRANK) REBAJES 1907-1990

MERRY RENK 1921-

FLORENCE RESNIKOFF

RUTH ROACH 1913-?

CAROLINE ROSENE

GEORGE K. SALO

CHRISTIAN SCHMIDT d. 1974

H. FRED SKAGGS d. 1983

OLAF SKOOGFORS 1930-1973

ART SMITH 1917-1982

HENRY STEIG 1906-1973

BILL TENDLER 1924-1981

ED WIENER 1918-1991

BYRON WILSON 1919-

BOB WINSTON 1915-

20TH CENTURY AMERICAN COSTUME JEWELRY MANUFACTURERS/DESIGNERS

Accessocraft c.1930-present

ART c.1950-1980

McClelland Barclay c.1930-1940

Beau (sterling) 1947-present

Bergère 1947-c.1965

Les Bernard 1962-1996

Bogoff c.1946-?

Boucher 1937-1971

Marcel Boucher

BSK c.1948-present

Nadja Buckley c.1940-1950

Calvaire 1935-c.1960

Hattie Carnegie 1918-1970

Castlecliff c.1938-1970

Alice Caviness 1945-present

Chanel 1914-1939, 1954-present
(most early, some later pieces unmarked)

Ciner 1892-present

Cini (sterling) 1922-c.1970, 1993-present

Coro 1919-1979
Corocraft (sterling pre-1950)1933-1979
Vendome 1944-1979
(Coro, Inc. Canada, to present)

Sarah Coventry 1949-c.1984

Danecraft (sterling) 1939-present

Wm de Lillo 1967-present

DeMario 1945-1960

R.[Ralph] De Rosa 1935-1970

Di Nicola c.1960-1970

Christian Dior 1955-present

Eisenberg Original
c.1935-1945
(sterling 1943-1946)
E. (script mark)
c.1942-1945
EISENBERG (block letters)
c.1945-1958
EISENBERG ICE © (block letters) 1970-present
(no mark 1958-1970)

Eisenberg "E" Mark

Emmons 1949-c.1980

Eugene c.1950-1960

Florenza 1956-1981

Givenchy 1952-present

Leo Glass c.1938-1957

Stanley Hagler 1953-1996

Miriam Haskell 1924-present
(most pieces not marked 1924-c.1948)

Hobé 1903-present

Hollycraft 1948-c.1965

Joseff of Hollywood 1938-present

Kramer 1943-c.1980

Krementz 1884-present

KJL/Kenneth Lane 1963-present

Laguna 1944-?

Lang (sterling) 1946-?

Ledo 1948-60 / Polcini 1960-?
(DBA Leading Jewelry 1911-1949)

Lisner 1938-c.1985

Marvella 1911-present
(1982-present: a division of The Monet Group)

Mazer Bros 1926-1951
Jomaz/Joseph Mazer 1946-80

Monet 1937-present
(1989-1994: a subsidiary of Crystal Brands Jewelry Group; 1994-present: Chase Capital Partners, Lattice Holding)

Napier 1922-present

Original by Robert 1942-1979
(Fashioncraft Jewelry Co.)

D'Orlan c. 1960-?

Panetta 1945-1995

Pell 1941-present

Pennino (pre-1950 sterling) 1930-1961

Rebajes 1932-1960

Regency c.1950-1970

Réja (pre-1950 sterling) 1940-1954

Renoir 1946-1964/ Matisse 1952-1964/ Sauteur 1958-1963

Nettie Rosenstein c.1935-1975

Sandor c.1940-1970

Schiaparelli 1931-1960
(most pre-1949 unmarked)

Schreiner N.Y. 1944-1977

Staret c.1941-1947

Yves St. Laurent 1966-present
Tortolani c.1960-1975

Trifari (pre-1950 sterling) 1920-present
TKF (Trifari, Krussman & Fishel) 1925-1938
(mark in use from 1935)
(1975-1988: subsidiary of Hallmark;
1988-1994: Crystal Brands;
1994-present:
Chase Capital Partners, Lattice Holding;
a division of The Monet Group)

KTF.

Trifari, Krussman & Fishel

Van S Authentics c.1935-1969

Vogue 1936-c.1975

Weiss 1942-1971

Whiting-Davis 1876-present

OTHER MANUFACTURERS: DATES OF OPERATION UNKNOWN

HAR

Ramé

Reinad

Warner

Wiesner

References: Joann Dubbs Ball, *Costume Jewelers, The Golden Age of Design*, Schiffer Publishing, 1990; Deanna Farnetti Cera, ed., *Jewels of Fantasy*, Harry N. Abrams, 1992; Maryanne Dolan, *Collecting Rhinestone & Colored Jewelry*, 3rd ed., Books Americana, 1993; Harrice Simons Miller, *Costume Jewelry Identification and Price Guide*, 2nd ed., Avon Books, 1994; Dorothy Rainwater, *American Jewelry Manufacturers*, Schiffer Publishing, 1988; Fred Rezazadeh, *Costume Jewelry, A Practical Handbook & Value Guide*, Collector Books, 1998; Lucille Tempesta, ed., *Vintage Fashion & Costume Jewelry Newsletter*, various quarterly issues; back issues of *Vogue* and *Harper's Bazar* magazines (researched by Pat Seal).

Advisors: Pat Seal, Lucille Tempesta.

MARKS & NAMES ON MEXICAN SILVER JEWELRY & METALWARE c. 1930-1990

(DATES OF OPERATION / MARKS IN USE)

FREDERICK DAVIS
(c.1925-1960)

Frederick Davis

WILLIAM SPRATLING
(1931-1945)

Wm. Spratling, c. 1931-1935

Wm. Spratling, c. 1940

Wm. Spratling, c. 1940-1945

WILLIAM SPRATLING
(c.1949-1967)
[SPRATLING DE MEXICO in a circle bisected by STERLING across center]

William Spratling, c. 1949-1967

William Spratling, c. 1955-1967

LOS CASTILLO
(1939-present)
[block letters across or in circle]

ANTONIO PINEDA
(1941-present, crown mark in use since c.1950)

Antonio Pineda

HÉCTOR AGUILAR
(1939-c.1965)

Héctor Aguilar

MARGOT van VOORHIES [MARGOT DE TAXCO]
CARR CASTILLO
(1948-c.1975)

ENRIQUE LEDESMA
(1950-c.1980)
[L underlining EDESMA]

SALVADOR TERÁN
(1952-1974)
[Salvador in script]

SIGI PINEDA
(1953-c.1975;
c.1985-present)
[Sigi in an oval, surmounting TASCO in an oval]

FELIPE MARTíNEZ [PIEDRA Y PLATA]
(1950-?)

HUBERT HARMON
(c.1943-1948)

Hubert Harmon

ISIDRO GARCíA
(1943-1986)
[Maricela in script, surmounting TASCO]

BERNICE GOODSPEED [B]
(1940-1972)

MATILDE POULAT
(mark since c.1950-1960)
[Matl in script or block, 925]

RICARDO SALAS POULAT
(c.1960-present)
[Matl Salas in script]

LOS BALLESTEROS (c.1940-present)

Los Ballesteros

SPREAD-EAGLE MARK - 925
c.1945-1979 (assay mark)

Government Assay "Spread Eagle" Marks

Mark used on non-sterling (pewter or silverplate) copies of Spratling designs by Victor Silson, c. 1940

"Silson" Mark

SERAFÍN MOCTEZUMA

Serafin Moctezuma

[XX] - [00] GOV'T-ISSUED REGISTRY NO. ASSIGNED TO WORKSHOPS SINCE 1979 (e.g., **TS-24** for Spratling workshop)

LESSER-KNOWN WORKSHOPS & SILVERSMITHS

IN TAXCO & MEXICO CITY D.F.

(DATES OF OPERATION/MARKS IN USE IF KNOWN)

CARMEN BECKMANN
(c.1960-1980)
[BECKMANN or BEKMANN]

PEDRO CASTILLO
(1948-present)
[superimposed P over C]

RAFAEL DOMÍNGUEZ
(1943-1980)
[RD in a circle]

DORIS
[block letters]

FAR-FAN
[FAR
FAN in rounded block letters]

DÁMASO GALLEGOS
(1941-1980)
[script DG]

GERARDO LóPEZ
(c.1950- ?)
[LOPEZ
TAXCO in an oval[]

MACIEL
(c.1930-1970)
[block letters]

EMMA MELENDEZ
(1953-1971)
[Emma in script or block]

MIGUEL MELENDEZ
(c.1955-present)
[large script M in a circle]

POPOWSKI
[popowski, all lower case]

RANCHO ALEGRE [block letters]
(c.1960-1980)

REVERI - REVERIANO & MARÍA CASTILLO
(1952-1989)
[Reveri in script]

SANBORN'S [block letters]
(c.1930-present)

TANE [block letters]
(1953-present)

EZEQUIEL TAPIA [EXEL-TAPIA]
(1961-present)

JANNA THOMAS [JANNA]
(1965-1980)

VALENTÍN VIDAURRETA
(1935-1955)
[large over smaller V]

VICTORIA - ANA NUÑEZ BRILANTI
(1940-1978)
[VICTORIA in block letters]

ALFREDO VILLASANA
[AV or A. VILLASANA in block letters]

20TH CENTURY JEWELRY DESIGNERS AND MANUFACTURERS IN SCANDINAVIA

Dates refer to births/deaths of individuals or founders of manufactories; initials of major companies follow names of designers who worked for them

DENMARK

JUST ANDERSEN 1884-1943 (mfr) [JUST A]

MOGENS BALLIN
1871-1914 (mfr)

Mogens Ballin

THORVALD BINDESBØLL 1846-1908

C.M. COHR (mfr)

NANNA & JØRGEN DITZEL (AM, GJ) [N J inside large D]
NANNA 1923-, JØRGEN 1921-1961

A.[AAGE] DRAGSTED 1886-1942 (mfr) [AD surmounted by a crown]

N.E. FROM (mfr)

BENT GABRIELSEN (HH, GJ) 1928-

GRANN & LAGLYE (mfr)

HANS HANSEN
1884-1940 (mfr)

Hans Hansen

KARL GUSTAV HANSEN (HH)
1914-

Karl Gustav Hansen

BERNHARD HERTZ 1834-1909 (mfr)

PETER HERTZ 1811-1885 (mfr)

GEORG JENSEN 1866-1935 (mfr)

Georg Jensen c. 1904-1920

Georg Jensen c. 1915-1930

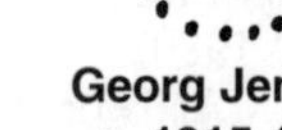

Georg Jensen c. 1915-1930

Georg Jensen 1933-1944

Georg Jensen post-1945

JØRGEN JENSEN 1931-
(mfr)

Jørgen Jensen

JØRGEN JENSEN (GJ) 1895-1966

SØREN GEORG JENSEN (GJ) 1917-

ANNI (1927-) & BENT (1924-) KNUDSEN (HH) [BENT K]

HENNING KOPPEL (GJ) 1918-1981 [HK]

HOLGER KYSTER 1872-1944 (mfr)

ERIK MAGNUSSEN 1884-1960
(DENMARK/U.S.)

ARNO MALINOWSKI (GJ)
1899-1976

Arno Malinowski

A.[ANTON] MICHELSEN
1809-1877 (mfr)

Anton Michelsen

EVALD NIELSEN
1879-1958

Evald Nielsen

HARALD NIELSEN (GJ) 1892-1977

JAIS NIELSEN 1885-1961 (AD) [JAIS]

JOHAN ROHDE (GJ) 1836-1935

HARALD SLOTT-MØLLER 1864-1937

KAREN STRAND (AD, AM) 1924-

POUL WARMIND 1929-

FINLAND

(Finnish mfrs' names after individuals who designed for them)

AURAN KULTASEPPÄ (mfr)

Auran Kultaseppä

KAIJA AARIKKA 1929- (mfr)

BERTEL GARDBERG (GJ) 1916- [BRG or GARDBERG]

E. [ERIK] GRANIT 1930-1988 (mfr)

PAULA HÄIVÄOJA 1929- (Kalevala Koru, Kaunis Koru)

MAUNO HONKANEN 1931- (Tillander)

SAARA HOPEA-UNTRACHT 1925-1984
(Ossian Hopea - OH)

KALEVALA KORU (mfr)

Kalevala Koru

KAUNIS KORU (mfr)

Kaunis Koru

KULTAKESKUS OY (mfr)

KULTATEOLLISUUS KY (mfr)

Kultateollisuus Ky

KUPITTAAN KULTA OY (mfr)

Kupittaan Kulta Oy

ELIS KAUPPI 1921- (Kupittaan Kulta)

LAPPONIA (mfr)

Lapponia

PEKKA PIEKÄINEN 1945- (Auran Kultaseppä)

BöRJE RAJALIN 1933- (Kalevala Koru)

EERO RISLAKKI 1924- (Kalevala Koru)

JAN SALAKARI 1932- (Kaunis Koru)

FINLAND (cont.)

MIRJAM SALMINEN 1918- (Kaunis Koru)

PENTTI SARPANEVA 1925-1978
(Kalevala Koru, Turun Hopea)

SEPPO TAMMINEN (Turun Hopea)

TILLANDER (mfr)

Tillander

TURUN HOPEA (mfr)

Torun Hopea

BJöRN WECKSTRöM 1935- (Lapponia)

WESTERBACK OY (mfr)

TAPIO WIRKKALA 1915-1985 (Westerback, Kultakeskus)

NORWAY

DAVID-ANDERSEN (mfr)

c. 1888-1930

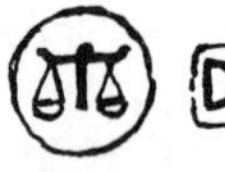

since 1939

David-Andersen

UNI DAVID-ANDERSEN (DA)

MARIUS HAMMER 1847-1927 (mfr)

Marius Hammer

AKSEL HOLMSEN (mfr)

Aksel Holmsen

FRANK & REGINE JUHLS [JUHLS]

THORBJØRN LIE-JØRGENSEN (DA) 1901-1961

GRETE PRYTZ KITTELSEN 1917-

BJØRN SIGURD ØSTERN (DA) [B.S.Ø]

HARRY SØRBY (DA) [H.S.]

J. TOSTRUP (mfr)

TONE VIGELAND 1938-

Tone Vigeland for PLUS

SWEDEN

SIGVARD BERNADOTTE (GJ) 1907- ?

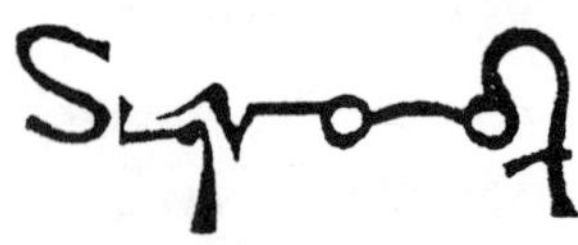

Sigvard Bernadotte

W.A. BOLIN (mfr)

INGA BRITT [IBE] DAHLQUIST (GJ) 1925-

WIWEN NILSSON (GJ) 1897-1974 [script signature]

SIGURD PERSSON 1914- [SIGP]

TORUN [BÜLOW HÜBE] (GJ) 1927-

Company codes:

AD = A. DRAGSTED

AM = A. MICHELSEN

DA = DAVID-ANDERSEN

GJ = GEORG JENSEN

HH = HANS HANSEN

BASIC HALLMARK IDENTIFICATION

Hallmarks have been in use in England and France since the 14th century. Most other European countries also use hallmarks. The United States has never used hallmarks per se. Indications of fineness or karat have been required since 1906, but fineness marks were sometimes stamped on silver jewelry in the 19th century ("coin" or "standard" for 900 silver, "sterling" for 925).

Hallmarks are most often found on objects made of precious metals. Jewelry is exempted from hallmarking under certain circumstances. However, when a piece of jewelry *is* hallmarked, the marks can yield clues to country of origin and, sometimes, date of manufacture, as well as indicate the metal content of the piece. Makers' marks are not strictly considered hallmarks by themselves, although a maker's mark may accompany a hallmark on a piece (see Glossary for definition).

Every country has a different system of hallmarking, ranging from simple to complex. The most commonly found marks will be discussed here. Others can be found in Tardy's *International Hallmarks on Silver* and *Poinçons d'Or et de Platine* (hallmarks on gold and platinum, French text).

FRENCH HALLMARKS

The French have what is undoubtedly the most complex system of hallmarks in the world, and the most difficult to read. If you can learn to recognize the French marks for gold, silver and platinum, you will have done well. The difficulty lies in the fact that the French never use numbers. Symbols in the form of animals and heads of animals and people, insects, and birds have been used to indicate fineness, place of manufacture, imports and exports. These have changed over the centuries. Tardy's *Hallmarks on Silver*, in English, can help decipher most of these marks, and help with understanding the book on gold and platinum marks, which has not been translated from the French.

The most easily recognized and commonly seen French mark is the eagle's head, in use since 1838, indicating 18 karat gold. Assayed French gold is never lower than 18k. The mark can be found on jewelry in any number of places. Look for it on clasps, side edges, galleries, and pin stems as well as on the back surface of a piece.

On French silver jewelry, the most often-seen mark is the boar's head, the mark of the Paris Assay Office, indicating a fineness of 800 or higher on small articles (such as jewelry). This mark was in use from 1838 to 1961. Outside of Paris, the crab mark was used from 1838 to 1961, and since 1962, has also been used by the Paris Assay Office.

After 1838, a maker's mark in a lozenge (diamond shape with four equal sides) was also required on French silver and gold.

From 1829, items made of both gold and silver were stamped with a conjoined boar's and eagle's head.

Platinum was not officially recognized by the French government as a precious metal until 1910, at which time the eagle's head for gold was also used for platinum. In 1912, a special mark for platinum was introduced, a dog's head.

OTHER EUROPEAN HALLMARKS

Many European countries mark silver and gold with numerical fineness marks in thousandths, e.g., 800, 830, 900, 935, etc. for silver, 333, 500, 585, 750, 875, etc. for gold. Other symbols may be used in combination with these numbers.

Austro-Hungarian items may bear the head of a woman, animal, or bird with a number inside a cartouche or reserve. The most commonly-seen mark on silver and silver-gilt jewelry is the dog's head with the number 3 inside a coffin-shaped reserve, indicating 800 silver, in use 1866-1937.

In Russia, two-digit numbers refer to *zolotniks*, which convert to thousandths, e.g., 56 = 583 (14k), 84 = 875 (silver or 21k gold). Between 1896 and 1908, the national mark was the left profile of a woman's head wearing a diadem ("*kokoshnik*"). From 1908 to 1917, a right-facing profile was used. After the Russian Revolution, the mark was a right-facing worker's profile with a hammer, and the fineness in thousandths.

Swedish hallmarks after 1912 include a triple crown mark, in a trefoil for local manufacture, and in an oval for imports, along with an S in a hexagon for silver indicating 830 or higher. Gold will bear a karat mark in a rectangle. There will also be a date letter and number, a city mark and a maker's mark.

Finnish hallmarks are similar to Swedish. A crown inside a heart indicates local manufacture, a crown in an oval for imports. Place of assay, maker's mark and date letter/number may be added.

BRITISH HALLMARKS

The British system of hallmarking is somewhat complex, but relatively easy to follow once the system is deciphered. British hallmarks include a fineness or purity mark, an assay office mark, a date letter, and usually but not always, a maker's mark. A royal duty mark was added from 1784 to 1890 (not always found on jewelry of this period). The sequence of marks on a piece is arbitrary.

Fineness or purity marks:

On gold, a crown plus the karat (spelled with a "c" in Britain, abbreviated "c" or "ct") was used from 1798 until 1975 (22 ct was marked the same as sterling silver until 1844). In Scotland, a thistle was used instead of the crown. From 1798 to 1854, only gold assayed at 18 and 22 ct was permissible and hallmarked. In 1854, 15, 12, and 9 ct were legalized. The fineness in thousandths was added to these karat marks from 1854 to 1932.

In 1932, 15 and 12 ct were abandoned in favor of 14 ct, which was also marked 585. 9 ct continued to be legal, also marked 375. In 1975, all gold marks were standardized, and the crown mark and the fineness in thousandths became the only marks to be used in addition to place of assay and date letter.

On English silver, the lion *passant* (walking lion) is the symbol for sterling silver (925). Scottish silver before 1975, like gold, bears a thistle mark. A higher silver standard, Britannia silver (958.4) was required to be used for a short period at the end of the 17th century, bearing the figure of Britannia instead of the lion. Britannia silver is still legal, but has been seldom used since the reinstatement of the sterling standard in 1720. The lion *passant* was retained in the Hallmarking Act of 1975, but the Scottish thistle was changed to a rampant lion.

Place of assay marks:

Assay offices have been located in a number of British cities. The ones still in operation today are in London, Birmingham, Sheffield and Edinburgh. Most jewelry will bear a London, Birmingham, or Chester place of assay mark (the Chester assay office closed in 1962). The mark for London is referred to as a leopard's head (crowned before 1821). The mark for Birmingham is an anchor. Most hallmarks books indicate an upright anchor for silver and a sideways anchor for gold, but this was not strictly adhered to. The mark for Chester is a shield bearing the town's arms, a sword and three sheaves of wheat.

Date letters:

Each place of assay has its own cycles of hallmarks which include a letter of the alphabet for each year, beginning with the letter A, and continuing through to Z (sometimes the lowercase letter j is omitted, and some cycles end with a letter before Z). The style of the letter and the shape of the reserve or shield background changes with each cycle. A letter can be upper or lower case and of differing type faces, in order to distinguish it from the same letter in an earlier or later cycle.

It is not necessary to memorize these letters. Pocket-sized editions of British hallmarks books make it possible to look up the date letter found on a piece "in the field." All that is necessary is to determine the place of assay from its mark and look up the date letter in the tables given for that city. It is important to remember to match the style of letter and shape of its surrounding shield. Occasionally there will be a discrepancy between what is in the books and the mark on the piece, in which case the style of the letter takes precedence over the shape of the shield. With practice, and book in hand, you can learn to read British hallmarks quickly and easily.

PSEUDO HALLMARKS

Because of the association of British sterling with quality, some American manufacturers emulated the British, making sterling objects and jewelry long before the United States government nationalized the sterling standard in 1906. Not only were British styles and metal quality imitated. Some American maker's marks bear a striking resemblance to British hallmarks. The most well-known of these is the mark of Gorham Manufacturing Co., featuring a walking lion, an anchor and an Old English style capital G, looking very much like a Birmingham hallmark for 1830. Most American maker's marks can be found in Dorothy Rainwater's *American Jewelry Manufacturers*.

MEXICAN HALLMARKS

After World War II, with the rising popularity of silver jewelry and objects made in Taxco, Mexico, the Mexican government issued an assay mark guaranteeing the fineness to be 925 or higher. This mark is referred to as the "spread eagle" mark. The original mark did look like an eagle, but with modifications over the years, the mark was simplified. The number inside the mark is a workshop or city designation. In 1979, this mark was abandoned in favor of a series of registry letters and numbers assigned to individuals and workshops.

MARKS REFERENCES

Bly, John, *Miller's Silver & Sheffiield Plate Marks* (English, Continental European, and American), Reed International Books, Ltd., 1993

Divis, Jan, *Guide to Gold Marks of the World* and *Guide to Silver Marks of the World*, English translation reprints, Promotional Reprint Co. Ltd., 1994

Pickford, Ian, ed. *Jackson's Hallmarks*, pocket edition (English, Scottish, Irish silver and gold marks), Antique Collectors' Club, 1991

Pickford, Ian, ed. *Jackson's Silver and Gold Marks of England, Scotland and Ireland*, Antique Collectors' Club, 1989

Rainwater, Dorothy, *American Jewelry Manufacturers*, Schiffer Publishing, 1988

Tardy, *International Hallmarks on Silver*, Tardy, Paris, 1993

Tardy, *Poinçons d'Or et de Platine* (French text), Tardy, Paris, 1988

Wyler, Seymour B., *The Book of Old Silver* (English, European, American), Crown Publishers, 1937 (still in print)

STYLES AND PERIODS

STYLE/PERIOD	TYPICAL MOTIFS/ DESIGN ELEMENTS	TYPICAL JEWELRY FORMS	TYPICAL MATERIALS
Late Georgian			
c. late 18th century-1835	Acrostics of gemstones, bows (*sévigné*), cameos, intaglios, and other neo-classical motifs, *cannetille* gold-work, feathers, floral and foliate sprays, girandoles, Maltese and other crosses, memorial and mourning motifs and symbols, portrait miniatures, scrollwork, stars, crescents and sunbursts; closed-back settings (stones often foil-backed), large stones set *à jour* (open back)	Bracelets, brooches, buckles, chains, chatelaines, pendent earrings, hair ornaments, lockets, necklaces (esp. gemstone *rivières*), parures, pendants, rings, watch chains, fobs, and seals	Diamonds, emeralds, rubies, sapphires; amethysts, citrines, coral, pearls, topaz, turquoise; chalcedony, garnets, marcasites; enamel, glass, hair, ivory, mosaics, paste (faceted glass), hardstone and shell cameos; gold, silver (all-silver or silver-topped gold for diamonds), Berlin iron, cut steel, pinchbeck
Victorian			
Early (Romantic) Period, c. 1840-1860	Sentimental motifs: hearts, hands, REGARD and other acrostics, (language of) flowers, snakes, crosses, anchors; Order of the Garter (strap/buckle), Scottish, Algerian knot, cameos and miniatures	Bracelets, brooches, buckles, chains, chatelaines, hair ornaments, earrings (1850s), lockets, necklaces, parures, pendants, rings, watch chains, fobs, and seals	Diamonds, emeralds, rubies, sapphires, chalcedony, garnets, pearls, Scottish "pebbles" (agates, jaspers, cairngorms, citrines, amethysts), turquoise; coral, enamel, hair, ivory, glass, mosaics, mother-of-pearl, hardstone and shell cameos, tortoiseshell; gold, silver (silver-topped gold for diamonds), gold-filled and electroplate, cut steel
Mid (Grand) Period, c. 1860-1880	Revivalist (Etruscan, Egyptian, Renaissance, Celtic, Gothic, Greco-Roman), amphoras, motifs from nature, cherubs, tassels and fringe	As above, plus pendent earrings, esp. with tassels or fringe, corsage ornaments, bullas (Revivalist), bookchain necklaces	As above, plus jet, "French jet" (black glass), vulcanite, bog oak, onyx, lava, tiger's claws; lower karat gold after 1854 in U.K.
Late (Aesthetic) Period, c. 1880-1900	Stars, crescents, birds, insects, lizards, sporting motifs (foxes, dogs, horses, etc.), Japanese designs and motifs, mottos, names, good luck symbols	Longchains with watches or pendants, chatelaines, small drop or button earrings, hatpins, lavaliers, lace or "handy" pins, bar brooches, narrow bangle and link bracelets, fringe and festoon necklaces, cuff links, scarf/stickpins	Alexandrites, amethysts, demantoid garnets, diamonds, moonstones, opals, pearls, peridots, reverse crystal intaglios, sapphires, turquoise; celluloid, enamel, glass, "gunmetal" (blackened steel), horn, mother-of-pearl, niello; gold, silver, platinum

STYLE/PERIOD	TYPICAL MOTIFS/ DESIGN ELEMENTS	TYPICAL JEWELRY FORMS	TYPICAL MATERIALS
Turn of the Century			
Arts & Crafts, c. 1890-1920	Emphasis on handmade appearance, crafted designs with hammered, patinated and/or acid-etched metal surfaces (Am.), motifs from nature with stylized, simplified lines, Celtic knots, strapwork, abstract designs	Bracelets, brooches, buckles, cloak clasps, festoon necklaces, hatpins, "paper clip" chains, pendants, rings, watch fobs, sash ornaments, scarf/stickpins	Brass, bronze, copper, silver, gold; amber, enamel, glass, blister and freshwater pearls, mother-of-pearl, cabochon gemstones such as turquoise, agate, opal, moonstone
Art Nouveau, c. 1895-1910	Flowing, graceful lines, "whiplash" curves, stylized motifs from nature: flowers, vines, insects; female faces and figures (draped and nude)	Bracelets, bangles, brooches, cuff links, dog collars and festoon necklaces, hair combs and ornaments, hatpins, lavaliers, lockets, pendants, sash ornaments and buckles, rings, scarf/stickpins, watch pins	Enamel (esp. *plique à jour*), cabochon gemstones, amber, glass, horn, ivory, tortoiseshell, gold, silver, gilt base metals
Edwardian (*Belle Époque*), c. 1890-1920	Lacy, delicate openwork, filigree, knife-edge and millegrained settings dominated by faceted stones, esp. diamonds, and pearls; the "garland" style: foliate swags and wreaths, ribbons and bows, flower baskets; stars and crescents, smaller scale figural motifs	Aigrettes, bar brooches, lace and watch pins, corsage ornaments, cuff links, dog collars, pendent earrings, longchains and sautoirs, *négligée* pendants and lavaliers rings, scarf/stickpins, tiaras	Diamonds, pearls, platinum, yellow gold, white gold after c. 1915; amethysts, black onyx, demantoid garnets, emeralds, moonstones, opals, peridots, rubies, sapphires; "imitation" jewelry in silver, glass, and paste (rhinestones)

STYLE/PERIOD	TYPICAL MOTIFS/ DESIGN ELEMENTS	TYPICAL JEWELRY FORMS	TYPICAL MATERIALS
Twentieth Century			
Art Deco & Streamline Moderne, c. 1920-1935	Simplification and stylization of forms; abstract and "Machine Age" designs, geometric, symmetrical, zigzag and stepped motifs, e.g., fountains, sunbursts, ziggurats, straight and curved parallel lines; speed motifs, including animals, e.g., gazelles, borzois; Oriental and Egyptian motifs; pavé settings, carved (engraved) gemstones.	Bangle, straightline, flexible/ link, and charm bracelets, bar and plaque brooches, buckles, cuff links and dress sets, dress clips, elongated pendent earrings (screwback or stud findings), jabot pins, short and long necklaces, esp. tasseled beads (sautoirs), pendants, rings	Diamonds, emeralds, rubies and sapphires (often synthetic or simulated), pearls (natural, cultured, and simulated), platinum, white gold; enamel, coral, jade, onyx, carnelian, chalcedony, chrysoprase, and other quartz family gemstones, marcasites, silver; for avant-garde designer and costume jewelry: "modern" materials, e.g., chrome or rhodium plated metal, celluloid, Bakelite; glass, rhinestones and white "pot" metal, gold- or silver-plated brass
Plastics & Other Novelties, c. 1920-1960	Whimsical figural motifs, e.g., cartoon-like animals and people, Western/ cowboy motifs, fruit, vegetables, flowers; geometric and stylized, laminated in two or more colors, or carved and reverse-carved naturalistic motifs	Bangle, hinged bangle, charm, link, and "stretchy" bracelets, brooches, buckles, clips, cuff links, earrings, necklaces, rings	Bakelite, celluloid, Lucite (after c. 1937), other plastic, ceramic, brass, chrome, glass, rhinestones; natural materials, e.g., cork, feathers, felt, pods and seeds, string, wood
Retro Modern, c. 1935-1945	Stylized and exaggerated, curvilinear, asymmetrical or opposed, three-dimen-sional floral, scroll, bow and ribbon, bird motifs; "tank track", brickwork and honeycomb patterns, other geometric forms; "gas pipe", "mouse tail" or snake chain; "invisible" settings, large emerald-cut stones	Large hinged bangle, cuff, flexible strap, and link bracelets, brooches, clips, double-clip brooches (convertible), "chatelaine" pins, cuff links, clip and screwback earrings, necklaces, rings, suites	Rose, yellow, green and white gold (two or three colors often combined), rubies and sapphires (often synthetic), small diamonds used as accents, amethysts, aquamarines, citrines, moonstones, topaz; sterling vermeil
Mid-Century Modern, c. 1945-1965	Geometric, biomorphic ("amoebae" shapes), non-representational abstract or highly stylized figural designs; large and unconventional forms, forged or cast metal	Cuff and link bracelets, brooches, cuff links, earrings, necklaces and neckpieces, pendants, rings, tie bars	Sterling, gold, copper, brass, enamel, cabochon and irregularly cut gemstones, enamel, glass, Lucite
Designer/Mfr Signed Costume, c. 1935-1975	Nonprecious jewelry marked with the name of the manufacturer and/or designer, often copied from or inspired by fine jewelry of the same or an earlier period; extravagant use of materials	Bracelets, brooches, clips, double-clip brooches, "chatelaine" pins, earrings, necklaces, rings, suites, sweater guards	Gold- and rhodium-plated base metals, sterling and sterling vermeil, rhinestones, glass, plastics, painted enamel

STYLE/PERIOD	TYPICAL MOTIFS/ DESIGN ELEMENTS	TYPICAL JEWELRY FORMS	TYPICAL MATERIALS
Special Collectibles			
Native American (Indian)	Primarily Southwest tribes, each with its own trademark techniques and designs, e.g., Navajo: metalworking techniques, tufa casting, forged ingots, large stone setting, leaf and feather motifs; Zuni: lapidary techniques, clustered stones set in patterns, channel inlay, rainbow god, knife-wing and other symbols; Santo Domingo: shell *heishi* and mosaic work; Hopi: silver overlay, animal and geometric symbols; Fred Harvey "tourist" jewelry stamped with swastikas, arrows, thunderbirds, and other "Indian" symbols	Squash blossom and *naja* pendant necklaces, bead, fetish and heishi necklaces, *ketoh* (bow guards), cuff bracelets, *jacla* (earrings), buckles, *concha* belts, brooches, bola ties, rings	Silver, copper, turquoise, shell, coral, mother-of-pearl, jet, fossilized ivory, petrified wood; battery cases, 78 rpm records, plastic toothbrush handles
Mexican (Taxco), c. 1930-1970	Pre-Hispanic and traditional Mexican motifs, along with popular modern designs of the period; often marked with the stamp of the designer or *taller* (workshop)	Bracelets of all types, brooches, buckles and belts, bola ties, clips, cuff links, earrings, necklaces, pendants, rings, suites, tie bars	Sterling silver used alone or in combination with brass, copper (married metals), alpaca, amethyst, azur-malachite, obsidian, sodalite, tiger's eye, turquoise, abalone, ebony, rosewood, tortoiseshell, enamel, synthetic gemstones
Scandinavian (Danish, Finnish, Norwegian, Swedish)	Early twentieth century Arts & Crafts (*skønvirke)* designs with repoussé floral, foliate, and animal motifs; mid-century modernist abstract designs; traditional Scandinavian (Nordic) symbols, filigree	Bangles, plain or with decorative front-hooked clasps, link bracelets, brooches, cuff links, earrings, necklaces, neckrings, pendants, rings, suites	Silver, bronze, gold; amazonite, amber, amethyst, chrysoprase, citrine, rock crystal, smoky quartz, labradorite (spectrolite), lapis lazuli, enamel, porcelain, damascene (metal inlay)

GLOSSARY

In order for us to understand each other when talking about antique and period jewelry, we must have a common vocabulary. A great many jewelry terms are French. French jewelers were the leaders of the jewelry industry, and France is where the language of jewelry-making evolved. The terms used there were adopted by English and American jewelers and thus are part of our jewelry vocabulary today. Included in the list below are the most commonly used French jewelry terms with their approximate phonetic pronunciation (nasal and glottal sounds are difficult to transcribe) in brackets, and jewelry-related definitions. Words in SMALL CAPS are defined elsewhere in the Glossary; foreign words are italicized.

à jour [ah ZHOOR] an open setting which allows light to pass through

alloy mixture of two or more metals

alpaca yellowish silver-colored metal composed of copper, zinc, nickel, and 2% silver

amber fossilized resin from extinct trees; lightweight and warm to the touch; can be translucent to opaque, imitated in plastics

amphora ancient Greco-Roman two-handled jar or urn with a tapered base, popular mid-Victorian Revivalist motif

annular ring-shaped

articulated having segments connected by flexible joints or jump rings

assay analytical test to determine metal content

attributed not SIGNED, but considered likely to have been made by a particular person or firm

aurora borealis an iridescent coating applied to faceted glass beads or rhinestones, developed by Swarovski Corp. in 1955

baguette narrow rectangular faceted stone

bail pendant loop finding through which a chain or cord passes

Bakelite trade name for thermosetting phenol formaldehyde resin, first entirely synthesized plastic, patented in 1909 by Leo H. Baekeland

balustered swelled section (as in the posts in a balustrade, or railing for a staircase)

bandeau ornamental band worn around the head

bangle rigid circular or oval bracelet

baroque in reference to pearls, having an irregular shape

base metal a non-precious metal

basse-taille [bas TIE yuh] enamelling technique: translucent or transparent ENAMEL applied over a decorated (engraved, chased, stamped) metal GROUNDPLATE, similar to *CHAMPLEVÉ,* but with a pattern or design visible through the enamel; when the groundplate has an "engine-turned" pattern, it is known as *GUILLOCHÉ* enamel

baton narrow, stick-shaped

bead set setting in which stones are held in place by beads raised from the surrounding metal

beauty pin small brooch/pin, also called handy pin, lace pin

bezel metal band with top edges burnished over to hold a stone in place

biomorphic amoeba-like, organic shape

blackamoor depiction of an African man or woman

bloomed gold karat gold which has been treated with nitric acid, causing the alloy to dissipate from the surface, leaving a thin matte surface layer of pure gold (has a "frosted" appearance)

bog oak fossilized peat; found mainly in nineteenth century Irish jewelry

bola string tie of braided leather with a decorative slide and ornamental tips, usually silver

bombé having swelled or bulging sides

bookchain chain necklace with folded-over square or rectangular links, often engraved or stamped, popular mid to late 19th century

bouquet pin brooch with bowed-out center and a spike mounted on reverse, designed to hold a small flower bouquet

box clasp fastener for bracelets and necklaces, a slotted box into which a V-SPRING catch is inserted

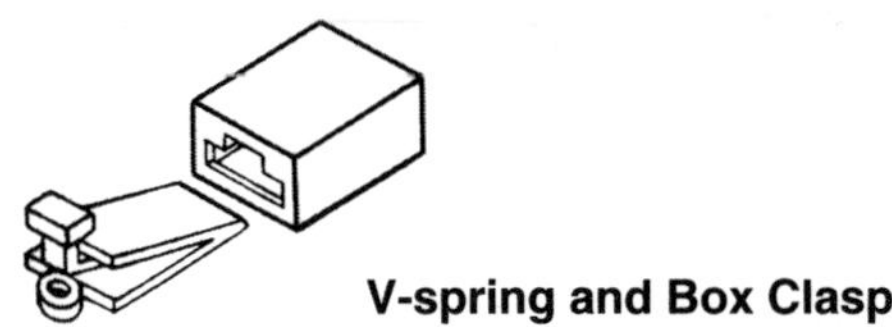
V-spring and Box Clasp

brilliant circular gemstone cut, especially for diamonds, with fifty-eight facets; the modern brilliant is a mathematically designed cut published in a treatise by Marcel Tolkowsky in 1919, also called the American or ideal cut; see also OLD MINE CUT and OLD EUROPEAN CUT

briolette gemstone cut, a three-dimensional faceted pear-shaped drop with small triangular facets

buff top gemstone cut, low cabochon top with a faceted pavilion (portion below the GIRDLE)

bulla ancient neck ornament made of two hinged convex plates, usually circular, suspended from a cord or chain; revived in the mid-Victorian period

bypass a bracelet or ring with open ends crossing parallel in front

cable-link chain oval links formed of round wire

cabochon an unfaceted, domed cut for stones or glass, with a flat base (a *double cabochon* has a convex base)

calibré small faceted gemstones, usually four-sided, cut to fit a setting, often in rows or groups

cameo a design carved in relief, often (but not always) from stone or shell with layers of more than one color forming background and foreground; a cameo carved within a concave depression of a gemstone, with the highest part of the design level with the edge of the stone, is called a *chevet* or *chevée*, *curvette* or *cuvette* (British term: "dished")

cameo *habillé* [ah bee YAY] depicting the head or bust of a person wearing jewelry set with diamonds or other gemstones (literally, "dressed up")

cannetille [kan ne TEE yuh] a type of metal ornamentation using thin wires to make a filigree pattern, often in tightly coiled spirals or rosettes, used in the early nineteenth century

carat unit of weight for gemstones

carbuncle cabochon cut almandite garnet

carré set a circular stone set within a square, flat-topped setting

casting molten metal poured or forced into a mold made from a design model

catch closure finding for brooch/pin that holds the pointed end of the pinstem. A *C-catch* is a simple C-shaped hook. See also SAFETY CATCH

C-catch

celluloid trade name for semi-synthetic pyroxylin-camphor thermoplastic, invented by John Wesley Hyatt in 1868

Celtic knot also known as *entrelac*, an intricate interlaced motif common in ancient Celtic ornamentation, revived by the British Arts & Crafts movement

chamfered having cut or beveled corners

champlevé [chaw le VAY] enamelling technique: opaque or translucent ENAMEL fills recesses or depressions which are stamped, etched or engraved into a metal GROUNDPLATE

channel setting a row of same-size square or rectangular stones fitted into a continuous metal channel or trough which holds the stones in place

chasing technique of decorating metal from the front, usually by hand, without removing any metal, forming a relief design by raising and indenting

chatelaine ornamental clip worn at the waist from which implements or trinkets are suspended by chains

choker short necklace that fits snugly around the neck

circa within ten years before or after a given date; literally, "around"

clip a type of brooch with a hinged double-pronged mechanism for attaching to clothing, sometimes called a "fur clip" to differentiate from a DRESS CLIP

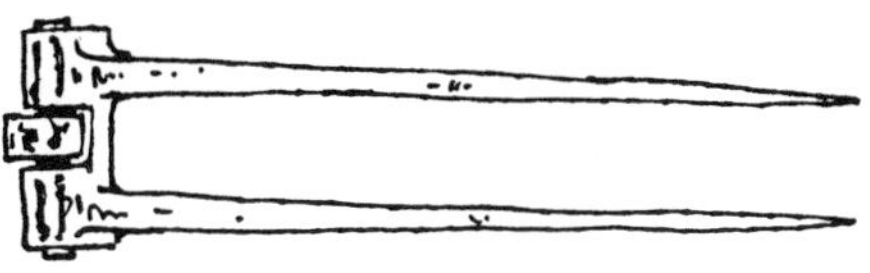
Clip

clipback earring finding for unpierced ear with a hinged clip for clamping earring to ear

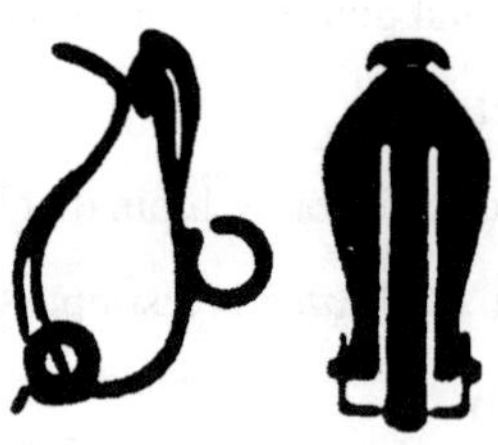

Clipback

cliquet [klee KAY] lit., catch. Type of pin having two ornamental terminals, one at each end of a pinstem, the pointed end having a snap closure or other mechanism for attachment. When worn, the pinstem is invisible. A.k.a. JABOT PIN, SÛRETÉ.

cloisonné [klwah son NAY] enamelling technique: a design or pattern is formed of wire soldered on to a GROUNDPLATE, creating cells or *cloisons* which are filled with ENAMEL

collet a short tubular band or collar of metal enclosing a stone

compass points (North, South, East, West) to indicate position of stones or design elements: top, bottom, and two sides

costume jewelry made from nonprecious materials, esp. since c. 1920

crystal < see **lead crystal, rock crystal**>

cuff bracelet a PENANNULAR rigid bracelet, usually wide with rounded ends

cultured pearl pearl produced by insertion of an irritant (small glass of mantle tissue and mother-of-pearl bead) into a mollusk (a *natural* pearl is formed around a foreign particle which occurs in nature)

curb chain twisted oval links forming a chain that lies flat

cushion cut rounded corner square faceted stone

cusped coming to a point, pointed end

cut-down collet or setting a method of setting gemstones in a collet or bezel with vertical ribs of metal holding the stone in place

cut steel small faceted steel studs, riveted closely together on a metal backing

damascening decorative technique, the embedding of gold and/or silver wire and/or cutout sheet metal shapes into a blackened iron or steel base (a.k.a. "inlaid metal")

demi parure [pah ROOR] two or three matched pieces of jewelry; a partial SUITE

déposé **[day poe ZAY]** registered (trademark or design), mark found on French items, and on items imported into or exported from France

die rolling repeating design created by rolling thin metal sheets between two steel rollers incised with a pattern

die striking or stamping method of mass production, a relief design produced from a flat sheet of metal with a two-part steel die forming the pattern under pressure

dog collar a wide ornamental choker necklace worn tightly around the neck

double clip brooch a pair of clips joined with a detachable pinback mechansim

dress clip an ornament attached to clothing by means of a hinged clip with a flat back and small prongs on the underside

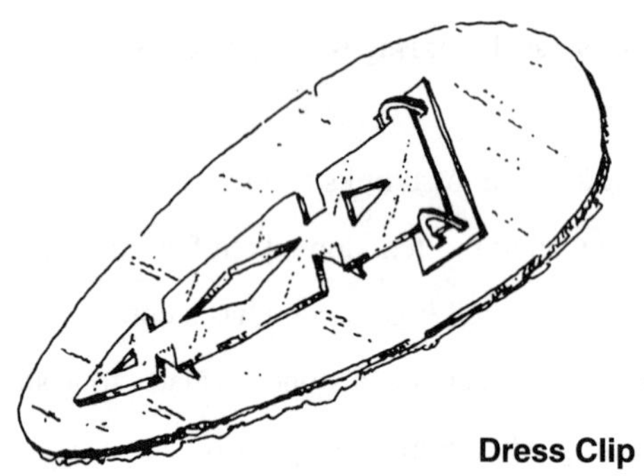

Dress Clip

ebonite <see **vulcanite**>

échelle [ay SHELL] lit., ladder. Series of graduated gem-set brooches or dress ornaments (often a bow motif) worn vertically (large to small) down the front of a bodice, 17th - 18th centuries.

electroplating electrolytic process of depositing a layer of metal over another metal

embossing technique for creating a raised decoration on metal using punches and hammers on the reverse side; also known as REPOUSSÉ work

emerald cut square or rectangular cut stone, square table, chamfered corners, step cut sides

enamel powdered pigmented glass fired onto a metal GROUNDPLATE using a variety of techniques <see *BASSE-TAILLE, CHAMPLEVÉ, CLOISONNÉ, GRISAILLE, LIMOGES, PLIQUE À JOUR, TAILLE D'ÉPARGNE*>

engraving decorative technique, the application of a design or pattern to the front surface of metal or stone by incising and removing material from the surface; differs from CHASING (in metal) in that material is removed with a tool called a graver, or a burin

en esclavage [awn es kla VAJH] lit., enslaved. A necklace or bracelet of identical or graduated plaques joined by swagged chains, usually three or more.

en résille [aw ray ZEE yuh] lit., in a hair-net. A flexible trellis or network, usually of diamonds and platinum, often forming a dog collar or other close-fitting necklace, originated by Cartier, early 20th century.

en tremblant [aw trã BLÃ] a brooch or other ornament with a motif (often a flower) mounted on a wire or spring, which trembles with movement of the wearer

equilateral all sides of equal length

estate jewelry previously owned, not necessarily antique, period or vintage

essence d'orient [door ee Ã] (**pearl essence**) coating used on glass or plastic to imitate pearls, made of fish scales

etching process for creating a design on metal or glass using acids

Etruscan jewelry ancient ornaments from central Italy (western Tuscany), usually of gold, reproduced in the nineteenth century

extended pinstem extends beyond the body of a brooch/pin; found on some nineteenth century brooches with C-CATCH closures, used to secure the brooch by weaving back into the clothing

fabrication hand construction using soldered sheet and wire

facet plane cut polished surface of a stone

faux [foe] French: false or fake

faux pearl artificial or imitation pearl, a glass or plastic bead coated with *ESSENCE D'ORIENT* (pearl essence)

ferronière [fair own ee AIR] lit., blacksmith's wife. A narrow band, usually with a central jewel, worn around the forehead, originally worn in the 15th century, popular c. 1830.

fetter chain elongated oval or rectangular links, often combined with short lengths of TRACE, CABLE, or CURB link chain

fibula ancient style brooch, used to close garments, resembles a modern safety pin

filigree metal decoration made of twisted thin wires

findings the functional metal parts used in construction and wearing of jewelry: catches, clasps, clips, jump rings, spring rings, etc.

fine jewelry made from PRECIOUS METAL and gemstones

flanged hinge brooch finding, a hinge (called a *joint* by jewelers) with projecting metal sides and a hingepin or internal posts to which pinstem is attached

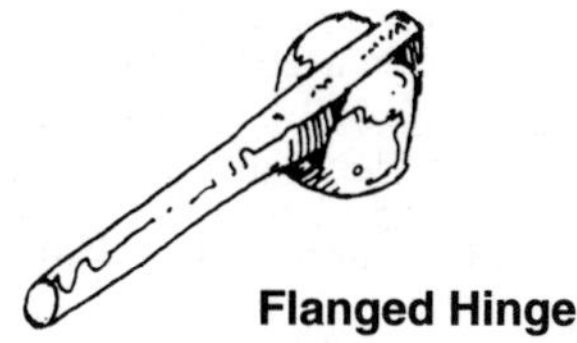
Flanged Hinge

Florentine finish textured brushed surface created by engraving cross-hatched lines on metal

fob a decorative ornament or seal suspended from a watch chain; also, a ribbon or metal band attached to a pocket watch

foiled back a thin sheet of metal backing a gemstone or paste, sometimes colored to enhance the appearance of the stone, used in closed-back settings; also, in reference to a RHINESTONE with painted-on metallic backing, as on a mirror, which can be set in an open setting foliate

foliated any leaf or plant design

forging the shaping of metal by heating and hammering

French jet black glass

gadrooned, gadrooning decorative oval beading on a border or edge

gallery a strip of metal with a pierced decorative pattern, used for settings

garter motif (Fr, *jarretière*) a strap with a buckle design

German silver an alloy of nickel, copper, and zinc, also known as NICKEL SILVER

gilding process by which a base metal is plated or coated with a thin layer of gold (called *gilt* metal)

girandole [[jhee rahn DOLE] lit., chandelier. Brooch or earring in which three pear-shaped drops are suspended from a center stone or motif

girdle widest part of a stone, part usually grasped by the setting; in a BRILLIANT-cut stone, the widest circumference where the crown (upper) and pavilion (lower) facets meet

gold filled a mechanical process using heat and pressure to join a layer of gold to a base metal; by law in the U.S., the gold layer must be at least 1/20th of the total weight of metal

gold plated layer of gold of less than 1/20th of total weight, can be applied by any process, but often ELECTROPLATED

gold wash a very thin coating of gold over base metal

graduated arranged in ascending or descending order of size

granulation ancient decorative technique of applying minute spheres of gold to a gold surface without visible solder, used in ETRUSCAN JEWELRY, a technique approximated by Victorian goldsmiths

grisaille [gree SIGH yuh] painted enameling technique, monochromatic, usually in shades of gray and white and/or black

groundplate the metal base on which enamels are fired; the method of decoration determines the name given to the technique (see ENAMEL)

guilloché [gee oh SHAY] lit., engine-turned. Machine-engraved decoration on metal, over which a translucent enamel is often applied (called *guilloché enamel*)

gypsy setting a one-piece mount for a stone which is recessed into the metal, with the table (top facet) of the stone level with the metal surface; also called STAR SETTING when lines radiating from the stone are engraved in the metal

hair jewelry ornaments made of, decorated with, or containing human hair

hallmark the mark(s) stamped on gold, silver, or platinum indicating fineness or karat; depending on country of origin, hallmarks can also include symbols for place of assay, date of assay (in the form of a letter or letter and number), maker's mark, and importation mark if applicable.

handy pin <see **beauty pin**>

intaglio Ital.[in TAHL yo] an engraved stone, opposite of a cameo, with a recessed design carved into the surface, common for signet rings and fob seals

invisible setting (*serti invisible)* a type of CHANNEL SETTING using specially cut square or rectangular colored gemstones (usually rubies or sapphires) which are notched to slide onto metal tracks and fit closely together in rows; no metal is visible from the front of the piece

jabot pin [zhah BOW] a pin with ornamental elements at both ends of a long pinstem which is invisible when worn at the collar (formerly worn on a jabot, a front ruffle on a shirt), see also CLIQUET, SÛRETÉ

japonaiserie [zhah po nay zair EE] decorative motifs in the Japanese style

jarretière [jhar et TYAIR] <see **garter motif**>

jet a type of fossilized coal, used primarily for mourning jewelry in the nineteenth century

jump ring a round or oval finding for linking or attaching other parts, made of round wire

karat 1/24th of the total weight in a gold alloy, a measure of fineness (24 karats is pure gold)

kidney wire <see **shepherd's hook**>

Kidney Wire

lace pin <see **beauty pin**>

lavalier, lavaliere, lavallière a neckchain suspending a gemstone or small pendant set with gemstones, popularly worn at the turn of the century

lead crystal colorless glass with a high percentage of lead added to enhance clarity and brilliance; resembles and is confused with ROCK CRYSTAL

Limoges [lee MOZH] enamelling technique: layers of finely ground colored ENAMEL fired after each application resulting in an image resembling a painting (without metal borders)

locket a two-part pendant or brooch with a hinge and cover, often containing a photo or lock of hair

longchain a very long metal chain worn around the neck with the end attached to the bodice, forming a swag, often terminating in a SWIVEL hook for suspending a watch or pendant

lorgnette [lorn YET] a pair of spectacles with an attached handle, usually suspended from a neckchain

loupe magnifying lens used by jewelers

lozenge an equilateral four-sided shape with corners at compass points; diamond-shaped (as in playing cards)

Lucite Du Pont trade name for acrylic thermoplastic

mabé pearl a pearl with a flat MOP bottom and rounded top (hollow, filled with epoxy or cement)

marcasite iron pyrite with a silver luster, cut in small faceted circular stones and often PAVÉ-set in silver or other white metal

marquise cut a gemstone cut that is oval or elliptical with pointed ends; the shape is also called NAVETTE

marriage a piece put together with two or more components from different sources, not as originally made

millegrain a method of setting stones using a tool around the top edge of a COLLET to form minute beads of metal which hold the stone in place; also a decorative technique

mosaic an object or jewel decorated with many small pieces of multicolored stone (called *PIETRA DURA*) or glass (TESSERAE) inlaid flush into stone or glass to form a design, motif, or scene; often called "*micromosaic*" when the glass tessarae are very small

mother-of-pearl the iridescent inside lining of mollusks

mourning jewelry jewelry worn in memory of a deceased loved one, most often black, sometimes containing the hair of the deceased

naja a horseshoe- or crescent-shaped silver pendant used in Navajo jewelry, often suspended from a SQUASH BLOSSOM necklace, sometimes set with turquoise or coral

navette <see **marquise**>

neck ring a rigid circular metal ornament worn around the neck

négligée [nay glee ZHAY] lit., negligent, careless. A pendant or necklace with two drops suspended unevenly

nickel silver <see **German silver**>

nicolo a variety of onyx with a thin layer of bluish-white over black, from which a cameo or intaglio is carved

niello a metallic form of enamelling using a powdered mixture of silver, copper, and lead which is fused by heat into an engraved design in silver, or occasionally gold, creating a grayish-black contrast with the metal ground

old European cut brilliant cut for diamonds with a circular GIRDLE, otherwise similar to OLD MINE CUT; the circular shape, developed c. 1876, was more easily produced with the invention of the steam-driven bruting, or girdling machine in 1891

old mine cut old style brilliant cut for diamonds, a cushion-shaped stone with a small TABLE, high crown (top facets) and an open, or large culet (the small flat facet at the base, virtually eliminated in a modern BRILLIANT)

open back setting setting which permits light to pass through a transparent or translucent stone (same as À JOUR)

painted enamel enamel applied in liquid form and baked on at lower temperatures than required for firing powdered enamels; used on costume jewelry

parure [pah ROOR] a complete set or SUITE of jewelry, matching pieces of three or more

paste high lead content glass which has been cut (faceted) to resemble a gemstone; also known as *strass*

patina color change on the surface of metal, esp. silver, copper, bronze, resulting from age and exposure to the atmosphere; a type of oxidation. Patina may be artificially applied using acids and/or liver of sulphur; color is usually green, brown, or red on copper, brass, or bronze (called PATINATED), grayish-black on silver

pavé [pah VAY] lit., paved. Method of setting many small stones very close together (literally, paved)

pebble jewelry Scottish jewelry set with multicolored agates in silver or gold

penannular open-ended ring shape

pendeloque [paw d'LOKE] lit., drop or pendant. Pear-shaped drop earring, suspended from a circular or bow-shaped surmount

pendant (noun) decorative element suspended from a necklace, chain, or cord

pendent (adjective) hanging, suspended

pietra dura literally, hard stone. A type of MOSAIC made of small pieces of stone which form a picture or scenic design, also known as *Florentine mosaic*

pinchbeck alloy of copper and zinc, developed in 1720, used to imitate gold

piqué [pee KAY] lit., pricked. The inlaying of gold or silver in patterns, usually into tortoiseshell or ivory. *Piqué posé* [poe ZAY]: floral or ornate patterns of inlay; *piqué point* [pweh]: geometric shapes or dots.

plaque de cou [plak de KOO] lit., plate of the neck. Central ornamental plaque of a dog collar necklace.

plique à jour [pleek ah ZHOOR] enamelling process in which the GROUNDPLATE is removed after firing; the end result resembles stained glass, the translucent enamel framed in metal

polychrome three or more colors, multicolored

"pot" metal base white metal, tin and lead alloy, greyish in color, used in early twentieth century costume jewelry

precious metal gold, platinum, or silver

prong set stones held in place by metal claws or prongs

provenance the origin and history of a piece, including its former owners

quatrefoil decorative element having four lobes

regard ring finger ring set with a variety of gemstones, the first letters of which spell "regard" (ruby, emerald, garnet, amethyst, ruby, diamond)

relief raised or standing out from the background

repoussé [ruh poo SAY] lit., pushed back or out. Raised design in metal. *Repoussage*: a technique of hand-raising a design in metal, working with punches and hammer from the back of the piece

rhinestone faceted colorless or colored glass, cut like a gemstone and usually with a fused metallic backing for light reflection (like silvering a mirror); used in costume jewelry

rivière [ree vee AIR] lit., river or stream. A short necklace of graduated gemstones of the same kind (e.g., diamonds), each stone COLLET-set and linked in a row without further decoration

rock crystal colorless quartz, occurring in nature as a six-sided (hexagonal) crystal

rolled gold a thin layer of gold fused over base metal

rondel, rondelle thin disk-shaped metal ornament, sometimes set with rhinestones, strung on a necklace between beads

rose-cut circular gemstone cut with triangular facets coming to a point at the top and a flat back

rose gold gold of a pinkish color (alloyed with copper)

safety chain a chain attached to a piece of jewelry which prevents loss if clasp opens

safety catch brooch finding with a swiveling closure which prevents it from unintentionally opening

Safety Catch

St. Andrew's cross an "X"-shaped motif, Scottish national emblem

sautoir [so TWAHR] a very long necklace or strand of beads or pearls, often terminating in a tassel or pendant

scarab Egyptian symbol of immortality, the *Scarabaeus* beetle, usually carved or molded in stone, clay, or glass

scarf pin, stickpin, tie pin decorative pin with a long pinstem and ornamental top, inserted into a scarf, cravat, or necktie

screwback earring finding for unpierced ear with a screw mechanism for securing earring to ear

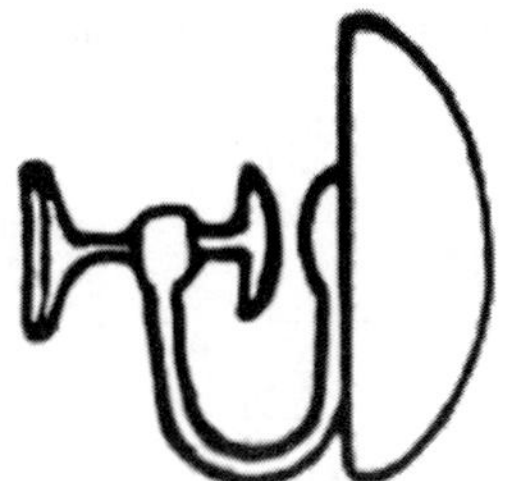

Screwback

seed pearl a natural, cultured, or artificial pearl weighing less than one quarter of a grain

sévigné [say veen YAY] a bow brooch set with diamonds, worn on the bodice (three or more worn *EN ÉCHELLE*), popular from the 17th century, named after the Marquise de Sévigné (1626-96), of the court of Louis XIV

shank the part of a ring that encircles the finger

shepherd's hook, fishhook, kidney wire earring findings for pierced ears, primarily for pendent or drop earrings

Shepherd's Hook, Fishhook

shoulder area of a finger ring where the SHANK and BEZEL or head (top) meet

signed marked (engraved, stamped, impressed) with the name, initials, logo, or trademark of the maker, designer, or manufacturer

slave bracelet a link bracelet of glass and silver or brass, often enameled; also a bangle worn on the upper arm, popular 1920s

slide movable decorative and functional element of a LONGCHAIN which adjusts its opening; when longchains went out of fashion, collections of slides were strung together and made into bracelets

solder metal alloy used to fuse pieces of metal together with the use of heat; *hard* solder requires high temperatures, is made of an alloy of the same metal being joined, and creates the strongest bond; *soft* or *lead* solder fuses at a lower temperature; it is considered unsuitable (and damaging) for use on PRECIOUS METAL

solitaire the mounting of a single stone, usually in a ring

spacer decorative or functional element used to separate pearls or beads

spectacle setting a ring of metal around the girdle of a stone, like an eyeglass frame, often used for setting diamonds or other transparent stones linked at intervals on a chain

spring ring type of clasp finding used with a JUMP RING to connect one part to another

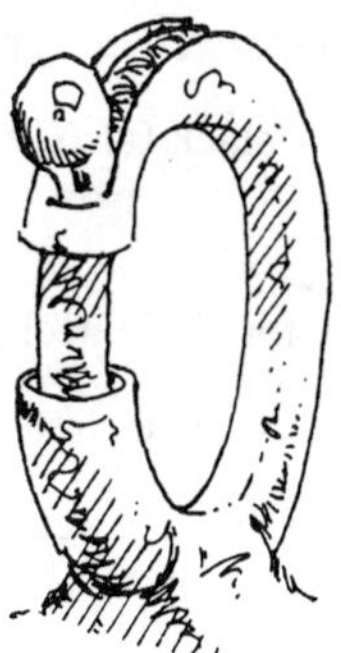

Spring Ring

squash blossom necklace Native American, hollow silver beads interspersed with floral motifs resembling blossoms, sometimes set with turquoise, with a central NAJA pendant

sterling silver an ALLOY which is 925 parts pure silver and 75 parts copper

stomacher large, usually triangular, bodice ornament, also known as a *corsage ornament* or *devant de corsage*

strass <see **paste**>

stud or post & clutch or nut earring findings for pierced ears

Stud or Post & Clutch or Nut

suite several pieces of jewelry similarly designed to be worn together <see also PARURE>

surmount the decorative top part of an earring

sûreté [soor TAY] (pin) lit., safety, security. See *CLIQUET.*

swivel a type of finding, a hook with a hinged spring closure joined to a swiveling base with a jump ring for attaching watch, PENDANT, item, a chain

Swivel

synthetic gemstone laboratory-created gemstone which is chemically, physically, and optically identical to its natural counterpart; in contrast to an *imitation*, which is only similar in appearance (e.g., purple glass imitating amethyst)

table the top facet or surface of a cut stone

taille d'épargne [tie yuh day PARN] lit., saving (economical) cut. Enameling technique: engraved design partially filled with opaque enamel, usually black (also known as *black enamel tracery*)

T-bar clasp a closure, usually for chain necklaces, consisting of a T-shaped bar that slips through a circular ring; when the chain is worn, the bar is held in place against the ring

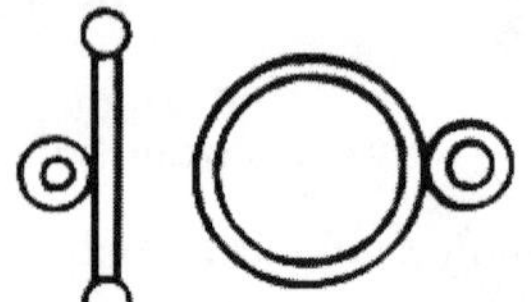

T-bar Clasp

tesserae [TESS er ee] tiny colored glass pieces used in MOSAIC (sometimes called *Roman mosaic)*

Tiffany setting a four- or six-prong elevated setting for a solitaire stone introduced by Tiffany & Company in 1886

torsade multi-strand twisted short necklace, usually beads or pearls; cabled or twisted cord

trace chain chain with oval links of equal size

trefoil decorative element having three lobes

trombone catch a two part sliding tubular closure finding for brooches

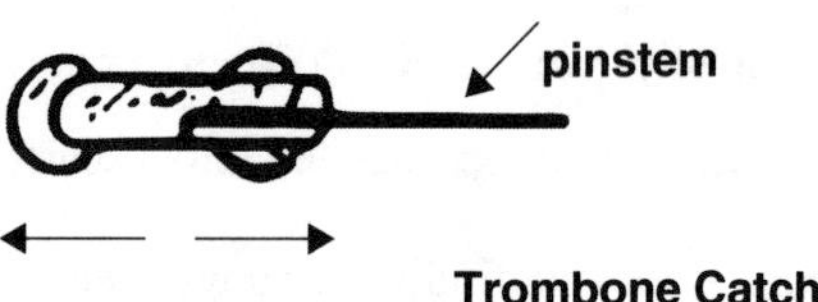

Trombone Catch

tube hinge brooch finding, an elongated tubular hinge (called a *joint* by jewelers) to which pinstem is attached

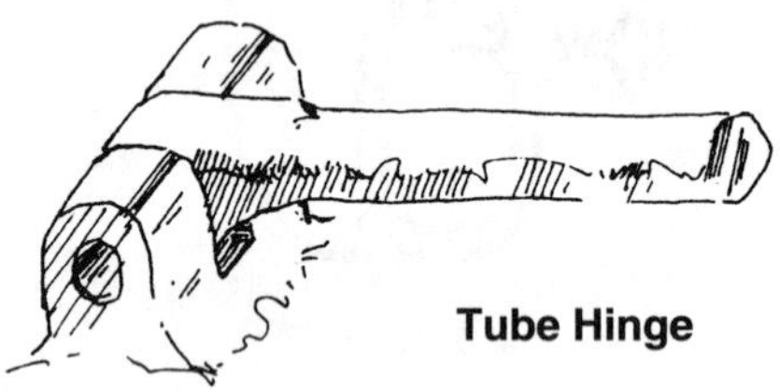

Tube Hinge

v-spring part of a BOX CLASP closure finding in which a wedge-shaped element fits into a metal box

vasiform vase-shaped

vermeil [ver MAY] gold-plated silver, silver gilt

volute spiral, snail shell-shaped

vulcanite vulcanized (hardened) rubber, used for mourning jewelry in the nineteenth century, also known as EBONITE

watch pin a small brooch/pin with a hook at the base of the reverse with its open end up, for suspending a small watch; worn on women's bodices at the turn of the century

white gold alloy of gold with nickel, palladium, or platinum (various formulae) which produces a silver-white color, approximating platinum, for which it is substituted

wirework twisted wire decoration applied to metal ground

yellow gold alloy of gold with silver and copper, most common color of gold

ziggurat stepped triangle or pyramid shape

INDEX